COLLECTED PAPERS ON ACCOUNTING

This is a volume in the Arno Press collection

THE DEVELOPMENT OF CONTEMPORARY ACCOUNTING THOUGHT

See last pages of this volume for a complete list of titles.

COLLECTED PAPERS ON ACCOUNTING

William T. Baxter

ARNO PRESS
A New York Times Company
New York • 1978

Publisher's Note: This book has been reproduced from the best available copies.

Editorial Supervision: LUCILLE MAIORCA

Reprint Edition 1978 by Arno Press Inc.

THE DEVELOPMENT OF CONTEMPORARY ACCOUNTING THOUGHT
ISBN for complete set: 0-405-10891-5
See last pages of this volume for titles.

Manufactured in the United States of America

Library of Congress Cataloging in Publication Data

Baxter, William Threipland, 1906-
Collected papers on accounting.

(The Development of contemporary accounting thought)
Reprint of 26 articles published between 1932-1976 by various publishers.
1. Accounting--Addresses, essays, lectures.
2. Inflation (Finance) and accounting--Addresses, essays, lectures. I. Title. II. Series.
HF5629.B34 657'.08 77-87311
ISBN 0-405-10924-5

ACKNOWLEDGMENTS

"An Investigation into the Dissolution of a Medieval Italian Partnership," "The Study of Balance Sheets," "The Inadequacy of Financial Accounts," "Inflation and Partnership Rights," and "Depreciation Assets" were reprinted by permission of *The Accountant's Magazine.*

"History from Old Accounts—John P. Cushing, Merchant and Investor," "A Note on the Allocation of Oncosts Between Departments," "Accounting As An Academic Study," "Recommendations on Accounting Theory," and "The Future of the Accountant" were reprinted by permission of *The Accountant.*

"Credit, Bills and Bookkeeping in a Simple Economy" was reprinted by permission of the American Accounting Association.

"Accountants and the Inflation" was reprinted by permission of the Manchester Statistical Society.

"Theory of Foreign Branch Accounts," "Partnership Rights," "Inflation and the Accounts of Steel Companies," and "Valuation of a Practising Accountant's Work-in-Progress" were reprinted by permission of *Accountancy.*

"A Colonial Bankrupt: Ebenezer Hancock" was reprinted by permission of *The Business History Review.*

"Inflation and Accounting Profits" was reprinted by permission of National Westminster Bank Limited.

"The Accountant's Contribution to the Trade Cycle" was reprinted by permission of *Economica.*

"Accounting in Colonial America" was reprinted by permission of Sweet & Maxwell, Ltd.

"British Transport Commission v. Gourley" was reprinted by permission of *The Modern Law Review.*

"Approaches to Pricing" was reprinted by permission of *Business Horizons.*

"General or Special Index?" was reprinted by permission of *Journal UEC.*

"Depreciation, Replacement Price, and Cost of Capital" was reprinted by permission of the *Journal of Accounting Research.*

"Monetary Correction" was reprinted by permission of Lloyds Bank International Limited.

P R E F A C E

I was apprenticed to a firm of accountants in 1924, and in 1928 I began to coach foreign class-mates. So I have been learning and teaching the trade for half-a-century. This collection of old writings may at least serve to give some notion of how accounting practice and training have changed in that time.

To keep up the profession's tone, the Society of Chartered Accountants of Edinburgh made the new apprentice pay one hundred guineas to his employer, and another hundred to the Society when he qualified five years later. My salary for this five years mounted up to exactly nil: my widowed mother somehow managed to pay the hundred guineas premium, and this was returned (after a bit of prodding by me) in three-monthly instalments, starting at £2.10s. But jobs were scarce, and so - despite the lack of pay - firms could recruit more apprentices than they could find useful work for.

My firm was biggish for the time and place, yet had a staff of under twenty. The partners busied themselves with investment trusts (which enabled us apprentices to pick up something about finance) and left our work in charge of an unqualified clerk. Perched on high stools, we started with endless adding and ticking. Then we graduated to the single-entry accounts of small shops. Also we drafted "accounts charge and discharge of the intromissions" of so-and-so (medieval documents peculiar to the Scots law of testamentary trusts, etc.); we wrote, ruled and sewed perhaps four copper-plate pages a day, merely as drafts for the typist to copy. This did at least instil a strong sense of accounting style. For formal training, we went to evening classes, where I learned compound interest (long before DCF became modish) but little else. Probably because I was bored and therefore careless, I was given no responsible audit work; and double-entry mystified me till half-way through my training, when a crammer coached me for the intermediate examination.

In those days, and indeed till the 'sixties, most British accountants relied on correspondence courses when studying - tired after a day in the office - for their examinations. That was the sum-total of their formal education. They had no contact with a university, and usually were scornful of academic accounting. But the Scottish societies were more enlightened, and from about 1920 made apprentices attend university courses in accounting and law. I wanted more than this, and took the B.Com. by part-time study. The University of Edinburgh provided feminine company, debating societies, and a gym; such study as office hours allowed me was vastly more interesting than my struggles to balance the petty cash.

Though I was (and still am) grateful for my university courses, they now seem far inferior to those of today. They lacked any tutorial work. Professors were not subject to an age limit; many were old and wise, but inaudible and preoccupied with bygone issues. The economics course lasted for only two terms, and - if memory is to be trusted - was mainly concerned with farm rents and bimetallism; one of the lecturers likened our text-book to clotted wool. Economic history was enjoyable history, but illuminated few economic truths. Commercial law was planned for mature LL.B. students, and left me bewildered. "Organisation of Industry and Commerce" was the most popular course in students' eyes, because we felt it was so entirely "practical". In other words, it was descriptive, and avoided all hint of the problems and paradoxes that beset economic affairs.

I owe an immense debt to William Annan, the part-time professor of accounting. He was a fatherly and competent man with wide professional experience, and his course taught me a great deal. But, as he later admitted to me, he laboured under two constraints. First, the course catered for both apprentices in their final year and students with scant knowledge of accounts. Second, he was a partner in a busy firm, and his university work was limited to three lectures a week; lack of time thus made it impossible for him to do as good a job as he wanted.

His strength as a teacher came mainly from his love of the law. He had taken classes in this when young, and later was often an expert witness in court. He taught us the rules underlying the conduct and accounts of partnerships, trusts, "judicial factories", and bankruptcies, and also something of the human frailties that we should meet in these spheres; he gave much time to tax; and he made us look on the Companies Act as our second Bible. He bade us suspect the wording of routine papers such as dividend warrants ("probably drafted by some underling"), and look instead to the original contract. In short, to him (like most other sound teachers of the subject then), accounting was a twin to the law.

After qualifying, most Scottish C.A.'s had to hunt for jobs in London (at £250 a year) or abroad. However, Annan gave me a post in his office in Edinburgh. Here the standards were high, and I found myself suddenly switched from trivial tasks to ones that were almost too exacting. Then Annan astounded me one morning by suggesting I should put in for a scholarship to America - a preposterous thing for an accountant to do. I duly sent off applications. On the way to the selection committee, I saw a street accident, and thus had something to talk about; a few days later I received a letter (which I still treasure) telling that the Harkness Fund would give me two years of graduate study.

The Fund was a fairy godmother if ever there was one. With its generous help, I did a year's work at the Wharton School in Philadelphia and a second at Harvard Business School.

In my application for the fellowship, I had sketched out a plausible research project: I was to compare the economist's version of the firm's cost and price strategies with what the accountant sees in real life. The idea was good, but I failed to carry it out. (Had I possessed the needed ability and training, I might have anticipated the famous paper by Hall and Hitch). So I was mightily relieved when Professor N.S.B. Gras and his colleagues, at the business history department of Harvard Business School, suggested that I might instead study old firms whose records lie in Boston.

For this task, an accountants' training proved helpful. Some of the incidental results are described in papers in this book. But my main effort was on the Hancock ledgers and letters, and I spent a hard year straining to decipher and understand the book-keeping of a semi-barter economy. If the trade of medieval Italians was at all like that of the colonial New Englanders, then the latters' credit transfers must go far to explain the birth of double-entry. Much later, after I had searched through other Hancock records in London, I tried to piece their story together in _The House of Hancock - Business in Boston 1724-1775_.[1.] My material had all the ingredients

---

1. Harvard University Press, Cambridge, Mass. 1945.

of a romantic film scenario: bluff Uncle Thomas rose from shop-boy to merchant prince, and made a fortune supplying the British forces during the Seven Years War; Nephew John tried to corner the oil market, was caught smuggling, was the object of the redcoats' famous march to Lexington (where he was courting his future wife), and was the first to sign the declaration of independence.

After my two years of affluence in U.S.A., I found myself back in a depressed Britain where a record of graduate study was deemed a disqualification in applications for an accounting job. Luckily my worst worries did not last long. Annan had contrived to reorganise the B.Com. at Edinburgh, splitting accounting into elementary and advanced courses; and he offered me a part-time lecturership (at the high rate of £300 a year) to run the elementary course.

During a year of unemployment before I took up this post, I worked on Hancock records in the British Museum, and went to the London School of Economics as an "occasional student". I chiefly remember Professor Plant's undergraduate seminars, where (I was startled to find) economic theory was used as an aid to understanding

"Commerce", and undergraduates were already so steeped in the theory that they kept running to the blackboard to illustrate their views with cost curves, etc.

These autobiographical ramblings are not intended merely to give the flavour of quaint old days. Their point is this: after a good professional training, plus study at some of the world's best schools of business, I still had no inkling of the problems that are now central to a sound course in accounting theory, and also to much practice.

There were several reasons for my blindness. The most important was professional attitudes. For decades, accountants had enjoyed mounting esteem. By and large, our methods met the needs of the time, and we felt no call to question or amend. The spirit of reverent acquiescence was nearly as strong in the office as in the church, and hampered all discussion of principles or reforms.

This spirit soon infected a new recruit. My immediate superiors did their best to lick me into shape, but stressed the *how* rather than the *why*; and office discipline did not encourage one to question still more important persons. The highest praise went to the clerk whose tenacity and skill could ferret out the error in a trial balance. Few asked what (if anything) the figures meant.

Looking back, it seems to me that our smugness reflected a certain insulation from economic forces and ways of thought. As earlier pages have suggested, a good accountant tended to see himself as the ally of solicitors and financiers rather than managers. Our text-books concerned themselves with legal rules, not economic analysis. Often our interest in management accounts was less than it is today. True, our examinations contained questions on costing; but many years were to pass before they dealt with accounts "as aids to decision making" (a <u>cliche</u> with which I was long unfamiliar).

Our indifference to economic forces was strengthened by our use of historical cost. In pre-inflation days, this seemed quite adequate for measuring assets (and anyway, published balance-sheets often hid even the historical costs, by lumping them together or deducting secret reserves); likewise, the measurement of income could safely be left to the historical figures - the more so because tax was low. In short, we were not concerned with <u>alternative values</u> and all the uncertainties that beset them.

What then did I teach when, full of zeal to improve accounting education, I started to lecture? Well, I explained the historical background of accounting and thus the casual way in which it evolved. I drummed in compound interest as a prelude to finance. And, if I had not new ideas, I could at least put the old ones across more efficiently. I tried to present the material in simple style, with systematic exercises. In this spirit, I wrote a book on income tax that took gross liberties with the legal rules, but was comprehensible to beginners. (To write a book on tax was naive, as it goes out of date at the next budget. But it was to get me my first chair). I happened to review an American text-book (by Harry H. Wade) that took the balance sheet as the starting point of book-keeping, and I switched my lectures to this order (then an innovation in Britain); the method made my students more friendly to debits and credits, and also led me later to treat income as growth in wealth rather than the residue of selected revenues and costs.

In the mid-thirties, the effects of Plant's teaching began to percolate to accounting. Three of his ablest pupils - R.S. Edwards, R.H. Coase and R.F. Fowler - took to writing, notably for *The Accountant*. I can still remember reading Edwards' first article. It was on reserves; it argued that investors need good information if a free economy is to flourish, and so secret reserves are harmful. Such was the power of the conventional training that this attack on accepted practice struck me as semi-blasphemous. And Annan (it shows the man's calibre) shook me further by telling me, rather pointedly, that such stuff was just what a young lecturer ought to be writing.

Worse was to come. I had of course scampered across the pages in an economics text-book that dealt with joint-products: where a single process lends to several products, the notion of average total cost of one of the products has no significance; thus a planter cannot sensibly separate the costs of growing his cotton-lint and cotton-seed. But the words had not sunk in. Edwards and Coase saw their relevance to allocation in accounts - the trick of splitting overhead between departments, jobs, etc.

If a firm has two departments, A and B, its accounts can usefully show the variable costs revenues and each, as in lines (1) and (2) below:

		Total £	A £	B £
(1)	Revenue	2 000	1 200	800
(2)	Variable costs.. ..	1 200	700	500
(3)	Gross profit	800	500	300
(4)	Overhead	200	w	x
(5)	Net profit	600	y	z

All is plain-sailing down to line (3). But thereafter the conscientious accountant feels he cannot just rule off columns A and B, and then leave well alone. Somehow or other, he must at (4) split the £200 joint costs (general management expenses, etc.), though these are unaffected by doings in each department. So he hunts for ways in which to produce £*w* and £*x* by dividing the £200 in some ratio that seems good to him (e.g. as the variable costs of A and B). And costing, I had been taught, should go still further than departmental accounts, by splitting a factory's fixed costs among all the separate jobs, in proportion to say direct labour.

I could not but see logic in the attacks on allocation.

Yet I was not quite convinced by them, mainly because the accountant's rituals seemed to go hand-in-hand with efficient business. I puzzled endlessly over this paradox, and engaged in much debate with an Edinburgh colleague (Kenneth Boulding, later to be a professor of economics in America). In 1937, I sailed to Cape Town to be professor there; and I recall much argument with economists in the sun on the third-class deck.

At my new university, I was the first and only full-time accountant. Luckily for me, a colleague in the Commerce department, G.F. Thirlby, was so perturbed by my ignorance that he appointed himself my private mentor, and drilled me in L.S.E. doctrine till I saw the light (though I still harboured doubts over his suggestion that depreciation charges were yet another instance of the accountant's misplaced love of allocation). These discussions led to the 1938 paper on oncost, and later - with more stimulus from Professor Oxenfelt at Columbia Business School - to the 1961 paper.

I was not an unmixed success as a young professor. This was partly my own fault: I did not at first grasp that, as my friendly South African students were a year or two younger than their British counterparts, they would see no reason to do any work when under the light rein that befits mature students. I needed time also to hit on an adequate technique of lecturing, to work out a stock of illustrations and exercises, and - most important - to decide what a good accounting course should contain. I was determined not to stick to the established text-books (which, despite great length, contrived to evade all the interesting problems). But what to substitute? In part, my answer was to stress the difference - well shown in such matters as par values and bonus shares - between the label and the goods inside the parcel ("The song is called 'Ways and Means': but that's only what it's _called_' you know ...... the song really _is_ 'A-sitting on a Gate')". I still think this is one of the most worthwhile bits of an accounting education; and it is what eventually led to the 1954 paper (with Professor L.C.P. Gower) on shares of no par value. Another topic that cried for treatment was the style of final accounts. In those days, most published reports still looked like double-entry exercises; only a few British companies were trying to set out their income statements and balance sheets in single-column form, and to use words that the lay reader could understand. I taught my students to experiment with the reformed methods. When news of this confusing innovation reached the ears of the local chartered accountants, they sent a protest party to the vice-chancellor. There were grumblings too about my teaching on allocation, which certainly handicapped students who were preparing to sit the C.A. examinations. When my three years of probabtion were up, it was touch-and-go whether the university confirmed my appointment. Fortunately there had recently been much unpleasantness over the non-confirmation of another professor, and senate shrank from more trouble in my case.

Edwards had by this time founded the Accounting Research Association, a short-lived body that tried to boost the level of accounting thought with research papers and critical reviews. One of his reviews praised Professor J.C. Bonbright's _Valuation of Property_. Thanks to this book, I came to see that asset values could be fitted into a meaningful framework - the "what difference does it make" approach of alternative budgets. I applied these new ideas in costing lectures, to discredit the usual practice of charging material at historical cost. They were invaluable too when

I had to advise in cases over compensation for expropriated shops. Later, when inflation began to give a tired look to historical value, they offered the obvious means for refreshing the balance sheet. As they equate value with the loss suffered when the owner is deprived of an asset (through use, accident, etc.), "deprival value" seemed a good name for the concept. Bonbright's work has not perhaps received full recognition in America ("a prophet is never .....") , but now, forty years after publication, is central to British proposals for inflation accounting. What would its fate have been without Edward's review?

Edwards in 1938 wrote also "The Nature and Measurement of Income", as thirteen weekly articles.[2] They explained the forward-looking concept of income, and pointed out the crudities of accepted measures. Like many other of his readers, I had not till then thought that the definition of income raised much problem: my training suggested that any difficulties could be solved by the dry

2. Reproduced in Studies in Accounting Theory, Sweet & Maxwell, London, 1950 and 1963.

rules of trust and tax law. Thus I had dutifully learned how to apportion a testamentary trust's receipts and costs between the beneficiaries entitled to a life-interest and those entitled to the final residue; so I had come to view "capital" and "income" more in terms of contending claims than of wealth and growth. I gave no lectures on income theory, and (I blush to recall) had earlier written that its problems could usually be solved "by a simple analogy, such as the running of a farm". Once again, I now had to supplement law with economics. It took me a long time to accept that rival measures of income can each be useful, and that conceptual purity must be weighed against ease and sureness of measurement.

In 1947 the London School of Economics took the brave step of creating Britain's first full-time chair in accounting, and of translating me to it. My new department mustered about a dozen specialist students in each year, one lecturer (David Solomons), and me.

At L.S.E., I had to think afresh about my lectures. These continued to provide beginners with a solid dose of book-keeping. But the advanced courses turned more and more to management budgets, asset values, and income.

I see that I wrote little during my early years at L.S.E. I employed some of the idle time usefully: accounting students were starved of good reading, and by editing Studies in Accounting, and its second edition (with Professor Sidney Davidson, of the University of Chicago as its joint-editor), I made perhaps the first attempt to assemble articles by lively writers in a handy book. Since then, the device has been repeated by any number of accounting professors who, like me, wanted to extend their publications list without undue exertion.

My slowness to produce articles was due in good part to lack of both ideas and facility at writing. But also I wanted to feel sure of my case, and to make it sound simple and persuasive. In this, I sometimes failed sadly and irritated my readers. Thus the 1962 article on inflation and partnership was rejected by one editor, who quoted his technical adviser (a partner in an eminent firm) as saying that practical accountants had no need to be told how to run their affairs. Again, the 1953 articles on "recommendations" (stimulated by the lectures of Sir Karl Popper) provoked an ex-president of the English Institute to reply in derisive verse. (I suspect that even academic accountants mostly fail to share my distrust of *ex cathedra* pronouncements on the nature of truth). Let me hasten to add that I have also received great kindness and encouragement.

Nowadays it is easier for young academics to spread way-out ideas. (Indeed, the rumour is that some of them do little else, so that their students stay innocent of all acquaintance with book-keeping). Several forces have helped to mellow attitudes. Inflation has undoubtedly been the most potent. I read my 1949 paper on inflation accounting to a meeting of the Manchester Statistical Society. As I left the hall, I overheard the talk of two men in front of me. Obviously one was a member of the society, and the other his guest; the latter's dress and bearing proclaimed him an accountant of some note. The member asked nervously whether the discussion of inflation accounting had proved interesting. "Interesting, yes" came the judicial reply" ... but of no practical importance". At the time, this was reasonable enough. But mounting inflation was soon to show up the absurdities of the historical cost system, and led financial journalists to poke fun at the defenders of orthodoxy.

My own thoughts on inflation accounting were largely conditioned by the analogy of foreign branch accounts (see the 1951 article, written with my Cape Town student and present colleague, Professor Basil Yamey). This was a good starting-point: if one views the problem in terms of translation of all the figures from one currency to another (old £s into today's £s), one may avoid the traps attendant on piecemeal thinking. One also sees asset values as a problem that is independent of the translation: and deprival value solves this problem.

Later, depreciating assets suggested themselves as good material with which to test the deprival approach. But when I tried to clarify my thoughts on the calculation of their value, I floundered hopelessly in arithmetic that had to embrace the long-run effects of technical improvement, real price chance, inflation, nominal interest, and interest filleted for inflation. Once again I was saved by a colleague: Mr. N.H. Carrier (a demographer) made short work of such complexities in our 1971 article.

The writings on depreciation were a useful but lengthy distraction from my main effort of recent years, a book on accounting theory and price-change. Articles of 1952, 1955, 1959, 1967 were examples of work-in-progress. Not till 1975 did the book at last achieve publication.

Looking through the papers, I can see plenty of inept and clumsy work that cries for revision; but perhaps it is just as well not to tamper with one's early efforts. I see too how much I owe to others. Joint-authorship acknowledges only part of the debt. Young students have sometimes given great help: thus a seminar talk by Mr. H. Attarzadeh (of Persia) gave me an excellent lead on depreciation, and Mr. J.E.S. Hammond's pained questions during my lecture on "goodwill" finally made me see what nonsense my orthodox exposition was. Discussion with L.S.E. colleagues has pointed out many errors, and supplied much good matter in replacement. The collection is dedicated to all these kindly critics.

W.T. Baxter
January 1977.

CONTENTS

THE INADEQUACY OF FINANCIAL ACCOUNTS: From the Standpoints of Shareholders and the Public (Reprinted from *The Accountants' Magazine*) Edinburgh, February, 1957

BRITISH TRANSPORT COMMISSION V. GOURLEY (Reprinted from *The Modern Law Review*) London, July, 1956

PARTNERSHIP RIGHTS: The Valuation Problem (Reprinted from *Accounting Research*, Vol. 9, No. 3) London, July, 1958

INFLATION AND THE ACCOUNTS OF STEEL COMPANIES (Reprinted from *Accountancy*) London, May/June, 1959

APPROACHES TO PRICING: Economist *vs.* Accountant. With Alfred R. Oxenfeldt (Reprinted from *Business Horizons*) Bloomington, Indiana, Winter, 1961

INFLATION AND PARTNERSHIP RIGHTS (Reprinted from *The Accountants' Magazine*) Edinburgh, February, 1962

THE FUTURE OF THE ACCOUNTANT, I-IV: Dilemmas Facing the Profession (Reprinted from *The Accountant*) London, July/August, 1964

GENERAL OR SPECIAL INDEX?: Capital Maintenance Under Changing Prices (Reprinted from *Journal UEC, European Journal of Accountancy*, No. 3) Dusseldorf, 1967

VALUATION OF A PRACTISING ACCOUNTANT'S WORK-IN-PROGRESS, I-II (Reprinted from *Accountancy*) London, March/April, 1968

DEPRECIATING ASSETS: The Forward-Looking Approach to Value (Reprinted from *The Accountants' Magazine*) Edinburgh, April, 1971

DEPRECIATION, REPLACEMENT PRICE, AND COST OF CAPITAL. With N. H. Carrier (Reprinted from *Journal of Accounting Research*) Chicago, Autumn, 1971

MONETARY CORRECTION: Adjustments to Inflation in Three South American Countries (Reprinted from *Bank of London and South America Review*) London, April, 1976

AN INVESTIGATION INTO THE DISSOLUTION OF A MEDIEVAL ITALIAN PARTNERSHIP

AN INVESTIGATION INTO THE DISSOLUTION OF A MEDIÆVAL ITALIAN PARTNERSHIP.

BY W. T. BAXTER, B.COM., C.A.

ON 1st December 1458 three merchants of Florence agreed, "in the name of God and of profit," to enter into partnership as dealers in woollen goods. Their names were Bernardo d'Antonio de' Medici, Giovenco di Giuliano de' Medici and Giovanni de Leonardo Bencini. Bernardo and Giovenco were cousins and distant connections of the main de' Medici family. Giovanni was not related to the other two, but was originally a clerk in their employ; evidently he was a man of sterling qualities, for in the fulness of time he was admitted to the partnership and was entrusted with the keeping of the firm's books and accounts. The partnership agreement also explains that Bernardo was more or less a sleeping partner, while Giovenco had to "work in the store and to go to the dye vats and to the place where cloth is stretched and anywhere for the good of the company."

Other clauses in the deed of copartnery were:—

(1) "The capital of the partnership shall and must be 4000 florins, and this sum must be placed in the said company in cash within twelve months and half within six months as follows:

"The said Bernardo d'Antonio, 3075 gold florins; the said Giovenco di Giuliano, 425 florins; the said Giovanni Bencini, 500 florins, within the time aforementioned, which in all makes the sum of 4000 gold florins."

(2) "The profit that our Lord God through his pity and mercy may grant" us shall be divided in the following manner: ". . . Bernardo d'Antonio shall draw on the basis of 2000 florins" [*i.e.*, 50 per cent of the profits, since the total capital was 4000 florins], "Giovenco di Giuliano shall draw on the basis of 1000 florins" [*i.e.*, 25 per cent], "and Giovanni 1000 florins, and likewise in case of a loss, from which God protect each one; and they may draw their share of any profit each time that a balance is made."

It was unusual at that period to prepare periodical Profit and Loss Accounts, and in this instance none was drawn up until after the dissolution of the firm. Until that time the partners lived on their drawings. The copartnership deed permitted the senior partner to withdraw eight florins per month, and each of the two juniors four florins per month. All of them did, in fact, exceed these limits.

This particular partnership agreement was not the first of its kind which had been made by the three Florentines, but was one of a series. Mediæval merchants evidently took a gloomy view of copartnery contracts, and usually stipulated that such a contract should expire after a short term of years had elapsed; if desired, it could then be renewed for another short term. Bernardo and his two friends therefore prepared the usual type of deed (written in the approved 'business Italian' of the period), and stipulated that the agreement should come to an end in 1461, or in the event of one of the partners dying. It was the latter contingency which actually brought the partnership to a close, for early in 1460 Giovanni, the accountant, possibly worn out prematurely by the intricacies of his duties, departed from this earth to a land wherein, we trust, accounts are kept no longer.

It now became necessary for the survivors to balance off the books and to settle with Giovanni's heirs. While most of these books have disappeared during the subsequent centuries, it so happens that by some extraordinary chance there have been preserved for us the aforementioned copartnership agreement and the firm's 'secret book' or private ledger. These are now part of the Selfridge Collection of Medici MSS. in the Baker Library, Harvard University. The private ledger contains references to debtors' and creditors' ledgers, books of receipts and payments (presumably the equivalent of a general ledger), and a cash book, so it is evident that a pretty complete system of accounts was kept. Judging by other early Italian merchants' books which have survived till our time, the general appearance of the various accounts would be much the same as that of modern ones, except that the figures in the effective column would be Roman numerals (possibly as a protection against fraud—the more convenient Arabic symbols were well known and often appeared in the narrative); also, when it was desired to close off an account, instead of balancing it in the approved text-book fashion, the book-keeper would simply draw his pen right across the folio. It is sometimes suggested that this procedure is not entirely unknown even to-day. The monetary units employed in Florence were florins, soldi and denarii, which bore the same mutual relationship as do the present British pounds, shillings and pence. A florin was worth roughly £2, 10s. at the period in question.

Let us now consider the private ledger and the peculiar method of dividing the partnership assets there revealed. As in most other account books of the period, on the fly-leaf are the sign of the cross and a commendably pious inscription, presumably written by the worthy Giovanni :—

"In the name of the Omnipotent God and of his Mother, Madonna Holy Mary and of St Peter and St Paul and St John the Baptist, apostle and evangelist, and of St Nicholas and St Stephen the Martyr and of all the celestial Court of Paradise, may they by their grace and mercy grant to us a profit with well-being of soul and body."

On folio 1 of the private ledger are written the following notes :—

"This book is the book of Bernardo d'Antonio and Giovenco di Giuliano de' Medici and Giovanni di Leonardo Bencini, partners and wool merchants in the Convent of St Martin in Florence, and it is called 'Secret Book K.'"

(According to the Articles of Association drawn up in December 1458, Bernardo was to put 3075 florins into the partnership, Giovenco 425, and Giovanni 500 florins. This partnership was the last of a series made between the three partners from 1434 on. The death of Giovanni ended the partnership in 1460).

As we have seen, the above note is in exact accordance with the agreement.

Folios 2, 3 and 4 contain accounts showing how each partner contributed approximately his prescribed share of the firm's capital. Lumping together all Bernardo's and Giovenco's cash payments—which were, as a matter of fact, made in small instalments over the whole period of the partnership—these accounts appear as follows :—

	Bernardo.			Giovenco.			Giovanni.		
	Fl.	*s.*	*d.*	Fl.	*s.*	*d.*	Fl.	*s.*	*d.*
Assets from the preceding business (stock and debtors) . . .	1553	14	3	214	20	4	252	17	5
Cash	1521	14	4	206	8	4	247	11	7
	3074	28	7	421	8	8	500	9	0

These totals were transferred, with slight discrepancies, to the credit of the individual partners' capital accounts.

On the succeeding three pages of the private ledger are listed the assets owned by the firm at the date of its dissolution.

	Fl.	*s.*	*d.*
The debtors, including the partners' drawings, amount to	2881	0	1
The inventory of cloth and other merchandise, plus cash, amounts to	2160	5	9
Total assets	5041	5	10
Less : Partners' drawings included therein . .	564	2	10
	4477	3	0

Folio 5 relates that the firm had creditors to the extent of Fl. 48, 18s. 4d., but explains that these liabilities may be ignored, since Giovenco has been given cash with which to make settlement.

On folio 7 appears a Statement of Affairs showing how much profit had been earned by the firm during its lifetime ; this statement is here reproduced in the same general form as the original :—

1460

Here below we shall list all our debtors and merchandise and cash in a statement in order to close off the books. March 24, 1460. They appear in this book on p. 4, that is five thousand forty-one florins, five soldi, ten denari .				Fl. 5041	5	10
Deducting for Bernardo's share of the capital	Fl. 3074	19	8			
Deducting for Giovenco's share, &c.	420	19	10			
Deducting for Giovanni's share	500	0	0			
Total of capital to be deducted				3995	19	6
Our profit is				Fl. 1045	6	4
Bernardo's share of the profit [50 per cent] is .				522	13	2
Giovenco's share of the profit [25 per cent] is .				261	6	7
The share of the heirs of Giovanni is . .				261	6	7

So far the modern accountant has nothing much to

quibble over. But mark what follows. We should anticipate that settlement would be made thus :—

	Total.			Bernardo.			Giovenco.			Giovanni.		
	Fl.	*s.*	*d.*	Fl.	*s.*	*d.*	Fl.	*s.*	*d.*	Fl.	*s.*	*d.*
Capital contributed, as shown in the partners' capital accounts . . .	3995	19	6	3074	19	8	420	19	10	500	0	0
Profit, as shown in the Statement of Affairs . .	1045	6	4	522	13	2	261	6	7	261	6	7
	5041	5	10	3597	12	10	682	6	5	761	6	7
Less : Drawings, as shown in partners' accounts .	564	2	10	257	15	7	169	19	3	136	8	0
Balance due by the firm to the partners . . .	4477	3	0	3339	17	3	512	7	2	624	18	7
Proportions in which one would have expected the assets to be divided . .	4477	3	0	3339	17	3	512	7	2	624	18	7
They were not, however, divided in these proportions, but thus . .	4477	2	9	2262	16	9	1090	7	10	1123	18	2
Apparent over-payments .							578	0	8	498	19	7
							1077	0	3			
Apparent under-payment .				1077	0	6						

A discrepancy of a few soldi or denarii was neither here nor there in those happy days.

At first sight this method of paying out the partners seems without rhyme or reason ; we get a clue, however, as to why such a peculiar procedure was followed if we consider each partner as an ordinary outside debtor in respect of his drawings. Their shares of the assets then become :—

	Total.			Bernardo.			Giovenco.			Giovanni.		
	Fl.	*s.*	*d.*	Fl.	*s.*	*d.*	Fl.	*s.*	*d.*	Fl.	*s.*	*d.*
Share of the general assets .	4477	2	9	2262	16	9	1090	7	10	1123	18	2
Add : Drawings . .	564	2	10	257	15	7	169	19	3	136	8	0
Amount received by each partner	5041	5	7	2520	12	4	1260	7	1	1260	6	2

It becomes apparent at once that the total assets have been divided in the ratio 50 : 25 : 25—*i.e.*, in the same proportion as profits were to be shared.

One's immediate impulse is to declare that either the person who supervised the division of the assets made a mistake in his methods—a mistake which most of us make when we first tackle similar problems—or else that Bernardo, the sleeping senior partner, was badly swindled by his unscrupulous junior. Neither of these theories is correct, however. The partners' capital accounts show the discrepancy perfectly clearly: appended by way of example is a translation of Bernardo's account:—

1460

Bernardo d'Antonio de' Medici himself should have as his share of the capital of this partnership	Fl. 3074	19	8
And he should have as his share of the profit .	522	13	2
Total . . Fl. 3597 12 10			
He has received for his current account of withdrawals	257	15	7
He has received in cloth and other merchandise cash and thirty debtors, and his share of the division as appears in Book .... p. 52 . .	2262	16	9
Total . . Fl. 2520 12 4			

Only a very sleepy sleeping partner would fail to wake up when he saw such a statement, so it appears as if we may rule out both fraud and error. And this view is confirmed by the copartnery agreement, the relevant paragraph of which runs:—

"And at the end of the said partnership Giovenco and Giovanni must remain in the store until all the cloth which is being prepared has been returned to the stock. And they must remain two months longer at the request of Bernardo, until all the debts are paid, except the partners' shares of the capital. And then they shall divide the cloth and all other merchandise and fixtures and debtors, according to the division which is mentioned above: that is, Bernardo shall receive on the basis of 2000 florins" [50 per cent], "Giovenco on the basis of 1000 florins" [25 per cent], "and Giovanni on the basis of 1000 florins" [25 per cent].

It would therefore appear that this peculiar transaction was perfectly legitimate. And as far as can be ascertained from other surviving copartnery agreements, such methods of dividing the assets between a sleeping and one or more active partners were quite customary at that period. This being so, we are left wondering how often a sleeping partner gained any advantage from his business connection. In this case, for example, by paying in more than three-quarters of the total capital, and only ranking for one-half of the assets at the dissolution, Bernardo automatically lost one-third of his original capital. Of course, the longer the partnership lasted, the greater would be the chance that the sleeping partner's gains in respect of profits would compensate him for his automatic loss of capital. Moreover, the sleeping partners possibly consented to the insertion of such one-sided clauses into the agreements because of the many other clauses which were in their favour—*e.g.*, in this instance, Bernardo was not only free from the necessity of taking an active part in the business, but he was also entitled to participate in other outside ventures, a privilege which was strictly forbidden to Giovenco and Giovanni. But even so, the arrangement was clearly very haphazard and clumsy, and it would be interesting to discover how long a period elapsed before the mercantile community evolved a more precise and satisfactory form of partnership contract.

The writer gratefully acknowledges the fact that the information on which this article is based was obtained through the kindness of members of the staff of the Baker Foundation, Harvard University ; in particular, he must thank Miss Florence Edler, Ph.D., the translator of the Selfridge Collection of Medici Documents.

HISTORY FROM OLD ACCOUNTS —JOHN P. CUSHING, MERCHANT AND INVESTOR

HISTORY FROM OLD ACCOUNTS —JOHN P. CUSHING, MERCHANT AND INVESTOR—I

At the present time, much emphasis is being laid upon the need for preserving the more interesting type of business records, in order to provide us with the raw materials for preparing histories both of accounting practice and of general economic development. The following article may accordingly be of interest to our readers. It shows the kind of story that can be gleaned from what at first sight appears to be a very ordinary set of accounts and records, a bundle of ledgers and papers now at Harvard Business School. The general papers were examined by Dr. H. Larson, of the Business History Department of that School, and the accounting material by a Scottish Chartered Accountant, Mr. W. T. Baxter, now Lecturer in Accounting and Business Method at the University of Edinburgh.—ED.

Probably most of us have, at one time or another, wondered how some wealthy and old-established family came by its property. John P. Cushing, an American born near Boston at the end of the eighteenth century, is one of the few self-made men who have left us full details as to how they made their fortunes, and as to what they did with them. His life is interesting for several other reasons. Not only was he an adventurous and picturesque figure, but his career illustrates certain trends in economic development with extraordinary clearness; to follow his story is to obtain a vivid picture of early nineteenth century business and social history.

GENERAL

Up to the middle of the eighteenth century, when the Industrial Revolution began to turn everything topsy-turvy, the outstanding figure in the business world was probably that of the general merchant—the *entrepreneur* who bought and sold not one but many types of goods, and who in addition risked his money in shipping or other kinds of commercial adventures. The Industrial Revolution has to a great extent swept away this picturesque person, and replaced him by a less versatile type. The business man of the next century was a specialist who concentrated exclusively on the manufacture or distribution of one small class of articles; not only so, but very often this specialist provided managerial ability alone, and looked to a new class of investors for all the capital that he might need.

John Perkins Cushing was a man who contrived to play a part in both the first and the second forms of business. He started on an office stool and rapidly became a merchant-prince of the old order, and then, wearying of wharf and market place, washed his hands of business, bought a large garden and some cows, and settled down to comfortable inactivity. But first he entrusted his wealth to another Boston merchant, called William Sturgis, who invested it judiciously in securities of the companies that were just then being formed to run the railroads, canals, banks and factories of the new era. And, as a *rentier*, Cushing was as fortunate as he had been when a sedentary merchant.

However, his career provides an illustration of several other trends besides this transfer of financial supremacy from the active merchant to the idle capitalist. For example, his life neatly epitomises the decay of New England's commerce with the Far East (leaving Old England supreme at last in this long-contested field) and the simultaneous shifting of America's interest from the clipper trade to the opening up of the West. Again, his story is bound up with the early phases of investment banking, and, in addition, he was one of the first Americans to practise the art of "conspicuous consumption."

BUSINESS CAREER OF CUSHING

Cushing entered business, whilst still a mere boy, as a clerk in the counting house of his uncles, James and Thomas Handasyd Perkins. The Perkins firm, established in Boston in the early 1790's, at first engaged in trade between America and Europe, but soon began to trade with the North-west American coast and China, and in 1803 sent a resident agent to Canton. John Cushing, still only 16 years old, accompanied this agent as a clerk. Because of illness, the agent was forced to leave Canton in the autumn of 1805, and so young Cushing unexpectedly found himself in charge of the Canton business. His work proved so satisfactory that in 1806 he was made resident manager, and a partner in Perkins & Co., a commission house established by the Perkinses to handle their rapidly-growing Canton trade.

With remarkable rapidity, Cushing became the most wealthy and highly respected foreign merchant in Canton, and for a time acted as American Consul there. His success was no doubt in large measure due to an infinite care in handling the details of the business. He seems to have stood well with the native merchants, and made friends with men whom he described as remarkable for their wealth, culture and high business ethics.

Except for a brief visit home in 1807, Cushing remained in China until 1828. We do not know exactly why he then left Canton, but a reasonable explanation would be that he had had enough of living in the foreign quarter. The Chinese officials forbade foreigners to bring their wives to Canton, and imposed other restrictions on them which made it impossible to establish homes there. A reflection of his own attitude toward the life of the factories may be seen in Cushing's advice to young Thomas Forbes (a nephew of T. H. Perkins and a cousin of Cushing), that the latter should remain in China no longer than necessary for financial reasons. The immediate cause of Cushing's return to America, however, was probably the fact that he was not well; he spoke in his letters of the unsatisfactory state of his health, which necessitated his seeking a good climate.

Before Cushing left Canton, Perkins & Co. was dissolved, and the aforementioned young Thomas Forbes was left to close the firm's affairs. After returning to Boston, Cushing arranged to withdraw $180,000 from the firm at Canton. He instructed Forbes to invest $80,000 of this in such goods as the latter thought would pay, suggesting $12,600 in teas and the rest in silks and nankeens (cottons), to be consigned to Bryant, Sturgis & Co., of Boston, on Cushing's account. $100,000 was to be lent to Russell & Co. of Canton and Manila, from whom 8 per cent. might be obtained, or to a native merchant-prince called Houqua, if the latter were safe; this should, however, be placed so that it could be withdrawn on three months' notice.

CUSHING'S RETIRAL

When Cushing returned to Boston he was 41 years old. Shortly after, he estimated that his wealth totalled $637,908.40. What should he do with his time and capital? The logical thing would have been to continue in the China trade. This he considered. A reorganisation was about to take place in the Boston Perkins firm, and T. H. Perkins, together with his son-in-law, Samuel Cabot, asked Cushing to join them in forming a new partnership. Cushing was at first willing to do so on condition that he was left free of all work, that the capital was strictly limited to $1,000,000 contributed equally by the three partners, and that the activities of the firm were confined to the China trade. He proposed that the Canton end of the business should be in the hands of a new house, with a working capital of $200,000 furnished by Cushing at 5 per cent. a year; Forbes would manage this branch in return for a quarter share of its profits. Considering how lucrative the China trade then was, this seems to have been a promising plan.

But the longer Cushing stayed in Boston, the less inclined he became to join the Perkins firm, and he finally decided not to enter into any definite partnership agreement. He discovered that his views about the business differed from those of Perkins and Cabot; the latter, he said, was unpopular, and the former too old to take his full share of responsibility. In those circumstances, much would have rested on Cushing, who was tired of "fagging," and wanted to be free to go where the climate best suited him. Moreover, he found that he had the strongest dislike of business as it was done in Boston, which he characterised as "totally different from what I have been accustomed to." He would not "for all the money in the universe" carry on business in Boston's way—it would kill him in a month. In fact, he seems to have felt disgusted with everything pertaining to business.

Cushing planned to continue in the China trade to a certain extent by taking occasional ventures with Perkins & Co., and some old friends, Bryant, Sturgis & Co., Forbes looking after his interests in Canton. He accordingly wrote voluminous letters to Forbes with instructions about what to purchase for him. During 1829 he also joined Perkins and Cabot and Bryant, Sturgis & Co. in sending three ships to China in which he took a quarter share.

CUSHING WITHDRAWS CAPITAL FROM CHINA TRADE

Since he was to a great extent withdrawing from foreign trade, Cushing was now faced with the necessity of finding investments at home. He wrote Houqua that he was planning to put some of his means into public stocks. Shortly after returning to America he had turned a goodly amount over to his friend, William Sturgis, of Bryant, Sturgis & Co., who was instructed to pay his bills and make investments for him, and by 9th January 1829 this company held $50,000 on his behalf. About a year later he wrote to Sturgis: "The 150 th. dolls. ($150,000) which you have invested I wish to remain active and on no account to be employed in any other way, however flattering prospects may be, this I consider as a 'nest egg' and apart from my business concerns."

Who were William Sturgis and his company? William Sturgis had entered a Boston counting house in 1796, at the age of 16, and two years later went to sea on a Perkins boat. He became an able captain, an American-Indian diplomat and a merchant thoroughly familiar with the North-west Coast and China trade. In those years he also struck up a close friendship with Cushing. In 1810 he settled in Boston as an importing and wholesaling merchant, and within a couple of years had acquired a family and shares in four ships and three brigs.

Bryant & Sturgis became one of the greatest American foreign-trade houses. They acquired ships and shares in ships, and leased ships from others or leased their own to others, depending on the state of the trade. They had correspondents in Oriental ports, many European cities, Havana, and the chief American trading centres. Their ships loaded American goods for Europe, exchanged these for European goods, and then went East; or they took goods to the North-west Coast to sell to the Indians, bought hides or furs, and then returned home or went to the Orient. In Asia they got spices, coffee, hemp, or China goods (tea, nankeens, &c.), all of which were in turn distributed in America or Europe. Cushing, as a member of Perkins & Co., had served as one of their Canton agents.

For a decade or more the partners turned most of their profits into the expansion of the business. Though their account books for the middle 'twenties are lacking, we know that this firm, like Perkins & Co., must by then have been making some investments at home. In 1824 William Sturgis was president of the bank which handled his business. The journal of the firm, beginning in August 1828, shows that Bryant & Sturgis were by that time buying stocks in insurance and manufacturing companies to be held jointly for the partners. A very considerable portion of their profits was being invested in this way—a fact possibly accounted for by the breakdown of the North-west Coast trade.

Bryant & Sturgis were by no means doing a general investment business, nor even what one might call a banking business. In the course of their mercantile dealing, they had indeed come to carry accounts with numerous persons, such as their correspondents, captains, captains' wives, and those who shared ventures with them. But, judging from the records, Cushing seems to have been the only person for whom they made extensive investments.

(To be concluded)

A Puzzler

A correspondent writes: "Quite recently I was explaining to one of my young sons that an entry placed on the left hand side of an account was called a 'debit' and that an entry placed on the right hand side was known as a 'credit.' Try to imagine the extent of my amusement when the little chap inquired—'And what would you call an entry placed in the *middle* of the account, daddy?'"

Increase in Telegram Traffic

During the week before August Bank Holiday nearly 1,200,000 inland telegrams were sent. This is a record since the introduction of the sixpenny telegram. It is 6 per cent. higher than in the corresponding week last year and no less than 54 per cent. higher than in the corresponding week of 1934, before the sixpenny telegram was introduced. Of the 1,200,000 telegrams, 380,000 (32 per cent.) were dictated to the Post Office by telephone. Throughout the whole country the traffic was handled without difficulty or delay. The special measures taken during the last six months to cope with the increased traffic have proved entirely successful.

HISTORY FROM OLD ACCOUNTS —JOHN P. CUSHING, MERCHANT AND INVESTOR—II

(*Continued from p.* 256)

The Search for a Wife and Home

It has already been said that Cushing found Boston's business habits distasteful after those of China; he soon discovered additional reasons for not liking America. He thought the climate was bad for his health. He was no more at home socially than he was in business. Try as hard as he could to feel and think like the good people in Boston, he could not get reconciled to " this detestable country " or the people and ways of his home city. The heathens of Canton did not suffer from comparison with his Boston acquaintances, although he had, of course, a few close friends in America, like Sturgis and the Forbes family. He had a mind to marry, but in his two years' stay at home he met only two women who interested him, and one of those, he said, was too young.

He decided to try living in Europe. In the summer of 1829 he crossed to England with the immediate object of making purchases for the " Margaret Forbes " and the " Bashaw," which were being sent to the East by himself, Perkins & Co., and Bryant, Sturgis & Co. These boats were loaded in England with iron, English cloths and opium. While in England, Cushing made some interesting observations on the China trade. It will not do, he said, to ship silks or nankeens to the United States or Europe, as these could be " made cheaper in this country and France than in China, to say nothing about the difference in duty." In the future teas would have to be looked to as a return cargo; when tea exports were not excessive and Canton prices moderate, there was a chance of profit.

The Last Trip to China

In the autumn he sought a better climate on the Continent. It is unlikely that he would have stopped there long—he did not care a " pin " for Europe—but his stay was interrupted by the news of young Forbes' death in Canton, on receiving which Cushing promptly boarded the " Bashaw " for China. He gave various reasons for going. One was to manage the sale of the Canton-bound cargoes and look after his own and the Perkins firm's interests; moreover, he saw the possibility of making " a cool 100 th. ($100,000) by an expedition to France and Holland," arranging with the Barings and Hopes to send out two ships to carry back tea cargoes. To his friend Sturgis he confided his homesickness for Canton, and the fact that he did not care much for " being amongst the good people of this hemisphere " among whom " I feel as much a stranger now as I did when I first reached home."

Before leaving London Cushing made some disposition of his affairs. He asked Sturgis not only to look after the $150,000 Sturgis had already invested for him, but in addition to manage all remittances on account of completed ventures and the liquidated Perkins firm. By this time he had $200,000 in the hands of Sturgis, and planned that the latter should receive $180,000 more from Canton in the ensuing six months, and eventually should be entrusted with the profits of the season's ventures and the remainder of Cushing's interest in the Perkins firm. And altogether by the end of 1831 Sturgis did in fact receive about $800,000 in these ways.

After a voyage of over four months which more than tried Cushing's patience—" of all the troubles of this life deliver me from talking men and women, calms, light and head winds, and a dull ship on a long passage "—he finally landed in Canton late in August 1830. He remained there until March 1831.

During his few months in Canton, Cushing succeeded in selling a portion of the European goods, though for much less than he had expected. He bought a considerable quantity of Chinese goods to be shipped to the United States on his own account. In addition he made arrangements for the purchase of tea cargoes to be sent to Europe, and for the settling of other matters concerning his interests in the East.

Cushing found the Canton market rather unsatisfactory in 1830-31. There was too much competition in the trade, and too many ships were bringing British goods and opium. He believed the export of British goods to Canton should be discontinued except for small amounts of certain things, and recommended that shipments be suspended altogether during the following year. A serious problem was the growing scarcity of specie, which the opium trade was draining out of China. In his letters he emphasised that the only goods worth taking from China to the West were teas—if they could be purchased cheap. Nankeens superior to the Chinese product were made, he said, in Germany and France at little more than half the price. The cargoes he ordered for the " Bashaw " and the " Margaret Forbes," costing $397,930.55, consisted almost exclusively of tea.

Cushing becomes a Country Gentleman

In the summer of 1831 Cushing returned to Boston, bringing many gifts. Not long after his return he married " the very pretty and amiable Louisa Gardiner," a daughter of the rector of Trinity Church in Boston, and settled down to lead the life of a country gentleman. He quit " fagging " to live.

The first step was to acquire a very beautiful estate, named Belmont, a few miles out of town. Here Cushing blossomed forth into an epicure. He had Chinese servants, and filled his home with delicate Eastern furnishings, until its atmosphere became one of Oriental beauty and luxury. His wine cellar must have been superb, judging by the inventories of the wines which he carefully set down in a Miscellaneous Account Book. He acquired a considerable library, and had a standing order with London book-dealers for the latest books and the best periodical publications. A French manufacturer of rolls for a " self-performing organ " (music box) supplied him regularly with classical music and popular works, like Mozart's, and a piano was imported from Europe.

Cushing made much of his gardens, which became known far and wide. He spent a fortune in importing flowers, shrubs and fruit trees from China and Europe. He also imported Chinese hogs, cattle—which gave little milk, but were " beautiful animals "—goats, fowl, geese, &c., peacocks and the best milk cows obtainable in England. Like Mr. Lloyd George, he turned to farming when other interests began to pall. He wrote to a friend, " I have become quite a farmer and find it affords me both occupation and amusement."

Organised Laziness

Cushing's skill in organising his laziness was equal to that with which he had formerly organised his business. Everything connected with his finances was thrust into the hands of Bryant & Sturgis. This firm was not only given complete charge of his capital and income, but also looked after his living expenses. Thanks to the careful accounts that were kept, we can obtain full details as to how Cushing's excess revenue accumulated, and as to the extent of his private outlays. These expenses amounted to about $50,000 per annum.

Cushing took very little active part in business after his return from China; as has been said, he left his affairs more and more in the hands of William Sturgis. The latter's firm continued in the China trade until in the late 'thirties, importing mainly teas. The opium war between Britain and China, 1840-42, put a final stop to this activity, and in 1841 Bryant, Sturgis & Co. was dissolved. Bryant and Sturgis therewith withdrew altogether from trade, but formed a new partnership principally for the investment of their own capital.

William Sturgis had come to be looked upon as one of Boston's soundest capitalists. He was a man of considerable wealth, wide acquaintance with domestic investments, and conservative business principles. From his early years as a Boston merchant we find such statements in his letters: "We do not hold goods on speculation for a rise, but believe in a quick turnover with low profits; we do not trade in the East on credit." He gave advice to railroads in the 'forties which modern accountants might well re-echo to some of their clients. "You ask our opinion as to the expediency of reducing dividends, to conform to diminished receipts. Upon this subject *we have not the shadow of a doubt*. Our rule of action for ourselves, and our advice to others, always is, to *earn* money before dividing it, and to let corporations *get out of debt, and keep out of debt*, so far as the nature of their business will permit." Another bit of advice to a railroad is interesting: "It is often said (and sometimes truly) that the increase of business upon railroads is sufficient to justify an increase of capital to absorb these additional earnings, but it is much better policy to invest the surplus earnings in improvements on the road without resorting to increase of capital for this purpose, and when the increase becomes too great (an event not likely to happen very often) let the rates of transportation be reduced, and thus most effectually stave off competition."

An Early "Investment Trust"

Bryant & Sturgis now became in a very real sense a private investment house, and as such they illustrate one of the main sources of modern American investment banking, a very large proportion of which had its origin in mercantile business. Except for themselves, however, the only persons for whom they acted were Cushing and a few relatives. They invested in loans to railroads and individuals (many in the West) and stocks and to a smaller amount bonds, in insurance companies, banks of New York and Boston, eastern railroads, and New England manufacturing concerns. Their purchases were made directly or through brokers.

By far the largest outside account they handled was that of Cushing, the whole of whose affairs they managed throughout the rest of his life. Cushing, indeed, seems to have avoided money like the plague; Bryant & Sturgis paid his private debts, sent off his subscriptions to charities, managed his investments, and re-invested income as it accumulated. From the records of these transactions it is possible for us to watch the workings of what was practically an early investment trust, and also to see how Cushing's financial stature was greatly added to, despite his lavish spending.

Cushing's Experience as a Capitalist Investor

To show how Cushing's fortune grew, there are given below statements that have been prepared from the accounts kept by Bryant & Sturgis on his behalf. The accounts cover almost all the years of Cushing's life, and so, for the sake of brevity, only one or two sample years are dealt with here. In the statements that follow, an arrangement has been adopted which shows not only the amounts invested in each of the different groups of securities, such as railroads, banks, &c., but also the division as between "fixed-interest" and "fluctuating-interest" securities. Personal loans made up the greater part of the fixed-interest securities, for bonds were not bought till the 1840's, and no preferred stocks were ever held—indeed, such stocks only became usual at a later period.

A.—*Balance Sheet showing Cushing's investments soon after he settled down.*

Balance Sheet, 31st December 1835

Assets

	Fixed Interest Securities $	Stocks and Real Estate $	Total $
Bills and Personal Loans— Cash in the hands of Bryant, Sturgis & Co.:			
In the United States	310,272.58		
In London, England	8,604.24		
	318,876.82		
Bills of Exchange ..	167,636.10		
	486,512.92		486,512.92
Securities—			
Banks		41,003.41	
Manufacturing.. ..		149,204.42	
Railroads and Canals ..		33,712.50	
Insurance		36,990.10	
		260,910.43	260,910.43
Real Estate		37,734.77	37,734.77
Shipping*..		153,496.46	153,496.46
	$486,512.92	$452,141.66	$938,654.58

Liabilities

	$
Capital	755,606.80
Profits accumulated to date	183,047.78
Total Value of Cushing's Assets	$938,654.58

*This is a net figure, representing the amount invested in ships and opium, less some profits not yet carried to profit and loss.

B.—*Annual Accounts for* 1851, *showing the position after* 16 *years.*

Balance Sheet, 31st December 1851

Assets

	Fixed Interest Securities $	Stocks and Real Estate $	Total $
Bills and Personal Loans— Amounts due by Bryant, Sturgis & Co.	8,372.81		
Bills of Exchange	326,550.00		
	$334,922.81		334,922.81

	$	$	$
Securities—			
Banks		149,701.86	
Manufacturing ..		427,169.63	
Railroads and Canals	30,684.92	392,023.17	
Insurance ..		58,608.42	
Government Bonds	24,920.00		
	$55,604.92	$1,027,503.08	1,083,108.00
Real Estate ..		156,899.53	156,899.53
	$390,527.73	$1,184,402.61	$1,574,930.34

Liabilities

	$	$	$
Original Capital— Balance as in 1835			938,654.58
Profits—			
Net gains from shipping as at 31st Dec. 1837		65,680.38	
Interest and Dividends up till 31st Dec. 1850 ..	1,263,241.80		
Additions during year 1851 ..	97,515.80	1,360,757.60	
		1,426,437.98	
Less Net Loss on Assets sold—			
Up till 31st Dec. 1850 ..	6,003.68		
Losses 1851 ..	24,375.00	30,378.68	
		1,396,059.30	
Less Private Drawings—			
Up till 31st Dec. 1850 ..	719,547.78		
Additions during year ..	40,235.76	759,783.54	
			636,275.76
			$1,574,930.34

A sample statement as to the income and expenditure of this early "investment trust" may be of interest:

C.—Profit and Loss Statement, 1851

	$	$	$
Expenses, Postage and Commission ..			2,537.08
Net Revenue			97,515.80
			$100,052.88

Revenue—	Bonds	Stocks	Total
Bills of Exchange ..	21,454.25		21,454.25
Investments—			
Banks		11,847.00	
Mfg. Securities ..		15,336.75	
Railroads & Canals	1,820.00	32,364.08	
Insurance ..		8,020.00	
Government Bonds	*		
	1,820.00	67,567.83	69,387.83
Real Estate		9,210.80	9,210.80
	$23,274.25	$76,778.63	$100,052.88

*Arrears paid in 1852.

The figure for the value of the investments in the balance sheets above shows book values, i.e. cost less a certain amount of depreciation written off. A truer view of the progress is obtained when current market values, so far as they are ascertainable, are substituted. The following statement shows these figures for 1851 and for 1858. It should be remembered that the year 1857 experienced a severe panic.

D.—Statement showing Securities at Current Market Values

	1851		1858	
	Book Value	Market Value	Book Value	Market Value
	$	$	$	$
Fixed Interest	382,154.92	382,154.92	791,975.93	766,935.00
Fluctuating Interest	1,027,503.08	958,035.52	1,218,401.12	987,078.00
Grand Total	1,409,658.00	1,340,190.44	2,010,377.05	1,754,013.00

It will be observed from the above that the market value of the holdings, when compared with their book values at the same date, showed some depreciation, despite their non-speculative nature. When Bryant & Sturgis bought a security, they almost always held it for a long period; apparently they did not aim at capital profits, and the few sales they made resulted in a loss. In this way, most of the original investments of 1835 were still held at Cushing's death. The majority of the undertakings in which Cushing invested were located in the East of America (although it is believed that many of the private persons to whom loans were made lived in the newly-opened Western districts). He staked his wealth upon the then unknown potentialities of New England, and when that region developed into an important manufacturing centre, he found himself the recipient of an enormous unearned increment.

Interest Yields in the Early Nineteenth Century

It may be of interest to show the percentage yields of the different classes of securities. For the period 1836-1851, these were approximately as follows:—

Fixed Interest—	
Bills of Exchange	5.6
Government Bonds ..	6.3
Railroad Bonds	6.0
Fluctuating Interest—	
Bank Stocks	6.6
Manufacturing Stocks ..	8.1
Railroad and Canal Stocks	8.5
Insurance Stocks	12.1
Real Estate (net rents) ..	5.9

Incidentally, very little was known on this subject until the Cushing papers were investigated.

Cushing's Death

When Cushing died (in 1862), the inventory to his will showed that, despite his epicurean mode of life, his wealth had tripled during his retirement. The actual figures were as follows:—

Assets as at 1862

	Fixed Interest Securities $	Stocks and Real Estate $	Total $
Notes and Personal Loans	669,213.32		669,213.32
Securities—			
Banks		204,260.00	
Manufacturing ..		305,210.00	
Railroads and Canals	343,785.00	423,831.00	
Insurance		67,520.00	
Government Bonds	109,522.00		
	453,307.00	1,000,821.00	1,454,128.00

Real Estate		$176,600.00	$176,600.00
	$1,122,520.32	1,177,421.00	2,229,941.32
Note.—In addition, Cushing owned			
Private Estates, &c., valued at ..		109,000.00	
Furniture, &c.		27,000.00	
			136,000.00
Grand Total			$2,435,941.32

In terms of hard cash, Cushing's life had been satisfactory. Had it been a success where things more subtle than accounts were concerned ? Probably not. He remained an unobtrusive and retiring figure till the end, regarding himself as a misfit in Western society, and finding what consolation he could among his books and cows.

A NOTE ON THE ALLOCATION OF ONCOSTS BETWEEN DEPARTMENTS

A NOTE ON THE ALLOCATION OF ONCOSTS BETWEEN DEPARTMENTS

by W. T. Baxter
(Professor of Accounting, University of Cape Town)

THE PROBLEM

When departmentalised accounts are being prepared, there are two ways of treating the "oncosts" of running the whole business. Such overhead expenses may either be split up between the departments, in accordance with any basis that seems good to the officials concerned (e.g. rent in proportion to floor space, &c.); or they may simply be deducted in total from the combined profits of the different departments. Which of these two systems should be preferred?

Some of the considerations that will lead to a correct decision are probably well understood by many experienced accountants, but textbooks are usually vague on the point, and the present writer has recently come across at least one case in which important questions of policy were settled by directors who were obviously being misled by faulty departmental accounts. Accordingly, some attempt to set out and illustrate the principles at stake seems worth while, particularly when the matter affects not only ordinary profit and loss accounts, &c., but also costing methods that are based on these accounts.

THE RELEVANT THEORY

A clue as to the type of reasoning to be adopted is provided in recent articles by Mr. R. S. Edwards (e.g. "The Rationale of Cost Accounting," published in "Some Modern Business Problems," Longmans: London, 1937), which have called attention to certain dangers that are inherent in the arbitrary allocation of "overhead" expenses. Mr. Edwards has concentrated chiefly upon cost accounts, but his arguments probably apply with equal if not greater force to simple departmental accounts.

The gist of Mr. Edward's contention is that the cost accountant's allocation on oncosts is apt to be unhelpful and misleading. Any operation is worth carrying out so long as it yields a surplus over its prime costs; for, whether or not an allocated proportion of the "fixed overheads" is covered, the enterprise in question is richer as a result of undertaking such an operation. Accordingly, there is little point in allocating overheads in the manner recommended by the normal textbook on cost accounting.

It should be noted that the expression 'prime costs" is in the preceding paragraph used in a broader sense than that usually given to it by accountants, and means all the costs which would be avoided if the operation were not carried out; part of the so-called "fluctuating oncost" is therefore included. Also, an assumption is of course made that the business could not follow any more profitable policy, e.g. by doing other kinds of work, or even by closing down all or part of its permanent assets.

A fuller summary of these contentions, with some critical comments, appeared in *The Accountant* of 23rd October 1937.

USES OF DEPARTMENTAL ACCOUNTS

When departmental accounts are concerned, it would seem to follow from Mr. Edwards' contentions, that expenses incurred for the benefit of the business as a whole should not be split up between the departments. The reasons for preparing departmenta statements are presumably as follows:—

(1) *To find out whether each department is sufficiently profitable to justify its continuance.*

Where this is the aim, no allocation should be made of those overhead expenses which are fixed and which would therefore remain undiminished even if a department were abandoned. (Logically, only items of expense which satisfy this condition should be called "overheads" or "oncosts"; but in everyday speech the terms are used more generally). If such expenses are allocated, the directors or owners may be given an unreasonably bad opinion of the departments that are not earning large profits. These departments will appear to be running at a loss; yet, if they are given up, the overhead expenses will not be substantially reduced, and so the combined profits of the whole business will sink.

(2) *To find out whether the heads of the individual departments are avoiding unnecessary expense.*

Where this is the aim, there is no point in splitting up general expenses over which the departmental heads have no control.

(3) (*In some cases*) *to find out suitable selling prices for the individual articles in which the department deals.* Thus, the selling price might be fixed at:—

(*a*) The "direct" cost of making or buying each article;
(*b*) An allocated proportion of the expenses of the particular department;
(*c*) An allocated proportion of the general expenses of the whole business; and
(*d*) a margin for profit.

Sometimes additional steps are introduced, as when the expenses of a department, plus part of the expenses of the whole business, are split up over different processes within the department.

The objections raised above to a simple allocation

between departments apply with all the greater force to more complicated procedures. We may sympathise heartily with the business man who wants some easy way of fixing on a suitable selling price for his goods, but we are not helping him very much if we give him a cost figure that is the result of an elaborate averaging process, the implications of which he probably does not fully understand. In strict logic, he is no further forward when his cost accountant tells him that the "cost" (including averaged overheads) of an article is 4½d. than he would be if a statistician, fresh from population tables, were to inform him that he had 2.843 children in his family.

We are here face to face with a problem somewhat similar to that of joint products. When a butcher has bought the carcass of a cow, can he separate the cost of the steak from the cost of the kidney? He could only do so if he were able to allocate the total purchase price between the different parts of the animal. But on what basis could he do this? In proportion to weight? Or in proportion to sale price? Or in proportion to calorific value? Or in proportion to vitamin content? Clearly, he would land himself in an absurd position if he tried any of these systems. In practice, he very sensibly does not attempt to find the costs of the separate organs, but is content when the total sale money exceeds what he paid for the whole carcass. He will at best experiment with different scales of charges, varying the price for each class of meat until he finds out how to secure the maximum total return.

Similarly, in a complex business there is not necessarily any connection between the overhead expenses and the expenses of one product or one department. The sale price of each line of goods should be fixed so as to maximise profit, and not with reference to an averaged cost figure. True, the business will never go bankrupt so long as all its products or departments cover their averaged costs; but it might make much bigger total profits by decreasing some prices and increasing others. The manager must ask, not whether the sale price of an article exceeds its average cost, but whether the business is making more profit by selling that article at that price than it could by adopting any other policy. After all, a "cost" which can be varied enormously by altering the method of calculation (e.g. by allocating rent in proportion to cubic space instead of area) cannot be regarded as especially sacrosanct.

The Defence of Allocation

Despite the apparent strength of the foregoing arguments against the practice of allocating overhead expenses, the fact remains that it is very common, not only where departmental accounts are concerned, but also in most kinds of cost accounts (e.g. it is met with in a highly developed form in job costs, in guises such as the "machine-hour rate"). We should therefore expect to find that, if the logic of the practice were shaky, many businesses would have noticed bad results, and vigorous criticisms would have followed. But the reverse is the case. There has been no public outcry; on the contrary, many of the most successful and profitable enterprises rely on costing methods that involve allocation, and attribute their prosperity at least in part to such systems. This fact is a telling argument against the theory which has been developed above, and is not to be set aside lightly; the proof of the pudding is in the eating. The British constitution can be made to look silly on paper, but nevertheless works quite well (presumably because deep down it has merits which escape the superficial theorist's notice, and which more than compensate for all its obvious shortcomings). Is cost accounting in the same position? Clearly, we must hunt for explanations of the seeming contradiction.

The Counter-Argument

It might, of course, be maintained that costing is still a young science, and that business men have not yet had sufficient experience of it to see its weaknesses. This line of argument is, however, not very convincing. A more reasonable way in which to approach the problem is to consider whether the processes of costing and of analysing expenses by departments do not bestow benefits big enough to counterbalance defects in the methods employed. The most important points to emerge when we adopt this approach seem to be as follows:

(1) *Costing involves certain non-controversial advantages.*

The criticisms that are levelled against costing apply only to parts of the systems. Nobody in his senses would deny the value of many of the functions performed by cost accountants. The advantages of, say, store and wages control are so well known as to require no underlining. Similarly, calculations as to prime costs, and as to the changes in expense that would follow increases or decreases of output, may be most useful guides to business policy.

(2) *Elaborate accounts may necessitate general efficiency.*

Before departmental accounts can be prepared, or a costing system can be set up, a thorough examination of the whole structure of the enterprise in question must usually be made. What is more, elaborate accounting methods will often not run smoothly until the various activities of the business have been reduced to some sort of economical routine. The extent of this reorganisation must frequently be considerable, and it may well result in substantial savings.

The present writer was recently shown over a works in which not only were the oncosts departmentalised, but they were further split between different processes and then between different sizes of product. The accountant who had planned this costing system was himself dissatisfied with it, since he had been instructed by the proprietors to "load" the overheads with what seemed an unreasonably large provision for possible maintenance expenditure. Yet the enterprise was unquestionably far more profitable than it had been before cost accounts were kept. The story of the change was illuminating. The accountant was a man with a thorough technical knowledge of the particular industry, and he had been given a free hand to reorganise the whole works. Before he could get departmentalised accounts, he had had to change the production methods root and branch. "Setting up a costing system" here involved, among other things, the buying of coal with a higher calorific value, the smoothing of floors to prevent breakages, the remedying of staff grievances concerning salaries, the inspection of work-in-progress at each stage, the hiring of a watchman to keep up the furnace temperatures at night, and so on. A marked increase in general efficiency followed these reforms, e.g. the amount of spoilt work sank from nearly 50 per cent. to under 10 per cent. of the total output. The cost records probably helped to improve matters; but even if the new accounting system had been thoroughly misleading, the business could scarcely have done other than benefit on balance from the changes.

It is sometimes suggested that the introduction of expensive office machinery is worth while, not because the machines themselves justify their cost, but because they cannot be used until the whole office procedure has been surveyed and planned afresh (often by an outside person who has plenty of time for his task, and who is free from the petty jealousies that may exist among the permanent members of an office staff). Could not the same suggestion apply to some accounting methods?

Arguments (1) and (2) above probably go a long way to explain why an accounting system may be illogical and yet prove useful to a business. Still another consideration is, however, available:

(3) *Allocated oncosts may correspond to "opportunity costs."*

One of the biggest "costs" of performing any operation involves no bookkeeping entries, and so is apt to be overlooked. It is the loss that results from some other work not being done instead. In a barber's shop, for instance, the cost of cutting one customer's hair may seem negligible, since the assistants are probably paid a fixed sum per week; but, if other customers walk out rather than wait for the chair to become empty, the real cost is clearly the lost sale money (which may be more than the revenue actually earned, as when the barber loses the chance of doing a two guinea permanent wave because he is busy on a half-crown "cut-and-trim"). Similarly, if a section of a department store were not being used for umbrellas, it could be used for bicycles or garden tools. This kind of sacrifice is sometimes called an "opportunity cost," presumably because it is the cost of a lost opportunity. True estimates as to the expense of running a department or of doing a job ought clearly to include something for this factor, even though accurate estimates may be impossible. (Incidentally, costing on such lines, if practicable under any circumstances, would be out of the question where the cost accounts were "tied in" with the financial books.) When overhead expenses are allocated between departments or jobs in what seems a defiance of logic, may the resultant charge not in some cases correspond closely to the neglected burden of opportunity costs? Thus, while the general manager's salary might not be reduced if department Z. were given up, he would then have more free time to improve the working of the other departments, or to start a fresh department; and the profits from his new activities might roughly equal the part of his salary that is allocated to Z. If this were the case, we should have an interesting example of compensating errors; the error of omission (the leaving out of opportunity costs) would neutralise the error of commission (the putting in of overheads). Needless to say, however, accountants ought not to rely on this possibility, but should try to estimate the opportunity costs when working out the possible results of changes in policy.

Conclusions

We may perhaps summarise matters as follows:—

Where costing calculations are concerned.—There seems to be good grounds for concentrating on prime costs and for ignoring the overheads when calculations as to the cost of any job, &c., are under consideration. But the expression "prime costs" must be given the very broad interpretation already indicated, and so made to cover far more than the conventional textbook definition of "material, labour, and direct charges," e.g. an allowance for opportunity cost must be included. (It would be extremely interesting to know how the resultant figures would compare, over a wide range of enterprises, with the figures now being worked out by the accepted methods. The writer would be grateful for any views on this matter.) The extent to which the selling price should exceed the prime cost so found would be a matter of selling policy; the amount of competition, and the customer's ability to pay, would be the usual guides. These guides may seem disappointingly vague and woolly beside the crisp "total cost" figures that averaging can produce; but in business, after all, there must often be a large element of chance and risk-taking, and we are perhaps in a better position if we admit this fact than if we take refuge in an illusory appearance of certainty.

Where departmental accounts are concerned.—The wisest course is probably to say that departmental accounts should normally show only expenses (and income) that can be traced simply and directly to the various departments. If any items require to be allocated according to some theoretical basis (e. g. in proportion to sales, or area), there are strong prima facie grounds for *not* departmentalising them. The acid test is usually this: Will the business be able to avoid the particular outlay if the department that is debited is closed down? Sometimes, of course, border line cases will present themselves (e.g. delivery van expenses may be of a "semi-fixed" nature, and would sink to some extent if a department were given up); in such cases, the best plan is probably not to allocate under normal circumstances, but, whenever changes in policy are being considered, to prepare special budgets, which need not be tied up to the ordinary accounts, and which would show the estimated saving from closing a department.

A numerical example may illustrate the matter. For the sake of simplicity, all the figures have been kept smaller than those which would be used in practice.

Illustrative Problem

The Departmental Store Co., Ltd., owns a retail shop with three departments, A, B, and C. Its cashier has prepared the annual accounts as follows:—

	Department A	Department B	Department C	Total
	£	£	£	£
1. Cost of materials	2,620	2,330	1,050	6,000
2. Wages of assistants	640	400	220	1,260
3. Miscellaneous expenses	220	170	70	460
4. Rent	240	140	170	550
5. General management salaries and expenses	450	300	150	900
Total expenses	4,170	3,340	1,660	9,170
Net profit	630*	140*	60	430
Sales	£4,800	£3,200	£1,600	£9,600

* Losses.

Notes:—

(*a*) Items 1, 2, and 3, consist entirely of expenses that can be traced directly to the various departments.

(*b*) The total rent is allocated in proportion to the space occupied by each department.

(*c*) The office salaries are allocated in proportion to the sales of each department. The item includes the manager's salary of £500, directors' fees of £100, and cashier's salary of £250.

In view of the results shown above, the directors are inclined to discontinue departments B and C, particularly as they believe that the space occupied by these departments could be sub-let to two other companies at rents of £125 and £300 respectively, without any bad results on department A.

What advice ought an accountant to give to the directors?

Suggested Solution

The way in which the accounts are drafted is misleading, since the allocation of items 4 and 5 has been carried out on an entirely artificial basis, and, if a department were closed down, the outlays would not fall to the extent of that department's "total expenses" figure shown above; probably items 4 and 5 would hardly sink at all if departments B and C were abandoned.

The correct manner in which to draft the accounts is therefore:—

Redrafted Profit and Loss Statement

	Department A	Department B	Department C	Total
	£	£	£	£
Materials	2,620	2,330	1,050	6,000
Wages	640	400	220	1,260
Expenses	220	170	70	460
	3,480	2,900	1,340	7,720
Sales	4,800	3,200	1,600	9,600
Surplus yielded by each dept.	1,320	300	260	1,880
Deduct—Expenses applicable to business as a whole—				
Rent			550	
Management			900	
				1,450
Net profit				£430

We see from this revised statement that all the departments are in fact yielding some surplus, and that accordingly the company would (if no more profitable alternative use were available for the vacant space) be the poorer as a result of discontinuing either B or C. To find out whether B and C should be given up, we must consider, not the figures shown in the original accounts, but a comparison of the true surplus with the alternative revenue from sub-letting, i.e., we must depend on budgets, not on historical accounts:—

Comparison of Actual with Possible Revenue

	Department B	Department C
	£	£
Surplus at present, per redrafted profit and loss account	300	260
Alternative revenue (rents from sub-letting)	125	300
Gain by discontinuing		£40
Loss by ditto	£175	

The company's best policy is therefore to give up C but to keep B. This change will increase the net earnings by £40, thus:—

Estimated Revenue after Discontinuance of C.

	£
Surplus or rent:	
A, surplus per redrafted profit and loss account	1,320
B, ditto ditto	300
C, rent	300
	1,920
Less Fixed expenses, as before	1,450
Estimated net profit after change	470
Present net profit	430
Gain by change	£40

The Crisis

A French contemporary, *Le Chef de Comptabilite*, produces the following topical conversation between a little girl and her accountant papa:

" Conversation entre une petite fille et son papa (C.C.C.):

— Dis, papa, ce n'est pas possible qu'il y ait la guerre?

— Mais non, tout cela s'arrangera. . .

— Tu en es bien sûr?

— Mais oui.

— Tant mieux, parce que 'ça en ferait encore une de plus à apprendre' . . .

Evidemment. M. Chamberlain n'avait pas pen séàc et argument. . ."

CREDIT, BILLS, AND BOOKKEEPING IN A SIMPLE ECONOMY

For instance, credit may be allowed to a debtor who promises to pay later with one-third money and two-thirds goods (which are always valued and recorded in terms of money).

THE DEVELOPMENT OF CREDIT TRANSFERS

Crude barter has two glaring defects: (1) if A and B are to exchange goods, their wants must be simultaneous; and (2) each must want what the other has.

Bookkeeping and credit enabled the New Englanders to surmount the first defect. To some extent, they contrived to overcome the second also. This was done by *triangular* barter. A sells goods to B; if B does not have what A wants, but is owed a debt by C, he may send A to look for acceptable things in C's store; a purchase there will mean that C has paid B, and B has paid A, although the goods in fact move only across the base of this triangle of traders. Such three-sided settlements were common as witness waste-book entries such as the following, in which Hancock fills the rôle of B:

Brown and Son Dr to Joseph Rhodes
for 15 boxes Tin plates

Were similar transfers made in the Middle Ages? Common sense suggests that the New Englanders probably inherited their technique of settlement from an earlier generation. And we know at least that transfers of goods took place when the goods had been deposited in a warehouse. Before the Christian era, the Egyptians could transfer rights to grain stored in granaries (with the help of a document corresponding to a cheque);[13] and transfers of hemp were made in the government rope factory of Venice in the fifteenth century.[14] Here are exact analogies to certain warehouse dealings that are mentioned in the Hancock MSS. For instance, Hancock had to hand over gunpowder for safekeeping to the official powder house; his account with this institution shows that he would then give orders to third persons entitling them to withdraw barrels. Much the same sort of thing happened when he had sent molasses to a distillery to be made into rum.

But if C is a warehouseman or a similar agent, perhaps we should be wary about speaking of triangular settlement. C is not here a fully fledged third party, but merely B in thin disguise. The goods still belong to B; thus Hancock did not always keep a money account with C (the powder house) but merely a stores account in terms of barrels. Happily for our theory, however, such warehouse transactions make up only one in a hundred of his triangular settlements. C was far more often an independent trader.

EARLY BILLS OF EXCHANGE

Should it prove that triangular settlements in kind were common in the Middle Ages, they may well explain the birth and popularization of double entry. What is more, they may perhaps throw light on the origins of bills of exchange.

Medieval scholars have shown us that recognizable ancestors of our bills had appeared by the fourteenth century. The very first evidence, we are told, consists of references to "letters of payment" in correspondence (dated 1291) from a Florentine company to its branch or agent in London. The bulk of the early evidence suggests that bills were used chiefly in foreign exchange; that they were somewhat complex in nature, often involving four parties; and that they became usual

[13] W. L. Westermann, "Warehousing and Trapezite Banking in Antiquity," in *Journal of Economic and Business History*, 1931, p. 49; A. T. Olmstead, "Materials for Economic History of Ancient Near East," *ibid.*, 1930, p. 224.

[14] F. C. Lane, "Rope Factory and Hemp Trade of Venice," in the same *Journal*, 1932, p. 836.

in home trade only at a much later date (in England, the seventeenth century).[15] In the Hancocks' own times, Acts of Parliament and Lord Mansfield's judgments were still reducing the law governing bills to order.[16]

This history does not seem altogether complete or convincing. It can say little with assurance about the *birth* of bills. It cannot yet be supported with any of the actual documents, which naturally are extremely scarce; and, as resounding legal deeds and important foreign letters are far more likely to be preserved than homely trade papers, there must surely be some risk of giving too much weight to the former types of evidence. One is left wondering whether the bill's origins should not be sought in something more simple and informal than letters to a foreign agent, and whether these early foreign bills had not some domestic parallel. On the face of the matter, evolution from foreign exchange to local payment, from the elaborate to the easy, does not appear likely. To my mind, the Hancocks' triangular transactions (especially those in goods), and the papers by which such transfers were engineered, suggest that our history of bills is one-sided. And it must be remembered that the Hancocks' legacy of MSS includes many papers of a type so informal that they would normally have been destroyed.

Yet I scarcely need to emphasize that what follows is intended as nothing more than a tentative line of research for the medieval scholar. It would indeed be absurd if, in an article that starts by taking to task theorists who prefer doctrines of evolution to facts, I were to make the same blunder. In the field of biology, "evolution" is merely growth, not necessarily from inefficient to efficient, or from simple to complex; sometimes the growth may seem degeneration to us. The same may well hold of human institutions like exchange. At the beginning of the Middle Ages, the written, as contrasted with the verbal, contract was looked on with suspicion; so the first bills may well have been hedged around with formalities. Further, the medievalist can counter my suggestions by reminding me that the New Englanders had the very advanced English practices of the seventeenth century to build on; that foreign exchange loomed unnaturally large in the minds of the early merchants, because it was often a useful cloak for usury; and that the medieval merchant was at many points held back by conservatively minded jurists, whereas the new Colonies were relatively unhampered by legal aid. Let me describe the Hancock papers, and leave the reader to judge for himself.

The simplest group of "orders" to reach the Hancocks was part of their two-way flow of goods. A wants wares from B; instead of going for them himself, he sends a servant or agent. This was very usual in the case of a country customer, who would write to Hancock for goods, and add that these should be given to some carrier or to the captain of a coasting boat for delivery. Such transactions are no more than mail orders at a time when there was no parcel post. The Hancock MSS contain many examples; a slight variant, which I found on the other side of the Atlantic, may be seen in:

January the 25th 1763.

Loving Child,

please at your conveniency to allow to the poor wydow Bearer hereof and her Orphans one Bole of the Moulter of your Mill of Benbeculla, which Shall be Sustained at accounting with

[15] Usher, *op. cit.*, p. 73 *et seq.;* R. de Roover, "Early Accounting Problems of Foreign Exchange," ACCOUNTING REVIEW, 1944, p. 381; W. S. Holdsworth, *History of English Law*, VIII (London, 1923), p. 113.

[16] R. D. Richards, *Early History of Banking* (London, 1924), pp. 46–9; C. H. S. Fifoot, *Lord Mansfield* (Oxford, 1936), p. 91.

Dear Sir
Your affectionate father
Ronald McDonald Clanronald Senior[17]

Often the third person was a partner, since a great deal of trade consisted of joint-adventures by casual and short-lived partnerships.

The next group of orders was part of the triangular trade. Here the third person is no mere agent. When A asks B for goods, B gives him a written order on C. C then makes an entry such as:

T. Atkins Dr to Merchandize
for his note paid John More in Pork and Flour 4. 12. 3.

B's entry will be like this:[18]

Andrew Symmes Dr to Capt John Matchett
for my order on him for 6 Bushells of Indian corn at 3/- —18.—

An example of the note is:

Boston Decr 30 1769

John Hancock Esqr

Sir please to pay Mr. Joseph Moffat or order in goods One pound thirteen Shillings and 3d Lawful Money and charge your humble serv^t.

Thos Dawes

£1. 13. 3

A suitable receipt is often written on the back.

Great numbers of such notes have been bequeathed to us among the Hancock MSS. These survivors include forty-four from a single customer, for a period of only four months. Though there were many individual vagaries, most of the notes tend to use much the same word formula, and even to be on paper of a standard size and shape, resembling our cheques. These facts, and the use of phrases such as "on demand" and "or order," emphasize the likeness of the notes to bills of exchange. And perhaps it is worth recording that the "bank" and provincial monetary notes, on the other hand, leaned towards the bills payable in kind, for their wording mentioned a *weight* of metal.[19]

Another, perhaps smaller, group of papers consists of bills payable in money. A lot of these, particularly the more formal documents, were for foreign trade, thus supporting the views of the writers mentioned above. On the other hand, many of the papers used at home were the same in effect as bills, although the informality with which they were sometimes drafted may disguise this fact. For instance, an order to pay one-third goods and two-thirds money would not now be classed as a bill by a lawyer, yet the results are the same.

EVERY MERCHANT A BANKER

The essence of our triangular settlements among A, B, and C is that C gives something of value to A on behalf of B. That something, as we have seen, was usually goods; it would have been idle to draw on C for cash if cash was not to be had. In the typical triangular settlement of to-day, C has blossomed into a banker, and the something is usually a credit in his books that is transferred from B's account to A's; settlement is made by the magic of a cross-entry. The question naturally arises: could the New Englanders also make settlements aithout moving goods or cash.

[17] Clanronald MSS, Register House, Edinburgh.

[18] A doubtful example is:
Expence Dr to Joseph Scott
for my note payable to Wm Warllan.
This may either be "two-way"—i.e., Warllan is an agent, or Warllan has rendered some service and is rewarded with the note, without any account being opened for him.

[19] Davis, *op. cit.*, p. 158, reproduces a note: "This bill of twenty shillings, due to the possessor thereof, from the province of Massachusetts Bay, shall be equal to three ounces of coined silver, Troy weight, of sterling alloy, or gold coin, at the rate of four pounds eighteen shillings per ounce and shall be so accepted in all payments, and in the treasury. Boston 1741."

The answer is that they could and did. This is proved by their odd use of the word "discount." Discount's original meaning was "abatement" or "deduction," e.g., by way of a counter-claim against a sum due. (Discount on a bill was one special type of abatement: "interest discounted.") Instead of taking goods from C, A might build up a credit with him (or lower an existing liability). So a variant to the notes runs:

> Pay into (or Discount with)
> Mr. James Dennie, or Order,
> Twenty Pounds.

Such "checks" might be endorsed and circulate from hand to hand.[20] I am not sure whether any "usance" was normal; probably, as in the above example, the drawer did not bother to specify when the payment or cross-entry was to be made. My impression is that a month here or there meant nothing in that easy-going society. Nobody seems to have fussed about "discount" in our sense. Perhaps the exchange rates tendered for foreign bills took the time factor into account, though the risk factor loomed a great deal larger in the mind of the buyer, who was willing to pay substantially more for bills drawn by merchants with first-class reputations.

Like the orders payable in kind, the notes may well have had their genesis in very simple requests, with the third person acting merely as agent or messenger. One possibility is shown by this letter:

> Boston Jan[y] 10, 1769.
>
> Sir,
>
> Please to pay my Wife Mary Anderson Five doll[s] per Month on Acco[t] Wages due to me on board the Schooner Lucy & charge the same to
>
> Your humble Serv[t]
> Charles Anderson.

That the orders were widely understood is suggested by entries in Henchman's ledger for two carpenters, one his debtor and the other his creditor; he puts through "discount" entries to set off their balances. On occasion, a verbal order might be a good enough authority for such a cross-entry. Apparently anyone who kept a ledger might be called on to transfer credit; every bookkeeper thus performed one of the banker's functions, and clearance was not yet centralized.

Most merchants of standing probably performed several other of the banker's functions. In telling the story of the Hancocks, I have explained that any large firm of repute would naturally be called on to deal in bills, to finance military campaigns, to take charge of other people's funds, and to invest these in securities such as provincial loans or lottery tickets.[21] But much less important men also carried out many of the banker's tasks for their customers. Because there were no specialized bankers and little cash, trade and finance were perforce tightly intertwined. Henchman was mainly a bookseller, but an account for one of his country correspondents tells this tale. In four months, the correspondent makes eleven deposits (eight in the form of cash delivered by captains, or others, and three by notes). On the other side are shown a series of payments at the correspondent's order (e.g., for pasturing a horse); finally about £500 of cash is withdrawn, together with £950 made up of a wedge of gold and 25 double doubloons.

INTERNATIONAL CREDIT AND EXCHANGE

Importing provides another instance of the union between trade and banking. The

---

[20] Henchman's journal contains:
9 Sept 1732 Ebenezer Gennings Cr
By a note to disc[t] with Mr. Beecham from Apthorp £20
David Mason Dr
To Mr. Apthorp's Note to pay Beecham endorsed to me for £20

[21] *The House of Hancock* (Boston, 1945), p. 204.

main financial burden of Anglo-American trade was shouldered by British exporting houses, which might give the Boston importer a year's credit, free of interest, and extend the loan for a further period at 5 per cent. The Boston merchant distributed the goods to country shopkeepers and chapmen, noting in his journal "to pay in 4 [or 8, or 12] months." If the customer's account was not squared after a long time, the balance might be converted into a bond carrying 6 per cent interest. When the account was next reviewed, this bond might be replaced by a fresh one (including compound interest).[22] Like most other commercial documents, the bonds were informal. They might contain a clause stating that the debt was to be doubled if not paid when due. Probably they were not normally mortgages over land, etc., though on occasion even a share in a ship was conveyed as security; in some instances, a church pew was mortgaged.[23]

It will be seen that the Boston merchant was doing much work that has since been delegated to bankers, shippers, and other agents. He was the central link in a chain of credit that stretched from London to the frontier. A loan seems a great favor before we have obtained it; after, we are apt to regard it as an injury. The heavy load of debt of merchants to Britain was probably a major cause of the Revolution.

An account-current between a Boston merchant and his London creditor would provide an object lesson to those who believe in tariffs or exclusive trade agreements between two countries. It shows us the stark realities of international trade, unobscured by money or bankers. The British exporter had to be an importer too, or go without payment. As in home dealings, the basis of trade was bookkeeping barter, often with triangular or more complex geometrical embellishments. If the Boston merchant had nothing that his London suppliers wanted, he would send provisions to Newfoundland, the West Indies, or Europe, and after one or more exchanges would get goods (or coins, or bills) that were acceptable in London.

Bookkeeping barter was by no means the only feature that was common to both local and international trade. Indeed, the New Englanders could probably see little distinction between the two trades. Foreign coins were everyday fare in Boston, and dealings with the next-door province involved currency exchange. Country trade must have shaded smoothly into interprovincial, interregional, and international trade.

As we have seen, country customers were forced by bad communications to appoint a Boston supplier as their general agent and banker. In overseas dealings, this dependence was the more complete; even the British government had to rely abjectly on Hancock for many supplies of credit, coin, and victuals, and for innumerable small services. Foreign exchange was not confined to specialists. Anybody might dabble in it; illiterate fishermen on the Newfoundland Banks provided Boston with many sterling instruments drawn on their Devonshire homeland. A merchant was always willing to deal in sterling bills on Boston 'Change, in general as a buyer,

---

[22] Thus on 22 June 1767, the journal shows a man being charged with:

Interest on his book debt after one year's credit on goods sold him	£ 4.11.9
Bond dated 27 September 1764 now given up	421. 8.6
Interest on this bond, 2 years, 8 months, 24 days	69. 2.2

After giving credit for some pork, a new bond was issued for the balance.

[23] Hancock wrote this letter to three men:

"The Pew [of the] late Capt John Bulkley in the meeting house whereof the Re^{d} Mr Saml Cooper is minister Being mortgaged to me the subscriber in 1754 which I have taken Possession of.

I am to Desire the fav^{r} of you Gent^{n} to apprize the same that I may give the Estate Credit for it. Note there is an Incombrence of Two Grand Children of Mr. Bulkleys sitting in s^{d} Pew which I can't well Refuse."

but occasionally as a seller if he had somehow managed to build up credits abroad (e.g., by a lucky sale of whale oil). It is hardly surprising that bills, even those on the British Treasury,[24] were by no means certain to be honored; each depended on a circle of transactions, and a ship might be lost, or another bill might not be due, or a clerk might make an error in posting. A creditor was apt to get his dues only after exasperating delays, bickerings, and rebates.

As in home trade, slight distinction was drawn between goods and money. Each was a "way of remittance." Money might be preferable, but the creditor could often be bullied into taking goods; thus Hancock, after telling a London firm that no gold or bills are to be had, asks in what form they would like a debt in local money to be remitted, "and the longer it lyes the worse it will be as our money is daily sinking." Among the bills sent to Jamaica was one "payable on demand in Molasses."

The Hancock MSS are worthy of study by monetary theorists on many grounds. They illustrate the working of an economy whose money, as we have seen, was largely made up of goods, private or external paper, and private paper based on goods. The quantitative importance of these seems to call for investigation. Perhaps a clue to the matter may be obtained from the effect of the great public note issue of 1741–9; the volume of Massachusetts notes jumped from some £220,000 to £2,200,000, but the price of silver, and exchange rates, merely doubled.[25]

EARLY TEXTBOOKS AS EVIDENCE

So much for eighteenth-century colonial accounts. To what extent were they typical of other places and dates?

Europe was at that time producing a fair number of accounting textbooks.[26] These were usually illustrated with full specimen accounts. There seems no reason to doubt that such specimens give an adequate bird's-eye view of contemporary trade methods, and provide us with fairly reliable standards of comparison.

A survey of eighteenth-century books swiftly dispels any theory that the Hancock records were like those of western Europe. True, casual partnership, joint-ventures, and consignments are often met with, and some authors still talk of barter; but bookkeeping barter seems to become rare about the end of the seventeenth century (especially in home trade), and cash transactions abound throughout that century. The only triangular transfers spring from bills of exchange—and the latter are payable in money. In short, the textbooks are in some respects far more modern in flavor than the Colonial accounts. We may perhaps risk two generalizations:

(1) Textbooks and Colonial accounts are alike in their stress on joint-ventures, etc. (because companies had not yet replaced partnership as an outlet for the speculative), and on bills (because banks were not yet the staple agents for credit transfers). Incidentally, day books had nowhere won their complete victory over the journal, which suggests that the volume of straightforward transactions was too small to call for grouping in specialized books of original entry.

(2) On the other hand, textbooks differ from Colonial accounts in assuming that money is always available, and payment in kind a rarity.

The further back we go, however, the less seems to be the gulf between the two sets of evidence. Textbooks dated 1718,

[24] Nettels, *op. cit.*, p. 201; Baxter, *op. cit.*, p. 104.

[25] Davis, *op. cit.*, p. 367; *Proc. of American Acad.*, p. 211.

[26] The library of the Society of Accountants in Edinburgh (where I made this survey) contains ten works of the eighteenth century, and four of the seventeenth.

1635, and 1610 show signs of bookkeeping barter. And Jan Impyn (1547) lists the following ways of buying and selling, whose kinship to Boston methods is patent:

"The first is with ready money. The second by tyme and daies of paimente. The third in geuyng wares for wares the whiche we call Bartery, and in Italien Barratto. The fourthe is with money, and part tyme. The fifth, with money and some wares, or other exchaunge. The sixt is by wares, and the rest for tyme. The seuenth by assignacion of one debtor to another. The eight one part by assignacion of redy money, and the other parte in wares, and tyme. And the nynth and last is by all condicions together, in geuyng money, wares assignacions, and for tyme.[27]

The researches of scholars lend color to the view that some of the Hancock methods had long been commonplace. "A general rule of Roman Law recognized transfer of obligation in books of account as a valid means of payment. Such operations were practiced by private persons as well as by the silversmiths (*argentarii*) who discharged many of the functions of the banker."[28] Professor Postan has mentioned medieval triangular transfers as substitutes for money.[29] And an able study of Italian accounts at the close of the Middle Ages confirms this; there was, we are told, a well-developed system of debt settlement based on substitutes for money—"the 'setting over' of debts was a common practice despite the absence of negotiable instruments. Local payments were often made by transfer in bank or by transfer of credit on the books of an ordinary merchant or a merchant-banker. Transfer orders were given not in writing, but by word of mouth."[30]

Let us now review our evidence. The Hancock MSS prove conclusively that, under Colonial conditions at least, any analysis of exchange into sequential phases of barter, money, and credit is indefensible; all three elements existed side by side, and were often interdependent. A comparison of the Hancock MSS with bookkeeping records of the Renaissance suggests that Europe was at that date emerging from a somewhat similar stage. We are thus not without justification if we regard Colonial accounts as clues to medieval practice; but conclusions based on the analogy must be very guarded until many more medieval records have been unearthed and studied. The last word obviously rests with the medieval scholars. I look forward in particular to further discoveries in the early story of bills. How is that story to be linked up with the innumerable notes that the Hancocks have left us? These seem to show that (a) orders in kind were an essential part of home trade; (b) bills could readily have developed out of the simple letters that shoppers would use daily when ordering goods; and (c) there was no marked gulf between home and foreign trade in the matter of payment methods.

If we discard the barter-money-credit theory of exchange phases, dare we hazard any alternative?

The phases suggested by accounting history are perhaps:

(1) *Pre-accounting age.* Presumably this is a time of crude barter, sometimes with credit.
(2) *Bookkeeping barter.* The "two-way flow" of goods allows traders to evade the worst drawbacks of crude barter. Some of the goods are commodity money. "Money of account" is the common denominator for reckoning, but the corresponding coins may not circulate much.
(3) *One-way flow.* Metallic and paper money are met with so freely that payment in kind is unnecessary. A merchant can divide his personal accounts into two groups, for suppliers and for customers. His transactions become so simple that he can segregate them in specialized day books.

---

[27] *Op. cit.*, p. 24.

[28] Usher, *op. cit.*, p. 4. Later pages mention many medieval analogies to the Hancocks' oral and written transfers of money.

[29] *Op. cit.*, p. 246.

[30] R. de Roover, "Early Accounting Problems of Foreign Exchange," ACCOUNTING REVIEW, 1944, p. 382.

(4) *Bank settlement.* Finally, the advantages of payment by cheque reduce cash settlements to a negligible scale. Clearance is centralized.

Such stages do not, of course, correspond crisply with successive periods of time. There must always have been some overlapping; probably all stages existed to some extent even in the Middle Ages. But each may well typify the procedure that was dominant in certain centuries.

Perhaps these accounting phases merely reflect steps in the evolution of the merchant. In the first, there are presumably few merchants, because craftsmen sell straight to customers without intervention by middlemen. In the second, the middleman has appeared, but he must be omnivorous, buying and selling almost everything, and so making his profits in a tediously roundabout way.[31] In the third, he can concentrate on one type of goods. In the fourth, he rids himself of the work of settlement, leaving it to professional bankers. If this analysis is correct, the key to exchange phases is *the merchant's degree of specialization.*

[31] A counterpart of the unspecialized Boston trader is suggested by E. F. Heckscher: "Natural and Money Economy as illustrated from Swedish History," *Journal of Economic and Business History*, III, p. 12.

ACCOUNTING AS AN ACADEMIC STUDY

Reprinted from *The Accountant*—6th March, 1948

ACCOUNTING AS AN ACADEMIC STUDY

by W. T. Baxter

IT is fitting that a new professor should be made to defend his subject, and doubly so when his subject is new too. We should always look cautiously at thin ends of wedges. Further, the custom gives a slightly sporting flavour to inaugural lectures; there is always just a chance that the raw professor may fail to make out a case for his subject, and so may feel forced to end his address by handing in his resignation. Unfortunately, academic history does not tell us of many cases in which this has happened.

While accounting managed to win its way into some British universities several decades since, its place has so far been small and uncertain. Mine is, I think, the first full-time chair to be created in Britain; and many universities are only this year appointing their first full-time—or even part-time—instructors. So a heavy responsibility lies on this tiny group of teachers. What are we going to make of our new subject? Accounting, as practised, may well include many things both interesting and useful; but can we select from and arrange these things in such a way as to build a stiff academic discipline? Can accounting contribute something to a student's mental training that will be worth having even if, after graduating, he never again sets eyes on a balance sheet?

In part from lack of courage, in part from lack of time, I propose to evade the fundamental question of whether a university should have any truck at all with professional subjects. These have for centuries been forcing their way into the syllabus. Sometimes the gate-crasher has ended as an honoured guest; latin was, I fancy, at first taught largely in order that professional men might earn their bread and butter. But this is far from meaning that every professional subject has an automatic right to a place. Nor would I suggest that such subjects ought not to be balanced by work in very different fields if we are to give a liberal education. Techniques, sciences, even languages do not

> 'provide a sufficient educational background for citizens of a free nation. For such a programme lacks contact with both man's emotional experience as an individual and his practical experience as a gregarious animal. . . . Unless the educational process includes *at each level of maturity* some continuing contact with those fields in which value judgments are of prime importance, it must fall far short of the ideal. The student in high school, in college, and in graduate school must be concerned, in part at least, with the words "right" and "wrong" in both the ethical and the mathematical sense. Unless he feels the import of those general ideas and aspirations which have been a deep moving force in the lives of men, he runs the risk of partial blindness'.*

Accounting Blends Several Subjects

The nature of accounting is such that its teacher is in the happy position of being able to range far and wide over everything related to financial administration. For the most remarkable thing about accounting as a field of study is that it is not so much a subject by itself as a synthesis of other subjects. The sole original contribution of accounting—narrowly defined—to man's mental store-cupboard is double-entry book-keeping. If, as I believe to be the case, accountants have built up a not unimpressive fabric of practice, they have done so by their skill in adapting, and perhaps improving on, what has been learnt in other spheres, notably the law and commerce.

The role of double-entry is to fuse together the different elements into one amalgam; and this it does neatly and well. Perhaps some genius may eventually hit on a better basis for keeping records, but such a system is hard to imagine. The first aim of the serious student of accounting must then be to master double-entry.

The task is not easy, and all too often it is long and dull into the bargain (though I do not concede the dullness to be inevitable). Therefore it seems a thousand pities that the syllabus of most schools, and even of higher institutions, never gets beyond the double-entry stage. One would feel sorry for the student of a language who did not pass from the memorising of conjugations to the delights of the new literature; in the same way, a short course in accounting is apt to be all pill, no jam.

It is therefore natural for a university to ask whether there is no method of side-stepping this first stage—no by-pass to the advanced studies that are, after all, what the business administrator will be mainly concerned with.

The answer is that such an approach is perfectly feasible, and in some cases may be justified. Your budding director would get great help from a short course of lectures in which, say, general finance is explained with the aid of balance sheets, and trends are analysed with consecutive profit and loss accounts. Such an outline may cover his likely minimum needs, and will certainly be immensely more useful to him at the board-room table than a smattering of beginner's book-keeping alone. Indeed, one could argue that too much familiarity with double-entry may in some ways be a handicap. Thus there was an unpardonable delay before companies took to publishing accounts in a form that was likely to be intelligible to their average shareholder; to-day, some companies still pay scant attention to this duty, and even their more scrupulous neighbours tend to show little imagination or taste for experiment. The reason is probably that the men responsible cannot shake themselves free from the technicalities of double-entry; forgetting how innocent of book-keeping are their readers, they frame accounts that are crude reflections of the debit and credit skeleton rather than attempts to interest and inform.

I have tried in the preceding paragraph to make out the strongest possible case for a short-cut training that skips drill in double-entry and deals only in principles. But I must confess that I have failed to persuade myself. Such a training is apt to be preten-

Inaugural address delivered at the London School of Economics and Political Science (University of London) on 2nd December 1947. Sir Harold M. Barton, F.C.A., was in the chair.

* J. B. Conant, in Harvard University *President's Report* (1946), p. 9.

tious and even dangerous. It can, I think, be justified only when extreme pressure on time rules out anything more thorough. All figures for costs, values, and the like are full of pitfalls. They are profoundly influenced by the machinery that gathers them; unless the manager of a business has the feel of this machinery in his very bones, he will frequently be misled, and will always be at the mercy of his subordinates.

An analogy may make my attitude plainer. The lover of music may enjoy concerts without having learnt to play a note; and his enjoyment may well be increased by listening to talks on the instruments of the orchestra or the lives of the great composers—with no drudgery at five-finger exercises. But one scarcely supposes that such a training will produce many first-class critics, still less composers or performers.

Because of this need for a preliminary training, I question whether a short course in book-keeping and accounting is worth putting into a university's commerce syllabus. Students whose main aim is not to become managers of business (e.g. engineers) may be none the worse for a superficial survey; but with commerce students it is surely a case of all or nothing. Unless the subject is taken for, say, two years (so that a grounding in double-entry can be followed by an introduction to the higher flights), the student can probably use his time better in other class-rooms and will be spared the dangers of a little learning.

The Influence of Business Organisation

One important factor in determining whether or not a subject is worth a place in a scheme of education is the degree to which it demands prolonged attention to a core of principles. It makes good food when it gives the student something that he can chew on for a long time. All too often, alas, accounting is presented as a series of disconnected fragments, without any underlying theme except double-entry, and governed by isolated and arbitrary rules rather than sustained reasoning.

Even in the elementary stages, when the beginner still flounders in double-entry, his work can be lightened and given point if he is taught to view book-keeping as the handmaid of the business manager. As each new problem is introduced, the sequence of reasoning should be, first, 'What does a business man want to know about this?' and, next, 'How then should the facts be dealt with by the book-keeper?' Our students should also be shown that the accountant's task is not only to record, but to plan a business in such a way as to stop error and fraud. In other words, the lecturer ought to discuss the procedures that we name 'internal check'. Strong reasons prompt the young administrator to learn this subject thoroughly. Excellent mental training is given by study of the principles of embezzlement; for here success demands mastery of the whole financial structure in all its ramifications, and a crystal-clear insight into the remotest effects of any transaction. If he comes to the counting-house armed with a knowledge of internal check, the administrator can make fraud next to impossible; what is more, he will be able to save expense and work by bringing in short-cuts. Thus he may at once increase his profits and spare his staff from drudgery and temptation. Seldom do self-interest and humanity lie so close together.

The Influence of Law

But businesses are not isolated. They have dealings with the outside world. So, if the first strand in accounting is internal management, the next is law. Much of accounting might be called legal arithmetic. Historically, indeed, it was probably this strand that came first; the most pressing reason for keeping accounts is to remember what you owe and are owed. At a slightly later stage in business history, a wish to record the legal rights of partners in their joint wealth gave another push to book-keeping. I quote from the earliest accounting text-book in English:

> 'negligence of kepyng bokes hath caused more striefe in lawe and variance of children and frendes than any one thyng in the world; seruantes and factors haue vndone their Masters, riche men hath sodenly become beggers and could not tell how it should come to passe. . .

The writer warns us of the troubles that plague executors if the dead man kept no accounts

> 'whiche leueth to the world all thynges rawly and vnperfectly, and causeth some in the place of "God haue mercie on his solle" to saie *the deuill gnaw the bones of hym*, and a vengeance on suche a keper of a boke'.*

These early needs were, however, child's play compared with what has come since. An accountant must now be at home with the law of companies, of bankruptcy, of executors and—above all—of taxation. A university training in accounting must accordingly have a heavy bias towards law. This is by no means a matter of regret. For the law—rightly taught—is a discipline that blends well with accounting. Especially among the older generation of accountants, one often sees the happy results of the union—in a keener and surer grasp, not merely of the legal aspects, but of all other branches of our subject.

I think that this is a particularly appropriate place at which to pay tribute to my predecessor, the late Mr. S. W. Rowland. For he was an obvious case of an accountant whose abilities had been quickened by a legal training. His lectures and his many articles in the accounting press had a strong legal flavour; and his books are enriched with illustrations from case law, and are specially useful in showing how book-keeping reflects legal relationships. It is a matter of deep regret to me that Mr. Rowland's sudden death has robbed me of his friendship and guidance.

The Influence of Economics

I have tried to show that the teacher of accounting needs to work hand-in-glove with his fellows in the departments of commerce and law. A third contribution to his task could come from economics.

The lack of any liaison between accounting and economic theory is so marked and so astonishing as to call for a whole lecture to itself. Each subject has grown up in serene indifference to the other, although both try to solve much the same problems, and in certain places the degrees of overlapping is remarkable.

Some of these common topics occur readily to the mind; the theory of costs and of revenue are cases in point. Less obvious, but perhaps of more importance, is valuation. If the teacher of accounting is seeking a backbone for his lectures, I suggest that valuation supplies it to a surprising degree. For, if an accountant

* Jan Impyn, original printed 1547, quoted in 'Economisch-Historisch Jaarboek', Vol. 18, 1934, p. 58.

is worth his salt, he will not be content merely to know how to insert given figures into his records; he ought also to have ideas on what these figures should be. And almost all the less simple business transactions involve valuation.

Valuation Theory

His text-books warn the young accountant that he is no valuer, and doubtless this is true enough so far as single physical objects go. But he may be called on to value less tangible things. Examples are:

(1) *Shares*. Where a company's shares are not quoted on the Stock Exchange, they must sometimes be valued artificially. An accountant may be called upon to make the appraisal—either because he is the company's auditor, or simply because he is deemed to be knowledgeable in such matters.

(2) *Partnership rights*. Almost all the problems of partnership hinge on valuation. When a new partner is to be admitted, the existing partners will naturally form some idea of what his admission will mean to them in terms of increased gains to the firm, less his share of the gains. For his part, he will doubtless compare the benefits of partnership with his prospects elsewhere. Some of the factors can scarcely be appraised in terms of money, for they include prestige, friendship, and loss of freedom; here, as in the partnership of marriage, it is perhaps just as well that most men are not given to weighing the endless pros and cons too nicely or decision might never be reached.

Again, when a partner dies or retires, he is presumably entitled to withdraw some of the wealth that he has helped to create. But how much? Logic may suggest that he or his heirs should receive the capitalised value of:

(*a*) what the remaining partners will earn without him; less

(*b*) what they would have earned had he stayed in the firm.

But here a clash arises between the ideal and the expedient. Such a concept may gratify logic, but it does not lend itself readily to conversion into a crisp and final sum of £ s d. It involves guesswork about future prospects; if his payment depended on such a highly subjective estimate, the retiring man might well be startled to discover how weak was the faith of his partners—who have to foot the bill—in the firm's future. He would find it hard to coax them round to his own cheerful views; his widow and orphans would find it even harder. Plainly then, some rule that is objective, and leaves scant scope for bickering, is a much better means for determining his compensation than one that is right in theory—or even equity—but which hinges on personal feeling.

(3) *A whole business*. When a business is bought, expropriated, appraised for death duties, or amalgamated with another business, accountants may be asked to suggest a value. Here, again, the question arises of whether the answer is to be found by speculating about future earnings or looking backwards at past results. The latter process, with its seeming certainty and objectivity, is the more tempting; but the answer so found is apt to be brushed aside contemptuously when buyers and sellers come to grips. Here we are not trying to deal justly with a widow or orphans, but to recreate the conditions of the real market. The latter seems to look forward, not back. However unsubstantial and controversial may be our guesses about the future, they are the stuff that prices are made of. The accountant is therefore forced willy-nilly to don the prophet's mantle if he becomes a valuer.

He is at once confronted with two more problems. First, to what extent can he use old data as guides to future earnings? Common sense suggests that there is normally some continuity between the past and the future—that to-day is a link rather than a barrier between yesterday and to-morrow—and that accordingly profits are likely to follow a trend. Secondly, what is the relationship between future earnings of the whole business and the present market values of its separate assets? If the value of the business is a function solely of future income, does this mean that we can shut our eyes to the individual assets? I think not; but a clear exposition of the relation between these two aspects of wealth has yet to be made. Much is being said about the need for accounting research. I can imagine no more useful field than this.

Capital and Revenue

We pass almost imperceptibly from the string of problems that have valuation as their common theme to those that find unity in the need to measure capital and revenue. For is not revenue a growth in value? There is, I know, a strong school of thought among accountants that does not altogether accept this view. It prefers the profit and loss account to the balance sheet as the basis of approach, that is, it deems net revenue to be the difference between incomes and costs rather than a 'value accretion'. But can incomes and costs be divorced from value? 'Income' is surely something that has been gained; and 'cost' seems to imply that something has been sacrificed. Now, what are these somethings if they are not changes in the value of wealth? It is hard to conceive of water flowing into or out of a tank without altering the quantity in the tank. Similarly, I cannot understand incomes and costs that do not affect the value of the net assets.

In any case, nobody denies that we must pay heed to the values of at least some assets, such as stocks, before we can find profit. So, whichever approach we favour, we cannot shirk this issue of valuation entirely. It raises intriguing problems. For instance, how should a manufacturer value his work in progress, and what figure should a building contractor place upon unfinished structures? How should we measure the depreciation of a wasting asset? I must humbly confess that I do not know of any adequate answers. Many have been suggested in writings on accounting; all fail to satisfy. The reason is, I think, that they deal with different assets piecemeal, without first trying to give a general definition. Reason will never be content with rules for valuing each specific asset unless they harmonise with an overall principle. The first thing that we must do, then, is to produce our fundamental definitions of capital and revenue. Till we have such definitions, we can only agree with the sad comment on present-day practice:

> 'What is set out as a measure of net income can never be supposed to be a fact in any sense at all except that it is the figure that results when the accountant has finished applying the procedure which he adopts.'[*]

---

[*] J. B. Canning: 'Economics of Accountancy' (New York, 1929), p. 99.

Here, surely, is another problem beckoning to the would-be researcher. I must, however, warn him of two important but somewhat contradictory needs. First, as I have just said, his only hope of creating a satisfactory body of rules is to start by finding a basic principle. Second, his principle and rules are not likely to be of much use unless they can be fitted into current practice without too harsh a shock. He may indeed tell us to mend our ways within reason; few of us would deny that there is room for improvement. But his hope must be to perceive, thanks to a freshness of insight, some germ in existing practice that can be fairly easily developed and extended to cover all cases.

It may sound confused to plead for a profound new principle in one paragraph and to give conservative warnings in the next. Let me try to clear up the muddle. One can conceive of a vast range of definitions of revenue, all of which would be thoroughly pleasing to the mind. The difference between them would lie in the *time* at which approaching gains are deemed to have reached us; what sign shall we require to prove that the bird in the bush has become the bird in the hand? I doubt whether any answer to this question can be found in detached thought. In other words, when we are faced with the job of turning a revenue concept into definite figures, we are apt to get bogged among many rival definitions, none of which seems capable of proving its superiority on abstract grounds. We must therefore test the definitions in the light of their usefulness. Why does a business man want to know his income? Various answers come to mind—for instance, to measure efficiency, to see how his investment is paying, to find what surplus should be shared among the joint owners (including that ever-present though invisible partner, the Chancellor). Probably the best definition of revenue is the one that yields the best answer to these questions. Important corollaries are that the answer must not cost too much to find, that it will be understood by as many people as possible, and that it will not leave endless room for squabbling. This can mean only that our basic principle must not be too alien to existing notions.

Cost

The theory of cost is another topic that may well be used to tie up scattered bits of accounting. It is the best introduction, not only to the many and important problems of cost accounting, but also to some phases of ordinary financial accounting. Examples are the accounts of departments and branches, i.e. of the subdivisions, for which separate data are recorded, that go to make up a large business. For here we are brought up against the problem of allocation. How should you split a common cost between departments? Ought you indeed to do it at all?

I would suggest that a plausible line of approach to the problem of allocation would be to try treating the departments of a business as if they were separate and competing units, i.e. as if the four walls of the firm enclosed an internal market. Economists have given us a fairly clear picture of how firms behave in the real (or 'external') market. Might not the same rules be extended to cover the subdivisions of a business—whether they be departments or processes or machines? We should then see that, although the money outlay on what is bought by the firm may be fixed, the corresponding services are not necessarily so. For instance, the rent paid for the whole shop may be fixed by a ten-year contract; but the manager is still free to rearrange the space between his departments. The latter will doubtless make 'bids' to him—whether in the form of vague cajolery for more space, or of forthright offers to raise sales by £x if given another hundred square yards. When services can in this way be allocated as a matter of hard physical fact, the objections to allocating their cost seem to me to grow less. Instead, the process of allocating may serve to make the internal market more real, and to raise profits by ensuring that the firm's resources are split up between departments according to the best possible scheme of priorities. Of course, we might then find that our costs had been transformed. For a department's 'bids' for space and so on will presumably be less influenced by the actual costs—e.g. the rent paid to the landlord—than by what that space is nowadays worth, both in the outside and inside markets. The normal earning power of rival departments may well loom larger than the cost figures of the ledger. Once again we must choose between a backward- and a forward-looking approach. These two conflicting viewpoints seem indeed to lie at the very heart of nearly all our controversies.

The Contributions of Accounting to other Subjects

So far, I have tended to stress what the teacher of accounting can gain from his colleagues in nearby departments. Perhaps I may without too much immodesty drop some hint of the returns that accounting might make to its neighbours. What, for instance, might students of law and economics learn if their courses included accounting?

On the technical level, the returns seem so plain as to need no emphasis. Thus most lawyers will be helped if they can interpret company affairs or income-tax rules in terms of figures. Again, statisticians are now experimenting with double-entry as a means for measuring national wealth, while economists seem to be adopting the balance sheet and other accounts as tools for their researches.

But I believe accounting to be capable of more positive contributions. Might it not, for instance, give the economics student a clearer picture of how the business man's mind works—in particular, by showing in which fields his decisions can normally be guided by figures and in which by nothing less misty than his feelings. If I have grasped the matter aright, the economist explains the business man's activity by relating it to a quest for the level of output at which profits are at their peak. This view seems just as incontrovertible as the notion that a man tends to marry the person who will, he thinks, bring him most happiness. What should be made clear is that the business man is often no more likely than the suitor to be guided by schedules of costs. It is always risky to generalise on such topics; whatever one says, some member of the audience is fairly sure to reply: 'Our firm has for years done the exact opposite of what you suggest.' However, I venture to submit that most firms have not yet found the formal measurement of marginal costs and revenues to be feasible. This is not to say that the economics text-book is wrong to use such figures; they make the issue plainer, just as a psychologist's weighing of emotions might help us to understand other kinds of choice. But, being beset by so many unknowns, the business man can hardly do more than feel his way towards the output level that is suggested by common-sense modifications of past experience; he may reject alternatives by mental processes that do not reach the level of conscious thought, far less figures on paper. If his plans for the coming year ever reach the accounting stage, it will probably be only as a broad budget, showing the costs and revenues of what he assumes to be the best output.

Now comes another important point. A firm seldom makes the single product with which the teacher of economics—very rightly—introduces his disciples to the problem. Accordingly, when the business man has decided, however roughly, on his best general level of output for the future, he still has to allocate his efforts between his various products and departments. Here his accountant—and still more his cost accountant—does make formal comparisons of revenues and sacrifices. The cost accountant's usual method is, however, not to list all the possible alternatives and to show the most profitable; the number of unknowns and the range of permutations are so vast that such a procedure is often out of the question. If I am not mistaken, the cost accountant ought to sum up his work thus: 'You have given me—in the form of a master-budget for the year or some vaguer estimate—a picture of the total revenue that the best output may win; with the help of that picture, I must first express our varied products in terms of some common standard (such as the man-hour) and then show what revenue each of these units of work is expected to contribute towards our costs and dividends; armed with this figure of normal revenue, I shall test each activity to see if it is worth while.' In short, the cost accountant will feel much more at home with the economist when the latter is talking about normal revenue than when he is making marginal calculations.

In this matter—as in many others—accountants are influenced largely by their views on what is practicable. A university course in accounting must often follow this formula: First, what is ideal? Second, what data are at our disposal? Third, how far can we get towards the ideal on our limited material? Accounting may thus give a training whose attitude differs somewhat from that of its sister subjects; the student may receive a certain sense of urgency, of the need for reaching decision with the help of knowledge that is necessarily imperfect. In many branches of learning, a state of suspended judgment may well be the hall-mark of high scholarship; an accountant's clients expect advice by the first post to-morrow.

From what I have said about revenue, values and costs, it will be clear that, when the student of accounting is dealing with those parts of his subject, there is little risk of his being spoon-fed with something that has already been settled and reduced to cut-and-dried finality. But, if he will not be given the thrill of introduction to a complete and polished doctrinal structure, at least he may have the fun of ruminating over the questions that we—his elders and betters—have so far failed to answer, and of knowing that he may be the lucky prospector who will first strike gold. Most of the answers depend for proof, after all, not on advanced technicalities but on what men in general feel to be reasonable and useful. A student's mind is as good a jury as any on such points. Take for instance the fundamental question of value. I have said that man esteems things because they will yield him future benefits. But is it always so? Professor Bonbright tells us:

> 'A squirrel which betrays a high valuation for the nuts that he stores in the ground cannot confidently be said to base his conduct on the discounted present value that he attaches to the opportunity of securing a series of nourishing meals therefrom during the winter. Instead, the squirrel is apparently motivated by some impulse of a non-anticipating nature to get that nut, to avoid eating it now, and to bury it in the ground.
>
> 'Human beings are doubtless more anticipatory than squirrels in their valuation processes. But it is an open question whether even men and women do not base their bids and offers for commodities partly on a similar impulse of desire for or aversion from the commodity itself, rather than on a process of valuing the prospects of a flow of future benefits. Can we be confident that the impulse of a woman shopper which leads her to pay a certain price for a pretty dress or a delightful bottle of perfume is governed by her calculation of a series of future receipts of warmth and decoration, and a series of future receipts of pleasant smells and favourable social responses?'*

Please note, too, that values, costs and so forth are homely matters that the student will go on meeting long after he has left the class-room, and even if he does not earn his living at accounting. One hopes that he will be brought afresh to these topics every time that he makes his income-tax return or invests some money or even reads his newspaper, and that, accordingly, the issues will remain alive in his mind.

Conclusion

How shall I sum up this survey of accounting? A wit has said that the three fundamental questions of philosophy are 'how?' 'why?' and 'so what?' We might do worse than consider the way in which accounting deals with these three questions.

'*How?*' should present no difficulties. If instruction in accounting were merely a matter of describing a technique, any conscientious teacher could create a sound course out of the material at hand. But I have already made clear, I hope, that descriptive teaching is of inferior value. Only when the student is led to ask '*why?*' does he receive satisfactory stimulus to thought; this, too, he may get from accounting, but only if the teacher has a deep understanding of the administrative and legal aims that have moulded our mystery. Most important, is the student imbued with that power of making cool and detached criticisms which is implied by '*so what?*'? This is probably our weak point. Yet, when I remember how much of an accounting student's time may be spent in analysing the meaning of familiar but woolly ideas, in deciding whether the answer to an imposing mathematical calculation has any real significance, and in wrangling over these matters in the light of theories that themselves invite controversy, I feel not unhopeful about our future; I cannot but think that, with such a wealth of disputatious problems, accounting should be able to put students on guard mentally—though the instructor may well feel humble as he considers how hard it will be to create the body of principles that will act as his students' loadstone.

In short, I have little doubt that the subject of accounting is capable of becoming a worthy member of the academic syllabus. Whether it can do so in the hands of this particular teacher is of course another matter.

* J. C. Bonbright: 'Valuation of Property', p. 222.

ACCOUNTANTS AND THE INFLATION

MANCHESTER STATISTICAL SOCIETY

Accountants and the Inflation

By PROFESSOR W. T. BAXTER.

Read 9th February, 1949.

No statistical topic to-day interests accountants more than price-level changes. We have known for years that such movements affect accounts ; until the end of the war, however, most of us tended to take the line that these effects were hardly important enough to warrant improvements in our methods. How swift and marked has been our change of heart ! To-day the subject is being "plugged" in all accounting journals. It has become the central theme in the annual speeches of countless company chairmen, who, suddenly finding their firms short of liquid funds, are questioning our time-honoured methods of providing for depreciation, and of computing profits and taxes. Bodies such as the Federation of British Industries, the Institute of Chartered Accountants, and the American Institute of Accountants—none of which could be accused of undue preoccupation with the abstract—have felt obliged to re-appraise accepted doctrine, even if they have so far stoutly refused to give their blessings to any of the proposed reforms.

ORIGINAL COST AND CHANGING PRICE LEVELS.

The reason for all this concern among practical people is that the post-war years have shown how serious are the consequences of our concept of profits—or, perhaps one should say, of asset valuation. By and large, our method has been to value assets at original cost permanently ; the cost of wasting assets is however written down to allow for depreciation, and current assets are revalued downwards (never upwards) to allow for losses such as bad debts and falls in the price of stock-in-trade. The arguments for using cost as our measure are strong—when the value of money is stable. When price levels change, any given cost figure may represent very different quantities of real wealth—*e.g.* a house bought for £10,000 in 1932 is very different from one bought for the same number of 1949 pounds. So the maintenance of net assets at a constant figure does not guarantee that real capital is intact. When prices are falling, the newer cost figures in a balance sheet represent a growing quantity of assets per pound invested. When prices are going up, the opposite holds ; a constant net asset total means a fall in real wealth—for instance, because assets bought during the last year have a real value lower than that of the stock or plant used up in the year's operations, despite an equality of cost.

If these arguments are correct, it follows that a firm's profits during a spell of inflation may be—in part at least—a mirage. An imposing paper surplus may have been obtained by cutting off slices from the firm's original capital. But taxes and dividends are based on these false figures ; and so, even where some of the paper surplus is prudently added to reserve, part of the original capital may be dissipated unknowingly. When the time comes for major replacements, the firm suddenly finds that its seemingly unimpaired resources are inadequate, and fresh capital must be raised.

Something of this sort probably happened during the war ; and our troubles were aggravated by the stiff increase in prices that has marked the post-war years in which we had hoped to replace our jaded and bomb-battered assets. That is why the limelights are now focussed on accounting theory, and why so many voices exhort the Chancellor of the Exchequer to mend his methods. This wave of interest, and a consequent wider understanding of our problems, are to be welcomed—even though there is perhaps some risk of the pendulum swinging too far. In my young days, a manufacturer of munitions was apt to be regarded as a gross fellow who grew fat on public funds ; now we paint him as one whose substance has been bled away by the tax-gatherer's too scanty wear and tear allowances.

Though the demand for a reform of accounting and tax procedure draws its main strength from the present embarrassments of business, milder voices from another quarter have for some years been saying much the same thing. Theorists interested in accounting have discussed possible improvements in our methods—in part from a disinterested desire for truth, in part from a hope that accounting reform might lead to social reform. For false profits—so it is argued—may help to accentuate the trade cycle. On the upswings, accounting profits are unduly rosy, and so give an extra fillip to hopes already extravagant ; on the downgrade, the figures are even more depressing than the facts warrant. New accounting methods might accordingly help to curb the trade cycle and lessen the menaces of boom and bust.

The issues facing us to-night are thus by no means insignificant. Let us, then, look more closely at accounting, and test the criticisms with the help of the simplest possible figures.

TYPES OF ACCOUNTING ERROR.

Most of the current debate centres on depreciation and methods of stock valuation. These may well be the most important facets of the problem. But, to be satisfactory, surely new methods and theories must be sufficiently general to cover *all* our figures ? So far as I know, the only serious attempt in English to show how the whole range of data—in both balance sheet and revenue account—may be put on a comparable basis is Mr. H. Sweeney's *Stabilized Accounting.*[1] His suggestions will not seem wholly unfamiliar to accountants. We have already a technique for converting the results of foreign branches into home currency ; and, if we can translate francs or rupees into sterling, it should not be impossible to convert the pounds of a post-war year into the stabler units of, say, 1938.

If we analyse the false impressions which may, following price-level movements, be conveyed by ordinary accounting procedure, and which "stabilized" figures should dispel, we find three main kinds of distortion :

A. The ordinary figures (*i.e.* revenue accounts drafted according to the accepted methods of to-day) change,

[1]Henry Whitcomb Sweeney : *Stabilized Accounting* (New York, 1936).

but in step with the general price movement. If simply adjusted to allow for this movement, they would show no real change in the firm's wealth.

B. The ordinary figures change more or less than the price index. Simple adjustment would here reflect a real change in wealth.

C. If the ordinary figures relate to different periods, they give, when compared with one another, a distorted picture that persists even after simple adjustment. Somewhat more complex adjustment is needed if a true picture is to be obtained in stabilized accounts. I shall call this the "time-lag error." It is much more formidable than errors A and B (if "errors" these can indeed be called); whereas anybody with his wits about him can detect and make some allowance for A and B, the existence and extent of C cannot be perceived readily.

But it is not the revenue figures alone that give false impressions. The balance-sheet becomes twisted too; appreciation or depreciation in capital values may be super-imposed on any or all of the revenue errors, and may far surpass the latter in size. One great advantage of stabilized accounting is that it covers this somewhat neglected factor, as well as errors A, B, and C.

I assume that *general purchasing power* is what most of us have in mind when we speak of keeping capital intact. In what follows, therefore, I ignore price changes that are confined to particular assets; "replacement cost" does not here mean what it would actually cost to replace the given asset, but original cost adjusted to allow for changes in a general price index.

A. *Ordinary figures change in step with price movements.*

If my income rises from £1,000 to £1,200 at the same time as the price index moves from 100 to 120, my real income has plainly remained constant. Being illogical, I may feel a glow of exhilaration because of the larger money inflow. But I ought to see that no real change has occurred—unless the general price index does not reflect my own peculiar tastes as a consumer ; and, alas, it will certainly not allow for one type of outlay—my income tax payment will, under a progressive scale, rise by more than 20%.

Income is however not my only form of wealth. How has my capital fared in the monetary upheaval? To find out, I must split my possessions into two sharply contrasted groups :

(1) *Property rights that are defined in terms of a fixed number of pounds.* Cash, debtors, and my life assurance policy are the obvious examples. War loan and fixed-interest securities are closely allied, but the link is a trifle more elastic. I shall call this class "money-assets." Almost all liabilities, be it noted, obey the same rules.

(2) *Property rights that are not defined in terms of a fixed number of pounds,* so that their current market value is free to move with the general price level. Stocks, plant, and investments in ordinary shares are the obvious example. I shall call these "non-money-assets."

The distinction between these two groups is far more real and (for our present purposes) important than that between "current" and "non-current" items, according to which our normal balance sheets are drafted. The latter scheme of division was evolved in a stable world where credit-soundness was the main matter that a balance sheet should demonstrate ; now that inflation-soundness has suddenly become more vital to most of us, the line must (mentally at least) be drawn somewhat differently—for example, stocks must be separated from money-assets, while preference share capital must be torn away from ordinary capital and put much closer to creditors.

So far as my money-assets are concerned, I automatically lose $\frac{20}{120}$th of my capital if the price index rises from 100 to 120. However, I may have been holding no money-assets (or my mortgage may exactly equal my cash and War Loan, so that the net money-assets are *nil*). In this case, my real wealth is unaffected by the change ; for my non-money-assets will—other things being equal—rise 20% in money value.

How could an accountant show the position when presenting the annual statements of a business ? I dislike the idea of his tampering with the ordinary accounts. But he might supplement these with a second set of statements, in which he tries to "translate" the new figures into stable units.

Suppose that expenses and gross income have been £1,000 and £1,400 for many years, and that the physical level of activity has remained normal. If the price index now changes smoothly by 20 points over the year, and this firm's revenue figures follow suit exactly, each item of expense and gross income must on the average rise by 10 points ; if you like, you can think of all transactions as taking place on 30th June, the middle of the business year, when the index stands at 110. The same sort of reasoning holds if prices have instead dropped. For purposes of exposition, it seems better to use the "normal" opening pound, rather than the closing pound (which Mr. Sweeney prefers), as the basis of stabilization ; the ordinary accounts, and their stabilized counterparts, therefore run :—

TABLE I

	Normal years	Prices increase		Prices decline	
		Ordinary accounts	Stabilized accounts	Ordinary accounts	Stabilized accounts
Revenue account :					
Expenses ...	1,000	1,100 × $\frac{10}{11}$	= 1,000	900 × $\frac{10}{9}$	=1,000
Income	1,400	1,540 ,,	1,400	1,260 ,,	1,400
Profit	400	440	400	360	400

Thus the stabilized accounts show the unreality alike of the increase and the decrease in earnings.

Because we are starting with the easy assumption that this firm has no net money-assets, stabilization does not much affect its capital. The ordinary balance sheet still shows the other assets at their "aboriginal cost," and so gives no illusion of loss or gain; and its units are the same as those of a stabilized balance sheet. But what about the new assets that have been won during the year, *i.e.* the profits? These may have been withdrawn, or retained as money-assets, or invested in other assets. Let us first consider the last case, for simplicity assuming that the profit was all earned on 30th June and at once used to buy plant, etc. This new plant is bought when the index stands at 110; its cost must therefore be deflated by one-eleventh if we want to take for our measure the pounds circulating on 1st January. Similarly, if prices are falling, the new plant figure must be raised by one-ninth. The various statements run:—

TABLE II

	Prices increase		Prices decline	
	Ordinary accounts	Stabilized accounts	Ordinary accounts	Stabilized accounts
Non-money-assets:				
Original—say ...	1,000	1,000	1,000	1,000
New	440 × $\frac{10}{11}$ =	400	360 × $\frac{10}{9}$ =	400
	1,440	1,400	1,360	1,400

B. *Ordinary figures change more or less than the price index.*

Let us next consider the more probable case in which some of the figures do *not* change in step with the price index. Their failure to do so may be partial, *e.g.* our system of price control puts a drag on most firms' selling prices. Or their rigidity may be complete, as when a price is fixed contractually or by unusually stern controls; thus a landlord's income may be held down forcibly by a long lease or government decree, while, unfortunately for him, the costs of maintaining his property show a delicate awareness of monetary trends.

If the net income does not alter at the same rate as prices in general, obviously real income is affected. Here stabilized accounts are useful for measuring the gain or loss, and for understanding its causes. Let us examine the situation of a firm that normally wins a revenue of £4,000 (which figure will fluctuate exactly with prices), but has to pay fixed rents and interest of another £4,000, so that its net profit is nothing before prices begin to move. Assuming an average change of 10 points during the year, our figures are :—

TABLE III

	Normal year	Prices increase		Prices decline	
		Ordinary accounts	Stabilized accounts	Ordinary accounts	Stabilized accounts
Revenue account :					
a. Gross revenue	4,000	4,400 × $\frac{10}{11}$	=4,000	3,600 × $\frac{10}{9}$	=4,000
b. Fixed expenses	4,000	4,000 ,,	3,636	4,000 ,,	4,444
Net Profit ...	—	400	364	—400	—444

Here the stabilized figures show that the firm's changes of fortune are real ; they spring, however, not from the obvious changes in gross revenue (line *a*), but from the concealed lightening or aggravation of the fixed burden (line *b*).[2]

[2]Some readers may prefer statements based on the *closing* price level, rather than that prevailing before the year started. To convert our revenue figures into closing pounds, they must be multiplied by $\frac{120}{110}$ or $\frac{80}{90}$.

	Normal year	Prices increase		Prices decline	
		Ordinary accounts	Stabilized accounts	Ordinary accounts	Stabilized accounts
Revenue account :					
Profit	4,000	4,400 × $\frac{12}{11}$	=4,800	3,600 × $\frac{8}{9}$	=3,200
Fixed expenses ..	4,000	4,000 ,,	4,364	4,000 ,,	3,556
Net profit ..	—	400	436	— 400	— 356

One reason for preferring an earlier date as basis is that this facilitates comparisons as year follows year ; as has however been said already, Mr. Sweeney prefers the closing pound as basis.

Capital appreciation may conveniently be considered here (though, of course, it may equally well occur in conjunction with errors A or C). Suppose that the same firm started the year with £10,000 of non-money-assets, and a like amount of money-assets. The closing position is :—

TABLE IV

	Prices increase		Prices decrease	
	Ordinary accounts	Stabilized accounts	Ordinary accounts	Stabilized accounts
Non-money assets ...	10,000	10,000	10,000	10,000
Money-assets :				
At start	10,000	$\times \frac{10}{12}$=8,667	10,000	$\times \frac{10}{8}$= 12,000
Due to profits ...	400		— 400	
	20,400	18,667	19,600	22,000
Accounted for thus :				
Original capital		20,000		20,000
Net profit on trade		364		— 444
		20,364		19,556
Capital loss on money-assets :				
On £10,000, for whole year ...		1,667	(appreciation)	2,500
,, profit, ,, half ,, ...		30	(on a loss)	— 56
Total loss		1,697	(gain)	2,444
Total assets, as above		18,667		22,000

In this example, a rise in prices gives a small trade profit but causes a large capital depreciation ; with a comparable fall in prices, capital appreciation far outweighs the trading loss.

The reverse situation obtains where the money-assets are negative. This situation is by no means unusual. Thus a company with a "highly geared" capital structure may well have creditors, debentures, and preference shares that in total exceed money assets. Here inflation spells capital appreciation to the ordinary shareholders—as well as lower real interest charges.

C. *Ordinary figures suffer from the time-lag error.*

So far, we have been considering examples in which there is close synchronisation between (*a*) an expense, and (*b*) the relevant gain. However, with certain transactions a long time-lag between (*a*) and (*b*) is inevitable. Merchandise may be bought many months before being sold ; plant may be bought years before a given act of production. Accounting makes no effort to allow for these delays, and, as a result, sales in terms of current prices are matched with costs (purchases and depreciation) measured in much earlier pounds.

This subtraction of unlike pounds inevitably distorts the revenue account. Nor can it be defended on grounds of cost logic. If, for instance, a man buys shares for £100, and ten years later decides to give them to an orphanage, what is his generosity costing him ? He is sacrificing, not £100, but the current market value of the shares. Similarly, when a grocer sells a tin of sardines, he is not sacrificing its original cost but its present value—of which replacement cost is probably the best measure.

Suppose that, in a time of rising prices, a man buys goods for £1,050, and later sells them for £1,100. Whether or not he has made a real profit depends on how much the value of money has sunk during the turnover period. Stabilized accounts would have to convert the £1,050 and the £1,100 with the help of different indices—those for purchase date and sales date. For example :—

TABLE V

		Ordinary figures	Index no.	Stabilized figures
31 March	Purchases	1,050	105	1,000
30 June	Sales	1,100	110	1,000
	Profit	50		—

Here the true profit is *nil.*[3] More realistic figures would allow for some profit in the stabilized accounts. Suppose this is 40% on cost. Then our statements become :—

TABLE VI

		Ordinary figures	Index no.	Stabilized figures
31 March	Purchases	1,050	105	1,000
30 June	Sales	1,540	110	1,400
	Profit	490		400

Tables V and VI show two important things. *First,* we are here dealing with an additional error that could not be detected by simple tests, such as deflating profit by the price index increase at 30 June; in the extreme case shown in V, this error can even produce an illusion of profit (or loss) where none exists. *Second,* this additional error is due to the time-lag between the two transactions that are compared ; it need not have anything to do with "inventory profits" on stocks

[3]It may be objected that, if the man is financing himself with a loan, he is really better off to the extent of fifty (closing) pounds. But is this gain not from capital appreciation rather than trade ? It will be shown as appreciation in the stabilized balance-sheet.

held at balance-sheet date—here these are *nil*[4]. I fancy that the reformers who plead for new methods of stock valuation overlook this point at times. True, our example is somewhat improbable in that few firms would let their stocks sink to zero at balance-sheet date. But there are many firms, surely, whose stocks rise during the year to meet seasonal needs, and decline again towards the end of the year. Tinkering with stock values will not correct the whole time-lag error in such cases ; some of the error has by balance-sheet date become "cash" or "plant" or other assets. To attack the whole error, we must increase the expenses in the revenue statement by charging a replacement cost provision that is based on the whole turnover —not merely on the opening and closing stocks[5] ; in bad years, a corresponding sum of "revenue" will be brought back to finance purchases. A replacement provision thus acts as a useful pendulum.

When there are opening stocks, the index number for their average purchase date must be used to find the stabilized figure, and similarly with closing stock. Table VII (on page 13) shows the statements that might result if the turnover time is three months, purchases and sales flow evenly throughout the year, and the stabilized stock figure is always £250.

[4]The issues can perhaps be shown better algebraically.

Let S = sales, P = purchases, and p = net profit, in stabilized figures, and let the corresponding unstabilized figures be S', P', and p'. The rate of inflation, if smooth throughout the year, may be expressed as i, a fraction ; and the average times of purchasing and selling as x and y (fractions of the year). Thus $P' = P(1 + ix)$, and $S' = S(1 + iy)$.

Where there are no stocks at beginning and end, p is the difference between S and P, and :

$$\begin{aligned} p' &= S' - P' \\ &= S(1 + iy) - P(1 + ix) \\ &= S - P + i(Sy - Px) \\ &= p + i(Sy - Px) \end{aligned}$$

But $p' - p$ is the excess of the ordinary over the stabilized profit. Thus $i(Sy - Px)$ is the extra profit due to inflation, when there are no stocks.

If there is no time-lax, x moves on and coincides with y ; accordingly, here $p' - p = i(Sy - Py)$.

Thus, when there are no stocks, the error due to the time-lag alone is :

$$i(Sy - Px) - i(Sy - Py) = i\,P(y - x)$$

or inflation in the purchases for the average turnover period.

[5]To show the position algebraically, the terms used in footnote ([4]) must be supplemented by B and E, the stock-at-beginning and stock-at-end, bought respectively when w and z (fractions of a year) have elapsed since the index left 100.

Expanding the material of footnote ([4]), we see that, where there are stocks, the time-lag error becomes

$$i\,(P\,(y - x) + E(z - y) + B(y - w)\,).$$

TABLE VII

	If prices increase			If prices decrease			
	Ordinary figures		Stabilized figures	Ordinary figures			Stabilized figures
	FIFO	LIFO		Cost (FIFO)	Cost or Market	LIFO	
Trading account :							
Stock-at-beginning	250	250	250	250	250	250	250
Purchases	1,100	1,100	1,000	900	900	900	1,000
	1,350	1,350	1,250	1,150	1,150	1,150	1,250
Sales	1,540	1,540	1,400	1,260	1,260	1,260	1,400
Stock-at-end	294	250	250	206	200	250	250
	1,834	1,790	1,650	1,466	1,460	1,510	1,650
Gross profit	484	440	400	316	310	360	400
Suggested provision for extra replacement cost ...	— 44			+ 44			
Corrected gross profit ...	440			360			

EFFECTS OF STOCK VALUATION METHODS.

Table VII also illustrates various methods of valuing stock.

The Last-In-First-Out method yields profit figures lying between those found by the FIFO and stabilized methods. I have assumed that it means, in practice, valuation of each physical unit of stock at the price of the base year ; the resultant figure is thus the stabilized version of the normal First-In-First-Out figure. Except where stock always consists of exactly the same types of goods, it is difficult to see what other procedure is feasible ; and this procedure is in fact the one accepted by U.S. income tax law as a result of the *Hutzler Brothers v. Commissioner of Internal Revenue* case.

LIFO puts a low value on stocks just when prices are going up, and a high value when prices are sinking again. This scarcely seems realistic. We could get the same profit figure, and see much better what we were doing, if we valued stock by the ordinary (FIFO) method, and inserted into the revenue account what I shall call a "special LIFO provision" ; this would be the excess of FIFO stock over LIFO stock, and would be used like a replacement cost provision. Under the ideal conditions assumed for Table VII—an even physical flow of purchases and sales throughout the year, and a constant stock—the LIFO provision is exactly equal to the replacement cost provision, and thus results in profits that are inflated only by the 10 point price change, *i.e.* by errors A and B, not C[6]. Conditions in many businesses are probably not very far removed from those of Table VII.

[6]If FIFO is used, $p' = p + i\,(Sy + Ez - Px - Bw)$ ......(1)
while if LIFO is used, $p' = p + i\,(Sy + Ew - Px - Bw)$ ......(2)
Subtracting (2) from (1) gives the extra provision charged (in effect) by LIFO, namely $i\,E\,(z - w)$.

Under what conditions will this LIFO provision extirpate the time-lag error ? It will do so if

$$i\,E\,(z - w) = i\,(P\,(y - x) + E(z - y) + B(y - w))$$
$$\text{i.e. if } P\,(y - x) + (w - y)\,(E - B) = 0$$

The most likely circumstance in which this holds is where the average purchase and sales dates are the same (so that $y = x$), and the physical stock is constant (so that $E = B$).

Similarly it can be shown that the LIFO provision equals the whole inflationary profit $(p' - p)$ if

$$Sy - Px + w\,(E - B) = 0$$

This could be true if, in addition to the even flow envisaged in the preceding paragraph, the gross profit rate is *nil*, so that $S = P$.

We must therefore concede LIFO to be a useful corrective in many cases. It has also the merit of simplicity. On the other hand, the charging of a replacement cost provision would be a more precise corrective. Further, it would be applicable to all cases, and so be fairer from the tax standpoint.

The limitations of these two methods must be clearly understood. They are aimed merely at the time-lag error, and ignore the other forms of error listed on page 4, which can be shown up by stabilization only. Further, they both would bring in their trail a disconcerting—and perhaps dangerous—situation if they were first adopted when prices were dropping. For they would then lead to a somewhat artificial addition to the assets and an equally dubious addition to profit. I must confess that I should hesitate for a long time before recommending any firm to adopt such a course, though perhaps the results would not be bad if *all* firms made the change together. But clearly any change towards a new stock basis or stabilized accounts would cause less misgivings if introduced on the up-grade.

When prices are falling, ordinary accounting practice is to value stock, not on a cost basis, but at "the lower of cost or market." As Table VII shows, this may lead to even more eccentric profit figures than unadulterated FIFO. The difference will be most marked in the years when the peak or trough are just passing ; when a boom begins to falter, we move abruptly over to the pessimistic basis, and we shift back to the more cheerful basis as soon as the downward sweep flattens out. Slight changes are thus amplified enormously. The cumulative effect on public opinion of these simultaneous jerks to tens of thousands of profit figures is beyond compute. I am astonished that social reformers have not seized on this point long ago.

DEPRECIATION.

The time-lag error arises, as we have seen, when assets are charged to "production" at costs of an earlier price level. So far, we have taken stocks of merchandize as our example. But the same distortion can occur with any kind of asset that has a long "turnover period," *e.g.* consumable stores. It may reach its biggest proportions with plant, since here the time-lag stretches out for years.

Possible methods of attacking this error are :—

(1) An extra provision for the increase in replacement cost may be charged against profit, being shown in the balance-sheet as an addition to a capital reserve.

(2) The asset may be revalued, and the depreciation charges increased proportionately. I notice that a number of companies are now doing this, though before the war we should have looked askance at such a step. The objection to revaluation is that, if the price-movement has not come to its close, another balance-sheet upheaval will before long be necessary. Further, most of us are prejudiced against uncontrolled revaluations, since they offer scope for window-dressing. Accordingly there seems a good deal to be said for "revalorization," *i.e.* the changing of asset figures, by all firms, in step with official indices published by government from time to time—a procedure adopted in France and Italy[7].

The analogy with a "replacement cost provision" for stocks is obvious.

Table VIII shows specimen depreciation figures, assuming that by the middle of the year the value of money has halved since the base year in which the wasting asset was bought.

TABLE VIII

	Ordinary figures	Replacement or revalorization figures	Stabilized figures
Profit before charging depreciation	500	500	250
Depreciation—say	200	400	200
Net profit	300	100	50

[7]See *e.g.* articles by B. M. Berry and John Kennedy in *The Accountant* respectively of 21st February and 11th December, 1948. The book-keeping of replacement cost provisions is set out in "Income—True or False," by D. Solomons, in *The Accountants' Journal*, October, 1948.

There has been some argument about whether "replacement cost" means (*a*) current price, or (*b*) the price likely to be payable when the plant is worn out—a bigger sum than (*a*) if the inflation lasts. I prefer (*a*)—on the assumption that the depreciation quotas will not be left to waste away as money-assets, but will be promptly invested in non-money assets and so will grow in value as fast as prices rise. To take the most vivid example, the quotas may be invested outside the firm in ordinary shares ; these should in theory appreciate, and yield enough money, not perhaps to replace any given asset at its ultimate replacement cost, but to maintain the owners' capital in terms of general purchasing power. Even if the quotas are retained as money-assets, it seems advisable to show that any short-fall is due to this faulty investment programme rather than to depreciation policy.

Let me end this discussion of depreciation by quoting from an admirable American pamphlet on the same topic :

> "That we are dealing here with a substantial problem is indicated by the fact that for corporations alone under-depreciation runs around $1·5 billions a year, with an equal overstatement for income before taxes and a resultant annual tax penalty (at the present 38 per cent. rate) of nearly $600 millions. This says nothing of the effects of under-depreciation in unincorporated industry."[8]

CONCLUSIONS.

What are we to do about this matter ?

First, a strong case has, I feel, been made out for correcting the time-lag error at once—by making extra replacement cost provisions ; if these are based on current changes in a general price-index, most of the practical objections to them seem to disappear. Such a change could be made within the framework of ordinary accounts, and is not likely to cause much confusion. We have already come to regard many departures from pure cost figures as normal—*e.g.* allowances for depreciation, bad debts, and so on ; if we provide for bad debts, why not for

[8]Machinery and Allied Products Institute pamphlet : *Depreciation Policy and the Post-war Price Level* (Chicago, 1947), p. 6.

bad money? The Inland Revenue would, of course, disallow these new items. In the long run, however, our tax machine would probably have to adapt itself to accounting practice that had become a proven success; we might then be given official price indices, which would make the new procedure less liable to abuse.

Second, I should like to see companies experimenting with the issue of stabilized accounts, as statistical appendices to their ordinary reports. Such a step would have to be very cautious. Great pains would have to be taken to keep the new statements simple, and to explain them in plain words; the danger is that, if drafted with all the complexity shown in Mr. Sweeney's book, they would be completely unintelligible to anyone except a qualified accountant with his Ph.D. in statistical science. If understood properly, stabilized accounts should go far to remove false views on the state of trade, and should encourage more equable dividend policies. Remembering the unanimous burst of praise that greeted the Dunlop Company when it bravely published its first consolidated accounts, I am surprised that no pioneer has so far ventured upon this other change[9].

It is, however, doubtful whether such experiments would completely realise the bright hopes of those who now plead for them. No doubt unsuspected difficulties would show up in practice. We can already detect some drawbacks to the scheme. For instance, if prices had during recent years been based (say, by the price control authority) on replacement instead of original cost, they would have spurted up, and the inflation would have been more obvious. Again, if tax law came to recognize the new procedure, during inflation the taxable profits of many traders and manufacturers would be less than by the ordinary system. Presumably the Chancellor would thereupon increase his rates or inflict new taxes. However, the new burdens might well be less unjust and harmful than our present ones.

[9]There can be no doubt about the usefulness of stabilized accounts for explaining the issues, and for special economic studies, *e.g.* that by R. C. Jones of nine U.S. steel companies during 1941-7, in *Journal of Accountancy*, January, 1949; this shows that the biggest companies have not really earned their dividends during the war years, although their published statements show dividends to have been earned by a substantial margin.

Or consider the argument that truer accounts would lessen the evils of the trade cycle by showing its ups-and-downs in more sober colours. The trouble is that the various types of error may work dead against one another. In particular, a company with negative money-assets may, during inflations, fare on balance even better than is suggested by its ordinary accounts, since the latter ignore capital appreciation. An investigation into a group of Swedish companies during World War I shows that ordinary accounts *understated* the profits (including capital appreciation) in about 40% of the cases.[10] The 60% with overstated profits included the banks and finance houses, whose policy of investing in solid, gilt-edged securities was at that time the reverse of safe. The wider use of stabilized accounts might therefore force us to re-write our proverbs, to show the twentieth-century child that inflation's harvest is garnered, not by the cautious ant, but by the improvident grasshopper who is up to the antennae in debt. One trembles to think of the social consequences of this realisation. And again, stabilized accounts would make us more index conscious, and thus might accentuate our stampedes from money to non-money-assets and then back again, so that the cyclical surges might grow worse than ever.

However, these reservations should not deter us from attacking the problem. The inquiry into Swedish companies suggests that, in an inflation comparable with our own, the profit-and-loss statements of three-quarters of the companies contained "errors of more than 50% of the account figure . . . many have errors considerably over 200%."[11] When mistakes can be as big as this, plainly we accountants must act at once if our craft is not to be gravely discredited.

[10]R. Kristensson : "Errors in Accounting due to Inflation," *Economic History*, February, 1940, p. 382.

[11]*ibid.* p. 383.

THE STUDY OF BALANCE SHEETS

THE STUDY OF BALANCE SHEETS

By Professor W. T. BAXTER, B.Com., Ph.D., C.A.

(Being a Lecture delivered to the Chartered Accountants Students' Society of Edinburgh on 13th October 1950)

I. THE SHAPE OF THE BALANCE SHEET

If a paper on this subject had been written some years before the Second Great War, there would have been no doubt about its content and tenor. Thoughtful accountants of that date were at one in feeling unhappy about published statements; for instance, some of Professor Annan's best teaching was on their shortcomings. The man who had to lecture on style in balance sheets usually began by deploring their lack of style. He would probably illustrate his argument with an imaginary set of figures, arranged as in the usual published balance sheet of the period—*i.e.*, with little attention to order and still less to grouping or completeness. Pointing to this indigestible jumble, he would show how limited were its uses, and how many pencil jottings the reader would have to make in order to see the company's position even in outline. Then he would shuffle the figures into what he regarded as good style; and the company's situation would suddenly emerge from the fog.

Though the general standard was very poor until the late 'thirties, there were some noteworthy exceptions. A number of companies were already—without any legal compulsion—pioneering in better ways. Their example received much praise; conceivably indeed it would have been followed voluntarily even if the law had not stepped in. Be this as it may, the Companies Act of 1948 re-enforced the example of the pioneers and made obligatory what had hitherto been an act of virtue.

So to-day we take it for granted that a balance sheet should be well arranged in groups, with the individual items marshalled in a helpful order; we also expect candour and full disclosure. Perhaps, indeed, the swing has gone to the other extreme, and the reader may now be confused by the excessive detail that the law demands. Perhaps, too, the completeness and rigidity prescribed by the Eighth Schedule, while admirable for dealing with the laggards, may act as a strait-jacket and cramp further experiment by pioneers.

It may make my later argument clearer if I give simple specimen figures (omitting much of the detail that would be desirable, and indeed compulsory, in practice). I accordingly attach an outline balance sheet—Appendix A. This seems to me to be in a form that is fairly typical of present-day published balance sheets.

Future Developments

Does the vast improvement of recent years mean that there is now no scope for further steps ?

In general, I think we may say that the needs of the technical reader (*e.g.*, the financial editor, or the accountant on the staff of an investment trust) are tolerably well satisfied already. No doubt further detail is needed—and badly needed—in some directions (*e.g.*, there is still no compulsion to state the bases on which stock is valued or depreciation allowed—often vital matters). No doubt, too, we shall continue to argue about the precise form in which certain items should be presented (*e.g.*, whether the credit for a remote income tax liability should be classed as a long-term liability or a reserve). Further, the revenue picture can hardly be regarded as complete yet; some accountants (including me) can see no very good reason why figures for sales, &c., should not be shown in British (as in many American) accounts.[1] A more extreme view is that the full tax computation should be published, since this gives, in respect of many items of expense and revenue, alternative figures; these figures may be less " right " than those of the company, but have the merit of being drafted by an independent person who follows fairly objective and well-known rules. However, important though such issues are, they are small compared with the victory that has already been won.

My suggestion is that the needs of the non-specialist (the shareholder who knows little of finance and nothing of double-entry) are more clamant. These needs might well be our guides in discussing further developments; we should think of the ignorant shareholder as our employer, or as the customer who is always right. How can the main features of the company's progress be shown to such innocents with maximum clarity ? Are we who have grown familiar with an existing pattern of accounts, and with the intricate apparatus of debit and credit,

[1] Incidentally, the precise definition of turnover is a matter of some difficulty. For instance, what is the " turnover " of a travel agency—ticket sales or commission ?

perhaps apt to ignore our customer's needs and to overlook obvious means for helping him? What follows is largely concerned with the task of making our figures more suitable for the layman.

WHAT SHOULD A BALANCE SHEET SHOW?

When we ask what the job of a balance sheet is, we probably all agree that it is to give as good a picture as possible of the firm's property and finances. For instance, we want to know how big the firm is, and whether it owns machinery or shops or mineral seams. This basic work is already done fairly well, so far as the figures go, but a short verbal statement on the nature of the company would often be a useful addition to published reports (which sometimes neglect to give any inkling of the trade carried on).

Before considering how the figures can best be presented, it may be helpful to ask how balance sheets got their present form. They almost certainly began as mere trial balances (*i.e.*, as the book-keeper's private proofs of accuracy). When they came to be employed for external purposes such as testing credit and informing absentee owners, much the same form was still used. With time, less crude and stilted arrangements have been adopted, but our present model still shows its descent very clearly. Only recently have we begun to wonder whether this form is not archaic—a lingering trace of servility to the trial balance—and to ask ourselves whether we need reflect in any way the double-entry structure of the ledger. Might not our two-sided balance sheet be replaced with advantage by a " report form " of account?

To decide how our figures should be arrayed, we must know what our aims are. We want to focus attention on the more important aspects of the firm's finances. Two approaches seem possible:—

(1) We may feel that the man who consults a balance sheet is more likely to be concerned with the intricacies of the share capital and reserves than with anything else, and that accordingly they should come first. Such would seem to be the general opinion of British accountants; at least, the overwhelming majority of our balance sheets begin, as you know well, by giving this group the place of honour at the top left-hand corner.

(2) We may instead decide that what readers are most likely to look at—particularly if they are the non-specialists—is the liquid position of the company. Nobody can deny that this is important in many contexts. Further, such things as cash and

debts are understood by everyone, and so form a good jumping-off place for the timid reader. Many American reports begin with the liquid assets—and American companies have been far more progressive than others in making their reports palatable to the general public.

On the whole, I am inclined to think that this second view is the better one, and that it should at least guide us in our experiments. As you will see from my later remarks, this treatment also seems to fit in well with some other ideas about the best way to explain the nature of a company's finance.

Certain other desiderata may be taken for granted, and I shall not mention them in any detail. Plainly, the balance sheet should look attractive. Whenever such a device leads to simplicity, complicated sets of figures should be put into appendices. The lay-out should make for easy comparison with the results of earlier years. Perhaps, too, the lay-out should let us show consolidated figures for the group on the same page as the holding company's figures; but I am not sure that this arrangement may not seem too complex.

The Two-sided Balance Sheet

If we feel friendly towards the criteria that I have just suggested, but are not yet convinced of the need to jettison such an old and faithful servant as the two-sided balance sheet, what mild changes in its form might we consider ?

To stress the liquid position more, we might make the connection between current assets and current liabilities closer by deducting the latter on the assets side, bringing out a figure for net working capital. This is already done by many British companies.

Again, we might reverse the vertical order of the items so that the assets begin with cash and other current items (*i.e.*, familiar and important things which the laymen would like to see first), the order of the liabilities being reversed to match. This is the lay-out favoured by Aspro, Ltd.—and, of course, by innumerable non-incorporated firms.

Finally, we might well consider switching the sides round, bringing the assets to the place of honour on the left. I think that this arrangement would on the whole appear more logical to the non-accountant, though it seems to make the British accountant's hackles rise; in this matter, as with the "rule of the road," all countries are out of step except Britain.

Need for Clearer Wording

Such changes in design might help the unsophisticated shareholder to understand what has happened to his money. But we could also give him help in another important way—by paying more attention to the *wording* of our statements. At present, our wording is over-technical, and is often out of line with normal speech. If we want to get our meaning across, we may have to scrap our recondite expressions and substitute ones that are well understood. This would probably result in shorter words but far more of them.

I have redrafted Appendix A. in a form that may illustrate my suggestions (Appendix B.). The wording is a fairly close copy of that used in explanatory supplements to the accounts of Jantzen (Australia). Though we may feel that some of the phrases are unfortunate (*e.g.*, " what we were worth " might give rise to some queer ideas), this company's experiment seems a courageous attempt to help its shareholders.

The One-sided Balance Sheet

If we once admit that our present balance sheet calls for improvement, we must face the question of whether we should not be wiser to go the whole hog and abandon the two-sided statement in favour of the report form (*i.e.*, a single-sided document with suitable narrative).

Such an arrangement gives a welcome elasticity. In particular, it leaves more room for columns in which to show previous years' results, consolidated figures, &c. But it has the demerit of not showing all the liabilities in a compact list; for some purposes, such a list is handy for comparing with the gross assets.

While most accountants will probably not share my predilection for a balance sheet in report form, they must admit that this style is gaining favour for the appropriation account. In such accounts, small groups of debits and credits may with advantage be set off against one another so that we can see, *e.g.*, profit before tax, profit after tax, and so on. The two-sided account is far too clumsy for this purpose. Appendix C. gives a good example of a well-worded revenue and appropriation statement in one-sided form; it is taken (slightly shortened) from the report of the Industrial and Commercial Finance Corporation. The example is interesting in a second way—the statement appears as an integral part of the directors' report, no other profit and loss account being published.

Is this a good plan ? I think so. To give figures twice is surely untidy; also, on meeting the figures for the second time, the layman may well scratch his head and ask, " Is this the same sum that I ploughed through on page one, put in again for fun, or is it new stuff ? "

If we vote for the report style, I suggest that our specimen balance sheet might be arranged somewhat as in Appendix D.

APPENDICES.

I have already said that appendices are a useful means for getting clumsy detail out of the balance sheet. Needless to say, however, they can be used to show any other material that is likely to interest shareholders. In particular, the main figures from the revenue account and balance sheets of a number of years may be given with great advantage; a ten-year summary is likely to cover the whole of a trade cycle. Some American companies also give the profit and dividends *per share*, the more important percentages and ratios (*e.g.*, profit as a percentage of sales), and even the high and low Stock Exchange quotations for the shares. At least one British company does this sort of thing admirably—I recommend you to study the statements of Harding, Tilton & Hartley Ltd.

THE TEST OF SUCCESS

Supposing that we accept, as our ideal, the need for helping the average shareholder to understand our figures, and that we make some of these experiments. How are we to know whether our experiments are a success ? How are we to decide which method is best ?

Adequate tests would be expensive. I suppose professional diviners of public opinion would be willing to conduct a poll on the subject. But, to be convincing, a test would have to be on an almost impossible scale. We should have to take a fairly large sample of persons who know nothing of finance. We should split them up into groups, and give one form of balance sheet to each group. After a suitable time for digesting the figures, each person would sit an examination on the financial state of the company. The group that won the highest marks could be presumed to have received the best form of balance sheet.

As such tests are out of the question, accountants are in a real difficulty. With diffidence, I suggest that the views of teachers should carry some weight, for teachers know—all too well—how perplexing a balance sheet seems to beginners. And we must gather what we can from the opinions of the press, and of such shareholders as may volunteer their views; this is not very satisfactory, however, because the man who does not understand is usually shy about showing his ignorance, and he is the man whom we should plan to aid.

II. THE OWNERS' BALANCES

The Problem of Capital, &c.

To my mind, the section in our balance sheets that is most hard to explain is that containing the owners' balances (*i.e.*, capital, reserves, profits, and so forth).

Let us start with the balance sheet of a small trader. It will look something like this :—

Creditors . . .	2	Sundry assets . .	9
Capital . . .	7		
	9		9

Now, why is it arranged just so ? For no better reason than because such an arrangement echoes the ledger balances. If the trader had never heard of a ledger, he would most likely have put down the data thus:—

Sundry assets	9
Less Creditors	2
Net assets—*i.e.*, capital . . .	7

This is short, direct, and free from confusing repetitions. The figure 7 is shown in its simplest guise—as the (net) total of the other items. From the viewpoint of the owner, 7 is the answer to the whole sum, not a step in the calculation. A book-keeper must unhappily in his ledger treat the 7 as an item in its own right, because he needs such a counterweight to balance his books; but to show it as a separate item in balance sheets is to drag in complication needlessly. Much ingenuity has been expended on explaining to students why capital is like a liability; a rather more truthful plan is to say that it is nothing of the kind (in the owner's eyes, at least), and that its appearance on one side of a balance sheet is just a quaint survival of early practice. Or am I overstating my case ?

No great harm may be done where the small trader is concerned. The capital section of his balance sheet can remain simple; each year, profits (less drawings) are merged with opening capital. But company law makes the position much worse. A company's " capital " may be changed only if great formalities are observed, and therefore growth in real capital—in the form of profits, &c.—must not be merged with the figure for share capital. The quantity corresponding to the sole trader's 7 gets elaborated into a series of items—share capital, various reserves, profits, and so on—sometimes not even put next to one another in the balance sheet. A lay reader may well be pardoned if he is confused—if, for instance, he supposes that a reserve betokens the existence of wealth over and above what is shown among the assets (a common mistake among not unintelligent people).

This is not to suggest that our re-analysis of the owners' wealth serves no useful end. In other fields, a double analysis of data is often helpful; thus the trucks in a railway yard might be classified twice—by:

(1) physical type (*e.g.*, size) and
(2) their place of origin (*i.e.*, the station that may be able to claim them back).

In the same way, we analyse the given net asset figure *first* by asset type and *second* by source (and here, too, the source may, in the eyes of the law, affect the destination). The point I am striving to make, then, is not that we should scrap the analysis, but that we should make clearer what we are doing—namely, examining the same wealth from different points of view. Whatever the faults of Appendix D., it does at least grapple with the problem.

Descriptions of the Group

How are published statements trying to meet the difficulty of describing the ownership group ? Some of the headings are:—

Shareholders' Capital, Reserves, and Profits.

Shareholders' Interest.

Net Worth.—This otherwise convenient Americanism conveys a suggestion of revaluation, which is most unfortunate.

Ownership evidenced by.

Sources of Net Assets.

Members' Funds.—Perhaps " funds " may be ambiguous (cf. " reserve fund ").

Lever Bros. start their balance sheet with:—

> *Capital Employed.*—The share capital, &c., follows. Next comes:
> *Employment of Capital.*—The various assets are then listed.

This is bold, but perhaps over-subtle.

Who are Owners ?

We have seen that, if we list the gross assets of a firm, and then strip off the claims of " outsiders," we are left with the answer that interests the owner (*i.e.*, the total of his wealth in the business).[1] But, you will object, a company may have many types and grades of " owners." What are the tests that we should apply to candidates for admission to the ownership group (*e.g.*, why do we put debentures under some other head, such as " long-term liabilities ") ?

From the standpoint of economic analysis, all persons who are represented by a credit balance can be regarded as contributors of capital, in the sense that all of them—trade creditors, debenture-holders, and shareholders, &c.—make up the structure by which finances are mobilised for business. However, for many purposes we can distinguish at least an outer and an inner group, using the following tests:—

(1) *Permanence.*—The temporary trade creditor is much less likely to be interested in our balance-sheet analysis than the man whose claims have been " funded " into some more permanent form.

(2) *Control.*—Particularly in the eyes of lawyers, the main test is that of control, as expressed by the right to attend meetings and to vote. By this criterion, preference shareholders are owners, whereas the holders of debentures, and of the " notes " that have recently become so important (for reasons not unconnected with the rules of profits tax), are mere creditors. Yet it sometimes happens that preference shares carry no votes. Again—particularly if the company gets into difficulties—the holders of debentures may be given control; thus debenture-holders took over many cotton companies during

[1] Of course, the size of the total depends on the method of *valuing* the assets. Whether the balance-sheet method is " right " is a big question demanding separate treatment; but we should be well advised to avoid expressions like " net worth," " what we were worth," &c.

the depression. This test is accordingly not so significant as appears at first sight.

(3) *Deferability of Claim.*—A man's place in the queue for benefits (annual interest and ultimate repayment of capital) gives a better clue to his degree of ownership. A creditor's interest *must* be paid each year; the preference dividend may be withheld. At winding-up, creditors rank before shareholders. However, the preference shares probably rank before the ordinaries, and also may be redeemable; so the position of the preference shareholder is again not free from ambiguity. The ordinary shareholder is normally at the end of the queue (*i.e.*, his is the " residuary claim ").

(4) *Fixed-money Claims* versus *Equities.*[1]—A Stock Exchange security is essentially a set of promises—of yearly payments and a final return of capital. Creditors insist on promises that are defined in terms of so much money. But the ultimate owner cannot promise himself a fixed sum of money; the uncertainties of life make the surplus unpredictable, so the last man in the queue merely gets what is left over, be it large or small. An ordinary share's rights must be defined as a promise to pay, not so many £s, but an arithmetical proportion of whatever number of £s may be available.[2] Ordinary dividends and quotations are thus apt to be mercurial, and to jig up and down in tune with the company's fortunes. On the other hand, ordinary shares may have stability in real terms when the value of the £ is changing. The inflation has underlined the enormous difference between " fixed-money rights " and " equities." For instance, companies financed by fixed-money claims have since 1939 in effect carried a shrinking burden, and their fortunate ordinary shareholders have become correspondingly richer (though our balance sheets give no inkling of this change, unless the assets have been revalued). True, the quotations for such equities have appreciated less than might be expected, for two reasons: the first is dividend limitation, and the second is our failure to charge replacement cost provisions, with a consequent rise in tax to a point at which many equities are subject to a yearly capital levy.

[1] " Equity " has unfortunately several meanings, but that of residual claims (in contrast to fixed-money claims) is now widely recognised.

[2] It follows that a *pro rata* issue of bonus ordinary shares to all ordinary shareholders cannot affect their rights in the slightest; the fraction of the total belonging to each shareholder is unaffected.

To-day the distinction between fixed-money claims and equities is often, I venture to say, immensely more important than any other test that can be applied in a balance sheet.

Perhaps the four criteria given above are, at bottom, only aspects of the same test—the amount of risk borne. The man who risks his wealth most deeply will normally insist on having the final say in management, and on getting accounts that photograph the enterprise from his standpoint. However, there are innumerable degrees of risk-bearing; and many schemes of ownership, which at first sight seem surprising, may work quite well. Thus the surplus of a consumer's co-operative goes not to the capitalist but to the customer; and a nationalised industry has no residual owners, unless you and I count as such.

The Unity of Ordinary Capital and Reserves

Ordinary capital, reserves, and profits constitute a unity, whatever statutes may say. The true capital of the ordinary shareholders is thus an elastic figure, rising as reserves and profits accumulate. Its total should be shown plainly.

Our logic suggests that we should put reserves, &c.—not preference shares—next to ordinary shares in the balance sheet. Instead of:—

Ordinary shares . . .	£ —
Preference shares . . .	—
	£ —
Reserves, &c.	—

we should have:—

Ordinary shares . . .	£ —
Reserves, &c.	—
	£ —
Preference shares . . .	—

The case for this rearrangement would be weakened where preference shares participate in either profits or surplus on winding-up.

The splitting up of true capital is unfortunate in many ways. For instance, when a student of book-keeping is working on holding companies, the separation of the subsidiary's capital from reserves and profits gives him needless trouble. In most cases, the rule is simple: you add together the three items (as at the date of acquisition), and so find the true capital that must be set off against the cost of the investment—the difference being the so-called " goodwill " (if a debit) or " capital reserve " (if a credit).

Again, the directors of companies with large reserves find it hard to explain to critics—perhaps among their workpeople or in Parliament—that a dividend of, say, 40 per cent on share capital may be only a small yield on true capital. If we always treated share capital, reserves, and profits as an indivisible trinity, the explanations would be a lot simpler. Big Business is usually credited by its foes with great skill at bluffing the public; here it has in fact failed to do itself bare justice.

The cause of all these troubles is the nominal (or par) values with which we endow our securities. What is the meaning of " nominal value," and what good purpose does it serve ?

The Unimportance of " Nominal Values "

A security that has £1 printed on its certificate may be issued at 21s. (*i.e.*, at a premium of 1s.), be redeemable at 22s., and be currently quoted on the Stock Exchange at 35s. £1 is not its issue price, or its redemption figure, or its market value. Why, then, should we use the " £1 " at all ?

When label and contents are at such odds, many people are likely to be deluded. They may be confused when buying shares; " it was thought that the engraving of $100 upon a share of stock oftentimes led the investor to pay, if not the full $100, at least a larger sum than he would have paid if freed from the hypnotic effect of the $100 emblazoned upon the certificate." [1] Again, the holder of shares may be lulled into a false sense of security when his investment is sinking in value, or he may fail to recognise its true worth when it appreciates. The longer the time since the original issue, the greater is the extent to which market value may diverge from par. True, with fixed-money securities the divergence tends to be slow and slight (though dramatic moves are not unknown); the chief factors making for price changes are rates of interest in general (*e.g.*, a rise in these depresses prices) and the level of the particular company's earnings (which can push the price to below the normal figure for shares in other companies of the same type, but not raise it much above). Equities are far more sensitive, at least to

[1] Henry Rand Hatfield: ' Accounting: Its Principles and Problems,' p. 189.

the latter of these factors, and their prices go up and down freely; the link with nominal value is here excessively elastic.

Anyone who has tried to explain this matter to, shall we say, an old lady who owns some shares, will know how extraordinarily hard it is to do so. I feel certain that very large numbers of simple people attach a wholly false significance to the printed symbol, and are thereby sorely handicapped in their investment policies.

You may object that nominal value has at least one use from the shareholders' standpoint—it enables the dividend to be stated quickly as, *e.g.*, a dividend of 5 per cent. But the directors might declare a dividend of 1s. per share equally well—indeed, even more conveniently; the *amount*, and the current *yield*, are of far more importance than a percentage based on par, which can at most have a historical interest.

THE SHARE OF NO-PAR VALUE

There seems to me to be an extremely strong case for the share of no-par value. As you know, most American states permit the issue of such shares, and, after a good many teething troubles, the practice now appears to work satisfactorily. A layman, if his shares were not called "£1 shares" but "shares of no-par value," would appreciate far better than at present the nature of his wealth. "A purchaser of such stock, because of the fact that it carries no designated par value, is at once put on notice to investigate the values back of it." [1]

Why, then, does our Parliament not countenance the share of no-par value? [2] The main argument against it is that some minimum value per share ought to be paid to the company when shares are issued, and maintained permanently, to safeguard creditors. But surely this difficulty could be got over with carefully drafted rules, based on American experience. Shares of no-par value, like other shares, are issued in

[1] Roy B. Kester: 'Principles of Accounting' (New York), p. 352.

[2] The Cohen Committee sets out the case for shares of no-par value extremely well; but it concludes a little lamely: "While there is, in our view, much logic in the arguments put forward in favour of shares of no-par value, there is little public demand for, and considerable opposition to, the proposal. We have also had some evidence that in practice this class of share has given an opportunity to the unscrupulous to manipulate accounts which could be defeated only by a series of elaborate provisions, the substantial effect of which would be to re-introduce a capital account and, with it, most of those same complications which the no-par-value share was designed to avoid. Nor would the proposal bring any of the other major subjects of our enquiry nearer to solution. We therefore refrain from recommending any change in this matter." —'Report of the Committee on Company Law Amendment,' Cmd. 6659, p. 12.

return for a consideration. This can be made subject to a legal minimum; also it can be credited to a special account—as can any premiums on later issues—and then treated as non-distributable. In the event of no-par preference shares being issued, their rights to annual dividends, and final repayment on winding up, could surely be stated without undue difficulty (see, *e.g.*, the rules governing the Mexican Eagle issue). Protection of creditors need not depend on the befogging of shareholders.

One of the few British advocates of no-par shares was the late Lord Melchett.[1] He proposed that, as industrial plant has often little or no value in uses other than those for which it is designed, industrial companies ought to issue no-par shares up to the amount of their fixed assets. For my own part, I should prefer the test to be the legal rights of the shares, &c. If the shares are not to be redeemed within a short period, and at a figure near to par, the use of par is at best rather pointless and at worst a cruel snare.

Reserves

The layman must surely find that " reserves " are the most treacherous feature in a balance sheet. There seem to be powerful arguments for altering both wording and practice.

To explain reserves to a layman, one would have to trace the steps by which they come into existence. Perhaps the explanation might go somewhat as follows:—

" Suppose a company's balance sheet runs:—

	£		£
Capital	1200	Plant	1150
Profit	200	Cash	250
	£1400		£1400

Legally, £200 of cash may be paid as dividend. But the board does not want to distribute so much, as new plant costing £175 would be a good investment. In other words, the board wishes to plough back £175 of profit, and so expand the permanent ' capital ' by that sum.

Accordingly, by way of a polite indication to the shareholders

[1] His plea is reprinted in ' Studies in Accounting ' (editor, W. T. Baxter).

of this plan, the directors recommend that £175 be ' put to reserve. The accountant makes a journal entry:—

Appropriation Account	*Dr.*	£175	
Reserve	*Cr.*		£175

The appropriation account appears:—

	£		£
Transfer to reserve . .	175	Profit brought down from Profit and Loss Account	200
Balance of unappropriated profits carried forward .	25		
	£200		£200

The balance sheet will now run:—

	£		£
Capital	1200	Plant	1150
Reserve	175	Cash	250
Profit	25		
	£1400		£1400

If the shareholders take this hint, and at their general meeting confirm the directors' recommendations and accept a meagre dividend, the new plant can be bought. Suppose that in fact they decide to conserve cash by paying no dividend at all. Then, when the £175 has been spent, the balance sheet will run:—

	£			£
Capital	1200	Plant—		
Reserve	175	Original .	£1150	
Profit and Loss . .	25	New .	175	
				1325
		Cash		75
	£1400			£1400

" Reserve " thus tends to mean that certain profits are not available for dividend, in the meantime at least. The word helps to make balance sheets look impressive, for it vaguely suggests strength and stability—which doubtless explains why it has come to be preferred to " surplus " or " rest." (" Rest " is the pleasantly unexpected word still used by the Bank of England and one or two other old institutions.)

We must ask ourselves whether this procedure really indicates what is happening. What does the man-in-the-street mean when he talks about a " reserve " in everyday speech ? (I set an examination question in which I posed this question. One candidate answered that " company reserve " conveyed the idea of " shyness or an unwillingness to talk and mix with others.") In the layman's ordinary usage, the word probably suggests an excess of assets over normal or immediate needs (*e.g.*, he may refer to his spare can of petrol as his " reserve of petrol ") and his daily paper tells him of munition reserves, dollar reserves, and gold reserves. He will therefore tend to look for a company's reserve among its assets, and especially its liquid assets. He has ample justification for doing so. Even persons who are well skilled in accounts use the phrase in this sense; thus, when bankers append a " ratio of reserves to liabilities " to their balance sheets, they mean the ratio of cash, &c., to deposits.

But, in the language of accounts, " reserve " indicates something much more abstract—the line of our re-analysis that shows how much of the total is probably not destined for distribution. Emphatically, the word does *not* guarantee the existence of liquid assets; the savings may be ploughed back into fixed assets as in the above example.

Capital and Revenue Reserves

The position has become even more obscure since the 1948 Act forced us to split reserves into capital reserves and revenue reserves, giving us the following by way of definition:—

> The expression " capital reserve " shall not include any amount recorded as free for distribution through the profit and loss account and the expression " revenue reserve " shall mean any reserve other than a capital reserve.[1]

We are now wondering what " not free for distribution through the profit and loss account " means. Booklets published by the Institute of Chartered Accountants in England and Wales,[2] and by the Joint Committee of Councils of Chartered Accountants of Scotland,[3] discuss the issue and elaborate it somewhat, but end by stating (very properly) that the decision must in each case depend on the views and judgment of those responsible (*i.e.*, the directors and auditors). A wide range of items might be regarded as capital reserves:—

(*a*) We can be reasonably sure of a minimum meaning: not *legally* free because of some explicit rule in a statute or the company's

[1] Eighth Schedule, 27 (1) (*c*).
[2] The Companies Act, 1947, pp. 51-52.
[3] Memorandum on the Companies Act (1948), pp. 11-12.

own Articles. Thus the Act itself forbids the distribution of premiums on shares.

(*b*) Certain types of receipts may reasonably be earmarked as " capital," in the sense that their distribution would mean the shareholder was in effect getting back his original contribution. Thus, when the company buys up another business, any profit that the latter has already earned at purchase date is no increase in the buyer's wealth; again, profit accrued when shares are bought in a subsidiary is presumably also allowed for in the purchase price.

(*c*) Gains on sale of fixed assets may be deemed " capital." But the case law on the subject is notoriously elastic, the Courts being reluctant to interfere with the honest judgments of business men. Apart from the hazards of case law, there seem in general no very good reasons why such gains should not be divided.

(*d*) In (*a*), (*b*), and (*c*) a reserve was labelled by virtue of its *origin*. But " not regarded as free " might also imply consideration of the *purpose* for which the reserve is retained. Once this view is granted, the labelling of reserves becomes part of the directors' budget procedure, and any sum may be dubbed a " capital reserve " when the directors feel that its distribution would be inconvenient. And then, as the Scottish memorandum points out, " there does not seem to be anything in the Act which would prevent a change in the classification in a subsequent year." We might push the matter even further, and suggest that what was at 3 o'clock an entirely sensible estimate regarding the company's surplus cash may by 3.05 have become nonsense (*e.g.*, because of what the bank manager says about overdrafts).

Whereabouts in the above range of possibilities should we draw the line ? Probably we all agree that (*a*) and (*b*) are capital reserves; but (*c*), and still more (*d*), give plenty of scope for argument. And note how the Scottish memorandum concludes:—

> " In the definition a capital reserve is one not ' regarded as free for distribution through the *profit and loss account*.' This does not appear to preclude the distribution to shareholders of a capital reserve. For example, a profit on the sale of fixed assets may be classified as a capital reserve and may subsequently be distributed directly (*i.e.*, not through the profit and loss account)

to shareholders by way of capital dividend, provided that the Articles and circumstances of the company warrant such a distribution."

So we are in a pretty pickle. I suggest that no terse statement of reserves is likely to explain all that the balance sheet's readers (expert or lay) want to know about the company's financial policy. A full narrative is desirable, perhaps on the lines of Appendix D. Here is a point on which statute and accountants' "recommendations" may conceivably hamper progress. We must still give much thought to definitions, wording, and layout, and the more elbow-room we have for experiment the better.

III. TESTS OF FINAL ACCOUNTS

Analysis of Balance Sheet Changes

Even the best drafted of balance sheets, considered all by itself, cannot tell us much about a firm's progress. A *series* of balance sheets is immensely more informative.

If we take the balance sheets of this year and last year, and wish to analyse the changes that have taken place, we can do so in two ways. First, we may analyse the differences by considering why the changes were made—what sort of services were obtained by the firm from outside, and what it did in return. An analysis of this type is, of course, our old friend the profit and loss account. Secondly, we may consider how each kind of asset and liability has altered.

Various names have been proposed for this second calculation. One American suggestion, unfortunately abandoned, is the "Where-got-gone." More usual is the "Statement of source and disposition of funds." This is, besides being quite a mouthful, very vague. What are "funds"? The phrase can be used to mean almost anything, from cash in the till to reserves that are matched by an earmarked group of securities. Better phrases are: "Statement of balance sheet changes," or "Summary of 1950 financial operations," or "Source of net current assets."

While one associates these statements primarily with American practice (because many United States companies include them in their reports), they are being used more and more here. It would be interesting to know what proportion of our auditors makes a practice of supplying clients with such an analysis.

The method of preparing the statements is simple and is shown in Appendix E.; one merely finds the difference between each of the balance sheet items. In what form could the statement best be served up for presentation ? There is a good deal to be said for sticking to the full layout shown in E., which is self-explanatory. But usually the contents of the right-hand column are presented as an independent calculation. The exact wording of this is still a matter of experiment. Users of such statements may want to tackle the problem from either end—that is, they may be impelled by one or other of two questions:—

(1) The accounts show a profit of £X. Why is there not £X for us to spend ?

(2) Our cash (or net current assets) has gone up by £Y. Where did this come from ?

If you think that question (1) is typical, then you should arrange the calculation in such a way as to answer it, and your statement will run like Appendix F. If the aim is instead to show how the net current assets have been behaving, the figures will be arranged in the reverse order, as in G.

There is, I submit, a great field for accounting skill in adapting these statements to the needs of the particular client. Two examples of possible variations will suffice:—

(*a*) In F. I have glossed over the problem of depreciation. An alternative (and to my mind confusing) treatment is to add depreciation to profits, describing it as a " non-cash expense."

(*b*) The general aim is to show what new resources became available to the business during the year, and how they were invested in the plant and similar assets. But should we regard stock as a " similar asset " ? Usually business men do not share the accountant's feeling that a wide gulf separates stock from fixed assets (or such is at least my guess). Therefore changes in stock might well be put beside investments in plant, rather than beside the more liquid assets.

Appendix G. includes both these elaborations.

RATIOS

Appendix H. shows how the figures of E., together with the revenue accounts of the same company (shown in H.), might be subjected to a further analysis with the help of ratios.

Thus line (*a*) shows the working capital ratio. I suppose that normally we mean, by working capital, what I have been careful to call " the net current assets." The absolute amount of such assets is an important guide to the firm's liquid position. But for some purposes (*e.g.*, if we are comparing a big firm with a small one) the absolute amount is not very helpful; ratios may be more significant. Further, if an extremely exacting test of liquidity is desired, stock might well be deemed too inert for inclusion, and we should deal only with the more liquid assets that make up (*b*), the quick asset ratio.

A ratio of the owners' balances to other sources of finance may be a useful means of finding whether too great reliance is being placed on temporary sources. Hence (*c*), the proprietary ratio.

The investor who is anxious to hedge against the effects of the trade cycle will study the gearing of his companies. A highly geared capital structure is one in which the equity capital is insignificant in comparison with the preference and debenture capital. As we have seen, on the up-swing of the trade cycle the holder of ordinary shares tends to get better dividends; on the down-swing his dividends are apt to dwindle. The more highly geared the company, the more pronounced are these gains and losses; with high gearing a small increase in the total earnings means a very high percentage increase in the amount available to the ordinary shareholders. Hence the importance of (*d*).

The average credit periods can be tested with ratios (*e*) and (*f*).

The stock turnover may be shown either as a period of months, as in (*g*), or as a ratio. The former gives the more concrete idea, but it has one slight fault. Imagine that the various ratios, &c., are arranged in rows across a table, with monthly columns. The director who scans the table hastily can assume, where most rows are concerned, that a *rising* trend is a good sign; there is thus perhaps some risk that, when he comes to turnover, he will fail to note a danger signal.

It may be helpful to compare earnings with the quantity of assets employed. In particular, the comparison may suggest that further expansion of the business is not worth while, as such outlay may be yielding a lower return than can be got from alternative investments. Ratios (*h*), (*i*), and (*j*) try to test this aspect of the directors' policy.

Limitations of Ratios

Ratios, like other forms of mathematical expression, look impressive. One should, however, not be overawed by them, or go to the trouble of preparing them unless one is sure that they will be of some real use.

Perhaps it is hardly necessary for me to stress that any given ratio can, considered all by itself, scarcely be of much significance. The greatest statistician on earth, if told, say, that the working capital ratio is 1·8, could not glean much from this isolated figure. If he knows the corresponding figures for similar firms he may gain a useful impression. He is still more likely to learn something if he is shown how the ratio for this firm has been behaving over several years. Such a series may be the quickest and most reliable pointer to what is happening.

But even a series has its limitations. One can never say, simply because the figures sink (*e.g.*, from 1·8 to 1·5, and then to 1·3), that the position is getting worse. Such a conclusion would only be justified if all other factors had remained the same—and, in particular, if we could be sure that the directors had not embarked on a different trade policy. Thus the directors may have realised that their particular company would gain by holding a bigger selection of stock, or letting debtors pay at a more genteel tempo; in such circumstances an increase in the periods of turnover and credit would be an inevitable accompaniment to the change in policy, and a ratio series that looks deplorable might go hand-in-hand with rapidly growing net profits. In this sense, the net profit trend is more important than anything else. Mathematical fireworks never become a good substitute for commonsense and understanding.

APPENDICES

APPENDIX A. OUTLINE OF BALANCE SHEET IN PRESENT CONVENTIONAL FORM

Share Capital, Reserves, &c.—				Fixed Assets—			
Capital—				Premises . .		£3,500	
Ordinary Shares .		£3,000		Motor Vehicles .	£3,000		
5 per cent Preference Shares . . .		2,000		*Less* Depreciation	1,500	1,500	
		£5,000					£5,000
Capital Reserve . .		500		Current Assets—			
Revenue Reserves—				Stock		£2,500	
General Reserve	£1,000			Debtors . . .		2,200	
Profit carried forward .	500			Cash . . .		1,100	
		1,500					5,800
			£7,000				
Long-term Liabilities—							
Debentures			2,000				
Current Liabilities—							
Creditors			1,800				
			£10,800				£10,800

APPENDIX B. OUTLINE OF BALANCE SHEET WITH FULL NARRATIVE, AND WITH ASSETS ON LEFT

EXPLANATORY BALANCE SHEET

Listing what we owned, what we owed, and what we were worth at the close of our financial year 19

ASSETS—WHAT WE OWNED.		LIABILITIES—WHAT WE OWED.	
Cash.—This amount is the total of cash, stamps, and bank balances	£1,100	*Trade Creditors.*—Amounts we owed for the purchase of merchandise, supplies, and services . .	£1,800
Debtors.—Total owed us by our customers for merchandise, less estimated amounts which we may not be able to collect . .	2,200	*Debentures.*—This is the amount borrowed, at 5 per cent interest, from creditors, to whom we gave a bond over our premises as security	2,000
Stocks.—This is the value of the merchandise on hand . .	2,500		£3,800
Motor Vehicles—Depreciated Cost.—This is the amount we paid for motor vehicles (£3000), less an estimated allowance (£1500) for loss in value because they were gradually wearing out . .	1,500	SHAREHOLDERS' FUNDS—WHAT WE WERE WORTH.	
Premises.—This is what we paid for land and buildings . . .	3,500	*Capital, Reserves, and Surplus.*—This represents the investment in the business by 238 shareholders	7,000
	£10,800		£10,800

APPENDIX C.

REVENUE ACCOUNT IN NARRATIVE FORM
(Included in Directors' Report)

REPORT OF THE DIRECTORS

The Directors submit their Report for the year to 31st March 1950, together with the audited Balance Sheet at that date and the following Statement of Profit and Loss.

STATEMENT OF PROFIT AND LOSS

Previous Period				Year to 31st March 1950
	Interest and Dividends on Advances and Investments (gross), less Interest on Loan Capital amount to			£536,161
	To which has to be added Other Income (including Net Profits on Sales of Investments) amounting to			128,053
				£664,214
	There fall to be deducted :—			
	Administration Expenses		£106,025	
	Provision for Audit Fee		630	
	Directors' Remuneration—			
	Fees	£4,000		
	Salary	2,500		
			6,500	
	Depreciation of Furniture and Equipment and Amortisation of Expenditure on Alterations to Leased Premises		429	
			£113,584	
	Amount set aside for Doubtful Advances and Investments		190,000	
				303,584
	So that the Profit for the Year before taxation is			£360,630
	The estimated charge for Income Tax, based on the profit for the year after giving effect to relief—£36,566—in respect of losses of earlier years, is			126,226
	Leaving a Net Profit for the year of			£234,404
	The accumulated deficiency brought forward from the previous period has to be deducted			53,585
	Leaving a balance to the credit of Profit and Loss Account of			£180,819
	The Directors have decided to make a transfer to Reserve for Contingencies of			100,000
	So that there is a Surplus on the Profit and Loss Account to be carried forward of			£80,819

(Rest of Directors' Report follows)

APPENDIX D. OUTLINE OF BALANCE SHEET IN SINGLE-SIDED OR REPORT FORM

THE COMPANY'S ASSETS ARE :—		
1. Current Assets—		
Cash	£1,100	
Debtors	2,200	
Stock	2,500	
		£5,800
2. *Less :* Current Liabilities—		
Trade Creditors		1,800
3. Net Current Assets or "Working Capital"		£4,000
4. Fixed Assets—		
Motor Vehicles	£3,000	
Less : Depreciation	1,500	
	£1,500	
Premises	3,500	
		5,000
5. Total Assets less Current Liabilities		£9,000
6. *Less :* Long-term Liabilities—		
Debentures		2,000
7. Net Assets		£7,000

THE ABOVE NET ASSETS HAVE BEEN PROVIDED BY THE SHAREHOLDERS THUS :—			
8. Ordinary Shareholders—			
Original Capital of 3000 Ordinary Shares		£3,000	
Premium on issue of these Shares		500	
Trade Profits—			
Portion to be retained in business indefinitely	£1,000		
Portion not yet appropriated	500		
		1,500	
9. Ordinary Shareholders' Interest (the "Equity")			£5,000
10. Preference Shareholders—			
Original Capital of 2000 5 per cent Shares			2,000
			£7,000

APPENDIX E. SUMMARISED BALANCE SHEETS

	Last year		This year		Increase in assets during this year
Assets—					
Fixed Assets—					
Premises		£3,500		£3,500	
Motor Vehicles—					
1st Jan.—Cost less depreciation	£1,620		£1,200		
Additions	..		800		
	£1,620		£2,000		
Depreciation for year	420		500		
		1,200		1,500	£300[1]
		£4,700		£5,000	£300
Current Assets—					
Stock		£3,000		£2,500	− £500
Debtors		1,300		2,200	900
Cash		..		1,100	1,100
		£4,300		£5,800	£1,500
Total Assets		£9,000		£10,800	£1,800

[1] Made up of gross investment £800, less depreciation £500.

			Sources of finance
Less : Liabilities to outside Creditors—			
Short-term Liabilities—			
Creditors	£1,200	£1,800	£600
Bank Overdraft	925	..	– 925
	£2,125	£1,800	– £325
Long-term Liabilities—			
Debentures	..	£2,000	£2,000
Total Liabilities	£2,125	£3,800	£1,675
Net Assets	£6,875	£7,000	
Ownership—			
5 per cent Cum. Pref. Shares	£2,000	£2,000	
Ordinary Shares	3,000	3,000	
Reserve	1,500	1,500	
Profit and Loss Account	375 [1]	500	£125
Total	£6,875	£7,000	£125
			£1,800

[1] In preceding year, a loss of (£435 – £375) = £60.

APPENDIX F. ANALYSIS OF BALANCE SHEET CHANGES (*Simple Form*)

STATEMENT SHOWING HOW PROFIT, &C., WAS USED

Profits shown in Profit and Loss Account		£225
To this must be added money obtained from debenture issue		2,000
Total		£2,225
This has been used as follows :—		
Preference dividend		£100
Increase in motor vehicles		300
Increase in net current assets—		
Current assets	£1,500	
Current liabilities (reduction in)	325	
		1,825
		£2,225

APPENDIX G. ANALYSIS OF BALANCE SHEET CHANGES (*Alternative Form*)

STATEMENT SHOWING HOW QUICK ASSETS WERE OBTAINED

Quick assets (net)—		
At close of year		£1,500
At start of year (deficiency)		825
Increase during year		£2,325
This increase has been obtained as follows :—		
Profits		£225
Add : Non-cash expense—depreciation for year		500
Found from own resources		£725
Debentures issued		2,000
Available resources for year		£2,725
Less : Disbursements—		
Additions to motor vehicles	£800	
Preference dividend	100	
	£900	
Less : Reduction in stock	500	
		400
		£2,325

APPENDIX H. SUMMARISED TRADING AND PROFIT AND LOSS ACCOUNT

Year ended 31st December	Last Year	%	This Year	%
Sales	£8,000	100	£10,000	100
Stock, 1st January	£2,800		£3,000	
Purchases	5,960		7,000	
	£8,760		£10,000	
Stock, 31st December	3,000		2,500	
Cost of goods sold	£5,760	72·0	£7,500	75·0
Gross profit	£2,240	28·0	£2,500	25·0
Selling expenses	£120	1·5	£125	1·2
Distribution expenses (including depreciation)	545	6·8	750	7·5
Administrative expenses	840	10·5	1,100	11·0
Financial expenses	200	2·5	300	3·0
	£1,705	21·3	£2,275	22·7
Net profit	£535	6·7	£225	2·3

Year ended 31st December	Last Year	This Year
Preference dividend	£100	£100
Ordinary dividend	..	..
Added to carry forward	435	125
	£535	£225

RATIOS

	Last Year	This Year
(*a*) Working capital ratio— $\frac{\text{current assets}}{\text{current liabilities}}$	$\frac{4,300}{2,125} = 2·0$	$\frac{5,800}{1,800} = 3·$
(*b*) Quick asset ratio— $\frac{\text{debtors and cash}}{\text{current liabilities}}$	$\frac{1,300}{2,125} = 0·6$	$\frac{3,300}{1,800} = 1·8$
(*c*) Proprietary ratio— $\frac{\text{ownership}}{\text{liabilities}}$	$\frac{6,875}{2,125} = 3·2$	$\frac{7,000}{3,800} = 1·8$
(*d*) Capital gearing— $\frac{\text{pref. and deb. capital}}{\text{equity capital}}$	$\frac{2,000}{3,000} = 0·7$	$\frac{4,000}{3,000} = 1·3$

	Last Year	This Year
Average credit periods—		
(*e*) (i) Allowed—		
$\frac{\text{average debtors}}{\text{sales}}$	$\frac{1{,}300^{1}}{8{,}000} \times 12 = 2$ months	$\frac{1{,}300 + 2{,}200}{2 \times 10{,}000} \times 12 = 2{\cdot}1$ months
(*f*) (ii) Taken—		
$\frac{\text{average creditors}}{\text{purchases}}$	$\frac{1{,}200^{1}}{5{,}960} \times 12 = 2{\cdot}4$,,	$\frac{1{,}200 + 1{,}800}{2 \times 7{,}000} \times 12 = 2{\cdot}6$,,
(*g*) Average turnover period—		
$\frac{\text{average stock}}{\text{cost of sales}}$	$\frac{2{,}800 + 3{,}000}{2 \times 5{,}760} \times 12 = 6$,,	$\frac{3{,}000 + 2{,}500}{2 \times 7{,}500} \times 12 = 4{\cdot}4$,,
Earnings rates on [2]—		
(*h*) Total assets—		
$\frac{\text{net profit}}{\text{total assets (gross)}}$	$\frac{535}{9{,}000} \times 100 = 5{\cdot}9\%$	$\frac{225}{10{,}800} \times 100 = 2{\cdot}1\%$
(*i*) Equity interest—		
$\frac{\text{net profit} - \text{pref. div.}}{\text{ord. cap.} + \text{res.} + \text{profit}}$	$\frac{435}{4{,}875} \times 100 = 8{\cdot}9\%$	$\frac{125}{5{,}000} \times 100 = 2{\cdot}5\%$
(*j*) Ordinary capital—		
$\frac{\text{net profit} - \text{pref. div.}}{\text{ordinary capital}}$	$\frac{435}{3{,}000} \times 100 = 14{\cdot}5\%$	$\frac{125}{3{.}000} \times 100 = 4{\cdot}2\%$

[1] It is assumed that the debtors and creditors were approximately the same at the beginning and end of last year.

[2] Strictly, these rates should be calculated on average funds employed, &c. In practice it is common to use the year-end figure.

THEORY OF FOREIGN BRANCH ACCOUNTS

W. T. Baxter and B. S. Yamey

Reprinted from ACCOUNTING RESEARCH, Volume Two, Number Two, April, 1951.

THEORY OF FOREIGN BRANCH ACCOUNTS

By W. T. BAXTER and B. S. YAMEY

Like most other forms of "advanced" accounting, foreign branch accounts are much older than one might casually suppose. Thus the Fuggers had eleven foreign branches, strung out all the way from Lisbon to Danzig, and the book-keeper at their Augsburg head office has left us a record (dated 1518) of how he consolidated the branch returns into annual accounts for the whole undertaking.[1]

Yet despite this respectable antiquity the theory of accounting for foreign branches (and, nowadays, foreign subsidiary companies) does not seem ever to have been set down critically. The topic has extra interest at the moment because of the pound's devaluation (which must have set many British firms wondering just what their branch figures mean); and also because of our growing concern over the accounting effects of changes in the internal price level, which involve much the same issues and practices.

A set of rules for consolidating branch returns is well enough known—any properly primed examinee can rattle them off. You first take the branch trial balance and convert its various balances from foreign to home money; if the exchange is unstable (though not excessively so) you choose your rates thus:

(*a*) *Current assets and liabilities*—at the exchange rate prevailing at the trial balance date ("closing rate").

(*b*) *Non-current assets and liabilities*—at the rates prevailing when the fixed asset was bought or the liability incurred ("original rate").

(*c*) *Inter-office accounts*—Remittances by the branch are deemed exactly to equal the home currency received in exchange by the head office ("actual rate"). Similarly, the branch's "capital" (the balance on its account with head office) is considered to be the equivalent of whatever home currency balance is to be found on branch account in the head office's books.

(*d*) *Revenue balances*—These are converted at a rate or rates designed to reflect the general state of the exchange during the year (often an "average rate").

This done, you find yourself with a converted trial balance that does not balance. The difference must next be inserted—as the "profit on exchange" if a credit, or "loss on exchange" if a debit; and this figure must be treated with profound caution, being written off immediately if a loss but treated as a non-distributable reserve if a gain.[2]

It seems a defect in accounting textbooks that the theory and implications of this procedure are seldom amplified. How do the rules fit in with the main

[1] M. L. Hartsough, "Book-keeping under the Fuggers," *Journal of Economic and Business History, IV,* page 550.

[2] There are in practice many variants to this textbook procedure. But it may probably be looked on as the norm. *Accounting Problems Arising from Devaluation of Foreign Currencies,* Research Department, American Institute of Accountants (1949), supports this idea, and elaborates the steps to be taken in consolidation.

body of accounting principles? Do the home figures give a "correct" picture of branch activities? When an item must be put into *both* revenue account and balance sheet (that is, when it is an adjustment figure, such as closing stock), which of the two recommended rates should be used, or should debit and credit each have its own rate? These and many other accounting problems clamour for answers. And do not economic factors sometimes come into the picture, perhaps giving it very different colours? For instance, if the British-French exchange rates alter, the new rates may reflect a change in the relative buying power of the pound and franc in their home markets; but they may instead result from a political scare or high-level financial operations, and the price indices may therefore show little or no change. Would such a situation affect our rules?

Another set of questions centres on the significance of our "profit on exchange" figure. Precisely what does it show us? In current speech, the phrase seems to suggest gains from actual transactions with a dealer in foreign exchange—realised profits from remittances. But a "profit on exchange" might be needed to square a converted trial balance for a year when there were no remittances; so this meaning plainly does not fit the facts. Another possibility is that the "profit on exchange" strips away the whole effect of exchange movements from our statements, leaving the bare figures that would have been found had the exchange stayed rigidly at some normal level. As we shall see, this attractive notion will also not hold water.

When the complexity of the problem is realised, we can readily understand why textbook authors have shirked it. And obviously it would be presumptuous to hope that any brief essay such as this can avoid error, or tidy up all the issues.

Let us now consider each group of converted figures in turn. The balance sheet items are fairly plain sailing, so we shall start with them.

THE CONVERTED BALANCE SHEET

Fixed assets. Conversion at original rate (that is, the continued use of the first home figures in all later balance sheets) harmonises with the general accounting principle that fluctuations in non-current values should be ignored.

Long-term liabilities. Usually a fixed asset has a market value that is *not fixed in terms of money*—for instance, the realisation value of plant is not tied to a given money figure. But suppose that we are dealing with rights that are rigidly defined in terms of so many units of foreign money (a long-term liability, such as a loan on mortgage, being a more likely example of such a right than a fixed asset). Should we not get a clearer and more stringent view of the branch finances by converting such balances, especially redeemable obligations, at *closing* rate? A dangerous understatement of liabilities may result from showing loans at original rate if the foreign currency has appreciated.[3]

[3] The American Institute's pamphlet (mentioned in the last footnote) shows honesty and courage in admitting that an earlier pronouncement, taking the opposite view, now seems wrong. One hopes its candour will be noted by other bodies that make *ex cathedra* recommendations on the nature of accounting truth.

The last paragraph draws attention to something that cannot be too strongly emphasised: when changes in money values are being studied, the significant line of demarcation in the balance sheet does not lie between current and fixed items, but between (a) rights and obligations that are defined in terms of money (including even preference shares), and (b) forms of wealth whose money value can alter freely.

Current assets and liabilities. Here the aim of recording historic transactions gives way (as in home balance sheets) to that of conservative revaluation. Past rates of conversion are therefore replaced by current rate—which is also a more reliable means of forecasting potential remittances. If the resultant "profit on exchange" is treated as a non-distributable reserve, the procedure harmonises with the general accounting canons for valuing current assets: (i) pending losses should be anticipated by immediately reducing the asset values; but (ii) appreciation should be sternly ignored till the gain is realised.

REVENUE FIGURES—CONVERSION AT A SINGLE AVERAGE RATE

What is the object of converting figures in the revenue account? Presumably to give a description of branch trading in homely terms, to save head office directors the trouble of wondering "What does this figure mean in my currency?" A second aim may also be present—to show the size of any potential remittances from earnings.

There would be no doubt about the size and meaning of the figures if the goods for every branch sale could, just at the moment of sale, be sent out specially from head office, and if every penny of receipts could be sent home again at once. The real procedure must be far removed from this ideal case: but we can obtain statistics that mean much the same (if branch operations are simple) by keeping up a pretence that money is remitted back and forth for each transaction, that is, by converting every figure at the rate of the day concerned.

Where the flow of trade is brisk, such detail would be a nuisance, and so we substitute the average rate for the year. "If the exchange is only subject to moderate fluctuations, and if the profits of the local branch or office are earned more or less evenly over the whole financial year, then it will probably be found quite sufficient to convert the profits . . . once a year at the average daily rate of exchange prevailing during the year."[4]

If exchange rates have been sedate, we may reasonably plead that the converted revenue account gives a not-too-blurred snapshot of branch behaviour. The photographer would be unwise to pretend that the likeness is exact in every way; but he may fairly claim that it gives a good enough idea of the size of branch costs and revenues—particularly as judged by the earnings that *might have* been remitted (or spent locally) during the year. Should the rate no longer stand at average level, the profit figure will not show how much home money could now be got by remitting profits still abroad. The figure is thus a less conclusive guide for dividend policy than home profit

---

[4] A. E. Cutforth, *Foreign Exchange* (London, 1925), page 40.

figures, nor in a just world would it be used mechanically as a basis for levying taxes.

If the course of trade or the exchanges does not run evenly throughout the year—for instance, where there is much buying and selling just before Christmas—the average should presumably be weighted to reflect the peaks and valleys. An alternative plan would be to find the branch profits "every three months or even every month, and to convert such quarterly or monthly figures . . . at the average rates of exchange applicable to each quarter or month as the case may be."[5]

In the pages that follow immediately, we shall assume that the procedure is to use one single rate—a suitable average for all revenue transactions (both debits and credits); and we shall try to see what the converted figures mean under this condition. Later we shall have to cast a glance at the results of using other kinds of average, and different rates for costs and revenues.

WHEN DOES "PROFIT ON EXCHANGE" ARISE?

The nature of "profit on exchange" is best seen with the help of ultra-simple examples, such as those in Table A. We there suppose that head office is in a country called Homeland, whose money unit is the Home (H); and that the branch is in far-off Foreignia, whose unit is the Forin (F). For a long time before our story begins, one Forin has been worth four Homes (that is, the rate has been F1 = H4). But during the current year the Forin suddenly appreciates, and the rate jumps to F1 = H5.

In example (1), the sole opening asset of the branch is F10 of cash. No trade is carried on, and (before the exchange alters) the F10 is invested in fixed assets. No "profit on exchange" results. Exactly the same figures would be obtained if the F10 were instead remitted (before the exchange alters).

In (2), cash is held until after the exchange movement. Here "profit on exchange" makes its appearance, thanks to the higher conversion rate of the debit balance—whether this represents cash left inert at the branch, or sent home, or invested.

In example (3), the branch has no "capital," but has for long earned and remitted F10 a year as net income (say, from a fixed royalty). Accordingly, head office has always received H40, and has come to regard this as the branch's normal earnings. In the present year, however, the exchange alters *before* the royalty is earned; the accounts, converted according to our rules, now show that earnings are no longer H40 but H50. Not a penny of "profit on exchange" is thrown up by our conversion process. This holds true whether the F10 is remitted, or kept as cash, or invested in fixed assets. Comparisons with earlier years' revenue become misleading, and a wholly false impression of the branch manager's "activity"—though not of his power to remit home money—is conveyed.

If head office wishes to excise the new exchange effect, it should adopt the less usual accounting device of converting at an unchanging "standard" rate.

---

[5] *Ibid.*, page 40.

TABLE A

Showing how and when "profit on exchange" arises.

Assumption: Opening rate: F1 = H4; changing to F1 = H5.	Branch results in foreign currency Dr. F	Cr. F	Conversion rate	Branch results converted into home currency Dr. H	Cr. H
Example (1). F10 of cash held at start of year, and invested before rate alters.					
Capital invested in branch		10	Opening rate, F = H4		40
Investment (*or* remittance)	10		Actual rate, F = H4	40	
Example (2). As in (1), but no transaction takes place till after rate alters.					
Capital invested in branch		10	Opening rate, F = H4		40
Cash (*or* remittance *or* investment)	10		Closing or actual rate, F = H5	50	
Balancing figure—"profit on exchange"					10
Example (3). Opening capital *nil;* income F10, earned after rate reaches F1 = H5.					
Income		10	Income rate, F = H5		50
Cash (*or* remittance *or* investment)	10		Closing rate, F = H5	50	
Example (3*a*). Variant of (3), using a method that removes the exchange effect from the income figure.					
Income: Normal equivalent ...		10	"Normal" rate, F = H4		40
Due to exchange alteration			Balance		10
Cash, etc.	10		Closing rate, F = H5	50	
Example (4). As (3), but income is not remitted until F = H5.5.					
Income		10	Average rate, F1 = H5		50
Remittance	10		Actual rate, F1 = H5.5	55	
"Profit on exchange" balance, being 10×(H5.5 − H5) = H5					5

Example (3a) illustrates this, and shows how the year's gains may be split between ordinary trade and exchange magnification. However, once men's minds grow used to the new rate, this device may be more of a puzzle than a help.

In fact, it is unlikely that all items in the branch revenue account will be fixed in terms of Forins. Particularly if the branch sells imported goods, its sale prices and volumes will tend to change as a result of the exchange movement. Then, unless there are some odd coincidences, any method of conversion is fairly sure to make branch activity look too big or too small. And "profit on exchange" is an imperfect instrument for restoring true perspective.

The answer to one set of the questions posed at the start of this essay now seems clearer. "Profit on exchange" can arise whether or not there are actual exchange dealings; thus it may or may not point to a *realised* gain. And it does not indicate to what extent larger trade profits are due merely to the flattering effects of a better exchange rate, as contrasted with greater physical turnover and similar factors.

WHAT DOES "PROFIT ON EXCHANGE" MEASURE?

What then *does* "profit on exchange" show? Consider the circumstances of its birth. It is a balancing figure, put into converted accounts when the owners' balances—capital, opening reserves, and income—do not equal the sum of the other balances, the net assets. No difference can arise if the net assets are still converted at rates the same as those used to show their "arrival" in the year's accounts, namely, original for opening assets, and average for the extra assets gained by earning income. So the difference has nothing to do with opening fixed assets (net), that have been kept throughout the year; similarly it has nothing to do with cash, and the like, that is remitted or invested before the rate moves from "arrival" level. It must be confined to items whose rate alters between "arrival" and conversion dates, that is, it must be confined (when there is no realisation of fixed assets) to:

i. *opening current assets* (net)—appreciation from start to close of year; and
ii. *additions to current assets* (normally equal to profit)—appreciation from income date to close of year;

less

iii. outgoings of current assets (remittances, or investments in fixed assets)—appreciation from remittance or investment date to end of year.

In the case of a trading branch with no capital transactions, then, "profit on exchange" is appreciation, springing from favourable movements in exchange quotations, in the home book-value of branch wealth while held in the form of current assets.[6] "Loss on exchange," it is hardly worth saying, is corresponding depreciation.

The same matter can be put in more generalised form with the help of algebra, and such proof seems desirable. In branch currency, let:

F be opening fixed assets (net) bought when rate was f.
C be opening current assets (net) to be converted at opening rate o.
R be remittance during year, when rate was r.
P be profit, to be converted at average rate of realisation p.

Closing current assets in this simple case equal opening current assets *plus* profits *less* remittances. They can be expressed as $(C+P-R)$. Let the closing rate be c. The opening balance on head office account, the branch "capital,"

---

[6] As will be explained, the above generalisation may require correction if income rate is not based on the date of income realisation. Again, fixed assets are for simplicity here deemed to be non-wasting; later paragraphs deal with depreciation.

equals $(F+C)$. At the end of the year the unconverted trial balance is therefore:

$$F+(C+P-R)+R=(F+C)+P \quad \ldots\ldots (1)$$

When converted, F becomes Ff, R becomes Rr, $(F+C)$ becomes $(Ff+Co)$, and so on; we must, to compensate, put in E (profit on exchange) as a balancing figure. Adjusting (1) in this way, we get the converted trial balance:

$$Ff+(C+P-R)c+Rr=(Ff+Co)+Pp+E \quad \ldots\ldots (2)$$

Our aim is to define E. Transposing, we get:

$$\begin{aligned} E &= Ff+Cc+Pc-Rc+Rr-Ff-Co-Pp \\ &= C(c-o)+P(c-p)-R(c-r) \quad \ldots\ldots (3) \end{aligned}$$

Thus, "profit on exchange" equals appreciation on opening current assets (between close and opening of year), and on the current assets won as profit (between close and profit date), but not on current assets remitted (from remittance date to close of year).

Equations (2) and (3) show plainly the rôle of p, the average rate at which profit is converted. If the rate chosen were lower, converted profit (Pp) would fall, and "profit on exchange" (E) would rise; and vice versa. Accordingly, if p does not truly reflect the dates on which profitable sales led to the arrival of extra current assets, some of the "profit on exchange" from holding such assets will seep into trade profit, and so confuse the trading picture.

Example (4) illustrates the issue more fully. Here the facts are the same as in (3), but the Forin goes on appreciating from profit date to remittance (or investment) date. As a result, there is a "profit on exchange" the growth in the home value of the income while lying in the branch till. It may be calculated by multiplying these Forins by $(r-p)$, where p is the rate when the profit was realised, and r at remittance.

The matter may be put more vividly as follows. Suppose that the branch's normal trade is the responsibility of a sales manager, while questions of when to make remittances (in either direction), and how much working capital to hold at the branch, are the concern of a finance manager. Neither "profit on exchange" nor any other converted figure is likely to tell us how much the sales manager's results have been affected by exchange movements. On the other hand, "profit on exchange" is some guide to the finance manager's genius at forecasting exchange movements—though he may reasonably point out that in fact a certain minimum of current assets *must* be kept at the branch and so is beyond his control.

"PROFIT ON EXCHANGE" AND FIXED ASSET TRANSACTIONS

How does our definition fare if branch transactions include dealings in fixed assets, instead of being confined to simple trading? Three main possibilities present themselves:

(1) *The branch may buy fixed assets.* The purchase money becomes frozen at investment date, and so thereafter drops out of our exchange reckonings.

Such investment thus affects "profit on exchange" in the same kind of way as remittances.

This fact may also be shown algebraically. In algebraic proof, I, an investment in fixed assets, etc., made when the rate is i, will lead to equation (3) becoming:[7]

$$E = C(c-o) + P(c-p) - R(c-r) - I(c-i)$$

(2) *The branch may sell fixed assets.* The sale thaws the book value (original cost or a written-down balance); any exchange appreciation on the book value, between dates of original investment and sale, swells "profit on exchange."

The algebraic statement must be enlarged to deal with F_1(the book value of the scrapped asset, bought when the rate was f_1) and C_1 (the sale money obtained when the rate was c_1). A revised equation (3) will show that the "profit on exchange" is swollen by $F_1\ (c_1-f_1)+C_1(c-c_1)$, that is, by exchange appreciation on the book-value between dates of purchase and sale, and on the fresh current assets (the proceeds) from sale date till the end of the year.[7] Thus the appreciation on fixed assets (unlike that on current assets) is "stored up" till the asset is sold.

(3) *The branch may hold wasting assets.* The using-up of an asset in the earning of revenue is very like case (2), the sale of an asset; the chunk of original cost written off can be thought of as a small fixed asset that has been sold—"realised" is our more usual word, and "disinvested" is also handy for our purpose as it covers both using-up and sale.

The annual depreciation charge can be converted in two ways, and we shall have to think about the rights and wrongs of this matter on another page. But we may now observe that, if we convert this charge at the same rate as we use for the sales, etc., on the other side of revenue account, we thereby stop any exchange appreciation (on the bit of original cost written off) from getting into trade profit—we guide such gains into "profit on exchange." So, under this method, conversion has much the same results as with the fixed asset sold in case (2). The extra "profit on exchange" is appreciation, on the Forins written

---

[7] The detailed algebra for the buying and selling of fixed assets (that is, for both paragraphs (1) and (2) above) is as follows. Closing current assets, hitherto $(C+P+R)$, become $(C+P-R-I+C_1)$. The unconverted trial balance now includes, say, a book-loss on the sale of F_1, namely (F_1-C_1), and runs:

$$F+(F_1-C_1)+(C+P-R-I+C_1)+R+I=(F+F_1+C)+P$$

If "loss on sale" is converted at the rate ruling at sale date, this equation becomes:

$$Ff+(F_1-C_1)c_1+(C+P-R-I+C_1)c+Rr+Ii=Ff+F_1f_1+Co+Pp+E$$

$$\text{Therefore, } E=F_1c_1-C_1c_1+Cc+Pc-Rc-Ic+C_1c+Rr+Ii-F_1f_1-Co-Pp$$

$$=C(c-o)+P(c-p)-R(c-r)-I(c-i)+F_1(c_1-f_1)+C_1(c-c_1).$$

If instead "loss on sale" is put into revenue account and converted at net profit rate, c, becomes p in the above, so the last two terms are $F_1(p-f_1)+C_1(c-p)$.

off, from the date when the asset was bought to the close of the year.[8]

To summarise. Provided all revenue account figures are converted at a single average rate, and this faithfully mirrors the arrival dates of current revenues, we may say: *"profit on exchange" is appreciation, springing from favourable movements in exchange quotations, in the home book-values of two forms of branch wealth, namely*

(*i*) *current assets* (*over such part of the year as they have been held*); *and*

(*ii*) *fixed assets disinvested during the year* (*from original date to disinvestment date*).

WHEN IS "PROFIT ON EXCHANGE" REALISED?

As has been said earlier, textbooks tend to advocate that "profit on exchange" should not be added to current revenue, but should be treated as a non-distributable reserve. So long as the current assets in question are still at the branch, much can be said for such caution.[9] But is the gain *never* to be thought of as "realised"? After the funds have been remitted, and so are no longer threatened by reverse exchange movements, surely the gain is as safely realised as a gain can well be? One might of course argue that it is a windfall, and not the result of deliberate income-making policy; but such a view seems slightly askew from reality when the circumstances of foreign branch management are considered, and might foster a dangerous indifference to the need for care and forethought in exchange policy.

Example (5) shows what is clearly an unrealised profit. Here part of the income is remitted as soon as earned (and so yields no "profit on exchange"), but $F1$ is still at the branch at the year's end. If closing rate is c, the profit on exchange is the sum retained in foreign money (here $F1$) multiplied by $(c-p)$.

Example (6) gives a more realistic case in which elements of (4) and (5) are both present, i.e. part of the income is remitted after a short time-lag, and part is left abroad. The exchange gains on both sums—despite the marked dis-

---

[8] Here a wasting asset (F_2, bought when the rate was f_2) is "realised" during the year, to the extent of the bit written off, i.e. the depreciation, C_2. P is now the net profit after charging C_2; so closing current assets may be written $(C+P+C_2)$ if there are no other transactions in fixed assets or remittances.

At the close of year, fixed assets are written down to (F_2-C_2), and the unconverted trial balance is:

$$(F_2-C_2)+(C+P+C_2)=(F_2+C)+P$$

Converted, this goes:

$$(F_2-C_2)f_2+(C+P+C_2)c=(F_2\ f_2+Co)+Pp+E$$

$$\text{Therefore, } E=C(c-o)+P(c-p)+C_2(c-f_2)$$

E thus now includes appreciation, on the bit of wasting asset written off, from the date of its original purchase till close of year. $C_2(c-f_2)$ might also be written $C_2(p-f_2)+C_2(c-p)$; the equation then seems to be merely a special case of that for a sale—footnote [7]—when "proceeds" equal original cost of the asset realised.

[9] Another reason for the procedure arises if fixed assets have been sold. Then, "profit on exchange" will include gain from the capital transaction, which may be deemed not available for dividends.

tinction between them in degree of realisation—are lumped together in "profit on exchange." To find what part of this omnibus gain is realised, one must multiply the remittance by $(r-p)$.

TABLE B

Showing when "profit on exchange" is realised.

Assumption: Opening rate: F1 = H4; F appreciates throughout year, the average rate being: F1 = H5; closing rate: F1 = H6.	*Branch results in foreign currency*		*Conversion rate*	*Branch results converted into home currency*	
	Dr. F	Cr. F		Dr. H	Cr. H
Example (5). As (3), but F9 only is remitted immediately, F1 being held at end.					
Income		10	Average rate, F = H5		50
Remittance	9		Actual rate, F = H5	45	
Cash	1		Closing rate, F = H6	6	
"Profit on exchange" being 1 × (H6 − H5) = H1					1
	10	10		51	51
Example (6). As (5), but the F9 is remitted after a delay, at F = H5.5.					
Income		10	Average rate, F = H5		50
Remittance	9		Actual rate, F = H5.5	49.5	
Cash	1		Closing rate, F = H6	6	
"Profit on exchange":					5.5
Realised: 9 × (H5.5 − H5) = H4.5					
Unrealised: 1 × (H6 − H5) = H1					
H5.5					
	10	10		55.5	55.5

If the situation is to be shown lucidly in accounts, both words and figures must be more ample than is usual—perhaps in some such style as this:

Exchange gains. Appreciation on branch current assets due to favourable movements in exchange rates:

Realised gains on remittances	4.5	
Unrealised gains on assets still at branch ...	1	
		5.5

DEFINITION OF CONVERTED TRADE PROFIT

Our definition of "profit on exchange" on page 122 enables us to define converted trade profit too. It is the sum that would reach head office if all trade profits were remitted at average rate.

Or let us put the matter in another way. Because profit cannot usually be sent home as soon as it is earned, remittance rate differs from average rate. If we want to know how many Homes would have been bought by remitting at average rate, we must skim off any appreciation that has taken place during the waiting period, and call it "profit on exchange." This is what we do automatically when we convert profit at average rate and stick in "profit on exchange" as a balancing figure.

What grounds have we for saying that average rate, and the above definitions, are "correct"? As with many other aspects of accounting, there hardly seem to be any grand first principles with which to blast advocates of other views. Rather must we modestly ask how and by whom the results are to be used, and then decide which rate will, all things considered, best fit these needs. Average rate has meaning, and renders the mild service of showing how many Homes could have been remitted immediately from profit. No great harm may result from using some other rate, for example, the arbitrary "standard rate" referred to below; trade profit then moves by so many Homes, "profit on exchange" by minus that number, and, as these two profits are often added together in the long run, we may well end up with the same net figure. But surely we should favour the system which can convey a significant idea to management, rather than one whose results are not much better than numbers pulled out of a hat?

If we plump for average rate, however, we must look a little more closely at the manner in which the average is calculated.

AN UNCHANGING "STANDARD RATE"

In passing, we may note a simple alternative to working out an arithmetical average—to choose some likely rate (in the hope that, as the months go by, it will prove to be not far from a more accurate average), and to stick to this arbitrary figure until it has obviously ceased to be suitable. Such a "standard" rate is advocated by many writers where the exchange is volatile. In effect, they are saying: "This nominal rate gives a better notion of the values at stake than the extravagant dealings of a crazy market"—a not unreasonable view.

A fixed rate is almost essential where monthly branch returns are tabulated and criticised at head office; fluctuating rates would here make comparison absurd. But one wonders whether it would not be still better to stick to the original foreign figures.

If, as the months go by, the standard rate proves to have been a bad guess —that is, if the average of the actual rates is very different—the converted figures hardly seem to have much meaning. Trade profit becomes a purely arbitrary amount, divorced from any notion of potential remittances; and the distinction between trade profit and "profit on exchange" melts away.

How should we define "profit on exchange" under this method? In equation (2), all the rates, except r, now become the same standard figure—call it s. So equation (3) shrinks to

$$E = -R(s - r)$$

Thus, with a standard rate, "profit on exchange" arises solely from remittances.

AVERAGE RATE AND THE TIME-LAG

How is average rate computed? So far, we have assumed that it reflects *all* trade transactions—for instance, purchases and expenses on one hand, and sales on the other. If these two sets of transactions take place at much the same dates (if revenue always follows hard at the heels of the corresponding cost), this method of averaging seems to fit our definitions. But costs and revenues may tend to have different dates (for example, the branch may lay in stocks in September for Christmas sales); and this time-lag may be marked by big exchange movements. What happens then?

Suppose H40 is sent to the branch on January 1, when the rate is H1 = F4, and the resultant F10 is at once used to buy goods or meet some other expense. During the year, the rate moves smoothly to H1 = F5, and on December 31 (that is to say, after a time-lag of almost twelve months) F11 is earned from sales, etc. The trial balance now shows:

	Forins		*Conversion rate*	*Homes*	
	Dr.	*Cr.*		*Dr.*	*Cr.*
Net profit		1	Average rate, F = H?		?
Capital		10	Original rate, F = H4		40
Cash, etc.	11		Closing rate, F = H5	55	
Profit on exchange			Balancing figure		?

What is "average rate" here? The figure that leaps to mind is F = H4.5 — midway between expense rate (4) and sales rate (5). Net profit is then revealed at H4.5, and "profit on exchange" at H10.5. In effect, we pretend that both purchase and sale took place on June 30, when the profit of F1 meant a potential remittance of H4.5.

This pretence is not too satisfying. In fact, there were no profits to send home till December 31; and then H5 (not H4.5) could be remitted. So the figure of H4.5 has no very palpable meaning. And if "profit on exchange" is the gain from holding a Forin asset from January 1 to December 31, the right amount is 10 × (H5 − H4) or H10, and not H10.5.

Our figures fit the facts better if we base average on the dates when transactions actually yield potential remittances, i.e. when profit is *realised* by a sale (or even the debtor's payment?). Thus, in our example, we get the desired H5 and H10 by converting at the sale rate of F = H5. So perhaps we should ignore the debit side of revenue account, and calculate average rate from the credits alone.[10]

It would seem to follow that, if sales vary from month to month, the average

[10] Put in a rather over-simplified form, the difference between realisation average, and average of expense and sale, is this:

P is net profit left after taking a debit (expended when rate is *d*) from a gross receipt (gained when realisation rate *p* prevails). Converted profit at realisation rate is *Pp*, *d* being ignored.

Expense-and-sale average reflects somewhat earlier rates than does *p*. It will tend, if transactions flow smoothly throughout the year, to be about $\frac{p+d}{2}$; in which case it will make converted profit sink to about $P\frac{p+d}{2}$, i.e. by $\frac{P}{2}(p-d)$, with a corresponding gain to "profit on exchange."

rate should be weighted: it should be found by multiplying each month's sales by the rate for that month, and dividing by annual sales.

DIFFERENT RATES FOR EXPENSES AND REVENUE

Sometimes debits and credits in the revenue account are converted at different rates, instead of at some single rate such as one of the averages. The most likely case is that in which transactions are so few that each is converted at its own rate.

What does this procedure mean? Example (7) shows a simple trial balance whose revenue items are converted by two alternative methods—first at realisation rate alone (let us call this method (*a*)) and then with separate rates for expenses and revenues (method (*b*)). F10 is sent to the branch and used to buy goods or to meet some other expense. After a delay, F10 is earned from sales, etc., so there is no trade profit in the Forin books.

F10 was worth H40 till after the expense date; by sale date it is worth H50. The branch revenue account shows no profit, but, as assets obtained for H40 have been sold for the equivalent of H50, the home accounts must somewhere register an H10 gain.

This H10 is exchange appreciation on stocks or pre-payments during their turnover period. If we put it into "profit on exchange," we shall be acting in nice accord with our definitions. Method (*a*) does so; by converting both sides of the account at the same rate, trade profit is purged of exchange variations. One might picture stocks as being kept in a branch warehouse until the day of sale; then they are charged to the sales manager at home cost multiplied by the current exchange rate; and any change in their home book-values while they lay in the warehouse is put into the finance manager's account, namely, "profit on exchange."

The alternative is to say that the sales manager is responsible for stocks, and that variations in their value in Homes should therefore go into trading account. Method (*b*) implements this view. Here expenses and sales each have their own rate. Exchange appreciation during the time-lag is in consequence lifted out of "profit on exchange" and put into gross profit—in practice, to be lost from view.[11]

[11] The matter can be re-stated algebraically. To the symbols used on page 123 we must add G, the gross revenue before charging D, the debit of an earlier time whose rate is d.

Therefore, $P=G-D$

The converted profit by method (*a*) is still Pp (if we convert at average realisation rate).

Therefore, $Pp=Gp-Dp$..............(4)

Let the converted profit by method (*b*) be P_b. We want to find the difference between Pp and P_b.

$$P_b=Gp-Dd$$

Subtracting (4) $Pp=Gp-Dp$

Therefore, $P_b-Pp=Dp-Dd$..............(5)

That is, converted profit, under the "two-rate" method (*b*), exceeds converted profit, under our single-rate method (*a*), by appreciation on the expense between expense date and realisation date. Similarly it can be shown, along the lines used to find (3), that "profit on exchange" (method (*a*)) exceeds "profit on exchange" (method (*b*)) by $D(p-d)$ also.

TABLE C

Showing possible methods for converting profit and loss account.

Assumption: Opening and expense rate: F1=H4. Income rate: F1=H5.	*Branch results in foreign currency*		*Conversion rate*	*Branch results converted into home currency*	
	Dr. F	Cr. F		Dr. H	Cr. H
Example (7). Income is F10 before charging an F10 asset consumed.					
(*a*) *Realisation rate alone used in P/L.*					
Profit and loss balances:					
Gross income		10	Realisation rate, F=H5		50
Expenses, etc.	10		” ” F=H5	50	
Net profit	—		Balance c/d.	—	
Balance sheet balances:					
Net profit		—	Balance b/d.		—
Capital		10	Original rate, F=H4		40
Remittance, etc.	10		Actual rate, F=H5	50	
Profit on exchange			Balancing figure		10
				50	50
(*b*) *Other rates also used in P/L.*					
Profit and loss balances:					
Gross income		10	Realisation rate, F=H5		50
Expenses, etc.	10		Earlier rate, F=H4	40	
Net profit	—		Balance c/d.	10	
				50	50
Balance sheet balances:					
Net Profit		—	Balance b/d.		10
Capital		10	Original rate, F=H4		40
Remittance, etc.	10		Actual rate, F=H5	50	
				50	50

Quite a lot can be said for either approach. In favour of (*b*), one could plead that the sales manager has in real life a considerable say in deciding when and how much stock is to be bought; and that, as some stock *must* be kept ready for sale, the distinction between trading and exchange profit is from the head office standpoint a bit too fine for common-sense. A single rate—method (*a*)—focuses attention on the influence of the exchange; and, if the rate selected is based on realisation dates, it fits in with our main definitions. More important, (*a*) preserves the general flavour and emphasis of the foreign account much more faithfully, being a multiple reflection of the original—thus in example (7) expenses and income remain equal after conversion and profit is still zero.

ITEMS COMMON TO REVENUE ACCOUNT AND BALANCE SHEET

When different conversion rates must be used for revenue and balance sheet figures, a student of accountancy may well ask: "which rate should I choose for an item that is common to *both* groups of figures?" The question covers all adjustments—opening and closing—but of course stocks and depreciation are normally the sole substantial members of this family.

Our textbooks answer that the balance sheet figure is converted at the rate usual for such an asset. But, so far as the revenue entry goes, they do not tell us how to decide between the two possible courses:

(*a*) *A single rate is used throughout the revenue account.* The two ends of the adjustment are converted differently; in revenue account, it shares the same average as all the other items, whereas in balance sheet the appropriate asset rate is used. Whatever the merits of this method, one cannot but deplore the resultant clash of figures; thus stock has one value in revenue account and another in the neighbouring balance sheet, while depreciation allowances may over the years mount up to more than their asset's cost. Such jarring inconsistency may be glossed over in several ways. In the revenue account, stocks can be concealed in a composite "cost of sales" figure. Alternatively (and more commonly) the foreign trial balance may be converted *after* profit has been struck. As a result, the problem seems to be neatly short-circuited. But in fact both method and profit are the same as before, since conversion of the balance at average rate is tantamount to converting the whole profit and loss account at that rate; all adjustments—including stocks and depreciation—are by implication converted at average.[12]

(*b*) *Balance sheet rate is used in revenue account.* For example, the closing stock is given the same value in both places, and depreciation is kept firmly linked with the original converted asset figure. Inconsistency in amounts is avoided—but at the cost of inconsistency in the rates used for the various costs and revenues, and a consequent distortion of their relative sizes and so of net profit.

This seems to be exactly the same matter as was considered in the preceding section—but in a more extreme form, the "purchase" having moved right outside the current year.

Much the same arguments therefore apply. Under method (*b*), exchange appreciation on the adjustment (that is, between expense date and income date, or income date and close of year) is taken from "profit-on-exchange" and confused with trade profit. If we want to keep the latter pure, we shall opt for method (*a*) instead.

The contrast between the two methods is well shown by 1949 British accounts for a branch in U.S.A. Method (*a*) treats the handsome devaluation

---

[12] Note that, where the full trial balance (including opening stock) is converted and average is applied to all revenue items, the correct balance of "profit on exchange" can be found only if closing stock is also inserted on both sides, at both its rates (closing rate for the debit, average for the credit).

gains on stocks as "profit-on-exchange"; method (*b*) raises trade profit—and tax.[13]

Moreover, (*b*) can lead to a rather dangerous breach—probably unsuspected by those who use the method—in our time-honoured principle of not taking credit for unrealised gains. Suppose the Forin appreciates just before the year's end. By crediting stock at closing rate, we jerk up profit somewhat prematurely; and, if the stocks consist of imports, Forin prices of such goods are not unlikely to drop in sympathy with the exchange movement (perhaps too late for our "lower of cost or market" rule to rescue us), so that the stock may next year be sold at a loss. Conversely, if the forin falls in exchange, (*b*) infuses the revenue account with gloom that may prove unwarranted. Method (*a*) gives more temperate results in both situations.

Once more, the balance of the argument would seem to support the use of a single average rate for every figure in the revenue account.

* * * * *

In conclusion, may we again stress that the chances of our having erred in this discussion seem not inconsiderable? Our views must be regarded as suggestions rather than dogmatic statements, and as an invitation to persons engaged in this kind of work to tell us what they do and why they do it.

London

[13] In general, the British tax authorities would seem content to follow the treatment adopted in a trader's own accounts, provided that he adheres consistently to the same treatment every year. Whether or not "profit on exchange" bears tax thus depends on how the trader has treated it for his own purposes.

Printed by Jordan & Sons, Limited, Chancery Lane, London, W.C.2

A COLONIAL BANKRUPT:
EBENEZER HANCOCK
1714-1819

A Colonial Bankrupt: Ebenezer Hancock, 1714-1819

This is the tale of a nonentity and failure. Were it not for the fame of his brother, the great John, we should know nothing of Ebenezer Hancock. As it is, a handful of his papers have been handed down to us, mixed up with the letters of Brother John the statesman and Uncle Thomas the merchant prince. Because he played poor relation to these celebrities, we can follow the life of a mediocre man who would in the ordinary course of events have been utterly forgotten; what is perhaps more interesting, we can trace his ill-starred business doings, which were probably a great deal nearer to the norm than were memorably successful ventures.

Ebenezer Hancock was born on November 15, 1741, some five years after his brother John.[1] Their father was the minister at Braintree, Massachusetts, and he died before Ebenezer was three years old.[2] The mother remarried—again to a minister. Uncle Thomas adopted John (a comely lad) and whisked him off to the splendours of a Beacon Hill mansion, leaving the other children to their mother and clerical austerity. Poor little Ebenezer was thus outstripped by his brother from the very start.

As the years went by, it became plain that Thomas meant to bequeath his fortune and business to John, who was given the best of schooling and then carefully trained in the countinghouse. When Ebenezer was eighteen, however, Thomas suddenly decided to give this neglected nephew a trial in business. Ebenezer had so far planned to follow in his father's footsteps and become a minister, but a little experience in Boston soon convinced him that an office stool held out brighter prospects than the pulpit; as John put it, in a letter from London, "I am glad to find that my Brother's conduct is so pleasing to my Uncle . . . clergymen have not the defference paid them, nor are they supported as they deserve, which is but poor encouragement

[1] S. A. Bates, *Records of the Town of Braintree* (Randolph, 1886), p. 784.

[2] L. R. Paige, *History of Cambridge* (Boston, 1877), p. 343.

to a young fellow." To our ears, John's language to his young brother has a priggish ring: "I am glad to hear you are well, and earnestly beg you will give great attention to business and let your conduct be such as to merit the esteem of all about you, and remember that the diligent hand maketh rich. I expect on my return to find you a compleat merchant."[3]

Uncle Thomas died four years later (1764). He left a vast fortune to John, and a modest gift to Ebenezer: £666.13s.4d. in cash, and some three thousand acres of frontier land in Maine. Apparently Ebenezer did not relish the prospect of being employed by his brother, for he at once left the firm. However, if John was a difficult man to work with, he proved not ungenerous. The brothers parted on good terms, and, when Ebenezer set up a shop of his own, John at once recommended him warmly to various British suppliers.[4]

Ebenezer's new venture was made in partnership with one Edward Blanchard. The latter is described by John as a frugal, honest, and industrious man in the "Braziery Business." In fact, however, the partners kept a general store. Admittedly, their main line was hardware (tools, pewter, glass, and so forth); but, like most of their neighbours, they were thoroughly unspecialized, and stocked many other lines such as cloth and cheese. The semibarter conditions of their times—concerning which the Hancock manuscripts are such a mine of information—meant that they also had to handle occasional payments in rum, beef, butter, and other forms of commodity money. Nor can the firm be described clearly as either wholesale or retail. The partners bought the bulk of their manufactured stock direct from British dealers, but some of it came via John Hancock's warehouse. Part of their sales went in small driblets to Boston customers; one order, which also shows the queer triangular pattern of much of the trade in a bankless society, comes from John and runs: "Let Daniel Barker [a shipwright] have iron to the amount of £2.13s.4d. and charge my account." But other customers included storekeepers scattered all along the New England seaboard, who obviously

---

[3] Bostonian Society MSS., March 2, 1761, John Hancock to Rev. D. Perkins; and John to Ebenezer, December 27, 1760, quoted in Massachusetts Historical Society, *Proceedings*, 1909–10, p. 194.

[4] Suffolk County Probate Records, 13,484; Hancock MSS., letterbook (Baker Library, Harvard Business School), November 17, 1764.

looked on Blanchard and Hancock as their wholesale suppliers.[5]

The first problem facing the partners was how to get the sterling with which to pay their British creditors—a task that was always something of a nightmare to colonial traders. Here John Hancock again proved helpful. He was at this time sending big cargoes of whale oil to be sold in London, and so had ample funds in the hands of his agent there; he disposed of the money by drawing bills on his agent and selling them to other Boston men. Blanchard and Hancock in this way got at least £1,500 sterling—a very substantial sum.

Hardly had the new firm celebrated its first birthday when it faced a crisis. The boom period of the Seven Years' War had come to an end a year or two earlier, and had been followed by the usual postwar slump. To make things worse, Britain chose this untoward time to start tightening up her mercantilist plans for bringing the Empire nearer to economic self-sufficiency; for instance, a much sharper watch was kept on New England's smuggling trade with foreign ports. And now (1765) came the Stamp Act. Leading Boston merchants showed their indignation by adopting a nonimportation agreement, which was expected to hurt trade still further. What ought Blanchard and Hancock to do in this embarrassing situation? As far as I can see, they decided that theirs was not to be the path of sacrifice. The nonimportation agreement was in force from October, 1765, till the following spring; the partners' invoices from Britain show that hundreds of pounds worth of goods—including luxuries like raisins and tea—were nevertheless sent to them in the closing months of 1765.

It was a well-established policy for Boston merchants to supplement their local trade with shipping ventures; Thomas Hancock, for instance, had laid the foundations of his fortune by arranging huckstering voyages round Newfoundland and the West Indies. Blanchard and Hancock decided to follow his lead, though conditions were probably no longer so good as they had been in his day. First they

---

[5] Hancock MSS. (Baker Library, Harvard Business School), especially case 28. For fuller details regarding the machinery of barter, see my *House of Hancock*, Cambridge, 1945. As a further example of the triangular method of debt settlement, consider Davis' account (Hancock MSS., 20, 1). Davis sold twine and duck to the partners. He got back some of his debt in odds and ends of goods, and also with the help of "my order on you in favour Jos. Hamond for 12 shillings," i. e., by drawing a bill, for an insignificant sum, possibly payable in kind.

sent a vessel with ironware, fish, etc., on a modest trip to Philadelphia, whence she brought back gunpowder and ship's bread. Next came a much more ambitious scheme. In company with one Samuel Gray, who held a half-share, they bought a brig called the *Neptune*. Having stocked her with New England farm produce and so on, they sent her off on a triangular course that covered the whole North Atlantic. First she headed for Newfoundland, and there the captain traded her beef and rum for codfish. She took this cargo across to Portugal, where the captain delivered it to a firm of English agents at Oporto. They sold it, though in a poor market. With a small part of the proceeds, they bought a load of salt for the return voyage; the rest of the money was remitted on behalf of Blanchard and Hancock to a Bristol creditor. The *Neptune* then recrossed the Atlantic, sighting Boston after an absence of six months. Her captain sold the salt and subtracted his outlays for wages, and then the partners divided their gains.[6]

Without delay, the *Neptune* was sent off once more to Newfoundland, with her hold full of the usual farm produce and her decks crowded with livestock; if prices were good, she herself was to be sold as well as her cargo. Her half-owner, Sam Gray, this time went with

---

[6] Hancock MSS., 23, 4, give much data on the voyage, but not enough for us to find the amount of profit:

1815 quintals of fish were sold in "Porto" for	Milreis	4760
Return cargo of salt (450 milreis), agency and expenses came to	"	1272
Net proceeds	"	3488

This was equivalent, in New England currency, to about	£1,300
The salt (495 hogsheads) was sold for	300
	£1,600
Known expenses (wages paid by captain £330, insurance, etc. £70) are	400
	£1,200

From this profit, Gray and the partners would have to deduct expenses that we do not know, viz., the cost of the original "outsets" from Boston.

her. Thanks to letters from him to his partners (written in language of resounding scriptural richness), we have an eye-witness account of the voyage. What follows is a summary of his correspondence.

The *Neptune* had a long and tedious passage of nineteen days. When she reached St. Johns (Gray tells), markets proved so uncommonly bad that he did not even bother to have the hatches opened. Too many of his countrymen from New England had also come to trade. There were more vessels for sale than had ever been known before at one time. As the *Neptune's* hay and corn were falling very short, he sold two oxen and a number of sheep, and was obliged to buy forty bushels of corn for the cows.[7] Hearing that a rival trader called Prince had sold three cargoes to the northward (i.e., at Bonavista), Gray made up his mind to go there too. With prices as they were, he thought it unlikely that he would be able to buy a return cargo, so he would instead engage a freight to Alicante or Leghorn when the first fish had been cured.

But his plans miscarried. Seven weeks later he writes that for three days the boat has been lying to in a very heavy gale, trying to get into Bonavista harbour to take 1,500 quintals of fish aboard and to collect some bills, but at last they feel obliged to bear away. "We shall not tarry here but return the first wind and push off the remains of the cargo at some price or other (being near half). . . . Trade grows worse daily, however I have the thing to comfort that I shall do as well as anyone except Prince who had made a good voyage out of my customers before I arrived. I lose every farthing of £350 sterling upon the Alexanders."

Winter was now uncomfortably close, and so the *Neptune* headed southwards. We next hear of her in February (1768) laden with fish, and far down in the West Indies. The voyage from the north (Gray tells his stay-at-home partners) has been made in extremely bad weather, which continued for six weeks and nearly caused the *Neptune* to founder in the ice. For the last two weeks there has been such a short allowance of water and food that the crew could not have subsisted much longer. Happily they have now spoken with a sloop and been able to supply themselves with several necessaries. A considerable part of the fish has been damaged in the storm. Gray intends to go to Barbados and then to the Leeward Islands, where he will do his utmost for the voyage.

---

[7] Hancock MSS., 27, 1, Gray's letters of August 5 and September 20, 1767.

Three days later comes a letter from Barbados. Gray is plainly worn out by the hardships of the journey, and his pen is bitter. It is now too late for him to make his usual voyage to Newfoundland in April. Much of the fish is bad; in any case, fish will not sell. As for the captain, he would "see the vessell, cargo and all sunk rather than loose the selling of half a gallon of his own rum." (It was usual to let the captain take a few goods on his own account.) Finally, Gray has suffered a great deal at the hands of "that Dambd Ignorant V-l-n-z," possibly the firm's correspondent at Barbados.[8]

Gray next tried to get admittance to the neighbouring French islands, and succeeded in reaching St. Lucia and in opening negotiations with possible buyers. After a week or two, he managed to arrange for the sale of his whole cargo to merchants from the nearby island of Martinique. The price was poor, but he was satisfied that he would never make more as the fish was very much damaged and daily growing worse. The French buyers agreed to send a small schooner from Martinique to take the fish; payment would be made soon after. Then, Gray concludes with relief, he will fill the *Neptune* with molasses and make for home.

But alas for poor Gray's hopes! The very next day "The Craft Returnd from Martinico and Finding Severall Vessells Arrivd here with Fish in Casks and Sold on much worse Terms than mine they Began to Baffle, and Finaly left the Harbour" without taking the fish. Gray now showed himself a man of metal:[9]

> I pursued 'em to Martinico and Brought 'em here where they tarried Some few Hours and then went to another Harbour. I then applyd for a Warrant which was Granted and Brought 'em here and commenced a Law Suit which was thought would have been desided in One day But the poor Damb'd Hungery Unjust Judge put it off from time to time till the 12th Instant when he thought my whole cargo was perisht gave it against me with 3,000 Livers Damages and as much more Court Charges, Secretary's Charges, Lawyers fees etc., etc., etc. Insted of giving it 20,000 Livers In my Favour (which God Reward him for) he further after keeping me 42 days In Suspense not admitting me to Sell gave me only two Hours to Raise the Money and after the Expiration of 2 Hours disappointed Me of Runing Out in the Night, by sending a file of Men on Board.
>
> Upon which I wrote to an acquaintance an English gentleman at a Near Harbour who upon receipt of my letter Travelled on Foot to Lend me the money

[8] Boston Public Library MSS., G.41.8. III 142, February 6, 1768.

[9] Hancock MSS., 27, 1, April 25, 1768.

> to make up the whole Sum which Never till this day has Been in my power to Repay him, for had I lost my whole Cargo I would not have left the Harbour without paying him as he Never Even askt a Receipt of me. . . .
>
> I have now no other Chance than going to St. Eustatius and St. Cruize and there Barter the Remainder the fish for sugars or anything that will Answer.

Gray went to St. Eustatius. His luck did not turn, and his rotting fish were still unsold a month later. The last we hear of him is that he is on the point of sailing for Demerara, where "the worst of bad fish will fetch three pieces of eight."

It is hard for us to tell whether these business disasters could have been avoided or not. Were Blanchard and Hancock incompetent traders (showing, for instance, little flair in choosing either cargoes or the men who were put in charge of them)? Or were they victims of a general depression? The latter question leads one to wonder whether a born merchant would not have seen that trade was bad, and refrained at such a time from sinking large parts of his scanty capital in hazardous shipping ventures.

Colonial traders do not impress me as having been remarkably efficient, but Ebenezer Hancock's standards seem to have been slovenly even when judged by the lax standards of his era. The correspondence on the Portuguese voyage, for instance, suggests muddle and incompetence. Again, his Philadelphia agent writes: "I am Surpriz'd you send your Goods without Mark and Number as they are lyable to be Chang'd." The luckless Gray ends his last letter from the West Indies with: "Being Fairly Tired Out with Writeing to you and Never a Single line in Answer, I Remain."

Whether we choose a charitable explanation or not, there can be no doubt that Blanchard and Hancock were getting into difficulties. Within three years of their start in business, they were receiving dunning letters from many creditors. Any British exporter in the North American trade took it for granted that he would have to give long credits; but the size of Blanchard and Hancock's debts, and their delays in paying, were unusually worrying. Throughout 1767, one of their London suppliers was begging for remittances (though he also pressed for more orders). Their debt to their Bristol supplier ranged between £1,000 and £1,700 sterling. They owed nearly £700 to their Philadelphia correspondent. By the beginning of 1768, John Hancock was very explicitly cautioning Hayley, his chief London agent, not to send too much to the struggling partners, and emphasizing that he would not be answerable for their debts. Their Bristol supplier took to sending their goods via John (so making him responsible). John wrote back that he could not speak freely about the partners, as he had a brother in the firm; he had examined "the state of their affairs," and as this seemed satisfactory had handed over the goods; but no more were to be sent to his address.[10]

Things were in this state when the partners got Gray's letters telling of his disasters in the West Indies. A less propitious moment could hardly have been found, for the political news was also becoming extremely bad. As a result of the Townshend Acts, there was another surge of bad feeling against Parliament. Growing severity on the part of the customs officials had aggravated the tension. Now one of John Hancock's ships was seized and he himself was arrested on charges of smuggling; the penalty demanded was at least £9,000 sterling. The partners thus found that their most likely ally was in some difficulty just when their need was greatest. Could they stand up to this double blow? Evidently not; their bill from the local newspaper contains the terse item: "To advertising Partnership dissolved, and Goods to Sell."[11]

After the dissolution, Ebenezer and his late partner possibly struggled for a time to start afresh, each in a shop of his own. As the second nonimportation agreement was now in full force, and trade was almost dead, their efforts were hopeless. A hoard of alarmed creditors hurriedly sent in accounts. Both men were bankrupt within a few months.

Further details are supplied in a letter from John Hancock to Hayley, the London merchant. Blanchard and Hancock "have not been so cautious and prudent as they ought to have been, in short, upon a[n] inspection it was found necessary that my brother should bring his affairs to a close, and he a few days ago shut his doors: I have done everything for him that a brother ought to do, and upon settling his affairs, I must put him forward in life again." John goes on to say (very handsomely, when one considers that he had warned Hayley not to trust the partners): "My recommendation to you of those gentlemen being the cause of your credit to them, and my regard and obligations to you are so great that I can't suffer your debt to come into an average with his other creditors, I therefore now engage to see you paid the sum my brother is indebted to you both principal

---

[10] Hancock MSS., letterbook, February and April, 1768.

[11] Hancock MSS., 20, 1, October 14, 1768, Fleet's account.

and interest." Hayley responded in the same spirit, declining to charge any interest.[12]

Blanchard showed grit in his way of making a fresh start. He packed up and sailed for London. Hayley had stated that he would never again supply goods to the bankrupt (whose creditors had so far been paid only 5/–in the £). But Blanchard called on him and somehow managed to talk him round, and so was able to return in triumph to Boston with a fresh stock of British wares.[13]

Ebenezer could not get onto his feet again with the same ease. Indeed, a note to him from John suggests that he had to hide from his creditors for some months: "Your affairs are now brought to such a close as that you are at liberty to come abroad and keep abroad." John adds that the best way in which Ebenezer can use his new-found freedom is to ride into the country, to collect debts that were owed to him by village shopkeepers and by traders in Providence. All his accounts, etc., were to be handed over to John—which probably explains how the materials for this article have survived. A final homily runs: "Reflect on your former imprudencies and resolve to quit yourself like a man . . . you are dependent on your own industry for your support and that of your family, and the greater the prospect of your family's increasing, the greater must be your diligence and industry. . . . [Be] always abounding in the work of the Lord."[14]

However, John gave much more than exhortations to Ebenezer. He was indeed most generous to his needy brother (perhaps being haunted by the feeling: "There, but for the grace of God, goes John Hancock"). We have already seen how he assumed the debt due to Hayley. He also guaranteed and took over a large liability to Ebenezer's Bristol suppliers. And not only did he settle the affairs of the old business, but he also set about planning how Ebenezer could be helped to start afresh. He decided that his brother's best course would be to set up shop in the hardware trade again, and he offered

[12] Hancock MSS., letterbook, July 26 and November 21, 1769, Hancock to Hayley.

[13] Massachusetts Historical Society MSS., December 29, 1770, Hayley to John Hancock.

[14] Boston Public Library MSS. 254, January 11, 1771. Ebenezer had married Elizabeth Lowell in 1767 (New England Historic Genealogical Society, *Register*, LIV, p. 316), and they had four children (*ibid.*, IX, p. 352).

to provide both stock and rent-free premises. He then wrote to Hayley for the goods, explaining that he was trying to re-establish Ebenezer, "Over whom I shall be careful to keep a Watchful Eye."[15]

After this chastening experience, Ebenezer seems to have led a placid life, and we learn little more of him. The Revolution interrupted his sober trading for a time; when the British evacuated Boston, we hear that he came back and cleaned out his house—which implies that he had to go elsewhere while soldiers were billeted in it. Shortly after, John again helped him, this time by making him deputy paymaster-general for the eastern department; Ebenezer's home was then used to store the French crowns sent with D'Estaing for the relief of the army, and had a guard of sentries posted round it.[16] But this pomp did not last long, and, after peace had been restored, we find Ebenezer back in his shop, humbly selling tea, chocolate, and sugar to John, who was now an immensely popular political boss and governor of the state.

Ebenezer died in 1819, having outlived his brother by over a score of years. John had not bothered to draw up a will; a third of his great fortune therefore went automatically to Ebenezer. The latter's portion included the Beacon Hill property; his son and eleven grandchildren were thus the last owners and occupants of Hancock House.[17]

W. T. BAXTER
London School of Economics

---

[15] Boston Public Library, Ch.M.1.8. 129, John to Ebenezer, December 5, 1771; Hancock MSS., letterbook, December 12, 1771.

[16] Boston Public Library MSS. 272, Warrant dated June 12, 1776; A. E. Brown, *John Hancock* (Boston, 1898), p. 250.

[17] New England Historic Genealogical Society, *Register*, IX, p. 352, and LIV, p. 316.

INFLATION AND ACCOUNTING PROFITS

Westminster Bank Review

May 1952 Issued Quarterly

Inflation and Accounting Profits

by

W. T. Baxter,

Professor of Accounting in the University of London.

I

THERE IS nothing like high taxation for kindling interest in accounting theory; and so the accountant's concepts of income are today being scrutinized as never before. Most of us expected profits and tax to be raised somewhat by inflation—say, in proportion to prices. In fact, however, the accountant's profit figures have in many cases shot up faster than prices. It is therefore natural to ask whether there may not be some flaw in his—and in the tax inspector's—methods, and to look more closely at the impact of inflation on accounts.

Changing price-levels influence accounts in two ways. First, there is what we may call the "money effect". Second, there are the results of the accountant's valuation methods; we may call these the "historic cost effect".

II

The Money Effect

We need not spend much time on the money effect. It is widely understood; and as inflation is an adroit teacher, understanding is spreading fast where ignorance has hitherto prevailed. We all recognize the present plight of the man with a small fixed income (let us call him the *rentier* for short). He lives on, say, £300 a year—a pension or interest on his savings in War Loan. Under inflation, he still gets these three hundred "safe" pounds, but they buy him a sadly reduced quantity of goods and services. In other words, rights defined in terms of so much money become, when prices rise, less valuable in "real" terms. If instead the man receives a variable money income (such as dividends on ordinary shares), it may now be rising above £300—conceivably, though this is not very likely, to a level at which he still can buy the same physical quantities of goods, etc., as before the inflation, so that he enjoys a constant real income.

The accounts of a business show that it can be harmed in the same way as a *rentier*. Its earnings may consist of fixed revenues, and its balance sheet may include fixed-money assets such as cash and debts; as prices rise, income and assets both dwindle in real terms.

On the other hand, inflation is kind in some cases. For fixed-money liabilities—such as creditors, debentures, and preference shares—are as much affected as fixed-money assets. The worse the lender of money is hit, the more his debtor thrives. At the start of the great German inflation of 1923-4 (so the story runs), a poor ex-princess pawned the family jewels and bought a small business. As prices soared up and up, her jewels rose in value as security, and she was able to get bigger and bigger loans—with which she promptly bought more non-money assets for her business. At the end of the inflation, she was able to pay off her depreciated debts with ease, and was left with both the jewels and a large business. Her tale summarizes the gains that may be wrested from inflation.

The biggest debtor is the State, and so the State quietly absorbs most of what the *rentier* sacrifices. Some firms benefit in a similar way. If we may judge from *The Economist*'s consolidated accounts for over 500 British companies, on average about one-third of the permanent funds of larger enterprises fall into the fixed-interest type. A company that was in 1939 "highly-geared" (i.e., had fixed liabilities, including preference shares, much in excess of its money-assets) has enjoyed a fairly effective shield against the assaults of inflation. On the other hand, fixed money liabilities carry an obvious risk: prices can fall. The highly-geared firm's gains of 1939-52 may conceivably be swept away during the next few years. Moreover, profits tax hits the ordinary shares in such companies particularly hard.

However, many firms were not deeply in debt at the start of inflation. Such firms have had no cushion against the losses that must now be described.

III

The Historic Cost Error

The distinction drawn above between money-assets and other assets suggests that the value of the latter does not seep away during inflation. Post-war experience has taught us that such a view is ingenuous. Certain business assets—notably stocks and plant—have proved almost as defenceless as money.

The reason for this paradox lies in our method of computing profit. If we kept no accounts, stocks and plant could not be touched by inflation. If however we keep accounts in the orthodox way, we treat the money-appreciation on these assets (to the extent that they pass through the annual revenue account, e.g., under the headings of stock or depreciation) as a realized gain. "Profits" are thereby vastly increased during inflation. Distributions of profits, by way of dividends, and still more surely by way of tax, also tend to grow; in time, these payments eat into all the assets.

How does this odd and unforeseen situation come about, and what can we do to cure it? The answers depend on our attitude to cost measurement. When for instance a barrow-boy is estimating his profit on a day's trade, what is he trying to do? The most plausible answer, it seems to me, is that he is guessing (*a*) how much money he must lay aside from the day's takings if he is to renew the wares that he has sold, and so keep his business going to-morrow; and therefore (*b*) how much remains for him to spend on consumption and extra investment. To find quantity (*a*), his costs, he must thus define the level of assets that he seeks to maintain. If he is like the rest of us, he will normally take refuge in a facile calculation based on historic cost:

> "I started the day with £5, and spent that sum on the apples; so my cost-of-goods-sold was £5, and I must set that much aside for to-morrow."

This calculation serves him well enough so long as prices are steady. If prices rise, he may find that it is much too slipshod; by setting aside £5, he maintains his money-capital, but his stocks and physical turnover may get so small that in the end he faces the collapse of his business. His plight may drive him to re-phrase his reasoning:

> "I started the day with £5, and this was the cost of buying my apples; but then their wholesale price rose to £7, and, as I must replace them to stay in business, I sacrificed £7 when I sold them; the cost of buying has no longer much interest, whereas the cost of selling (and replacing) is what I must put aside to maintain my real capital."

If this line of argument is correct, a method of calculating cost implies a method of valuing capital; and here the choice lies between money-capital and real capital. I doubt very much whether we can say that either concept is "right". We can however decide that one concept is more serviceable than the other.

In the accounts of a less simple business, the situation is obscured—e.g., prices may vary throughout the year; there are many different assets, inputs, and products; and opening and closing stocks are held. But in essence our problem is the same. Conventional accounts base expense on historic cost. Usually a longish time elapses between cost date and sales date. During inflation, therefore, the earlier "cost £" is worth more than the resulting "sales £"; there is a certain incongruity in subtracting such unlike quantities from one another.

The problem can perhaps be made more vivid with a diagram. (Diagram 1.) This tries to explain the figures of a hypothetical firm whose main costs and revenues come from dealing in stocks of merchandise. The diagram shows time along the base, and money on the vertical axis. Suppose that the accounting year runs from January to December, the year under study being the space between the two vertical dotted lines. The curve SS′ represents monthly sales for the year, and RR′ represents monthly purchases. Inflation began about the middle of the preceding year, as is shown by the rise in these two curves from then onwards. Physical turnover is constant from month to month, and opening and closing stocks are unchanged in physical volume; the upward slope of SS′ and RR′ (i.e., the increasing money figures for sales and purchases) is due solely to rising prices.

HH′ represents the historic costs charged for goods in the orthodox revenue account. Such an

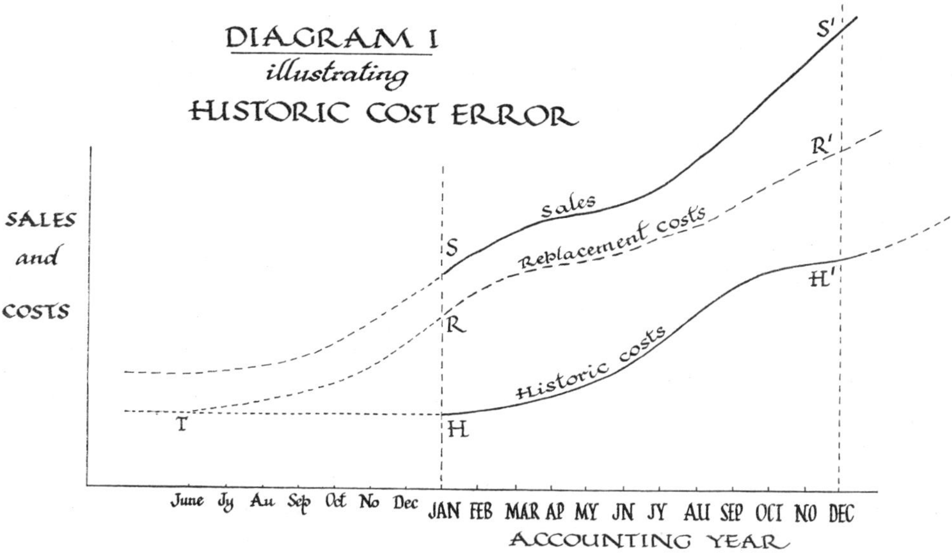

account would show the charge to be made up of:

(1) Stock on hand at 1 January. Given, say, a turnover period of six months, opening stock might roughly consist of the purchases of July-December in the preceding year, bought before prices had risen much.

(2) The year's purchases, *less* stock still on hand at 31 December. Roughly, the resultant net charge equals the purchases of the period January-June.

The costs, HH′, debited in the annual revenue account thus approximate to the actual purchases for a year beginning in fact at T, some six months before the current business year, and overlapping the current year for only six months.

Profit is, on the historic cost basis, represented by the area between SS′ and HH′. It has grown faster than prices and sales, i.e., the accounts suggest that the owner's income is more than keeping abreast of the inflation.

Should we decide to work instead on a replacement cost basis, we must rub out HH′ and use RR′ instead, i.e., we must treat the actual purchases for January-December (instead of those for July-June) as the current costs. Profit is thereby squeezed into a much smaller area; despite this compression, it is growing somewhat—as is evidenced by the slightly broader gap between S and R′ than between S and R; but, as we might expect, it has grown only in proportion to prices and sales, and the owner's real income is constant.

The area between RR′ and HH′ indicates the amount of the "historic cost error" found in orthodox accounts. In the early part of the preceding year, before prices began to rise at T, the error was *nil;* and it reaches its greatest size when the price index stands furthest from its level of six months earlier.

When prices are *falling*, replacement costs sink below the historic costs of an earlier period. Our conventional calculations then show a profit that is, in real terms, too low; in some cases, the accounts could even register a loss where real capital had grown during the year. Reported profits thus tend to be as gloomy in deflation as they were over-optimistic on the up-grade.

The man who wants to base his calculations on real capital, not money figures, will try to correct the historic costs produced by orthodox accounting. During inflation, he must seek a quantity corresponding to the area RR′HH′, and add it to his expenses (as a "replacement cost provision"); conversely he will deduct such a provision when prices sink.

How is such a figure to be found? If the firm has a costing system, some estimate of the replacement value of the materials, etc., devoted to each job can normally be made without too much trouble or inaccuracy. Even if the values are dubious guesses, they seem to be the best available basis for measuring the profitability of each job or other operation, and so constitute a useful guide in the firm's day-to-day decisions.

Does it follow, however, that the yearly profit figures also should be measured in this way—i.e., that the accounts shown to shareholders, workers, the Inspector of Taxes, and the public, should be based on guesses about the replacement costs of each firm's peculiar assets? The difficulties and complexity of such a method would be vast; most firms have not the necessary costing system; and tax measurement would usually be beset by wearisome squabbles and sometimes by downright fraud. Apart from these practical troubles and dangers, moreover, there are grave objections in theory to such a method. It would lead (since the input prices of various firms rise in markedly different degrees) to a somewhat undeserved tax favour for firms whose stocks happen to appreciate most. Further, "maintenance of real capital" is a phrase with several possible meanings; the thing that is to be maintained might be *either* the firm's physical assets *or* its earning power in real terms (i.e., its owners' future standard of living). Presumably the latter concept of capital is what interests most shareholders, and what they want to measure.

If these arguments are accepted, we must distinguish two types of replacement cost. There is the figure that should be used by management when making decisions about jobs, levels of output, and other internal matters; here the appropriate basis is the expense of replacing whatever assets are in fact sacrificed, so that the given firm's peculiar assets will be kept intact. There is also the figure that should be used for external problems, e.g., when annual profit is to be found for dividend and tax purposes; here the ideal is to show whether the assets have been kept at such a level that future earnings will always enable the owners to live at their wonted standard. A reasonably close approximation to the latter cost could probably be got by adjusting historic figures with the help of an *index of general prices*.

A scheme based on a general index would have many advantages. It would be fair, uniform, simple to understand, and easy to work. The index should be prepared by an impartial body such as the Board of Trade, and might well be a cost-of-living index reflecting the standards of a middle-class investor. True, no index is perfect. But the linking of adjustments to official figures would make the scope for window-dressing and profit manipulation very slight. The adjustments, one must admit, would be somewhat arbitrary; accounting experience suggests however that arbitrariness is a small price to pay for ease, speed, and absence of dispute.

Other schemes have been tried. Depreciation charges have been raised as a by-product of asset revaluation (e.g. by Imperial Chemical Industries); such monumental labours are however not to be embarked on lightly. Again, the "cost of goods sold" can be pushed up by valuing stocks at some artificially low figure; thus the disciples of "Lifo" (i.e., the "Last-in-First-Out" concept of stock flows) would in effect have us value stock, year after year, at the same prices—those prevailing at some given base-date. This trick is however only a partial cure where closing stock is not typical of the stocks held throughout the year. Further, it gives the balance sheet an antiquated and meaningless stock figure.

IV

Tax Reform

The above suggestions may be made more concrete if we set them out in a somewhat different way—as a summary of the procedure that we might press the Chancellor to adopt under a reformed system of tax assessment.

Method of income adjustment. Income would be found by adjusting the cost side of the revenue account with the aid of replacement cost provisions. The provisions would be based, not on the replacement costs of each firm's peculiar assets, but on an objective index e.g., a general index of wholesale prices, or (preferably) of the cost of living.

Accounting requirements. These are simple. Firms in the scheme would draft their revenue account on almost the same lines as at present. The charges in the revenue account for "cost of goods sold" and depreciation would however consist of two separately-stated parts:

(i) *Charge based on original cost*—exactly as in orthodox accounts.

(ii) *Replacement cost supplement*—the figures found in (i) multiplied by fractions based on the price index.

Thus the good features of historic cost records would be preserved, and the size of the adjustment would be shown clearly. During a spell of rising prices, the relevant parts of the revenue account might appear somewhat as below; the figures are chosen merely for illustration, and their magnitudes may well not be typical.

Cost of goods sold
(Opening stock, purchases, etc., less closing stock, detailed as usual)
Total, based on original cost .. £2,100
Add Replacement cost provision —say 200

Adjusted charge .. .. ——— £2,300

Depreciation
Normal charge based on original cost £1,000
Add Replacement cost provision —say 900
Adjusted charge .. .. ——— £1,900

The depreciation supplement is based on the following imaginary data: a machine with a life of 10 years was bought for £10,000 when the index stood at 100; depreciation is written off on the straight-line method; and the index stood on average at 190 during the current year. (Where assets are bought in different years, the calculation will be a trifle more complex, as the price index will have moved more for some assets than for others. A plant register will thus be needed—a useful thing anyway.)

The adjustment to "cost of goods sold" will normally be a smaller percentage than that to depreciation. Stocks lie unsold for a turnover period of months, whereas years may have passed since plant was bought; therefore the changes in the index over the two "turnovers" are very different.

Balance Sheet. Stock, plant, and historic depreciation could still be shown at historic cost exactly as in orthodox accounting; revaluation would be optional. The replacement cost supplements could be carried forward from year to year as capital reserves.

Deflation. When the price index drops, the firm must re-transfer a corresponding part of its accumulated replacement cost provisions to revenue account (until the provisions are exhausted). Such sums would then be taxable and available for dividends. They would thus serve as dividend and tax equalization reserves; they would probably be very welcome to shareholders, while the ultimate loss to the Treasury, taking good and bad times together, might not be great.

Voluntary adoption. The scheme would be optional, i.e., there should be no compulsion on firms to keep records or adopt a theory of cost measurement that they consider undesirable. Each taxpayer would estimate whether, in the long run, the trouble involved would be repaid in saving of tax. Many traders with inadequate records might well be ruled out; and those who are so optimistic as to foresee the end of rising prices would naturally not opt for the change. Where the change was made for tax purposes, its use in the ordinary published accounts should be compulsory. And, once the election was made, it should be irrevocable.

Past losses ignored? It would probably be impracticable—on the grounds both of the largeness of the sums involved, and of clerical difficulties—to grant retrospective relief (e.g., for the years from 1939 to 1952). However, the important thing is to make certain that the mistake never occurs again.

No outside control. Beyond seeing that the inflation reserve was carried forward in the balance sheet, the Inland Revenue would not need to supervise firms' policies in any way. The reserve is not a sort of bonus to be held in sacred trust, but the firm's own original wealth, which it can (subject to deflation) hold in any form it pleases, like ordinary depreciation provisions.

While unforeseen difficulties would no doubt arise in practice, the fact that a similar scheme appears to have worked fairly well in France and other European countries is encouraging. In U.S.A., too, something comparable in its effects—a "Lifo" system based on indices—has been in use for some years.

V

Equity Between Taxpayers

It is one thing to decide that a method of accounting will work, quite another that it is socially desirable. A reform that lightens the tax of firms subject to the historic cost error must put a heavier load on other taxpayers.* The latter will question the fairness and wisdom of the change. We must accordingly broaden our discussion, and pass from questions of accounting technique to those of social policy.

* This sentence supposes that the Chancellor is forced to raise some given minimum of tax. Perhaps, however, we could permit ourselves a rather more sanguine view. During inflation part of the Chancellor's budgeted figure for revenue is a surplus designed to check the rise in prices. Large-scale adoption of better accounting methods might itself furnish the needed check (see section (6) on "The Trade Cycle" later in this article) and make such a big surplus unnecessary. If so, tax could be cut somewhat.

We can divide the other taxpayers into two rival groups. First, there are the people whose income, while not subject to the error, has been free to rise with the tide of prices. Such taxpayers may be in business, and yet happen to own little or no plant or stock; they may be in the professions; in a sense, the wage-earner and the owner of durable non-business assets must also be thought of under this head. Because their rights are not of a fixed-money type, members of this group have not, in most cases, suffered excessively from the inflation. Their tax bills have no doubt grown—thanks to progressive rates, faster than their money incomes. But a member of this group will pay less tax than he would if he earned the same real income with the help of stocks or plant, and so had his nominal income swollen by the error. Or, to twist this statement round, the owner of stocks or plant must pay (*a*) as much tax as another man with the same real income; plus (*b*) an extra tax for holding stocks and plant. The justification for (*b*) is not clear. The stresses of 1952 may indeed make checks to investment necessary for the short-run; but the holding and even the expansion of stocks and plant would normally seem not to call for discouragement.

The second group consists of persons who own or receive fixed money incomes (e.g., the *rentier*). The suffering inflicted by inflation on these people rightly arouses great sympathy, and any plan that would put bigger taxes on them must give us pause.

The owner of plant and stocks stands somewhere between these two classes. His accounts blandly suggest kinship with the group to which inflation has been gentle. But tax (*b*) has for years been acting as a special Excess Profits Levy on him, and has gone far to bring him down to the level of the victimized second group.

Our verdict on the claims of the competing groups must partly depend on our views concerning social justice. However, for me to pronounce on what is just would savour of presumption; each of us must decide this issue in the light of his own beliefs. And justice is not the only factor to be weighed. We must, surely, keep economic welfare in mind too; conceivably our present way of measuring profit and tax does so much harm that all groups of taxpayers would gain by change.

From the standpoint of welfare, the case for reform is that the owner of stocks and plant will, failing some relief, in many cases cease to carry out his function. He will do so in part from choice, in part from necessity. He is probably not yet fully awake to the disabilities that attend the holding of stock and plant—to the fact that, if all goes well with his venture, his taxes tend to leave him not much better off than the *rentier*, while the ordinary risks of business may instead afflict him with losses that the *rentier* is spared. When he appreciates his situation, he will become less willing to handicap himself with stocks and plant; faced, say, with a choice between mechanical and hand methods, he will tend to choose the latter because of the tax saving.

However, even if he does not want to give up his stocks and plant, his finances may force him to do so. Notoriously, many firms today cannot, without raising fresh capital, pay both their tax and a modest dividend, and also maintain their physical assets. So far, the larger firms at least have been able to get the needed funds, largely by borrowing from institutions or issuing new shares. There are now ominous hints that this process is growing more difficult. The stock-market droops when a big new issue is made. The social accounts suggest that private savings have declined to a negligible figure. Such a drying-up of saving would be no matter for surprise. The investor's living costs are rising. Further, he must often feel that any investments he has contrived to make in recent years have fared badly; the fall in the buying power of money has robbed his gilt-edged securities of their worth, high taxes have probably kept down his equity dividends, and the rise in interest rates has further lowered the capital values of both types of security. He has scant inducement to save more.

Thus, unless some tax relief is accorded us, so that firms and private persons are once again likely to save, we may reasonably fear a slowing down process (if not something worse) in Britain's economic growth. Almost everyone would lose thereby.

Such are the usual arguments for reform, and they are powerful. But another argument also exists: that our accounting methods are bad because they aggravate the extremes of the trade cycle. We see at present how harmful the overstrain of the boom is to our society; and most of us can still remember the sombre years of unemployment and slump. We must briefly examine the contention that accounting intensifies these evils.

VI

The Trade Cycle

The essence of the historic cost method of drafting revenue accounts is that income of today is set against costs of an earlier date. Accordingly, if the peak of a boom is drawing near, and curves of prices and sales are beginning to flatten out, accounting costs for goods, etc., may still be rising with the steepness of a former period; thus accounting profit may be made to waver and fall prematurely. When prices pass their zenith and start to come down, shrinking sales are for a while matched with costs that are still rising, so that accounting profit is squeezed both above and below, and dwindles much faster than prices and correct profits.* In time, cost figures also reach the peak and start to fall; at this stage, the precipitate decline in accounting profit is checked somewhat; however, as the price-index now stands higher at input date than at sales date, accounting profit will tend to stay below correct profits as long as prices are falling steadily.

The same forces start working in the other direction whenever the fall in prices grows less steep. Reported profits may then begin to rise; after the lowest point of the price curve has been passed, the rise may become a violent spurt; and throughout the years when prices are climbing to their peak, accounting profits will tend to exceed correct profits.

* By "correct profit" I mean money-profit that fluctuates in proportion to prices. We should expect such fluctuation—and no more—in cases where the physical volume of trade (and real profit) did not vary during the cycle.

These movements are illustrated in Diagram II. The dotted line represents the movement of prices over the whole of an imaginary trade cycle. Given a constant physical volume of activity, this curve will also show correct profits. The lightly-shaded columns show the profits produced by the annual accounts of an imaginary firm dealing in goods. The vertical distance between the dotted lines and the tops of the columns gives an idea of the extravagant fashion in which accounts tend to overstate some profit items on the up-grade, and to understate them on the down-grade.

To make the movements stand out clearly, I have used hypothetical figures that are perhaps more subject to the error than cost figures are likely to be in practice; and in any given firm's accounts there may be other factors that modify the scale of distortion. In one particular, however, accounting methods are likely to impart a more pronounced irregularity to the reported profits of the down-grade. We have so far presumed that stocks are always valued at cost, found on the customary "First-In-First-Out" basis (Fifo). But the usual procedure of accountants is to modify Fifo when prices fall, in accordance with the maxim that stock should be valued at "Cost Or Market, whichever is lower". Various interpretations are placed on this formula (which we may

DIAGRAM II
ACCOUNTING PROFITS
over a complete TRADE CYCLE
(Hypothetical data)

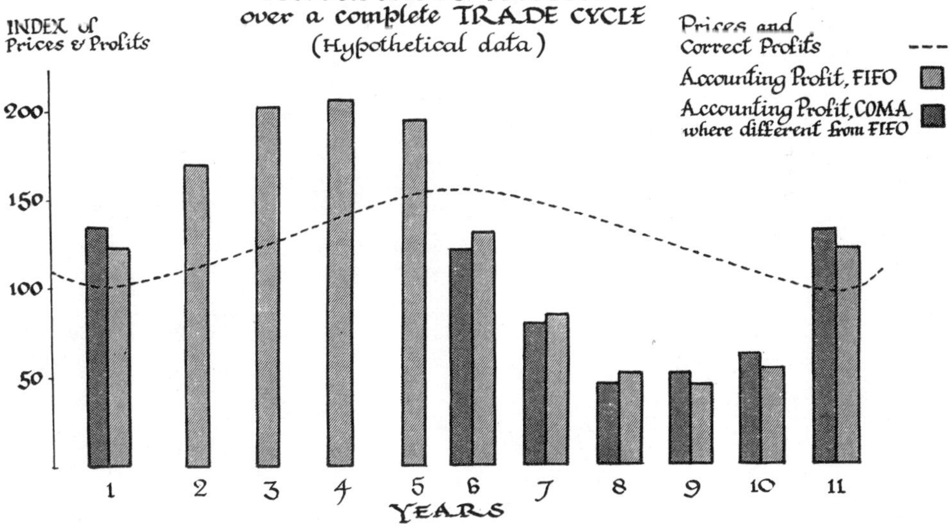

perhaps call COMA, somewhat disrespectfully, for the sake of shortness). It is, however, meant to make stock values cautious when prices are falling; at such times, all interpretations are likely to yield more recent stock values than those obtained by Fifo. In consequence, reported profits react still more sharply to the initial drop in prices, to any change in trend during the slump, and to the first year of recovery. This extra sensitivity is suggested by the heavily shaded columns on the diagram.

It is sometimes argued that in the long run the over-statement of profit on the up-grade cancels the under-statement on the down grade. This might well be true if over a long period (including many cycles) the course of prices were free from any marked upward or downward trend; in fact, the long-period trend is upwards. And even if the two errors do cancel, their effects on our society could be substantial. A business-man's outlook can hardly fail to be influenced in some measure by his accounts. On the up-grade, they flatter him; on the decline, they belittle his achievement. His own results tend to be echoed in the figures of other firms, in dividend news, and in share prices. We may well suppose the cumulative effect on his judgment and expectations to be considerable. The expectations of business-men presumably colour their demand for goods and labour. Thus the synthetic element in accounting profit could alter the level of employment and prices, and intensify further the forces making for the extremes of the cycle. We may not unreasonably conclude that the accountant bears some responsibility for the ills of boom and slump, although, as the factors at stake are intangible, we shall do well to reserve judgment on the extent of his responsibility.

We must, however, note at least one flaw in the above thesis. If accounting methods raise profits during inflation, they also raise tax assessments; therefore, at the very moment when the Chancellor should drain off funds to check buying, he is given an easy means of doing so. During a depression, similarly, tax assessments fall in a convenient fashion.

This counter-argument has some force, but I doubt whether it outweighs the main argument. The brilliant profit figures of booms are likely, despite the high tax, to make banks and other lenders more willing to provide a firm with the money it needs for both tax and expansion. Under British law, moreover, tax payment takes place so long after the profit has been earned that the cycle may have entered a different phase by then, so that the payment may do little good and even some harm. A quick change in the tax rates payable by everyone would probably be more effective. It would certainly be more just; there seems no reason why owners of stocks and plant, any more than men with red hair, should be forced to serve as the valves through which the Chancellor adjusts the supply of money.

The extremes of the trade cycle are, next to war, probably the gravest threat to Western society. Any device that offers hope of moderating them seems well worth a trial. Here surely is a major reason why Parliament should reform our tax law.

VII

Conclusions

To sum up. The case against our present tax system seems on balance strong enough to warrant experiment with reforms. These might not only remove a threat to our country's productive resources, but also iron out the trade cycle somewhat. However, even if the Chancellor declines to act, there are good reasons why a firm should on its own initiative recognize price movements in its accounts. The change would be fairly simple, though not so simple as its advocates suggest. Two kinds of adjustment would be needed: the replacement costs of the firm's assets must be grafted on to management calculations, while an index of general prices should be used to correct the annual profit and loss account. Such a change would make for more balanced judgment by managers, for better relations with workers and the public, and for the preservation of the firm's assets. It would also, if taken up by many firms, do more than anything else to compel a corresponding reform in our tax system.

RECOMMENDATIONS ON ACCOUNTING THEORY

Recommendations on Accounting Theory[1]

By W. T. Baxter

Professor of Accounting, London School of Economics.

I. *The need for a review*

Various societies of accountants have now for some years been issuing official statements on our profession's problems. What I have mainly in mind are of course the " recommendations " and " bulletins " published by the Institute of Chartered Accountants in England and Wales, and by the American Institute of Certified Public Accountants. These started to come out in quantity soon after Hitler's War, and they now add up to a substantial volume covering a long list of subjects. Their influence on accounting and auditing is great, and is likely to become greater. So some review of this development seems not out of place.

Almost every accountant must find the recommendations exceedingly useful in his day-to-day work. They provide him with a code of rules on all sorts of difficult points (notably where the law leaves awkward gaps); and they save time, thought, and worry. They have also served the general public well by raising the quality of published statements.

In view of these benefits, it may seem churlish, and academic in the worst sense, to attack the recommendations. Nevertheless I shall try to argue that at least in one aspect (which could be changed) they are doing a great disservice. And many other accountants—even if they do not share my feeling that the recommendations have already gone too far—may perhaps like to discuss how much further the process of recommending can with propriety go. Where is the limit? Are we to look forward to the day when every detail of our work has been dealt with? Should our goal be—as high authority has hinted apropos the question of price levels—super-recommendations by a massed assembly representing *all* the professional bodies?

Another reason for airing the matter is this. Some accounting societies have so far made few or no recommendations. Their

1 Based on an article in *The Accountant* of October 10, 1953.

members may well have some feeling that the omission betokens lack of zeal and public spirit. They should recognise that a policy of official silence has in fact much in its favour. However, this most emphatically does *not* mean that inertia should be lightly excused, or that accounting societies need take no part in furthering knowledge. On the contrary, they should do everything in their power to encourage education, debate and research. For instance, they could give great help by setting up much-needed scholarships (perhaps to be awarded on the results of the professional examinations) to enable their brilliant young men to study further.

II. Scope of the review

A recommendation tends to contain three types of ingredient:

(1) A description of the given problem;
(2) A reasoned discussion, often based on fundamentals, on how best to solve the problem; and
(3) The recommended solution.

It is mainly (2) that seems objectionable. For here the accounting society weighs intellectual principles, analyses the *pros* and *cons* of the alternative arguments, and decides that one view is better than the others; in short, here authority tells us what is true. Is it wise for any group of men to say what is " true " or " right " in matters of theory?

By " theory " I mean the attempt to explain, in terms of fundamentals, what accounting is and what it tries to do; I thus assume that accounting is a branch of knowledge, like law or physics, with basic principles that are worth exploring. (One might use phrases like " scientific laws " instead of " principles " or " theory," but that would suggest work among test-tubes. Other phrases, employing " abstract knowledge " or " scholarly learning," might sound a bit pompous. On the whole, " theory " seems the neatest word to cover what we have in mind.)

The distinction between (2) and (3) can best be seen by contrasting our recommendations with a set of *working rules*, for instance the Companies Act or the Football Association's rules of play. Such rules are a framework designed to make something run smoothly; unlike the recommendations, they consist only of (3), and do not start off with a discursion into the philosophy of, say, companies or football. The test of a good law is that the institution works well; it is not educational but practical.

Consider, for instance, the problem of how assets should be dealt with in a balance-sheet. When a writer on accounting tries to show us the best method, he probably builds up his case by discussing and judging various theories. But when a law says that company accounts must show the values in such-and-such ways, it does not analyse all the theories and then tell us which satisfies logic. It merely issues orders. It tells us *what*, and perhaps *how*, but not *why*. So we can obey this kind of law without feeling that we are being forced to accept a particular theory, and that our freedom of thought is being lessened. Besides, few citizens of a lively democracy grow up believing that everything in their laws is sensible; we hear much criticism of laws, and we accept that we have the right—indeed the duty—to try to repeal or reform bad laws.

Of course, even the answers to *what* and *how* can be influenced by theory. Normally the makers of a law must have some theory in mind when they draft it. A legislature may even be forced to choose between scientific theories, *e.g.*, public health law assumes that the views of Pasteur and Fleming are right. But the choice is made merely so that hopeful lines of development can be tried without delay, and should not imply that the official seal of approval has been put on any theory; if the experiment fails, it can be promptly scrapped without loss of face. Legislators who went further—to the point of explicitly endorsing a theory—would exceed their function, and would indeed be threatening our freedom of thought. Similarly, if an Act of Parliament includes definitions, these are not meant as revelations of final knowledge, but only as tools for making effective the particular set of rules; a judge may even hold that the definitions in one Act do not apply in the context of another Act on a dissimilar subject.

An obvious corollary seems to follow. When rules are prescribed for published accounting statements, they should not only avoid *why*, but should be chary about *how*. The stress should be on *what*. Authority can set minimum standards of disclosure without dragging in much theory; if it prescribes methods—particularly in the context of valuation—it must inevitably choose between theories. A terse list of minimum requirements, such as is given in the British Companies Act, works well and leaves honest men tolerably free to think and experiment. It provides a floor, not a ceiling.

Our views on recommendations may thus depend on whether we look on them as law or research; we may indeed regard a rule in (3) as useful, and yet object to its preamble in (2). In many cases, the tenor of the recommendations suggests that contributions to both theory and law are the aim. Whatever the intentions of their framers, there can be little doubt that they have been accepted by wide audiences as official and definitive pronouncements on theory.

We shall thus restrict the scope of our review to the parts of recommendations that pronounce on theory, or imply adoption of a theory, and shall say little about the other parts that proffer rules for minimum action on technical problems. Likewise we are not concerned with recommendations that adopt a different pattern, or deal with non-technical problems. They may for instance be concerned instead with *public policy*. A professional body sometimes advises its members to follow a common policy on questions that have little to do with the intellectual content of its members' work. For instance, it may make statements on "professional ethics," fees, registration by the state, and so forth. Such types of advice should be judged by standards quite different from those useful in our present review. If, for example, a body of architects or lawyers advises its members to charge a uniform scale of fees, or pay its assistants a standard wage, we judge the issue in the light of our views on the benefits or otherwise of economic monopoly; if it commends integrity to its members, perhaps we merely wonder whether it is not preaching to the converted in most cases, and wasting its breath in the rest.

Again, a recommendation may deal with *definitions* and *uniform practice*. To some extent these can be handled in ways that avoid theory—in which case they too fall outside our discussion. But such matters infringe on theory more often than might be supposed; and so we must give a little space to them.

One other matter should be made clear. Our review will make its point better if it omits all discussion of whether individual recommendations on theory have in fact been right or wrong. What is said here is thus not meant as criticism of any recommendation's content. Indeed, we may for our present purpose agree that every word in every recommendation seems entirely true; and yet we may think that a policy of making recommendations on theory will, in the long run, be disastrous.

III. Origins of recommendations

I should like to admit that, when official statements on accounting principles were first published, I was enthusiastic about them. My doubts have arisen since, on seeing how the new venture has developed.

Looking back, one remembers certain features in early statements that have unfortunately not usually been copied since. Consider the *Statement on Accounting Principles* of 1938. It was published by the American Institute, to whose members it was commended in a foreword; but it bore the names of three distinguished authors—Messrs. Sanders, Hatfield and Moore—who had been formed into an independent committee to do this bit of writing (and who were not even members of the Institute). Under such an arrangement, the Institute was plainly doing its duty to foster discussion, and yet was itself not taking sides. That kind of procedure goes far to disarm criticism.

Since this venture, the trend has been for the statements to be drafted by committees much more closely linked with the sponsoring body, and for the latter to back the conclusions in a much firmer way. The American Institute, for instance, set up its own Committee on Accounting Procedure to issue research bulletins. Bulletin No. 1 explained the aims and methods. It stressed the growth of corporate organisation, and therefore the social importance of good accounts; and it noted that there " has been a demand for a larger degree of uniformity in accounting." The committee stated that its rules were not intended to have retroactive effect; also they may be subject to exception, but " the burden of proof is upon the accountant clearly to bring out the exceptional procedure and the circumstances which render it necessary."

This has perhaps a somewhat mandatory ring. But the American bulletins have in fact used two safeguards that make their tenor less authoritarian: the members of the drafting committee are named in recommendations, and any member who disagrees with the majority is entitled to have the fact of his dissent recorded in the document. At least one American committee has had the courage to say bluntly that an earlier pronouncement by itself now seems wrong.[2]

The Institute of Chartered Accountants in England and Wales announced its first recommendation as follows:

> " The Council has requested the Taxation and Financial Relations Committee to consider and make recommendations to it on certain aspects of the accounts of companies and it is proposed from time to time to publish approved recommendations for the information of members. It is, of course, a matter for each individual member to consider his responsibility in regard to accounts presented by directors, but it is hoped that the recommendations to be made will be helpful to members in advising directors as to what is regarded as the best practice."[3]

These words are as modest and cautious as anyone could wish. They show how undogmatic the original plan was; and

[2] *Accounting Problems Arising from Devaluation of Foreign Currencies*, Research Department, American Institute of Accountants (1949).
[3] *The Accountant*, December 12, 1942, p. 354.

they suggest that the Council did not foresee the eventual scope of the recommendations, or the deference with which they would be treated.

IV. The case for recommendations

It would be ungenerous not to set down at length the good that has been done by the recommendations. Their benefits have obviously been great.

Recommendations have been so widely accepted that they have in fact acted very like a supplement to the law. What we may call extra-parliamentary control can often eke out statutes in a useful manner, particularly at the experimental stage; the rules of a stock exchange are another example of such control. In England, the early recommendations did much to prepare the way for the 1948 Companies Act, and indeed have in fact been absorbed into that Act. In America, the interplay between the Institute's bulletins and the S.E.C. regulations clearly is close; and the absence of a counterpart to the Companies Act enhances the bulletins' value as a code of standards.

The recommendations may thus serve as private forerunners and reinforcements to the law. Their record in this work has on the whole been excellent—notably in procuring full, frank, and consistent accounts.[4] The auditor has special cause to be thankful for them; the task of persuading his clients to comply with high standards in published accounts is sometimes delicate, and the recommendations have greatly strengthened his hand. They have also aided the analyst by fostering uniformity.

Though the recommendations have been less successful in the realm of theory, they have yielded some benefits. As each recommendation is first suggested, amended, and then adopted, undoubtedly it gives rise for a time to discussion and interest. Again, many of us used to deplore the fact that our profession's leaders never could spare time to write about their work; whatever the faults of the new system, it does prompt these men to tell us a great deal about what they think, and what they regard as usual practice.

We thus have cause to feel grateful to the drafters of recommendations; and this review should on no account be construed as an attack on them. Obviously they have devoted much time and

[4] Some other writer may like to examine the question of what safeguards (if any) are needed if a private group is to make rules, almost with the force of law, that affect non-members. Already one company has felt impelled to try to stop publication of a statement (alleged to have been prepared without normal opportunities for hearing objectors) that seemed likely to damage the company's borrowing status: *Appalachian Power Company* v. *A.I.C.P.A.*, 268 Federal 2nd 844 (Court of Appeals for the Second Circuit).

care to their task, and have been prompted by a high sense of public service. If harm should in the end come from their work, the blame should attach more to disciples who have accepted their teaching too eagerly, and have invested it with an *ex cathedra* quality that could not perhaps have been foreseen.

It is not unusual in human affairs for a thing to be started with the best intentions, and yet to develop aspects that threaten harm. My plea is that we should now review the good and bad alike, and see whether we cannot guide future growth in directions that are wholly good.

The recommendations' benefits are clear and present. Their ill results are hypothetical, and will show—if at all—in the future. Moreover these ill results are suggested by experience in other fields of study; and conceivably accounting is unlike these in nature and difficulty. If accounting differs from other subjects in its nature, then the arguments that follow may be weakened. But I see no reason to think that it is different.

V. The case against recommendations

The case against official recommendations on theory is threefold. First, men do not always become better at research when they work as a group. Second, if authority takes direct part in the pursuit of truth, it may hinder rather than help. Third—and most important—there are no sure signs by which truth can be recognised.

The first objection need not keep us long; admittedly it is not always a strong factor. To judge from experience in most fields of learning, men tend to do their best research when left to their own devices. There are many exceptions; a large team of chemists may be the quickest means of dealing with a laborious task, and a government committee may be admirable at sifting evidence and assessing opinion. In general, however, thinkers are apt to be hampered by close connection with a team or with a powerful institution. The link may curb initiative, or bring a need for diplomacy and compromise. The welfare of the institution may seem more important than truth; thus the authorities of the Church could not deal fairly with the ideas of Copernicus and Galileo because these ideas clashed with official pronouncements of the past.

The second objection is much weightier. It is an indirect way of saying that freedom is necessary for progress. " Freedom " here means the absence, not merely of crude tyranny, but also of benevolent authority that makes us respectful to some ideas and hostile to others. Man should be able to think freely and without bias, so that the stream of new ideas can flow strongly; and he should be able to discuss and experiment freely and without bias, so that all ideas can be criticised and tested with rigour. If authority intervenes—by joining in the quest itself or by giving its *imprimatur* to some favourite idea, let alone by making attacks on personal liberty—the chances of progress are lessened. Men cease to think so freely—whether from fear, or powerful preconceptions, or belief that others can do the job better; and therefore the stream of new ideas dries up. They cease to discuss and experiment so freely; and therefore criticism loses its edge, and ideas are not put to a stern test.

This train of reasoning leads to the third objection. How can we tell what is true? Even the objective tests of the laboratory are not final (and pronouncements on accounting must surely be based on discussion, and so be far from objective). Under strong criticism, many ideas soon prove false. Others satisfy all immediate tests, yet should be accepted as tentative only, for they, too, are likely to show flaws as the years go by. Even after an idea has survived triumphantly for centuries, some critic may shatter it, or else show it to be capable of improvement. Einstein was able both to generalise Newton's theory and to correct it for conditions that had not previously been considered. No human being—however distinguished—can certainly foretell which idea will become a casualty. As Bacon says: "Truth is the daughter, not of Authority, but of Time."

The root of the matter, surely, is man's fallibility. Only if we believe a statement to have divine inspiration can we treat it as beyond doubt.

It may be helpful to ask why learned bodies do not in general issue official solutions to questions puzzling their members. Why, for instance, does the Royal Society not organise a team of Fellows to solve this or that intractable problem of physics? All three objections suggested above are relevant to the answer. The Fellows may perhaps feel that they work better apart. Their training in science has made them sceptical, and more apt to test and attack than to defend ideas. They have learnt from the experience of centuries that their "laws" can never be regarded as final. If the Society gave official approval to theories, its members would probably soon be rent by a schism between an orthodox and a dissenting party; and sooner or later (the chances are) the Society would be proved wrong, and would be forced to utter an embarrassing recantation.

Similarly, official recommendations by an institute of engineers would have to be framed with some care. Assume, for instance, that it advised its members to build bridges in a uniform way, based on the best current knowledge. For a while, standards might well be raised. But research would in time point to better bridges; nonconformist bodies of engineers would be free to build these, while the orthodox would be denied the fruits of advancing science.

Exactly what do we mean by " authority " in this context? A wide sweep should be given to the word; it here includes all forces that can give weight to some ideas at the expense of others. Privilege is bad for ideas as for men; only if they can jostle one another in a democratic way is the best likely to reach the top.

Authority may thus rest (at one end of the scale) on prestige only, and (at the other) on power. Occasionally the brilliance of a single thinker can cause his views to be treated with deference. A close-knit school of able thinkers may well dominate opinion to an unhealthy point—even if they lack organisation and can impose no sanctions. The harm becomes vastly more formidable when the authority controls education, or can mould adult opinion. It reaches its worst when authority has total power. In its extreme forms, we are all agreed that it is evil—and that the evil persists whether or not the views that it promulgates happen to seem true or false.

Happily, we are here concerned with authority at its mildest and most benevolent. Nevertheless, we may wonder whether, in the realm of mental freedom, even a slight degree of control must not lead to harm.

VI. Training and innovation

With our recommendations, the basis of authority is of course mainly the prestige of the bodies concerned. But this is of a high order. We all know in what respect such a body is held by the bulk of its members. Moreover, its drafting committee will include many of the profession's best-known men. It gives the recommendations its whole-hearted backing and much publicity. In consequence, the issue of a new recommendation is treated as a matter of great moment by the accounting Press; this attention is fitting, though one could wish that the notices were a shade less passive and fulsome.

The recommendations must therefore have a considerable influence on the thought of the mature accountant. On the immature mind—that of a young man in training—their impact must be deep. They are given conspicuous place in his textbooks and correspondence courses, and so play a large part in moulding his views when he is still impressionable and uncritical. They naturally appeal to the feebler type of teacher, who finds it easier to recite an official creed than to lead a brisk argument. Even before the days of recommendations, accounting textbooks and teachers preferred in general to state facts rather than explore theories. Their main concern was painstaking description of normal practice; scant space was accorded to the reasoning behind the practice, and next to nothing was said of controversy. This dull and sterile approach has now been made far more likely. If an official answer is available to a problem, why should a teacher burden his examination candidates with other views? Further, the body that gives the answers also controls the examination. A young man has thus good cause for minute and respectful study of its statements. And his question paper does not often include such items as: "Discuss Recommendation No. —. Set out the grounds for supposing that its reasoning is (a) correct, and then (b) fallacious; and give your own views on this point."

Thus the recommendations tend to rob our young men's education of its power to enrich and stimulate. On such a spare diet, they may perhaps still train well enough to master the techniques of today. But their minds will be less fit to solve the new problems of tomorrow; and such fitness is no bad test by which to judge an education.

Recommendations must also to some extent cramp the mature accountant's thought. They relieve him of responsibility for intellectual decision—a state that is comfortable, but hardly stimulating. They may hinder him if he wants to try out new ideas or make experiments. In America, one important experiment has already been stopped because it offended "accepted accounting principles" as set forth in a bulletin: the S.E.C. compelled the U.S. Steel Company to amend 1947 depreciation figures based on the current price level, and so prevented all further experiment in this field by companies under S.E.C. control.

Even where there is no legal prohibition, recommendations could endanger a thoughtful auditor if they were used as evidence in lawsuits. Consider for instance a case that hangs on questions of auditing theory—say, the valuation of stocks and wasting assets when price levels change. Suppose that a company follows the advice of an auditor who sincerely believes a recommendation to be wrong; that the company thereafter runs into financial trouble, and that it sues the auditor for negligence. In such a case, the determining test would probably be the standard of behaviour followed by good professional practice. Hostile counsel would treat the recommendations as powerful evidence, and could make the most damaging use of the auditor's deviation.

The defence might have some difficulty in proving that many conscientious but inarticulate accountants still regard the issue as open to argument. A judge or jury might well be swayed decisively by the recommendations, and give a verdict against the auditor.

An analogy is tempting. Suppose that the medical profession's first dislike of antiseptic surgery had crystallised in a hostile recommendation; that one of Lister's patients had died; and that the deceased's relatives had brought a suit for negligence. What would have been the effect on surgery?

Such cases must inevitably crop up sooner or later. Where an auditor is faced with this risk, the temptation to play safe—by abandoning his independence of judgment—is very great. Yet a pliant attitude in such matters is scarcely compatible with the dignity of his profession.

VII. Other kinds of recommendations

Section II suggested that there are some kinds of recommendations which may seem to avoid theory, but in fact are apt to be entangled with it. Let us consider these briefly:

(a) *Definition.* If precise and uniform meanings can be given to our terms and figures, then doubtless we shall be able to exchange ideas with more ease and clarity. Also, accounting data will be more consistent. (The Royal Society *has* set up a standing committee to make recommendations on the symbols, signs and abbreviations used in scientific publications.)

Standard definitions are, however, not without their drawbacks. If speech is made rigid, it cannot evolve to meet new needs. There may be a clash between the ordinary and the technical use of a word. Both the American and the English Institutes have pointed out the ambiguities of " reserve " (which in everyday speech can mean something quite different from its sense in a balance-sheet), and have tried to restrict its meaning helpfully; yet even this restricted use may still bewilder rather than enlighten the public.

Further, words are seldom quite neutral in the battle between ideas. With " goodwill," for instance, the ordinary meaning stands out so strongly that it obtrudes when we are trying to unravel the technical concept, and thus colours our understanding of " goodwill " in accounts. Again, choice of a definition often demands a choice between ideas. For example, any definition of " depreciation " is almost sure to be tendentious.

Thus an official link between a word and an idea is likely to bias our minds. What is almost as bad, some definitions have an air of finality that checks inquiry, and leaves students with no exciting sense of being explorers in a great and unknown territory.

(b) *Standard practice.* Uniformity in presentation of published data (minimum content and method of layout) has strong arguments in its favour—provided it neither cramps honest business nor begs ideas. If a choice between words or methods clearly is arbitrary and free from any pretence of research, it is not likely to damage future thinking or to act as a straitjacket; for example, whether traffic keeps to the left or right of the road is an arbitrary matter, and uniformity yields a gain in convenience, so no one regards a standard rule as an attack on freedom. Therefore, when we are attracted by uniformity, a good test is perhaps this: if a decision between possible terms or practices can be reached by tossing a coin or pulling words from a hat, then uniformity is unlikely to do harm.

However, it is one thing to say that such-and-such items must be shown and explained, and quite another to say how their size must be calculated. The size of the figures is a matter of valuation theory; and, as is shown by our hot debates on such matters as depreciation, income measurement, asset valuation, and the effects of changing price levels, this is certainly an area in which we are far from knowing where truth lies. Rules for standard practice should not prescribe valuation methods. Even rules on how items should be grouped in a balance-sheet may impinge on principle; thus, if they say that allowance for deferred tax must be shown in (or out of) the owners' capital group, they are in effect forcing us to swallow a particular view on the valuation of capital.

Perhaps " standard " should here mean " usual," *i.e.*, what is normal but not necessarily right. For convenience, the reader of published accounts should be able to rely on their compliance with standard practice—unless he is given clear warning to the contrary, and (where this would not mislead) a note of what standard practice would have shown. An accountant should always reserve his right to depart from the standard, on giving notice, if he thinks the standard does not fit the particular case, or the reader's current needs, or his own views on theory.

(c) *Legal opinions.* Counsel's opinions, given at the request of an accounting society and sent out to its members, are not usually classed as " recommendations." To round off our review, however, we should ask ourselves how such statements fit into our reasoning.

The opinions do not seem so dangerous as recommendations on theory, on two grounds.

First, no wise man tries to be expert in everything; outside his own province, he can to some degree accept ideas from others without sapping his mental independence. *Second*, as we noted in Section II, the law does not pretend to state absolute principles. When a lawyer is trying to find what is " true " or " false," he is mainly concerned with the arbitrary—though no doubt exacting—task of interpreting words (especially those in statutes) according to the intentions of their users and the rules of his craft.

VIII. Conclusions

If the above arguments are sound, where do they lead us? Perhaps the recommendations that should be made on recommendations are:

(a) Official statements on accounting cover a number of very different things, which are often hard to separate. They include:

Working rules, *e.g.*, for company reports.
Guidance on professional policy.
Definitions.
Suggestions for uniform accounting.
Legal opinions.
Abstract theory.

None of these is without its pitfalls. However, given due care and caution, the risks seem worth taking—except in the case of theory. Official quests for the abstract are apt to bear little fruit and to run into great hazards. No human being, however impressive his trappings, knows what the truth is.

(b) Recommendations should not only confine themselves to rules for action, as contrasted with principles, but should stress this restriction in their scope. For instance, if a recommendation suggests a definition of "current assets," it might expressly disclaim any attempt to elucidate principles, and describe the rules as being based merely on convenience or custom.

(c) The more concerned a statement is with theory, the stronger is the case for not treating it as an official recommendation. A group of distinguished accountants who have debated a subject, and who wish to help us by announcing their conclusions, would not have the least trouble in finding a publisher.

(d) A recommended " standard practice " should be explained in terms of normal behaviour—something that the user of published accounts can take for granted if nothing to the contrary is said. The accountant, acting in good faith and with due warnings, should feel free—indeed obliged—to vary the practice when he deems it unsuitable. Final responsibility should still rest on the accountant's own judgment; where possible, the rule should be cast in the form of minimum standards, thus leaving room for improvement.

(e) The objections to a recommendation become much less marked if it is described as the work of certain named persons. We all know that individuals can err; we all tend to look on institutions as infallible. Therefore recommendations should—following the American example—be signed by the men who approve the final draft.

(f) A dissenting opinion at once adds a valuable extra dimension, making the recommendation far more useful as an aid to the mind. Therefore great pains should be taken to foster and express minority views.

To conclude. Recommendations by authority on matters of accounting theory may in the short run seem unmixed blessings. In the end, however, they will probably do harm. They are likely to yield little fresh knowledge; "the best test of truth is the power of the thought to get itself accepted in the competition of the market." [5] They are likely to weaken the education of accountants; the conversion of the subject into cut-and-dried rules, approved by authority and not to be lightly questioned, threatens to reduce its value as a subject of liberal education almost to *nil.* They are likely to narrow the scope for individual thought and judgment; and a group of men who resign their hard problems to others must eventually give up all claim to be a learned profession.

[5] Dissenting opinion of Judge Oliver Wendell Holmes in *Abrams* v. *United States*.

SHARES OF NO PAR VALUE

No Par Value

I—*The Theory of No-Par-Value Capital*

The setting up of the Departmental Committee on Shares of No Par Value suggested that the Government was not ill-disposed to this form of capital. Now that seven of the Committee's eight members have signed a report that is very favourable to such shares, only the misgivings of organised labour seem to stand in the way of an amendment of the law, and these misgivings—as it is hoped to show—appear to be based on a misunderstanding. Accordingly, accountants may before long be faced with a set of problems that are new to British practice. The problems will involve points of (1) theory, (2) accounting, and (3) law ; and so we shall marshall our views under these three heads.[1]

MONEY RIGHTS AND NON-MONEY RIGHTS

The man who puts £100 into a savings bank makes an investment whose terms are both familiar and certain. He receives a pass-book that clearly shows £100 at his credit ; he is sure to earn an annual sum of interest that is a percentage of £100 ; and he is also sure to get back his £100 when he decides to close the account. The symbol " £100 " thus conveys an accurate picture of his rights, since these are defined strictly in terms of money. He can aptly speak of his " £100 investment," for his asset is not very different from cash.

Next, suppose instead that he contributes his £100 as a share in some private trading venture or partnership. Here the facts are quite different. But they are still familiar, and he is not likely to have any doubts about the nature of his investment. He knows, even if he is not expert in law or business, that he no longer has something that can certainly be changed back into £100 of cash ; instead, he has rights in an enterprise. He knows, too, that these rights depend on the terms of his agreement with his partners ; and that the value of the enterprise—and therefore of his share in it—may vary from day to day according

[1] Parts I and III of this article are developed from a memorandum submitted by the authors to the Departmental Committee.

to all the countless circumstances and hazards of trade. His grasp of these truths will probably be undiminished even if he is shown a balance sheet in which his capital is stated in print to be " £100 " ; his common-sense tells him that the figure is history, and not a guarantee of present worth or future repayment. In short, he is well aware that his rights can no longer be defined in terms of money, and that the symbol " £100 " has largely lost its meaning where his investment is concerned.

In this second case, however, the man's perception of the nature of his investment might not always remain so clear if great stress were often put on the term " £100." If he received a certificate with " £100" printed on it, and if his dividend were always expressed as a percentage of £100, and if all the partnership accounts linked his share with the sum of £100, and if legal documents described his share as being of £100, and if common speech dragged in the £100 on all occasions—in short, if the money label were used as incessantly as if it really meant something—then his understanding might pardonably be clouded. Suggestion on this scale is hard to withstand.

Here in a nutshell is the case for shares of no par value. A holding in the share-capital of a company is in nature like the second investment in the partnership ; but the use of par value obscures the facts, and suggests instead the deposit in a savings bank. Only somewhat sophisticated investors are able to shake off all the effects of this suggestion.

Fundamentally, the issue at stake here is the distinction between the *name* of a thing and what the thing *is*. A stock exchange security is a set of rights—for example, to yearly payments of income and a final return of capital. These rights are defined, not by the name of the security, but in a set of rules that forms the basis of contract between company and investor. Let us look more closely at the rules governing the various kinds of securities, and see how far nominal values are apt.

DEBENTURES AND NOTES

To the extent that a company is financed by debentures and notes, the use of par value seems defensible ; here our analogy with the deposit in the savings bank is fairly close. Thus a debenture may involve payment of £5 a year and a final return of £100 ; particularly if this £100 is well secured, and redemption date is not too remote, the phrase " £100 of debenture stock " is a reasonably accurate name for the rights in question, and the printing of " £100 " on the certificate is not likely to do much harm.

EQUITY CAPITAL

Some portion of a company's capital, however, must be raised on less rigid terms. The underlying wealth of the business (whether thought of as present assets or as future receipts) has hardly ever a fixed value in terms of money ; this becomes plain if an inflation occurs or if the business is unusually fortunate or unfortunate, for the money-value of the business then changes—perhaps to a dramatic extent. Because of this changeability, a business cannot be entirely financed by investors with rights defined in terms of fixed sums of money. Someone must be willing to bear the risks—that is, to accept rights of a more elastic type. This class (let us call it the " equity shareholders ") voluntarily takes its stand at the tail-end of the queue for benefits, and is content to receive an unpredictable residue (both of annual income and of ultimate return of capital).

An interest in a company's equity must therefore be defined as a right, not to so many pounds, but to an arithmetical proportion of whatever surplus is left—be it large or small—after money-claims have been met. The most usual type of equity interest is of course Ordinary capital. Ordinary dividends and prices are therefore apt to be mercurial, and to move abruptly up and down with the company's fortunes. However, although the equity-shareholder assumes the risks of his company, he sheds some of the risks of money; when the value of the £ is changing, his shares may (in real terms) be more stable than debentures.

Thus the whole *raison d'être* of equity capital is to absorb changes in the money-value of the company; and the very essence of the rules governing such capital is that it is not tied to a fixed quantity of money, but can change its money-value with complete freedom. That being the case, any name that implies a fixed money-value is peculiarly unsuitable. Just as a partner in an unincorporated firm can say " I have a half share in Messrs. X and Y," so an ordinary shareholder might say " I have a $\frac{213}{100,000}$ share in X.Y. Ltd." Unfortunately this accurate phrase is too cumbersome for general use.

PREMIUMS AND DISCOUNTS

So far, we have assumed that par value can at least be justified on historical grounds—that it is the price paid for shares at their first issue. But even this may not be true. Shares are often issued at a premium, and sometimes at a discount ; in these cases, the meaning of par may well elude definition.

Our argument has also so far assumed that the equity-shareholders contribute a certain quantum of real assets (admittedly with a changeable money-value) to the business, and stop at that. In fact, they usually keep on contributing more and more real assets, by ploughing back profits. Where firms are untrammelled by company law, they show this process for what it truly is—additions to equity-capital; thus a private trader who begins the year with £10,000 of capital, and who then earns (and leaves in his business) £4,000 of profit, normally drafts his end-of-year balance sheet in some such way as :

Capital :	£
Opening balance	10,000
Add : Profit for year	4,000
Closing balance	£14,000

and £14,000 becomes the opening capital at the start of next year. But the rules of company law prevent such informal changes in capital account, and so, when a company retains current earnings in the same way, the additions must go under some other heading, for example, " reserve," and must be kept permanently apart from capital in the balance sheet :

Interest of equity-shareholders in the business :

Share-capital	£
10,000 ordinary shares of £1	10,000
Revenue reserve	4,000
	£14,000

The true capital has now risen, thanks to the savings of the equity holders, to £14,000. Indeed, two sets of cheques for £4,000 might equally well be exchanged between company and shareholders, and then 4,000 new shares could be issued as evidence of the capitalised profit. Yet in practice the figure of £10,000 tends to stand indefinitely, even though the equity holders continue to save each year, and so increase their investment until reserves perhaps exceed the original capital of £10,000. In these circumstances, phrases such as " a £1 share " and " a 10 per cent. dividend " are most unhappy, and the case against the use of par value is strengthened still further.

The issue of free bonus shares can to some extent overcome the objections to par-value shares. The large number of such issues in recent years (when inflation has brought the anomalies of par value into sharp focus) stresses the extent to which par values have diverged from earning power. But the issue of bonus shares is a costly, rough-and-ready, and temporary cure. Moreover it is one which is peculiarly liable to cause misunderstanding; and in so far as it tends to encourage realisation of the bonus by shareholders, and the spending of the proceeds on consumption, it may decrease national saving.

PREFERENCE SHARES AND PAR

When we pass from Ordinary to Preference capital, the distinction between money rights and non-money rights becomes less clear. Into which group do Preference rights fall ? The arguments here are nicely balanced. The Committee has recommended that freedom from the shackles of par value should extend only to Ordinary shares (including shares " by whatever name called, such as ' preferred ordinary ' or ' deferred ordinary,' which do not have either a fixed dividend element or a fixed element of repayment of capital ") ; but the *pros* and *cons* are still worth consideration.

With Preference capital, the links with money may be close. In particular, the maximum rights to annual dividend are defined in money terms. On the other hand, dividends are sometimes not declared. And the stock exchange price varies considerably, in tune with general rates of interest and the circumstances of the particular company (for example, the cover-margin given by profits).

In the case of redeemable Preference shares, the link with money is strengthened by the possibility of redemption—though the date may be variable and remote, and the redemption figure need not be par. With irredeemable shares, final repayment may or may not exceed par, according to the vagaries of the company's rules and of case law. Recent cases have shown that the articles governing the redemption of Preference shares may be very vague, and that at redemption the rights of Preference shareholders may be surprisingly weak. And, whatever the holders' rights on paper, the company may in fact not have enough money left, after settling with creditors, to repay even the par figure.

Thus Preference shares combine a strong suggestion of fixed-money rights with a possibility that the rights may in the event prove watery. In such circumstances, potential investors should surely be warned not to bank on appearances, but to get to the heart of the matter by studying the company's rules with care. And this is precisely the intention underlying no-par-value capital.

Furthermore, the difficulties attendant on the Committee's suggested definition seem considerable. Preference and equity shares shade off imperceptibly one into the other, and any dividing line is necessarily arbitrary and liable to produce anomalies. The Committee suggest excluding from the ambit of equity shares any which have " either a fixed dividend element or a fixed element of repayment of capital." This excludes many types which have such a considerable stake in the equity that nominal value is clearly misleading ; for example a share conferring a 10% fixed dividend and a right of full participation on repayment of capital. Moreover, as it stands, the definition is ambiguous: Is a share with a right to a fixed 4%, and a right to participate up to a further 5%, to be regarded as having " a fixed dividend element " ? If not, why should it be treated differently from a share with a right to a fixed 10%? If, on the other hand, the imposition of an upper limit (however high) on the extent of participation brings us within the meaning of " fixed dividend element," then a preferred share which may participate without limit has to be distinguished from one in which the possible participation is " limited " to 1,000%. Again we ask, why ? Yet, under the Committee's recommendation, a share which falls on the " preference " side of this arbitrary line cannot be converted into no-par, whereas one which falls on the "equity" side must be converted if any other class of equity shares is to become no-par capital.

There thus seems to us to be a valid case for the use of no par value with Preference shares, and we are somewhat regretful that the Committee takes the contrary view. Other countries have legalised such shares without any bad results.

EARLY THEORIES REGARDING PAR

We can readily understand why early legislation and practice put such stress on par value. When the limitation of liability was still a hazardous experiment, to warn potential creditors that the " contributories " need pay only some maximum amount of capital, and to stipulate that this amount could not be reduced, or (once paid in) could not be withdrawn, would seem obvious precautions. No doubt par appeared a suitable device for achieving these ends. We now know that it is not. Shares may in fact not only be issued at a premium or discount, but also as a consideration for assets other than cash. Moreover, share denominations are now very different from what the founding fathers of our company law expected. In place of the £100 or £10 share, partly paid, we now generally find shares ranging from £1 downwards, almost always fully paid; uncalled liability (the only really solid protection for creditors) has been practically eradicated except in the case of the banks, insurance companies, and similar financial institutions. And the nadir of "capital" as a guarantee fund is reached when we find a company on the register with a share capital of ½d. divided into two ¼d. shares !

Time has modified our notions on the permanence and size of the guarantee fund in other ways. New statutes and decisions have made drastic changes in what is treated as non-distributable capital—sometimes strengthening the original concept, sometimes weakening it. And views on the worth of shares have perhaps been altered by a century's experience of stock exchange transactions, and by developments in the theory of value; our theories now tend to recognise that the market fixes prices in the light of expected future receipts, not of figures with historic significance only.

CONFUSION CAUSED BY PAR VALUE

No one would suggest that persons highly-skilled in financial matters are likely to be misled by par values. On the other hand, the great majority of people obviously have little opportunity of getting such specialist knowledge. We may reasonably suppose that such people, when confronted by words that seem quite familiar but in fact have meanings very different from those of everyday speech, jump to wrong conclusions. Judging for example from the prior misconceptions of persons who have come to us for advice on investment matters, we think that misunderstanding is widespread.

While we do not in general suppose that the class-room provides faithful evidence of what goes on in the outside world, perhaps students' difficulties over par value are worth mentioning. We find that university students—even those specialising in law, accounting, and allied subjects—have much trouble in understanding par value ; and that their trouble may persist even when they have read those subjects to a fairly advanced stage, under teachers who put stress on company finance. Their confusion shows unmistakably in their written work. A straightforward question on the nature of equity rights may perhaps be sensibly answered after adequate training ; but a slightly more difficult problem—dealing, for example, with the consequences of bonus issues or reconstruction schemes—is apt to trip up quite intelligent students. The experience of examiners of professional accounting bodies would, we fancy, confirm this.

Public pronouncements regarding bonus shares and reconstructions provide perhaps the best available evidence that confusion is not confined to persons unversed in worldly affairs. Things said during Parliamentary debates on bonus shares suggest remarkable misconceptions on the part of Members of Parliament having a deep interest in our economic life ; and these things are echoed in journals written for educated readers.[2] And the approval given by our Courts to reconstruction schemes of dubious fairness can often be explained, we are tempted to suppose, only on the assumption that even Judges may have a less than perfect realisation of what is at stake.

ILL RESULTS OF CONFUSION OVER PAR VALUE

If misunderstanding is as common and grave as we believe, it must lead to many unfortunate results.

Par value gives unnecessary trouble to investors, and exposes them to unnecessary risks. Many people are likely to be deluded when buying shares ; to quote an American writer :

> It was thought that the engraving of $100 upon a share of stock oftentimes led the investor to pay, if not the full $100, at least a larger sum than he would have paid if freed from the hypnotic effect of the $100 emblazoned upon the certificate.[3]

They may also be lulled into a false sense of security when their investment is sinking in value, or fail to recognise that it has appreciated. Such artificial obstacles to understanding are specially unfortunate at a time when national welfare depends so much on the appearance of fresh sources of risk capital, and on investment becoming more democratic.

Again, most people have difficulty in making a fair appraisal of the annual performance of business when dividends are expressed as percentages of nominal capital. Of course, companies are not bound to declare dividends as a percentage of par-value capital ; but even if they—very sensibly—state the dividend as " *x*d. per share " (and this is seldom done) the public will inevitably tend to relate the dividend to par value if the share has one.[4] Much criticism by politicians and

---

[2] Even members of the Cohen Committee did not seem wholly immune ; see, for example, questions 1310 and 1311 during the oral evidence of Mr. Acworth.

[3] Henry Rand Hatfield : *Accounting : Its Principles and Problems*, page 189.

[4] Note that, with par-value shares, the percentage size of a dividend remains the same even if the shares are sub-divided and so the absolute size of the dividend per share falls rateably. Thus the sub-division of par-value shares does not, as is sometimes claimed, give an escape route from misunderstanding.

labour springs from false impressions caused in this way. A dividend can with justice be called " excessive " only if it is unduly high as a percentage of *total equity*—that is, capital, accumulated profits, and reserves (including reserves that are—or could be—formed by revaluing assets at current replacement cost).

ILL EFFECTS ON CAPITAL REORGANISATION

Par value puts a severe handicap on companies that wish to raise more capital at times when their shares are quoted below par. Though the Companies Act permits issues at a discount under certain conditions, the market does not seem to take kindly to them. The use of no-par-value shares would thus remove a disability that is often as irrational as it is embarrassing.

Schemes for the reconstruction of existing capital give a particularly good example of the false impressions that par-values convey. Thus the issue of bonus shares can evoke ludicrously unsound criticism. If a man's one-half share in a partnership is for some odd reason re-named a two-fourths share, nobody will suppose that his rights have improved; but if the number of his Ordinary shares in a company is doubled by a one-for-one bonus issue, he will probably congratulate himself, and the company may come under heavy political fire.

Similarly, the writing down of capital may be surrounded by misunderstanding and injustice. Such reconstructions tend to be unfair to Preference shareholders. When the value of a business has fallen and the assets are to be written down, an equal sum must also be subtracted from share capital, etc. The proposal may then be made that part of this loss should be deducted from the Preference capital, and the remainder (perhaps a far bigger sum) from the Ordinary capital. Such a scheme has a plausible air of fairness—indeed, even of generosity on the part of the Ordinary shareholders. However, if a £1 Preference share is written down to say 10s., rights to fixed-money dividend (and probably to ultimate capital repayment) are thereby halved ; whereas if a £1 Ordinary share is written down—no matter to what extent—its rights to all the residue remain completely unaffected. Thus the Ordinary shares here sacrifice nothing, and gain what the Preference shares give up. The Committee do not stress this point, but it seems to us that the fact that such schemes have been proposed by directors, accepted by the Preference shareholders, and even approved by a Court[5] whose role is to protect shareholders from

[5] For an example, see *Re Mackenzie Ltd.* [1916] 2 Ch. 450.

injustice, is the most telling argument that can be advanced against par values. It is also a strong argument for extending the no-par system, if introduced, to Preference shares.

THE MINORITY REPORT

The only hostile memoranda submitted to the Gedge Committee came from the Trades Union Congress and Mr. Martin Coles Harman (somewhat incongruous allies). Organised labour again expressed its hostility—much more ably this time—in the Minority Report of the Trades Union representative, Mr. W. B. Beard, O.B.E. This Report makes the following main points :

(1) While it is true that the no-par system represents the ordinary share for what it really is (an aliquot part of the equity), nevertheless this confers no " advantage on no-par-value shares which is not possessed by par-value shares . . . it might, indeed, even be argued that the constant relationship between an investor's holding and the whole of a company's capital is more faithfully represented by the stable nominal value of a par-value share than by the ever-fluctuating market value of an N.P.V. share."

(2) Percentage dividends may be misleading, but " there is no need to amend the Companies Act to make possible the declaration of dividends in pence or shillings per share or, more generally, to enable companies to educate their shareholders—or workers—in the difference between nominal and real capital and between yields and dividends."

(3) The majority of the Committee are right in saying that no-par-value shares would simplify matters analogous to bonus issues and share sub-division. But this would not necessarily be advantageous to the wider public interest. Trade unionists consider that " splits " would be used to hide the fact that dividends were being raised. Statistical evidence suggests that bonus issues have in the past usually been followed by bigger dividend payments. Such increases—in some cases " excessive" —could be " camouflaged " under no par value. As the increases are to some extent the consequence of " restraint by the trade union movement in demanding wage increases," the legalisation of no par value would have bad effects on industrial relations.

(4) There is no appreciable demand for no-par-value shares.

(5) While the administration of no-par-value shares " could be entrusted with perfect safety to most Boards of directors," the control exercised by shareholders over Boards is too weak to eliminate all chance of abuse.

Plainly the crux of the matter lies in paragraph (3). We feel that here the argument—despite protestations to the contrary—still implies that " excessiveness " in dividends can be measured by simple figures such as nominal percentages. Unfortunately there neither is, nor can be, any easy statistical trick for determining what is " excessive." Certainly nominal percentages are a gross failure as a yardstick ; in some cases a 50 per cent. dividend may satisfy all canons of moderation, while in others (for example where many of the assets have been lost) a one per cent. dividend might be too much.

After a stiff inflation, modest dividends must sound high when their rate per cent. is compared with the rates prevailing before inflation; and stock exchange values will also tend to exceed nominal values. Thus the par system gives labour an easy and effective weapon to use in current wage negotiations. A natural dislike of losing this weapon must inevitably colour labour's attitude to reform of the system.

It should be noted that no-par-value shares could not stop a Labour government from freezing dividends if it felt so disposed. Nor could such shares make it any less easy for a trade union negotiator to say " You have raised your total dividend from £10,000 to £12,000." They would merely make it somewhat harder for him to say " You are paying *a 50% dividend* "; and this way of expressing mathematical relationship has a rare power to whip up our emotions of indignation or guilt.

CONCLUSIONS : THE ILLOGICALITY OF PAR

To sum up the main argument. A share on whose certificate the printer has put " £1 " may :

(*a*) Be issued at say 25s., i.e. at a 5s. premium. Thus, in the period of unpaid calls, £1 is *not* the limit of the contributory's liability; nor is it the sum that creditors can rely on the company receiving and retaining.

(*b*) Have a balance sheet value, thanks to the piling up of reserves, of say 50s. Thus par does *not* reflect the holder's investment in the business even as measured by the accounts.

(*c*) Be quoted on the stock exchange, thanks to its prospective earnings, at say 62s. Thus par is a most imperfect guide to current price. The longer the time since the original issue, the greater is the likelihood that market value will diverge from par.

(*d*) Be repaid (if the company is wound up) at say £2.

So £1 need not be any of the value figures that are relevant. Why then should we use the " £1 " at all ?

It is reassuring to note that foreign experience of no-par capital has on the whole been satisfactory. Belgium long ago legalised *parts sociales sans valeur nominale* on an optional basis ; more recently, the U.S.A. and Canada have followed suit and at least forty-six of the forty-eight American States today permit the issue of such capital. The Report confirms that the system, after a good many teething troubles, now works well, and has indeed ceased to be a matter for controversy (any decline in its use being largely due to tax discrimination rather than its own defects). The one abuse cited by our correspondents arises where the law permits part of the issue price to be credited to " surplus " (instead of " capital "), with the result that some of the issue price may be repaid as dividends. This would not be permitted in Britain under the majority's proposals.

We appreciate that politically a weakness of the case for reform is that though the dangers of the present system to investors and the public have always existed, business as a whole has hitherto shown little concern. It is only in recent years, when par values have encouraged ignorant criticism of business profits, that there has been any general enthusiasm for the no-par-value system. Nevertheless it would be lamentable if a reform, desirable in the public interest, could not be implemented merely because some of its belated advocates have shown themselves to be more easily moved by considerations of self-interest than of altruism. Neither company law nor commercial morality insists on altruism, and few reforms would ever be made if the reformers had to prove themselves completely disinterested.

Advocates of any reform are prone to overstate the benefits that their pet schemes would secure. Far be it from us to suggest that no-par shares would bring in a financial millenium. We do not for a moment suppose that such shares would make confusion and mistakes impossible. The fundamental problem would still remain—namely, how are we to teach people to look beyond the symbols on a certificate or balance sheet, and to study instead the facts and rules which alone confer value? But the phrase "no par value" at least carries no spurious suggestion of familiar and stable rights, and so should act as a warning of the need for such study. To quote again from an American authority : " A purchaser of such stock, because of the fact that it carries no designated par value, is at once put on notice to investigate the values back of it."[6]

In short, the no-par system cannot force investors to take safe paths. But it would remove a signpost that at present points the wrong way.

[6] Roy B. Kester: *Principles of Accounting* (New York), page 352.

II—Accounting Aspects

THE LEDGER

In principle, the ledger entries for no-par-value capital will normally be much the same as for par value. In some ways, indeed, the book-keeping can be simpler than for par value, since the number of accounts is reduced.

Capital. The usual practice, in countries that have permitted the use of no-par-value shares, has been for capital account to be credited with the " stated values " of the shares (that is, with a figure that is either the issue consideration or a substantial part of it) ; if British law adopts the Committee's recommendation that the whole issue price must be treated as capital (paragraph 45 of the Report), then this figure will presumably all be credited to capital account.

With no-par-value capital, the allotment, calls, and so forth can be dealt with much as at present. A permanent uncalled liability on shares of no par value is unlikely ; but there is nothing to prevent such a thing where it is deemed desirable (for example, banks and insurance companies might still use the device to strengthen their standing).

Premium and discount. A premium will no longer be kept in a capital reserve account, since the whole consideration for share issues is credited to capital account. Similarly, " discount on capital " no longer calls for a separate account ; if no-par capital is issued on terms equivalent to a " discount," the exact price can be credited to capital account without ado.

Capital reserves. Capital reserves, other than the premium reserve, will be unaffected by no-par-value rules, i.e. will not be merged with capital account but will continue their separate existence as at present.

Revenue reserves. These too will be dealt with as at present, and not merged with stated capital. Thus credits to the latter account will be restricted to the proceeds of share issues ; it will still unfortunately fail to show the whole investment (including profits ploughed back) by the shareholders.

Preliminary expenses, etc. If the Committee's recommendation in paragraph 45 is put into effect there will also be no need for separate accounts for preliminary expenses, commissions, and expenses of issue; these can be debited to capital account. (But presumably the details of the preliminary expenses, etc., ought still to be compiled separately in the first instance—simply as a matter of statistical clarity. See page 28, footnote 11).

Sub-headings in an omnibus capital account. We may well feel that the Committee, in recommending the merging into a single account of capital, premiums, and preliminary expenses, was acting reasonably enough—so long at least as only one class of shares is in question ; the balance on the account is then the net contribution of opening capital by that class of shareholders. But should this wholesale merging be extended to cover dissimilar classes of capital ? In explaining its proposals, the Committee recommends (paragraph 52) :

> (*Sub-paragraph* (3).) When a company converts its ordinary shares having a nominal value into shares of no par value, it should carry to stated capital account, under appropriate headings, a sum equal to the amount of its paid-up share capital (whether Preference or Ordinary) plus all amounts standing to the credit of share premium account, including premiums on the issue of Preference shares,

and again

> (*Sub-paragraph* (5)). When a company having shares of no par value issues Preference shares, the whole of the proceeds of issue, or value of the consideration as assessed by the directors, should be carried to stated capital account, expenses and commissions being charged to that account.

If the phrase " should carry to stated capital account, under appropriate headings " refers in fact to balance sheet arrangement, the interpretation presents no difficulties. But the words suggest instead that the reference is to book-keeping : that Ordinary and Preference shares —the former of no par value, the latter presumably with a par value— together with all the incidental reserves and preliminary expenses, etc., should be dealt with in a single ledger account. This omnibus treatment would plainly be contrary to normal book-keeping, and we may feel that such an inconvenient and alien method should not be prescribed by law.

Our objection is not however based merely on a dislike of congested book-keeping ; if capital account was ruled with columns for total, Ordinary shares, Preference shares, etc., the book-keeping would become easy enough. A weightier objection is conceptual: we cannot see that the no-par system gives any more grounds than the present system for uniting different classes of capital (especially Ordinary shares of no par value and Preference shares with a par value).

THE BALANCE SHEET

In general, the balance sheet will not change much if shares of no par value are used.

One point, however, calls for stress. With par value, the balance sheet must preserve a rigid ratio between the number of shares and the money figure for capital (that is, 1,000 shares with a nominal and paid-up value of £1 each must obviously lead to a figure in the effective column of £1,000). With no par value, this ratio need not be maintained. Thus capital acquires a flexibility which may be very useful (for example, as has already been pointed out, capital can be increased by what is in effect an issue at a discount).

The procedure can perhaps best be explained with the help of balance sheets illustrating the various stages and alternatives that might arise. For simplicity, we have assumed in all our examples that there are no preliminary expenses, etc., to set off against capital.

(*i*) *First issue*

Assume that a company's first issue of capital is made up of 100 Ordinary shares of no par value, issued for £1 each in cash. The balance sheet would then show :

	£		£
Capital		*Current Asset*	
Ordinary shares of no par value : 100 shares ...	100	Cash	100

Here capital account is credited with a " stated value " that is the full issue price. As we have already noted, part of the stated price may instead, under some American and Canadian company laws, be credited to reserve. If the recommendations of the Gedge Committee are implemented, however, this latter procedure will not be permissible in Britain.

(*ii*) *Issue for consideration other than cash*

Here the value to be placed on the consideration raises some interesting problems. Suppose, for instance, that our company (introduced in (*i*) above) at once acquires some intangible asset too—say, a trade mark—in return for another issue of 100 no-par-value shares. The balance sheet figures should then be expanded as below. (Neither North American practice nor the Committee's report in fact demands that the different capital issues should be shown separately, as in our examples. But such details are helpful for purposes of exposition; further, as we shall point out (on page 28), they give a useful safeguard which, we feel, might well be made obligatory.)

The new balance sheet runs :

	£		£
Capital (Ordinary N.P.V. shares)		*Current Assets*	
100 shares (issued for cash)	100	Cash	100
100 shares (issued for trade mark) ...	100	*Intangible Asset:* Trade mark	100
200 shares	200		200

The immediate issue of 100 more shares for the trade mark implies (in conjunction with the first issue of shares at £1 apiece) that the market value of the trade mark is £100. There are accordingly strong grounds for insisting that the directors should put that value on record in the balance sheet. Such is the Committee's recommendation ; and on page 27 we stress the case for this procedure.

However, let us in passing note an interesting counter-argument—that intangibles, etc., should be shown (as is possible with no par value) at extremely conservative figures. There is plainly something to be said for laying stress on the uncertainty of any money figure for intangibles, and for mineral rights (whose value depends solely on working receipts in the future). Some advocates of no-par shares have indeed argued that the whole of the fixed assets of a manufacturer should be shown at low values : " There is now nothing which is harder to dispose of, nothing that is, in a way, a bigger ' white elephant ' than a factory that cannot make money. It is far from being an asset ; it is very likely a liability, and it is certainly not worth the money that has been spent on it. . . . Write your fixed assets down to scrap values."[1]

If the director of our company were allowed by British law, contrary to the Committee's wish, to show the trade mark (acquired in return for

[1] Lord Melchett : " The Share of No Par Value and its Effect on Company Finance," on pp. 149-150 of *Studies in Accounting* (*edit.* W. T. Baxter). This article recommends that fixed assets be written down to scrap from the very beginning, even where the shareholders subscribe in cash and the assets are bought for cash. The exact book-keeping procedure is not explained.

100 shares of no par value) at a nominal value—say £1—the above balance sheet would instead run :

	£		£
Capital (Ordinary N.P.V. shares)		*Current Assets*	
100 shares (issued for cash)	100	Cash	100
100 shares (issued for trade mark) ...	1	*Intangible Asset :* Trade mark	1
200 shares	101		101

This illustrates very clearly the lack of a rigid ratio between the number of shares and the money figure for capital.

Some Canadian companies show the whole of their no-par-value capital at negligible values, or even at *nil.* Thus the balance sheet of *Western Leaseholds, Ltd.*, includes, besides the usual items, the following :

	$
Under " Capital Assets "	
Petroleum and natural gas leases in respect of which 100,000 shares of the company's capital stock were issued, at no recorded value	—
Under " Capital Stock and Surplus "	
Capital stock :	
100,000 common shares of no par value authorised, and issued as a consideration for petroleum and natural gas leases acquired, on which no monetary value has been placed...	—

The arguments for low asset figures, and therefore for low stated values per share, are worthy of respect. But most legislatures have insisted on a substantial minimum figure being credited as stated capital. There are two reasons for such insistence. First, most of us like a balance sheet to give some notion, however imperfect, of the sizes of the various assets. Second, a high stated capital brings the safeguards that we mention on page 27.

(*iii*) *Issue " at a discount "*

Suppose that, after the company mentioned in (*i*) above has been in existence for some time, its shares are quoted on the Stock Exchange at only 15s.; and that the company desires to raise further funds by issuing 100 more shares for 15s. each in cash. With no par value, there is no reason why this should not be done. After the second issue, the balance sheet would run :

	£		£
Capital (Ordinary N.P.V. shares)		*Assets*[2]	
100 shares—first issue ...	100	From first issue	100
100 shares—second issue ...	75	From second issue ...	75
200 shares	175		175

(*iv*) *Issue "at a premium"*

If instead our company is able to make a second issue "at a premium," the whole of the consideration may be credited to capital account (instead of being split between capital and a capital reserve as with par-value shares). For instance, a second issue of 100 shares might be made for 30s. in cash per share. The balance sheet will then run :

	£		£
Capital (Ordinary N.P.V. shares)		*Assets*[2]	
100 shares—original issue	100	Proceeds of first issue	100
100 shares—second issue	150	Proceeds of second issue	150
200 shares	250		250

(*v*) *Reserves*

Reserves, other than those arising from share capital transactions, are treated in exactly the same way as with par-value shares. Thus a revenue reserve of £1,000 could be shown as in (*vi*) below ; unlike the premium reserve, it would *not* in the ordinary course of events be combined with the capital account. Special considerations apply at a reconstruction (paragraphs 63-65 of the Committee's report) ; we shall touch on these in Part III (pages 28-9).

(*vi*) *Split of shares*

When shares of no par value have risen in exchange value to what is, judged by marketability on the Stock Exchange, an inconvenient height, they can readily be split. On the other hand, if prices fall to an inconveniently low figure, they can equally well be consolidated.

[2] In practice, the assets should of course be classified in the usual way ; they are here classified according to the various issues merely for simplicity.

Thus, if the company mentioned under (*i*) found eventually that its shares were being quoted at an unduly high figure, it might decide to split each share into 10 new shares. Let us suppose that revenue reserves have by this time accumulated to £1,000, but that the directors decide not to capitalise these. After the sub-division, the balance sheet would run :

	£		£
Capital (Ordinary N.P.V. shares)		*Miscellaneous assets* ...	1,100
1,000 shares	100		
Reserves	1,000		
	1,100		1,100

Alternatively, the directors may decide to transfer some or all of the reserve to capital when the split takes place. We deal with this matter on page 34.

(*vii*) *Preferred shares*

If there were more than one class of shares of no par value, the balance sheet might run somewhat as follows (to cite an example from Canadian practice) :[3]

Capital issued

Shares of no par value and non-assessable—	
854,770 participating preference shares	Can. $ 2,551,488.66
23,163,855 ordinary shares ...	Can. $ 83,447,928.06

[3] This example is an excerpt from the consolidated balance sheet of the *Canadian Eagle Oil Company Ltd.* as at December 31, 1952. " Non-assessable " is the term habitually used in North America to indicate that the shares, being fully paid, carry no liability to further calls. As explained above (p. 8) the question of whether, under the Committee's recommendations, the preference shares could be no-par would depend on the exact nature of their participation.

III—Legal Aspects

EXTENT OF LEGISLATIVE CHANGES

In this country the traditional method of limiting the personal liability of members of an incorporated company has been by means of shares with a fixed nominal value. Our company legislation presupposes that all companies with a share capital have shares of this type, and accordingly a considerable number of verbal amendments to the Companies Act, 1948, will be required if no-par-value shares are introduced. Nevertheless, as is recognised in the report of the Committee, this consideration would not involve any widespread alterations to the Act (which indeed already includes in its scope companies without any share capital at all). Substantial amendment would be needed only to those Sections which relate to the raising, maintenance and reduction of share capital. Moreover, the incidental verbal amendments needed elsewhere might materially add to the clarity of the Act as a whole. For example, Section 213 of the Act defines " contributory " as " every person liable to contribute to the assets of a company in the event of its being wound up," thus leading the reader to suppose that the expression is restricted to holders of partly-paid shares. But he will be mistaken, for it has been held that the term includes all members, both present and past, even though their shares are fully-paid so that they have in fact no liability to contribute anything.[1] If a new amending Act is passed introducing no-par-value shares, it will be necessary for the draftsman to go through the existing Act with a fine tooth-comb to see where consequential alterations are called for ; and it is to be hoped that he will take the opportunity of correcting blemishes of this sort.

The major changes would, then, be confined to those Sections in the Act which relate to share capital. The task of the Gedge Committee was to recommend how these Sections, and the rules which the courts have deduced from them, should be adapted to legalise no-par capital without weakening present safeguards.

---

[1] *Re Anglesea Collery Co.* (1866), L.R. 1 Ch. App. 555 ; *Re Aidall* (1933), Ch. 323, C.A. ; *Re Consolidated Goldfields of New Zealand* (1953), Ch. 689.

VALUE OF EXISTING RULES REGARDING SHARE CAPITAL

Before discussing the recommendations, it is necessary to decide what the present position is and what practical benefits are in fact secured from it. The following rules are thought to be an accurate summary :

(*a*) Uncalled capital cannot be reduced without the consent of the Court. Where such capital exists, it constitutes a source of potential funds that is of great value to creditors.

(*b*) Where shares have been issued for cash, those dealing with the company can rely upon its having at some time received assets to the full nominal value of its issued share capital and premiums (except where the Court has consented to an issue at a discount).

(*c*) Creditors are protected by the rule that the company cannot (without the consent of the Court) deplete its assets by repaying capital to the shareholders. The accounting corollary is that the company must maintain the share capital and share premium figures shown as " liabilities " in its balance sheet (unless the Court consents to a reduction) and this even though the corresponding assets have been irretrievably lost.

(*d*) The existing shares cannot (without the consent of the Court) be " watered " by an issue of the same class below par.

The real value of these rules must not be exaggerated ; indeed, an examination of each in turn will show how restricted their ambit is.

(*a*) *Uncalled Capital*

Rule (*a*) is rarely applicable, for today uncalled capital seldom exists for longer than a few months after allotment, except in the case of banks and similar institutions. For the most part, therefore, the rule has ceased to give any protection

(*b*) *Issues at a Discount*

Nor does protection (*b*), the prohibition of issues at a discount, amount to much. Its only value seems to be to prevent the figure of nominal capital being used to give a false impression of size or solvency. Such a deception, however, would hardly be possible if the whole balance sheet were studied. Moreover, as we have said above, this safeguard can be relied on only when the issue is for cash. When it is not, there are no arrangements for checking the valuation of the non-cash consideration (as there are in most Continental countries) and hence (unless there is evidence of fraud, or unless inadequacy of consideration appears on the face of the transaction) the company's valuation must be accepted as conclusive.[2] Accordingly, shares may in effect be issued at a discount. Moreover, it is easy to disguise such an issue as an issue for cash, either by an exchange of cheques or by a book-keeping set-off without that subterfuge.[3] And even a genuine cash issue may be made at a discount of 10 per cent. plus brokerage.[4] Furthermore there is at present no requirement of any minimum capital—nominal, issued or paid-up—or minimum par value per share.[5] If a company can have a total capital of ½d., made up of two ¼d. shares, it is clear that par values mean very little—either here or elsewhere.

(*c*) *Maintenance of Capital*

As regards rule (*c*), which expresses the so-called principle of the maintenance of capital, the only formal exception is in the case of redeemable Preference shares (and even there the purity of the principle is maintained by provisions regarding the " capital redemption reserve fund "). But the weakness of this rule as a protection to the creditors is that it prevents only an open return of capital as such. It insists on the maintenance in the accounts of share capital, share premium, and capital redemption reserve fund as " liabilities," but in the nature of things it can do little to ensure that the corresponding assets (which alone are of any use to creditors) are also maintained. It cannot secure that assets are not lost in trading ; and, once assets are lost, it does not prevent dividends being paid to shareholders out of the current year's profits notwithstanding that past losses have not been recouped. Moreover, the existence of rule (*c*) encourages companies to make a formal reduction of capital and so to circumvent the rule. As we stressed on page 11 of this article, one class of shareholders (usually Preference) is often penalised unjustly by a reduction; and the consent of the Court has not always proved a very effective safeguard in such cases. Normally the Courts refuse confirmation only if there is some breach of the procedural rules ; in other circumstances they take refuge in the facile, but fatal, rule that the shareholders are better judges of what is in their interests than Judges can be. Indeed, a

---

[2] *Re Wragg* (1897), 1 Ch. 796, C.A. ; *Re White Star Line* (1938), Ch. 458, C.A.

[3] *Spargo's Case* (1873), 8 Ch. App. 407.

[4] Companies Act, 1948, Section 54. In more than one recent case this Section has been relied on for the making of an issue of £1 shares less a commission of 1s. to all subscribers.

[5] Hence the rule fails to ensure that a company does not get under way while inadequately capitalised. In so far as this is secured at all, it is by the requirement in Section 47 of the Act that the minimum subscription shall be raised on a public issue of shares.

recent case[6] seems to be unique in this century in that there the Court actually refused (although as an alternative ground for its decision) to confirm a reduction that it regarded as unfair.

Nevertheless, rule (*c*) does prevent an open repayment of capital, and without it there might be a temptation, for tax reasons, to repay capital rather than to pay dividends out of income. Further, it does exercise a restraint (as a matter of practice rather than strict law) on the payment of dividends until past losses have been recouped.

(*d*) *Share-watering*

As regards rule (*d*), par value as a protection against share-watering is obviously only of slight value. If 1s. shares are now worth 5s., they are diluted by any issue at a price of less than 5s. Par value is thus a protection only in that it puts a limit to the dilution. Where new shares are not offered to all existing shareholders, the only real protection is the good faith of the directors, which normally requires that they should obtain the best possible price.

Accordingly, it seems that the value of all our existing rules is slight. But such benefits, however slight, should certainly not be abandoned. What safeguards, then, must be introduced to ensure that they are preserved under a no-par system ?

SAFEGUARDS NEEDED TO RETAIN THESE BENEFITS

Maintenance of Capital

It must first be stressed that it is only rules (*a*), (*d*) and, in part, (*b*) which really still depend on the *nominal* value of capital. After the reforms relating to share premiums introduced by the latest Companies Act, the most valuable of these rules (rule (*c*)) is today aimed at ensuring, so far as practicable, the maintenance of total capital receipts (including premiums) rather than the maintenance of nominal capital as such. Hence the no-par system makes no difference, provided that it is laid down that the whole consideration received on the issue of the shares must be allocated to capital. This, in effect, is what the Gedge Committee have recommended. They rightly reject the practice, adopted in some American States, of allowing part of the proceeds of issue to be credited to " surplus," and recommend that the whole shall be credited to " stated capital," which will take the place of both the capital account and the share premium account of a company with par-value shares. Such a rule—simple, but drastic in comparison with the rules

[6] *Re Old Silkstone Collieries* (1954), 1 Ch. 169, C.A.

adopted by many legislatures—is enough to preserve fully the principle of capital maintenance.

As a corollary, the Committee also recommend that, if a company converts its Ordinary shares[7] having a nominal value into shares of no par value, it should carry to stated capital account, under appropriate headings, a sum equal to its existing paid-up capital (whether Preference or Ordinary) and all amounts standing to the credit of share premium account, including premiums on the issue of Preference shares.[8] Again, if a company with no-par Ordinary shares issues Preference shares, the whole proceeds of issue or value of the consideration should be carried to stated capital.

The Committee recommend that the "stated capital" rule should apply whether the shares are issued for cash or for a consideration other than cash.[9] As we have already pointed out (pages 19-20), it has sometimes been urged as one of the great advantages of no-par-value shares that they would avoid the necessity of placing a monetary value, which may be arbitrary and misleading, on shares issued for a non-monetary consideration. But, unless some figure for this " capital " is inserted in the company's records, it is quite impossible to preserve any of the safeguards referred to above. In the absence of such a requirement, moreover, promoters might more easily be able to obtain excessive rewards and to conceal their extent. It is clear, we think, that abuses resulting from issues otherwise than for cash can never be wholly eradicated without adopting the Continental practice of requiring an independent valuation of the consideration. Failing this, it appears to us that the best procedure is to require the directors to place " a true and fair value " on the consideration, and for this sum to be credited to capital account. The recommendations of the Gedge Committee are phrased rather more vaguely ; they require the directors to assess " the value of the consideration," and do not actually use the well-worn formula " true and fair value." Reading the report as a whole, however, it seems clear that the intention is that the directors should not be permitted to value the consideration at an arbitrary figure either above or below its market price. This, it is submitted, ought to be made quite clear in any legislation implementing the proposals. It may be pointed out that in practice there will be at least some objective check, in that the valuation of all assets which do not pass by manual delivery will normally[10] have to be agreed with the Revenue for purposes of stamp duty on the sale agreement.

---

[7] As previously pointed out, the Committee do recommend that no-par Preference shares should not be permitted.

[8] Our comment on this omnibus type of account is given on page 17.

[9] Cf. *Head & Co.* v. *Ropner Holdings Ltd.* (1952), Ch. 124.

[10] Unless exemption can be obtained under the Finance Act, 1927, Section 55: *infra*, footnote 13.

To our regret, the Committee have not seen fit to adopt our suggestion that balance sheets should be required to distinguish between shares issued for cash, shares issued for a consideration other than cash, and shares allotted as fully paid by way of bonus issue. If this were required (as it is under the new Indian Companies Bill) it would make balance sheets far more informative about the development of the company's capital structure; and it would also do much to meet the argument of the Trades Union Congress that bonus issues enable the true position to be concealed, and that this concealment would be enhanced by the legislation of no-par-value shares.

Exceptions—(i) Preliminary Expenses

To this general principle that all share considerations are capital, the Committee are prepared to recognise two exceptions, both of which are more apparent than real. In the first place, they suggest that preliminary expenses, commissions and the expenses of issue should be charged to stated capital without this being regarded as a reduction of capital. In other words, stated capital would represent the net proceeds of the issue.[11] This admittedly differs from the present position where shares are issued at par. If, however, they are issued at a premium, these expenses may already be written off against share premium account.[12] For all practical purposes, therefore, this represents no change.

Exceptions—(ii) Reconstructions

Secondly, the Committee are prepared to relax the present rule whereby on a reconstruction or amalgamation the revenue reserves become " frozen " as capital. They recommend that, where the shareholders remain substantially the same,[13] revenue reserves should be allowed to remain as such, and that this should apply both to companies with shares of a nominal value and to those with no-par-value shares.[14] The rule requiring revenue reserves to be frozen on a reconstruction can cause unnecessary inconvenience ; it is really an

---

[11] The Committee suggest that a note of the charges for expenses (etc.) should be included in the balance sheets for the next two years.

[12] Companies Act, 1948, Section 56(2).

[13] The Committee suggest that a definition of reconstructions of the appropriate type should follow the lines of Section 55 of the Finance Act, 1927, as amended, which provides concessions as regards stamp duties.

[14] The Committee admit that this recommendation goes beyond their " strict terms of reference." This seems to be an understatement ; it is difficult to see how the recommendation has anything at all to do with no-par-value shares as such, and there can be little doubt that it is really made because the members feel that there is now an opportunity, which may not recur for some time, of instigating a much-needed reform. This is most commendable, and one wishes that they had gone even further ; there are other reforms which, as some would think, are more urgent than this, or indeed, than no-par capital itself.

example of the harm that can be done if a principle is extended to its logical conclusion without regard to the object which it was designed to serve. When investors put up capital to buy a going concern from someone else, they would deceive themselves if they treated any pre-acquisition profits as fruits of their own capital. But a reconstruction under which the investors remain substantially the same does not involve the purchase of a business from someone else (except in the most legalistic sense). Hence there seems no good practical reason why shareholders should not here treat pre-reconstruction profits as their own profits. The true test is not whether the profits are earned before or after the date of some formal legal act, but whether they have been earned before or after the investment of capital by the present proprietors. Certainly the purpose of the " maintenance of capital " principle will not be frustrated if this excrescence is lopped off, and its removal is unlikely to be deplored by any except a few legal and accounting purists.

Insistence on placing the whole proceeds of the issue to stated capital will thus preserve the most important of the present rules relating to share capital. What of the others ?

Uncalled capital

Although with shares of a nominal value the uncalled amount is based on their par values, the same margin can easily be achieved with no-par shares. Hence, as the Committee say, no-par shares need not prevent the retention of uncalled capital in the rare cases where it is wanted. All that is necessary is that the terms of issue, the share certificates and the like, should all clearly state that the holders are liable to pay further sums of a stated amount when called upon.

Issue at a Discount

The Committee conclude that the present prohibition of issues at a discount, except with leave of the Court under Section 57 of the Act, serves no good purpose. Indeed they think that the prohibition may have done more harm than good by forcing companies to overload their capital structures with prior charges when, but for the prohibition, they might have been able to raise finance by the issue at a discount of further Ordinary shares. In principle they would be prepared to favour a relaxation of this rule even in the case of shares of a nominal value, but they doubt whether companies would often make use of any such facility in view of the psychological unattractiveness of a share which has its devalued state branded on its face. With no-par-value shares the question of issues at a discount does not arise, and this they rightly regard as a considerable advantage.

This, however, does not mean that rule (*b*) above is altogether discarded. It will be observed that, in our statement of its practical effect, all we claim for this rule is that on an issue for cash it ensures that the company does in fact receive the full stated amount of the consideration. Under the Committee's recommendations this will be ensured equally effectively.

Share-watering

Similarly, the Committee do not consider that any legislative safeguard is needed to prevent share-watering by a further issue at an undervaluation. In our respectful submission, they are wise to reject the suggestion that rights of pre-emption shoould be given to the existing shareholders. In the United States of America, where, in most States, shareholders have been held to have such rights at common law, much difficulty has been caused, and the rule has now been generally modified or abrogated by Statute. We certainly would not favour the introduction here of an inflexible rule of law to this effect. But this, of course, does not mean that a rights issue to the existing shareholders will not often be the appropriate method of raising new capital—the growing popularity of such issues shows that this is already recognised in practice.

The Committee consider that matters of this sort should be left to the supervision of the stock exchanges; to the powers of investigation conferred on the Board of Trade; to the powers of the Court to wind-up if that is just and equitable, or to adopt the new alternative remedy under Section 210 in the event of oppression; and to the general law as to misfeasance. They may well be right. On the other hand, it must be recognised that the first of these safeguards is available only in relation to public companies with quoted shares, and the second is unlikely to be exercised in relation to any other companies. Private companies also, under the Committee's recommendations, will be at liberty to issue no-par-value shares, and we have an uneasy feeling that the remaining legal remedies are both too uncertain and too expensive to be really effective. It might have made it easier to establish a case of misfeasance or oppression if, as we suggested to the Committee, it were laid down as a legislative rule that when more capital is issued the duty of the directors is to get the best price reasonably obtainable. This, however, might cause complication unless also stock options were barred; personally, having regard to the use and abuse of such options in the United States, we should face the latter prospect with equanimity.

ADDITIONAL LEGISLATIVE CHANGES

Conversion from Par to No Par

The only further safeguard recommended by the Committee is that, if a company having shares of more than one class decides to convert its

Ordinary capital from par value to no par value, the conversion should be subject to approval by extraordinary resolution of each class. The report states that this is to remove any ground for apprehension that the rights of holders of special classes could be prejudiced by the conversion. This, we suspect, may be partly due to a misunderstanding of the fears which we ourselves expressed to the Committee. Our misgivings, however, were not that the conversion itself might prejudice anyone (we do not see how it could) but that the increased facility for splitting shares after conversion might do so. Our point, if it is a point, is hardly met by requiring class consents to the conversion itself ; we favoured requiring the separate consent of each class to any share-splitting, whereas the Committee recommend that splitting should be possible by a special resolution, without class consents unless required by the Articles.

Perhaps an example will show what we had in mind. Suppose a company has 5,000 Preference shares and 10,000 Ordinary shares, all of £1 each. The Preference shares confer the right to a fixed 7 per cent. preferential dividend. All shares have one vote, but the Preference shareholders can vote only on resolutions for winding-up, for reduction of capital, or affecting their special rights. Nothing is said about rights to return of capital on a winding-up, so that all shares rank equally in this respect.[15] There is the usual " modification of rights " clause in the Articles.

If, now, the company wishes to convert its Ordinary shares into no-par-value shares, this is harmless enough on the face of it, and the Preference shareholders may well approve. But suppose, once this has occurred, that the company decides to split each of its Ordinary shares into ten. The effect on the Preference shares is startling in the extreme, for their rights of voting and participation in capital may be degraded to a small fraction of their former value. Of course, if this is, in law, a " variation or modification " of the rights of the Preference shareholders, they are protected, for their separate consent will be needed under the modification of rights clause in the Articles. But, strange as it may seem, it is by no means clear that the law would regard this scheme as varying, modifying, or affecting their rights,[16] and,

---

[15] But, as we understand the Committee's recommendations (see p. 8 above), this would not make the preference shares "equity share capital" (which would also have to be converted into no-par shares if the ordinary were so converted).

[16] It is certain that the effect on voting power would not be so regarded : *Greenhalgh* v. *Arderne Cinemas* (1946), 1 All E.R. 512, C.A. ; *White* v. *Bristol Aeroplane Co.* (1953), Ch. 65, C.A. ; *Re John Smith's Tadcaster Brewery ibid* 308, C.A. ; nor apparently would the effect on their rights of participation, Cf. *Re MacKenzie & Co.* (1916), 2 Ch. 450 which was cited with apparent approval by the Court of Appeal in the above cases.

if it does not, their separate consent will not be needed, nor will they have any vote at all on the special resolution.

Admittedly the strictly legal position would not be very different if the Ordinary shares remained with a nominal value.[17] But there would be a slight difference, even in law, for so long as the shares had a nominal value the capital would be returned on the basis of this nominal value. Hence the Ordinary shareholders could not increase their slice of the cake on a winding-up merely by splitting ; a bonus issue would be needed.[18] With no-par shares, it seems that the Ordinary shareholders can increase their slice merely by a sub-division of the shares. Even if this is not so, and an increase of Ordinary capital is still required, it does not alter the fact that both " splits " and bonus issues will be facilitated by no-par shares. It is precisely this increased freedom that the majority of the Committee regard as the great advantage of no-par shares and the minority as their great danger.

Finally, it may be objected that no company would dare to treat its Preference shareholders so scurvily in the face of Press comment, and that the stock exchanges would not countenance such an abuse. To this, we can only say that, even if the objection holds true of public companies with quoted shares,[19] these desirable restraints will not be available where other companies are concerned.

In the light of these considerations, it is suggested that Preference shareholders should—failing safeguards—be very reluctant to consent to a conversion of the Ordinary share capital. In our view they will rarely be well advised to agree without making it a condition either that the modification of rights clause be so amended as to prevent any increase in the number of Ordinary shares (whether by way of a split or on a bonus issue) without their consent, or that they be given some fixed percentage of votes and some fixed amount or percentage of capital on a winding-up. And, similarly, investors should scrutinise very carefully the terms of any new issues of Preference shares by a company having no-par Ordinary shares.

---

[17] But, as we have pointed out, the Committee did not hesitate on another point to recommend a reform of the law relating to companies with par-value shares.

[18] But they could increase their votes without this: *Greenhalgh* v. *Arderne Cinemas* (*supra*). In any event, the Preference shareholders seem to have no legal right to object to the bonus issue ; the reserves could have been distributed as Ordinary dividend, and can therefore be used to pay up a bonus issue to the Ordinary shareholders.

[19] But note in *Scottish Insurance Corporn.* v. *Wilsons & Clyde Coal Co.* (1949), A.C. 462, H.L. and *Prudential Assurance* v. *Chatterley-Whitfield Collieries*, (*ibid*, 512), a type of reduction scheme was carried out which was described by *Imperial Chemical Industries* in a recent circular (May 20, 1954) as one which " stockholders of both classes would probably regard as unfair and inequitable."

It is also possible to imagine circumstances in which share-splitting of Preferred Ordinary no-par shares might be used to the grievous detriment of the non-Preferred shareholders. If the Preferred Ordinary shares were entitled to a fixed preferential dividend of £1 per share, and to a preferential right to a payment of £10 per share on a winding-up, the Preferred Ordinary shareholders, if they had voting control, might multiply the value of their holdings by splitting each of their shares into two or more. Here again, it is not clear that the law provides a remedy.

In the light of these examples, we submit that the Committee's proposals do not go far enough and that it is essential to provide, as we recommended, that the separate consent of all classes should be necessary before any class of no-par shares is sub-divided or increased. This, as we said, might be relaxed if the terms of issue expressly provided to the contrary, for then the investors would have had their attention drawn to this point and have only themselves to blame if they took the risk and suffered as a result. But under the Committee's proposals they might be led blindfold to their own destruction.

Registration Fees and Capital Duty

It will be appreciated that, under the no-par system, some change will be necessary in the present arrangements for levying fees and capital duty, which are at present based on the nominal capital. The Committee rightly points out that registration fees are of minor importance. As regards capital duty, they recommend that it should be imposed on the total issue price or consideration, that is, on the total amount of the stated capital as and when issued. And, here again, they recommend that this should apply to all companies—to those with par-value shares as well as to those with no-par shares. As we suggested in our evidence, this seems infinitely fairer than the present system; fairer to the Inland Revenue, which at present is virtually cheated out of its dues whenever a company issues its shares at a premium, and fairer to the company, which will not have to pay the duty until it actually raises its capital.

This recommendation would remove the main restraint on the overstating of the original authorised capital by companies with par-value shares. Hence a company might register with an authorised capital of £20 million and refer to this as its capital, notwithstanding that only a few pounds of it was actually issued. The Committee suggest that this might be prevented by making it an offence for a company with a nominal capital to refer to its authorised capital without stating the issued and paid-up capital with equal prominence. We should feel greater confidence in the adequacy of this safeguard if we did not know that many people who have dealings with companies are quite oblivious of the distinction between authorised, issued, and paid-up capital. While it is clearly desirable that the two types of company should be treated alike (tax discrimination against no-par shares has had unfortunate results in the United States), there may be a real danger of fraud unless some effective sanction is found to prevent the inflation of authorised capital once the restraining influence of the capital duty is removed.

Capitalisation of Reserves on Share Splitting

Under a no-par system, it seems likely that share splitting will frequently be used instead of a bonus issue. Under the present system, a splitting of shares has no effect on the apparent rate of dividend, since the nominal value of the shares is reduced to the same extent as their number is increased. A company wishing to reduce the apparent rate of dividend is therefore forced to make a bonus issue. With no-par shares, this more cumbersome and expensive method is not needed. Hence, an incentive to the capitalisation of profits will be removed ; and, further, the Inland Revenue will not obtain the capital duty payable on an increase of capital to provide for a bonus issue. In our evidence to the Committee, we accordingly suggested that, if the Committee thought it was in the public interest for companies permanently to plough back profits, they might like to recommend that an increase of stated capital should be obligatory whenever there was a splitting of shares. However, the Committee considered that this should be left entirely to the discretion of the directors.

Minimum Capital

As we expected, the Committee ignore our further suggestion that companies should be required to have a minimum paid-up capital or, better still, a compulsory deposit with the Board of Trade. A similar proposal was rejected by the Cohen Committee on the ground that it would discriminate unfairly against persons of small means. This seems to us to be unrealistic. Limited liability is a dangerous thing, and when it is abused it is " persons of small means " who suffer most. To require those who want limited liability to provide some safeguard to third parties seems to us to be no more a discrimination against the poor than the requirement of third-party insurance for those who want motor cars. Clearly, a deposit with the Board would be a far more effective safeguard than a minimum paid-up capital, but even the latter would be some restraint on the formation of mushroom companies and on consequent abuses, and would be a small price to pay for the advantages of incorporation. The absence of any minimum share capital leads directly to the defeat of creditors, for it enables the proprietors to finance the business by lending to it on debentures, and thus to rank ahead of the business creditors. Clearly a company with a ½d. capital is not in fact working on ½d., and its proprietors must in fact provide working capital in the form of loans; thanks to the existing law, the proprietors may run less risk, as regards this balance of working capital, than do the unfortunate members of the public who have dealings with the company.

We appreciate that our proposal, if applied to companies generally, might be regarded as beyond the Committee's terms of reference ; but this, as we have pointed out, has not deterred the Committee in relation to another reform. It is significant that most Continental systems, even though they do not permit shares of no par value, insist on a minimum capital as an essential condition of incorporation with limited liability. Moreover, the case for a minimum capital, already strong, becomes overwhelming as regards companies with shares of no par value. Such companies could, in the absence of this safeguard, be formed without the proprietors putting even a ½d. share capital into it ; they could just subscribe for two (or seven) shares for no consideration, and put up the entire working capital in the form of loans. Any rules for the maintenance of capital would thus be defeated, for there would be no share capital to maintain.

We therefore recommended that a company should not be allowed to issue no-par-value shares, or to convert into such shares, unless it had a total capital paid-up in cash of (say) at least £1,000, with the proviso that this limit might be reduced to not less than £100 if the company deposited with (or secured to) the Board of Trade half the difference between the actual paid-up capital and £1,000. Any sum deposited or secured would then be treated as " reserve capital " and shown in the balance sheet as :

Reserve Capital (deposited with the Board of Trade) ... £—

or

Reserve Capital (secured to the Board of Trade) ... ... £—[19]

As indicated, the Committee did not take kindly to this suggestion, and we are not altogether surprised. But we remain unrepentently attached to it, and are continuing to advocate it.

---

[19] The money value of the " secured " capital would be ruled off, that is, would not be extended into the effective money columns of the balance sheet.

CONCLUSION

This concludes our survey of the theoretical, accounting, and legal aspects of no-par-value capital. We think that the matter is already full of intellectual interest, and we hope that it may become of practical value also.

Should the no-par system in fact be introduced, its effects on company practice will be interesting to watch. One likely result, for reasons already pointed out, is that capitalisation of reserves by bonus issues will become less common, its place being taken by the cheaper expedient of share-splitting. This may or may not be a good thing.

Another likely consequence is that on any future trade recession we shall not see so many applications for formal reductions of capital. Where the only real purposes of a formal reduction after a loss of capital are to acknowledge the loss openly and to enable the company to resume payment of dividends of a normal size per share, these results can be simply achieved by a consolidation of shares if these are unhampered by a par value. The latter procedure appears to us to be wholly desirable, since it may avoid the undoubted hardship that one class of shareholders often suffers on a formal scheme of reduction.[20]

---

[20] This does not mean that asset values could not, or should not, be written down after losses have occurred. A corresponding sum might, for instance, be shown as a deduction from the " capital and reserves " section on the other side of the balance sheet. For example, suppose the unrevised balance sheet runs :

	£		£
Capital and Reserves		*Assets* (*net*)	
1,000 Ordinary N.P.V. shares	1,000	Book values	1,200
Reserves	200		
	£1,200		£1,200

The assets are now worth only £100 ; and the shares are for convenience to be reduced to 100 in number. After consolidation, etc., the balance sheet might be shown thus :

	£		£
Capital and reserves		*Assets* (*net*)	
100 Ordinary N.P.V. shares	1,000	As revalued	100
Reserves	200		
	1,200		
Less Loss in asset values ...	1,100		
	£100		£100

The Committee are to be commended for their refusal to countenance any relaxation of the principle of capital maintenance. Perhaps, however, they may not be sufficiently alive to the possibilities of abuse in other directions—particularly in cases where the restraining influence of the stock exchanges does not make itself felt. We ourselves think that the Committee's recommended safeguards do not go far enough, especially as regards restraining the possibility of prejudice to class rights by share-splitting. In our view it would be better to err on the side of strictness than on that of laxness, even if this diminishes the attractions that no-par shares might otherwise offer. If the rules are not made stringent from the very start, no-par shares may unnecessarily acquire an ill-repute and lose their attractions altogether. This would be a pity, for potentially they should provide the ignorant investor with greater protection than he enjoys at present.

Subject to this doubt, we fully share the Committee's view that the belated introduction of this form of capital would be in the interests of business, investors, and the public generally.

THE ACCOUNTANT'S CONTRIBUTION TO THE TRADE CYCLE

The Accountant's Contribution to the Trade Cycle

By W. T. Baxter

I

It is well known that changes in the price-level can alter the accountant's figures for cost and profit. A firm's inputs are normally charged in accounts at their acquisition price; and so—unless inputs and sale are simultaneous—the cost side of a revenue account must reflect an earlier price level than the revenue sale. When prices are rising, accounting costs tend to be low relative to replacement costs, and so profit looks large; when prices are falling, accounting cost is relatively high and profit small. Perhaps we may—rather tendentiously—use the phrase " historic cost error " to describe the gap between accounting profit and the profit figure that would be found if inputs were charged at the replacement prices ruling at sale dates. This latter profit may be called " corrected profit ".

The historic cost error has been widely advertised during the post-war inflation, mainly by businessmen who feel their taxes—based on accounting profit—to be unreasonably high. But it has other aspects of importance, and notably its possible influence on the trade cycle.[1] Its alternate over- and under-statement of profits seems likely to affect the size of the cycle—in particular, through its influence on mental attitudes, on the supply of credit, and on policies of consumption and investment.

II

There are accordingly plausible grounds for agreeing with the critics who accuse the accountant of *intensifying* an established upswing and downswing. Little has, however, been said so far about the *timing* of the accounting error. This point seems to demand study—since, if the error's size alters much at times of instability, its impact is likely to be the greater.

A scrutiny of the error's anatomy is necessary for this argument. The error arises if, during a time of changing prices, the date of buying any input precedes the sale date of the resultant output. By far the most important inputs with such a time-lag are plant and materials; and so the accounting costs that are suspect are those under the heads of depreciation and " cost of goods sold ".

The error can in theory be measured easily enough, since it is the difference between the replacement and the historic costs of inputs.

[1] The trade cycle effects have been explored, in particular, by Mr. K. Lacey—see e.g. his *Profit Measurement and Price Changes* (London, 1952). They are also discussed in G. Haberler: *Prosperity and Depression* (New York, 1952), pp. 49–50, and in Erich Schiff: *Kapitalbildung und Kapitalaufzehrung im Konjunkturverlauf* (Vienna, 1933), pp. 113–34.

Let H be the historic cost, c the reading on an appropriate price index at the date of the input's purchase, and s the reading at sales date. (" Appropriate " obviously evades a lot of questions; but, difficult and relevant though these are in other contexts, they scarcely seem to demand answer for the narrow purpose of our present study.) Then the accounting error is $H(\frac{s}{c} - 1)$—i.e. this is the amount by which accounting profit exceeds corrected profit.

III

Let us take depreciation first. Here H is that part of the asset's historic cost which is shown each year as an expense in revenue account —and is, by the straight-line method, a constant quantity in all years of the asset's life; c is the price-index of the asset's acquisition date, and therefore is also a constant throughout the asset's life; and s varies each year, since it represents the price-level at which output is sold during that year, i.e. it is the average of the price-indices at the dates of all sale transactions, weighted by their sizes. The error, $H(\frac{s}{c} - 1)$, thus alters in step with the price-level.

It may be helpful to get a rough picture of the error's results through diagrams. In Diagram 1A, we assume that plant is bought at the start of Year 1, when prices have just reached the median level of an imaginary cycle, and the index stands at, say, 100. Their course is then assumed to follow the unbroken curve AB. The annual depreciation charge in accounts, being based on original cost, will follow the straight line CD. The vertical distance between AB and CD suggests the error's movements from year to year. When s exceeds 100 (as in the years till the end of 6), historic cost is less than replacement cost—for instance, at the middle of Year 1—by AC; accordingly the accounts now understate costs and overstate profit. The error's contribution to the profit figures for each year may perhaps be best shown by the height of the pillars at the foot of the diagram. Those pillars which rise above zero indicate a positive error, i.e. an increase in the accounting profits; such an increase is found during all years with prices above 100. In Years 7 to 12, prices are below 100, and the error becomes negative and depresses low profits still further. The positive and negative errors will—in these improbably symmetrical conditions—exactly cancel over the years.

We can speak of the error's effect on costs with some certainty. However, its size relative to profit must vary from case to case. Depreciation may be large or small compared with profit; thus the error will be negligible where a firm owns little plant, but substantial in e.g. an electric power undertaking. Again, the given firm's profits may not move in proportion to price changes. But perhaps we are not over-simplifying too grossly if we picture corrected profits as following

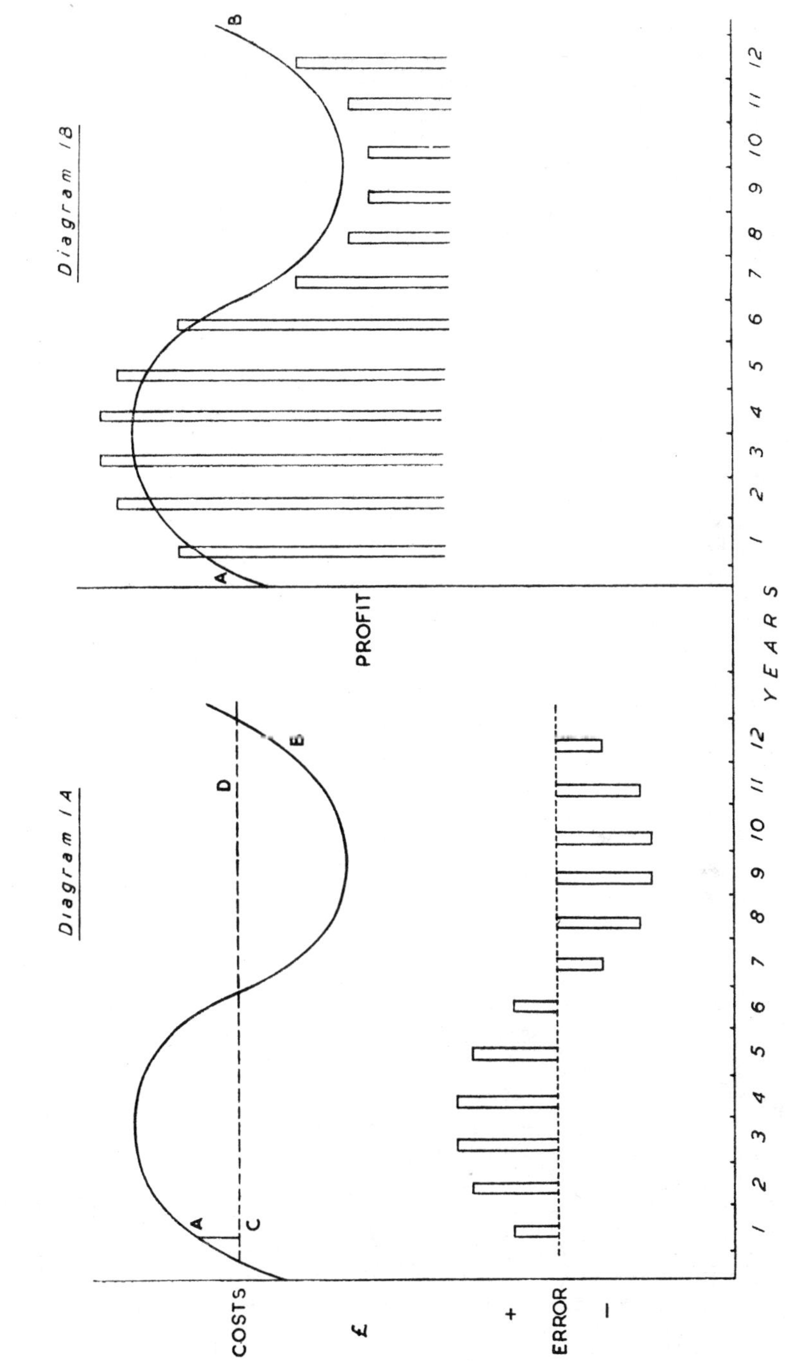
Diagram 1A
Diagram 1B
COSTS
£
+
ERROR
−
PROFIT
YEARS
A
B
C
D
1 2 3 4 5 6 7 8 9 10 11 12

much the same pattern as the price-index. Then the pillars in Diagram 1B represent accounting profits of the various years; were it not for the error, each pillar would rise to the price curve *AB*. The error extends the pillars somewhat in good years, and cuts them short in bad years.[1]

Had the plant not been bought at the mid-point of price movements the error's pattern in Diagram 1A would not be symmetrical about *CD*, and the positive and negative errors would be less likely to cancel over the years. For instance, if the plant is bought at a price peak (as in Diagram 2), *s* will never rise above *c*, the error will always be

Diagram 2

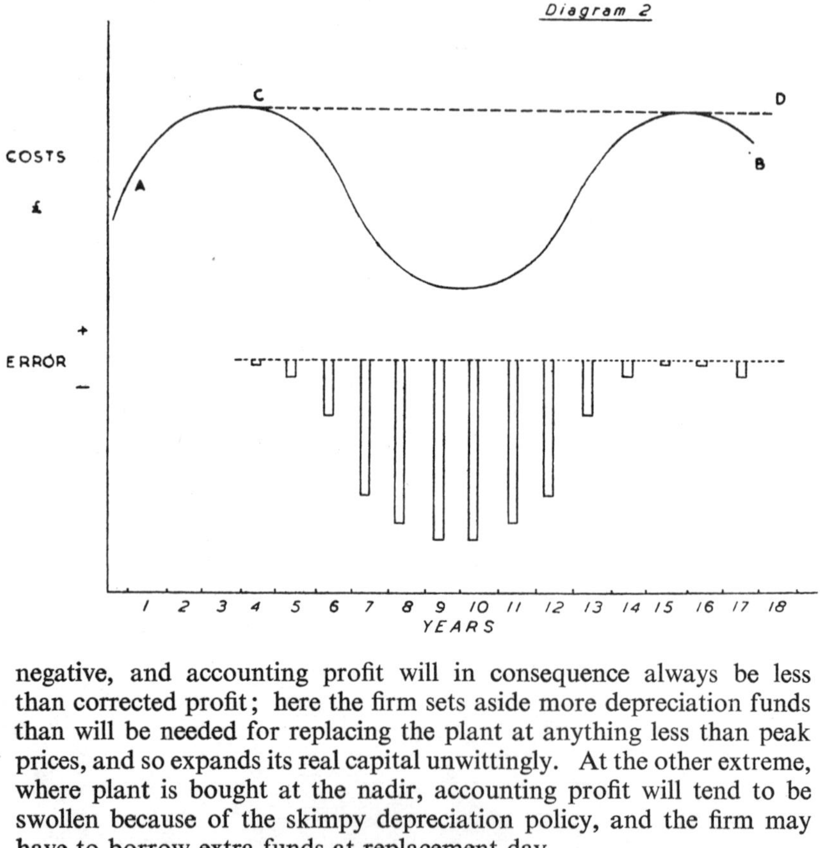

negative, and accounting profit will in consequence always be less than corrected profit; here the firm sets aside more depreciation funds than will be needed for replacing the plant at anything less than peak prices, and so expands its real capital unwittingly. At the other extreme, where plant is bought at the nadir, accounting profit will tend to be swollen because of the skimpy depreciation policy, and the firm may have to borrow extra funds at replacement day.

There seems to be a general impression that the error is substantial only when prices are still going up; thus the agitation for tax concessions dies down as soon as a rise in prices is checked. In the case of plant,

[1] In Diagram 1A, the heights of the pillars show the extent of the error relative to historic depreciation. In 1B, the difference between the pillars and *AB* suggests the extent of the error relative to correct profit. The vertical scales in 1A and 1B are therefore not the same.

however, a large error can obviously persist for a long time. For instance, at present (1955) the price increase seems to have been slowed and the curve may now form the contour of a fairly level plateau (perhaps as in Year 9 onwards in Diagram 3). But much of our plant was bought long before the plateau was reached, at prices far below those now current; $\frac{s}{c}$ is therefore still a sizeable quantity, and will continue to be so until the plant has been replaced at plateau prices (when, as in Year 11 of Diagram 3, historic cost *CD* rises abruptly and once

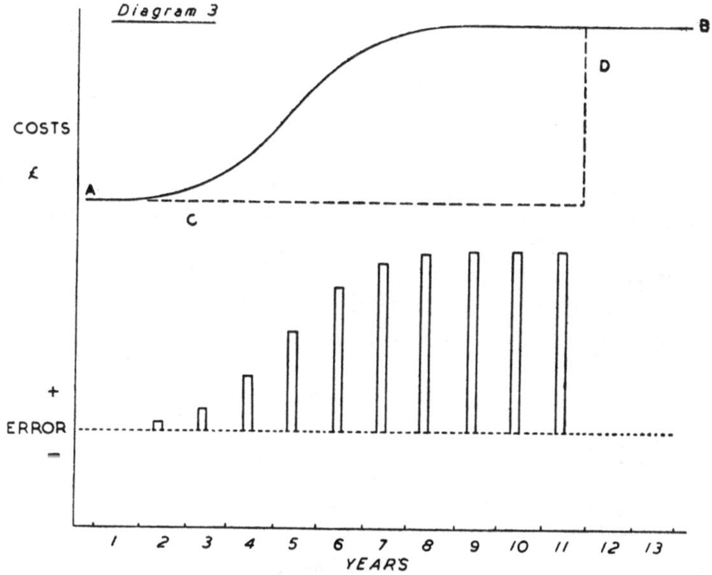

more blends with replacement cost *AB*, thus dragging accounting profit down to its correct level). The depreciation error must be substantial in firms with large old plants; the owners of such firms have still as strong a case as ever for tax concessions. A recent estimate suggests that in 1952 replacement cost depreciation was still, for the plant and machinery of manufacturing firms as a whole, *nearly double* historic cost depreciation.[1]

We may conclude that movements of the depreciation error will—in timing and pattern—approximately coincide with movements in prices, and perhaps with those in correct profits. Thus the error is likely to serve the cycle as a prompt and often powerful ally by intensifying the prevailing mood.

IV

In any discussion on stocks, one should keep in mind the form of calculation through which stocks alter accounting profit. A

[1] Philip Redfern: "Net Investment in Fixed Assets in the United Kingdom, 1928–1953" (a paper read before the Royal Statistical Society, 19th January, 1955), Table 12.

merchant's trading account (for, say, a calendar year in a spell of rising prices) is set out somewhat like this:

	£		£
Cost of Goods Sold—		*Sales*—1,000 units	1,456
Opening Stock (400 units) ..	380		
Purchases (1,000 „) ..	1,090		
	1,470		
Less Closing stock (400 units)	460		
Total	1,010		
Gross Profit	446		
	£1,456		£1,456

The important things to note are that closing stock must mainly consist (on the usual "First-In-First-Out" assumptions) of those purchases which were made in the later months of the trading year; and that, by subtracting closing stock at its original cost, we deprive these later purchases of all influence over this year's trading cost and profit. The "cost of goods sold" might be set out more clearly by showing the various blocks of purchases in detail—for example, as under (supposing that extra stocks are built up in the spring to meet a sales peak in the autumn):

	Physical Units		*Average Price*	£	
Cost of Goods Sold—					
Opening stock (bought July–December, last year)		400	·95		380
Purchases:					
January–June (this year) ..	600		1·05	630	
July–December (this year) ..	400		1·15	460	
	1,000			1,090	
Less Closing stock (bought July–December, this year)	400		1·15	460	
		600			630
Total		1,000	1·01		£1,010

Thus the £1,010 charged against the sales of the current accounting year is the cost of purchases made between the preceding July and the current June. (Where the units of stock are not homogeneous, some items will not be sold in strict order, and the figures will overlap a trifle; but the argument is not changed substantially.)

The error is produced by this discrepancy between "cost year" and "revenue year". If the average replacement price—weighted to allow for the pattern of sales over the year—is 1·12, then the error is:

	£
Replacement costs, at average price for January–December, 1,000 units at 1·12	1,120
Historic costs, at actual purchase prices, July–June	1,010
Error	£110

It will be seen that " inventory profit " is scarcely a happy phrase with which to label the error. " Inventory profit " is commonly used to mean the increase in the value of the given physical quantity of stock between opening and closing dates. Here this increase is only £80, whereas the error is £110. If the physical quantity of stock is kept fairly constant at all times throughout the year, inventory profit gives a handy approximation to the error.[1] But many types of stock, even though they may return to the same level at the year's end, have seasonal peaks. Where, for instance, a firm builds up stocks for the Christmas rush, or a country's store of wheat diminishes as harvest recedes, the difference between annual inventories will not exactly equal the error save by coincidence; usually it will be less than the error, since the accounting year tends to end at a time of low stocks. To fall back on the *reductio ad absurdum* method: there could be a substantial error if a firm buys all its goods in the spring and sells out completely in the autumn, and yet its opening and closing stocks (and presumably therefore its " inventory profit ") would be zero.

How does $H(\frac{s}{c}-1)$ behave when we pass from plant to stocks? For most firms, the annual cost-of-goods-sold is a far bigger figure than depreciation, and so H is normally substantial. s is again the cost index at the weighted average date of the year's sale transactions—say, mid-year. c is the cost index at the weighted average date of the year's purchases of stock. Because stock is normally sold within a few months from its purchase date, the cost of a batch of goods is not likely to be split up and charged against several years (as is the case with the cost of a machine), and so c is here a far more volatile quantity than when it relates to depreciation, and usually follows hard on the heels of s. The stock error may thus have a pattern quite different from the depreciation error.[2]

In Diagram 4, the curve AB represents the current (replacement) cost of goods; it can also represent purchases if physical activity is constant. The curve for historic cost can be got simply by shifting AB to the right, by the space of the turnover period; it is shown as the dotted line CD. The error is due to the vertical distance between the two curves (e.g. in Year 6, EF). The total contribution by the error to each year's accounting profit may again be shown by the heights of

[1] The stock error can be expanded to $s(B+P-E)-(Bb+Pp-Ee)$ where B, P, and E are respectively the physical quantities of stock-at-beginning, purchases, and stock-at-end; and the average prices at which each of these quantities was bought—at beginning, purchase, replacement, and end—are respectively b, p, s, and e. If stock is kept constant, however, $B=E$. Then the error is $sP-(Bb+Pp-Be)$; whereas inventory profit is $B(e-b)$. Error and inventory profit are equal if $P(s-p)=0$. This condition is satisfied if $s=p$, which is perhaps most likely to be the case where goods are replaced at the same time as they are sold, i.e. where stock is always constant.

[2] The difference would shrink if the life of the machine is short; for instance, where the life is only two years, c tends to catch up with s in a series of biennial hops. Where a range of long-lived machines is being steadily replaced throughout the cycle, c (based on the total cost of all the machines) is very stable.

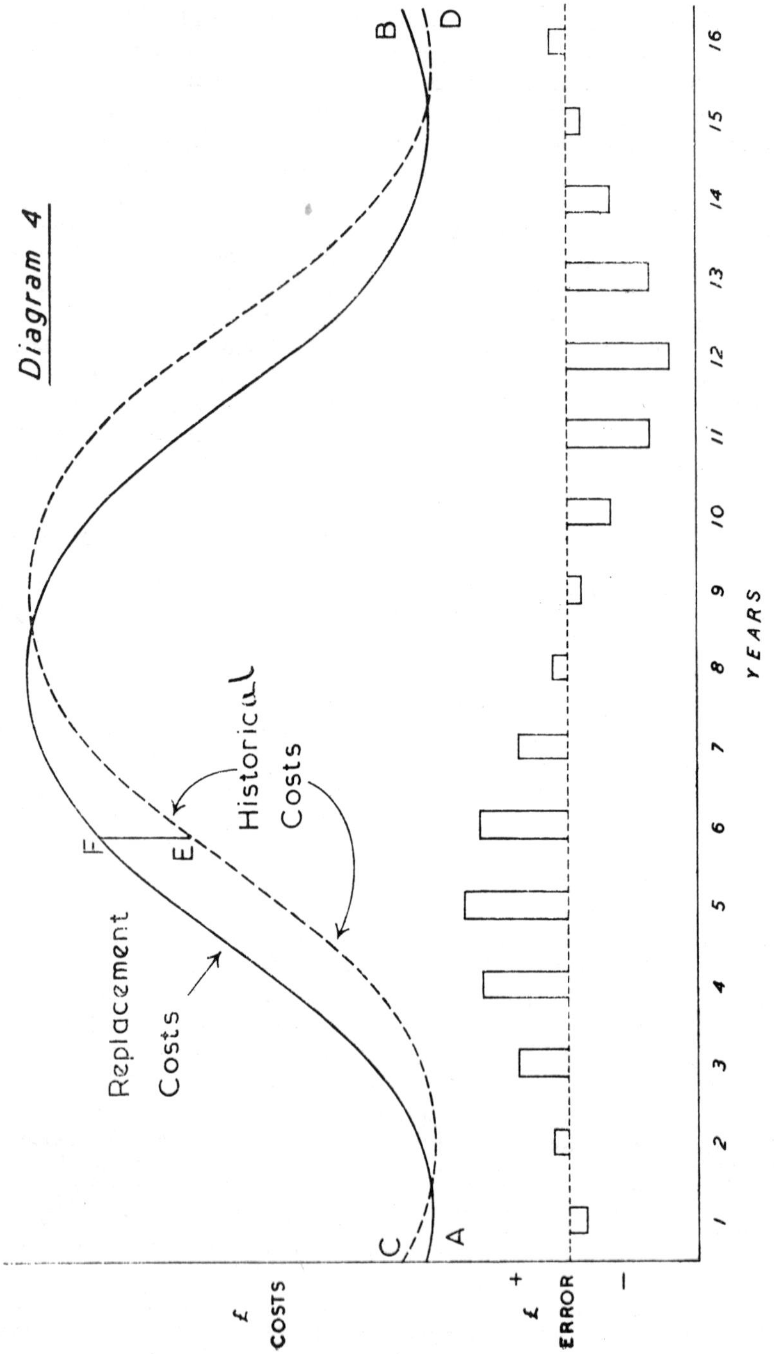

Diagram 4
Replacement Costs
Historical Costs
A
B
C
D
E
F
£ COSTS
£ ERROR
+
–
YEARS
1
2
3
4
5
6
7
8
9
10
11
12
13
14
15
16

the pillars at the foot of the diagram. In years of rising prices, $H(\frac{S}{C} - 1)$ is positive and so the error restrains accounting cost and thereby lifts accounting profit. If prices stop rising, the error shrinks to *nil* in a time not longer than the turnover period (as in the months about the end of Year 8). On the down-grade, the error is negative.

The stock error can move from its positive to its negative extremes either slowly or abruptly, according to the shape of the price curve. (With the depreciation error, this transition lasts from peak to trough.) Our curve in Diagram 4 rises at its fastest in Year 5, thereafter rises at a decelerating pace, and culminates in a gently rounded peak ; corresponding movements take place on the down-grade. With such a " sine-shaped " curve, the error's upward trend is reversed (in Year 6) well before the peak is reached, at the point where *AB* and *CD* cease to run parallel and start to converge ; and the new trend lasts till the curves are once more parallel (Year 12). When the price curve has a less rounded peak and trough than in our example, the error's trend will change more steeply. In extreme cases, where the curve culminates in a sharply pointed peak (i.e. where *AB* and *CD* are triangular or cusp-shaped) the transition from positive to negative is violent, and its damaging impact is concentrated on the period just after the peak ; similarly a pointed trough may herald a sudden improvement in the accounts.

Whether the stock error has noteworthy effects will depend on both the price curve and the methods of the firm in question. The impact on costs is the more likely to be big if any of the following conditions obtain:

(*a*) The price change is violent.
(*b*) The turnover period is long.
(*c*) Material costs form a large part of total costs (as e.g. where the firm deals in commodities).

Yet another condition must obtain before the change in costs is likely to have a dramatic effect on profit trends: the rate of gross profit must be low. Given suitable circumstances, accounting profit might be distorted as in Diagram 5. Here we assume the course of the price-index—shown as the unbroken curve *AB*—and the error to be the same as in Diagram 4; we also assume that corrected profit follows much the same pattern as the price-index. The height of the pillar for, say, Year 6 shows the correct profit for 6 (from the base up to the line *AB*) and then the error (from *AB* upwards—corresponding to the distance *EF* in Diagram 4).

In this particular example, accounting profit starts to wane in Year 7, although the peak in prices and profits is not reached till the middle of 8. The circumstances needed to bring about this premature fall are:

(1) As the summit draws near, prices must rise at a decelerating pace. And

(2) The error must be large relative to profit, so that the decline in the error outweighs the rise in correct profit (see Years 7 and 8).

Condition (1), it seems reasonable to think, will obtain not infrequently. Condition (2) depends on the factors listed in the preceding paragraph; however, even if these are not strong enough to make accounting profit fall, they will certainly damp its upward trend.

On the down-grade of prices, our example reflects the same forces. In Years 14 and 15, the negative error moves so steeply to zero that it raises accounting profit (though the nadir of prices and correct profits is not reached till the mid-point of Year 15)—and this merely because prices are now falling at a decelerating pace. (The dotted lines in Diagram 5 will be explained later.)

If our diagram correctly shows a tendency found in a fairly large number of cases, then surely the error should play a bigger part than it has done hitherto in discussions of the trade cycle. Such changes in the trend of reported profits might well affect business opinion decisively. Just as the " accelerator " is said to alter the demand for capital goods before general activity reaches its turning points—perhaps thereby causing the general crisis or the recovery—so accounting may alter mental attitudes prematurely, and thus contribute to changes in activity.

It is not hard to find flaws in our diagram. In real life, the pattern of profits will doubtless not correspond closely to our curves. One reason is that firms are unlikely to carry constant physical stocks throughout the cycle; if stocks are reduced in the slump, the error will also dwindle at that stage.[1] Another factor that may vary physically is sales; if, as seems likely, these grow in the boom and fall off in the slump, they will probably give a bias to corrected profit; but the error would not seem to be affected thereby (save by any consequential changes in physical stock). Again, selling prices may not be adjusted promptly when general prices change; in particular, they may lag because the firm fixes them at historic cost plus a constant mark-up—a policy likely to cause further changes in customers' demand, and so in physical volume of sales. Thus we cannot—till many empirical studies have been made—treat any abstract diagram as an accurate photo of profit patterns. The case against conventional accounting is not so clear as Diagram 5 suggests.

However, though we cannot say that accounting profit always anticipates the general trend of the cycle, we can hardly avoid the conclusion that accounting cost may have a most unfortunate influence at crucial points in the cycle. Just when confidence begins to waver, delayed high charges for goods find their way into the accounts; the stock error has its least desirable effect at the worst possible moment.

[1] In general, stocks appear to have a cycle very like the sales cycle, but with a narrower amplitude and a lag of some months (the number of months varying with different types of stock)—M. Abramovitz: *Inventories and Business Cycles* (New York, 1950), pp. 93–6, 144–5.

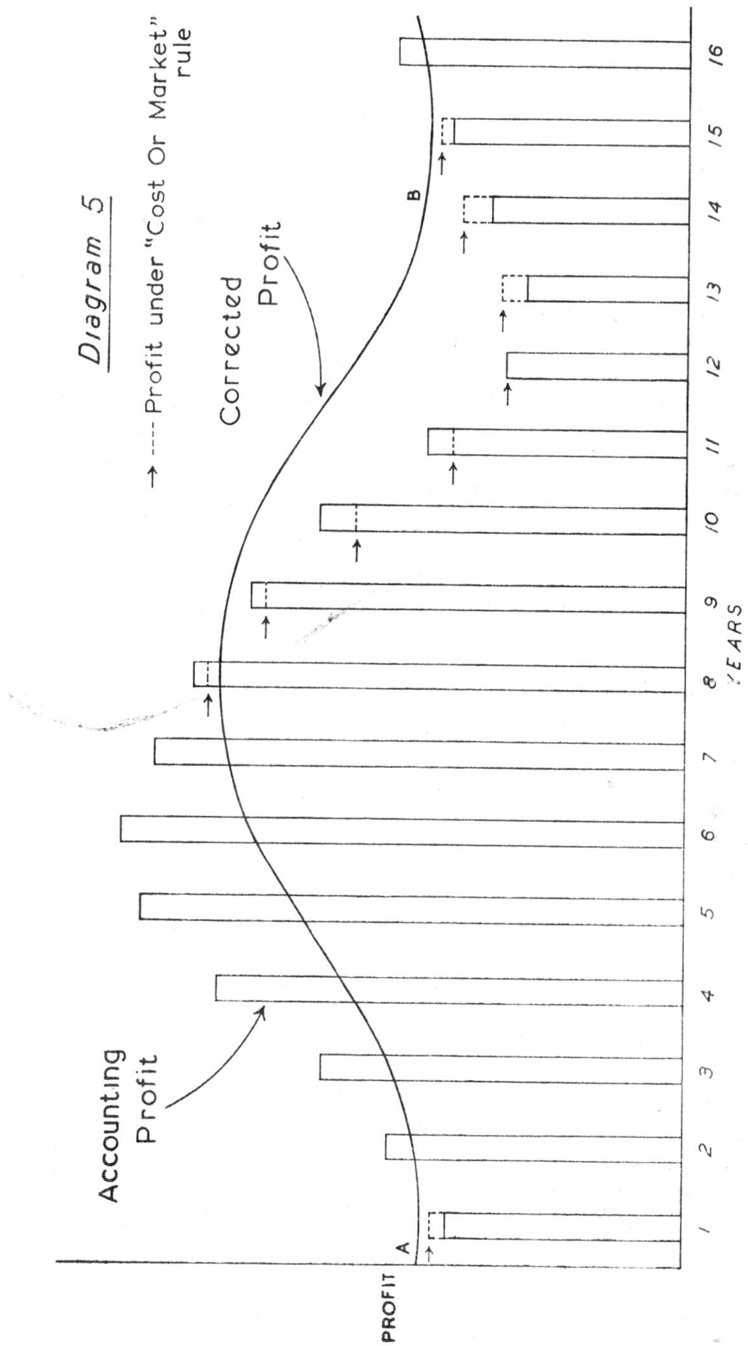

Diagram 5
→ ---- Profit under "Cost Or Market" rule
Corrected Profit
Accounting Profit
A
B
PROFIT
YEARS
1
2
3
4
5
6
7
8
9
10
11
12
13
14
15
16

V

Another practice of accountants may aggravate the stock error's effects at the start of the down-grade. Our discussion has so far supposed that the closing stock figure in revenue account is always valued at historic cost (found on " First-In-First-Out " assumptions), i.e. at the price level of a date preceding the end of the business year (on average, by half the turnover period). In fact, this may well not be true on the down-grade of prices. For then the normal practice of accountants is to abandon historic cost, in accordance with the over-riding rule of " Cost or Market, whichever is the lower ". The precise interpretation of this cautious formula varies from firm to firm; but its general effect must on the down-grade be to depress stock values to below their historic cost. For example, if the business year ends on December 31st and stocks were bought in August, the unsold items will at closing stocktaking be valued at the market prices of December 31st if these are lower than the cost prices of August.

This rule leaves our argument unchanged so far as the up-grade of prices goes. In the first year of falling prices, however, Market is substituted in the revenue account for the (higher) Cost value of closing stock, though opening stock is—somewhat inconsistently—still shown at Cost. Thus a smaller sum is deducted from the charges, and accounting cost is increased; in effect, the cost-of-goods-sold is loaded with both (i) the usual error for the year, and (ii) a bit of next year's error. Profit, under this double assault, may well fall abruptly. In Diagram 5, this decrease is shown by the dotted line cutting off the top of the profit column for Year 8.

In subsequent years of the down-grade, both opening and closing stocks are valued at Market. This pessimism at both ends of revenue account puts a brake on the rule's working. The net effect of the rule seems to be substantially as follows (assuming physical quantity of stock does not change violently, and the price curve is free from kinks). Profit is reduced so long as the replacement cost curve is falling at an accelerating pace (Years 8 to 11 in Diagram 5). If the pace becomes constant—for the space of an accounting year plus the preceding months during which opening stock is bought—profit is the same as if the rule did not exist (Year 12 in Diagram 5). If prices fall at a decelerating pace (Years 13 and 14), the rule actually makes accounting profit less conservative, and so speeds up the illusion of recovery—and perhaps the actual recovery too.[1] In the last year

[1] Let E and B be the physical quantities of stock-at-end and -at-beginning in a revenue account for Year n. Let c_n and c_{n-1} be the prices at which stock-at-end and -at-beginning are valued at Cost, and m_n and m_{n-1} at Market. Then the inclusion of stocks in a revenue account raises profit by :

If stocks are valued at Cost.......................... $Ec_n - Bc_{n-1}$
If stocks are valued at Market........................ $Em_n - Bm_{n-1}$

So switching from Cost to Market depresses profit by .... $E(c_n - m_n) - B(c_{n-1} - m_{n-1})$

Suppose that physical stock is constant. Then E and B are equal : therefore the rule depresses profit if $(c_n - m_n)$ exceeds $(c_{n-1} - m_{n-1})$—i.e. if prices are falling

of the rule's operation, closing stock reverts to Cost, but opening stock stays at Market and so keeps down the cost-of-goods-sold.

Thus, on the down-grade, the rule's effect is to reinforce the error, and to make accounting profit respond more sensitively to each change in price trends.

VI

There is an important counter-argument to the whole case against the error. When profit rises and falls on paper, tax rises and falls in fact. Thus the elation of good years is damped by stiff extra payments to the Treasury, while poor results bring compensation in the shape of lower imposts.

With tax rates at their present level, this counter-argument should plainly make us pause. However, though it may weaken the case against conventional accounting, it does not seem to destroy it. Various factors lessen the compensating effect of tax. Tax is not usually included in cost calculations; if costs are distorted by the error, tax will not save the management from faulty decisions. Tax is not assessed at 100 per cent.; some part of a profit increase remains to cheer the appropriation account. Moreover, high profits convey a comfortable suggestion (to all save the knowledgeable) of correspondingly high cash resources; and this is rational at least to the extent that high profits make banks more ready with loans. Again, the date at which tax is paid may seem remote—under British tax law, a spurt in profit is unlikely to raise tax payments until a year or more has passed, and so there is a long period before the cash is drained off.

For these or more elusive reasons, tax does not appear to neutralise the error's effects. Everyday observation suggests that, despite tax, high profit figures bring elation and low figures gloom.

Another counter-argument deserves note: firms that make inadequate provision for replacing assets will soon find themselves short of funds, and so their expansionist policies will be pulled up sharp. This argument also merits respect. Many firms did get into a sorry cash position while rebuilding stocks after the war.[1] Once again, however, the counter-effect does not seem strong enough to check the inflationary trend. Probably the firms short of cash can usually manage to borrow (especially as those worst hit by the error will tend *ipso facto* to show the most glowing profits); bankers are not immune from the general optimism.

---

at an accelerating pace; the rule raises profit if $(c_n - m_n)$ is less than $(c_{n-1} - m_{n-1})$; and it has no effect when $(c_n - m_n)$ equals $(c_{n-1} - m_{n-1})$.

If E and B are not equal, the pattern is modified. For example, if physical stocks sink during a depression and so E is less than B, the switch from Cost to Market depresses profit less than if stocks are constant; the dotted lines in Diagram 5 become higher in all years. But the modification seems to be slight unless physical stock changes to a remarkable degree.

[1] See the consolidated balance sheets of some 1,500 sample companies dependent on banks, in the British Bankers' Association's *Memorandum to the Royal Commission on Taxation*, 1951.

VII

To sum up. The accountant's devotion to historic data begets cost figures that lag behind prices. In consequence, accounting profits overpaint the state of trade. The depreciation error tends to make the high-price years (both before and after the peak) look better, and the low-price years look worse. The stock error instead lifts profits in all years when prices are rising, and depresses profit throughout the down-grade; it seems likely to exaggerate the rate of change in the trend of correct profit, and may on occasion produce falling profit figures before the price rise has ended, and rising figures before recovery has begun.[1]

It appears reasonable to conclude that an error so widespread and so emphatic in its rhythm must have a considerable influence on business sentiment. In particular, the error is likely to strengthen the factors that link demand and investment (after a time-lag) with the rate of change of prices; it probably introduces a relationship analogous to the accelerator principle. If this argument is correct, the error must reduce the stability of the economy.[2]

Reform of accounting thus seems to offer one of the simplest and safest devices by which we might try to combat instability. Many businessmen have already suggested that the Chancellor should permit the use of replacement costs in computing their firms' taxable profit. By granting this privilege, on condition that replacement costs are also used in the ordinary revenue accounts, widespread reform could be achieved with little opposition from business.

The London School of Economics.

[1] Where accounts include both depreciating assets and stocks, the errors' *composite* pattern will probably look rather like the pillars in Diagram 4, but the depreciation error will push each pillar somewhat to the right (so that the highest error is nearer to, but still comes before, the price peak); the depreciation error will also give the accounting cost curve a greater amplitude than the replacement cost curve.

[2] See A. W. Phillips: "Stabilisation Policy in a Closed Economy", *Economic Journal*, June 1954, pp. 311–4, for a mathematical demonstration that, when one component of demand depends on the rate of change of prices, the system is made less stable. The accounting error is presumably one of the reasons for such dependence.

ACCOUNTING IN COLONIAL AMERICA

Accounting in Colonial America[1]

W. T. Baxter*

MOST people who have lived in a small country town can still remember cases of " book-keeping barter." Perhaps for instance the dairy-farmer sent milk each day to the tailor. The latter did not bother—and was hardly expected—to pay cash, but ran up his account indefinitely. Then, when the farmer needed a new suit, he ordered it from the tailor. With luck the two sets of sales would more or less cancel over the years, so that both men avoided the distasteful task of settling accounts by paying money.

This modified version of barter seems to have been the essence of much colonial trade, to judge from surviving account-books.

BARTER

In the eighteenth century, barter was still practised to some extent in Britain [2]; in America, it was very common. For this there were several reasons. First, each community was small in numbers; and, if a market consists of few dealers, the chances are high that A will both sell to and buy from B—particularly as both men may be somewhat unspecialised and so have a wide range of wares on offer. Second, money was scarce and bad.[3] Britain would not let the colonies make their own coins; and any British coins that reached America were soon sent home again to pay for much-needed manufactures. So, though the colonists calculated and bargained in terms of pounds, shillings, and pence, these were somewhat abstract moneys of account

---

* Professor of Accounting, London School of Economics and Political Science.

1 My interest in this subject was roused by research on the records left by the Hancocks of Boston; a description of that firm's accounts is given in my *House of Hancock* (Cambridge, Mass., 1945), and " Credits, Bills, and Bookkeeping in a Simple Economy " in *Studies in Accounting* (London, 1950), edited by me. To find whether the Hancock's methods were typical, I have lately looked at over fifty other sets of accounts, for firms scattered from New Hampshire to Virginia—and in one case at Nevis. The evidence appears consistent and convincing. However, there are few sets of records that include, for any one firm, both (a) correspondence, orders to pay, etc., and (b) complete accounts, *i.e.*, day-book and ledger for the same period. Particularly for (a), the Hancock MSS. are still the least fragmentary collection that I have seen.

2 The writers of accounting textbooks deemed it worthy of mention, *e.g.*, John Mair's *Book-keeping Modernized*, 6th ed. (Edinburgh, 1793) has a section on " Debtor and Creditor applied in Bartering," p. 28.

3 See, *e.g.*, C. P. Nettels, *The Money Supply of the American Colonies* (Madison, 1934); A. M. Davies, *Currency and Banking in the Province of Massachusetts Bay* (New York, 1901); and W. B. Weedon, *Economic and Social History of New England, 1620–1789* (Boston, 1890).

rather than real coins; their nearest equivalents today are perhaps the "guineas" that generous British donors send to charities, or the "bits" that sometimes crop up in American speech. When hard money was in fact available, it was likely to consist of a motley collection of foreign coins, such as Spanish dollars, which the colonists gained by trade with the West Indies. The dollar, worth 4s. 6d. in sterling, was declared by each colony to be worth such-and-such a number of its own imaginary shillings (for example, Massachusetts at one stage valued a dollar at six local shillings). The colony that put the biggest value on the dollar hoped to attract most coins to its ports; they argued that this kind of inflation would lure silver from Spaniards, pirates, and other holders of dollars. But the inflow of coins proved erratic. Moreover they were often light-weight and mutilated; their sizes did not make up a convenient range of values; and in any case they seldom circulated in a colony for more than six months before they too were exported to pay British debts.

In an attempt to make good the shortage of coins, the colonists issued various kinds of paper money. Their schemes were apt to be ingenious rather than sound. In Virginia "tobacco notes" were based on tobacco in warehouses. In Massachusetts, groups of private persons formed a "land bank" and a "silver bank" to emit notes. The provincial government might issue notes—with no special backing, but with a promise that they would be accepted in payment of tax. These flows of paper sometimes led to inflation, and widened the disparity between the money-units of the different colonies.

Under such handicaps, even a rich and provident man was apt to be perennially short of sound money. He might look on coins not as the inevitable means of paying for commodities but as one of the commodities themselves—and one whose supply was exceptionally fickle. "Bring all the money you can for it is scarce and in good demand" wrote a Canadian settler in 1773.[4]

In these circumstances some form of barter was inevitable.

"Barter" is apt to call up mental pictures of a savage trying to swap a pig for a spear. Such an exchange, simple though it sounds, must in fact present awkward problems. The savage has to find a seller who

(a) owns a spear just equal in worth to the pig; and

(b) wants a pig on just that day.

The value of colonial accounts is that they show how men overcame these difficulties. Barter became plain sailing when traders could appraise goods in common terms, and still more when they

---

[4] Frederick Moore, a loyalist *émigré* whose letter is preserved at the East Pulteney Tavern, Vermont.

could stretch the exchange over a long time. Money—even though it was too scarce to be always available as the unit of exchange—provided the common unit of value; and book-keeping gave the means for remembering and proving the details of a lengthy exchange. Thus the farmer of colonial New England was able to sell his pig in Boston for a money-credit in the storekeeper's books; he could then take supplies as and when he wanted them, while the storekeeper charged up his account. If the farmer could also on occasion *assign* his credit to third persons—so that the storekeeper acted in effect as his bank—then barter became a tolerably flexible and efficient means of trading.

In discussing colonial trade we must evidently distinguish between what we may call:

(1) truck, *i.e.*, the simultaneous exchange of goods; and

(2) book-keeping barter, *i.e.*, an exchange with a time-lag.

Both types of barter appear to have flourished. The colonists were not much given to compiling statistics of their doings, and so a quantitative description of their different ways of trade is hard to come by. But one exceptional man did make and bequeath to us an analysis of his sales. He was Adam Stanton, who kept a general store at Clinton, Connecticut. His surviving records [5] include pages ruled with columns in which he splits up his "sails" for each week from 1796 to 1801. The columns are for:

"Truck" — presumably straightforward barter;
"Charged" — presumably credit sales, which might be paid for later either in cash or by book-keeping barter.
"Cash" — presumably cash sales.

His total for the three items averaged about £40 a week. A little more than 10 per cent. of these sales were for truck, over 60 per cent. were charged, and under 30 per cent. were for cash.

Unfortunately, Stanton does not tell us what fraction of his charged sales was eventually paid for in cash and what by barter. This was a bit of information that could hardly be foreseen at the date of sale. Even a search through the accounts in many ledgers, long after they have been ruled off, does not yield satisfactory statistics on the point (mainly because the involved nature of some transactions defies analysis). But, as a rough guide to the quantities at stake, I would hazard a guess that about one-third of total indebtedness was discharged in cash, and two-thirds by more roundabout means such as book-keeping barter.

The books of most traders seldom mention truck; men less fond than Stanton of statistics may have thought that crude barter called

[5] At Yale Library.

for no entries. But Ninian Boog of Virginia kept a household expenses account,[6] which shows that much of his food was got by bartering wares from his store:

	£	s.	d.
To 1 dozen pipes for 1 dozen eggs			4
4 penknives 2s. 1 lace 9d. for 2 turkeys		2	9
1 quart rum for 4 chickens		1	3

and so on, at the rate of about twenty purchases a month. When the wares from the store did not quite balance the food received, a little cash was thrown in as the needed make-weight.

Book-keeping Barter

If most traders did not trouble to mention truck in their accounts, they were at pains to record more sophisticated exchanges. Indeed, I fancy that the main purpose of colonial book-keeping was to lubricate barter.[7] Ledgers contained practically nothing save accounts for persons; apparently colonial merchants for the most part saw no point in keeping any other records. Further, these accounts cannot readily be divided between those of debtors and creditors. A modern firm can split up its personal accounts into two clear camps: its debtors (goods on the left, cash on the right), and its creditors (goods and cash the other way round). The colonial merchant bought from, and sold to, the same man, and so an account in his ledger might well have goods on both sides. Perhaps he could mentally distinguish between " suppliers " (often the British exporters who sent manufactures to him) and " customers " (*e.g.*, the smaller storekeepers of the villages); and it may be that he tended to be in debt to his suppliers, and that his customers were usually in debt to him—though a balance might well swing the other way after a large remittance in kind. Perhaps too he could divide goods into (i) those which it was his primary aim to handle, and (ii) those staples—beef, timber, tobacco, etc.—which passed more as commodity-money than as merchandise.[8]

The evidence on this point is overwhelming. Though cash is

---

[6] His ledger (1748–1751) lies in the library of William and Mary College.

[7] It would be an interesting task, if one had the skills of a medievalist, to find out whether the same generalisation holds for the earliest examples of book-keeping in Europe. There is a certain plausibility in the notion that the American colonies were, in such matters as currency shortage and lack of specialisation, nearer to the thirteenth than to the twentieth century. And European textbooks of the seventeenth—still more, those of the sixteenth—century suggest that the colonists were faithfully copying the ways of European traders—with a time-lag of a century or so.

If there is anything in this idea, it may help to explain the development of both double entry and bills of exchange.

[8] Strictly, " commodity money " means goods that were acceptable by government in payment of tax. Here I use the phrase to describe goods that were commonly taken and given by merchants to square off debts. For such settlements, the goods were valued at the current market rate; so a journal may show them being " bought " and then " sold " *without any profit.*

CAPTAIN JOHN

Dr.			£	s.	d.
1730					
		To Sundries as per ledger A fol. 192	36	18	4
May	28	Wheat, corn and bacon as per waste	22	15	10
June	4	Cash paid £50 (5) 1 pen knife 2/6	50	2	6
		[There follow numerous items of stationery, etc.]			
Feb.	3	1 ream paper 45/– (6) To 3 account books 66/–	5	11	0
	6	Cash £20	20	0	0
		1/4 part of oil and bone the 16 June	51	17	2
	13	100 quills, 12/–. Mar. 9 1 quire paper 2/–		14	0
		1 barrel pork omitted Oct. 2nd	9	0	0
		1/5 of 6 bags cotton	29	14	0
		1/8 of the balance of sloop Dolphin	15	4	6
		Captain Harris's set of books	3	0	0
			434	6	1
Mar.	10	Balance due per adjustment	129	9	9
			£563	15	10

BENJAMIN HORROCKS O

Dr.			£	s.	d.
1730					
Apr.	22	To Mr. Clark's bill of exchange on Mr. Wilks	19	15	0
Feb.		Mr. Caner's bill on Tryon	20	0	0
		Gold and silver sent per Carey	33	18	0
		53 oz. silver sent per Captain Homans (Boston May 10)	14	7	0
1731					
Aug.	3	My note on Messrs. Sam Sheafe account to pay	50	0	0
Feb.	24	1 bill of exchange drawn by Apthorp	20	0	0
Mar.	20	1 do. drawn by ——— on F. Mills Jr.	25	0	0
Feb.	28	91½ oz. silver 16 moidores,* 1 guinea sent per Alden			
1734					
May	18	Oil and bone sent per Homans			
Nov.	9	80 oz. silver sent per Homans			
	22	16 barrels oil per Bennett			
Mar.	7	48 barrels oil sent per Scott			
May	15	5 tons logwood per Homans			
June	14	10 moidores 5 pistols and 11/– sterling per Bennett			
		tons cwts. qrs. lbs.			
		12 14 0 21 logwood per Quince			
Sept.	19	2 notes of Gordon for £5 9s. 9d. sterling			
Dec.	8	Sundries as per waste per Shepherdson			
1736					
Dec.	3	Bill of exchange of J. & J. Gerrish £55 5s. 4d. sterling			
1737					
Oct.	29	Cash to Saint, New England currency £50			

Note that the calendar year does not end on 31 December (but on 25 March).

* One Moidore was equal to 6 Spanish dollars.

This account was kept in sterling, and the fact that many of the figures are not enter at balancing is of course impossible. The names are chiefly those of ship's captains.

GERRISH & COMPANY

		Cr. £	s.	d.
1730				
	By foot of account in ledger A fol. 192	525	11	4
	Short credit in invoice of books	4	10	0
	So much due on guns		8	4
	Russian linen	2	0	9
	1 barrel oil	3	15	0
	6½ yards Whitney	3	5	0
	My part of fitting out sloop Raven	23	17	9
	Omission		7	8
		£563	15	10
Mar. 10	By balance due per adjustment	129	9	9
May 4	1 barrel bread	2	0	1
		131	9	10
'eb. 21	By balance due as per adjustment transferred to fol. 120	14	9	8
		£145	19	6

.ONDON, STERLING ACCOUNT

		Cr. £	s.	d.
729/30				
⁄Iar. 12	By balance due	83	14	1¼
	Interest to Feb. 10th	4	10	3
730				
'eb. 20	Freight of money per J. Carey		13	10
731				
⁄Iay 6	A parcel of goods per Bayley	70	9	1
une 23	Freight of silver per Homans		5	6
26	Goods per Capt. Foster	19	13	0
ug. 3	do. Capt. Homans	8	3	0
19	do. Capt. Crocker	22	18	4
ept. 29	do. Capt. Webster	9	13	2
ondon				
'eb. 3	do. Capt. Bonnor April	97	5	11

nphasizes the difficulties of keeping accounts when exchanges were uncertain; any attempt

mentioned in most accounts, its appearances tend to be erratic, belated, and inadequate. Innumerable accounts display a jumble of goods or services on both sides. An innkeeper charges his customer with "a bowl of toddy," and credits "a bushel of rye" [9]; a blacksmith charges for ploughing and gets back molasses [10]; and the accounts of a trader had to encompass not only his sober merchandise but also such items as "a little pig," "one day's mowing," "writing a very long petition to the General Assembly," "seven fowls to balance," and the like.

As an example of the roundabout flows that seem to have been normal, consider the accounts kept by Daniel Henchman. He lived in Boston from 1689 to 1761, and was a bookseller of note.[11] Besides books, he imported a wide range of wares from London. His customers were both fellow-Bostonians and village storekeepers. The latter might pay in country produce, *e.g.*, by sending rye and pork on a coastal sloop; in such cases the accounts show a fairly clear flow of manufactures out of Boston, and of produce into Boston. The flow between Henchman and other Boston merchants is not so clear; probably it depended on household wants, the need to settle old debts, and the fitting-out of joint trading ventures. Often the ventures were voyages to the West Indies, where the produce of New England was exchanged for Spanish and other foreign coins, logwood, and bills on London. These provided Henchman with a means of repaying part of his debt to his British supplier; the rest of the debt might be squared with exports of whale oil.

Two personal accounts from Henchman's ledger are given on pages 276 and 277); they have been slightly simplified and modernized. (See also Plate VIII for a reproduction of the first account.) The accounts are, respectively, for Captain John Gerrish, a Boston merchant, and Benjamin Horrocks, a Londoner. Gerrish's account is mainly concerned with the fitting out of a joint-venture; the debits seem to be a mixture of genuine sales (of Henchman's stationery) and of commodity-money and cash (perhaps transferred to Gerrish to finance the venture). The British agent is credited with supplies, freight, and interest; he is charged with bills, specie, and the proceeds of goods (such as whale-oil) consigned to him for sale in London.

Accounting Methods

As trade was so largely based on book-keeping barter, many people (including petty shopkeepers and farmers) had to keep accounts. What sort of system did they use?

---

9 Stratton's ledger (1788–1814), Essex Institute.

10 Harvey's ledger, in New York Public Library. These entries are as late as 1837.

11 W. T. Baxter, "Daniel Henchman," *Essex Institute Historical Collections*, LXX (1934).

The answer is clear. Everyone in business had some inkling of standard double entry, and took its form as his model; but remarkably few seem to have had the skill—or felt the need—to push the system to anywhere near its full perfection. Crude single entry was overwhelmingly the rule. I have not come across any colonial ledger that is certainly complete.[12] In the great bulk of cases a trial balance was patently impossible, as most of the impersonal accounts are lacking, the personal accounts are not ruled off, and the work abounds in arithmetical slips and other blemishes. Some of the accounts may be in the currency of a sister province or of Britain, or a debit may be in £ s. d., and the credit in lbs. of tobacco.[13] Even in the rare cases where full and logical entries in a copper-plate journal hold out promise of completeness, the ledgers do not in fact fulfil this promise [14]—though the deficiency may conceivably be due to a book or pages having been lost.

There is, of course, nothing surprising about the colonists' nodding acquaintance with the standard ledger. European textbooks were available to them; for example, Obadiah Brown of Providence, R.I., used one entitled *A Guide to Book Keepers according to the Italian Manner* (London, 1729); his copy has survived, with his diary when a ship's captain written on its blank pages.[15] Further, the bigger firms had each one or more correspondents in Europe, whose frequent statements of account mirrored their ledgers. In some cases, a colonial merchant's son was sent overseas for a spell of training in the correspondent's counting-house.[16]

We can guess some of the reasons why colonial traders fell short of full double entry. Their whole method of business was often lax and careless, so precision in their accounts was hardly to be looked for; moreover, the snail-like pace of transport gave a good excuse for

[12] But possibly the sample offered by American libraries is biased. Mair, *op. cit.*, Chap. VII, describes how factors were shipped out from Britain to keep stores in Virginia, and then would send home accounts to their employers in complete double entry. In such cases there would indeed be unusually strong pressure to keep full records. On the other hand, Mair was apparently painting his picture of colonial trade from his study in Perth, Scotland.

[13] See, for instance, Ninian Boog's ledger, 1748–1751 (William and Mary College). This has a few personal accounts with double columns, in some cases headed " tobacco " and " cash," in others " sterling " and " cash." The tobacco and sterling balances may in the end be translated, at suitable rates, into the currency column.

[14] Thus an entry in Hancock's journal may debit cash or merchandise, and credit a person. But the items composing the debits are so odd and varied—sterling bills of exchange, cash collected in London, the cost of hiring a sloop or buying a house—that one suspects the words " cash " and " merchandise " were used ritually when the book-keeper could think of nothing else with which to round off the entry; if cash and merchandise accounts existed, they must have been meaningless hold-alls.

[15] James E Hedges, *The Browns of Providence Plantation* (Cambridge, Mass., 1952), p. 6.

[16] The general statements made in this and the next two paragraphs are supported in W. T. Baxter, *The House of Hancock*, especially in Chaps. XI and XVI.

dilatory book-keeping. Few if any professional book-keepers were at hand to help. And traders must have felt it pointless to record matters that they could, thanks to the tiny scale of business, keep under close watch.

Profit Calculation

There was another—and perhaps a more weighty—reason for not keeping full accounts: a colonial trader was not obliged to calculate his year's income in order to please tax officials or stockholders. So he had little need for sales and expense figures; nor was there much point in closing off his ledger at regular yearly intervals.

Some scholars have argued that profit calculation, and therefore double entry, are essential tools of the successful capitalist.[17] Such a theory naturally commends itself to accountants like myself, since it bestows still further prestige upon our craft. Unhappily the book-keeping of the colonial merchant (who was often a remarkably successful capitalist) does not lend colour to this flattering view. He apparently felt that profit figures were not worth their keep. True, he may conceivably have worked out his profit by drafting a single-entry balance sheet; but his failure to rule off ledgers once a year makes even this compromise improbable.

It might, on the other hand, be argued that for an eighteenth-century trader the annual profit of his whole business was not the vital figure—that what he needed to know was the outcome of various lesser enterprises as each reached its end. For, if he was a man of substance, he tended to engage in many short-lived ventures as side-lines to his principal business—perhaps to get rid of commodity-money, and perhaps because there was no stock-market through which to invest his surplus capital. From time to time he might send off a parcel of fish on consignment to his agent in Spain, or fit out a whaler, or experiment with the making of candles or potash; and he might well keep an account for the consignment, voyage, or manufactory.[18] Such atomised profit-and-loss statements may perhaps be regarded as the eighteenth-century counterpart of today's cost accounts. Yet even here we cannot be sure that profit calculation was always the motive for keeping the account. When such enterprises were afoot, the

---

[17] This view is explained and criticised by B. S. Yamey, " Scientific Book-keeping and the Rise of Capitalism," *Economic History Review*, second series, I (1949), reprinted in W. T. Baxter (ed.), *Studies in Accounting*.

[18] *e.g.*, Jenkins' day-book, 1747 (Rhode Island Historical Society) mentions accounts for voyages, Fowle's ledger, c. 1822 (New York Public Library) for consignments inwards, and Ridgeley's ledger, 1765–1769 (Maryland Historical Society) for shoe-making and a plantation. Apart from these venture accounts, there was not much liking for the many different merchandise accounts featured in contemporary textbooks.

A good example of an account for a shipping venture is reproduced in Richard Pares, *Yankees and Creoles* (London, 1956), p. 140. It cheerfully confuses successive voyages, and also capital and revenue items.

trader was apt for safety to join with other men; thus he might at any time hold shares in half a dozen brief partnerships. Or an agent or captain might be mixed up in the affair (*e.g.*, receiving a commission on the proceeds). In such cases profit had to be known—or, at least, a cargo, etc., had to be split up—in order that settlement could take place. In short, personal relations might here again be the chief spur for keeping accounts, not a love for profit figures in the abstract.[19]

One more question poses itself. How would a colonial accountant with a taste for theorising have defined profit? Clearly, there would be small point in his talking about realised gains and losses; debts were apt to turn into pork rather than cash. In such circumstances final " realisation " might take place only if the pork was transferred to the family dinner-table, or if a debtor furnished the trader's wife with a new bonnet. Nor could the theorist have taken refuge in phrases about matched flows of receipts and expenditure. To measure his profit, the trader would have had to estimate the net appreciation on a host of commodities and unfinished ventures, and appraise the probability that each debtor would pay in some acceptable medium. This approach might have left a salutary imprint on accounting theory. But the work and mental strain of the calculations would have been a sore burden. The colonists perhaps showed a true sense of economy in declining to measure profit.

Personal Accounts

From what has been said, it follows that the overwhelming majority of accounts in a colonial ledger are for persons. The degree of care with which they were written up varied greatly; occasionally they are elegant (notably in the books of the wealthier merchants), but often they are slovenly. Many contain wording that strikes the modern reader—used to the drab products of book-keeping machines and their operators—as quaint and pleasing. The narrative rambles over the small incidents of everyday life:

> To cash paid in the street,

or (from a kind of cash-book kept by Jefferson) [20]:

> Gave in charity . . . . . . 3d.

or, on the credit side of an account:

> The latter part of May my negro wench scoured at his house 3 days at 2 per day charged on other side

and, sure enough, the correct debit has been put in.[1]

---

19 But how (it may be asked) were good relations maintained when the main business was run by a permanent partnership? I do not know the answer. Perhaps the partners hoped to straighten matters out with occasional single-entry balance sheets. Perhaps—as the indices of ledgers suggest—such partnerships were rather rare, and tended to be confined to a closely knit family group.

20 Massachusetts Historical Society.

1 Evert Wendell's ledger (early eighteenth century), New York Historical Society.

Once a debt had been created, a quick settlement was hard to accomplish. Payment might consist of a long-drawn-out series of petty instalments. Thus a merchant credits Doctor Greenough with two year's service ($100), and the doctor then takes driblets of goods from the store, and cash in single dollars.[2] Accounts often span periods of many years—perhaps with long breaks during which the balance lies fallow. For example, the ledger of an Albany merchant has an account, starting in 1711, that drifts on—with many gaps—till 1757, when at last his heirs put in a note to say that settlement has been reached.[3] A contemporary writer describes a store's life as being endless—" the debts are so small and numerous that it requires posterity to finish a concern." [4]

Sometimes the two men concerned would meet to scrutinise the details in an account; and then—no doubt after a good deal of debate and head-scratching—the balance would be agreed by both the parties. A note might be inserted:

> He produced his book to me and found the balance due to him £1 10. 10,

or

> This I took out of his book.[5]

One or both parties might sign under the agreed balance, *e.g.*:

> Then made all accounts even from the beginning of the world to this day to our satisfaction as witness our hands
>
> Joel Canford
> Joseph Peck [6]

In one case, the parties must each have employed an auditor:

> Then we the subscribers reckoned and found due from Thos. Cobb Esq. to Mr. John Adam sixteen shillings and 3d. witness our hands
> On behalf of Mr. John Adam, Wm. Crocker.
> On behalf of Thos. Cobb Esqr., Joseph Crocker.[7]

Specialised Day-books

In general, traders do not seem to have kept any books of original entry except an omnibus waste and/or journal. But there were exceptions. The records of a Nevis planter include a cash book of 1703; receipts are listed at one end of the book, and payments at the other.[8] Special needs might give rise to other books, *e.g.*, an iron-founder's papers include a " time-book." [9]

By the start of the nineteenth century, cash-books were getting not

---

[2] Ledger of Parker, Aikens, & Co., in Essex Institute.
[3] Evert Wendell's ledger, New York Historical Society.
[4] Quoted by Albert J. Voke, in " Accounting Methods of Colonial Merchants in Virginia," *Journal of Accountancy*, XLII (1926), p. 5.
[5] Both from Evert Wendell's ledger, New York Historical Society.
[6] Peck's ledger (1793), Yale University.
[7] Cobb's ledger (1766–1784), New York Public Library.
[8] Pinney papers, University of Bristol, England.
[9] Ridgeley papers, Maryland Historical Society.

uncommon. Thus in 1816 a Salem firm had both a cash-book and a sales day-book.[10]

Credit Transfers

Notes payable in goods

Credit transfers, the historians of early accounting tell us, played an important part in the birth or growth of double entry. They certainly are an outstanding feature in colonial ledgers. Thanks to these transfers, colonies with little cash and no banks contrived to build up a supple system of trade.

Consider a simple transfer, involving three parties. A country storekeeper buys produce from Farmer Giles, and sells it to a city merchant. Neither creditor pays. When next the farmer goes into the city, the storekeeper furnishes him with a letter to the merchant: "Please let Farmer Giles buy £*x* of goods in your shop." So two debts are settled by a short-circuit, and not one penny of cash is used.

John Hancock kept a big store at Boston, and here is an example of the "orders" that he received by the dozen:

> Boston May 27 1766
>
> John Hancock Esq.
> Sir
> Please to let Mr. John Moore have Four pounds one shilling lawful money out of your store in such goods as he shall chose on account of your humble servant
>
> Thomas Atkins

On getting the goods, Moore signs the back of the order by way of receipt. Hancock's clerk methodically docquets it "Thomas Atkins note to John Moore," and debits Atkins "for his note paid John Moore."[11] Presumably Atkins must in his ledger credit Hancock and debit Moore; it is in just such a credit transfer (we may surmise) that double entry had its genesis.

Notes payable to order

It may be too that these notes to pay in goods—a blend of the modern cheque and the letter to a mail-order firm—can suggest the origin of the bill of exchange. They undoubtedly performed many of the bill's functions. Thus, by adding "or order" to the wording, the colonists could stretch the cycle of credit transfers:

> April 27 1770
>
> John Hancock Esq.
> Sir Please to pay out of your store to Captain Adino Paddock or order £13. 6. 8 and etc.
>
> Thomas Dawes

---

[10] Parker & Company's records, at the Essex Institute (which also has one or two other cash-books from different firms).

[11] Harvard Business School, Hancock MSS. This collection has also examples of even simpler letters, in which the creditor asks that goods be given to an agent (not to an independent third-party) such as his wife or a ship's captain.

On the back is written

> Please to pay the within to Mrs. Mary Hatch
> Adino Paddock
>
> Received the contents
> J. Hatch.

In Hancock's journal, the entry this time runs:

> Sundry accounts debtor to Merchandise
> Thomas Dawes—paid his order to Adino Paddock £13. 6. 8.

Orders often did in fact circulate from hand to hand; they thus provided a private source of paper-money, based on a merchant's credit and his goods. The resulting journal entries may be somewhat formidable (particularly as they were apt to stray far afield from our textbook precepts):

> A and Company dr. to B for their acceptance of a note drawn by C on them in B's favour and by him indorsed to me.[12]

The beginning of a series of order transactions can be seen in this narrative, written by Brown (of Providence) in his account for Chauncey (of Hadley):

> Settled the above account and there is due to balance £108—19—6 which I promise to ship in sugar @ £15 per hundred-weight on account of the said Chauncey to his order in Newport as witness under hand
> Obadiah Brown
> Josiah Chauncey.[13]

Later debits show that this arrangement was carried out—*i.e.* Chauncey from time to time sent orders, and Brown met these by issuing sugar.

Variants. Notes payable in money

The procedure varied greatly from case to case. The man who penned such primitive instruments felt himself free to change their wording according to taste and circumstance, and few of them (except those for foreign exchange dealings) fall clearly into the categories now recognised by bill of exchange law; nor had he any prim ideas about such formalities as presentation for acceptance, etc. Sometimes the notes were payable in unspecified goods up to a given value, sometimes in specified commodity-money at a given rate. Or a note might be payable in cash; when it was met, the drawee would charge the drawer's account with "cash paid—per your order." Occasionally the note was payable half (or some other fraction) in money and the rest in goods. Even if the note did not state that payment was to be made in goods, the journal may show that goods were in fact the final means of settlement. The drafter seldom

---

12 Brown's Ledger 4 (1740–1752), Rhode Island Historical Society, has entries in this style.

13 *Ibid.*

bothered to specify any payment time; when he did observe this formality, the order might be payable on demand or at a date as remote as three years later.[14] On occasion, all writing might be dispensed with, and settlement contrived by word of mouth alone—hence entries like:

To Timothy Gilbert's Verble Order [15]

By the beginning of the nineteenth century some accounts are treating the orders in a more orthodox way, suggesting that the formal bill of exchange has arrived in ordinary trade. The payee of a bill may on occasion be charged with an "advance" that varies with the nearness of the due date (*e.g.*, 8½ per cent. if the bill is payable at once, and 6 per cent. if in sixty days).[16]

Promissory Notes

Besides the notes ordering a debtor to pay, the colonists made some use of documents resembling promissory notes.

It was fairly usual, after two men had agreed the amount due between them, for the debtor to give a promissory note (or occasionally a bond) for the balance. This balance might be still carried forward in the creditor's ledger; the note was regarded more as a proof of debt than a guarantee of payment on a certain date. Thus Wendell remarks, when writing up Fitch's account, that the two men have settled and found that Fitch owed a balance of £14, "as may appear by his note of hand"; three years later comes the sequel: "I gave Fitch up his note of hand and he paid me in goods." [17]

There were many variants to the procedure. A promissory note might carry interest. Its holder might get paid by instalments (acknowledged on the back in some such words as "Received on this note six dollars by me"). It might be drafted specially for triangular settlement, as in this example addressed to one Hill:

I promise to pay Benjamin Hand two pounds lawful money. Charge me with the same and you will oblige

July 18, 1787 [18] David Lyman

---

14 See Ridgeley's accounts (mid-eighteenth century), Maryland Historical Society.

15 Cobb's ledger (1766–1784), New York Public Library.

16 See the books of Lawrason & Fowle (Alexandria, Va.) in the New York Public Library—for instance:

Nov. 14, 1816	Jacob Hoffman dr. to Sundries	
	Thomas Thaxter for our draft on him at 1 days sight in favour Jacob Hoffman	1200
	Advance 8½ p. ct.	102

17 Wendell's ledger (entries of 1791–1794), New York Historical Society. See also Pinney's Ledger 3, at the University of Bristol. In May, 1774, Pinney owes Stanley £232 "for which I gave my [promissory] note payable on demand"; in June, Stanley's account opens with this credit balance, and is charged with four payments (to third parties) of cash and rum; £106 of "balance due on my note" is carried down to the credit of the next account, which then starts: "By my note for the balance having taken up the above [note] ——— £106."

18 Examples from a packet of documents with the Lyman day book, Yale.

Settlement by book entry alone

On occasion, traders managed to effect a settlement by the neat device of book-transfer alone, *i.e.*, no goods or cash changed hands. Here some friendly merchant made a cross-entry in his books on behalf of the two parties; he thus acted exactly as a modern banker who, on receipt of a cheque, credits one customer's account and debits another. Such jugglery seems to explain entries like:

> To amount of your debt due this day to Anthony Gibbons on bond assumed by me,

and—to square off a long-standing liability for freight and turtles—

> To William Cohen paid him the amount of this account in full by a deduction from your bond to him.[19]

The use in notes of phrases such as "please to pay or discount with" suggest the same procedure. "Discount" is here used in its old sense of a set-off to debt:

> Sir Please to discount one dollar with Captain Strong if it is convenient and you will much oblige your humble servant
>
> Elizah Cornwal
>
> To Colonel David Lyman
> Middletown September 2 1800[20]

Other orders run "please to pay to or discount with ——."

Importance of notes

Credit transfers of one kind or another played a substantial part in colonial trade. Many accounts are freely sprinkled with references to them. Their number must have been great—*e.g.*, an important merchant like Hancock might well receive several notes in one day from the same customer. Even humble labourers (whose counterparts today would not recognise a bill of exchange in the unlikely event of their seeing one) were adepts at handling such papers; thus the ledger of a trader in Taunton, Mass., has an account for "Gambo Negro," who got advances of cash, rum, and iron; Gambo is then charged with "your order to Philip King, paid to John Adam"; and the account is ruled off when Gambo gives his note of hand for the balance.[1] At the other end of the scale, we find also a municipality using paper to settle for the shovels that it buys.[2]

The End of the System

What I have called "colonial accounting" in fact out-lasted the colonial period by many years. The transition to modern methods varied in its speed from case to case. By say 1820, the modern look

---

19 Pinney papers (c. 1770), University of Bristol.

20 Lyman MSS., Yale.

1 Cobb's ledger (1766–1784), New York Public Library.

2 This was the town of Newburyport (see its account in Greenleaf's ledger, Essex Institute). In 1814 it still paid with a "town order" and bills on third persons.

is beginning to creep in: cash appears more often, debtors can sometimes be distinguished from creditors, and the double-entry structure is less incomplete. Twenty years later the change has become marked; nevertheless colonial traits still crop up in some ledgers.[3]

The date at which a book-keeper switched from £ s. d. to $ was entirely a matter of his own whim. The change was usually made at some point during the fifteen years between 1795 and 1810. The break was not always a clean one; a few accounts might still be kept in the old units after the others had been changed to the new. An inner column was sometimes used for $s and an outer column for the £ equivalents; or the narrative might state the amount in $s, whereas the column translated these figures into the more traditional and respectable units.

We can readily guess what were the factors that put a stop to colonial methods. Growth in population encouraged more specialised trade. The currency was disciplined, and coins were issued in plenty; by the early nineteenth century, a cash account—or even a cash-book—was becoming feasible and useful. Banks appeared in the same period, and with them came bank accounts; the cheque drove out the order payable in pork.

Perhaps these economic factors tell us everything that is needed to explain the change. But I am not quite sure. May not the character of colonial life—for instance, a relaxed tempo in business, and a relish for negotiation—have had something to do with financial methods? Attitudes on such points still vary from place to place. The modern visitor to South Africa (where coins and banks are plentiful enough) is struck by the widespread habit of putting off settlement; shopkeepers politely assume that even well-to-do customers will not pay till the end of the month. In the American colonies, money cannot have been unobtainable always and everywhere. For instance, Massachusetts printed paper money wholesale to finance expeditions against the French; and Rhode Island was even more reckless in her emissions. Ledgers show the results of this inflation clearly—in the sense that prices soared to many times their former level; but, though the provincial notes must presumably have circulated freely and abundantly in those years, there is scant sign of any fall in the volume of barter. We are thus left wondering how far the colonists' roundabout trade sprang from economic forces, and how far it mirrored a more easygoing way of life.

---

[3] Thus an order in kind is mentioned in 1842 (Barbour's books, New York Public Library). A ledger from Hanover, N.H., still has the full colonial flavour at its end, in 1834 (E. Miller's books, in the same library).

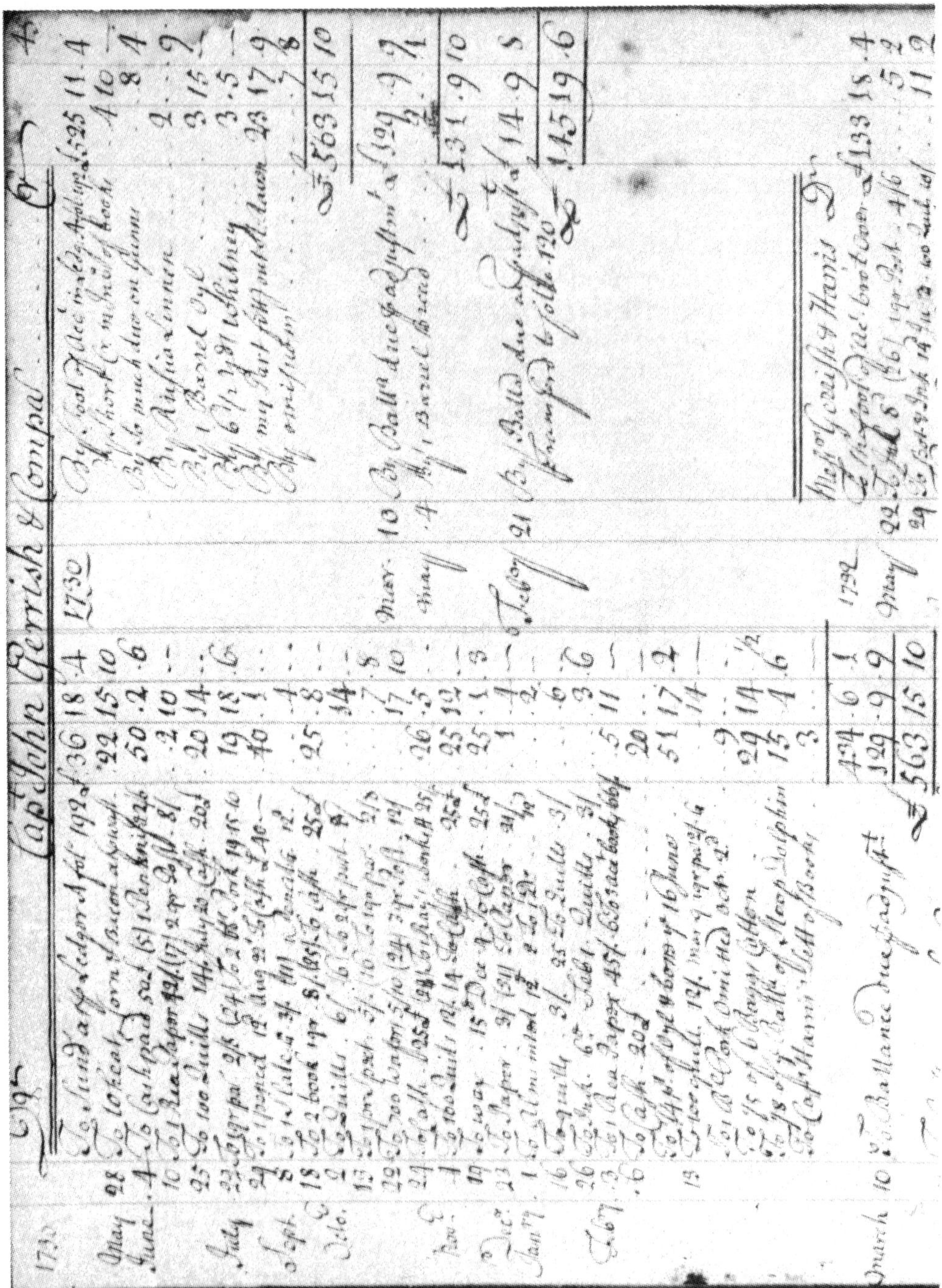

VIII. A PERSONAL ACCOUNT IN DANIEL HENCHMAN'S LEDGER, 1730

(see p. 278)

(*Courtesy of The Library, Harvard Business School.*)

THE INADEQUACY OF FINANCIAL ACCOUNTS

The Inadequacy of Financial Accounts *

—FROM THE STANDPOINTS OF SHAREHOLDERS AND THE PUBLIC

By Professor W. T. BAXTER, B.Com., C.A.

Professor BAXTER served his apprenticeship with Messrs Scott-Moncrieff, Thomson & Shiells, C.A., of Edinburgh, and qualified in 1930.
Subsequently he went to the U.S.A. as a Commonwealth Fund Fellow at the University of Pennsylvania and the Harvard Business School. When he returned to this country he became Lecturer in Accounting and Business Method at the University of Edinburgh. This appointment was followed by the Chair of Accounting at the University of Cape Town. Since his return from South Africa Professor Baxter has taken up an appointment as Professor of Accounting at the London School of Economics.

WHEN the Companies Act, 1948, came into effect, British accountants may well have felt a certain pardonable pride in their achievement; some may also have hoped that they could rest on their laurels for a spell.

Much had been accomplished in a fairly short time. One has only to look back at the published reports of the 'twenties and 'thirties to see how great the change had been. In the 'twenties, accounts had slight pretension to style, secret reserves were commonplace, and important detail could be submerged in a comprehensive blanket figure. And few accountants found much to criticise in such unhelpful reports. Our general view was that we had no call to make our statements interesting or candid; so long as directors avoided the sin of over-statement, they could be obscure and pessimistic to their hearts' content. Consider some of the evidence that we tendered to the Wilfrid Greene Committee, prior to the drafting of the 1929 Act. The memorandum sent in by the Scottish accountants says tersely, under the heading of " Secret Reserves ":

> " Legislation, however desirable, appears to be impracticable." †

The memorandum from the English Institute is more explicit:

> " The business done by Limited Companies is, on the whole, transacted by Directors and Managers who are honest, and if in some cases they disclose in the published accounts less than some people desire the absence of detail is in most cases wise and is generally supported by the Shareholders. To give in a Balance Sheet such detailed information as would afford full protection to creditors might mean the giving of a mass of detail of material value to competitors. . . . It is impossible by legislation to protect fools from their own folly. . . .

* A Paper read on September 24, 1956, at the Fourth Summer School at St Andrews University of The Institute of Chartered Accountants of Scotland.

† Departmental Committee on the Companies Act, 1925, lviii.

> " Secret Reserves or Inner Reserves are in certain cases desirable and in many cases essential. In the Council's opinion all such Reserves should be included in the Balance Sheet items and no Company by its Articles should be allowed to contract itself out of this obligation.
>
> " If businesses carried on by Joint Stock Companies are to be as successful in the future as in the past, too much disclosure should not be insisted on and the greatest possible freedom should be allowed to those responsible." *

If " recommendations " had been in vogue at that date, presumably the relevant pronouncements would have given their semi-mandatory force to the above views, and reform would have been vastly harder to achieve.

Many factors combined to break down the old attitude. Some of the larger companies realised how much a good report can do for public relations. The rules of the Stock Exchange were a strong influence for advance. But perhaps the most salutary force was the *Royal Mail* case. This, you will recollect, resulted in the acquittal of the auditor after leaders of the profession had testified that the sly re-transfer of reserves, to bolster waning profits, was a well-recognised and perfectly respectable usage. But by a very odd paradox—which perhaps shows the wisdom of dealing gently—the case proved hardly less drastic in its results than if its end had been harsh punishment. The secret reserve quickly fell from esteem; and auditors came to show a far greater sense of responsibility to their ultimate employers, the shareholders.

The new attitude fostered a voluntary improvement in the standards of many companies during the 'thirties and 'forties; and the 1948 Act pushed the laggards into line with the leaders. The stringent terms of the Eighth Schedule are too well-known to call for comment. Looking back, we can still describe the Act as a notable stride in the right direction.

But, alas, the reform of accounting seems to be a task that never ends. One is tempted to compare it to the repair of dykes during a flood. The engineers with great effort plug the obvious leak, and then pause to draw breath and congratulate themselves on their feat; and suddenly a flaw whose existence they have never suspected lets the flood come bursting in at a new place.

Our achievement in the first half of this century was to adopt rules compelling the full and frank disclosure of the ledger figures. Our limitation—subsequent experience of rising prices suggests—lay in our belief that such historic figures were adequate for all circumstances.

* *Ibid.* lxviii.

Defects of the 1948 Act

Before we go on to deal with this large issue of inflation, we should perhaps pause to consider what matters, if any, still call for reform in more homely fields. Has the 1948 Act succeeded in all its aims? Do the accounts of to-day give shareholders the whole range of historic facts about their business?

So far as the balance sheet goes, the Act has stood up pretty well to the test of the years. Certain small matters still seem to call for improvement; *e.g.* it would often be helpful if the basis of valuing stocks were stated. But in general there does not appear to be much need for more regulations—indeed one may feel, on seeing the formidable notes which embroider the hem of some balance sheets, that abandonment of the fussier regulations might be all to the good.

But when we turn to the revenue account, things are very different. Here the fight against concealment has still not been pressed to complete victory. Sales and all the basic costs can legally be veiled from the owners' gaze; and there is little tendency for the voluntary concession of what is not demanded by law. When so much is now laid bare—with none of the ill results that were foretold by the defenders of the old order—it seems hard to find logical grounds for the excessive modesty of directors in this particular. Leading American companies have long published a full revenue account, in part because of enlightened leadership by the New York Stock Exchange; and there is no suggestion that the practice should be abandoned—rather that it should be extended to a wider range of companies.

This matter is usually argued in terms of shareholder versus director, or of the given company versus its competitors. To my mind, the decisive argument is much wider. The whole system of free enterprise is now on trial. Even such a sober and conservative people as the British has already taken a long step into state-ownership; and a slight change in feeling would suffice once again to tip the electoral balance that way. Let me try to set forth the issues—no doubt with some bias. When the state is owner, all investment policy (*i.e.* the direction of new resources into possible projects) is in the hands of a small group of super-planners, who presumably take care to equip themselves with a full battery of statistics. Under free enterprise, the flow of resources is instead directed by a host of lesser investors, each making his independent decision after weighing the prospects and risks. The multitude of investors is more likely than the few planners to steer the economy to good results (or so the argument runs); for example, the small investors may have a closer knowledge of the outlook in their own area or trade, they may weigh risks better than officials with nothing to lose or win, they are not subject to political pressure, and their mistakes may tend to cancel one another. But clearly this case is in danger of becoming moonshine if the private investor cannot get good information. Without clear accounts, he is gambling in the dark, and is likely to do a worse job than planners armed with powers to extract the figures. Thus publication of fuller accounts is no narrow matter of company law, but a pressing social issue. In the long run, the question is not " shall we tell or conceal? " but " shall we tell the shareholders or the planners? " Tell we must.

Improvements in Wording

The most useful experiments now taking place are in the layout and style of published accounts. There is still much to be done in this field. We are apt to forget how little most laymen know about the tricks of our trade; almost every reference by public speakers to the " balance sheet " shows that they confuse this document with the revenue account. The company accountant is a public relations officer with the tough job of explaining the facts of business to folk who know little about it, dislike figures, and often are somewhat hostile.

Two points suggest themselves here. *First*, an account is not likely to inform the layman if it is primarily constructed to fit into the double-entry mechanism. *Second*, confusion will result from using familiar words in unfamiliar senses.

Under the first head, we must remind ourselves that, though published figures are derived from the double-entry system, there is no need to thrust this system into the layman's face. The medieval book-keeper found that two-sided accounts increased his accuracy; and all later experience has confirmed that debit-and-credit can be very useful within the privacy of the counting-house. Surely, however, when the accountant wants to present data to outsiders, he should clear his mind of all such technical tricks, and should set out the figures in a style dictated entirely by his readers' convenience. This view is steadily winning ground, and so the " report form " of published account is tending to displace the two-sided vestige of ledgercraft.

The report form is also helpful where my second point is concerned; for the extra space of the report enables terse technical phrases to be replaced by fuller descriptions. The place where these are most needed is in the owners' section of the balance sheet (share-capital, reserves, etc.). The prime source of confusion is, I think, that this section—particularly as set out in a two-sided balance sheet—seems to list *additional* items of the owners' wealth, whereas in fact it tries to re-analyse figures already shown elsewhere in the same account. A useful analogy may be got from railway statistics. If there are a hundred waggons in a marshalling yard, a clerk could helpfully describe them:

(*a*) by analysing them according to their size or other physical features; and also
(*b*) by re-analysing them according to the administrative regions to which they belong.

A balance sheet does much the same thing. It first classifies the owners' wealth by asset type; and then it re-analyses the same wealth according to its source.*

Our railway clerk's two lists should both add up to 100 waggons. If he designs his lists in a way that leads any reader to suppose the total number of waggons may be more than 100, then his arrangement is clearly faulty. Yet in fact this is exactly the risk to which the conventional balance sheet exposes its readers. Many laymen, I am convinced, do not clearly appreciate that we are attempting a double analysis of the same wealth, and so they are in some danger of falling into confusion.

It is mainly our special twist to the word " reserve " that exposes the layman to the risk of double-counting. The dictionary definition of the word is " something reserved for future use, extra stock or amount "—for example, military reserves are troops held as reinforcements, and a banker's reserve is the "amount kept on hand to meet probable demands." These definitions correspond closely with popular usage, in which a reserve is a supply of some asset over and above likely needs. In the context of finance, therefore, the layman may reasonably suppose that a reserve is a group of extra assets—very likely, liquid assets—which the company keeps somewhere in the background against sudden needs; and of course this comes very close indeed to what bankers and City editors mean when they talk about the " reserves " of banks and financial houses. Our use of the word, as the name of an item in the list of sources, is at best a cause of confusion, and at worst an awkward trap. Much the same sort of criticism can be advanced—though with less force perhaps—against our use of " provision ", " allowance ", and even " capital " itself.

* I am assuming that, because the draftsman is accounting to the legal owners, he deducts claims by non-owners (as negative assets) in the first list. But the argument would still stand if the report was intended for a broader group of " capital " providers.

What should we do to remove these ambiguities? There would be little point in trying to educate the layman in our own usage. After all, both logic and popular habit are on his side; when we finished our laborious explanations, he would probably murmur to himself: " assets are good things; reserves are good things; therefore reserves and assets ought to be added together." A better solution is to avoid the word "reserve", and instead to seek a clearer arrangement of the balance sheet and a fuller narrative. The sections of the balance sheet (and I think that there is less risk of confusion if they are placed underneath one another, rather than on opposite pages) should each start with a full and adequate sentence of explanation: the net assets section, with a statement that the company's assets, less liabilities to outside persons, consist of . . .; and the ownership section, with words indicating that the above total of net assets has been provided by the owners in the ways detailed below . . .

In the ownership section, there seems a good case for not grouping preference capital with the equity. The latter (*i.e.* paid-up capital, share premiums, and retained earnings, etc.) should be treated as a separate group, unless the preference capital has substantial rights to participate in any surplus. This would emphasise that preference claims are restricted to a fixed amount of money and so enjoy a status wholly different from those of the equity—an important matter in times of inflation.

I suspect that an incidental advantage would follow from a fuller description of reserves. We should be forced to think more clearly about their different categories. Where accumulated revenue is concerned, a distinction is usually drawn between unappropriated profits and general reserves. This distinction is apt to be fine—so fine, indeed, as to make one suspect that it partakes more of the æsthetics of window-dressing than logic. Is the division really worth making? Again, most of us would be hard put to it to give an adequate definition to capital reserves. Some amounts, such as share premiums, fall clearly into this category because of a rigid statutory rule. The more dubious rules of case law make it seem plausible to put other items under this heading (*e.g.* profit on sale of fixed assets). Sometimes common-sense may suggest further additions to the list, such as profits earned prior to the acquisition of a business. But there remain other items which might or might not be classed as capital reserves. The Act's definition—by which capital reserves are sums not " regarded as free for distribution through the profit and loss account "—is not over-helpful; in any case, creditors are just as interested in distributions made otherwise than through the profit and loss account.

It thus looks as if a full statement, telling in forthright terms what the directors think about each reserve figure, would make for more understanding. And greater mental clarity might in the end lead to a clearer statute.

Changing Price-levels

The points covered in preceding pages are doubtless interesting and important. But they pale beside the issues that have emerged since inflation came to plague us, and showed us how open to criticism are records and theories based on original cost.

I should like to discuss the effects of inflation under three heads:—

(1) The revenue account and the " historic cost error."
(2) Money-assets and creditors—the " money effect."
(3) Fixed asset values.

(1) *The Revenue Account and the " Historic Cost Error."*

This aspect of the matter has excited great interest—for the reason that it leads to higher tax on firms owning stocks and wasting assets, and some people see no very strong grounds for such discrimination.

Briefly, the cause of the trouble is as follows. Suppose a revenue account runs:

Sales	£1,000
Cost-of-goods-sold	600
Profit	£ 400

The sense behind this account (assuming it is meant as a guide to action, and not just as a means for tidying up the ledger) is surely to tell the owner: " You have made a gross income of £1,000. But you must not withdraw that sum, or you will be left with fewer assets than you had at the start, and so will be unable to trade on the same scale next year. You must instead use £600 to plug up the gaps that the year's trading has made in your assets; £400 is all that you can spend on yourself if you want to maintain your capital." In short, the essence of a cost is a reduction of the firm's assets—and a reduction that must be made good if the business is to continue to earn at a constant rate.

The calculation is plain-sailing when prices are stable. Then costs, sales, and opening assets are all measured in the same value unit; and so the retention of £600 in the business serves to keep the pile of assets up to its original level. But if prices are changing, £600 will *not* replace the used-up assets with ones of equal size (whether " size " is measured physically or in terms of the living standard that they will enable their owner to maintain). The historic figure of £600 is no longer the true measure of cost; instead, we must substitute whatever amount is in fact now needed to replenish the assets. Replacement cost is the proper charge to revenue account, not historic cost.

What are the arguments of those who deny this proposition? They pitch their objections at two very different levels. First, most of the apologists for conventional accounting disagree with my view that the capital to be maintained is a stock of " real capital." They substitute " money capital." In other words, if a firm starts with £*x* of assets, then it is deemed to maintain its capital intact so long as its assets, measured at cost, add up to £*x*—regardless of the assets' physical size or earning power. The weakness of this argument can be best shown, I think, by the *reductio ad absurdum* method. A German firm at the end of 1923 would have kept its money capital intact even if its physical stocks had shrunk to far less than one-millionth of their opening volume; the conventional revenue account would here be utterly worthless as a guide to what the owner could withdraw. And if the money-capital yardstick is nonsensical when inflation is severe, it must be less than wholly satisfactory when the inflation is mild.

I have much more sympathy with the second group of objectors. They concede money-capital to be sadly defective as a measure, but point to the difficulties of substituting a better one. These difficulties are certainly grave enough. Departure from the historic basis would make accounts slightly harder to read, and perhaps open to trickery. What is more serious, we do not quite know how to define " real capital "; and even if we did, no statistician could devise an index that would measure it perfectly.

These objections seem to me to be genuine but not insuperable. It is true that uncontrolled adjustment of costs might in some cases lead to window-dressing or dishonesty; the remedy is to control the adjustments—by insisting that they are made openly and in tune with an official index. It is also true that no index will assess real capital with complete precision; but the least satisfactory of the usual indices would yield expense figures vastly nearer to the ideal than does original cost.

If reform takes place, the new system should, I feel, be confined to the making of closing adjustments to the few items much affected—usually only two in number, namely cost-of-goods-sold and depreciation.

In our example, if the replacement cost of goods is shown by the index to be one-tenth higher than their historic cost, the adjusted revenue account will run:

Sales		£1,000
Cost-of-goods-sold:		
Historic cost	£600	
Provision for increase in replacement cost	60	
		660
Corrected profit		£ 340

Depreciation can be raised likewise from the historic to the replacement basis. Such adjustments, made voluntarily but in line with a prescribed index, would be simple yet adequate. More elaborate schemes, involving frequent alteration of all the ledger figures, seem to me to yield no worth-while extra benefits as compensation for the labour and confusion that they would entail.

If this reform were extended to the tax system, it would remove the extra impost on holders of stocks and depreciating plant. Corrected figures would be superior to the conventional ones as guides to pricing and dividend policy; more realistic profits would also make for better relations with labour and customers. And it is at least arguable that reform would do something to calm down the damaging hysteria of boom and slump. These are weighty arguments for change.

(2) *Money-Assets and Creditors—the "Money Effect."*

In any discussion of inflation, our thoughts may be clearer if we separate the historic cost error from changes in the value of money-assets. For it is one thing to say " You are counting your profits wrongly " and quite another to add " You need pay your creditors only half of what you owe them." The historic cost error is an abstract matter of how best to do one's own sums. Concepts of measuring wealth are here at stake, and not the wealth itself; if accounting had in 1939 been using a rather different method of calculation, no problem would exist to-day. But the changes in the value of money-assets (cash, government stocks, debtors, etc.) and of money-liabilities (including debentures and preference capital) are genuine and objective; they alter a firm's ability to buy real assets, and they upset the rights of outside creditors. Accountants could correct the revenue figures with a stroke of the pen. Only if government stops the inflation can the other trouble be cured.

Let us again illustrate the issue with an ultra-simple case. Suppose that a firm starts in 1939 with an ordinary capital of £10,000, buys offices or other non-wasting fixed assets for £9,000, and keeps £1,000 as cash; its profits thereafter are all paid out as tax and dividends; by 1956 the price-level has trebled. The closing balance sheet, on conventional lines, is shown in column A below. If the company revalues its assets, the results will be as in column B. To show what has happened to the money-assets, we should also have to revalue the opening capital in terms of 1956 £s, as is done in column C; I shall for convenience call such calculations—where *all* the undervalued items are altered by reference to some index—" stabilized accounts."

1956 Balance Sheets

	A *Conventional*		*B* *Assets Revalued*		*C* *Stabilized Accounts*
	£		£		£
Fixed assets	9,000	$\times \frac{300}{100} =$	27,000		27,000
Money-assets	1,000		1,000		1,000
	£10,000		£28,000		£28,000
Equity:	£		£		£
Original capital	10,000		10,000	$\times \frac{300}{100} =$	30,000
Revaluation surplus			18,000		
Loss on holding money					−2,000
	£10,000		£28,000		£28,000

The important fact shown by column C is that the company, because it was so ingenuous as to keep £1,000 of its original capital in liquid form throughout an inflation, has burned its fingers and lost two-thirds of that part of its capital. If instead it had put the £1,000 into fixed assets, these might have retained their real value, *i.e.* would now be worth £3,000.

In practice, ought the £2,000 loss to be measured, and then charged against revenue? I suppose that to be consistent I should answer " Yes "; for here is a clear case in which the owners' real wealth has been reduced by their business activities. Yet I must confess that the argument seems less strong than that for righting the historic cost error. The following points of contrast are perhaps relevant:—

(i) The cash, government bonds, and other money-assets in a conventional balance sheet are correctly valued in contemporary £s. Similarly, interest on the government bonds is shown correctly in the revenue account. Anyone with his wits about him knows, without being told, that these items will buy less than they would have done in earlier years, and that the company is losing wealth by holding on to its liquid assets. The revenue account patently ignores the £2,000 loss; it does not pretend—as it does with depreciation and cost-of-goods-sold—to allow for the loss without in fact doing so. The lack of an adjustment to make good the £2,000 money-effect thus seems far less likely to deceive and confuse than the failure to correct historic cost error.

(ii) The money-effect is an external reality. The historic cost error is something that we have brought upon ourselves; by a trick of accounting, we have deprived stocks and plant of their superiority over assets that must lose value in an inflation. Therefore the first step ought surely to be the righting of this home-made error.

(iii) Perhaps we should distinguish between the long-term and the short-term. A loss of *current* money-assets (net) may indeed mean that working funds have been impaired, and should be made good out of revenue. But consider, instead, a company with a big long-term debt (including preference shares). Here the money-effect is by no means unfriendly during inflation. For, as the whole scale of money transactions has gone up, the burden of fixed-interest payments is in effect scaled down; and the ordinary shareholder must gain what the debt-holder loses. A stabilized balance sheet here shows a gain, not a loss. This gain is the capital expression of the future improvement in net income. It is genuine enough; but it is certainly not yet a realized gain. If, then, it is recognized in the accounts, there is a powerful case for not treating it as current revenue.

(iv) The historic cost error arouses strong feelings among businessmen because of the tax burden it imposes. Change would be welcomed by such men, and the educational task of the accountant would in consequence be lightened. The money-effect arouses no such feelings, for the simple reason that most firms have a negative quantity of money-assets, and so have made a profit instead of a loss. As a matter of crude tactics, then, the reformer might do well to start with the historic cost error, and leave the money-effect till later.

Whatever the outcome of this debate, there must often be cases when a director or accountant would for his own information like to draw up a completely modernized balance sheet, *i.e.* one that revalues the capital as in column C above. In an example less simple than the one shown there, the various items under " owners' capital etc." will need to be revalued to different degrees, according to the date at which they were acquired; similarly, asset values must be raised to varying extents because of different dates of purchase. As a basis for discussion, I suggest the following treatment.

Suppose that the business starts on January 1, when the index stands at 100; that it earns its income from letting-out office premises, and on average receives all its rent (and pays all its costs) at the mid-year, when the index stands at 110; that the index reaches 120 at December 31; and that the transactions are:—

		£
1 January	Starts with:	
	Ordinary capital	100,000
	Debentures	100,000
	Buys office premises	150,000
30 June	Receives rents (less all expenses and interest)	10,000
30 September	Buys additional premises (index at 115)	46,000

Both original surplus cash (£50,000) and net earnings (£10,000) are kept in the bank; the September payment reduces the balance to £14,000.

The closing balance sheet might be served up in the same three versions—A, B and C—as before:

CLOSING BALANCE SHEETS

	A *Conventional*	*B* *Assets Revalued*	*C* *Stabilized Accounts*
Money Assets	£	£	£
Bank	14,000	14,000	14,000
Less Debentures	100,000	100,000	100,000
Net money assets	−86,000	−86,000	−86,000
Fixed Assets			
Cost: January 1	$150{,}000 \times \frac{120}{100}$	= 180,000	180,000
September 30	$46{,}000 \times \frac{120}{115}$	= 48,000	48,000
Total net assets	£110,000	£142,000	£142,000
Equity	£	£	£
Original capital	100,000	$100{,}000 \times \frac{120}{100}$	= 120,000
Revaluation surplus		32,000	
Profit	10,000	$10{,}000 \times \frac{120}{110}$	= 10,909
Gain from owing money			11,091*
	£110,000	£142,000	£142,000

* Loss on current assets (here cash only):

January-December	$50{,}000 \times \left(\frac{100-120}{100}\right)$	= − 10,000
July-December	$10{,}000 \times \left(\frac{110-120}{110}\right)$	= − 909
October-December	$-46{,}000 \times \left(\frac{115-120}{115}\right)$	= + 2,000
		− 8,909
Gain on long-term debt (= debentures):		
January-December	$-100{,}000 \times \left(\frac{100-120}{100}\right)$	= + 20,000
Net gain		+ 11,091

The treatment in C could, with a little ingenuity, be adapted to cover several accounting periods.

(3) *Fixed Asset Values*

Comparing columns A and B, we see how far historic values must be raised if the figures for pre-war assets are to be given some significance for to-day's reader. Now that we can no longer suppose that inflation is either slight or short-lived, the case for renovating the balance sheet seems unanswerable. There may be legal objections to the method shown in column C—since this alters the sacred capital figure—but the change illustrated in column B has in fact been carried out by several important companies, with no disastrous results.

A safe and simple procedure, I would suggest, is:

(i) Assets should be revalued on a replacement cost basis (less any depreciation).

(ii) They should be dealt with in broad groups, and revalued by reference to indices. The auditor would be helped, in testing the reasonableness of the write-ups, by the indices published by THE ECONOMIST, and by the company's insurance cover.

(iii) The re-appraisals should take place at intervals of say five years. They should be dispensed with when the price change is too small to alter the figures materially.

INSURANCE ACCOUNTS

What has been said so far acquires extra piquancy when it is applied to the accounts of such privileged bodies as insurance, shipping, and banking companies. These accounts are doubly defective in the investor's eyes; not only are they subject to the drawbacks common to all statements based on historic cost, but they are exempt from the 1948 Act's more stringent provisions regarding disclosure.

The demands for special secrecy by these bodies have never struck me as being particularly convincing. However, if foreigners are in fact more willing to trust our firms when their status is shrouded in mystery than when their strength is patent, then perhaps we should not quibble unduly over this source of invisible exports. The gratuitous handicapping of British savers is quite another matter; and so, I suggest, it is high time for our life offices to make their reports more informative.

We all know how important life insurance is as a means to saving. In this sphere, as elsewhere, the impact of inflation has been savage. The sufferers are mainly the old and the widowed; to many of these, long-term policies must now give back less—measured in real terms—than the premiums paid. The reason is that the non-profit policy has the same qualities and weakness as the trustee security; and even with-profit policies can scarcely behave better during inflation than preference shares enjoying meagre rights to participate.* Despite the clamant need, no insurance company has (so far as I am aware) felt able to launch a new kind of policy with the virtues—and of course the hazards—of the equity share; the difficulties would admittedly be great, and might well involve a new form of policy, perhaps based on the unit trust principle, or with some such device as a negative bonus for bad years.

Although we must still await a policy-model that is not behind the times, most life-offices have gone so far as to change their investment spread, and tend to include more equities in their portfolios. Accordingly, to take out a long-term with-profit policy is now rather like buying shares in an investment trust. The same kind of information is needed before one can pick a company that answers one's own circumstances and forecast of future conditions. The directors' prowess in managing the portfolio is a major factor. And the buyer of ordinary shares in an investment trust will, if he is hedging against inflation, also look for a trust with (*a*) a large part of its assets in equities, and (*b*) a high ratio between its liabilities and its own equity capital (*i.e.* if he thinks money will depreciate, he wants a trust that owes a lot of it). Similarly, a prospective policy-holder would like to weigh both (*a*) and (*b*) (as well as guides peculiar to insurance, such as bonus history and gross interest yield on book-value of assets). Under (*a*), different insurance companies have very different stories to tell, since they vary greatly in the courage and promptitude with which they took to buying equities. Presumably something analogous to (*b*) is provided in insurance by the gearing of the non-profit to the with-profit funds.

How far do published accounts help the would-be saver? They are helpful, so far as (*a*) goes, in that the balance sheet lists the portfolio according to type of holding; but, since the figure opposite each item is described with some such phrase as " at or below cost less reserve," the guidance is strictly limited. A note of current value, analogous to that supplied by investment trusts, would greatly help the reader. So far as (*b*) is concerned, no guidance at all is proffered.†

* With-profit policies may be legally entitled to 90 per cent of (or the whole) surplus. But this surplus will be too small to outweigh inflation if the company has played safe by investing the premiums in gilt-edged securities.

† Figures for the with-profits and without-profits funds are however published in the Fourth Schedule of the returns made to the Board of Trade, after each valuation (*i.e.* often at five-year intervals). They include actuarial valuations of the liability under each head—*i.e.* estimates that link up with asset values better than the historic fund balances.

It seems a pity that such data are not summarized in the annual accounts.

Thus insurance accounts are another of the casualties of inflation. In their present form, they fail to meet to-day's needs.

Take-over Bids

More than anything else, it is the take-over bid that has shown us how grave can be the consequences of antiquated values. Such bids would not have been feasible—or, at least, could not have been anything like so spectacular—if our figures were linked to present reality. They constitute a lamentable indictment of accounting convention—in their way, perhaps as damaging as the *Royal Mail* case.

Let me add that it is not the bids themselves that are the main evil, but the process that makes them possible. For reasons set out below, the bids should be regarded as the medicine rather than the disease; they act as the somewhat drastic cure for a malady that ought to have been checked much sooner.

When assets are shown at figures bearing no relation to their current worth, shareholders cannot tell whether profits and share-prices are in normal relationship to the assets' size. Sometimes the company's share prices remain absurdly low; and then a perceptive onlooker may decide to buy these bargains wholesale, in the hope of winning control of a good business at a low price. If he succeeds, he may then put fresh life into its existing activities, or he may deflect assets to new and more fruitful uses; in either case, his profit is likely to be great. If the directors defeat him—by revealing to gratified shareholders that their shares are worth keeping, as it has just emerged that dividends can be put up to a hitherto unsuspected extent—then the shares that he has already bought may appreciate sharply. Victory and defeat can both yield a prize.

The man who organises such a bid is apt not to be regarded by the public with much favour. There may be a case for thinking that his actions are sometimes anti-social—for instance, directors may have kept down dividends for patriotic motives, in response to government appeals for restraint; again, the manœuvres by which he raises ready-money are not always in the best of taste. In the main, however, shareholders have good cause to bless him. He it is who in the last few years has forced equity dividends—and capital values—to move up belatedly in the trail of general prices. If any group of shareholders has been exploited, it is not the members of a taken-over company; it is the members of the company that hid the full size of its wealth—the pensioners whose dividends failed to rise with the cost-of-living, and the men who sold shares at a fraction of their potential worth. Dividend limitation was defensible as a short-run emergency measure; eleven years after the war it is a sign of Treasury failure.

From the broader standpoint of national efficiency there is also much to be said for the organiser of take-over bids. Though his procedure may be novel in outward form, he is merely carrying on an ancient process—the switching of resources into more profitable employment. If assets yield more profit in another use, then they are probably of more social value in that use—unpleasant in the short-run though their transfer may be for some people. Again, where a firm's profits have not gone up more-or-less in step with prices, there are *prima facie* grounds for thinking that the firm is not being run vigorously; we owe a debt to the man who rouses it from its torpor. In short, the bad thing about all this reorganisation is, not that it is now upsetting so many comfortable apple-carts, but that it did not start years ago, when scarcities were more acute and the upheavals could have been less violent.

Attacks on the balance sheet have been stoutly resisted by defenders of historic cost. To my mind, take-over bids have given a final and unanswerable proof that historic cost alone is not enough. The case for reform is overwhelming.

BRITISH TRANSPORT COMMISSION v. GOURLEY

BRITISH TRANSPORT COMMISSION v. GOURLEY [1]

This case posed the question of whether tax should be deducted from compensation for loss of income. The decision—that tax should indeed be deducted—will in many instances change the amount of damages to a dramatic extent; further, the new principle may possibly be stretched in the future to cover loss of office and even compulsory acquisition. Accordingly, some comment by an accountant on the arithmetic of this case, and on its implications, may not seem altogether out of place.

Facts

The respondent, Mr. H. J. F. Gourley, was severely and permanently injured while travelling by train on September 21, 1951, owing to the negligence of the appellant's servants. He was sixty-five years old at that date, and, as senior partner in a firm of civil engineers, was earning a high income. For some months after the accident he was unable to take part in the firm's business. On his return to work an abatement was made—because of his disabilities—in his share of the profits; accordingly, from the date of the accident to the end of 1953 (just before the action for recovery of damages) his earnings were greatly reduced. Moreover, the firm's profits seemed likely to fall in future years because of his diminished working powers; and so his prospective earnings (from the trial until his hypothetical retirement date) might well be lower than they would have been but for the accident. Nevertheless, his expected income—despite his handicaps—still appeared large enough to attract surtax "at the highest rate."

The trial took place in March, 1954, and Pearce J. awarded damages of £47,720. Authorities binding on him and the Court of Appeal required him to ignore tax in assessing the respondent's loss of income, *i.e.*, the damages under this head were estimates of gross income lost, regardless of the fact that tax would have been paid on this income had it actually been received. As the appellants wished to bring this matter before the House of Lords, they requested Pearce J. to make alternative findings of the damages due if tax was deductible. The resulting analysis may for convenience here be shown as follows:

[1] [1956] A.C. 185.

	Gross amount £	*Tax on earnings* £	*Net amount* £
(*a*) Loss of earnings			
1951–3 (*i.e.*, till trial)	15,220	10,275	4,945
1954– (*i.e.*, prospective)	22,500	20,750 [2]	1,750
	37,720	31,025	6,695
(*b*) Pain and suffering	9,000	—	9,000
(*c*) Out-of-pocket expenses	1,000	—	1,000
	47,720	31,025	16,695

All these figures were accepted as correct. Items (*b*) and (*c*) were not challenged; the question under appeal was whether the judge ought to have taken account of tax in assessing (*a*), and so should have awarded £6,695, not £37,720, under that head.

It was agreed by both sides that the respondent would incur no tax liability on the award of either £6,695 or £37,720.

Reasoning

According to the judgments delivered in the House of Lords, the principle to be followed in assessing the damages is not in doubt: the injured person should get "such a sum as will, so far as possible, make good to him the financial loss which he has suffered and will probably suffer as a result of the wrong done to him" (Lord Reid). Plainly, such a calculation must often be fantastically difficult, uncertain, and arbitrary—and all the more so when prospective earnings of the distant future are at stake. Yet, however rough-and-ready the estimate may be, the court has to assess damages as a lump sum once and for all.

There is, however, a qualification to the principle. The loss suffered, and any compensatory gains, must not be too remote in the chain of consequences. The problem before the court in this case was therefore whether tax on income is too remote and uncertain to be taken into account.

When one reflects on the importance of tax, this problem seems to have featured in surprisingly few earlier cases. In these, the decisions (with one exception) all favoured the view that tax should be disregarded in assessing damages. Thus, Lord Keith in *Blackwood* v. *Andre* [3] examined the argument that the injured person's

[2] The increase in the rate of tax, as between the pre-trial and post-trial incomes, can perhaps be explained as follows. Suppose that a man was earning £10,000 a year; and that, after his accident, his income is zero in the first year, and then is £9,000 for the next ten years. Under a system of progressive taxation the average tax rate applicable to the £10,000 lost in the first year will be much lower than the rates applicable to the £10,000 lost over the next ten years; for the latter £10,000 consists of the top slices of each year's income, which attract tax at the stiffest rate.

[3] 1947 S.C. 333.

loss is merely the net sum that he would receive after deduction of tax, and decided that this view is illegitimate. "It would apply on the same grounds where a person had come under obligation to pay a proportion of his income away to somebody else. The fact that he would then be left with a net sum does not appear to me to be any reason for basing the assessment of damages upon the net sum which he would receive or retain and not upon the gross sum which should be paid to him and from which he would make the conventional deduction to which he had become bound. Further, the argument seems to ignore the fact that the only person who is going to benefit is the person who is liable in damages. There is no suggestion that he will account to the Revenue for the capitalised income tax which *ex hypothesi* has been taken into account in assessing damages. The court, in my opinion, has no concern with the incidence of taxation in assessing the damages of an injured taxpayer. The argument rests upon a consideration of facts that really are *res inter alios acta*, and for these reasons the argument must, in my opinion, be rejected." The matter was decided in the same way by the Court of Appeal in *Billingham* v. *Hughes*.[4]

The one case in which a contrary view had been taken was *M'Daid* v. *Clyde Navigation Trustees*.[5] Here tax was not so belated and remote as when it falls on profits; it was actually deducted from the income, for the injured person was a workman whose wages were subject to P.A.Y.E. Lord Sorn stated that to ignore the tax position at the present day was to be out of "touch with reality"—a phrase that echoes through the House of Lords judgments.

Counsel for Mr. Gourley put great stress on the remoteness argument. Income tax on profits is not usually paid until a year or more after the money has been earned; surtax is paid at an even later date. To estimate the future tax rate of the particular taxpayer is not easy, particularly as the rate will vary with personal and changing factors—such as the wife's earnings, covenants to pay annual sums to third persons, and so on. If based on net income, damages would thus vary greatly with the peculiarities of each taxpayer's circumstances. Further, if the chain of relevant consequences is to be lengthened till it includes tax, why should not regard be paid to other financial circumstances, *e.g.*, the injured man may have to give up his life insurance policy, or sell investments and real estate at a loss.

Counsel for the Transport Commission argued that the award is not a penalty, and therefore its only measure is fair compensation to the injured man for his losses. The man's gross income is part of the evidence, but so also are any disadvantages that go hand-in-hand with the income, such as expenses and liabilities; and the

[4] [1949] 1 K.B. 643; 65 T.L.R. 246; [1949] 1 All E.R. 684.
[5] 1946 S.C 462.

disadvantages must include tax imposed by statute. The *balance* between the gross income and its disadvantages is what is to be made good; if the injured person receives more than this balance, he reaps a profit from his accident. It is incorrect to assume—as was done in *Billingham* v. *Hughes*—that the defendant is in the position of a person who contracts to replace lost earnings.

Six of the seven judges accepted the appellant's argument. While some part of their speeches was given up to a survey of the earlier cases, their reasoning was not legalistic in any narrow sense; rather did it deal with the general problem of whether, under present-day conditions, tax is so remote and insignificant that it should any longer be left out of account in assessing lost income.

Three of the judges touched on the difficulties of calculating tax. Their opinion was that the calculation must of necessity be inexact; "but such an estimate will be none the worse if it is formed on broad lines, even though it may be described as rough and ready. It is impossible to assess with mathematical accuracy what reduction should be made by reason of the tax position just as it is impossible to assess with mathematical accuracy the amount of damages which should be awarded for the injury itself and for the pain and suffering endured" (Earl Jowitt).

The dissenting judgment was by Lord Keith of Avonholm. His argument was that the tax position of an injured person is no concern of the wrongdoer, and ought not to lessen the damages. A wrongdoer is not allowed to say that the injured person does not need full compensation because he has a wealthy wife or an independent income. "The law would say the wealthy wife and the independent income are not his concern. But by taking net income after payment of tax as the measure of damages the wrongdoer achieves by a back door precisely what is refused to him by the direct entrance." Further, to bring tax into the picture is to introduce many difficulties and complexities; for instance, if the injured person is a foreigner, British courts would have to pay regard to an alien tax system.[6]

COMMENT

The whole case manifestly turned on the question of whether, as a matter of common sense, tax is so closely bound up with earnings as to demand inclusion in any estimate of the loss suffered when a man cannot work. The expenses normally charged in his profit-and-loss account ought to be deducted from gross income in computing his true loss; and the tax that he must inevitably pay, as a direct result of earning his net profit, also seems a strong candidate for deduction. It is not "income after expenses" but "income after tax" which gives a man his spendable income.

[6] One can speculate on the labours that might follow the crash of a British aircraft full of assorted foreigners.

In the modern world, this has surely become part-and-parcel of our attitude to income. Further, it is a commonplace, to anyone possessing even a nodding acquaintance with business, that tax must be kept prominently in mind when almost any kind of financial decision is to be made. In these circumstances, one can hardly suppose that any group of knowledgeable men, if they were asked to comment on the issues of the *Gourley* case, would have been likely to leave tax out of an unbiased calculation.

An imperfect knowledge of the facts of the *Gourley* case might however suggest that the decision somehow involved the deduction of tax twice over, and so was unjust. There was not, in those particular circumstances, double deduction. But in other cases, with different circumstances, the danger might be real.

Let us use figures to illustrate the point. Suppose that an injured man loses £1,500 per annum of gross income, and that he pays tax on this marginal slice of income at an average rate of 6s. 8d. in the £, so that his net loss is £1,000 per annum.[7]

It will be convenient to distinguish three ways in which his compensation money might be "invested" by the injured man: (a) he might simply deposit this capital receipt in, *e.g.*, a bank, and then gradually withdraw the capital and treat it as income; (b) he might use the compensation to buy shares, and then live on the dividends; or (c) he might buy an annuity.

(a) *Capital treated as income*

Suppose first that the injured man's circumstances approximate to those in the *Gourley* case: he is already sixty-five, is expected to retire in a short period of say five more years, and so—given our imaginary figures—loses a total future income of £7,500 gross, or £5,000 net. Following the *Gourley* decision, he will receive £5,000 as damages. This money will not be taxed; so he can put the whole £5,000 in the bank and then withdraw it at the rate of £1,000 each year. He thus consumes capital over the five years, and pays no tax on the sums withdrawn; his spendable income for the period is the full £5,000, as it should be. He might in fact get rather more than £5,000, if he took the obvious step of depositing his damages at interest. This extra receipt (which might well attract tax) is not large where the period to retirement is relatively short. But in all cases the interest factor will lessen the lump sum which the defendants should pay; though the injured man keeps the money under his own control, his cash position over the five years will have the same advantages as if he had bought a five-year annuity-certain. In the *Gourley* case, the trial judge made a deduction (based on the 4 per cent. tables) of about one-ninth as a fair allowance under this head; tax on the interest was apparently

7 Doubtless no real case would be concerned with a tax rate so straightforward as this. For instance, the switch from profits to interest (on the compensation) may bring a limitation in earned income relief.

ignored—despite Mr. Gourley's high tax rate, which would reduce his effective receipts of interest almost at zero.

(b) *Income derived from dividends, etc.*

Now consider a different case in which the time period is much longer—say, the injured man is still only thirty, and is expected to lose forty years' income. If he is presented with all his income as a lump sum in advance, he will feel more than satisfied, even though he receives forty prepayments of his net income (£40,000), and not of his gross income (£60,000). With such a long span of years ahead of him interest is no longer somewhat insignificant as in (a). He will invest his £40,000 in shares or other securities; these may, on a 5 per cent. basis, yield him £2,000 a year. True, the £2,000 will be taxable, and so he will (on our assumption that his tax rate is 6s. 8d.) be left with only £1,333 to spend each year. He is still better off than if he lets his capital lie idle till he consumes it at the rate of £1,000 per annum; further, he has the full £40,000 left when he reaches seventy (and a larger sum if continuing inflation has pushed up the money-value of his equities).

Here it would not seem unfair to award a smaller lump sum. Its amount should, however, be big enough to allow for the deduction of tax from dividends, *i.e.*, it should yield a gross income of £1,500. Investments costing £30,000 would, on our assumptions, be enough to yield that income. After deducting tax from his £1,500 of dividends, the investor would be left with a spendable income of £1,000. To reduce the damages to below £30,000, by subtracting tax, would indeed be double deduction, and would leave the investor with less than the agreed figure of £1,000 as spendable income.

Thus, as the expected life grows longer, a point is reached at which it pays the defendants to abandon a literal interpretation of the *Gourley* case, and to offer instead a lump sum that yields the full gross income.

(c) *Income derived from an annuity*

The clash in methods under (a) and (b) above can be resolved if we refine the discussion by bringing in annuities. In (b), as in (a), the defendants might well argue that they would satisfy justice by paying the present value of an annuity-certain, *i.e.*, the sum with which the injured man could buy an annuity to run for a stipulated number of years. This arrangement would reduce the damages; in our examples, the purchase price of the five-year annuity of £1,000 would be (on a 5 per cent. basis) £4,330, and that of a forty-year annuity only £17,159. However, part of each year's instalment of £1,000 might be treated by the Inland Revenue as interest, and taxed. This interest-content is usually regarded as varying over the years; in the first instalment it is at its maximum (and is large relative to the £1,000 where the annuity will be paid over a long period), and it sinks in each subsequent instalment till it reaches a negligible sum in the last instalment. Provided the compensation is increased to a point at which the net annuity (after tax) is still £1,000, on average over the years, the argument for the annuity-certain has plausibility.

However, the defendant might now carry the argument a step further, and take expectation of life into account. The cost of the £1,000 annuity would sink if the insurance company had to pay it only till the annuitant reached seventy or to his earlier death; in the case of the man aged sixty-five the damages would fall to about £3,332, and in the case of the man aged thirty to £16,328. Prior to the proposals of the 1956 Finance Bill (under discussion at the time of writing) there was a grave objection to this approach; for the whole instalment of a life annuity (and not merely its interest-content, as with the annuity-certain) was normally treated by the Inland Revenue as revenue, and so tax was paid on the whole £1,000. If the Chancellor's new proposals become effective, this objection will presumably vanish, and the interest-content alone will be diminished by tax.

We have so far assumed retiral date to be the limit beyond which the annuity should not run. In some circumstances, however, the annuity should presumably run till the injured man's death, even if he lives to a hundred; where a post carries a pension, or the injured man will still need costly care after he retires, some or all of the annual payments might well continue so long as he lives. This would raise the cost of the life-annuity—in our two imaginary cases, to about £9,080 and to £17,060 respectively, for yearly instalments of £1,000.

An annuity that is terminated by death seems at first sight to resemble closely the stream of lost earnings, and so to be admirable as compensation. But it has one serious disadvantage (even if the burden imposed on it by the Inland Revenue is lightened). When an inflation takes place, profits and salaries tend to rise in step with prices, so that real income is maintained. Accordingly, damages for lost earnings—it can surely be argued—will be inadequate if they do not allow for the likelihood of changing price-levels; to ignore inflation nowadays seems fully as "out of touch with reality" as to ignore tax. The injured person might perhaps be content if his compensation was based on a scale of earnings higher than that prevailing at the award date; but a more satisfactory scheme would be one that let him invest a substantial sum in highly geared equities, so that he would have some prospect of maintaining his real income as prices rise. If this reasoning is accepted, an annuity (whose instalments are rigidly fixed in terms of money) is far too speculative for a man with a long life ahead. Whether or not a court would accept this argument is another matter; however, it unquestionably provides the only safe method for investing whatever compensation is received.

The above paragraphs boil down to a simple enough rule. The injured person should have as much to spend after the accident as before it. Where he will consume the actual lump sum awarded as compensation, tax can reasonably be deducted in fixing its amount. The amount can also be reduced where—because enough time passes between the award date and his spending of the money—the lump sum will itself be a source of earnings; but this deduction must be limited to allow for tax levied on the earnings by the Inland Revenue, *i.e.*, the discount rate used in the calculation should be the net rate left after the particular individual has paid tax.

OTHER TYPES OF CASE: UNEARNED INCOME

What light does this analysis throw on cases other than those for accident damages?

When compensation is paid for *loss of office*, the argument appears to be on all fours with what has been said above—provided that the lump sum is again not taxed by the Inland Revenue. Normally it is exempt,[8] being regarded as the capital equivalent of the lost future income. The *Gourley* decision has in fact been applied in *Beach* v. *Reed Corrugated Cases, Ltd.*[9] But it was here qualified in an important respect. The plaintiff's income was made up of (a) salary and fees from employment, and (b) a large private income from disposable investments (an element that seems to have been left out of account in the *Gourley* case). If (a) alone was considered, the tax rate was roughly 11s. in the £; if (b) also was considered, the rate rose to about 18s. The size of the award by Pilcher J. shows that he felt the appropriate rate to be much nearer 11s. than 18s., *i.e.*, that little regard should be paid to income of type (b) in estimating general damages.

In cases of *compulsory acquisition of property*, the reasoning of earlier pages again seems applicable; and, happily, this reasoning also fits in with the rules for valuing assets in normal cases. The loss of an asset usually involves loss of profits or other income, not for some limited term such as the years till the owner's retirement, but for an indefinite future period. The lost asset can be looked on as the capital that yields a perpetuity. Its fair value in the eyes of the dispossessed owner is presumably the amount that will, when reinvested in another asset carrying equal risks, yield the same receipts for as far into the future as the eye can reach. The whole of each year's receipts will be income, and taxable. So the compensation must not be diminished by deducting tax; the facts have here narrowed down until they somewhat resemble those assumed in case (b) on p. 370 (where the injured person lives on dividends). Or, to put the matter in another way, asset values

8 *Henley* v. *Murray* [1950] 1 All E.R. 908.

9 [1956] 1 W.L.R. 807.

fixed by the market or an appraiser have already been reduced to allow for the tax that will be levied on the asset's fruits, and must not be reduced further.

The analogy with a perpetuity may not always be apt. The diminution in the owner's income, following the loss of his asset, may seem likely to be temporary—for instance, the asset may be of the wasting type. Here the compensation should be regarded as an annuity-certain for a limited number of years. The *Gourley* decision has already been applied in a case that savours somewhat of this situation,[10] though in fact it was for *trespass* and *conversion*; compensation for loss of one year's rent of farm lands was restricted to the rent less tax (and, as the plaintiff was a company, " tax " here meant income and profits tax); damages for loss of a hay crop, etc. (being themselves possibly subject to tax by the Inland Revenue), were not restricted.

W. T. BAXTER.*

[10] *Hall* v. *Pearlberg* [1956] 1 W.L.R. 244.

* B.Com.(Edin.); C.A.; Professor of Accounting in the University of London.

PARTNERSHIP RIGHTS

PARTNERSHIP RIGHTS

THE VALUATION PROBLEM

By W. T. BAXTER

Though partnership is much older than the limited company, a partner's rights may well seem harder to evaluate than those of a shareholder. The reason is partly that the company divorces the rewards of capital and management more cleanly; and partly that company shares are dealt in more often and held more widely, and so have become familiar.

When a new partner is admitted, the men concerned have to assess arrangements that may involve a "capital", a "premium" and a "loan"; and the matter may be still further complicated by the use of "goodwill". What the men would find of assistance is a logical frame into which each arrangement can be fitted, so that they can compare alternatives—seeming to involve different kinds of rights and different sums of money—and, if possible, reduce them to some common basis.

Three ways suggest themselves as aids to understanding. First, we may see how far the analogy with companies is helpful. Second, we may use balance sheets as models. And, third, we may try the experiment of using diagrams.

Company Analogy

First, let us see how far the analogy with companies is helpful. The partnership contract may provide that profits are to be divided on a triple basis: "salaries" and "interest" form the first two slices, and then the surplus is split in some agreed fraction. However, it is doubtful whether the chosen figures for salary and interest are close to market rates (for example, to the sums foregone by the partners, as personal earnings and interest on capitals, when they join the firm). The figures often seem meant instead to allow for *differences* in each man's personal and financial contributions; and for instance a rate of interest that acts as a fair penalty on a small excess of drawings is likely to be much less than the full market rate for the whole capital.

For this and other reasons, partnership rights do not necessarily have close equivalents in the rights accorded to the men providing management and finance to companies. The slice of profit that goes as partners' salaries may or may not be comparable in size with the salary and fees of a company official; where a partner's salary differs from his market worth, one must assume that some remuneration classed under another head in the partnership contract is in fact personal reward. In many instances, a partner's loan (or "advance") may correspond fairly well with a first Preference share. So far as concerns the remaining rights, much depends on whether the partners' book-capitals are fully stated, in the sense of being complete and up-to-date values (a situation which I shall call "full valuation" and treat more fully on pages 173-5). Thus partner's capital bears some likeness to a second Preference share, but with "full valuation" lacks the capital cover given to such shares by Ordinary shares. Rights to surplus may sometimes compare broadly with Ordinary shares—particularly if the total of partners' capitals is well below full valuation, and if profit is shared in the ratio of those capitals. This matter of profit ratios is of great importance, and will dog our heels throughout the discussion. Presumably because personal qualities loom bigger in partnership than do capital contributions, surplus is often split between partners in ratios that do *not* correspond with their capitals; and so the analogy with Ordinary shares is weakened.

Balance Sheet Models

Balance sheet models may be short-cuts to understanding. Thus a useful trick for comparing two arrangements is to write down (or up) the balance sheet figures found in one arrangement (for example, by altering the "goodwill") until the totals in both arrangements are the same.

Diagrams

Sometimes one may grasp the facts more readily if one is helped by

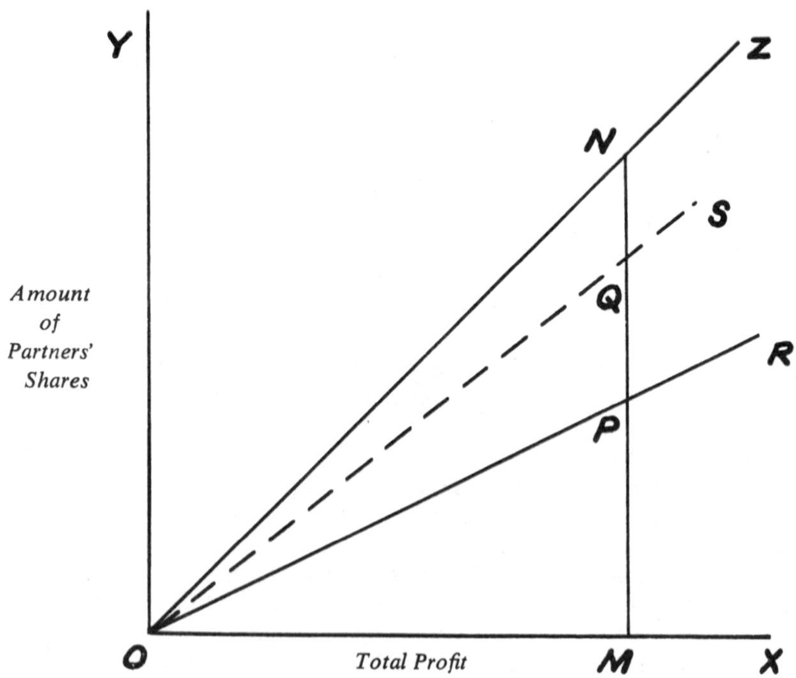

Diagram 1

diagrams like those used in an economics textbook. These diagrams seem well suited to show the facts where there are only two partners.

Division of Annual Profits

As an hors d'œuvre to heavier fare, let us now ask how the division of annual profits might be explained in diagrams.

In Diagram 1, annual profit is measured along OX; the parts of this total sum taken by each of two partners—call them A and B—are measured up OY. The line OZ is the "45-degree line", bisecting angle YOX. So if a perpendicular is drawn from OX at any point M, to cut OZ at N, then OM = MN; and if the total profit for a year is OM, it will be shown also by MN, and its division can conveniently be measured by points on MN. Where A and B split profits equally, A's share can be represented by MP and B's share by NP (= MP). Points corresponding with P, showing the sizes of the equal shares earned by A and B when total profits vary in other years, fall along OPR. A line such as OPR may be called a "share-line". If A and B share profits in the ratio 4 : 1 instead of 1 : 1, A's share of total profit rises to MQ, while B's share shrinks to NQ (where MQ = 4NQ); and the share-line moves up to OQS.

Partners' Salaries and Interest

In Diagram 2, the share line OR gives the division of profits if they are shared 3 : 2, and if (as in Diagram 1) no salary of the like is credited to a partner.

If now A is credited with a salary, the line OR in Diagram 2 moves up to S′S. (PQ, the growth in A's part of revenue, is not the whole salary, but is the salary minus his share of the fall in surplus due to charging the salary.)

When profit gets lower, M moves to the left along the X axis, and the resultant fall in A's share is shown by the shrinkage of the distance between OX and the share-line. If profit falls to nothing, A's share is OT; thanks to the salary, he still is credited with a positive sum. If profit moves still further left (that is, becomes negative), his share sinks till it reaches zero at M_2; and a bigger loss gives him a negative share (for example, M_3Q_3 if the results of the year are a loss of OM_3).

Similarly, B (whose share is the distance, such as NQ, between Z′Z and the share-line) has a share that shrinks to nothing at profit OM_1. If profit falls further, his share may be shown by a vertical line running up from a suitable point on $Z'Q_2$ to $S'Q_2$, and is negative. Thus, if the firm had a loss of OM_3, B's share is N_3Q_3. Here A's share of the loss (M_3Q_3) is, thanks to his salary, smaller than B's; but, as the loss increases, his share of it grows faster than B's, and eventually becomes the bigger.

Capital

A figure for the nominal Ordinary capital of a company means remarkably little. Do partners' figures mean any more?

The answer seems to be that, except where unequal capitals lead to material differences in profit-sharing through their effect on interest, capital balances are unimportant[1]—till a partner leaves. Then they suddenly acquire significance, as guides to final settlement. The partnership deed should be very

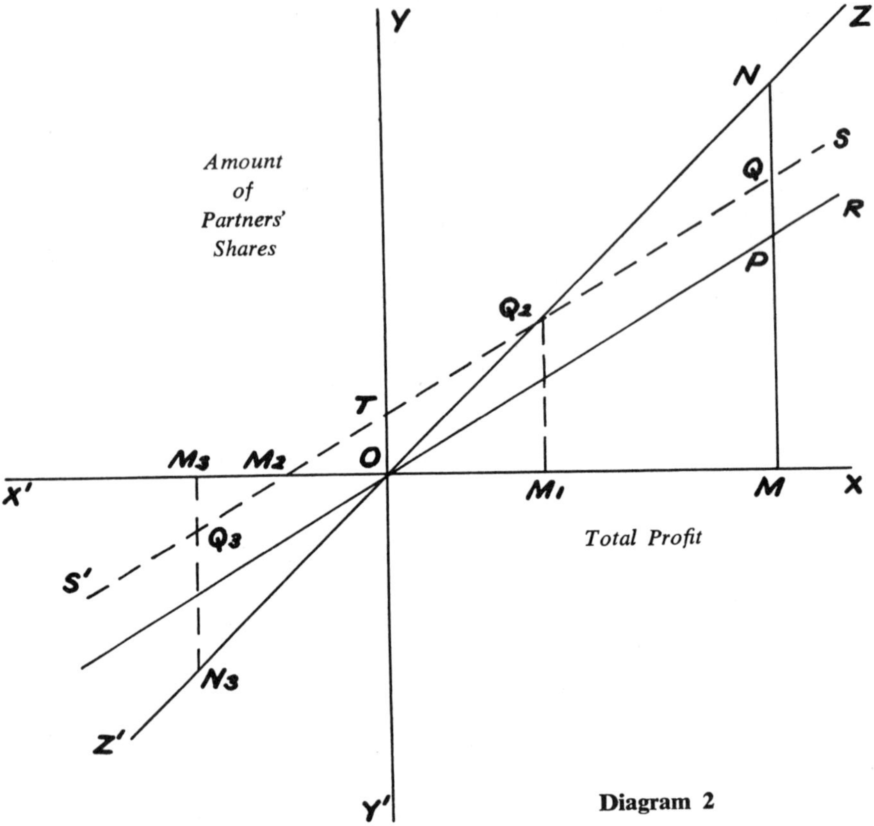

Diagram 2

clear on what happens at this stage, and, in particular, should explain precisely how capital gains and losses are to be split.

Diagram 3 tries to show how capital rights are shared. OX gives the firm's total wealth, and OY gives each partner's share of this total. When the balance sheet puts net assets at OM, partner A's capital account might amount to MP and partners B's to NP. The scale used in Diagram 3 is consistent with a balance sheet such as:

		£			£
A—Capital	...	5,000	Net assets ...	...	7,000
B—Capital	...	2,000			
		£7,000			£7,000

[1] I assume that there is, for our present purposes, no difference between a partner's capital account and his current account—that is to say, a partner's whole "capital" is here the total of his nominal capital and his current account.

OM can show whatever capital values seems most helpful to the partners —for example, existing book values, or full valuation (based either on income prospects or realisation proceeds).

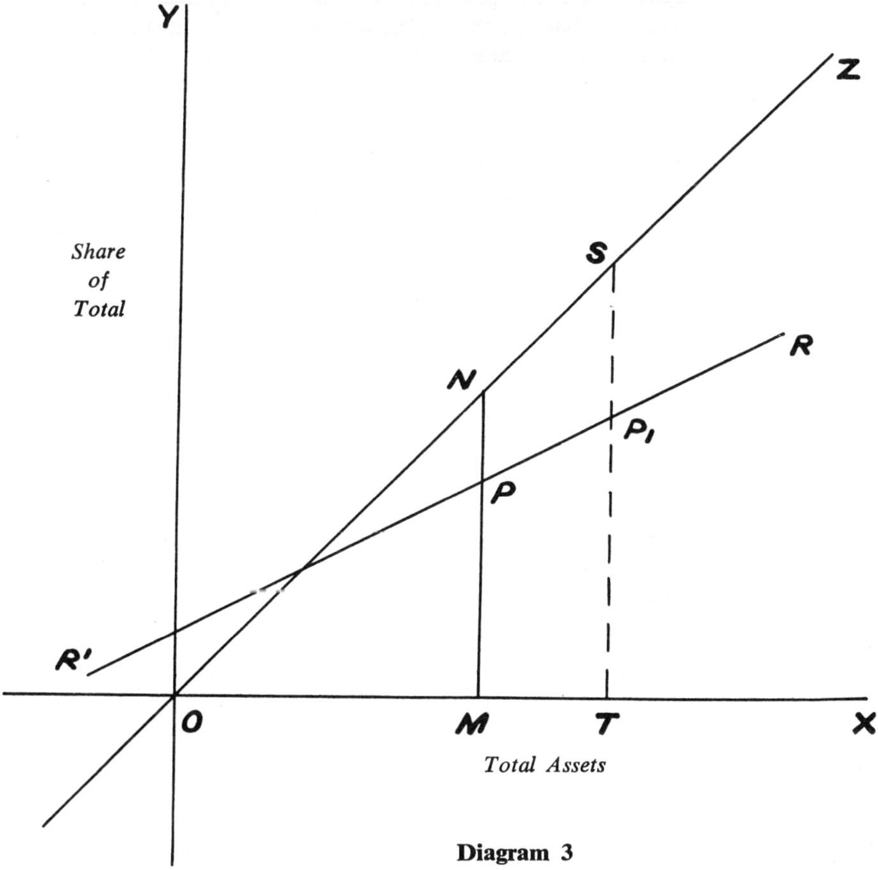

Diagram 3

The slope of the share-line depends on the ratio in which capital gains are divided. Diagram 3 assumes A and B share equally.

Where two partners are both active in management, and contribute material parts of the capital, there seems a good deal to be said for sharing capital gains in the same ratio as that used for sharing annual profits. However, there may be exceptional cases—for instance, where the sleeping partner contributes the whole capital and the active partner contributes only management. Here the active partner is given a share of annual profit to spur him to further zeal. His zeal may also be stimulated by the prospect of a capital profit when the firm winds up; but he will probably regard himself as ill-used if winding up results in a loss and consequent need for him to pay capital to his sleeping partner. If he objects to bearing a capital loss, should he forfeit gains too? At least the contract should be specific on the point.

Just as the nominal capital of a company plus its reserves are unlikely to reflect exactly the price that the enterprise will fetch if sold, so the partners' accounts may not predict the actual proceeds. Suppose that A and B (see balance sheet on page 164) sell their business, and it fetches £10,000. The gain of £3,000 must now be divided between A and B. If they have agreed to share capital gains equally, the balance sheet becomes:

	£		£
A (£5,000 + £1,500)	6,500	Cash, etc. (proceeds	
B (£2,000 + £1,500)	3,500	of realisation) ...	10,000
	£10,000		£10,000

On Diagram 3 we show the change by extending the assets from OM to OT; A's share, hitherto MP, goes to TP_1; and B's share NP to SP_1.

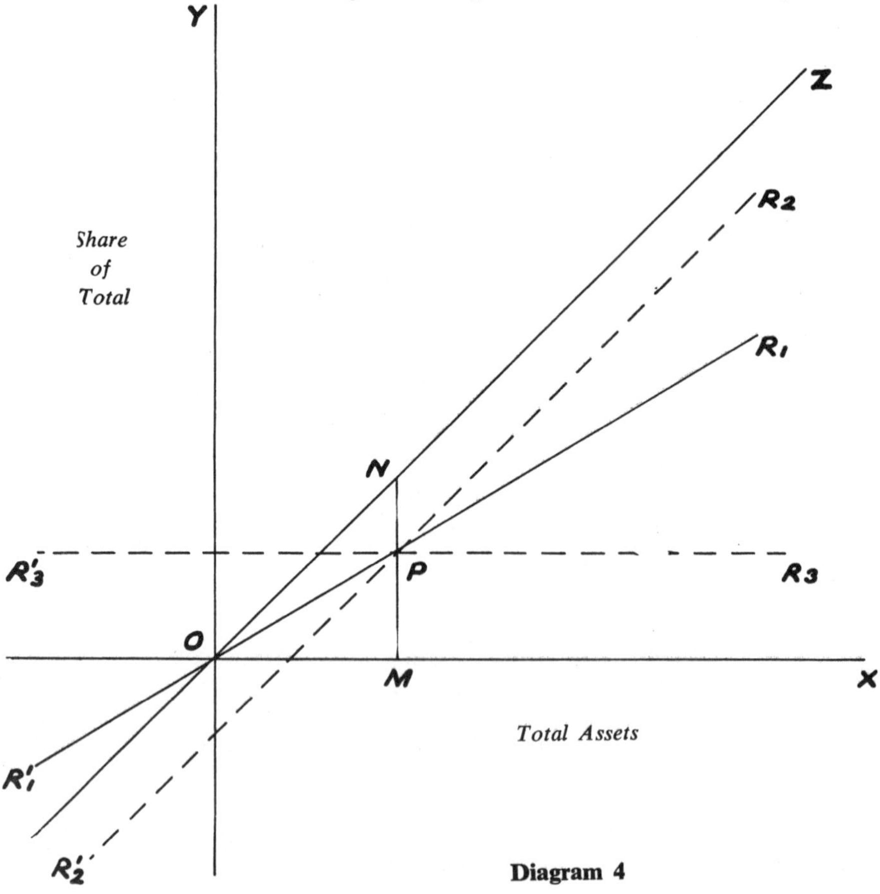

Diagram 4

Where partners can with some confidence forecast a big gain on realisation (that is, where MT is likely to be both large and positive), the slope of the capital share-line R′R is something worth bargaining over. The same holds where MT is likely to be both large and negative. However, OM may seem a good valuation in the sense that MT is likely to be tiny; then there is no point in fussing about the capital share-line. OM may also be a good valuation in the sense that MT, though it could be big, is just as likely to be negative as positive; here a partner might well feel sadly unsure about what slope to prefer, knowing that a handsome share of potential gain carries a handsome share of potential loss.

The share-line will pass neatly through O only if capital gains and losses are divided in the ratio of capitals. This situation is shown in Diagram 4. Here the balance sheet runs (at the point M):

		£			£
A—capital	...	3,000	Net assets ...	...	5,000
B—capital	...	2,000			
		£5,000			£5,000

Gains and losses are shared 3 : 2; so, if all the assets have to be written down to zero, A and B alike end with capitals of *nil*. The share-line is R'_1R_1.

The line swings round on P if the ratio is changed. The two limiting cases are likely to be those in which, first, the senior partner A takes all the gains and losses (suggested in Diagram 4 by the share-line R'_2R_2, which shows that the junior partner B will take a fixed capital NP whatever the profit); and, second, where A has a completely fixed capital MP and lets B take the gains and losses (see R'_3R_3).

The role of the capital figures in the ledger is thus to provide the starting point for calculations at final settlement; they define the position of P—the pivot round which the share-line rotates. In a company with only two Ordinary shareholders, their nominal holdings give the slope of the share-line, which must go through O; in a two-man partnership, nominal capitals define the fixed point on the line, and its slope is a matter of agreement.

Valuation of New Partner's Rights

Now let us turn to the central issue of the value to be put on the rights transferred to a new partner. Assume that he agrees to pay the old partners a suitable amount of money as a price, in return for some given share in capital rights and in annual profits. (Owing largely to the weight of taxation, and the consequent difficulty of saving capital, nowadays the price in a professional firm is apt to be low or *nil*, or may in effect be treated at first as a loan to the newcomer, who pays it off by instalments out of his later profits. Our discussion, however, is not limited to the professional firm.) The price naturally depends on the value of the rights transferred. How is it fixed?

The Partnership Market

People are naturally secretive about their incomes, so it may be hard to find out what size of salary is commonly paid for a new partner's services. Again, the market for partnership capital, compared with the stock exchange, is minute and private; no list of yields is to hand. Accordingly, to use the word "market" in the context of partnership is perhaps to stretch the language of economics beyond normal usage. The word here means no more than that the existing partners in a firm, and its potential new partners, can make guesses about the prices paid elsewhere for services and capital. Because neither side is likely to get much outside guidance in fixing its terms, these can be reached only by a very imperfect process of private bargaining.

Presumably the yield on partnership capital should be: (a) the yield on shares in a company whose trade risks are the same, *plus* (b) an allowance for the acute difficulties of transfer. What about the further risk from unlimited liability? Compensation for this risk can hardly take the form of an extra percentage yield on capital invested. The risk is not necessarily proportional to the size of such capital; indeed, a partner who invests no capital has still to shoulder the full risk of losing his private assets. The compensation should probably consist of a lump sum added to personal remuneration.

Conceivably we are wrong to think of separate prices for a partner's services and capital. The hazards of investment in some firms may be such that the investor will not put in risk capital unless he can become a partner and so keep an eye on it—that is to say, man and money are in joint supply, and the two prices cannot be unravelled.

Alternative Budgets

As an illustration, let us take a case where A is a sole trader who is thinking of taking in B as a partner. A will naturally assess the *pros* and *cons* of this grave step. In part, they can hardly enter into a money calculus: for instance, A must weigh the chances of shedding strain and work against the chances of B's proving uncongenial. In money terms, he will try to compare his receipts (including capital on his retirement) after B's entry with the receipts he would obtain by carrying on in the best alternative way—which might, for instance, be to hire more staff, or to merge with a rival firm, or to sell off the assets and take a salaried job. Differences in risk may be a complication (for example, A's best alternative may be to withdraw money from an uncertain trade and invest in blue chips). Only if his satisfactions and money receipts from partnership with B seem likely to exceed those from the best alternative plan (that is to say, his opportunity costs) will A take in B.

Similarly B will compare his prospects within the partnership and outside (though perhaps in other partnerships). He will not join A unless benefits outweigh sacrifices. He, too, must weigh some factors that are hard to put in money terms: partnership means interesting work and social esteem; however, it also means worry, loss of freedom, and the embarrassments that may attend unlimited liability. (We can only guess the net effect of these conflicting factors. Possibly there is a balance in favour of being a partner where the risks are slight—for example, in a profession—and against where the risks are high—for example, in most trades.) He must also guess what his money receipts will be if he does not join A.

The drafting and comparison of alternative budgets involves many imponderables and some appallingly difficult judgments. Looking at the process in cold blood, we may well marvel that agreement is ever reached. Fortunately, most men are able to make decisions—about matters even graver than partnership—without undue analysis; at many points, no doubt, "judgment" serves instead of arithmetic. So it may well be that the actual calculations of potential partners do not split many hairs, never reach paper, and deal only in round numbers. Further, a wish to start the new association on good terms will doubtless temper each man's inclination to press for the last penny.

However, if we are to understand the issues at stake, we must analyse a set of figures in some detail—perhaps, indeed, with more refinement than is possible in practice.

Opportunity Costs and Economic Rent

Let us suppose that A and B, having considered all the possibilities, both decide that as partners they could jointly earn £5,800 a year (without extra capital being paid in by B); that A could earn £4,000 a year by carrying on the business without B, or £3,100 a year by dismantling the business (investing the proceeds in an equally risky trade and taking a salaried job); and that B on his own could earn almost £1,400 a year. A's alternative budgets thus run:

Table 1
ESTIMATES OF FUTURE ANNUAL EARNINGS

	(i) *Partnership* £	(ii) *A alone* £	(iii) *Sell out* £
(1) Firm's profit	5,800	4,000	—
A's revenue if he sells out:			
(2) Salary elsewhere			1,900
(3) Interest elsewhere			1,200
(4) Total			3,100
(5) B's salary elsewhere	1,400		
(6) Surplus after (5)	4,400		
(7) Surplus of (i) over other alternatives	—	400	1,300
	£4,400	£4,400	£4,400

Comparing the columns, we see that A will prefer the partnership. Column (iii) shows that selling out is the least rewarding of the three courses. Column (ii) shows that A's second-best course is to carry on alone; so his appropriate opportunity cost (for his decision about partnership) is the revenue from carrying on alone, that is, £4,000 a year, and the partnership will yield (see line (7)) a surplus or "economic rent" of £400.

Other things being equal, A will on no account consent to any arrangement that does not give him the benefit of at least the £4,000. For his part, B will insist on receiving at least (5), £1,400—without paying any price for this income. But who gets (7), the "economic rent" of £400?

Common sense suggests that A usually has the whip-hand here, since he is likely to control whatever scarce thing it is that yields the rent (for example, the firm's name, its connections, and its organisation); B might need years to build up a similar monopoly.

However, perhaps we should not feel too sorry for B. If he has a good training and ability, other firms will want him too, so his opportunity costs will be high. (Note that the estimates in Table 1 hold only for B or someone of the same qualities. If C, a lad of rare talent and connections, is the candidate, the firm's profits are likely to improve, that is, the £5,800 on line (1) must be changed into a bigger figure; but then the newcomer's demands—item (5)—may also go up; and thus the surplus on line (7) may go either up or down.) And there is no rigid rule that the old must necessarily enjoy all rents. One can conceive of situations—though they may be unusual—in which the young enjoy the monopoly (as where, in a small town, B is the only eligible person known to an elderly A in dire need of help or funds). Further, in practice A and B will not both draw up identical alternative budgets, or feel at all sure about their own figures. Such conflicts in expectations will strengthen the natural wish of the parties to bargain, giving plenty of scope for manœuvre and chaffering. Logic can lay down limits, but cannot tell us what the outcome should be within those limits: A and B will split the £400 according to their bargaining skill.

We shall suppose that A knows his strength, and declines to give away any of the £400. He may however be willing to *sell* income—so enabling B to receive more than the £1,400 in line (5). What is the maximum that A can sell? The limit may be hard to define in practice. B will dislike paying for more income than he is tolerably sure will be maintained in future years. Thus B will not want A's residue to be so low that A may lose interest in the firm, and grow slack or take a job elsewhere. Let us say that, in the case of A and B, the disposable income is total profit less the partners' potential earnings outside.

Table 2

PROFITS AT DISPOSAL OF A

	£	£
Partnership profit, as on line (1) of Table 1		5,800
Less Opportunity costs of services:		
A—as on line (2)	1,900	
B—as on line (5)	1,400	
		3,300
Disposable annual profit		£2,500

The discounted present value of this annuity of £2,500 is—by the test of market value—A's true capital in the firm.

For whatever part of the annuity he buys, B must therefore pay a suitable price. For simplicity, we shall assume that the whole of B's price is given privately to A, and is not used to expand the firm's resources and so change the future earnings given in Table 1.

It may be that B wants to invest a given amount of capital. In that event, A and B will bargain over what part of the annuity goes to B in return for the fixed amount; in practice, this slice of income in not stated in so many £'s (perhaps because the future size of the annuity is subject to the risks of trade) but is expressed in B's vulgar fraction of surplus profits. Or instead A may want to sell a given share of profits—in which event, it is B's price that emerges as the answer to the sum. It will suit our exposition better to take the former situation, and to suppose that B wants to invest a given amount, namely £3,600. What fraction of profits should the agreement give him?

Finding the Fraction of Surplus

As was noticed at the outset, rates of salary and interest in a partnership agreement tend to be conventional and unrelated to opportunity costs. This complication is unfortunate, but we cannot here ignore it if we are to be realistic.

Suppose that the contract between A and B lays down conventional rates —for instance:

Salary of A	£1,500 per annum
Salary of B	£1,000 per annum
Interest on capital	5 per cent. per annum

Neither man will consent to the contract unless his fraction of the surplus raises these figures at least to his full opportunity costs. So—even though the contract ignores the point, and A and B are hazy about how they reached their terms—we should look on part of their shares of surplus as hidden payments for services and capital.

The opportunity cost of the services of A is £1,900, whereas his nominal salary is only £1,500; therefore, £400 of his share of surplus is concealed remuneration. The hidden remuneration of B happens also to be £400 (£1,400–£1,000). Because profits fluctuate, the shares of profit are sure in fact to vary each year from the target of £400. Thus they are rather like the commission on profit that may be paid to managers, and so we can conveniently call them "commission".

Partner B must buy any income that he receives in excess of his £1,400 of salary and commission. All this excess is therefore—from his standpoint—return on his capital. The 5 per cent. allowed in the contract is a wholly inadequate yield if the trade is risky; in that case, B's share of surplus (after his commission) must in fact be the supplementary reward needed to boost 5 per cent. to the full market rate. Like commission, this income will vary from year to year, and may for convenience be called "dividend".

Let us put the current market price of partnership capital at four times the corresponding income. In other words, we suppose that a yield of 25 per cent. can be obtained by investing in firms whose trading receipts are equally risky, but whose assets offer the same security from scrap values. (The second point suggests that the assets mentioned in line (3) of Table 1 can be sold for £4,800.)

It follows that, as B is paying £3,600, he should each year get £180 (=5 per cent.) as interest, and also a dividend of £720 (=20 per cent.). Further, as the total disposable income is £2,500 per annum (see Table 2), the total capital value of the firm is about £10,000.[2]

The figures can be put in a table that readily shows each man's fraction.

Table 3

ANALYSIS OF RETURN IF PRICE=£3,600

	Total £	*A* £	*B* £
Capital	10,000	6,400	3,600
Profit	5,800		
Less Nominal Salaries	2,500	1,500	1,000
Profit after salaries	3,300		
Less Interest on capital (5 per cent. on £10,000) ...	500	320	180
Surplus after interest and salaries	2,800		
Commission	800	400	400
Balance—dividend	2,000		
B's share, 20 per cent. on £3,600			720
A's share, 20 per cent. on £6,400		1,280	
	2,800	1,680	1,120
Fraction of surplus		3/5	2/5

Thus the contract will give effect to the partners' wishes if it says that surplus is to be split 3 : 2.

If, instead, A began by deciding to sell a two-fifths share, then some of the lines in the table would be rearranged, and the price of £3,600 would be the end-product.

What happens if B wants to invest a smaller amount—say £800? If A and

[2] The critical reader may rightly point out that I am over-simplifying in assuming that the value of the firm is proportionate to the value of B's share; in the realm of value, the whole does not always equal the sum of the parts—for example, where one share in a company with a million shares sells for £1, the whole capital might sell for much more or less than £1,000,000. My answer is that a first exposition would be well-nigh impossible without the simplification; and, further, that as the aim is to show the partners' *relative* positions, an error is unlikely to be important unless one partner's proportion of a large firm vastly exceeds the other partners' proportions.

B act consistently, B should get much less surplus for this investment; the reduction in his fixed interest (now 5 per cent. of £800 instead of 5 per cent. of £3,600) is not sufficient to match the fall in his investment. On the 20 per cent. basis, his dividend must be reduced to £160, and so his fraction of annual surplus to one-fifth:

Table 4

ANALYSIS OF RETURN IF PRICE=£800

	Total	*A*	*B*
	£	£	£
Commission	800	400	400
Dividend	2,000	1,840	160
	2,800	2,240	560
Fraction of surplus		4/5	1/5

When B cannot pay any price at all, he should—given the assumption on which we have been working, that A declines to give away any of his economic rent—get merely his £1,000 salary and £400 commission each year; £400 is one-seventh of £2,800, so the surplus should be split in the ratio 6 : 1.

All our calculations and arguments have been based on an estimate of future annual profit put in the form of a single figure and, similarly, other estimated quantities each expressed as a single figure (see Table 1). We ignore the complication that, in theory at least, the profit and other quantities may be estimated at fluctuating figures over a period of years in the future.

Book-keeping on Admission—Real Capital not Expanded

We turn to deal with the various ways in which our friends A and B might record their partnership agreement in their ledger.

If a man buys existing shares in a company, he makes a private payment to a shareholder, and the wealth in the company does not rise. We shall therefore be on familiar ground if we start our study of new partners by taking a corresponding situation. A price is paid by B to A in return for some of A's rights in the firm; the price is handed over privately to A (or if paid into the firm is immediately withdrawn by A) so that, whatever the entries in the books, the real wealth of the firm does not expand.

We must distinguish between two possible treatments of book values: (a) the existing book values may be written up (for example, by the insertion of a goodwill figure) to bring them into line with the full current value of the firm, or (b) the book values may be left at conservative figures.

(*a*) *Book Figures Raised to Full Valuation*

Probably it is simplest to start a sketch of the book-keeping by assuming that the book figures are raised to the full valuation. Then, because the book values of the firm are linked with the market value of B's share in the firm, B's figure for nominal capital is the same as the price that he pays.

The values of existing tangible assets (for example, buildings) may be raised to present replacement level; further, to lift their total to the full current value of the firm, an amount must be inserted as an intangible, with some such name as "goodwill" (a rather inept term for a balancing figure that probably depends mostly on monopoly).[3]

Let us suppose that A duly raises the book value of his assets to a current replacement figure of £6,000. (This is not the same value as that implied in line (3) of Table 1 in the first part of the article. Here, we are thinking of buying prices, because the firm is staying in business; there, we were considering the (break-up?) proceeds that might be got by selling the assets for the next-best use. If the market for second-hand assets is imperfect the two prices will differ.)

The pre-admission balance sheet of A is:

A—capital ...	£6,000	Net tangible assets	£6,000
	═══		═══ .. (1)

As the full value of the firm is now agreed to be £10,000, a "goodwill" item of £4,000 may be inserted. In the ledger, the whole increase must in the first place be treated as A's property, and credited to his account; on the eve of B's entry, therefore, A's balance sheet is revised to:

A—capital ...	£10,000	Goodwill ...	£4,000
		Net tangible assets	6,000
	═══		═══ .. (2)

In Diagram 5, the assets of the firm increase from OM_1 to OM_2 at full valuation—that is, goodwill is M_1M_2. A's capital grows from M_1P_1 to M_2G_1.

In return for a price of £*x* (paid privately to A) A will transfer £*x* of his capital to B. If—taking the figure that we used before—the price is £3,600, then the balance sheet becomes:

A—capital £10,000−£3,600 =	£6,400	Goodwill ...	£4,000
B—capital ...	3,600	Net tangible assets	6,000
	═══		═══ .. (3)

In Diagram 5, A's capital falls from M_2G_1 to M_2G_2 and B is credited with G_1G_2. The 3 : 2 ratio (see Table 3) gives us the slope of the share-line in a diagram showing the division of annual income. If the partners decide to split

[3] To use this everyday word in a technical and difficult sense is so misleading that I think it should be abandoned. The trouble is to find a handy substitute. "Excess of Value of Integrated Firm Over Separate Asset Values" would not fit neatly in a balance sheet. "VIFO Surplus"? The phrase is terse, and odd enough to put the reader on his guard.

Mr. Patrick O'Leary has pointed out to me that goodwill may on occasion arise without monopoly (as "monopoly" is commonly used). The welding together of a new firm may take time, during which the profits are low. This sacrifice of profits amounts to an investment in intangible assets. Under competitive conditions, rivals are free to start similar firms; but "it would still be true that in a position of long-run equilibrium, earnings after the initial period would require to be sufficient to pay an appropriate rate of interest on this intangible investment; so the goodwill may be something other than monopoly profits capitalised".

capital gains in the same ratio, we can draw the share-line R'_1R_1 in Diagram 5.
Similarly a price of £800 results in:

A—capital	...	£9,200	Goodwill	...	£4,000
B—capital	...	800	Net tangible assets		6,000
		══			══ .. (4)

The dividing point is here G_3. If capital gains are split in the 4 : 1 ratio suggested by Table 4, R'_2R_2 (Diagram 5) is the expected share-line.

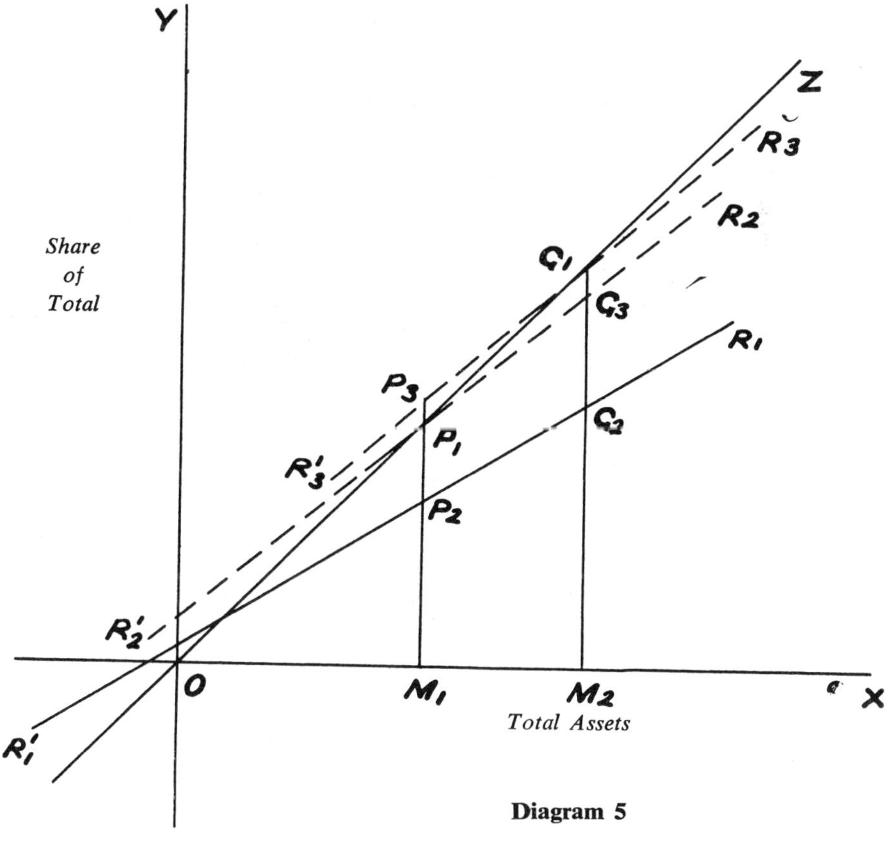

Diagram 5

If B is not able to pay any price at all, the balance sheet is:

A—capital	...	£10,000	Goodwill	...	£4,000
			Net tangible assets		6,000
		══			══ .. (5)

That is to say, the balances stay as in (2), and A's capital continues to be M_2G_1. In Diagram 5, G_1 shows B's capital at *nil*; and R'_3R_3, the appropriate capital share-line in the 6 : 1 ratio, runs at a steep angle.

(b) Existing Book Values Retained

In deference to the general bias against writing up assets, A and B may decide not to raise asset values to full value, as supposed under (*a*), but to keep them at a conservative figure—say the £6,000 in balance sheet (1). Accordingly no goodwill is inserted, and (since we still adhere to our assumption that A withdraws B's payment) both assets and capital stay at £6,000; in Diagram 5, the assets continue to be shown by OM_1, and capital by M_1P_1.

The buyer of shares in a company (particularly where capital has not been modernised by the issue of bonus shares) will hardly expect the price to be the same as the nominal worth of the shares. Similarly, a partner entering a firm with rigid ledger values should not be surprised if the price fails to match his book capital. If the firm is prospering, his capital will be less than the price; the difference may reasonably be called *premium* (or *bonus* in America).

How is the abridged book capital (£6,000 in our example) to be shared, and how big is the newcomer's premium? To understand the nature of their bargain, the partners must, I believe, always start by casting it in terms of full valuation; then, if they wish, they can deflate the figures. With either full value or conservative value, a given price should command the same set of real rights.

Diagram 5 again illustrates our problem. With full valuation we showed the assets at OM_2, and (with B's price at £3,600) used G_2 as the capital point. If now the small book capital of M_1P_1 is used, G_2 can be replaced by P_2; because P_2 is on R'_1R_1, each man's real rights are preserved at the same level. So long as the capital point lies on the agreed share-line, its position does not matter one jot.[4] It is used only when the firm ends; and then its whereabouts on the share-line are established afresh (as we saw in Diagram 3) by the proceeds of realisation.

In terms of arithmetic, the capitals of A and B can be found by starting with balance sheet (3), and then deflating it. We have to write down the assets by £4,000; this reduction is spread between A and B in the agreed 3 : 2 ratio for sharing capital losses:

A—capital £6,400 $-\frac{3}{5}\times$ £4,000= ...	£4,000	Goodwill £4,000−£4,000=	£ —
B—capital £3,600 $-\frac{2}{5}\times$ £4,000= ...	2,000	Net tangible assets	6,000 .. (6)

Thus B's £3,600 payment consists of £2,000 of capital plus £1,600 of premium; perhaps he is told that his £1,600 is the price for two-fifths of the goodwill—good arithmetic, but raising issues that a company prospectus wisely avoids. Whatever the book-keeping, B's whole payment is still in fact the composite price for his indivisible stream of future receipts. The pedant warns his pupils

[4] So far as the partners' capital rights go. It may be important for calculating interest and impressing the bank manager.

not to confound capital with premium; but at bottom the two are one, and their division is merely a trick to suit ledger conventions.[5]

The book-keeper will record a £2,000 transfer from A's capital—which has throughout remained in the ledger at £6,000, as in balance sheet (1)—to B's capital, giving the same balances as those extended in (6).

In general terms, suppose the newcomer buys a $\frac{1}{n}$th share of surplus. Then his premium is $\frac{1}{n}$th of the goodwill, and the rest of his price is his book-capital. Or, where the partners somehow or other contrive to start by agreeing that a premium of £x is the right price for a $\frac{1}{n}$th "share of goodwill", they should feel able to re-express these terms without inconsistency by switching to full valuation with goodwill at £nx.

Where the price is £800, the full valuation balance sheet (4) becomes:

A—capital			
£9,200 $-\frac{4}{5}\times$ £4,500= ...	£6,000	Net tangible assets	£6,000
B—capital			
£800 $-\frac{1}{5}\times$ £4,000= ...	—		
	═══		═══ .. (7)

In this example, the correct "conservative" capital for B happens to be *nil*; all his £800 is premium. Point P_1 gives his position in Diagram 5. Though nominal figures mean little, he may well show no enthusiasm for starting with such a modest capital; in that event, A has a strong inducement to adopt full valuation. The more painful the gap between price and capital, the more tactful is the use of goodwill.

The soothing effect of goodwill is seen where B pays no price at all. His appropriate "conservative" capital can be found from balance sheet (5):

A—capital		Goodwill	
£10,000 $-\frac{6}{7}\times$ £4,000= ...	£6,571	£4,000 − £4,000=	£ —
B—capital			
$-\frac{1}{7}\times$ £4,000=	−571	Net tangible assets	6,000
	═══		═══ .. (8)

---

[5] But all the circumstances must be borne in mind. Normally the newcomer's price is for an annuity that will, subject to business risks, go on indefinitely, until it is replaced by a capital sum (for example, at winding up). The circumstances may sometimes be different; for instance, Section 40 of the Partnership Act (in its sole reference to premium) states that where the partnership is "for a fixed term" the court may at earlier dissolution order the return of part of the premium. The stress on a limited term of years suggests such circumstances as:

(1) The newcomer so lacks skill or other qualities that he must pay for the chance to learn the ropes during a probationary period. Here his premium is like that of an apprentice. In our analysis, it fits in as negative salary rather than capital; and, if he retires before his training is complete, the return of part of his money may be reasonable.

(2) The trade is expected to fizzle out after a brief spell—that is, the annuity will be short-term and the assets of small value. Here the logic of the Act is harder to appreciate; however, if there is a risk that at the accounting between the retiring partner and the others the present values of the remaining annuity and assets will not be adequately measured, possibly the court should review the figures.

Thus B starts with a deficit of £571. Point P_3 reflects his negative wealth in Diagram 5. Though his real position is no worse than it was at G_1, he is not likely to relish the conservative arrangement; once again, hard feelings can be avoided by "raising goodwill".

A Note on the "Goodwill" Approach

We began this discussion of new partners by revaluing the firm fully; then we worked backwards to a smaller nominal capital. "Goodwill" emerged incidentally, as the mere balancing item—not necessarily having the slightest connection with "popularity"—required to raise the old asset total to full valuation.

Such is not the procedure envisaged in most textbooks. In them, it is usually implied that one can start with the old capital, and then find goodwill direct; full valuation is merely a by-product, which may or may not be used.

Even the more sophisticated theories of goodwill, based on the capitalisation of "super-profits", attract the heavy fire of thoughtful critics.[6] The method usually recommended for partnership is, however, far less plausible in logic, and is crude in its mechanics: goodwill is annual profit (or, in some trades, turnover) multiplied by a round number in the range one to six. Such a slap-dash calculation seems unlikely to give an adequate answer—that is, the partners will sooner or later feel that their bargain was not consistent with other opportunities for using capital.

Book-keeping on Admission—Real Capital is Expanded

In many instances, the assets of the firm are expanded when B is admitted; indeed, the main motive for bringing him in may well be to get extra funds. To use the company analogy again, we are no longer considering a transfer of existing shares, but have moved on to the creation of extra shares and their issue for cash.

It clearly would not matter, in the case of a company with full valuation, whether:

(i) An existing shareholder A sells some of his shares to B for £x, and then uses this £x to take up a new issue; or

(ii) B pays £x direct to the company for the new shares.

Similarly in full-valuation partnership; and, as (ii) is the simpler scheme, usually B is forthwith credited with his price (and gets no transfer from A). Without full valuation, however, we must allow for the premium, and something approaching (i) is needed.

---

[6] J. C. Bonbright: *Valuation of Property*, New York, 1937, pages 79-80; and H. C. Edey: "The Super-profit Methed", *Accountancy*, January, 1957, pages 15-18, and February, 1957, pages 52-54.

The case for the "goodwill" approach might perhaps be stronger if it followed the same principles as Table 1 in the first part of the article—and especially if it recognised the reassuring nature of scrap values by defining "normal profit" as interest on these (as in item (3) of Table 1); then "super-profits" would be the unsecured residual earnings—like the £1,300 in line (7). But in fact it computes "normal profit" on values that are less relevant (for example, replacement cost).

(*a*) *Book Figures Raised to Full Valuation*

Here the book-keeping seems straightforward. Our friends A and B must again start with balance sheet (2), showing A's full capital at £10,000. If B pays in £3,600, the balance sheet becomes:

A—capital ...	£10,000	Goodwill ...	£4,000
B—capital ...	3,600	Original assets ...	6,000
		New assets ...	3,600
	═══		═══ .. (9)

Similarly B will be credited with any other agreed price, such as £800.

However, is a price of £3,600 still consistent with a two-fifths share of surplus? The answer depends on the sizes of the various items that go into a revised Table 1, and in particular (since more assets should spell more profit) on guesses about the yield of the marginal £3,600. If A and B guess that the new capital will earn 25 per cent. (the market rate assumed in the first part of this article), the "profit after salaries" in Table 3 will grow by £900, from £3,300 to £4,200:

Table 5
RETURN IF PRICE OF £3,600 IS KEPT IN FIRM

	Total £	*A* £	*B* £
Surplus after salaries ...	4,200		
Less Interest on capital: £13,600 at 5 per cent. ...	680		
Surplus after interest and salary ...	3,520		
Commission ...	800	400	400
Balance—dividend ...	2,720		
B's share, 20 per cent. on £3,600 ...			720
A's share, balance ...		2,000	
	3,520	2,400	1,120
Fraction of surplus ...		$\frac{15}{22}$	$\frac{7}{22}$

Thus B should get only seven twenty-seconds (about 32 per cent. of surplus, as compared with the two-fifths or 40 per cent. that he was given in Table 1); total dividend having grown, B's £720 is now a smaller fraction of total. And there is in fact some presumption that the return on marginal capital is higher than the market rate of 25 per cent. (for otherwise A would not see much point in letting B bring in new capital); so perhaps B should receive an even smaller fraction of annual surplus, or the price should be raised (still on our assumption that A's bargaining position is such that he can obtain all the economic rent).

Let us agree to leave the price at £3,600, but to decrease B's share of profits from two-fifths to one-third (rounding off the vulgar fraction for convenience).

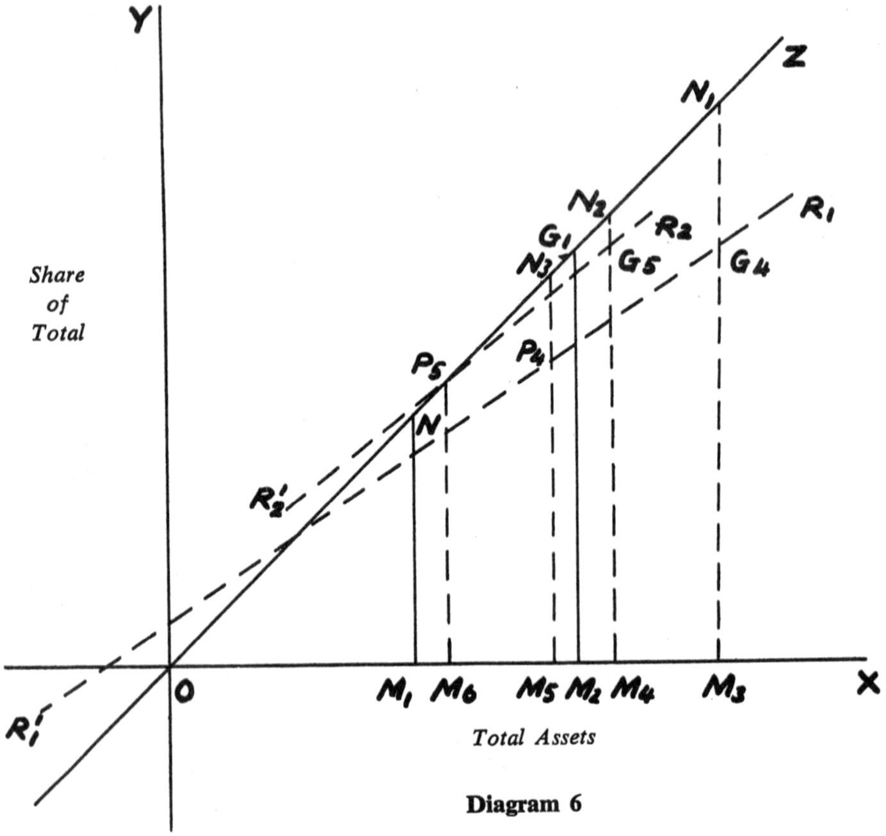

Diagram 6

The same line of thought applies with the smaller price of £800. But here the extra profits may be too small to have an appreciable effect on B's fraction.

Diagram 6 shows the effect of expansion. We use the same letters (where applicable) as in Diagram 5. So A's £10,000 of revalued assets are represented by OM_2. The introduction of B's £3,600 extends this line to OM_3; G_4 now gives the division of capitals, and R'_1R_1 is the share-line for capital gains and losses on a 2 : 1 basis.

With the smaller price of £800, assets expand to only OM_4, and G_5 shows the division of total capital. R'_2R_2 is drawn at the steeper angle consistent with a 4 : 1 division of profits.

(b) *Existing Book-values Retained*

If the original assets are to be kept at the conservative value of £6,000, book capital must become £9,600 when B's £3,600 is put into the firm. The problem is to find the right division of the £9,600 between A and B.

Once again, the simplest way to reach the answer is to start with the full valuation capitals—as in balance sheet (9)—and to write off goodwill in the agreed ratio of 2 : 1.

A—capital	£10,000−$\frac{2}{3}$×£4,000 =	£7,333
B—capital	£3,600−$\frac{1}{3}$×£4,000 =	2,267
		9,600

Of the price, £2,267 is credited to B. The rest (£1,333) is premium; it belongs to A, and is credited to his capital. Balance sheet (1) changes to:

A—capital £6,000+£1,333=	£7,333	Original assets ...	£6,000
B—capital ...	2,267	New assets ...	3,600
	9,600		9,600

..(10)

In Diagram 6, OM_1 shows the conservative asset value of £6,000, which expands to OM_5 when £3,600 is paid in. Capital shares are shown by P_4, on the original 2 : 1 share-line; the real facts are the same as when the capital point is G_4.

The lower price of £800 (for a one-fifth share of profit) must all be treated as A's property:

A—capital £6,000+£800=	£6,800	Original assets ...	£6,000
B—capital ...	—	New assets ...	800
	6,800		6,800

..(11)

The distance OM_1 expands merely to OM_6; P_5 shows that B's capital is *nil*; and 4 : 1 share-line goes through P_5, indicating that the real facts are the same as when the capital point is G_5.

Related Problems

Reasons for Making the New Partner Buy Income

It is in theory possible to offer the new partner a share of annual profit (salary plus commission) so small that it is just adequate as a personal reward (e.g., B's £1,400); in this case plainly he should not pay any price at all. But in fact the old partner tends to offer a larger income, and therefore to exact a price. Why should he do so?

Various answers are possible. The old partner may wish to withdraw money from the business, so as not to have all his eggs in one basket; or he may think that it will be profitable for him to expand the assets of the firm. Even if he does not want extra funds, he may well feel that the payment of a price makes sure that the new partner will treat his obligations seriously and not lightly withdraw from the firm; it thus serves much the same purpose as the entrance fee charged to new members of a club.

Inflation

Rising prices will expand the money income of the firm and its ultimate proceeds on realisation, even if its real value has stayed constant. The situation can be illustrated by a diagram similar to number 5; the money-value of the assets grows from OM_1 to OM_2. This may have serious and unforeseen effects upon the rights of the partners, if they do not share gains in the ratio of their capitals. The man whose fraction of gains exceeds his fraction of capital will profit at the expense of his partner; if B, for instance, starts (Diagram 5) at P_1 (that is, with no capital) he ends with a money-capital such as G_1G_3. Here is another example of the power of inflation to transfer wealth unobtrusively from one man to another. We may guess that in general the junior partner tends to gain at the expense of his senior.

The remedy might well be to write up each partner's capital (annually, or just before dissolution) with the aid of an index. Possibly the best index to use would be one reflecting general consumption costs.

Conclusion

The writer who uses mathematics to explain an economic problem is sometimes accused of merely repeating in symbols what has already been better said in words. There is a certain justice in this criticism. But the illustration of partners' rights with diagrams does seem to me to make at least a slight contribution to our understanding of the issues. It enables us to compare different schemes; it links book values to current values without dragging in the confusing term "goodwill"; and it shows, more clearly than words or even arithmetic, that payment of "premium" is not something completely different from payment of "capital". Finally, it draws our attention to the whole range of possibilities in a given scheme of division.

London

INFLATION AND THE ACCOUNTS OF STEEL COMPANIES

Reprinted from ACCOUNTANCY, the Journal of the Institute of Chartered Accountants in England and Wales, May, 1959, and June, 1959

Inflation and the Accounts of Steel Companies*

by W. T. Baxter, B.Com., C.A.

Professor of Accounting, London School of Economics, University of London

I INTRODUCTION

BY NOW, MOST of us know that inflation has certain effects on accounts; but we are still hazy about the *sizes* of the effects. So it seems worth while to find out what the figures are for various companies. If we know the quantities at stake, we are in a much better position to argue whether or not accounting and tax methods need reform.

Studies of this sort have been published in America by Professor Ralph Jones.† His most comprehensive survey deals with the impact of inflation on nine American steel companies in the years 1941/47. Accordingly, there are some grounds, in a British study, for also selecting a group of steel companies. This procedure allows us to make comparisons; further, though "steel companies" no doubt vary considerably in the nature of their work (for example, in the extent to which they do engineering), we can reasonably suppose them to be fairly like one another in asset structure.

In one particular, the choice of steel companies may not be quite happy: these companies were subject to some odd financial transactions when they were nationalised and denationalised. However, as our aim is to see the influence of inflation on ordinary trade profits, such manoeuvres in high finance do not appear to upset the study; though the companies were forced during the period to shed certain work (notably coal-mining), most of the assets seem to have been kept steadily at their normal task, regardless of who held the shares. In one respect, close relations between companies has been helpful: the industry has collectively given a good deal of attention to this matter of inflation, so that some companies themselves have figures that were useful in finding or checking my own.

Scope

While much of the information needed for a study of inflation is to be found in published accounts, some data (notably fixed asset values sub-divided by year of age) are not. Accordingly, the help of individual companies was essential for my task. Seven companies agreed to assist and possessed the needed data (either in full or with sufficient fullness to justify inclusion of their figures). I am grateful to the officers of those companies for giving me the extra information.

My results are in effect consolidated accounts of the companies—many of which are themselves groups with consolidated accounts. This aggregation serves to give a broad picture of the industry, and to conceal effectively anything that the individual companies may regard as confidential.

The period covered by the full study is 1949–57. There is a rift between the accounts for this period and those of earlier years. The change is partly due to the loss of coal mines and railway wagons on nationalisation, and partly to the Companies Act of 1948. A long survey of steel companies' accounts makes one keenly aware of the many good results of the Act; but the new standards broke the run of figures. Further, more thought seems to have been given in recent years to accounting for plant (perhaps because of interest in inflation), and some companies that have kept full plant records since the war cannot carry their figures back to earlier dates.

However, three of the seven companies also gave

* I must thank Mr. J. B. Selier, B.COM., A.C.A., and Mr. J. R. Gould, B.SC.(ECON.), for much help with the computations.

† R. C. Jones: "Effect of Inflation on Capital and Profits: The Record of Nine Steel Companies," *Journal of Accountancy*, January, 1949; see also his *Case Studies of Four Companies* (American Accounting Association, 1955).

figures stretching back to 1938. Three is a small sample; but the figures seem worth publishing to give some idea of the trend during the war. Accordingly, my tables fall into two sections:

I. Results of three companies from 1939 to 1947; and
II. Results of seven companies from 1949 to 1957.

Aspects Studied

Inflation affects accounts in several ways, and so a writer on this subject has some choice in deciding which aspects to select. But the topics all fall under one or other of two heads: (1) correction of recorded gains, and (2) valuation of assets and liabilities.

(1) *Correction of recorded gains*

Normal accounts carry most assets at historical cost. This results in higher income figures if prices rise. For, when the assets are used up in producing income, the accounts charge a low and out-of-date cost against an inflated current sale price. The difference is labelled profit. But this profit figure is too big—in the sense that the cost does not fully provide for maintenance of the real assets.

The most important expenses subject to time-lag are depreciation and "cost of goods sold." Corrected accounts must raise these to the price-level of the corresponding sales.

Exactly the same reasoning applies when assets are realised in ways other than normal trade—for example, when a steel company sells its coal mines or investments. I should have liked to correct the consequent profit figures. However, I deem this impracticable here. Such transactions are often looked on as top-secret; and, even if the facts of the sale are divulged, one would probably need much knowledge of the particular history and book-keeping to decide on the proper cost adjustment. Fortunately, these transactions are seldom mixed with trading results.

(2) *Valuation of assets and liabilities*

As normal accounts keep most assets at historical costs, the book values of assets (other than money and rights closely linked with money) fall below current market values when prices rise. On the other side of the balance sheet, book figures for the equity-holders' interest (for example, Ordinary shares and retained earnings) are correspondingly understated. To bring the figures up to date, one must raise the non-money assets and the equity; the write-up does not reflect any real gain—unless, and to the extent that, appreciation on these assets exceeds the general rise in prices.

Money assets do not need to be revalued after inflation; for their book values still match their market values. However, their failure to appreciate is a loss in real terms. Conversely, the rigidity of money liabilities (including Preference shares) is a real gain to the equity holders.

Indices Used

In this study, published figures are adjusted with the help of indices. The main index used is that for consumers' expenditure, as set out in the *London and Cambridge Bulletin.*

A consumption cost index is plainly an imperfect tool. But it has the great merit of showing in some degree whether the equity-holders have maintained their wealth—in the fundamental sense of ability to satisfy their daily wants. Column (*a*) of Table I summarises this index.

Though cost-of-living figures give a good index from the standpoint of private capital maintenance (and therefore, I suggest, of income measurement), they fail to show whether a firm is maintaining its physical assets. For this purpose, one needs other figures—indices that mirror the replacement costs of different types of assets.

I have therefore elaborated the main revenue tables, so that they show both:

(i) Figures based on the consumption index; and
(ii) Additional figures, needed to raise those under (i) to replacement cost of the specific assets.

TABLE I
Cost Indices

Year		(*a*) *Consumers' Expenditure*	(*b*) *Raw Material Prices (Steel Industry)*	(*c*) *Plant Replacement Costs (Steelworks)*
1938	..	100	100	100
1939	..	103	99	101
1940	..	121	118	122
1941	..	134	130	143
1942	..	144	133	150
1943	..	150	135	155
1944	..	153	138	160
1945	..	158	140	165
1946	..	164	150	183
1947	..	175	153	208
1948	..	189	171	226
1949	..	194	203	233
1950	..	201	198	244
1951	..	218	231	270
1952	..	230	316	297
1953	..	236	326	304
1954	..	239	302	315
1955	..	247	333	335
1956	..	259	392	361
1957	..	265	407	388

Sources:
(*a*) Index of consumers' expenditure, average value index, in *London and Cambridge Bulletins*, published quarterly in the *Times Review of Industry.*
(*b*) Raw materials price index (method 4) prepared by the British Iron and Steel Federation. Figures for 1939-45 are insertions based on index of wholesale prices of manufactures, table 287, *Annual Abstract of Statistics*, 1937-47.
(*c*) Index of replacement cost of industrial assets, steelworks, prepared by the *Economist* Intelligence Unit. Figures for 1939-45 are insertions based on index of wholesale prices of building materials, table 287, *Annual Abstract of Statistics*, 1937-47.

The physical asset structure of even a single company is always changing (for example, the proportions of different types of raw materials alter in each balance sheet). No index, or battery of indices, can deal faithfully with the assets of a whole industry. A fairly useful set of figures may, however, be got by using two specific indices—one for stocks of goods (index of raw material prices, published by the British Iron and Steel Federation) and the other for fixed assets (index of the cost of replacing steelworks plant, published by the *Economist* Intelligence Unit). Columns (*b*) and (*c*) of Table I summarise these figures.*

Comparison of the columns shows that the two specific indices, (*b*) and (*c*), are more erratic, and rise much further, than the consumption index.

However, though the specific indices are more extravagant in their movement than the consumption index, the three indices have usually followed the same trend. With rare exceptions, all three were going up throughout both periods (1939-47 and 1949-57). And the speed of increase followed a rather similar pattern in both periods—fast near the beginning and again near the end. Prices rose swiftly when the war began, less swiftly during the rest of the war, and then soared just after the war. During the 1949-57 period, the Korean crisis started a new acceleration; this disappeared in a year or two (and the stock index was actually *falling* for some months of 1953/54); thereafter the upsurge once again became fast. We should expect this variation in the pace to be reflected in our results.

Corrected Ordinary Figures *v.* Stabilisation

The results are organised into three kinds of tables:

A. Ordinary revenue figures plus corrections

In the tables marked A, the actual figures of the particular year are taken as the starting point. The unchanged figures are then interspersed where necessary with correcting adjustments geared to the price-level of that year. For instance, the figures of 1940 profit are copied from the original accounts of 1940, and then an extra cost is deducted to allow for inflation — leaving the reduced profit figure that might appropriately have been published at the end of 1940. In short, the revenue account is corrected but is still expressed in current £s; and assets still stand at their ordinary book values.

B. Stabilised Accounts

If the faults of historical cost are to be entirely cut out, each figure in a given year's accounts must be re-expressed in "stabilised"† terms, that is, in £s of some common date. This automatically brings costs into line with revenues, and so corrects net profit; further (if the common date is recent) it goes some way towards revaluing assets and equity in terms of current prices; and it shows the depreciation of money during inflation (a loss if money assets exceed liabilities, but a gain if liabilities exceed money assets).

Any convenient dates can be used as bases for stabilisation. If trends over a period are to be studied, the accounts of all years should be geared to a single base. To achieve this uniformity, the B tables stabilise each period's figures in terms of the £ at the close of the whole period.

C. Special asset revaluation

As has been said above, a simple method of stabilisation must content itself with the use of a single index—that for general consumption prices. However, there is no reason why somewhat more accurate values of fixed assets should not be calculated. In what follows, the stabilised B tables (general index) are supplemented with estimates—marked C—of plant values found by using the specific index of plant construction costs.

Gains and Losses on Revaluation

The corrections mentioned under A above—inflation charges for materials and depreciation—seem proper additions to costs, and are therefore used to reduce profits in the tables showing revenue.

Gains and losses due to the depreciation of money (see B above) present more controversial issues, as do the *extra* appreciation and depreciation on assets when revalued with a specific index instead of the general index (see C above). Though such gains and losses are genuine and worthy of measurement, they scarcely seem proper additions to the trade profit account—particularly when they are still unrealised.

The definition of "realised" in this context raises awkward problems. The fall in the real value of a long-term liability during inflation is a gain in the sense that annual interest and final redemption become less onerous. Is redemption date the time when the gain is realised? If so, does it follow that gain on current liabilities is realised during the turnover of each year? Until answers to these questions are clearer, the right course seems to be to show these gains apart from trade profit.

Accuracy

The best composition of an index number is a matter of opinion. The technique of stabilisation is still being explored. The data provided by the companies left scope for interpretation. For these and other reasons, my results should obviously not be looked on as figures whose accuracy to the last penny can be objectively proven. Rather should they be judged—like the figures for stock and depreciation in ordinary accounts—as general guides to the values at stake.

When faced with alternative ways of adjusting the figures, I have usually chosen the way that favours ordinary accounting—that is, the reduction in profits and reserves should possibly be greater than my tables suggest.

---

* I must thank the British Iron and Steel Federation, and the *Economist* Intelligence Unit, for supplying the data.

† The word is used here in appreciation of the pioneer work of Professor H. W. Sweeney, in *Stabilised Accounting* (New York, 1936).

II RESULTS—PERIOD 1939–47

Costs and Revenue

A. Correct profit in current £s

Table 2A sets out revenue figures, for three companies, from 1939 to 1947. These are current figures, as explained above. So lines *a* to *e* merely aggregate the data given in the original accounts for profit, normal depreciation, and interest.

Line *e* shows that the net profits, as originally reported, kept fairly steady at something over £2 million, except for temporary peaks in 1940 and 1946. From these profits, certain "distributions" were made—appropriations for tax and dividends; these are listed on *j*, *k* and *l*. Comparison of net profit (*e*) with total distributions (*m*) shows that distributions are always below profits (except in 1939); in other words, despite high tax rates and dividends that were fairly well maintained, apparently a solid and growing surplus was ploughed back.

To find correct profit, one must deduct "inflation charges" (line *f*) based on the consumption index. Details of this charge are appended in the note below Table 2A, on lines *r* to *y*. Line *r* tries to estimate appreciation on stock during each year. Here two factors govern the size of the figures—the rise in the consumption index during the particular year, and the quantity of stock held. Line *s* tries to estimate the extra depreciation needed for real capital maintenance. Throughout the period, most of the plant still consisted of assets bought before the war; ordinary depreciation figures (*b*) were therefore largely based on pre-war costs (though the high 1947 figure suggests a tendency to write down assets more quickly at the end of the period); accordingly *s* is governed mainly by the cumulative rise in the consumption index over all the years since 1938, and the figures grow each year till (contrary to what is often said) they far outstrip the stock charge.

Line *y* suggests how much further the inflation charges would have risen if specific indices for stock and plant had been used, instead of the consumption index. Line *v* shows the extra sums needed to raise the stock charge (*r*) to a level at which physical stocks of steel firms would be maintained; as the stock index in most years rose less than the consumption index, these extra sums are often negative. Line *w* suggests the extra sums needed to raise the depreciation charge (*s*) to a level at which physical plants of steel firms would be maintained. After 1939, the plant index always stood above the consumption index, so that the extra sums are positive; in 1946 and 1947, they became substantial.

To return to the upper part of Table 2A. Line *g* shows the corrected profits still left after deducting the main inflation charges (that is, those based on the consumption index). The figures in *g* diverge over the years more and more from reported profits (*e*); the right-hand column shows that the total fell from £22 million to £13 million. But, though the annual falls were substantial, in no year did they turn profit into loss.

Line *i* suggests that the results would not have been changed much by substituting specific indices for the consumption index—except in 1947, when the prices of materials and plant rose so sharply that a large uncorrected profit becomes a small deficit.

However, when the sums distributed (*j*, *k* and *l*) are brought into account, the picture changes. Distributions exceed corrected profit in every year. After extra charges to maintain physical assets, we are left with the deficits shown in *n*; over the period, earnings accumulated before 1939 were reduced in real terms by some £7 million. Tax alone is nearly 100 per cent. of corrected profit.

B. Correct profit in stabilised £s

Table 2B deals with the same revenue items (after correction) as 2A, but stabilises the figures with the aid of the consumption index (using the end of 1947 as the base). Because the data are expressed in the inflated £ of the period's close, earlier figures swell considerably, and the downward trend of profit becomes more noticeable (*e*). The deficit after distributions (*n*) is large in all years.

DIAGRAM 1

Revenue figures. accounting and stabilised versions of profits. and of surplus after distributions

1939-47

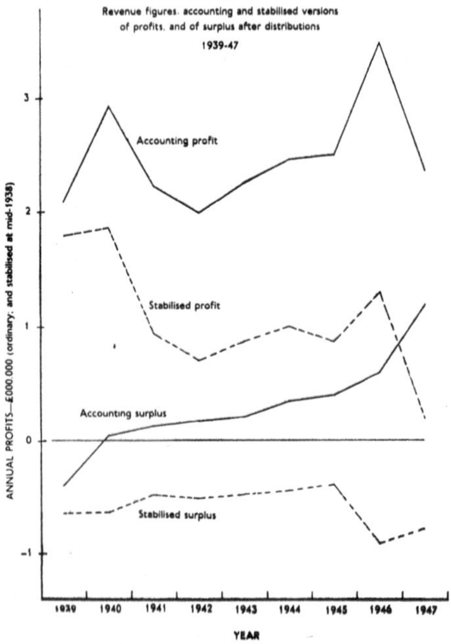

TABLE 2A

REVENUE ACCOUNTS OF THREE COMPANIES, 1939-47

Current £s. £000 omitted.

	1939	*1940*	*1941*	*1942*	*1943*	*1944*	*1945*	*1946*	*1947*	*Total*
a Trade profit, uncorrected	3,750	4,634	3,914	3,877	4,200	4,457	4,765	5,861	5,560	41,018
b *Less* Depreciation (uncorrected)	1,379	1,377	1,404	1,561	1,677	1,710	1,986	2,100	3,063	16,257
c Interest..	250	292	287	283	279	276	274	241	147	2,329
d Total of *b* and *c*	1,629	1,669	1,691	1,844	1,956	1,986	2,260	2,341	3,210	18,586
e Net profit (uncorrected)	2,121	2,965	2,223	2,033	2,244	2,471	2,505	3,520	2,350	22,432
f *Less* Inflation charges, consumption index	267	728	966	1,033	963	950	1,179	1,405	1,983	9,474
g Net profit (corrected)	**1,854**	**2,237**	**1,257**	**1,000**	**1,281**	**1,521**	**1,326**	**2,115**	**367**	**12,958**
h *Less* Extra charge to raise *f* to specific index	1	72	−213	−170	− 54	96	−188	677	620	841
i Corrected net profit after replacements ..	1,853	2,165	1,470	1,170	1,335	1,425	1,514	1,438	−253	12,117
Less Distributions:										
j Tax	1,509	2,194	1,342	1,154	1,291	1,361	1,301	1,981	67	12,200
k Preference dividends	127	108	96	94	94	94	94	133	209	1,049
l Ordinary dividends	877	628	653	635	653	668	713	811	824	6,462
m Total distributions	2,513	2,930	2,091	1,883	2,038	2,123	2,108	2,925	1,100	19,711
n Surplus (corrected net profit after replacements and distributions)	**−660**	**−765**	**−621**	**−713**	**−703**	**−698**	**−594**	**−1,487**	**−1,353**	**−7,594**
Details of inflation charges, f and h:										
Inflation charges, consumption index:										
r Stocks	231	459	524	405	218	177	246	395	492	3,147
s Depreciation	36	269	442	628	745	773	933	1,010	1,491	6,327
u Total inflation charge, consumption index, as in *f*	267	728	966	1,033	963	950	1,179	1,405	1,983	9,474
Extra charge to raise above to specific indices:										
v Stocks	26	61	−339	−258	−142	− 10	−306	348	−105	−725
w Depreciation	−25	11	126	88	88	106	118	329	725	1,566
x Total extra charge, as in *h*..	1	72	−213	−170	− 54	96	−188	677	620	841
y Total inflation charge, specific index ($u+x$)	268	800	753	863	909	1,046	991	2,082	2,603	10,315

TABLE 2B

REVENUE ACCOUNTS OF THREE COMPANIES, 1939-47

Stabilised in £s of December 31, 1947. £000 omitted.

	1939	*1940*	*1941*	*1942*	*1943*	*1944*	*1945*	*1946*	*1947*	*Total*
a Trade profit (stock corrected, consumer index)	6,218	6,280	4,604	4,388	4,831	5,091	5,205	6,066	5,271	47,954
Less										
b Depreciation (corrected, consumer index)	2,500	2,476	2,507	2,766	2,938	2,954	3,362	3,452	4,736	27,691
c Interest	442	439	390	358	339	328	316	267	153	3,032
d Total of *b* and *c*	2,942	2,915	2,897	3,124	3,277	3,282	3,678	3,719	4,889	30,723
g Net profit (corrected)	**3,276**	**3,365**	**1,707**	**1,264**	**1,554**	**1,809**	**1,527**	**2,347**	**382**	**17,231**
h *Less* Extra charge to allow for replacement (specific indices)	2	109	−290	−215	− 66	114	−217	751	645	833
i Corrected net profit after replacements ..	3,274	3,256	1,997	1,479	1,620	1,695	1,744	1,596	−263	16,398
m *Less* Distributions	4,440	4,407	2,840	2,380	2,473	2,525	2,428	3,246	1,144	25,883
n Surplus (corrected net profit after replacements and distributions)	**−1,166**	**−1,151**	**−843**	**−901**	**−853**	**−830**	**−684**	**−1,650**	**−1,407**	**−9,485**

The effect upon trends of all our adjustments can perhaps best be gauged by comparing accounting figures with figures stabilised in terms of 1939 £s. Diagram 1 shows the ordinary accounting profit (*e* in 2A) and surplus as unbroken lines, and the stabilised profits and deficits as broken lines; this arrangement is useful for contrasting the *trends* in the two sets of figures (but not for comparing ordinary and stabilised figures for any one year). The unbroken lines suggest that profits have been well maintained, and have indeed a slightly upward trend. The broken line for profit shows a downward trend ending in steep fall.

1939-47 Balance Sheets

The balance sheets are arranged in two different forms:

Table 3A. This gives the ordinary figures, without any correction.

Line *n* is a note suggesting what the effects of profit correction might have been. It accumulates the inflation

TABLE 3A

BALANCE SHEETS OF THREE COMPANIES, 1939-47

Ordinary figures. £000 omitted.

	1938	*1939*	*1940*	*1941*	*1942*	*1943*	*1944*	*1945*	*1946*	*1947*
a Fixed assets—cost	26,820	31,138	32,929	33,841	34,531	35,554	37,153	39,241	42,670	44,427
b *Less* Depreciation (uncorrected)	2,949	3,711	5,183	6,417	7,817	9,712	11,261	13,073	15,242	17,007
c Net book value	23,871	27,427	27,746	27,424	26,714	25,842	25,892	26,168	27,428	27,420
d Subsidiaries and associated companies, etc.	2,816	3,597	4,693	4,813	4,319	4,340	4,277	4,096	5,101	7,467
e Stocks	3,508	3,167	6,071	7,875	8,140	7,682	7,538	8,142	8,741	6,881
	30,195	34,191	38,510	40,112	39,173	37,864	37,707	38,406	41,270	41,768
f Current liabilities, less money assets ..	−927	486	3,716	5,267	4,102	−187	−1,218	−2,044	−266	−3,599
g Debentures	6,281	7,656	7,861	7,659	7,453	7,243	6,903	6,500	3,247	3,185
h Preference capital	3,302	3,302	3,302	3,302	3,302	3,302	3,302	3,302	6,686	8,399
i Maintenance provision	497	727	1,434	1,734	1,882	2,453	2,438	3,293	2,770	2,698
j Tax reserve	—	—	—	—	—	2,261	2,349	2,836	2,377	2,549
k Revenue reserves and misc. (uncorrected)..	4,625	4,775	4,952	4,905	5,189	5.547	6,144	6,730	8,627	10,416
m Ordinary capital plus premium	16,417	17,245	17,245	17,245	17,245	17,245	17,789	17,789	17,829	18,120
	30,195	34,191	38,510	40,112	39,173	37,864	37,707	38,406	41,270	41,768
n Inflation charges (cumulative) consumption index	—	267	995	1,961	2,994	3,957	4,907	6,086	7,491	9,474

TABLE 3B

BALANCE SHEETS OF THREE COMPANIES, 1939-47

Stabilised in £s of December 31, 1947. £000 omitted.

	1938	*1939*	*1940*	*1941*	*1942*	*1943*	*1944*	*1945*	*1946*	*1947*
a Fixed assets	48,088	55,718	58,384	59,607	60,404	61,493	63,315	65,562	69,285	69,856
b *Less* Depreciation (corrected)	5,288	6,699	9,304	11,552	14,041	17,092	19,774	22,778	26,223	28,356
c Net book-value	42,800	49,019	49,080	48,055	46,363	44,401	43,541	42,784	43,062	41,500
d Subsidiaries and associated companies, etc.	5,049	6,429	8,075	8,240	7,615	7,641	7,566	7,358	8,473	10,934
e Stocks	6,290	5,279	8,953	10,695	10,528	9,708	9,326	9,739	9,966	7,520
	54,139	60,727	66,108	66,990	64,506	61,750	60,433	59,881	61,501	59,954
f Current liabilities, less money assets ..	−1,662	789	5,303	6,895	5,078	−224	−1,424	−2,309	−286	−3,599
g Debentures	11,262	12,441	11,217	10,026	9,227	8,699	8,077	7,345	3,486	3,185
h Preference capital	5,920	5,366	4,712	4,322	4,088	3,966	3,863	3,731	7,180	8,399
i Maintenance provision	891	1,297	2,350	2,767	2,953	3,645	3,627	4,612	4,031	3,956
j Tax reserve	—	—	—	—	—	2,743	2,848	3,410	2,901	3,080
k Revenue reserves and miscellaneous (corrected)	8,292	8,085	7,255	5,880	4,943	4,209	3,789	3,106	3,653	3,450
l Gain from owing	—	1,850	4,372	6,201	7,318	7,813	8,107	8,440	8,946	9,590
m Ordinary capital, plus premiums	29,436	30,899	30,899	30,899	30,899	30,899	31,546	31,546	31,590	31,893
	54,139	60,727	66,108	66,990	64,506	61,750	60,433	59,881	61,501	59,954

charges (consumption index) that were shown separately in Table 2A, line *f*. If this degree of correction had been made from year to year, revenue reserves (*k* in Table 3A) would have fallen by the sums in *n*, and a new item—a capital reserve—would have risen correspondingly.

Table 3B. This re-expresses the balance sheet figures of 3A (after correction of cumulative revenue and depreciation) in terms of the £ of December 31, 1947.

Comparing the 1947 columns of 3A and 3B, one sees that the money items (*f*, *g* and *h*) are the same. Stock, being in the main shown at current values in ordinary accounts, is almost the same in both columns.* Otherwise the figures throughout 3B tend to be bigger than those in 3A, reflecting the depreciation of the pound between the "acquisition date" of each item and the end of 1947. Fixed assets, for the most part acquired before 1939, are much higher all along line *a*; the provisions for depreciation also grow (and are now "corrected" figures). Similarly equity capital (*m*) is up substantially; its 1947 size shows roughly what the nominal capital might have been in that year if bonus shares had been issued to match the price change.

Because 3B is stabilised in terms of a single base-date, trends can be seen readily. Thus physical growth of assets is here much easier to gauge than in 3A. Further, accumulated revenues are corrected sums. Line *k* (revenue reserves) gains much in significance; whereas this line in 3A suggests growth, the corrected figures of 3B stress the inroads made by over-distribution of real profit.

Gain from owing

When all the balance sheet items, save the rights defined in terms of money, are increased, a new balance emerges—the loss or gain in the value of the money items. This important factor is shown in 3B as "gain from owing", on line *l*. The three companies have fairly high capital gearing (see *g* and *h*), and their current liabilities sometimes exceeded money assets (see *f*); so the net result is here a substantial gain, amounting to over £9 million by 1947.†

Balance sheet trends contrasted

The ordinary and the stabilised balance sheets (A and B) suggest very different trends. The contrast is best seen by listing the changes between 1938 and 1947:

Changes in balance sheet items 1938-47
(£000 omitted)

	A. Ordinary	*B. Stabilised* (£ of Dec. 1947)
Asset growth:		
Fixed assets, less depreciation and maintenance	1,348	—4,365
Subsidiaries, etc.	4,651	5,885
Stocks	3,373	1,230
Liquid assets, net	2,672	1,937
Total growth	12,044	4,687
Obtained by increase in:		
Loans and preference capital ..	2,001	—5,598
Ordinary capital	1,703	2,457
Reserves: Tax	2,549	3,080
Revenue	5,791	—4,842
Gain on owing ..	—	9,590
Total reserves ..	8,340	7,828
	12,044	4,687

In A (the ordinary accounts) the trend is good. Each group of assets has grown somewhat; the total growth is substantial. It mainly results from retaining profits; for the rest, it comes from raising more ordinary capital and long-term money liabilities.

In B, the upward trend is much less clear. Asset growth is small; fixed assets have not been maintained. But there has been a great reduction in long-term obligations; despite some net borrowing, inflation has whittled down the total. Accumulated reserves have grown about as much as under A—but for very different reasons: retained trade earnings are negative, but the gain from owing far outweighs that deficit.

In short, A and B both agree that the equity-holders' wealth has grown, and by roughly the same amount. But A paints a robust picture of physical assets and trade profit; B shows that physical assets did not expand much, and that the equity-holders' gain sprang mainly from shrewd financing rather than trade. The equity wins what the *rentiers* lose.

Valuation gains in real terms

Table 3C tries to estimate the real appreciation on the fixed assets—that is, the extent to which their values rose beyond the general rise in money prices.

Line *a* revalues the fixed assets by applying the specific index to the historical cost of plant and to depreciation. The results give some notion of what the ordinary balance sheet figures would have been if they had been shown at current replacement cost (for example, in 1947 the current value was some £47 million, compared with £27 million in the published accounts). Line *b* shows fixed assets raised with the general index; the difference—*c*—is thus the cumulative real gain. It reaches over £5 million by 1947.

How far do the real but rather remote gains from

* I have ignored the slight value rise that takes place under mild inflation between acquisition of stocks and the end of year. Thus the figures in the two tables would be identical but for the fact that part of the ordinary figure happens to be a LIFO valuation.

† Unfortunately, accounts are not required to distinguish between the money and non-money parts of composite items. Thus it is impossible to split line *d* into the two components that here interest us. I have treated the whole of this item as non-money, since a large part of it is equity investments. But in some years the money advances to associated companies must have been substantial; so the figures in *d* and *l* are somewhat too big.

TABLE 3C

Real Valuation Gains (Cumulative) of Three Companies, 1939-47

Current £s. £000 omitted.

		1939	*1940*	*1941*	*1942*	*1943*	*1944*	*1945*	*1946*	*1947*
	Fixed assets, less depreciation, raised by:									
a	Specific index	30,403	36,170	39,087	39,506	38,800	39,202	40,956	45,827	47,485
b	General consumption index	30,166	34,394	36,704	37,451	36,964	37,206	37,853	40,109	41,500
c	Real appreciation (cumulative).. ..	237	1,776	2,383	2,055	1,836	1,996	3,103	5,718	5,985
	Gain from owing (cumulative):									
d	On money assets less current liabilities..	28	272	689	1,008	1,120	1,127	1,108	1,118	1,049
e	On debentures and preference capital ..	1,111	2,793	4,044	4,904	5,381	5,795	6,353	7,211	8,541
f	Total gain on owing	1,139	3,065	4,733	5,912	6,501	6,922	7,461	8,329	9,590
g	Total, $c+f$	1,376	4,841	7,116	7,967	8,337	8,918	10,564	14,047	15,575

appreciation offset deficits on trading profit? To show the whole story, we add *d* and *e*—the gains from owing money.* The grand total of the two types of appreciation, *g*, is double the cumulative trade deficit (about £7 million by 1947—see Table 2A, foot of total column). Thus real capital rose by some £7 million over the period.

However, gains due to plant appreciation and the scaling-down of obligations are somewhat far-off and contingent, whereas a trade deficit could spell speedy and concrete shortages.

* Here analysed by kind of obligation, as gain on the *current* items can perhaps be regarded as realised, whereas gain on the *non-current* items is a long-term benefit.

III RESULTS—PERIOD 1949-57

Changes in Pattern

Part III deals with a bigger sample of companies—seven instead of three—and a more recent period, 1949 to 1957. Because the sample has grown, and still more because steel plants expanded wholesale during recent years, our figures now have a different size and pattern. The pattern of inflation also changes somewhat: the general index of consumers' expenditure rises at a relatively slower pace; the index of fixed asset costs is a shade more sedate than during 1939–47; but raw material prices go up much faster than before, notably in 1952 and 1956.

Arrangement of Results

We shall arrange the figures in the same order as before, namely:

Costs and revenue

(A) The ordinary figures from revenue accounts, with possible corrections, still in current £'s.

(B) Corrected figures, converted into 1957 values.

Balance sheets

(A) Ordinary figures.

(B) Corrected figures, converted into 1957 values.

(C) Gains from appreciation of fixed assets, and from owing money.

Costs and Revenue

(*A*) *Corrected profit in current £'s*

Table 4A, lines *a* to *e*, gives consolidated revenue figures of the seven companies, as shown in their published accounts, for 1949–57.

TABLE 4A

REVENUE ACCOUNTS OF SEVEN COMPANIES, 1949–57

Current £s. £000 omitted

	1949	*1950*	*1951*	*1952*	*1953*	*1954*	*1955*	*1956*	*1957*	*Total*
a Trade profit, uncorrected ..	25,049	29,254	31,799	43,805	45,704	56,796	72,216	72,705	90,397	467,725
b *Less* Depreciation (uncorrected)	4,358	4,813	5,321	7,684	9,581	10,577	12,344	13,804	16,699	85,181
c Interest	755	1,258	1,717	1,988	2,163	2,806	3,649	4,953	6,125	25,414
d Total of *b* and *c*	5,113	6,071	7,038	9,672	11,744	13,383	15,993	18,757	22,824	110,595
e Net profit (uncorrected) ..	19,936	23,183	24,761	34,133	33,960	43,413	56,223	53,948	67,573	357,130
f *Less* Inflation charges, consumption index	2,689	3,614	5,159	5,271	4,114	5,087	6,152	7,882	8,287	48,255
g Net profit (corrected)	**17,247**	**19,569**	**19,602**	**28,862**	**29,846**	**38,326**	**50,071**	**46,066**	**59,286**	**308,875**
h *Less* Extra charge to raise *f* to specific index	5,390	−558	7,903	14,052	−2,256	−3,768	11,796	12,650	6,033	51,242
i Corrected net profit after replacements	11,857	20,127	11,699	14,810	32,102	42,094	38,275	33,416	53,253	257,633
Less Distributions:										
j Tax	10,297	11,927	13,677	21,570	20,247	21,333	26,715	23,622	30,494	179,882
k Preference dividends ..	447	444	356	324	298	492	732	739	828	4,660
l Ordinary dividends ..	2,236	2,217	1,965	2,284	2,642	7,704	4,800	5,000	8,204	37,052
m Total distributions	12,980	14,588	15,998	24,178	23,187	29,529	32,247	29,361	39,526	221,594
n Surplus (corrected net profit after replacements and distributions)	**−1,123**	**5,539**	**−4,299**	**−9,368**	**8,915**	**12,565**	**6,028**	**4,055**	**13,727**	**36,039**
Details of inflation charges, f and h:										
o Allowance made in original accounts. Stocks			1,008	385	300	−136	700	1,000	1,100	4,357
p Depreciation	1,981	2,090	575	750	1,000	5,141	7,975	9,196	10,467	39,175
q Total, *o* and *p*	1,981	2,090	1,583	1,135	1,300	5,005	8,675	10,196	11,567	43,532
r Further allowance needed, consumption index, Stocks ..	1,001	1,898	2,088	1,863	303	1,921	1,807	2,183	2,240	15,304
s Depreciation	−293	−374	1,488	2,273	2,511	−1,839	−4,330	−4,497	−5,520	−10,581
t Total, *r* and *s*	708	1,524	3,576	4,136	2,814	82	−2,523	−2,314	−3,280	4,723
u Total inflation charge, consumption index, as in *f* ..	2,689	3,614	5,159	5,271	4,114	5,087	6,152	7,882	8,287	48,255
v Extra charge to raise above to specific index. Stocks ..	4,616	−1,343	6,981	12,472	−4,023	−5,936	8,968	9,733	2,074	33,542
w Depreciation	774	785	922	1,580	1,767	2,168	2,828	2,917	3,959	17,700
x **Total extra charge, as in *h*** ..	**5,390**	**−558**	**7,903**	**14,052**	**−2,256**	**−3,768**	**11,796**	**12,650**	**6,033**	**51,242**
y **Total inflation charge, specific index ($u+x$)**	8,079	3,056	13,062	19,323	1,858	1,319	17,948	20,532	14,320	99,497

TABLE 4B

REVENUE ACCOUNTS OF SEVEN COMPANIES, 1949-57

Stabilised in £s of September 30, 1957. £000 omitted

	1949	*1950*	*1951*	*1952*	*1953*	*1954*	*1955*	*1956*	*1957*	*Total*
a Trade profit (stock corrected, consumer index)	33,123	36,452	35,652	48,605	50,955	61,755	77,119	71,823	88,049	503,533
Less										
b Depreciation (corrected, consumer index) ..	8,327	8,700	9,172	12,523	14,791	15,581	17,689	19,115	21,893	127,791
c Interest	1,040	1,676	2,132	2,325	2,444	3,150	4,037	5,117	6,195	28,116
d Total of *b* and *c*	9,367	10,376	11,304	14,848	17,235	18,731	21,726	24,232	28,088	155,907
g Net profit (corrected)	**23,756**	**26,076**	**24,348**	**33,757**	**33,720**	**43,024**	**55,393**	**47,591**	**59,961**	**347,626**
h Less Extra charge to allow for replacement (specific indices)	7,424	−743	9,817	16,435	−2,549	−4,230	13,050	13,069	6,101	58,374
i Corrected net profit after replacements	16,332	26,819	14,531	17,322	36,269	47,254	42,343	34,522	53,860	289,252
m Less Distributions	17,878	19,439	19,871	28,279	26,197	33,149	35,675	30,333	39,977	250,798
n Surplus (corrected net profit after replacements and distributions)	**—1,546**	**7,380**	**−5,340**	**−10,957**	**10,072**	**14,105**	**6,668**	**4,189**	**13,883**	**38,454**

DIAGRAM 2

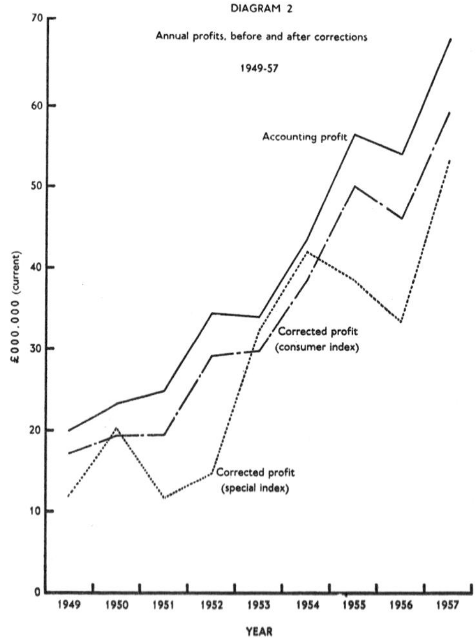

DIAGRAM 3

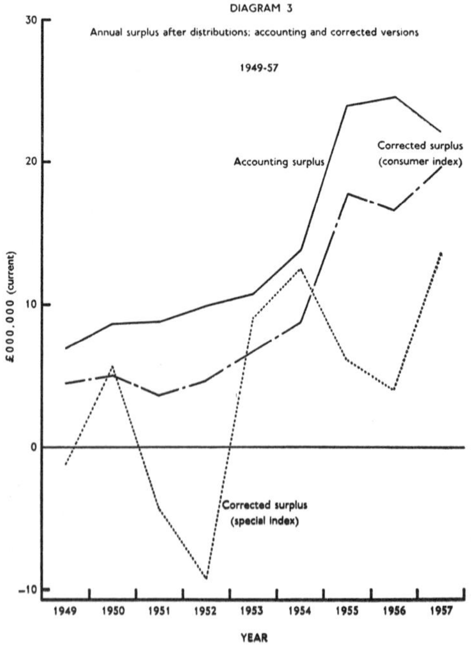

These are years of booming output; trade profits (*a*) rise by some 250 per cent. Plant is greatly increased, in part with the help of fresh loans; and so depreciation (*b*) and interest (*c*) rise steeply. Net profit (*e*) more than trebles over the decade. About half of this profit is paid out as taxes (*j*), and dividends raise the fraction distributed to some two-thirds (*m*); so the published accounts depict about one-third of the profits as being ploughed back.

Line *f* deducts "inflation charges" on stocks and depreciation in order to correct profits. Details of the charges are given below the table (lines *o* to *u*). One contrast with the 1939–47 figures is notable. By 1949, some of the companies had themselves recognised that ordinary depreciation was inadequate, and in their own accounts were making transfers to replacement reserves. Stock allowances soon followed. These appropriations are listed in *o*, *p*, and *q* (and so form part of my total charge, *f*). By 1957, they had grown to nearly £12 million a year, exceeding by £3 million (*t*) the charges suggested by the general index, but still falling nearly £3 million short of the total based on specific indices (*y*); both tests suggest that inflation charges made by the companies themselves for depreciation have in recent years been more than adequate, while those for stocks remain too small.

As in the earlier period, the depreciation charge ($p+s$) exceeds the stock charge ($o+r$).

In this second period, the inflation charges (*f*) average about 13 per cent. of uncorrected profit (compared with roughly 40 per cent. in 1939–47). This decrease is due in part to better trade, in part to the slackened pace of inflation. Moreover, because of the lavish purchases of plant, later depreciation figures in line *b* are based mainly on up-to-date values, and need only a relatively small inflation charge to raise them to corrected current costs.

Because the inflation charges are small, corrected profit (*g*) remains substantial. The extra "specific" charges to maintain physical stocks and plant (*h*), though slightly bigger in total than the charges based on the consumption index, are nevertheless covered in comfortable fashion by the corrected profit.

However, the impact of the charges on "surplus" is more serious (line *n*). Plainly the "distributions" of tax and dividend (*m*), though reasonable enough compared with uncorrected profit, are somewhat too big when both charges are taken into account; surplus is turned into deficit in three of the early years.

Diagram 2 repeats the three versions of profit:

(1) Ordinary accounting figures, as in *e*—unbroken line.

(2) Profit corrected with the consumption index, as in *g*—broken line.

(3) Profit corrected with specific indices, as in *i*—dotted line.

There are three corresponding versions of "surplus"—that is, profit after distributions. They are shown in Diagram 3:

(1) Accounting surplus—that is, uncorrected figures (unbroken line).

(2) Surplus after deducting inflation charge based on consumption index (broken line).

(3) Surplus after deducting inflation charge based on specific indices, as in *n* (dotted line).

Even the mild correction of the consumer index reduces the accounting surplus considerably. The more stringent effects of the special indices are shown by the dotted line.

In both diagrams, the ups-and-downs of the dotted lines are very noticeable. Desire for stability thus reinforces theoretical grounds for preferring the consumption index to the specific indices when determining correct profit.

(B) Corrected profit in stabilised £'s

Table 4B repeats many of the items in 4A, but converts the figures into £'s of September, 1957. Thus the 1957 column has nearly the same figures as the 1957 column of Table 4A (the latter being slightly smaller because transactions took place on average at about March 31, not September 30). The columns for earlier years contain larger numbers than in Table 4A—because the measuring-rod has shrunk.

Table 4B shows the trend of earnings better than Table 4A. The impression of upsurge is confirmed, though it is less marked; net profit (*g*) rises by about 150 per cent. over the 10 years (compared with 240 per cent. in 4A).

Balance Sheets

(A) Ordinary figures

Table 5A sets out the published figures. Line *n* adds a note of the cumulative inflation charges—that is, the overstatement in revenue reserve.

The remarkable thing about the figures is the growth of plant (*c*), which goes up to nearly five times its opening size; see also the unbroken line in Diagram 4. Stock values (*e*) rise at almost the same pace.

Line *f* shows that the companies managed, after the first three years, to operate with money-assets below current liabilities. Line *j* stresses the size of the Chancellor's claims; if current tax is also considered, these claims rise in the later years to about one-sixth of the asset total.

Window-dressing by the Iron and Steel Holding and Realisation Agency has deprived the credit balances of much of their normal meaning, and one must be cautious about interpreting them. In particular, revenue reserve (*k*) cannot be treated seriously; large slices of it were removed (for example, to provide bonus capital and loan stock) during the reorganisations that preceded public issues.

(B) Stabilised figures

Table 5B re-states Table 5A in terms of the £ of September 30, 1957. Thus its 1957 column has some figures also

TABLE 5A

BALANCE SHEETS OF SEVEN COMPANIES, 1948–57

Ordinary figures. £000 omitted

	1948	*1949*	*1950*	*1951*	*1952*	*1953*	*1954*	*1955*	*1956*	*1957*
a Fixed assets—cost	106,894	132,792	164,283	196,138	222,648	259,457	298,855	337,448	389,635	458,700
b *Less* Depreciation (uncorrected)	32,102	35,908	42,745	47,229	54,020	62,991	69,839	81,012	94,029	111,073
c Net book-value	74,792	96,884	121,538	148,909	168,628	196,466	229,016	256,436	295,606	347,627
d Associated companies, etc.	15,016	14,850	13,280	16,520	16,098	13,318	8,776	8,893	7,637	6,760
e Stocks	32,079	39,307	42,064	44,199	60,650	69,494	71,186	77,833	101,567	120,749
	121,887	151,041	176,882	209,628	245,376	279,278	308,978	343,162	404,810	475,136
f Current liabilities, less money assets	−15,753	−1,175	−2,468	1,331	12,953	13,985	12,413	3,717	23,970	21,068
g Debentures and loans	22,066	28,346	46,654	56,630	61,200	73,780	96,301	103,703	117,732	121,798
h Preference capital	15,012	15,012	15,012	15,012	11,399	11,399	25,097	24,097	24,097	27,097
i Maintenance provision	7,878	6,947	7,383	6,168	6,784	7,880	9,317	11,087	13,004	14,864
j Tax reserve (non-current)	6,387	8,875	11,155	16,108	27,674	29,893	35,374	44,586	45,147	52,280
k Revenue reserves and miscellaneous (uncorrected)	34,793	41,482	47,715	57,844	64,876	75,141	57,461	70,978	87,923	90,143
m Ordinary capital and capital reserves	51,504	51,554	51,431	56,535	60,490	67,200	73,015	84,994	92,937	147,886
	121,887	151,041	176,882	209,628	245,376	279,278	308,978	343,162	404,810	475,136
n Inflation charges (cumulative)		2,689	6,303	11,462	16,733	20,847	25,934	32,086	39,968	48,255

TABLE 5B

BALANCE SHEETS OF SEVEN COMPANIES, 1948–57

Stabilised in £s of September 30, 1957. £000 omitted

	1948	*1949*	*1950*	*1951*	*1952*	*1953*	*1954*	*1955*	*1956*	*1957*
a Fixed assets	216,060	249,320	289,931	327,290	354,013	393,976	435,642	474,825	521,736	586,026
b *Less* Depreciation (corrected)	78,842	84,662	98,511	104,627	112,451	125,067	134,436	147,918	160,354	178,846
c Net book-value	137,218	164,658	191,420	222,663	241,562	268,909	301,206	326,907	361,382	407,180
d Associated companies, etc.	20,955	20,726	18,634	22,658	22,164	19,022	13,923	14,052	12,754	11,867
e Stocks	45,768	54,345	55,489	53,095	69,707	79,018	78,914	83,495	104,727	120,749
	203,941	239,729	265,543	298,416	333,433	366,949	394,043	424,454	478,863	539,796
f Current liabilities, *less* money assets	−21,983	−1,594	−3,193	1,599	14,888	15,901	13,761	3,987	24,715	21,068
g Debentures	30,793	38,446	60,346	68,035	70,343	83,888	106,760	111,242	121,393	121,798
h Preference capital	20,949	20,361	19,418	18,035	13,102	12,961	27,823	25,849	24,846	27,097
i Maintenance provision	10,994	9,712	10,293	8,784	9,504	10,742	12,355	14,313	16,293	18,173
j Tax reserve (non-current)	8,913	12,339	15,377	21,529	35,057	37,564	43,717	53,908	54,488	61,704
k Revenue reserves and miscellaneous (corrected)	48,554	53,192	52,874	58,844	60,284	67,106	41,002	48,558	60,186	52,234
l Gain from owing (cumulative)		1,276	4,590	10,607	14,650	15,612	18,912	23,640	29,181	34,383
m Ordinary capital, capital reserves, etc.	105,721	105,997	105,838	110,983	115,605	123,175	129,713	142,957	147,761	203,339
	203,941	239,729	265,543	298,416	333,433	366,949	394,043	424,454	478,863	539,796

TABLE 5C

REAL VALUATION GAINS (CUMULATIVE) OF SEVEN COMPANIES, 1949–57

Current £s. £000 omitted

		1948	1949	1950	1951	1952	1953	1954	1955	1956	1957
	Fixed assets, less depreciation, raised by:										
a	Specific index	110,090	132,526	159,856	203,212	233,943	262,888	301,650	342,419	395,296	467,249
b	General index	98,332	121,407	147,997	185,351	210,177	236,496	271,668	304,700	350,447	407,180
c	Real appreciation (cumulative)	11,758	11,119	11,859	17,861	23,766	26,392	29,982	37,719	44,849	60,069
	Gain on owing (cumulative)										
d	On money assets less current liabilities		−229	−336	−422	−176	−44	294	446	654	1,387
e	On debentures and preference capital		1,170	3,885	9,251	12,924	13,767	16,770	21,585	27,647	32,996
f	Total gain on owing ..		941	3,549	8,829	12,748	13,723	17,064	22,031	28,301	34,383
g	Total, *c*+*f*		12,060	15,408	26,690	36,514	40,115	47,046	59,750	73,150	94,452

found in the same column of Table 5A (lines *e* to *h*, for items shown at current values in ordinary accounts), but figures based on historical cost are raised with the consumption index. For instance, the fixed assets in the 1948 column—consisting largely of pre-war purchases—are revalued at over double their cost figure, and depreciation also grows; in later years, when some of the older plant has been scrapped and much new plant bought, the increase in value becomes relatively less important.

Revenue reserves (*k*) fail to grow much during the decade (even though they rise considerably in Table 5A, despite window-dressing transfers), because Table 5B corrects for short-falls in depreciation and cost-of-goods-sold—some £50 million by 1957.

Table 5B shows *trends* in better perspective than 5A. The expansion indicated in Table 5A is confirmed. But the upward surge is gentler; assets have in real terms grown by roughly 170 per cent., not the 290 per cent. suggested by historical cost figures. This trend is also portrayed by the line for stabilised values in Diagram 4.

Line *l* traces the *gain from owing* over the decade. As the companies normally met some 30 per cent. of their financial needs with fixed-money loans (*f*, *g* and *h*), erosion of these loans was a large gain—£34 million. (Pre-1948 lenders in addition had lost some purchasing-power before 1948; such early transfers to the equity are not included in *l*, but in the figure for ordinary capital, etc., on line *m*.)

How was the expansion in assets financed? If various transfers from reserve are added back (and the corresponding bonus issues and additions to capital reserves are excised), the sources may be set down roughly as the following percentages:

	Ordinary accounts		Stabilised accounts	
		Percentage		Percentage
New issues:				
Loans		29		36
Ordinary capital		9		9
		38		45
Internal sources:				
Depreciation and maintenance	20		25	
Trade revenue	31		18	
Tax reserve	11		12	
		62		55
		100		100

In real terms, 45 per cent. of the growth came from outside;* internal sources provided 55 per cent. Corrected depreciation stands higher, and corrected profit much lower, than uncorrected figures.

(C) *Valuation gains in real terms*

Table 5C summarises the valuation gains. Line *a* revalues the fixed assets, with the help of the special plant index. The results suggest the values that might have been put into ordinary balance sheets had the assets been re-stated each year at current replacement cost; thus

* The loans are stated at their "arrival" value—that is, before allowing for subsequent transfers to the equity *via* gains on owing.

DIAGRAM 4

Fixed assets, less depreciation: cost and current revaluations, and stabilised values

1948-57

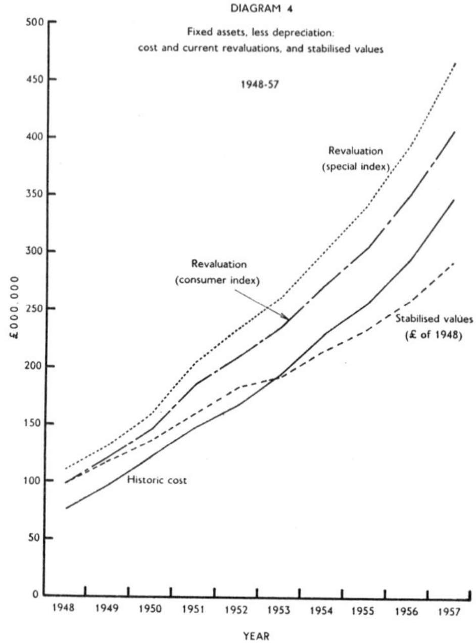

comparison of the 1957 estimate (£467 million) with the cost figure of Table 5A, line *c* (£347 million) shows appreciation of some £120 million, or approximately a third. The same two sets of values are shown in Diagram 4 by the dotted and the unbroken lines.

Line *b* gives a lower set of plant values, found with the consumption index; these are also represented in Diagram 4. The excess of *a* over *b* is given in *c*, and may be regarded as a real gain for the companies. It rises to £60 million over the decade.

Next in 5C comes the gain from owing—mainly unrealised benefits from the lessening burden of long-term debt (*e*).

The total of these two forms of gain is shown in *g*—and comes in the end to over £90 million.

Return on Investment

Did the vast investment in new assets give a commensurate return? Comparison of trade profits with asset totals, in both the A and the B tables, shows that assets and profits grew at much the same rate; indeed, the closeness of the correlation has a somewhat artificial flavour. Normal accounts suggest a steady yield of about 15 per cent. on the assets; stabilised accounts show that the real yield was about 13 per cent. The real earnings of the equity alone were roughly 13 per cent. in early years, but rose to some 17 per cent. by the close.

IV CONCLUSIONS

Data Summarised

Let us now review our findings.

The main features of the two periods, it will be remembered, are:

> 1939–47. General prices rose on average by some 8 per cent. each year. As might be expected during a war, plant did not grow much.
>
> 1949–57. General prices rose on average by some 4 per cent. each year. Plant was greatly expanded.

Our results for the two periods—it turns out—differ somewhat. It is useful that they do: the contrast gives a clearer view of the conditions under which ordinary accounting becomes open to criticism.

It may be helpful to ask questions about the alleged defects of ordinary methods, and then to state how far our survey bears out the criticisms. (Needless to say, the questions would have to be re-phrased in times of falling prices.)

(1) *Does ordinary accounting seriously overstate profits?* In 1939–47, correction of the ordinary figures cut down profit to an extent that varied over the years—12½ per cent. at the start, some 40 per cent. in the middle period, and over 80 per cent. in 1947. Throughout 1949–57, the percentage kept fairly close to 13.

(2) *Does ordinary accounting fail to maintain capital?* After payment of tax and dividends, there were deficits on trade revenue account (corrected figures) throughout 1939–47. In 1949–57, there was always a surplus on the corrected figures (unless maintenance of physical stocks and plant is taken as the test—if it is, there were deficits in three years).

(3) *Does ordinary accounting understate assets seriously?* By the end of the first period, revaluation of plant would have raised net book values by some 70 per cent. (special

index) or 50 per cent. (consumption index). The corresponding percentages at the end of the second period were 34 and 17.

(4) *Does ordinary accounting alter trends?*
Comparison of uncorrected with stabilised results shows that ordinary accounts impart a flattering upward bias. This bias was marked in 1939–47, less so in 1949–57.

(5) *Is the "gain on owing" sizeable?*
A loan for the whole of the first period was in effect written down by nearly 9s. in the £; for the second, by some 5s. 8d. Thanks to these transfers to equity-holders, their final investment was raised by about one-quarter (1947) and one-tenth (1957). In neither period were these gains sufficient to wipe out the shortfalls in depreciation and cost-of-goods-sold (though they came near to so doing in the first).

Type of Index
Our two sets of results throw light on the question whether a general price index gives results that differ much from those obtained by using special indices for each type of asset.

In the first period (see Table 2A), the choice of method makes remarkably little difference to the resultant profits. But in the later period (see 4A), the special indices on average more than double the inflation charges found by the general index; and their impact in different years fluctuates wildly. The moral seems to be: use the general index for correcting profits, and the specific indices as guides for appropriating extra sums, in round numbers, based on long-term needs.

For asset revaluation, the special plant index seems the logical tool, and gave higher values than the general index in both periods.

General Application
The 1939–47 results agree fairly well with those in the study of American steel companies (which covered 1941–7).

How far would our findings apply to concerns other than those in the steel trade? The answer presumably depends on financial and asset structures. Thus low gearing lessens the gain from owing; but gearing of the steel companies seems not untypical of that of many large enterprises. Relatively little in stocks and plant reduces the inflation charges; perhaps steel companies are exceptional in that their depreciation charge exceeds their stock charge, but the total of the two must surely be substantial for any industrial concern.

In one particular, the figures of the steel companies for the second period probably fail to illustrate the weakness of ordinary accounting. As we have seen, the expansion of steel plants was so great that the ordinary depreciation charges for later years were in large part based on recent high-price acquisitions; and so these charges came unusually near to being adequate. Other types of firm may not have fared so well; and in a few years (unless inflation ends or plant goes on growing at an almost inconceivable pace) understatement of depreciation will again be a serious problem for steel companies.

Published by The Institute of Chartered Accountants in England and Wales at Moorgate Place, London, E.C.2, and Printed in Great Britain by The Shenval Press, Simson Shand Ltd., London, Hertford and Harlow.

APPROACHES TO PRICING

William T. Baxter and Alfred R. Oxenfeldt

WILLIAM T. BAXTER AND ALFRED R. OXENFELDT

approaches to pricing | ECONOMIST *vs* ACCOUNTANT

This article examines the part played by the cost accountant in fixing a firm's prices, and especially his assumption that cost plus or full cost is a useful and logical basis for price. It also undertakes the difficult task of reconciling the almost flatly contradictory views of the cost accountant and the economic theorist on pricing.

Generalizations about the two professions must, of course, be unsatisfactory. Since the terms "cost accountant" and "economist" cover many persons with a wide range of views, a short article must omit many desirable qualifications and do injustice to many individuals. However, few who are familiar with both costing and economics would fail to recognize the gulf that often separates the respective approaches to price. It is generally true that the cost accountant fails to state his assumptions about the firm's aims and pays scant attention to demand; he collects cost data and arrives at price by manipulating these. The economist, on the other hand, starts by assuming that the firm is trying to maximize something, for example, profit; he then shows how the firm should study demand as well as cost in an attempt to find this maximum output level.

Mr. Baxter is Professor of Accounting, University of London, and Mr. Oxenfeldt is Professor of Marketing, Columbia University.

COST PLUS

The cost-plus procedure is too familiar to need extended description.[1] In the multi-product firm, the formula for finding the price of a job runs somewhat as follows: (1) find the job's direct costs—mainly material and labor; (2) add a charge for indirect costs (by allocating these overheads as a rate on a unit such as the wages or hours of direct labor, or machine-hours); and (3) add a further sum for profit—often calculated as a percentage of the total under (1) and (2).

Objections to Cost Plus

It is not hard to ridicule the logic of the cost-plus doctrine. Its "cost" is objectionable on at least three grounds—time, jointness, and opportunity.

Time The avoidable cost of any job depends on the firm's degree of commitment at the time in question. Since this may change with each decision and act, a job has not one cost but a range of costs varying with its stage of completion and at best a cost figure can be right at only one stage. The cost accountant's sums, however, are based on historical records that do not change with changing commitments.

Jointness A job is normally a joint product in the sense that other jobs use the same resources. The cost of such resources is thus common to many jobs and there is seldom an unimpeachable basis for dividing it among the jobs (since the resulting figures rarely show what will actually be saved if a given job is not done). Yet full cost includes an allocated slice of common cost.

Opportunity Costing tends to concentrate on expenditures of a given work program. It seems to ignore the alternatives open to the enterprise, or to assume that the alternative is idleness. Yet displaced opportunities are vital in making a business decision, which might indeed be defined as the process of selecting among alternatives.

The objections to the "cost" in the cost-plus formula are only part of the problem; economists criticize the "plus," too. The use of a somewhat rigid margin suggests that the firm does not want to find the price levels at which its total profits will be highest—or at least that it is oddly indifferent to the power of demand and of competition. Yet competition in some cases may be strong enough to take price decisions right out of the firm's hands. In other cases, surely the starting point in pricing should be the study of demand (whether, for example, it is elastic or inelastic) and the realization that each possible price may entail a different output and profit.

Superficially, it appears that if a firm adds a margin to costs to cover overheads and profit, it thereby ensures itself some profit. But, of course, this is true only in favorable markets. If cost plus produces a price so high relative to customer valuations that few sales are made, losses will be sustained. No mechanical pricing formula can guarantee a profit, although, unfortunately, cost plus gives the impression of doing so.

Cost and Displaced Alternatives

Costing thus seems to violate a central cost principle of the economist, that cost can be measured realistically only by taking into account the alternative opportunities open to the firm. To find the sacrifices that will result from the decision to do a job (the economist argues), we must logically look only to the period that still lies in the future at decision date, and must estimate the changes in future expenses and revenues that result from the decision, a procedure

[1]Costing practices are described in countless textbooks. For a description of U.S. pricing practices, see Theodore Karger and C. Clark Thompson, "Pricing Policies and Practices," *Conference Board Business Record,* XIV (September, 1957), 434-42; Joel Dean, *Managerial Economics* (New York: Prentice-Hall, 1951), pp. 444-57; Alfred R. Oxenfeldt, *Industrial Pricing and Market Practices* (New York: Prentice-Hall, 1951), pp. 156-65; and A.D.H. Kaplan, Joel B. Dirlam, and Robert F. Lanzillotti, *Pricing in Big Business* (Washington: The Brookings Institution, 1958).

that obliges us also to estimate what these expenses and revenues would look like if the job is not done.

It will therefore be helpful to classify costs under two heads. The first agrees with what is commonly understood by "cost" (except that it insists on a cause-and-effect relation between decision and sacrifice), while the second differs from the everyday definition of the word in that it is concerned with potential gains displaced by the given job.

First, compare expenses if the firm does Job A, with its expenses if it does nothing. In this way, we find the expenses that should appear in an ordinary budget—the sacrifices that the firm can avoid by not doing A or anything in its place. We shall call these potential savings *avoidable costs.*

Second, compare the firm's balance sheet after doing Job A with its balance sheet if it instead puts its assets to their next best uses (for example, employs plant on other work, or lends cash at interest). The net revenue that the firm would gain by applying its resources to their next best use is part of the sacrifice of doing A. We shall henceforth use *opportunity cost* in this narrow meaning of net revenue foregone. The total sacrifice involved in doing Job A may thus include both avoidable cost and opportunity cost.[2]

Business Acceptance of Cost Plus

The objections to cost plus sound formidable in the classroom, but cut remarkably little ice outside. The cost accountant often concedes that they have some validity in private discussion; yet he ignores them in his published writings, and his accounts continue in the main to be filled with historical costs and allocations. These seem to impress executives and to serve as satisfying guides to policy. Cost plus is probably the primary method of fixing price in American industry (and is perhaps even more usual abroad).

The main attraction of cost plus is, of course, that it offers a means by which plausible prices can be found with ease and speed, no matter how many products the firm handles. Moreover, its imposing computations look factual and precise, and its prices may well seem more defensible on moral grounds than prices established by other means. Thus a monopolist, threatened by public inquiry, might reasonably feel that he is safeguarding his case by using cost plus; also when the "just price" of part of a firm's output is at issue (as in contracts for military supplies), cost plus may be the best short-run method of fixing price. For these and other reasons, the appeal of cost plus to harassed executives is plain, even though some of them may look on it privately as no more than an expedient ritual. We must indeed ask whether those of us who are its spoken critics would in fact wholly reject it if we were ourselves responsible for pricing.

The gulf between practice and doctrine is thus extremely wide.[3] In an effort to appraise the issues, we shall now look more

[2] This approach to cost assumes that the cost figures are to be used only for decision on pricing or the like. Some accountants now say that the merits of costing lie more in *control* (of waste, and so on) than in pricing. For control, the right cost may well be historical cost, possibly compared with standard or budget figures.

[3] Considering the size of the gulf, it has excited surprisingly little comment. Costing authors are usually too swamped in massive computations to say what their end-figures mean. Economists tended to ignore costing until the late thirties, when articles by R. H. Coase and R. S. Edwards—republished in David Solomons, ed., *Studies in Costing* (London: Sweet & Maxwell, 1952)—criticized costing theory; and when, for example, R. L. Hall and C. J. Hitch, "Price Theory and Business Behaviour," *Oxford Economic Papers,* No. 2 (May, 1939), pp. 12-45, pointed out that businessmen's descriptions of their own behavior fail to tally with those in economic writings. P.W.S. Andrews in *Manufacturing Business* (London, 1949) went on to suggest that the economist's description is therefore wrong. Such backsliding evoked many retorts, including: Austin Robinson, "Pricing of Manufactured Products," *Economic Journal,* LX (December, 1950), 771-80; and Fritz Machlup, "Marginal Analysis and Empirical Research," *American Economic Review,* XXXVI (September, 1946), 519-54. The virtues and limitations of the economist's approach are ably set out by R. A. Gordon, "Short-Period Price Determination in Theory and Practice," *Studies in Costing,* pp. 183-208.

closely at the cost accountant's figures under various circumstances. We shall, for instance, compare different market structures and contrast single-product with multiproduct firms.

SINGLE-PRODUCT FIRMS

Where a firm makes only one product, the cost accountant generally summarizes his results as averages. Average cost seems at first sight to serve many useful ends. In particular, it can readily be compared with price and for this reason it is a handy test of whether the firm is earning profits—provided the implied guesses at total cost and volume prove correct. However, average cost becomes less attractive when we distinguish various markets in which the one-product firm may find itself, and consider the pricing problems that these markets sometimes pose.

WHERE MARKETS ARE PURELY COMPETITIVE

Although examples of pure competition are probably not to be found anywhere, rough approximations to the economic theorist's model do exist. Agriculture, organized commodity markets, and some branches of the textile industry come fairly close. In such purely competitive markets, the businessman needs no cost data for pricing purposes. He has no power over price, being compelled to accept the prevailing one, or wait to sell his wares at another time, since price is determined by the interaction of all buyers and sellers, and is not subject to perceptible influence by any one of them. Therefore, cost cannot be the basis for price.

Accounts, however, may still be guides to business policy. Every firm should consider whether it can better itself by altering its scale of operation; the cost accountant would be doing useful work if he drafted budgets of total cost and revenue at various levels of activity. These would show which level is the most profitable, or even that none of the levels is profitable, in which case the firm would do better to switch to other products, or go right out of business. With change in scale comes change in cost; thus, under pure competition, it is price that fixes cost rather than vice versa.

WHERE THE PRODUCT DIFFERS FROM COMPETING PRODUCTS

A firm making a single product that differs from the offerings of rivals generally has some discretion over price.[4] Its price decisions will influence, perhaps strongly, its physical volume of sales. It should presumably try to find the price and volume that bring the highest profit; it may decide to charge a price far below what its rivals ask for competing wares, or to sell at a premium. Only rarely will its best price be the same as its rivals' prices. More important, only rarely and by accident will its most profitable price (in the short run or the long run) be average cost plus a constant conventional margin. Sometimes the firm with the lowest unit costs can command the highest price because of attractive features in its product. To reap the rewards of its skill, such a firm must depart from routine cost plus. As a minimum, it should raise its "plus" when it produces an outstanding product; conversely, when its model is a failure, it may be forced, in order to get rid of the batch, to shift from cost plus to cost minus.

WHERE DIFFERENT PRICES ARE CHARGED

Under the two kinds of markets outlined above, we have assumed that the firm sells all units of its one product at the same price. In practice, however, a firm often sells at different prices. The price may be changed rhythmically over time (with seasonal shifts in demand, for instance), or different prices may be charged at the same time in different markets—customers being ostensibly distinguished by location, size of order, or promptness of payment, but in fact by intensity of demand. Many firms believe that

[4]Certain market imperfections have the same result. Firms may, for example, be too widely scattered to experience severe competition.

they raise their profit by varying price in this way; indeed, there seems to be a trend in retailing away from the one-price system and back to old-fashioned higgling.

On occasion, the prices of some units may with advantage be put *below* average cost; as long as sales in the low-priced market exceed the avoidable costs of the extra goods, the firm's net profit is raised. For instance, hotels and airlines sometimes gain by cutting off-peak rates to less than average cost. Comparison of the cut rates with average cost serves little purpose, except perhaps as a clumsy reminder of the deficit to be made good at the peaks.

When one-product firms vary price in such ways, they have presumably rejected cost plus. Here then are cases where our opening statement about the widespread use of cost plus does not apply, and where firms apparently agree with the view that cost plus can impair profit.

For the reasons just given, one might almost say that any reference to average cost will be downright harmful at the pricing stage. Average cost becomes useful after the firm has chosen the best price for the given output program, because comparisons of price and average cost then form a handy miniature budget for predicting period results, and may well suggest a need to change the program. But a miniature budget of this kind cannot give a more accurate financial picture of total revenue and cost than a full budget; in fact, it is likely to be less accurate.

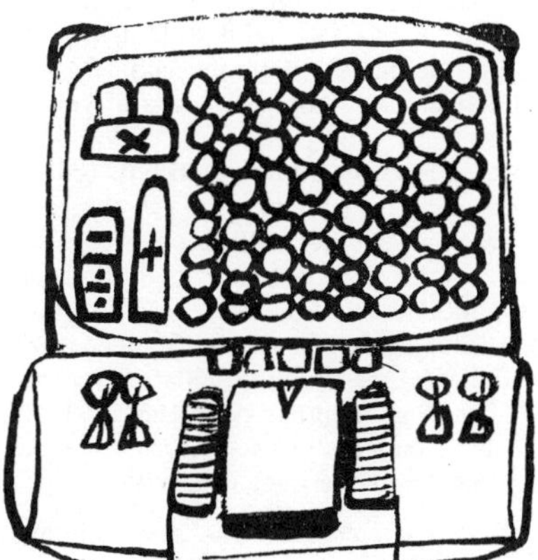

MULTIPRODUCT FIRMS

The firm with many products is, in its extreme form, the individual job shop that makes unique goods to order—for instance, the engineering shop that bids for special projects. Most common is the firm producing substantial numbers of several standardized products. In such firms, both cost accountant and price fixer are confronted by far harder tasks and, consequently, are all the more apt to take refuge in cost plus.

Demand Difficulties

As we have said, the economist insists that demand should be consciously weighed when price is being fixed. But the labor and skilled guesswork needed for making detailed demand studies for a wide range of items would generally be prohibitive. Systematic comparison of the firm's prices with those of rivals is perhaps the simplest part of the task, and yet this is often burdensome and confusing. Even the firm that is a price leader might well throw up its hands at the costs of fully estimating demand for each product. Clearly, no firm selling hundreds of products could afford to make careful demand estimates for each; in any case, many of the estimates would be out of date by the time they could be used.

Thus the accountant has a strong argument in that his system is simple, quick, and cheap. Moreover, and this is a most important point, it lets a manager delegate pricing. Such advantages, coupled with the inevitable vagueness of demand estimates, no doubt go far to explain its wide acceptance.

On the other hand, inability to estimate demand accurately and in time scarcely excuses the substitution of cost information for demand information. Crude estimates of demand might substitute for careful estimates of demand, but a cost gives remarkably little insight into demand.

Allocation of Indirect Cost

If asked to explain his charges for indirect costs, the accountant will perhaps explain that a job makes a drain on the firm's manufacturing resources—its plant and space, supervisors, design talent, and the like—and this drain is a cost of the job. Since a big job makes a big drain, cost varies with size.

Here the views of accountant and economist are poles apart. The accountant in effect believes that the total historical cost of providing the plant can be divided up into separate sacrifices for each job. The economist contests the worth of such figures and offers instead his opportunity cost argument: If the firm has excess capacity (plant, supervisors, cash, and so on), *no* sacrifice is involved in using these idle resources on the particular job;[5] if the firm has other uses for the resources, then the cost of assigning them to this job is the sum they would earn (less avoidable costs) in their best alternative uses. Opportunity cost in a range from zero to a large sum is very different from the accountant's layers of overhead.[6]

Overhead allocation is arbitrary in that the choice of any particular basis (for example, direct wages or machine-hours) is hard to justify; in addition, each of the possible bases gives figures that may differ greatly from those found on another basis. Moreover, allocation invests the "fixed costs of the job" with an air of reality that at times deceives some managers, who may, for instance, let plant stand idle rather than use it on jobs that yield less than its full slice of overhead. However onerous—even disastrous—fixed commitments like rent and interest are to the firm, they are not sacrifices for which the individual job is responsible, and are irrelevant in pricing it.

Costs bind the firm, not its customers. In the case of a product, if the avoidable costs exceed its price, the firm can at least stop making it, but where allocations of fixed costs are concerned, this remedy may not help. A firm that cannot turn to more remunerative jobs should carry on with those that fail to cover their share of overhead; such a firm can only hope that the gross margin (revenue minus avoidable cost) on all jobs will meet fixed cost and leave a profit.

Relevance of the Master Budget

In a firm of any sophistication, job costing (whether in forward-looking budgets or backward-looking accounts) is intimately linked with the firm's plans as stated in its master budget, the budget of total revenue and total cost for the next period. Sometimes such budgets merely give combined figures for the firm's total operations, but generally—if subdivision is feasible—they allow individually for each of the main products. The master budget's projection of revenue implies a specific level of price (hopefully resting on the most competent analysis of market conditions that management can make). Both revenue and cost figures similarly imply forecasts of volume and mix.

From the master budget, with its implicit price and cost per unit, one can derive an average margin per unit. In other words, it is the master budget that gives the rates of allocated overhead and profit for each job. This holds whether the budget is full and formal, or merely a tentative forecast.

If costing and pricing are integrated with a master budget, then several extremely important corollaries seem to follow.

Pricing Objectives The master budget presumably states the firm's realistic plans

[5]Any extra expenditure due to the extra wear and tear on equipment and so on *is* a sacrifice caused by the job, and should be included in avoidable cost. This is a good example of the way in which the accountant's direct cost (based on the arbitrary classification of the ledger) can differ from true avoidable cost.

[6]A job's full cost may include, besides the load for factory overhead, a second load for more remote overheads such as administration (usually found as a percentage of the job's direct cost plus the first load). The second is even harder to justify than the first, since a given job is not likely to add much to administrative expense or make much drain on administrative services.

and expectations, and reflects what it is trying to maximize. The economist summarizes the relevant forces in his diagrams of total or marginal cost and revenue, and suggests that the firm will trim its output until it arrives at the point of maximum profit. The master budget seems to be the firm's forecast of its costs and revenue at that point. The maximand may in fact be profit—probably for the long run rather than the budget period alone; more likely, it is some compromise among such advantageous factors as profit, a safe cash position, growth, and prestige.

Considering the importance of the master budget, costing writers are curiously silent about its construction, and add little to our scant understanding of the mental steps behind the big decisions. Their reticence compels the critic to put his own interpretation on this fundamental part of costing theory, but it is doubtful that these writers seriously challenge the economist's view of the firm's aims and methods *at the budget stage.*[7] They must surely regard maximum long-run profit as an important part of the goal at least in the sense that the less costly method is better than the more costly, and a very low profit is a danger sign.

Measures of Activity and Size of Job With Diversified Output Some multiproduct firms have no obvious unit with which to measure the size of jobs. Such firms cannot readily link budget figures with units produced, or speak of unit cost and unit price, nor can they in any direct way compare the profits and costs of different jobs.

[7]For instance, the concept of profit target as a round percentage on past investment may strike many accountants as no more than a convenient simplification, which can be amended without inconsistency when circumstances demand something less crude. Again, the accountant (like other practical men) sometimes illustrates the master budget with a break-even chart whose lines are straight, in contrast to the economist's curves—thus seeming to imply that output and profit can expand indefinitely. If pressed on the point during discussion, the accountant will freely agree that the implication is absurd; he may explain away the absurdity by saying, for example, that nonmonetary factors, such as strain on management, will in fact check expansion.

We suggest that the one object of job costing is to overcome this difficulty, and to find units where these are not provided by the nature of the job. In a few cases, an artificial unit of output can be devised, such as the "bus mile" or "passenger mile" of a motor bus. Where no common unit of output can be found, the accountant for want of something better may take a unit of input, like wages or hours of direct labor, or machine-hours. The master budget can thus be regarded as a plan for a certain volume of activity measured in man-hours, or some other selected unit. The cost estimate for each job likewise makes use of the same unit for allocating indirect costs and finding price; in this way, cost and price are linked with the job's size.

Average Cost per Unit With Diversified Output If this interpretation is right, then the accountant's measure of indirect costs for a job is often akin to an average that is weighted to allow for the job's size, measured in the chosen input units. It has therefore much the same demerits and merits as average cost in the one-product firm. It fails to show the real sacrifice involved in doing the job, but it serves under some circumstances as a miniature forecast of the firm's annual results, and so gives advance warning of a need for revising, say, the scale of operations.

The Costing Margin as a Processing Charge Again, just as the one-product budget shows both the number of units to be produced and total revenue, so a multiproduct budget shows planned production in input units and total revenue. But the one-product budget may sensibly deal with unit price whereas to speak of average price per unit in the multiproduct firm usually does not mean much.

If the margin added to direct cost to arrive at price is explained as so much indirect cost and profit per input unit, it has little to recommend it. But if it is regarded as a price per unit—for example, the firm's estimate of the best average price to charge per man-hour for the service of converting direct materials into finished goods—it may be both useful and intellectually defensible. The price quoted for a job could then be regarded as avoidable cost plus a processing charge—with no mention of overhead cost. This idea comes close to the method called "contribution costing," which is used by certain cost accountants when they express the margin on a job as a rate per machine-hour, that is, as the earnings per hour of some key machine that the job utilizes.

A firm in its master budget should presumably try to forecast the number of input units and the average price for each that will give best results. Then, in its day-to-day decisions, it should implement the budget strategy. Suppose, for instance, that the planned costing margin is $\$m$ per man-hour. A job needing x man-hours is priced at $\$mx$ (plus direct costs), not because $\$mx$ measures meaningful slices of overhead, but because this is the price that the firm must charge if it is to carry out its budget decisions. Cost plus, then, represents an administrative trick for putting a price policy into action.

The Costing Margin and Opportunity Cost Our interpretation thus implies that a costing margin should be regarded as a tacit allowance for opportunity cost, among other things. The firm first decides that it can maximize profit by selling so many input units of service at a certain price; given this assumption, to do Job X at a lesser rate is to lose greater potential revenue. The loss may arise because X's buyer would in fact be willing to pay more, or because X displaces a better job, or because the firm would need to cut prices all round when X's price became known.

This view, if correct, would go far to explain why costing seems to serve business needs despite its shaky logic. It does not do what it professes to do, but it may do something better; the traditional costing margin —overhead plus profit—may serve as a rough guide to opportunity cost. On the other hand, if costing derives its virtue in this way, then recognition of its true nature would prevent errors based on misinterpretation and would enable accountants to improve their figures.

There are obvious objections to our interpretation of the costing margin, to which we shall return shortly. It does, however, stress one important point; in real life, the alternative to Job X is usually not a known Job Y that neatly duplicates X in everything save profit. The alternative, which may still be unknown when a price is put on X, may consist of several small jobs or part of a large one; it may demand more or less time, space, and money than X. Job-by-job comparisons of profit may, in fact, be impossible or meaningless. Conceivably, operational research will someday help to simplify this issue; in the meantime, probably the best the firm can do is to allow roughly for X's displacement power by means of a load that depends —like the costing margin—on how much of the firm's resources are engaged in the production of X.

JOB COSTS AND MARGINAL ANALYSIS

A further conclusion may perhaps follow if the foregoing argument is correct. The conflict between accounting and economics seems, in this area, somewhat unreal; both may simply be dealing with different stages of the production program.

When the economist considers the problem of profit maximization, he is generally thinking of the stage at which the firm is still trying to find its best scale of operation for the next period. He considers, for instance, the results on expected cost and revenue of expanding the next period's ouput from n units to $n + x$ units. (x is here the marginal quantity, and its avoidable cost is the relevant marginal cost.)

Costing is more often concerned with what happens after these plans have been made. As we have seen, estimates for single jobs or small batches assume that the master budget for the period has already been drafted and that the figures of the budget (including planned physical activity of n units, however these are measured) have been used to find rates for burden and profit at the start of the period. Later, at some point during the period, a given job is considered. Costing tries to estimate inputs of this job, its size (x units), and, thus, its weighted average cost. But the master budget is not changed by the job; output is still expected to total only n (not $n + x$) by the close of the year, for x is merely a part in the planned flow of output. Consequently, the job, its cost, and its revenue do not appear to be marginal in the economist's usual sense; a textbook diagram whose horizontal axis shows total output is helpful for explaining the composite program, but is irrelevant to any job within that program. We suspect that, when economists question businessmen on how the fundamental decisions are made, there may be sad muddling of budget strategy with costing tactics.

Objections to the Costing Margin

In our attempt to interpret the costing margin as a measure for pricing, we have deliberately passed over the flaws in the argument.

1 One weakness is that the interpretation has never to our knowledge been put forward by a cost accountant.

2 Another lies in the notion of omniscient budgets and clear-cut budget periods; plainly, a costing margin found by a master budget cannot measure opportunity costs at all closely, for the budget assumes such costs to be the same for every date during its period and for all the products. The day-by-day state of the market ought to change a manager's views on the period's possibilities; if he gets a big order, he must, at least mentally, revise his budget totals somewhat. Consequently, a cost margin found at the budget stage may soon be out of date.

3 Again, the argument makes sense only where the firm can in fact switch from one product to another. This is often difficult or impossible, because for instance the products emerge in fixed proportions, or plant is built to do only one job. If there is no alternative, there is no opportunity cost.

4 Further, the argument assumes that the chosen input unit correlates with costs and demand in much the same way as the output units of the single-product firm. This is a tall assumption. In some firms, any given input unit seems likely to vary too much with each job's peculiarities to be a good general index of size for all jobs, and there may be no common denominator for size if each job is a distinctive bundle of materials, skills, and services.

5 A customer, to take the demand point of view, will not base his valuations on any internal unit used by his supplier. His test of a job's size is how much he wants it, and his price ceiling is the lower of this subjective value and the price he must pay for a similar article elsewhere, or for substitutes. This composite force on the demand side, and not the supplier's cost and effort, is what enables the supplier to charge more for the big job—and indeed to earn any revenue at all. Accordingly, a prime criterion in choosing a unit should be that it serves as a guide to the bids of rivals; the more their productive methods differ from those of the given firm, the less sound will the latter's input units be as guides.

6 Finally, just as one-product firms may find that it pays to charge different prices in different markets, so the multiproduct firm may benefit by varying its margin per unit on its different products. A firm of jobbing engineers, for example, may make each of its tenders in somewhat different demand conditions; here the case for flexible pricing is very strong.

Although these objections to the use of the costing margin as an indicator of opportunity cost and price are formidable, the pricer in the multiproduct firm must have some measure of the size of each job in order to determine how much of the firm's productive resources (man power, machinery, space, and executive direction) the job will consume. Even when these resources involve no added expense or outlay, they do represent the firm's opportunity to create net income, and some price must be placed on their use if the firm has alternatives. The costing margin may be a crude and imperfect tool, and yet be the least objectionable one that is available.

Perhaps the correct attitude toward the costing margin is to regard it in practice as the best starting point for pricing. When the appropriate price for the size of the job has been found by this omnibus formula, management can consider whether the master budget's assumption about the general state of trade still applies or whether demand for the particular article warrants a change in the margin. Considering such factors, they may, perhaps without realizing the extent of their intervention, modify the costing price substantially.[8]

The Firm With a "Line of Products"

A good example of the need to modify prices found by means of a costing margin occurs when a firm sells many different products to the same customer. Such firms may be said to sell a "line of products." A new customer means sales of many products; a lost customer means lost sales of many products.

Cost plus, strictly applied, would often rob the firm of the benefits that come from pricing its wares as a "team" in which some items clear the ground for others. The price line, with the low-price, low-margin items whose function is to "build traffic" and arouse customer interest, and the high-price, high-margin, and high-quality item that brings prestige to the entire line and aids the medium-priced items, is commonplace in many industries. Other firms use the variation of periodically cutting prices of some items for a short time.

Could costing at least show which items to promote and which to drop? There are several difficulties in using accounts to this end. First, the cost side would include some arbitrary allocations; many of the overheads charged to the item under scrutiny would not be reduced to nil by dropping it. Second, the revenues are likely to understate the item's contributions; inclusion of an item in the line may well explain how important customers have been won and held. Finally, the decision maker must look to the item's future rather than its past.

Accordingly, this kind of firm is likely to be led astray—both in fixing prices and in deciding whether to promote, drop, or maintain items—if it relies on traditional accounts. It is far better for an expert price fixer to guess clumsily at the right factors than to measure precisely those that are irrelevant. He should estimate the demand for those products that are unique in some degree and arrange prices on the team principle; when he is considering whether to drop an item, he should guess at what it adds to revenue by boosting the sale of other products. The mechanical application of a generalized budget formula is here most unlikely to measure opportunity costs. A cost estimate of the savings from dropping the item may be useful, but it should be an *ad hoc* estimate, confined to costs that will in fact be changed by the omission.

SUGGESTED PROCEDURE

Early in this article, we posed two problems. Why is cost plus so popular, despite its crude logic? And, would we, if we were in positions of business responsibility, reject this approach? We shall now try to answer both questions by outlining the way in which we think the cost accountant should help with pricing.

Formula vs. Individual Analysis

The central problem is whether any general formula, such as cost plus, suitably reinterpreted, can with advantage be put in the place of individual decisions about each price.

The two main factors to be weighed by a pricer are demand and cost. Demand should ideally be studied with the utmost care by persons of outstanding discernment. We believe that no formula can accurately assess all the pulls and shifts of the living market, and that management must in the end bear

[8]I. F. Pearce showed in "A Study in Price Policy," *Economica*, XXIII (May, 1956), 114-27 that in one firm, whose managers firmly believed they worked on cost plus, job prices found by cost plus became actual prices in only a minority of cases.

full responsibility for estimating demand. A formula can be defended only on the grounds that careful judgments on each separate price are either not feasible (because of the need for quick decisions on many articles) or not worth while (because of the high risk of error). The retail shop provides an apt analogy: its owner might well maximize profit by bargaining afresh with each customer on each visit over each unit of stock, but in practice he is usually forced by the difficulties of doing otherwise to put the same price ticket on all like units.

Cost may at first sight seem easier to reduce to a formula. If however it is looked on as a choice between alternatives, it too becomes subjective and hard to weigh. Ideally, a job's cost should be estimated by senior managers after full consideration of the likely alternatives and all their impacts on future possibilities. We accept that no formula will do justice to a host of dimly foreseen and hypothetical events, and that management must shoulder the task of choosing between alternatives. But a formula may still be defensible, if only on the grounds that it winnows out the obviously unattractive plans, and leaves managers free to work on plans that offer a good prospect of success.

In short, the formula can be defended only as a last resort. Our task is to consider the circumstances in which it is most likely to be a useful supplement to special studies, and the means by which its defects can be minimized.

Building the Master Budget

As we have seen, the formula implies the existence of some sort of forecast—at its best, a full budget of the firm's revenue and costs. Such a budget seems desirable in any case. Before it is drafted, certain basic questions might well be explicitly posed. Is it the firm's aim to win maximum profit, at least in the long run and with various provisos? Is there a point on the firm's scale of activity at which profit is maximized, and on either side of which profit declines through the combined action of cost and demand forces? Practical men will know that such questions cannot be answered without qualifications, and that no one can pinpoint the quantities at stake. The important thing is to be clear on the objective and plan of attack.

Demand and price should play a big part in the plan. Our discussion has stressed the major influence of demand, and how this varies in different markets. In some markets, the firm has no discretionary power over price; the only major decision concerns scale of output. In others, the firm must simultaneously envisage price, demand, volume, and cost as interrelated parts of the budget problem.

In firms facing several types of demand, or making several products with very different cost patterns, the budget should be split up between home and foreign markets, or time of year, or type of product, and so forth. The firm must study demand in each market, and try to map out the best price policy in each; it must also draft separate budgets for each department that has a fairly uniform cost pattern.

The Task of the Formula

The budget establishes the general plan—scale, level of prices, and so on. The formula tries to put this plan into effect when the minor decisions are later made on each job.

One must in each case ask whether the firm can foresee the future clearly enough to establish such an all-embracing plan. If conditions change so fast that even supplementary budgets soon lag behind events, then a predetermined formula seems likely to do mischief. The same holds if the various jobs differ greatly, whether on the side of demand or costs. The formula presumably assumes stability and sameness in day-to-day operations; it relies on "what things usually cost" or "what we can usually charge," and thus breaks down if there is no "usual."

For reasons set out earlier, we cannot accept the normal wording of the formula in terms of allocated overhead and so on. We prefer to interpret it as a measure of contribution, that is, what the firm believes to be its best price, per unit of activity, for converting direct inputs into finished goods.

If the formula is to work well, it must allow for three quantities that would otherwise need to be found by special estimate:

1 Concealed and remote avoidable costs

2 Opportunity costs, that is, the contribution to overhead and the profit that could be obtained by doing other jobs instead

3 Any further contribution from this particular job.

The formula's claims may be tested by following the build-up of a price, step by step; we shall, if we do not state the contrary, deal with single jobs rather than large flows.

Building a Price The first step is to find the avoidable costs. Though the direct costs of the accountant may often be very similar to the obvious avoidable costs, the accountant's figures are based on clerical convenience rather than a cause-and-effect relationship between decision and sacrifice.[9] They will thus on occasion need amending in two ways: The money values attached to some ingredients must be changed, for example, by substituting current for historical cost; and the list of direct costs must be extended to include those avoidable costs that accounting classes as indirect. By their very nature, items on this extended list may be hard to detect and evaluate; even a special study for the job might end with a very vague guess at the sums in question. Therefore it does not seem unreasonable to allow for them roughly with a rate per unit of size, unless the job has individual peculiarities that call for a special estimate. Size in this context seems more likely to be a function of time (man-hours or machine-hours) than of direct expenses.

If we ignore odd cases like the loss-leader, avoidable cost will be the lowest price at which the firm will ever take on work. This minimum will, however, need to be raised if the given job displaces other profitable opportunities. Accordingly the next step is to estimate opportunity cost.

Opportunity Cost The alternatives to the given job may be known and clearly measurable. If they are, straightforward comparison between the job and the best alternative should be easy, and will show which work yields the biggest margin. If they are not, then a margin based on normal yields per unit of activity seems likely to be helpful, at least as a starting point. However, since such a margin cannot be more correct than the master budget from which it springs, the pricer should consider whether the budget still holds good. There may be a temporary change in activity, or new trends may be emerging, in the light of which the load for the given job should be trimmed. Unless the margin rate keeps pace with the order book, it is a poor guide to opportunity cost.

Which unit of activity from contenders such as direct labor cost or machine-hours should the formula employ to measure opportunity cost? Presumably the firm must find out by experience which unit best satisfies a double test: (1) prices based on this unit must attract the desired volume of activity; and yet (2) the items bought at these prices must not displace more remunerative items. The right unit is thus part of the price mechanism that equates demand with supply; customer reactions to the unit are important as well as the firm's internal workings. When one starts to find out whether a given job will displace other work, one's first inclination is perhaps to look for any scarce factor that acts as a bottleneck in production. Such a factor may exist; if, for example, labor is short, man-hours may be a good index of displaced jobs. Under imperfect competition, however, a firm may have plenty of "slack" in a physical sense, and yet continue to charge a margin. Here the bottleneck is not physical; it is the firm's own policy of restricting sales volume by keeping up prices. In this case, therefore, one should not search for bottlenecks in the plant, but should use the unit that rations sales most

[9] For instance, a clerk can trace the historical cost of raw materials through his records from their purchase until they enter the final product, but the resulting "direct cost" may not show the sacrifice due to the decision to use materials in stock. This decision probably causes the purchase of new materials; if so, the sacrifice is not a figure already in the books, but the outlay on replacement.

profitably (particularly in markets that are subject to destructive price cutting). Once again, a unit based on time seems most likely to work well; but conceivably the best unit for measuring opportunity cost is not the best for measuring concealed avoidable cost.

Profit Margin When the pricer has estimated the job's avoidable and opportunity costs, his next and final step is to ask how much more can be added as pure profit.

In many cases, the ceiling is obvious—the price charged by rivals (adjusted to allow for any special features in the firm's own product). If this is less than total cost, the firm will withdraw from the race. If it is more, the pricer must judge how near it to pitch his figure, a calculation for which direct comparison would seem a better guide than the formula.

But, where the product is new or a tender has to be made for a special job, the firm may not yet know the competing prices. Here one of the chief aims of the cost department might be to guess the prices charged by rivals. If the latter rely on a formula, then a formula may be a useful tool for predicting their prices; indeed, the normal full-cost estimate may be defensible on the grounds that it suggests not the firm's own costs, but the prices of competitors (actual or potential). Presumably the formula should not be used blindly, but should be adapted in the light of what is known of the rival's ways. For instance, a special estimate might be needed if the rival has a different method of production.

There may be a wide space between the cost floor and the demand ceiling. In that case, bargaining skill rather than economic factors may fix the position of price, or the firm may gain by charging a low price, perhaps because this will mean many future sales. An omnibus formula can scarcely respond to situations of this type. Nor can it weigh the eagerness of particular customers or the merits of a particular product. Such factors strengthen the case for using individual decisions to modify the formula's figure for profit.

Cost and Price for Large Batches Our approach must obviously be modified when we pass from the individual job to many sales of like units. Here the pricer faces nearly all the complexities of the complete budget in a single-product firm: cost may vary with volume, which may vary with the price that he is trying to find. No mechanical approach that relies on the use of a formula can do justice to such a problem.

The accountant can help by providing cost estimates at several points of the scale of output; the pricer must try to guess demand at corresponding points, and so find the optimum scale of operations. As the drafting of many precise estimates would involve much work, there may be good reason for using a formula in the preliminary stages. When the choice has been narrowed, special studies of avoidable and opportunity cost may become worth while, particularly if the given batch of new articles is big enough to suggest that it amounts to a change in the master budget.

Importance of Demand Our review of the forces at stake has emphasized the supreme importance of demand. Though this force is hard to gauge, the pricer's success must in the long run depend on his flair for assessing it.

Part of his problem stems from the effect that frequent price changes may have in the long run on customer relations. He should be equipped with a clear statement of the firm's policy on this point. Does the firm feel that isolated price concessions will involve a serious handicap in the future? The top executive might even be called upon to set a figure that measures the size of the handicap; for instance, he might estimate that price stability would in the long run justify a drop in current profits of up to $25,000.

The pricer may sometimes get helpful impressions from other members of the firm. If, for example, he is trying to set prices for a line and to employ the team-pricing concept, men in the sales department are likely to be the best source of information about which items to treat as promotional numbers, how much to charge for a prestige model, and the probable gain in general sales from having a particular item in the line.

The pricer should gather data and impressions from others within the firm, including data from specific studies specially undertaken for him by the market research department. In the end, however, he must size up all the relevant forces for himself. He cannot move directly from cost to price; he cannot even assign clear values to many of the forces. He can probably do his job best by drawing up a schedule covering the main factors at stake, and by making his own estimate, however crude, of their values. Such schedules would call for different information according to the type of product and market. Once prepared, however, they would be helpful starting points the next time a price decision for the same product was needed.

In the procedures described above, costs are still important, and it is to be hoped that the cost accountant will help to make the estimates. Since he is the man most at home with the firm's cost structure, he can give much useful information.

However, if the cost accountant is to play his full part, he must adopt an approach that is still alien to his tradition; any attempt to kill two birds with one stone (that is, to use his ledger balances for pricing as well as for their more fitting task of control) will fail. He must abandon a classification that depends on clerical traceability; he must look forward rather than back, and must cease to imagine he can perform the miracle of splitting common cost. Further, he must recognize the need for a wider range of information, much of it subjective; opportunity cost depends on factors about which the accountant in many firms is at present not kept informed, such as the nature of the market and the state of the order book. Thus, he must keep in close touch with other departments, notably the sales department.

Such a task would be an exacting challenge to the cost accountant. But it would make for much closer ties between him and the managers, since he would have to be privy to their intentions and alternative plans, and, in consequence, it would greatly enhance his status.

Our approach can in part be summarized as a plea for cost statements with more precise words and less precise figures. The words ought to serve as clear explanations of the different kinds of sacrifice—obvious avoidable costs, hidden avoidable costs, and opportunity costs. Many cost figures must inevitably be guesswork, and this should be made plain; on occasion, they will be none the worse for being expressed as a range of probabilities, or for being sprinkled with question marks. Such vagueness accords with the facts of business life better than a facade of precision.

Clear words would also show the nature of each computation, whether it is the passive product of a formula, or a special estimate. A pricer must choose between the two. The special estimate is plainly superior in the sense of being more logical and flexible; but, as none of us has boundless wisdom, time, and energy, there may often be a sound case for the critical use of a formula.

INFLATION AND PARTNERSHIP RIGHTS

Inflation and Partnership Rights

BY PROFESSOR W. T. BAXTER, B.COM., C.A.
Professor of Accounting, London School of Economics

THE effects of price level changes upon accounts are usually discussed in the context of *companies*. This is natural enough, since companies take the bulk of public investment. But inflation also affects *partners'* accounts; its impact should thus be of some interest to the many owners of small firms, particularly in professions such as accountancy.

THE COMMON PROBLEMS

Inflation (or deflation) has results that are common to all firms, regardless of their ownership form. We need not dwell on this familiar topic longer than is necessary to sketch the territory within which the special area of partnership is found.

The well-known effects are:

CHANGES IN REAL WEALTH

Inflation lessens not only the purchasing power of money assets, but also the real burden of money liabilities. Because of these changes in the firm's power to buy outside resources, its real wealth falls if its net liquid assets are a positive quantity, or goes up if it is highly enough geared.

These real gains and losses bring special problems for a partner if some of his investment takes the form of a fixed " advance " or " loan " In return for the right to prior repayment of such investment, he gives up its chance (retained by his equity investment) of immunity from inflation; in post-war Britain, he has in real terms lost about 4 per cent per annum (compound) on loans (less his share of the equal gain by the firm).

DISTORTION OF REPORTED PROFIT

Profit on the turnover of assets tends to be overstated during inflation (and understated during deflation). When trading stocks and fixed assets are sold, or any deferred expense such as depreciation is "realised", the accounts charge historical costs against revenue measured in current £s; the difference is not real profit.

So far as trading profit goes, this distortion seems likely to be insignificant for professional firms, since their expenses include little depreciation and less cost-of-goods-sold. But such firms are more apt than companies to engage in "capital reconstructions"—if that term is used for any revision of the partners' holdings that leads to an evaluation of their rights; in particular, the death or retiral of a partner (which could happen, say, every few years in a large partnership) may bring such a review, and with it the recognition of capital gains whose size is, in inflation, likely to be exaggerated. I shall try to show that such reconstruction, whether or not the relevant book-values in the ledger are altered, can lead to a somewhat unexpected transfer of real wealth.

Analysis of Owners' Remuneration

So much for the types of inflationary effects. We now come to our main concern—the *shares* in which the resulting gains and losses are split between partners.

In a company, the arrangements for rewarding owners usually conform to a clear and fairly sensible analysis of each man's various contributions. Thus, if a shareholder takes part in management, he gets a salary, fees, etc.; and these sums tend to reflect the current market value of his services (though tax considerations may in a small private company lead to distortion). He receives also a separate reward for capital investment. Each ordinary shareholder's dividend is proportionate to his stake in total ordinary capital. And so capital appreciation and similar gains—real or nominal—are likely to accrue to the shareholders both in full and in exact proportion to their holdings.

In a partnership, however, the analysis is seldom so satisfactory:—

1. The entire annual surplus available to partners may be split in some agreed ratio, with no attempt to distinguish the rewards of service and capital. *When one ratio is used to determine jointly the rewards for both services and capital, we shall call it a "composite ratio"*. Or
2. The agreement may instead provide for appropriations under separate heads such as salary, interest, and then surplus divisible in some agreed ratio. Though surplus is here smaller than in 1, it is again likely to contain some reward for *both* services and

> capital; it makes good shortfalls in the salaries and interest,[1] which partnership contracts tend to state at rather low and unchanging rates. So here again we have a composite ratio.

Such a ratio may—by chance or design—be the same as the ratio of the partners' capitals. One must however expect those cases to be rare and to be short-lived, unless the partners impose rigid conditions on one another; thus their capitals are likely to vary over the years because of differences in each man's drawings.

A composite ratio may be entirely defensible—in the sense of giving a partner his appropriate total reward—so long as profits follow their expected pattern. But it seems less likely than the more flexible analysis of the company to deal properly with abnormal and unforeseen profits, including the dubious gains of inflation.

Thus the novel point for discussion is that many partnerships—unlike companies—split inflation's profits in a ratio other than that of the owners' capitals.

An extreme example of the composite ratio will stress the point. Occasionally a sleeping partner provides all the capital, and an active partner does all the management. Thus suppose a financier and an engineer become partners in a new venture, the financier putting up the money and the engineer acting as manager. Their capital ratio is 1 : 0; yet a composite profit-sharing ratio of say 1 : 1 may well seem just to both men, having regard to their sacrifice of alternative opportunities of gaining dividends and salary.

Division of Capital Gains and Losses

Even an elaborate partnership agreement may ignore capital gains and losses. The omission seems to invite subsequent bickering. But, if such gains are distinguished, should they be split in the composite profit-sharing ratio, or in the ratio of the partners' capitals? For the former viewpoint, one could argue that hard work and careful judgment are often as necessary as wealth for winning capital gains, so that a prospect of reward for service is calculated to create such gains; this argument will plainly appeal to partners with small means, such as the engineer in the example above. Wealthier partners may argue instead that capital gains come from shouldering the risks of investment, so that

[1] The point is more fully illustrated in my "Partnership Rights—the Valuation Problem", Accounting Research, July 1958.

the fruits should go to the risk-bearers. Some sort of compromise may be desirable; but a happy solution to the problem perhaps depends more on each partner's feelings about failure than about success. Thus, when the agreement is being drafted, the possibility of heavy capital losses should be discussed; the engineer in our example would probably object to bearing a large part of a loss on the final sale of the assets. When the treatment of capital loss has been agreed, a like treatment of capital gains may seem reasonable to all.

The arguments seem accordingly to favour the use of the capital ratio for capital gains. This view holds for real capital gains at all times; but, as we shall now see, it is specially valid when the gains are nominal.[1]

The Composite Ratio and Nominal Gains

Under this heading we shall consider first the spurious addition that inflation brings to both annual profit (where there is a cost-of-goods-sold or depreciation) and capital gain (where a fixed asset is held for some time and then sold). This addition is in effect a transfer from capital to revenue.

X, an owner of capital, may not greatly care if his wealth receives a new name in this way; he will perhaps regret the distortion of a useful statistic, but otherwise is unlikely to object much—provided that his transferred capital goes to swell *his own* income figure. He will hardly welcome its conversion into someone else's income. It is the conversion of capital into tax that has caused the main outcry against orthodox accounting.

If X is a partner whose share of capital exceeds his share of revenue, he does not get back as revenue the whole of his transferred capital. Thus, during inflation, part of his real capital may be switched to his partners in the guise of profit.

On the other side, if Y (like our engineer above) is a partner whose share of revenue exceeds his share of capital, then he may take over some of X's real capital.

We may perhaps guess that, where the capital ratio differs much from

[1] If a fixed asset is sold during inflation, gain commensurate with the general price rise is merely nominal, but any excess is real. Inflation yields a real capital gain only if we define " gain on owing " as capital; such gain is of course never recognised directly in conventional accounts, but (as the experience of highly-geared firms shows) seeps out in the guise of profit on fixed asset dealings, or as extra annual profit due to the failure of interest charges to rise.

the revenue-sharing ratio, X is likely to be the senior partner and Y the junior. If this is true, there must in recent years have been a good deal of levelling as between junior and senior partners—none the less real because neither side planned or even detected the shift.

When a new partner is taken in, he and the old partners doubtless negotiate a price (*e.g.* his payment into the firm by way of capital) that approximately matches the benefits he will get (*e.g.* his annual share of profits in excess of remuneration for his labour). Just as the price of ordinary shares is high if dividends are expected to rise, so the partner's price will reflect any expected rise in money profit. Thus the obvious results of inflation can be allowed for in his price, and an upward trend in his profits—properly measured—may be regarded as a fair exchange for a stiff price. But one may reasonably doubt whether partners foresee a hidden transfer of capital between themselves, and allow for it in the price. Such a transfer probably violates their intentions, and would strike them as unfair if they found out that it was taking place.

Illustration to Nominal Gains—Individual Assets

Some examples may help to test the argument, particularly if they compare partnership arrangements with the clearer ones of a company.

Two investors, X and Y, join forces in a new project. X provides £12,000 of the capital, Y £4,000. They both take part in management; but X works only a small part of the time, whereas Y is full-time, and their services are worth about £400 and £2,800 a year by market standards.

Profit (before salaries) is £4,800 a year. If they form a company, the division of this income will be:

Table 1

	Total £	*X* £	*Y* £
Reward for:			
Services	3,200	400	2,800
Capital (balance)	1,600	(12/16) 1,200	(4/16) 400
Totals	4,800	1,600	3,200
Ratio of totals	(3)	(1)	(2)

The reward of capital works out at £1,600 p.a., for an investment of £16,000, *i.e.* 10 per cent.

If X and Y form not a company but a partnership, they may simply split total profit in the ratio of their totals above, *i.e.* 1 : 2, whereas their capital ratio is 3 : 1. If instead they have an elaborate agreement that provides for salaries, interest, and surplus, the composite ratio for surplus will probably still differ from the capital ratio.

Now suppose that this firm buys certain assets for £10,000, at a date when the general price index stands at 100—the same level as when the capital was paid in. After some time, the index rises to 160; whereupon those assets are realised, for £16,000. If regard is paid to the rise in the index, the whole gain of £6,000 is illusory. Contrast its treatment in the balance sheets of a company and of a partnership with a 1 : 2 profit ratio:

Table 2

	Company £	*Partnership* £
X:		
Share of capital	12,000	12,000
Share of surplus	(3/4) 4,500	(1/3) 2,000
	16,500	14,000
Y:		
Share of capital	4,000	4,000
Share of surplus	(1/4) 1,500	(2/3) 4,000
	5,500	8,000
Capital (£16,000) plus gain (£6,000)	22,000	22,000

The company credits X with three-quarters of the nominal gain [1] (which is the right thing to do, if his share of real capital is to stay at three-quarters). But the partnership credits him with a lesser sum; and so, as total real capital has remained constant, part of X's capital is in fact transferred to Y.

The illustration holds true whether or not the assets in question are realised by normal trade (when their historical cost of £10,000 would be charged as cost-of-goods-sold or depreciation), or by an abnormal transaction (as when the £10,000 is charged against receipts from the sale of fixed assets).

[1] For simplicity, profit on the other transactions of the firm is deemed to have been correctly measured and then paid out in full to the owners (covering the reward for services in the company's accounts).

Illustration to Nominal Gains—Whole Firm Revalued

If (as in the case of a professional firm) the partnership is not much given to selling individual assets, its nominal gains are most likely to arise when the firm as a whole is revalued. This is what happens in effect at a " capital reconstruction ", *e.g.* a partner's admission or retiral. Here, if the capital payments between the partners aie keyed to current levels of earnings, some element of nominal gain is likely during inflation (even though the book-values of all the assets are kept at conservative figures, and thus the ledger gives little help in measuring the appreciation).

To clarify the point, let us consider schemes for admitting a new partner. These can on the face of the matter take many shapes. But apparently different schemes would all seem to boil down to either—

I. *Transfer of existing capital*

> The analogy in company finance is a normal share transfer—the sale by an old shareholder to a new shareholder of existing capital. The old shareholder here gets all the price, and the firm's assets do not increase.

or—

II. *Issue of additional capital*

> Here the company analogy is the issue to a new shareholder of new shares. The firm gets his full price; real assets expand.

Each scheme must, however, be considered under two book-keeping methods, which do not alter its realities, but do give them very different looks: either (*a*) the book-capital may (by chance or revaluation of assets) reflect the market value of the capital sold; or (*b*) the book-capital may not reflect this market value (probably because assets are kept at conservative values). So we must in all consider four styles of balance sheet.

For illustration, let us revise the case of X and Y.[1] Again X and Y start in business, paying in as capital the sums of £12,000 and £4,000 in cash.[1] Their prospects and rights to income also remain as in the earlier example, so that their composite ratio is still 1 : 2; and the general index once more starts at 100. This time, however, suppose that they do not sell any asset; they sell services only. Their income (which exactly justifies their capital investment of £16,000) is all withdrawn each year.

[1] See Table 3 on pages 120 and 121.

Now the index rises, and profit keeps pace. When the index reaches 125, a newcomer—call him Z—agrees to invest £10,000, and to work full-time. Elsewhere he could get just under £1,000 p.a. as dividend on this investment, and he could earn £1,500 as salary. So his share of expected profit must be at least about £2,500.

Just before Z's admission, a normal balance sheet shows assets of £16,000, and capitals of £12,000 and £4,000. These figures appear in columns (1) and (2) of Table 3; they are historical figures, and thus appropriate for the " conservative values " of strip (*b*) (the lower half of the table).

Asset figures may now be put up to reflect the increased earnings, which have raised the firm's current value from £16,000 to £20,000. This extra £4,000 of capitalised earning-power may be recorded either by raising existing asset values or by putting in an intangible. The capital of X and Y must also go up by £4,000 (though this increase may nominally be treated as " capital reserve " in companies). The way in which X and Y share the £4,000 depends on whether it is divided—as in companies—in the capital ratio of 3 : 1, or in the composite ratio of partnerships, here 1 : 2. The (upper) " current values " strip (*a*) of Table 3 shows the two possible results. The damage done to X by the composite ratio stands out clearly in the contrast between columns (1) and (2). X as a partner—under (2)—no longer owns three-quarters of the unchanged real capital, and so the composite ratio has in fact transferred a slice of his wealth to Y; the purchasing-power of his new capital (£13,333) is less than that of his original capital (£12,000) at the date when he brought it in, and his annual profit may tend to shrink relative to Y's (*e.g.* if the two partners decide to allow interest on their revised capitals, or to change the composite ratio so as to reflect these revised capitals). The " conservative values " in strip (*b*) do not show this damage, but its impact is merely postponed, since current values must be recognised sooner or later—*e.g.* at the final settlement when X retires from the partnership.

The next step is for Z to pay his £10,000, either for existing or additional capital.

Columns (3) to (6) work out fully the possible arrangements of capital after the change. Readers who do not want to study the detail can see what matters—the results for X of the composite ratio—by glancing along the horizontal lines showing his net total after the change. The current values (strip (*a*)) give the best picture; as has been said, the conservative figures of strip (*b*) merely present the same facts in obscure form.

T

PARTNERSHIP

Before admission of Z

(a) Current Values		*Company* (1) £		*Partnership* (2) £
X Capital—Original		12,000		12,000
Revaluation surplus	($\frac{3}{4}$)	3,000	($\frac{1}{3}$)	1,333
Total, current value		15,000		13,333
Y Capital—Original		4,000		4,000
Revaluation surplus	($\frac{1}{4}$)	1,000	($\frac{2}{3}$)	2,667
Total, current value		5,000		6,667
Z				
		20,000		20,000
(b) Conservative Values				
X Capital—Original		12,000		12,000
Y Capital—Original		4,000		4,000
Z				
		16,000		16,000

NSTRUCTION

	After admission of Z						
	I. *Existing capital transferred*				II. *Additional capital issued*		
	Company (3) £		*Partnership* (4) £		*Company* (5) £		*Partnership* (6) £
	15,000		13,333		15,000		13,333
Transfer to z	—10,000		—10,000				
	5,000		3,333				
	5,000		6,667		5,000		6,667
Transfer from x	10,000		10,000	Paid in	10,000		10,000
	20,000		20,000		30,000		30,000
	12,000				12,000		
Current value, as above			3,333				13,333
Transfer to z	—8,000						
Share of £4,000 w/o		($\frac{1}{9}$)	—444			($\frac{11}{51}$)	—863
Share of premium reserve				($\frac{15}{30}$)	1,000		
	4,000		2,889		13,000		12,470
	4,000				4,000		
Current value, as above			6,667				6,667
Share of £4,000 w/o		($\frac{5}{9}$)	—2,223			($\frac{25}{51}$)	—1,961
Share of premium reserve				($\frac{5}{30}$)	333		
	4,000		4,444		4,333		4,706
Transfer from x	8,000			Paid in	8,000		
Current value, as above			10,000				10,000
Share of £4,000 w/o		($\frac{3}{9}$)	—1,333			($\frac{15}{51}$)	—1,176
Share of premium reserve				($\frac{10}{30}$)	667		
	8,000		8,667		8,667		8,824
	16,000		16,000		26,000		26,000

SIGNIFICANCE OF PARTNERS' CAPITAL FIGURES

Before one can check the mechanics of Table 3, one must be clear on the rules governing partners' capitals—particularly where these are book-figures far removed from current values, and in a ratio very different from the composite ratio.

Capital figures are the best that book-keeping can do to show the owners' relative claims. The older the figures, the feebler they are as guides to the absolute amounts at stake. The unimportance of par value is notorious; where, as in companies, the reward of management is an independent matter, par value can be scrapped entirely (both current and capital payments to shareholdeıs being measured in terms of *number* of shares). In partnership, par value is almost equally useless for run-of-the mill transactions. At dissolution, however, unless par is brought into the settlement, payments to partners would presumably be made in the composite ratio. That would seem contrary to the partners' intentions. For, when they agree to invest in the firm, they must expect each man's capital claim to be based on what he then puts in—at least, few rational men would accept terms below this standard.[1] They may decide that, at the end of the agreement, any surplus over their total contributions will be split in the composite ratio; but the contributions and not the ratio must be the starting-point of the sum. The task of partners' capitals is thus to serve as first line in the calculation of sums due at dissolution.

The book-keeping rules are obscure, but seem to bear out the above interpretation. They are thus simpler when the ledger shows new investments at current market value than when it deflates them to conservative figures.

I. TRANSFER OF EXISTING CAPITAL

First take the case (shown in columns (3) and (4)) in which the firm's real capital is not enlarged; Z buys existing capital—say from X—and pays his £10,000 price to X privately.

(*a*) *Current values*

Here a straightforward transfer from X to Z gives the final capitals

[1] An exception to this statement is known to economic historians. The accounts of the Medicis (who were no fools in business matters) show a senior partner repeatedly agreeing to division of capital at dissolution in the profit-sharing ratio. See R. de Roover: " Accounting prior to Luca Pacioli ", STUDIES IN THE HISTORY OF ACCOUNTING, edited by Littleton and Yamey, page 154.

for strip (*a*) of Table 3. X continues to be worse off as a partner than as a shareholder, and Y to gain what X loses.

Note that the capital ratio is now 1 : 1 : 2 in the company. In the partnership, the capital ratio does not matter; a new composite ratio must be agreed. Something on the lines of Table 4 may now give a new ratio acceptable to all three men. This table assumes that profits will run at about £7,500 p.a. (the Table 1 figures being raised to allow for the 25 per cent price increase and the services contributed by Z). The actual calculation of the ratio may well be less formal than Table 4; but, unless the three men have at least at the back of their minds some rough ideas about the figures, it is hard to see how they can reach a sane agreement.

Table 4

Reward of	*Total*	*X*	*Y*	*Z*
Services	5,500	500	3,500	1,500
Capital:				
Pre-admission [1]	2,000	1,333	667	
Transfer		−1,000		1,000
		333		
	7,500	833	4,167	2,500
	(9)	(1)	(5)	(3)

Thus X's composite share is 1/9, Y's 5/9, and Z's 3/9.

(*b*) *Conservative values*

If X and Y decide not to write up their capitals, Z must get a capital smaller than his price.

In a company, it is child's play to find Z's conservative capital; it is likewise easy to move direct from the conservative values (strip (*b*)) of X and Y in column (1) (*Table 3*) to those of (3) and (5). Given the desired total of £16,000, the 1 : 1 : 2 ratio supplies each man's new figure.

[1] These " interest " figures are 10 per cent of the current value capitals in column (2), Table 3. The amounts of £1,333 and £667 thus assume that, just before Z is admitted, X and Y give effect to the shift in their relative capitals. If they do, X's " reward of capital " falls, and Y's rises; so their composite ratio should change from 1: 2 to 1,833: 4,167, *i.e.* to 11: 25.

If conservative values are retained throughout, X and Y are less likely to recognise the real shift in their relative capitals, and may continue to think in terms of a 1: 2 ratio. This would lead to slightly different figures in strip (*b*) of column (4), but does not otherwise alter the argument.

After Z's admission, profits rise by some £1,500, and so the fraction of this bigger total going to X and Y should fall. X's fraction also falls because of his transfer of £1,000 p.a. to Z.

To understand a partnership, we are forced to take instead the current values (strip (*a*)) as the start of our calculation. We then in strip (*b*) write off the £4,000 " loss " on the revaluation from £20,000 to £16,000. By doing this in the composite ratio, we make sure that, at the next reconstruction, the present market values of strip (*a*) will in effect be restored as the basis of settlement. There seems no good way to avoid this roundabout approach *via* full current value. Often phrases such as " Z pays a £1,333 premium for a one-third share of goodwill " are used to describe the arrangement. Such a phrase sounds simple and knowledgeable; and it may correctly show the end-result of the roundabout calculation. But one may rightly feel sceptical of any agreement that is thought out from the start in terms so divorced from market values; only men blessed with uncommon intuition could divine the reality behind the words, and hit on conservative figures that are consistent with current ones.[1]

Therefore in column (4)—and also (6)—we move to the conservative values in strip (*b*) *via* the current values of strip (*a*). X continues to show a smaller capital in the partnership than in the company, and Y a larger one.

II. Issue of Additional Capital

We next assume that Z pays his money into the firm instead of to X. Assets expand by £10,000, and X's capital is not reduced.

(*a*) *Current values*

These are shown in columns (5) and (6), upper strip.

In the company, the capital ratio becomes 3 : 1 : 2. What happens to the composite ratio ?

Table 4 must now be varied slightly. There is no point in expanding total capital if profit is not raised in consequence—and by at least as much as the opportunity cost of capital, which we have taken as just under 10 per cent. For simplicity, let us say that this marginal gain is expected to be 10 per cent on the fresh capital, *i.e.* is £1,000 p.a. Then Table 5 runs—

[1] Thus, if conservative values are the sole guide to the entries, it would seem right in 4(*b*) to credit all the £1,333 premium to X, leaving Y's capital unchanged at £4,000. But then, if the business is now sold for £20,000, Y gets only his £4,000 plus five-ninths of the gain, in all £6,223—whereas 4(*a*) shows his correct part of " current value " to be £6,667. In other words, if it is just that Y's claim should reach a given sum in the final share-out, and his profit fraction is lowered, his starting point—conservative capital—must be put up. Probably his conservative capital should be left unchanged only when his fraction of total profit is the same before and after Z's admission.

Table 5

Reward of	*Total*	*X*	*Y*	*Z*
	£	£	£	£
Services	5,500	500	3,500	1,500
Capital:				
Pre-admission . .	2,000	1,333	667	
Additional . .	1,000			1,000
	8,500	1,833	4,167	2,500
	(51)	(11)	(25)	(15)

Thus the partners should now use the ratio 11 : 25 : 15 (which they might well in practice round off to something less ungainly).

(*b*) *Conservative values*

Z's conservative figure presents no difficulty in the company. Since his book-capital must be limited to half the total of X and Y (£16,000), his figure must be £8,000. The £2,000 premium (between his price and par) is normally kept as a reserve—but in effect raises all three partners' balances above their nominal figures, and so is split between the partners in 5(*b*).

In the partnership, we again write down the £4,000 " loss " from current values, using the composite ratio. Thus Z's £10,000 sinks to only £8,824 of conservative capital, and he will be told that the rest of his price is a premium payable to X and Y.[1]

[1] If X and Y stick to conservative values throughout, they simply add their shares of Z's premium to their opening capitals of £12,000 and £4,000; Z is said to pay a premium of £1,176 for a 15/51 share of goodwill. The final figures by this direct approach may with luck be close to those that we have reached in 6(*b*) by writing down current values ; the two results may indeed be identical if one-and-the-same sharing ratio (as between X and Y) is used throughout in both approaches. However, it is hard to see how the partners could divine the premium correctly by using conservative values alone. The latter seem likely to cause confusion and injustice, giving results at a final settlement (*e.g.* if the firm is now sold for its current value) inconsistent with well-informed intentions.

Because a company does not credit premium to the existing owners, the premiums of company and partnership differ in size (even if the same sharing ratio is used). Their relation can be generalised thus. Let the sharing ratio be $e : n$ for existing owners and newcomer, and G be the difference between current and conservative values of the firm. The premium is $\frac{n}{e} G$ for companies, and $\frac{n}{n+e} G$ for partners.

Results of Reconstruction

The final figures of partners in Table 3 show that, whichever of the possible forms Z's admission takes, X loses and Y gains as a result of the inflation.

It may be objected that the composite ratio used here differs from the capital ratio much more than is usual, and thus X's loss is exaggerated. That is true. In compensation, the degree of inflation has been limited to 25 per cent—far less than the degree that must actually have been experienced in the post-war history of all save the most short-lived of firms.

Much the same results follow reconstructions on quite different occasions—for instance, a partner's death or retiral.

It is not very plausible to suppose that any set of partners would knowingly agree in advance to possible transfers of existing wealth such as those forced on our friend X. We have already considered (page 114) the arguments for sharing *real* capital gains in the profit-ratio, and have seen that a partner has at least some slight grounds for feeling he may not be the loser if his juniors can hope for gains higher than their capitals would warrant. But this argument does not hold when applied to the nominal gains of inflation. We cannot conceive of a rational X wanting to present real capital to Y every time the Chancellor degrades our money. And, if we cannot accept such a nonsensical aim, surely we must say that it violates the spirit of the partners' agreement, and should be prevented by its wording.

Proposals

It is hard for a partnership contract to deal with price-level changes in a simple way. Fairly elaborate rules are needed. The following ones would each help; their adoption *in toto* would probably reduce the mischief almost to zero:

1. *Reform of the composite ratio*

The harm done by this ratio can be lessened in two ways:—

(*a*) The surplus profit divided *via* the composite ratio should be kept low. Annual profit appropriations should include partners' salaries (raised periodically to allow for growing experience and inflation) and perhaps a commission on the remaining profit. If these payments for service are realistic and variable enough to mirror current market rates, interest might well be abolished and the whole surplus divided in the capital ratio, or very nearly so.

(*b*) Capital gains should be given special treatment. Perhaps after a commission for partners' services has been deducted the gains should be split in the capital ratio.

2. *Accounting reform*

The illusory gains of inflation could be dealt with by two means.

(*a*) The firm could adopt the familiar proposals for using an index to raise historical cost in profit calculations. In this way, nominal gains on trading and fixed-asset transactions could be avoided. The credits created (treated by companies as capital reserves) could be divided among the partners in their capital ratio.

(*b*) To adapt the familiar proposals to the special needs of partnership reconstruction, capitals should be written up before a reconstruction, with the help of an index of consumption prices. (The corresponding debit could be added to undervalued fixed assets, or to a special intangible with some such name as " Increase in money-value of firm due to inflation ".) This would minimise the nominal gains on the revaluation of the whole firm.

Further, partners should use current values for their important calculations. By so doing, they would avoid much trouble and muddle.

A Gift for Full Consideration

By H. E. SMITH, LL.B.
Editor of HANSON'S DEATH DUTIES

(*Mr Wyzed, C.A., has received a call from his client, Mr Johnson, sole proprietor of a toy manufacturing business.*)

Mr JOHNSON (*indignantly*): The Revenue want me to pay death duty on a half of my business and on a half of that other business I sold two years ago.

Mr WYZED: I take it this has to do with the death of your father. Let me see, he died rather more than a year ago, did he not?

THE FUTURE OF THE ACCOUNTANT

The Future of the Accountant – I

DILEMMAS FACING THE PROFESSION

by W. T. BAXTER, B.Com., C.A.
Professor of Accounting, University of London

THE future historian of our profession will perhaps sum up the twentieth century in this way: the first half saw growth and smooth development; the accountant enjoyed prestige and felt confident. The second half saw an abrupt change in his prospects; new forces threatened him, competitors invaded parts of his kingdom, and he himself no longer felt sure that his training matched his opportunities.

The suggestion that we are at such a turning-point may prove too gloomy. Let us hope so. But the threats – and also the opportunities – seem real enough. I suspect that we must now either show ourselves capable of shouldering important new tasks, or else abandon some of those that we take for granted – and lose some of our prestige into the bargain.

It may therefore be sensible to take stock of our present position, to see just where our strength and weakness lie.

THE SUB-DIVISIONS OF ACCOUNTING

For this review, we can conveniently break up accounting into various sub-divisions. (Auditing shares in at least the first two of these, and so I have, for brevity, not treated it as a separate sub-division.)

Stewardship Accounts

In past centuries, the accountant's great contribution to economic life has been the orderly recording of business transactions. Thanks to his double-entry technique, he has been able to record and sort historical data with skill and efficiency, and in ever-growing quantities. We may well doubt whether trade, except in an elementary form, would have been possible without book-keeping. Personal accounts provided an easy way of keeping the records that were essential if credit transactions were to be remembered. Personal and related kinds of accounts also helped the growth of agency, consignments, joint-ventures, and partnership – the devices by which much trade was organized till, say, the early nineteenth century. Accounts for cash and other assets helped to control wealth.

All such accounts were specially useful as evidence to some other person that his affairs had been faithfully managed. This sort of work is therefore often called *stewardship accounting*. Nowadays, 'data processing' is being more and more used instead, but I shall stick to the older phrase.

Financial Reporting

Historical records were put to a new use from about the middle of the nineteenth century. Then firms began to raise capital on a large scale from the public. Further, the State greatly increased its say in business affairs – by its new bankruptcy rules, its company law, and (above all) its taxes on income. It demanded periodical accounts for shareholders and its own officials. The accountant responded by demoting his old consignment accounts etc. (which showed the profit on each kind of venture), and promoting statements that gave a view of the whole firm, i.e. the annual income account (hitherto a tidying-up device rather than a source of information) and the balance sheet (hitherto regarded as not much more than a trial balance). Thus the new reports grew out of the old methods of book-keeping; despite the change of function, the figures were still tightly linked with historical records.

This type of work has, of course, grown enormously in its scope and complexity – and seems likely to go on growing. It can conveniently be labelled *financial reporting*; but some such phrase as 'statutory accounting' would also be apt.

Management Accounting

The phrase 'management accounting' stands for two different things. First, there is an extension of control. Perhaps this should be treated under the heading of stewardship; some parts of the firm's accounts, notably costing, are the up-to-date counterparts of the eighteenth-century merchant's venture and voyage accounts, in that they show in detail the results of the firm's different activities. But there is now an important contrast with the earlier control methods. Many accountants have decided that historical book-keeping is not enough. Increasingly they are reinforcing their controls with *forecasts*, i.e. are using budgets to supplement historical accounts. Their forecasts include budgets for the whole firm and sections of it, and standard costs for many activities within a factory. This new approach has been welcomed by business; there is a general feeling that the budgets and good planning go hand in hand (notably because budgets foster team work), and that study of the variances between budget and actual data gives firmer control. Not unnaturally, the accountant has tended to arrange his new forward-looking figures in the same familiar style as the old backward-looking ones, and to incorporate the standards within double-entry.

Secondly, management has in recent years asked more and more for data that will help it with *decision-taking* – on problems such as whether to sell more of product X and less of Y; whether the time has come to replace an old machine; or whether to make or buy components. Accountants are striving to meet this demand. The question is whether we have gone far enough and whether we have grasped the principles that are needed. Decisions, like the new controls, demand budgets; the accountant's first impulse – again not unnaturally – has been to use his historical data instead. This may lead to error. So here the accountant's training is apt to be a handicap.

It is perhaps no exaggeration to say that the switch from historical figures to forecasts is the biggest change that has taken place in accounting during its first seven centuries.

Though it is convenient to put both types of budget (for control and for decision) under the heading of 'management accounting', there is some case for calling the second 'economic accounting'. This name would mark the need for fresh principles, and would underscore the debt that we owe in this area to the clear thinking of the economists.

ASSESSMENT OF THE THREE SUB-DIVISIONS

Having classified accounting under three heads – stewardship, financial, and management – we must next assess the degree to which each branch meets the demands now put upon it, and therefore the likelihood that it will endure or wilt in the future.

Stewardship Accounting in the Future

Stewardship, the oldest of the three, is plainly the most satisfactory. It sets itself the limited task of recording a narrow set of transactions that are governed by unambiguous rules (mainly of contract law). The figures are never in doubt. The double-entry system is simple and flexible. Given care and time, the accountant can here achieve perfection.

Accordingly, we may reasonably expect that stewardship records will retain their importance and that demand for accounting service in this field will if anything grow bigger.

Nevertheless, the accountant may not have everything his own way. He faces threats from rivals who have developed impressive new techniques for handling figures. The statistician has shown that results of high accuracy can be got from samples (whereas accountants are predisposed to record the whole of the transactions, even when such thoroughness is laborious and costly); moreover he can define the probable accuracy of his figures. The expert in operations research has shown that he, too, can often contribute something of value (e.g. in stock control); some of his techniques need more mathematics than the normal accountant can command.

Stewardship, Control and the Computer

Above all, more and more accounting work will probably be taken over by men who are experts with the computer. One American writer is prophesying that 'every one of the five million business enterprises in the United States will some day, within the lifetime of men now active, process all its business data on computer systems'.[1] Change on anything like this scale would be something of a threat to book-keeping skill. If even fairly small firms can keep their accounts by hiring time on a computer, and standard programs are available for every kind of trade, there will no longer be much scope for the man who now supervises book-keeping. However, there may be a gain if he can move away from routine and can take the historical figures for granted. He will then be free for more important work and more disposed to study other values and techniques. Understanding of double-entry principles is likely to remain a necessary part of his mental equipment – but he will be able to let it recede somewhat from the forefront.

This is not to suggest that the accountant can safely sit back and leave data processing to the

[1] John E. Johnson, 'E.D.P. as it Affects the Accountant', *N.A.A. Bulletin*, December 1963.

computer expert. If he does, he will abandon his function of control. Indeed, control is threatened in any case; whereas the old procedures fall readily into separate steps (each of which has visible results that can be checked), the computer is apt to jump from start to finish without any visible intermediate stages. So the accountant is abdicating responsibility if he does not help to build-in ample controls at the planning stage. A system is unsafe unless the accountant knows at least enough to participate in 'the detailed planning procedures and programmed internal controls, as well as in the detailed procedural changes and actual running of the programs'.[1]

The auditor, too, will become less effective if he fails to acquire an understanding of the computer. An ignorant auditor will be at the mercy of the expert; further, he will be insensitive to new types of error that may be bred by the new techniques. Computers may offer a golden chance to the expert with a taste for embezzlement. Is it unreasonable to guess that a second Coster will sooner or later try to bring off a devastating *coup*? If he succeeds, the profession will again lose face as it did after the McKesson and Robbins affair, and may have to accept reform from outside.

Financial Reporting in the Future

Mainly because it calls for artistry and personal judgment, the drafting of public reports is not likely to be done by computers. Here the accountant can keep his pre-eminence. However, although the financial accountant has not any obvious rivals, some parts of his approach are attracting a good deal of hostile comment from intelligent critics (particularly the investment analysts). This criticism, and his own obvious wish to produce better figures, should both impel him to review the traditional approach.

It is easy to argue that financial reporting, like stewardship, is a success. To do so, however, one has to use a rather artificial standard. If the final accounts are no more than the culminating proof of good historical book-keeping, then admittedly they deserve high marks. But if they are instead a means for telling managers and investors about the firm's progress and present state (i.e. if they are meant to show current economic facts), then they are open to criticism. After all, they were not designed for this latter end. They are summaries of historical data; they came into being, as we have already noted, not to give information, but as a by-product of clerical routine (the income account as a periodic bonfire for obsolete figures, and the balance sheet as a test of accuracy). It is expecting a lot to think that they can meet both purposes well.

[1] John E. Johnson, *ibid.*

Suppose that mankind knew nothing about final accounts, and had now to invent them *de novo*. Can anyone seriously contend that managers and investors would ask first for historical data? Surely they would instead ask for various up-to-date figures to show:

(1) how the firm's wealth has grown recently – as a test of efficiency in buying and selling assets, and in 'operating' them; and

(2) the current nature and value of the net assets – as a test, e.g. of the adequacy of the income: capital ratio.

In other words, desirable accounts would throw light on management's skill at dealing with the market, and at running the firm internally; and also at holding liquid and other assets in good proportions. Investors are concerned with the trend of the cash flow (and therefore of likely dividend patterns in the future); so they want up-to-date figures that bear on this matter. Only as an afterthought would they ask for supplementary statements to prove faithful stewardship; the latter may be a basic need, but – like many other basic needs – is surely something that a sophisticated society can take for granted.

Our existing (historical) final accounts thus pass muster mainly because the standard that we set for them is synthetic. We establish our own simple requirements (stemming from ease of book-keeping rather than economic reality), and then have not much trouble in meeting them. Accounting 'profit' is sound by the test of man-made law; it is less sound as a logical attempt to measure economic growth.

One gets support for this view when one looks at our textbooks' attempts to set out the principles that underly accounting profit. The best that they can do is to explain those principles in terms of splitting up historical costs and revenues appropriately between years. As a description of how to put the debits and credits in the ledger, this is satisfactory. But I cannot see that it says much in terms of economic measurement.

The same sort of difficulty arises when judges have to decide what is income. Not unreasonably, our Courts have come to accept something close to the accounting way of measuring income as right for tax – because that way is quick, simple, and normally leaves little scope for dispute. A judge might therefore end a case sensibly by saying: 'After listening to the argument on what is the proper income figure, I find that the one given by method *x* is correct. It is not much use as a measure of the firm's economic progress. But the evidence shows that it demands fewest man-hours in the book-keeping department, accords most closely with tradition, and affords little room for bickering.' In fact, the judge's words in such cases will sound more impressive than these, but may mean less.

However, it is easier to ask for satisfactory current values than to provide them. The book-keeper can reasonably argue, so far as small firms are concerned, that current values are not worth the trouble involved by their preparation. But managers of large firms, and investors in public companies, seem entitled to the best available figures – which need not in fact involve excessive trouble.

(*To be continued.*)

The Future of the Accountant – II

DILEMMAS FACING THE PROFESSION

by W. T. BAXTER, B.Com., C.A.
Professor of Accounting, University of London

THE first instalment of this article ended by suggesting that a balance sheet filled with historical costs cannot satisfy the critics of accounting. The latter maintain, with good reason, that current values are desirable; investors and managers are both entitled to the best available figures for asset values.

What are 'the best available figures'? For most assets, in most circumstances, current replacement cost is probably the answer; if this is hard to find, an adequate figure can normally be got by up-dating historical cost with a special price index for the particular type of asset. 'Money' assets and liabilities do not need any alteration, since most of them are automatically expressed in today's money values.

Alternative Forms of Balance Sheet

Table I suggests, in an ultra-simple way, how these rules might be put into effect. It compares three firms (A., B., and C.) that illustrate very different asset policies. We suppose that all three set up in business on January 1st. Their ordinary capital is £10,000; C. also borrows £20,000 on debentures. They at once invest all their money as follows:

A. and C. – in non-wasting fixed assets (e.g. land, equity shares).

B. – in money assets (e.g. bank deposits, Government stocks).

The special price index for the fixed assets then rises over the year from 100 to 120. (Unfortunately we must deal both with *special* price indices for each type of non-money asset, and with a *general* index for the purchasing power of money over all commodities and services.) For simplicity, we assume that profits are paid out (as tax and dividends) as soon as they are earned.

The top horizontal part of Table I – marked (1) – shows the balance sheet in our usual style. To judge by these statements, A. B., and C. have done equally well.

Part (2) suggests an alternative arrangement (already being used to some extent in Britain and also Holland), with the assets revalued. This suggests that A. and C. have grown richer while B. has stood still.

TABLE I
Different sets of balance sheet values

Firm:	A.	B.	C.
	£	£	£
(1) USUAL STYLE (based on historical cost)			
Fixed assets (still at cost)	10,000		30,000
Money assets		10,000	
Less Debentures			20,000
	10,000	10,000	10,000
Capital	10,000	10,000	10,000
(2) ASSETS REVALUED			
Fixed assets (revalued at 120)	12,000		36,000
Money assets		10,000	
Less Debentures			20,000
	12,000	10,000	16,000
Capital: Original ..	10,000	10,000	10,000
Appreciation on fixed assets	2,000		6,000
	12,000	10,000	16,000
(3) ASSETS AND CAPITAL REVALUED			
Net assets – revalued with special index as in (2)..	12,000	10,000	16,000
Capital: Original, adjusted with general index of 110	11,000	11,000	11,000
Real appreciation on fixed assets	1,000		3,000
Loss from holding money		—1,000	
Gain from owing money..			2,000
	12,000	10,000	16,000

But to get a complete picture, in real as distinct from money terms, we must consider also the behaviour of money since the firms began. We do so by trying to up-date the remaining bit of the balance sheet, i.e. the owners' balances for capital, retained earnings, etc. The best we can do with this record of past investment is to re-express it with the help of a *general* price index. Part (3) of the table shows this.

We assume that there has been a considerable inflation during the year, and the general index has risen from 100 to 110. Now we can see that firm A.'s non-money assets have indeed risen in value ('Real appreciation on fixed assets' is 120 per cent less 110 per cent on £10,000, i.e. £1,000) – but by less than (2) suggests. B. has *lost* wealth: these accounts show how much and why – it made the mistake of holding money during inflation (10 per cent of £10,000 = £1,000). C. has gained both from a real rise in asset values (120 per cent less 110 per cent on £30,000 = £3,000), and from being so highly-geared during inflation (10 per cent on £20,000 = £2,000).

I do not suggest that a new Companies Act should force companies to use this particular way of setting out a balance sheet. No doubt other people will – at once or in the future – think of better ways; so an Act should be persuasive but not rigid. Its right approach is perhaps to require that published accounts must either show current values in the best available way, or else must contain a statement by the directors explaining why they feel unable to use such values. This is very like the British 1948 Act's rule on depreciation; and few of our companies now fail to write it off.

Alternative Forms of Income Account

How can the profit and loss account deal in current values? Accountants have a strong objection to taking credit for unrealized gain, for two valid reasons: the size of the gain is seldom certain, and to show it may lead to demands for tax and dividends before enough cash reaches the till.

The answer probably is that this is one of the rare occasions on which one can both eat one's cake and have it. In other words, there seems no reason why we should not show both accounting profit (realized gains only) and also a less objective figure; they are not mutually exclusive. After all, profit is a measure of economic growth. If we were asked to measure the growth of, say, a child, we should have to admit that there are many excellent ways of doing so – by finding the increase in its weight, or height, or mental prowess, or so forth. Much the same applies to economic growth. And to give several measures is more informative than to give only one. An important book by Messrs Edwards and Bell[1] shows how two profits can be shown – in parallel as it were – within the double-entry structure. The two are accounting profit and what the authors call 'business profit'. The latter includes both unrealized and realized appreciation, for the current year only. (Oddly enough, it can be *smaller* than accounting profit, since the latter of course includes appreciation on realized assets for all the years during which they have been owned.) And because both calculations show appreciation (a test of management's skill in buying), they must as a balance state the other ingredient of profit, which the authors call 'current operating profit' (a somewhat notional figure that suggests skill in manufacturing, selling, etc.).

Table II tries to show, with simple figures, how this ingenious trick is performed. The data are as follows. Suppose I buy three units of like goods in year 1, at the wholesale price of £10 apiece. In year 3, I sell two of the units at the current retail price of £21. Accounting normally shows my results thus:

INCOME ACCOUNT	£
Sales: 2×21	42
Cost of goods sold: 2×10	20
Profit	22

BALANCE SHEETS

	Jan. 1st Year 1	*Jan. 1st Year 3*	*Dec. 31st Year 3*
	£	£	£
Cash	30	—	42
Stocks	—	30	10
	30	30	52
Capital	30	30	30
Accounting profit	—	—	22
	30	30	52

Now let us assume that wholesale prices have been:

	£
Year 1 Purchase date	10
3 January 1st	12
June 30th (sale date)	16
December 31st	17

The Edwards and Bell re-statement of the accounts runs:

Table II shows how the excess of unrealized over realized profit (£1 for the year, £7 for all years) can be segregated. This safety device seems to dispose of most of the risk in recognizing unrealized gain.

[1] E. O. Edwards and P. W. Bell, *The Theory and Measurement of Business Income* (Berkeley, 1961).

Price Changes and Income Measurement

Table II, for simplicity, deals only with special price change (in the particular assets) and ignores general price change. But the latter has unfortunate effects on income measurement.

We can use a simple short-cut to cure the error (nearly enough for practical purposes). As is well known, when there is general price change, the ordinary profit and loss account may subtract cost £s of one value from sale £s of another value, because some of the historical costs may date back to an earlier time than the corresponding revenue. For example, depreciation on plant bought in, say, 1948 is subtracted from sales of 1964, i.e. heavy £s from light ones – with the result that 1964 profit is too high by the test of real capital maintenance.

The short-cut cure is to revise historical cost – in my view, with the general index (and not the special index of 'replacement cost accounting'). For instance, if general prices rise 10 per cent in the year and average stock turnover takes a quarter of a year, then the historical cost of goods sold should be raised by 2½ per cent as an 'inflation charge'. If we go further than this (as when we use LIFO, or base depreciation on the current special value of plant), then we are also excising real appreciation from profit, i.e. reducing profit to its 'current operating' component.

For instance, suppose goods costing £100 are bought when both general and special indices stand at 100, and are sold for £110 when the indices stand at 102·5 and 104 respectively. The ordinary accounting profit of £10 merely maintains *money* capital – an exercise that people experienced in inflation may well deem pointless. If we want to maintain *real* capital, we must set

TABLE II

INCOME ACCOUNT showing two versions of profit, in parallel

(a) Current trading section.	£
Sales	42
Cost of goods sold (as at 30 June, Year 3). 2 x 16	32
Current operating profit	10

(b) Alternative treatments of profit:

	1. Only realized gains shown	£	2. Both realized and unrealized gains shown	£
i. Current operating profit, b/d		10		10
ii. Appreciation	Realized appreciation, during years 1-3, on assets sold 2 x (16-10)	12	All appreciation during year 3 only, on assets: sold 2 x (16-12) 8; still held 1 x (17-12) 5	13
Total	Accounting (realized) profit:		"Business profit":	
For year		22		23
Brought forward		-		6
		22		29

BALANCE SHEETS, year 3

	1. Jan.1 £	1. Dec.31 £	2. Jan.1 £	2. Dec.31 £
Cash	-	42	-	42
Stock	30	10	36	17
	30	52	36	59
Capital	30	30	30	30
Profit: realized		22		22
unrealized			6	7
				29
	30	52	36	59

aside £102·5; so we raise the £100 historical cost with an inflation charge of £2·5, and measure profit at £7·5. If, instead, we charge a replacement cost provision of £4 (or replace the goods for £104 and use LIFO), then we reduce profit to £6 and so maintain *physical* capital and increase real capital. The balance of argument seems to suggest that the most serviceable figure for profit is the one based on real capital maintenance (i.e. here £7·5).

I suspect that the pronouncements on inflation by accounting bodies – in both England and the U.S.A. – have done more than anything else to harm the accountant in the eyes of intelligent onlookers. A profession cannot claim to be a restraining and conserving influence if it publicly defends the over-stating of profits for the very times when this is most undesirable.

There are no signs that the Treasury has yet found how to stop inflation. Accountants may well have to get the knack of allowing for it in their figures, or else hand over this job to someone else. Apart from the need for better statistics for each firm, there are strong grounds for the Government prodding all firms into correcting profit – perhaps by letting them use the corrected figure (lower during inflation) for tax purposes, provided they use it also in the shareholders' accounts.

The argument for intervention is that the uncorrected accounting figures exaggerate the profit trend of booms and slumps, and so may be a weighty contribution to the social evils of over- and under-employment. We cannot be sure of this; who can tell what factors induce the mental states – of optimism or gloom – that influence investment decisions? But it seems reasonable to think that marked changes in the trend of published profits must have some effect on general confidence. When the disease is so grave, a wise Government will try any medicine that offers hope of even a partial cure. (*To be continued.*)

The Future of the Accountant – III

DILEMMAS FACING THE PROFESSION

by W. T. BAXTER, B.Com., C.A.
Professor of Accounting, University of London

Management Accounting in the Future

AS we have seen, 'management accounting' tends to mean both budgets-cum-control and special budgets for decision-making. The former (budgets linked with cost control) seems to be contributing much that is of value, and will no doubt be used more and more widely. Perhaps the main criticism that might be levelled against it is that standard costs tend somewhat to divorce management from markets – by stressing 'controllable costs' (narrowly defined in terms of internal efficiency) rather than input prices. There must surely be many firms in which buying prices are more than tiresome irrelevancies, i.e. whose profit depends largely on the price savings that come from clever buying (varying the mix of inputs, and the timing of their acquisition). Can a foreman in such a firm be really efficient if he is trained to think of inputs in terms of their fixed standard costs rather than volatile market prices? Perhaps standard costs will in time be modified so as to draw more attention to the choice of cheapest inputs.

Because of the vast importance of this work, the accounting profession should be at pains to make sure that most of its trainees have experience inside a factory. Something in the present training scheme may have to be jettisoned to give future industrial accountants the needed time; executorship and insolvency are perhaps the most promising candidates.

It is in the realm of special budgets for decisions that the accountant is likely to have most trouble. This is because our traditional training disposes us to start off on the wrong foot. A man trained as, say, an engineer or economist tends to think readily of the amount of *change* in total figures. So, if he has to budget for the cost of a possible new activity, he can easily shut his eyes to everything except the *extra* sacrifices caused by it; he rightly defines cost in terms of cause and effect. The accountant, on the other hand, is trained to record *all* transactions, and to analyse them by categories that can scarcely show extra cost due to extra work.

An obvious example of the accountant's difficulty is the problem of overhead allocation – in departmental accounts, costing, and so on. Suppose a firm rents space for two departments of equal area at a total cost of £10,000 per annum. The accountant's training prompts him to allocate £5,000 to each department's income account. But this suggests the firm could have saved £5,000 if it had rented only enough space for one department – which is not necessarily true. It also suggests that £5,000 might now be saved by giving up one department – again not necessarily true. We can, for instance, readily imagine a landlord insisting on the whole space being rented *en bloc*, or else charging more than £5,000 for half the space.

It is probably stretching stewardship records too far to revise its joint figures by allocation. The safe rule is surely not to split the total of a joint cost. If the cost is relevant to a decision, then one should draft a special budget showing the probable change in the total that would follow from the decision. If, for instance, the firm in the preceding paragraph is considering the closing of one department, then the rent saving can most likely be found only by some such step as sounding the landlord about the terms on which he would revise the contract; his answer may well be that he would take, say, £3,000 less if either department were given up. The position cannot be shown by allocating total rent.

These arguments suggest we shall see a big growth in the popularity of variable (or 'direct') costing, in contrast to 'full cost' allocation of overheads. The former is simple, cheap, and free from the false impressions that can be given by allocated figures.

The costing problem can perhaps best be illustrated by listing alternative ways in which the yield from a product can be expressed. In effect, the cost accountant has the choice of describing the gain from making one of a firm's varied products in four ways:

(*a*) 'Its net profit per unit is £*a*' (net profit being sale price less fully allocated costs). Or (*b*) 'Its net profit per hour is £*b*'. Or

(*c*) 'Its gross margin per unit is £*c*' (gross margin being sale price less variable cost only). Or

(*d*) 'Its gross margin per hour is £*d*'.

None of these statements is a perfect guide to management (because e.g. of problems of product mix). But (*d*) seems the least imperfect; it is the most likely to predict which product will contribute best to annual profit; (*c*) can mislead if the number of units (of the particular product that is being considered) made in an hour is not typical of all products; (*b*) can mislead because oncost allocation (particularly between products made in parallel) need not mean much; (*a*) combines the faults of both (*b*) and (*c*).

This is all part of a bigger problem – the extent to which we can trust averages. Suppose the annual profit and loss account is the best test of results. Then an average cost or profit *per hour* may have merit (if it is in fact a miniature version of the annual account). An average *per physical unit* (of product, or square foot of floor-space, etc.) is much more remote, and so may point the wrong way. It is too synthetic to be trustworthy. A manager's standing request to his cost accountant should perhaps be: 'Please multiply-up the data that you show me into likely annual equivalents.'

Allocation and Pricing

Many accountants who sympathize with the approach of avoidable costing are, however, worried about its effect on pricing, and for this reason hesitate to adopt it. They ask, for example, whether its low costs may not prompt salesmen to quote disastrously low prices.

This is a real problem, but there are several sound answers to it. Perhaps the most cogent is that the accountant can easily rank products in a league table based on their contribution (gross margin) per hour; the sales department should be able to see that a product low down on the list calls for a lot of awkward explanation. (And, after all, such a product may still be well worth making – e.g. during slack times).

But this is not always an adequate answer. Certain firms need a 'cost-plus' figure – or something that looks like it – if they are to get through the task of pricing; they may agree that in theory the manager should carefully weigh demand elasticity and marginal cost, but know that in practice this is out of the question. For instance, a jobbing engineer may have no existing prices to guide him in quoting for a single new article; and a firm that has to revise its catalogue for a thousand products must needs entrust the revision of these prices (in large part, at least) to subordinates using a rule-of-thumb.

Perhaps, here, the solution of future years will be to produce figures analogous to cost-plus, but to call them not 'costs' but 'prices'. Thus a product that uses a given cost centre would be charged with a sort of hourly price or rent (like the passenger in a hired car). The change of name from 'cost' to 'price' may not seem to mean much and often might not lead to different figures, but it would be a revolution in mental attitude, and would do much to encourage sound decisions. For instance, no one would hesitate to put 'prices' down or up if, for example, the cost centre's machines were becoming obsolete, or if it were on the verge of congestion because of high demand; yet these factors do not alter historical cost one whit.

If these arguments have any truth in them, they may explain why costing has sometimes to give ground to the clearer logic of operations research.

The Rules of Decision Budgets

Let us now turn to the special budgets that will probably be needed more and more for decisions (as distinct from control). This is to some extent unknown terrain, but perhaps the rules for such budgets can be set out as follows:

1. *Alternative budgets*

To forecast the results of a proposed activity (for shortness, call it a job), fundamentally one must try to guess what two alternative budgets for the whole firm's workings will look like if the job (*a*) is done, and (*b*) is not done; if budget (*a*) shows a net surplus over (*b*), the firm should do the job. Many of the firm's costs and revenues will be the same for both (*a*) and (*b*); these common items are irrelevant, and we can both save work and gratify logic by missing them out. Thus the budgets can concentrate exclusively on *items that the job will change.*

2. *Cash budgets*

Just as we can sum up historical results in various kinds of accounts (e.g. a profit and loss account), so too can budgets take various forms. The easiest form is based on cash; and the flow of cash for dividends etc. is precisely what interests most investors. So there are strong grounds for choosing cash budgets. Such budgets should be forecasts of potential changes in a future cash account – no more, no less.

We should, however, re-state the cash figures if they are spread over long periods, by using compound interest tables to reduce them all to common equivalents. Such manipulation of long-term cash flow with compound interest is the hall-mark of what is often called *capital budgeting*. Accountants will find it hard to play much part in this important new field if their training gives no practice with actuarial tables. The stress on compound interest in the syllabus of, e.g. the Scottish Institute, now seems doubly justified.

3. *Historical cost excluded*

A cash budget cannot include anything save future cash changes. This rule is simple, and helps us to think straight. Often it upsets accounting methods that have become ingrained in us.

Historical cost, for instance, cannot be used by the accountant when he is drafting a cash budget (except as a guide to the size of future costs). Thus historical depreciation is not found in a cash account, so neither should it be put in a cash budget; instead the future purchase price of new plant and the scrap value of the old are likely to be the useful figures. If obsolete plant has not yet been written off, this is just too bad; the manager should ignore the point when deciding whether to replace.

Again, if materials are taken from stock for a job, then their cost – in the sense of the present sacrifice due to the decision to use them on the job – is not (save by coincidence) the price once paid for them. Instead we must ask what effect their using-up will have on the future cash-book (see 5. below).

4. *Commitments*

Likewise a job cannot create a cost if the firm must make the payment anyway. So commitments, like historical costs, are not true costs for our present purpose, and should be ignored. (Or, if you will, they should be put into *both* budgets (*a*) and (*b*) of rule 1. above, so cancelling one another and having no effect on decisions.)

Thus even a future cash payment for input is irrelevant if the firm is already committed to make the payment; for instance, if goods are already on order, then their cost in today's budgets is no longer the future cash payment for the agreed price, but other future figures found by rules such as those in 5. Again, suppose that a firm will not in fact fire labour during idle spells; then wages are no cost to a job done at such times.

What makes cost is thus not 'directness' (in the sense that a cost clerk can trace the input to a job), but the fact that the firm could avoid the outlay by not doing the job.

A rather upsetting corollary of this rule is that a job's cost changes from date to date, according to stage of commitment. Thus at a late stage the firm may rightly decide to finish a job even though the expected sale price has fallen disastrously – so long as that price still exceeds the outlays to which the firm is not yet committed.

5. *Effects of using input*

The cost of using an input (already acquired) depends on future alternatives. We must adopt a 'what difference does it make' approach to find it. Consider further the materials mentioned in 3. Their cost could be one of several figures:

(i) If the goods are plentiful, and will in fact be replaced, then their use on the given job means that cash will as a consequence be burdened with their *replacement cost*. So the latter is normally the right figure at which to charge issues.

(ii) If, however, the firm does not want to replace the goods, because e.g. they are obsolete, then their use on this job merely deprives the firm of cash benefits (probably small) connected with other possible uses: the goods might be sold as scrap, or worked off on jobs for which they are not really suited. So their cost is now probably the higher of scrap value or the replacement cost of the other jobs' relevant materials. If they are no good for anything, then their cost to the job is nothing.

(iii) Both (i) and (ii) assume the goods to be plentiful. If instead they are in scarce supply, then other jobs may be handicapped because the goods are used on this job. Cash will then be burdened with e.g. higher payments for dear substitutes, or loss of net revenue because other jobs are squeezed out. The budgeter has here an awkward task.

It is, of course, in this sort of context that the economist's concept of opportunity cost is so helpful.

These rules, coupled with our earlier ones for average costs and pricing, are not at all palatable to those of us who have been through the mill of traditional training. (*To be concluded.*)

The Future of the Accountant – IV

DILEMMAS FACING THE PROFESSION

by W. T. BAXTER, B.Com., C.A.
Professor of Accounting, University of London

FUTURE ORGANIZATION AND TRAINING

OUR review of the accountant's changing work leads us to speculate on two further topics – his future training, and his future organization into professional societies etc. As the societies prescribe much of the training, these topics intertwine.

History of Professional Bodies

To get perspective, it may be worth while to see what happened to other professional bodies that lasted much longer than our modern accounting societies have yet done. Our societies have many points of resemblance to the old guilds. For the latter, too, were set up to foster the welfare of those in a profession or trade – e.g. the Mercers' rules were 'for the cherishing of unity and good love among them, and for the common profit of the mistery'.[1]

Guilds sometimes did much good in fostering education. We may, for instance, conjecture that the uniformity of our debit-and-credit system stems from the training rules of bankers' guilds in medieval Italy. Long apprenticeship was common; in this sense at least it is true to say that the accountant's 'training method currently followed in England is medieval rather than modern'.[2] The apprentice often had to pass a test before admission. It might take the practical form of showing a sample of his skill as a craftsman. When this 'masterpiece' demanded much time and expense, he was apt to grumble that the test was aimed at keeping the profession exclusive.

A group that started with common interests tended in time to develop conflicting interests. Members at first fairly equal in prospects would drift apart into groups of wealthy employers and permanent journeymen; they drifted also into different types of work, e.g. the more enterprising might give up manufacture for foreign trade. Then malcontents would in protest hive off and form their own sub-group within the guild; and this new body 'which at the beginning of the fifteenth century had been a prohibited organization of rebellious journeymen, had before the end of the century been gradually transformed into a recognized but subordinate branch of the livery company' with its own officers. Or there would be complete secession and the formation of new incorporations.

Often guilds tried to win the sole right of practice for their members. Their declared motives were unimpeachable. Thus some of the London guilds contrived to gain powers under the new monopoly rules of the Stuarts 'to guarantee the consumer a supply of sound and serviceable commodities at reasonable rates'. Where the guild won exclusive rights, the results were apt to disappoint; it has, for instance, been suggested that the guilds' great power in Germany led to stagnation or decline in the cities, as innovators were driven outside the walls.

All this suggests that the task of professional bodies is not easy. They are an attempt to solve a difficult and perhaps insoluble problem.

Comprehensive or Specialized Accounting Bodies?

The different groups within the guilds have obvious counterparts in our societies. The latter have the hard task of catering for several groups; and it is arguable that their omnibus approach cannot give the best training to each group. In particular, it hampers the growth of an *élite*. A scheme that is geared to the 'average' trainee may suit him admirably, and yet thwart the future specialist. There is an obvious contrast between the needs of, for example, the auditor and the accountant in industry.

One likely possibility, therefore, is that groups of accountants will hive off in coming years into different vertical divisions – for such specialisms as auditing, computing, costing, and perhaps new kinds of work about which we yet know nothing. (Engineers, with their specialized institutes for each branch of their science, provide an

[1] This and the other quotations are from G. Unwin, *The Gilds and Companies of London* (London, 1924). Perhaps the guilds were sometimes more successful in social relations and colour than we are. For instance, members bought a hood and gown (at cost) to wear at the annual feast, at funerals, 'and on other solemn and great occasions'; hence the livery companies.

[2] P. A. Towsey, 'Some Thoughts on the Teaching of Accounting', *Nigerian Accountant*, January 1964.

obvious lead.) The weakness of such an arrangement is that the trainee is apt to get too narrow an experience.

Another possibility is a common initial training, followed by more scope for specialization than at present; the proposals in Britain for a 'post-graduate' certificate and diploma in management accounting are perhaps a step in this direction (and are certainly encouraging signs of the profession's awareness of the need for change). Medicine, with its 'colleges' for those who specialize, suggests how this system might develop. But it, too, has its faults. The minimum common training might be too long. And it would involve some sort of apprenticeship, presumably to an auditor. This can scarcely provide much experience in management accounting and computing; moreover it is a slow way of learning and one that is apt to damp the spirit of inquiry and innovation. Despite its good points, it is therefore not ideal.

Probably it is presumptuous to suggest what forms of organization and training will work best in the future. Quite likely the computer will force our hand. The best advice that we can now give is not to check development by making rigid arrangements or setting up monopolies.

Changes in Auditing Firms

One rather spectacular feature of the last decade has been the expansion of the bigger auditing firms (an obvious echo of what was said above apropos of guilds). Their growth has, in part, been due to their clients' growth; particularly where the client has many branches, at home or abroad, there is an economy in the auditor having corresponding branches. When the client expands by take-over bid, his auditor also may gain more work – which the auditor of the taken-over company loses. We lack statistics on this point, but we can reasonably suppose that the growth of big audit firms has not been without effects on the medium and small firms.

In one way, at least, it seems socially desirable that the growth of big companies should be matched by a corresponding growth in audit firms. Only a big firm has the necessary prestige and wealth to maintain effective independence *vis-à-vis* the giant client.

The big audit firm has other advantages. It can afford to pay its trainees well. It can emulate the technical college etc. in laying on introductory courses for new staff; one such firm claims that its intensive three-week course for beginners matures them as much as nine months of practice. It has enough skilled manpower to carry out large-scale investigations quickly. It can also employ specialists. Thus it can run its own department for management consultancy. Such departments seem likely to grow further as more clients install computers or demand the services of advisers trained in operational research etc.

The main way in which a less big firm of auditors can respond is by linking itself with several similar firms in a loose consortium. Such a group can, for instance, set up an associated firm to deal with management consultancy. Again statistics are lacking, but there seems to be a rather marked trend of this sort.

Computers and the Company Accountant

A parallel change may be taking place in the accounting departments of large companies. The computer is mainly responsible. It is not likely to displace all accountants, but it may offer them a clear choice between demotion or promotion.

The reason is that even a cheap computer costs a lot; further, expensive ones can do far more than cheap ones. This leads to centralization.

> 'Even a small computer is such a glutton for work that a firm possessing one tends to centralize its accounting system once the E.D.P. department has settled in and starts looking around for more work.
>
> 'The larger the computer, the lower tends to be the cost of a particular data-processing step . . . this being so, there is a tendency to buy one large computer rather than a number of smaller ones, and this, in its turn, leads to centralized data processing and so to centralized accounting.'[1]

Thus accounting may in future be done by a compact, high-power department. And accounting may be only one part of that department's work; the computer can also handle very different jobs, e.g. sales and personnel statistics, production control, and scientific research.

Further, there is at least some evidence of correlation between the success of a computer department and the rank of its chief:

> 'The survey indicated that the manager of business-computer activity in the nine successful companies was generally only two levels below the president of the company, and that the manager of business-computer activity in the eighteen less successful companies was generally three or more levels below the president'.[2]

---

[1] T. W. McRae, 'The Demands of E.D.P. on the Accountant of the Future', *Accountants' Magazine*, March 1964, page 183.

[2] John E. Johnson, 'E.D.P. as it Affects the Accountant', *N.A.A. Bulletin*, December 1963.

So here the accountant faces, if not an 'all-or-nothing' situation, at least a 'lot-or-little' one. He can content himself with the minor job of feeding in the financial data. Or he can step into a new post with high potentialities and prestige. But the latter will demand considerable knowledge of the computer and some grasp of statistics that lie far outside the realm of book-keeping. Our orthodox training is not well-fitted to instil either type of expertise.

Formal Education

It seems inevitable that formal training (i.e. work in the lecture-hall and library, as contrasted with the office) will become an increasingly important part of the accountant's preparation.

As a country grows in wealth, its young people go more and more to universities and take a higher education as much for granted as driving lessons. A Welfare State makes such education still more attractive; in comparison, private training schemes are bound to strike young people as ill-rewarded and parochial. The accounting profession must therefore come to terms with the universities and technical colleges – not because they give more practical skill in book-keeping than the office (which they cannot, and should not, do), but simply to ensure an adequate flow of recruits of good potential.

Formal education can make a contribution of three different kinds. At the first stage of a university training, the subject does not matter and can be matched to individual tastes; the subject is only the framework in which the student learns how to learn. Once he has been well trained in this sense, he should – given diligence – not have undue trouble in mastering practical accounting, and then in whatever further learning and unlearning the future may make necessary.

Second, formal education is probably the simplest and quickest way of giving an introduction to book-keeping. A teacher's main concern is to take his students over the right ground fast; this aim must come a poor second in the master-apprentice relation.

Third, the theoretical background to important new techniques – and sometimes their practice too – cannot be taught in most offices. The majority of today's accountants have not yet got the needed knowledge, and the minority have not the time for giving detailed instruction. Further, few small firms (of, for example, auditors) own a computer.

If these arguments hold water and accounting development must to some degree depend on formal education, then a likely bottleneck becomes visible. A good teaching department cannot be brought into existence overnight. The teachers have to be taught and allowed to run themselves in – a process that may take many years. So, if we are to improve our training in the seventies, we should already be setting about the necessary first step of producing future teachers.

CONCLUSION

This article has tried to list the disturbing changes that now threaten accountants. Its catalogue of threats may well strike readers as too alarmist. Plainly there are also many factors to give us comfort. But, if even a small part of my argument is sound, the danger is real.

To maintain their position against rivals, and to convert rivals into allies, accountants need to learn various new skills. Unfortunately these are exacting and some of them go against the grain. Further, our method of training is singularly ill-adapted for quick and drastic change.

We can recapitulate the needs as follows:

(1) *Stewardship accounting* ('data processing'). The accountant's position will be weakened if he cannot deal with statistical methods and the computer. He must therefore have a better background in mathematical subjects, and learn a good deal about the theory and practice of E.D.P.

(2) *Financial reporting*. The chief attack here comes from financial journalists and analysts, who are dissatisfied with the principles underlying our published figures. To meet their criticism, the accountant must acquire the kind of mental ability that comes with study of economic analysis and accounting theory.

(3) *Management accounting*. Here the need is for experience in industry plus knowledge of compound interest and relevant economic principles.

In total, these requirements are formidable.

However, accountants have so far shown themselves able to acquire difficult new skills, and to deal not unsuccessfully with competition from other professions. Thus the British accountant has an eminence in income taxation that is the envy of the lawyers. I doubt if any one of the new subjects is much harder to master than are the complexities of tax law. Let us hope that it is not yet too late for us to meet the challenge.

(*Concluded.*)

GENERAL OR SPECIAL INDEX?

General or Special Index? - Capital maintenance under changing prices

by W. T. Baxter, Professor of Accounting, University of London

A book by Dr. Ray *Gynther** (head of the department of accountancy, University of Queensland) is a useful statement of the present state of play in the price change argument. But it also takes this argument a long step forward, by exposing the conflict between the two main schools of reform. These agree that conventional accounting, in seeking to maintain money capital, is inadequate to our needs. But they fall out over what to use in place of money capital. One group wants to maintain real capital in terms of general purchasing power, the other a given set of physical assets.

Income definition

Thus both schools define income as surplus over a capital that has been adjusted to allow for price change. But the former tells us to adjust capital (i. e. the whole equity, including retained earnings, etc.) with the help of a general index. The second wishes to do the adjustment by creating a revaluation reserve to match the totals of each individual asset's change in value, found by piecemeal reappraisal or use of a specific price index for the given class of asset. Dr. *Gynther* therefore labels the first type of reformer "the general index man" and the second "the specific index man". He makes no bones about being himself an enthusiastic specific index man.

Equity versus entity

He warns us in his preface that our views on this matter may be coloured by personal experience. "It seems that the attitude adopted depends on whether one tends to look on a firm from without or from within, and this depends on what one's environment has been. As the author's background includes 12 years as a company accountant, secretary and controller, he is an 'entity theorist'. He believes that the purpose of accounting is to account for the entity primarily, as in our society activities are carried on by entities (firms, corporations, government authorities, etc.)". (p. x). One's logic is thus coloured by one's environment and "one's subconscious ideas on for whom or for what accounting systems are maintained" (p. 44), i. e. by whether we look at the firm's wealth through the eyes of the outside equityholder or through those of "the entity itself". Accountants in public practice are concerned to protect the interests of shareholders, and tend to favour the general index. Accountants in business tend to favour the special index.

Dr. *Gynther* is quite happy to let the individual shareholder measure his income as a general index man. But, he maintains, the accounting of a company is not the accounting of its owners. For the company, the important thing is to preserve the physical structure; the special index group "comprising those who look on a company as from within, is not conscious of the shareholders in the first instance. They want to see the entity's (company's) physical stock of assets and operating capacity maintained from period to period before arriving at profit – thus involving the use of specific indexes. They want to see the capital 'increased' from period to period in order to keep pace with the rising prices of the company's assets. Their prime interest is that of the company itself" (p. 46).

In part, Dr. *Gynther's* attitude is due to his concern with a firm's need for figures that help with day-to-day decisions – i. e. for management accounting as contrasted with annual profit measurement. Here surely he is in a strong position; the main test of any accounting values (conventional or reformed) is their ability to answer questions – by managers faced with daily decisions, as well as by the investor and tax collector.

Arithmetical illustration – Balance sheets

The best way to set out the cases of the two schools is probably via an example (adapted slightly from one used by Dr. *Gynther* on p. 47).

Suppose that a firm starts a capital of $ 1,000 in cash, and uses this to buy a good for re-sale. The good is later sold at retail for $ 2,000, at a time when its wholesale replacement cost is $ 1,550 (i. e. the special index has increased from 100 to 155). During the holding period, the general index has increased from 100 to only 120.

These figures should be analysed first with the help of consecutive balance sheets. The relevant dates are:

1. Start of the venture.
2. During the venture, just after the increases in the asset's replacement cost and in the general index.
3. End of venture, after the sale is made.

The balance sheets at these three dates are shown in Table I. To give a complete picture, it starts with the conventional figures.

Table I

Asset and equity values by various methods:

	(1) *Start*	(2) *During period* (after appreciation)	(3) *End*
I Conventional Accounts			
	$	$	$
Assets			
Cash	1,000		2,000
Asset, at historical cost		1,000	
Equity			
Capital	1,000	1,000	1,000
Profit			1,000
			2,000

* *Accounting for Price Level Changes: Theory and Procedure,* by R. S. Gynther. The Commonwealth and International Library of Science Technology Engineering and Liberal Studies, Pergamon Press, Oxford, 1966. 21s.

II Reformed Accounts

Assets			
Cash	1,000		2,000
Asset, current value		1,550	
Equity			
(a) *general index*			
Capital – historical	1,000	1,000	1,000
Capital – inflation adjustment		200	200
Real holding gain		350	
Realised profit			800
	1,000	1,550	2,000
(b) *special index*			
Capital – historical	1,000	1,000	1,000
Capital reserve on revaluation		550	550
Profit			450
	1,000	1,550	2,000

Conventional accounts

These show no appreciation until the asset is realised. Then they register profit at $ 1,000.

The latter figure (say both schools of reform) is not a helpful pointer to the sum that can conveniently be paid out as dividend. By any test of real wealth, more than $ 1,000 must be kept in the business if capital is to be maintained.

Revised accounts

Assets

It is not essential to write up the assets at the column (2) stage, i.e. before realisation. But writing-up then is useful for our exposition – and very often for practical reasons too.

Again, it is not essential to the general index method to write up the asset to its market value of $ 1,550 – the value also used by the special index man. Reform can take many shapes; some general index men would be content with the synthetic figure of $ 1,200 (historical cost adjusted with the general index). But I prefer the good sense of using current market value; and I hope that special index men will not deem me unscrupulous if I graft this bit of their method onto its rival.

If the general index approach is modified in this way, one cannot fault it on the grounds that it revalues assets clumsily. The difference between the two reforms lies only in their treatment of the corresponding credit balances. i.e. in the equity section of our balance sheets.

Equity. (a) General index method.

Here the aim is to re-state the owners' investment figure at its equivalent in today's $s (so that today's assets can be compared with a base-line expressed in like units). An exact equivalent is impossible to compute; inflation plays havoc with our sums as well as with a lot of other things. But most people – the general index man avers – will be tolerably satisfied with an adjustment that re-states capital in terms of general purchasing power. So capital is raised in step with the general index. This has gone up from 100 to 120; the adjustment to $ 1,000 is therefore $ 200. One way of showing the last figure is as an "inflation allowance"[1] or a capital reserve.

The balance of $ 350 is a *real* gain. It comes from holding the asset while the latter's market value was rising faster than did the values of things-in-general. Caution suggests that, as the gain is still unrealised at stage (2), it should be kept apart from realised profit.

At stage (3), however, the gain is realised. So it can be merged with the extra $ 400 now obtained (which might be called real current operating profit) to give a total of $ 800 as realised profit.

Equity. (b) Special index method.

At stage (2), when the asset appreciates, the company has good cause to congratulate itself. But the treasurer's joy should be alloyed somewhat (particularly if the asset is indivisible) by the thought that replacement will now demand more cash. The special index man argues that this financial need cuts profit: appreciation is $ 550, so this sum must be put into a capital reserve (and kept there for as long as $ 1,550 is needed to finance the given asset structure). "The real surplus *to the company*", to use Dr. *Gynther*'s phrase, is only $ 450, compared with $ 800 under (a).

LIFO would (with stock replaced at the same physical level) also kut profit at $ 450. It thus tries – perhaps unawares – to use the special index concept Dr. *Gynther* prefers the less crude technique illustrated here.

[1] The journal entry might be:

Cost of goods sold	$ 200
Inflation allowance	$ 200

Arithmetical Illustration – Income Statement

The income statements for our example, prepared (at the end of the venture) according to the same alternative recipes, are set out in Table II.

Table II

Income statement by various methods

	(1) Conventional accounts	(2) Reformed accounts (a) General index	(3) (b) Special index
	$	$	$
Sale	2,000	2,000	2,000
Cost of goods sold:			
Historical	1,000	1,000	
Inflation charge		200	
Real appreciation		350	
Current		1,550	1,550
Current operation profit		450	450
Real appreciation (holding gain, 550–200)		350	
Realised profit	1,000	800	450

Conventional accounts

These show no profit until the gain is realised. The statement for the final period puts profit at the too-generous sum of $ 1,000.

Reformed accounts

(a) General index methods

The minimum reform is to raise the historical cost of $ 1,000 by adding the $ 200 "inflation charge" – giving a cost-of-goods-sold at corrected historical cost of $ 1,200. Realised profit is then ($ 2,000 – $ 1,200) i. e. $ 800.

But there are strong grounds, especially where costs are to be used for management decision, for measuring inputs at the full sacrifice consequent on their using up, i. e. current replacement prices; here Dr. *Gynther* is entirely right. If this rule is followed in the income statement, the cost-of-goods-sold rises to $ 1,550. Columns (2) and (3) use this figure. The increase of $ 350 (real holding gain) must also be credited to somewhere. It is a gain from good (or lucky) merchandizing policy; so the logical place for it seems to be as revenue in the same income statement (or perhaps, if the appreciation took place in an earlier period, in the earlier statement)[2]. The $ 350 is therefore brought back as revenue at the foot of column (2); and it cancels the extra cost, making profit once more $ 800. Thus the minimum reform of the preceding paragraph in fact gives the right answer (in the general index man's eyes) though less incidental enlightenment.

If the period of this venture covers several years, and appreciation is recognised in the earlier annual accounts (of the years preceding the sale), these accounts should carefully describe the gain as *unrealised*. Only after the sale is this warning withdrawn, and appreciation merged with current operating profit. Thus there can be no danger of paying a dividend bigger than realised profits. But there remains the danger of finally paying one big enough to hinder asset replacement.

(b) Special index method

Here the cost is again the sensible figure of $ 1,550. But all the appreciation – real and nominal – is treated as "capital". Thus profit is severely pruned, and dividends will not eat into the cash needed for asset replacement.

Replacement cost accounting

The example shows there is some ambiguity in the phrase "replacement cost accounting". It can be applied to the general index re-statement (provided the costs are raised to current level as in Table II), but to its cost figures only. It fits the special index method much better, since both cost and profit are here linked with replacement.

To avoid confusion, one should specify what is to be replaced – the given asset or the owners' real capital.

Aspects of the argument

To discuss the special index reform helpfully, one must first state one's views on a rather long list of points, many of which hinge on the meaning of words.

Definitions of "capital gain"

If both schools accept that inputs should be charged at current market value (as in Table II), then the

[2] This approach plainly owes much to E. O. Edwards and P. W. Bell, *The Theory and Measurement of Business Income*, Berkeley 1961.

debit side of the adjustment is not in dispute. It is the credit that prompts the arguments: should this gain be looked on as a form of income?

If the gain is not income, then it must presumably be called capital. But what does "capital" mean? Consider some of its more relevant meanings:

(1) Holding versus operating.

It is easy to slip into the habit of calling holding gains "capital gains". Then, by definition, appreciation is a capital gain — and our whole discussion becomes infantile.

This, I take it, is not the approach of the serious advocate of the special index. Indeed Dr. *Gynther* excludes some forms of appreciation from capital gain, e. g. "accretion, such as the natural increase of flocks or the growth of standing timber is definitely a real profit item and not 'holding gains' as such. With accretion there is an actual *physical* increase in inventories, or an increase in their *physical* qualities (as with spirits)" (p. 76). Some holding gains thus bear the stigmata of capital, others do not.

It may be worthwhile at this point to look more closely at holding gain. Edwards and Bell[3] have shown the usefulness of distinguishing between gains due to making, selling, etc. (conceived as almost instantaneous operations), and those due to the appreciation that accrues if inputs are bought when buying prices are low and held till they are high. Clearly the distinction must often be artifical; but figures for the two gains might for instance help to assess the skills of the works manager and the purchasing officer. Table II, column (2), uses this analysis.

(2) Unusual versus usual.

"Capital" can of course mean merely "unusual" or "non-recurring" or "unplanned". Thus gains on the sale of fixed assets are less expected and repetitive than gains on trading stock.

Accounts should certainly try to distinguish between the usual and unusual. But this is to clarify our expectations, and surely not because what is income by all other tests ceases to be income if its source is abnormal or its timing irregular.

There is a strong tending to regard gains on the sale of fixed assets as something different from income. I suspect this derives largely from the law governing life-interest in trusts, and this in turn from hoary concepts of the tree and the fruit. (3) below suggests circumstances in which the tendency may be justified; the general index argument provides some further justification when gain is an illusion created by price change; and we must admit the danger of consuming gain before it has been realised. Otherwise, the tendency seems to rest on nothing stronger than ill-considered habits of everyday practice and speech. According to the severe logic of the U.S. revenue code, capital gains are merely unusual income. This seems right.

(3) Change in interest rate.

Normally an increase in an asset's value betokens an increase in subsequent receipts. But this is not always true. Consider appreciation due to a fall in general interest rates — for example where the assets are long-term fixed-interest stocks. My existing holding of government stocks then rises in value, but my future income — the yearly interest — stays the same; and I cannot improve this flow by switching to other stocks. Yet I am in some ways better off; for example, I can recklessly sell my stock and go on a longer holiday or buy a bigger annuity than before.

There is a good case for putting this kind of gain into a special category. We may perhaps call it "capital"; but it seems rather to be a peculiar form of income of limited usefulness. The best plan is perhaps to show it separately, labelling it with some phrase that clearly describes it.

The special index man can justify his treatment of gain as "capital" by appeal to (3) only where the asset's appreciation cannot lead to higher trading etc. receipts. In theory, if input prices rise then sale prices must tend to rise too, and by enough to put up the firm's profit per product unit. Men whom I respect disagree with me here; but I should have thought this upward tendency of profit is strong enough (in normal market conditions) to remove most instances of appreciation on business assets from capital's sense (3), i. e. such appreciation is usually income.

(4) Wealth at an earlier date.

Having disposed of meanings (1) — (3), we are

[3] Op. cit. On page 73, they seem to treat "capital" as a synonym for "holding".

left with only a narrow meaning – that of capital as the wealth of a person or firm, etc., at some given opening date. In accounts, we take opening wealth as our base-line; if allowance is made for drawings and fresh investment, increase in net assets (compared with this base) is income.

One then says that a transaction is "capital" if it merely changes the nature of the opening wealth without changing its size. Thus, when our debtor repays a loan, a capital transaction takes place; our original wealth is replaced by new wealth, but the total is not affected.

I think that (4) is the correct sense for our present purpose. However, if this be true, the special index man is not much further forword when he says appreciation is "capital". He is merely repeating his view that the credit must be kept clear from income because the assets' total physical size has not changed. His statement does not *justify* his use of physical size as base-line.

Meanings of "physical size"

"Physical size" too can mean many things. Does it here mean the *number* of e. g. items of stock, regardless of other attributes? Or their *weight?* Or (where these are important) qualities such as calory or vitamin *content?* With plant, does it mean the machines themselves or capacity to produce physical units of product? And what does *total* physical size mean (e. g. as one machine grows old and inefficient, how does the firm fill up this physical gap)?

Further, as Dr. *Gynther* points out, special indices can be more or less special – i. e. can vary greatly in what they embrace. At one end of the spectrum, each is a close representation of one given asset; at the other, they reflect the replacement costs of the whole firm or even the industry[4].

But technological change is probably what worries one most in this context. When asset A grows old, it may be replaced by an asset B that bears little or no resemblance to A. Indeed, the whole system may be changed, as when an oil company replaces lorries with a pipe-line.

Dr. *Gynther* deals with the point thus (p. 49):

In any case, profit is for a period *ended* and it should measure the amount by which the firm is better off after taking into account the specific current costs of assets used up in producing the revenues of that period. Such profit is created by daily and monthly transactions and not just at the end of the period when the profit figure for the whole year is calculated. This profit is reinvested immediately throughout the period in other assets, *and it does not matter if these are of a different kind,* provided that the specific current costs of using up these during the remainder of the period are also taken into account in the profit calculation. In this way the creeping changes that occur within a firm through technological improvements, diversification, automation, etc., are taken care of in a correct manner while using specific indexes for profit determination.

I must confess that I cannot understand this.

All reformers who use replacement cost are faced with valuation difficulties. These can be very awkward – e. g. what is the value of a semi-obsolete and perhaps unsaleable machine that will soon be replaced by a new process? The general index man can try to value it by assessing the buying price of its remaining services – perhaps with trouble and doubt, but not (I think) with inconsistency of principle. Presumably the special index man must ignore such obsolescence, and base his assessment on physical wear alone. He began the year with one unit; he still has one unit (though it has suddenly become almost useless); so the firm has made no loss.

Liquidity versus profit

There is yet another point on which writers in this field should be explicit. What do they consider to be the relationship between liquidity and profit?

Accounting already goes a long way towards protecting the liquid position. Its income concepts usually refuse to recognise unrealised gains, and so ensure that cash equal to recognised gains is still – or could have been – available at balance sheet date for dividends. In fact, the cash may already have been re-invested, or it may be earmarked for future re-investment; if so, its non-availability can

[4] The general index also takes many forms, as Dr. *Gynther* rightly points out on page 59. Probably the best for income measurement is the one that most nearly reflects the consumption of the average shareholder.

be explained to the shareholders in the annual report. Sometimes the explanation takes the oblique form of a transfer to reserve; but then the charge in the income statement is an appropriation, not a cost.

As Tables I and II show, the general index reform treats the inflationary part of the replacement outlay as a cost; any addition for replaçement would be an appropriation. The special index reform treats the whole as a cost: the shareholders "have no claim to profits until such time as dividends might be declared, and profits from the viewpoint of the firm can only exist if they can be distributed without impairing the physical capital" (p. 142).

Finding the cash for desirable or essential investment can be acutely painful and indeed crippling. But are we getting more helpful statistics by treating it as a cost? Suppose a salary-earner runs a vintage car, and its market price goes up steeply. He thus suddenly find himself wealthier – in just the same way (I suggest) as if he had won a second car in a raffle. He must now choose between various plans for the future. He can enjoy his expensive car while it lasts, and then revert to his usual more modest kind of car; or he can maintain the new level after replacement, by putting aside more of his salary to meet the high cost of another expensive model. If he opts for the second plan, his position is probably best explained by saying that he now needs to *save* more – not that his net income is down. The reason for his saving is his decision to live henceforth with an asset structure that has expanded in money and real terms. His position seems on all fours with that of a firm which decides to sustain real appreciation from its own finance. But, using the test of physical change, the special index man would treat the latter form of extra investment as a fall in income.

The "going concern" viewpoint

Dr. *Gynther* suggest (p. 45-6) that the general index reformers "think of paid-up capital as if it were actually back in the hands of the shareholders themselves, and hence they want to see this capital "increased" in order to keep pace with the movements in general purchasing power of money." Their concern is thus to safeguard the shareholder in the event of liquidiation, i. e. they do not subscribe to the "going concern" convention.

This seems a mis-interpretation. As I see it, both conventional and general index accounting accept the going-concern premise. Their concern with capital arises solely because they want an investment total (the owners' various contributions, including retained earnings) that they can treat as the baseline from which progress to date is measured. (General index accounting then takes an extra step, and quizzes these old figures through today's spectacles.) A person who looked instead to the firm's death (as may be proper if this tragedy seems imminent) would value assets at their likely scrap proceeds.

Appreciation on Money

So far, I have said nothing about the real gains (or more likely, in modern conditions, the real losses) that come from holding money. These are important, and Dr. *Gynther* devotes a long chapter to them.

If, after inflation, a balance sheet is fully "stabilized" in end money units, (i. e. if every item is converted into its modern equivalent) the "non-money" items (such as plants, stocks, and equity) tend to go up in value – by both the general index and the special index methods. But "money items" (cash, debtors, creditors, preference shares, etc.) cannot be raised, since they are already stated automatically in today's values. Unless the net money total happens to be zero, the two sides of the balance sheet will no longer be equal; the difference is a loss on holding money or a gain on owing money. Such loss or gain can be big. So there is much to be said for some type of reform that shows them in the accounts. "This is essential if real profit is to be known, and if the efforts of managements in such times are to be evaluated" (p. 137).

Example

Table III gives an arithmetical illustration. A firm starts a year with $ 1,000 of capital, all in the form of cash. During the year, there are no transactions (i. e. the cash balance stays at $ 1,000), and the general index rises from 100 to 120.

Table III

Loss on holding money

	(1)	(2)	(3)	(4)
	At start	At end		
		Con-ventional accounts	General index method	Special index method
Balance sheet	$ (start)	$ (end)	$ (end)	$ (end)
Money	1,000	1,000	1,000	1,000
Equity -historical	1,000	1,000		1,000
– adjusted for inflation			1,200	
– adjusted for special needs				550
– loss on holding money			– 200	– 550
			1,000	1,000

Columns (2), (3), and (4) show how the closing position is interpreted by various methods:

Column (2) – conventional accounts

These fail to show that a sizeable slice of wealth has been allowed to evaporate.

Column (3) – reform by general index

The firm started the year with wealth appraised at 1,000 $s of that date. This expression of opening wealth should at the close be interpreted as 1,200 end $s, because this last figure now gives the clearest available picture of the opening magnitude.

Thus the firm's inaction has cost it $ 200.

Column (4) – reform by special index

If one talked about a special index for money, one would have to say that it always stays dead still at 100. On this view, the loss by the special index method would presumably again be $ 200.

Dr. *Gynther* is pioneering (so far as I know) when he advocates a different view. He maintains that we should use the special index of something other than money – namely, the asset that the money is being held to buy eventually (p. 155–8). Column (4) assumes our firm plans to buy an asset whose index has gone from 100 to 155 during the year; so the loss from holding money is, if I have read Dr. *Gynther* aright, $ 550 by his approach.

This is an intriguing idea. The failure to buy the asset when it cost only $ 1,000 certainly is important; we should learn a lot about bad managers if such failures could be shown in reports.

But is the – $ 550 a form of income? In other words, did the firm's capital rise to $ 1,550, only to be frittered down again?

Consider a gain (instead of a loss) from delay in asset buying. A year ago, a business-man would have had to pay $ 1,550 for a machine; today he got it for $ 1,000. Is his income $ 550, i. e. has wealth gone up $ 550 during the year? Should he really pay tax on $ 550? Surely this is stretching the special index case too far. His $ 550 seems to be a potential payment averted, not something that came in. It can best be shown as a variance between budget and actual outlay, rather than in the income statement.

Practical difficulties of money adjustment

Dr. *Gynther's* theory would manifestly be hard to apply. A firm keeps cash to make many kinds of future purchases, some still not seen clearly. So its money index would be complex, uncertain, and subjective. Dr. *Gynther* admits this, but finds reassurance in G. O. May's comment:

"You would be more nearly right if you used any one of the indexes than if you made no adjustment of the figures at all"

and in Keynes' remark:

"It is better to be vaguely right than precisely wrong"

I feel strongly that we should not damn theories solely because practical difficulties hinder their application. Life would get very dull if we did. Besides, if we can establish what is right in principle, we may then be able at least to move towards some workable compromise. So my opposition is based on principle, not practical difficulties.

Long-term money assets and liabilities

Dr. *Gynther* thinks that inflationary gain from the whittling away of long-term money liabilities should not be recognised. He again bases his case on the entity theory: the gain leaves the permanent resources of the firm unaffected, though there is a shift in wealth among the lookers-on – from loan-holders to equity-holders. I should have thought our capital concept (3) – page 14 – is perhaps a better reason.

On the other hand, he recognises loss on long-term money assets. I must confess to finding this inconsistent.

Some wider issues

To treat our topic properly, we must venture far beyond the frontiers of accounting, and into less familiar subjects.

The real group-person

Thus we ought to find out more about the concept of the entity. When Dr. *Gynther* appeals to this, clearly he does not mean that splitting up figures in accounts, as between a trader's business and his home, etc., somehow endows the business with special status. The analysis implies no more than that classified figures are useful: the trader is helped by knowing for instance how much he spends on the shop and how much on his wife. In much the same way, the economist is helped in his reasoning when he unravels man the consumer from man the firm.

The law goes a long step further; there is plainly much convenience in the legal fiction that a corporation is a person. But the entity's status presumably derives mainly from the view that a business is run by more than one man, and that a *group* of men – working together as say a church, gild, or firm – acquires a personality of its own, demanding our special respect.

This line of argument leads us into the realm of political philosophy, where an accountant like me must soon be floundering out of his depth. Apparently some serious philosophers, as well as demagogues like Mussolini, have attributed "the red blood of real corporate personality" to the group, asking whether it has a "personality beyond the persons of its members, and a will beyond their wills". An opposing view is stated by Ernest Barker. He sees in the group not an extra person but merely an *organising idea*. "What has happened is that this idea has entered into a continuous succession of persons ... a new personality has not arisen, but a new organising idea has served as a scheme of composition for existing personalities." He thus cuts down the group's status. "When we talk of real persons, we attach to them an intrinsic value as such, because we feel that all personality has value. At that rate we should see value in the Mafia or Camorra. If one talks rather of ideas, one can keep something more of critical poise ... one can deflate a bubble idea with a prick of logic."[5]

The problem is acute when the measurement of wealth is at issue. For wealth is a matter of satisfactions, which can be savoured by human beings but hardly by abstract creatures. The general index reformer can rest his case on the welfare and emotions of the human owner – things admittedly vague, but at least capable of being argued about. But how does one argue about a *company's* reactions to wealth? Do we mean in fact the reactions of its managers? Or of some part or the whole of the people – employees, customers, owners, etc. – who have dealings with it? Or can we somehow weigh the emotions of the abstraction itself?

Economics and physical quantities

Much the same doubts are engendered by one's reading in economics. The end of production is consumption; production is not a matter of physical size, but of power to satisfy human demands in the context of scarcity. "There is no quality in things taken out of their relation to men which can make them economic goods ... wealth is not wealth because of its substantial qualities. It is wealth because it is scarce. We cannot define wealth in physical terms as we can define food in terms of vitamin content or calorific value."[6] Such home-truths make one look askance at any income concept that is founded on physical capital.

Conclusion

The urge to maintain a firm's physical structure is strong. True, the assets of many firms are available in different quantities and sizes, so that a change of scale at replacement can be achieved smoothly; and, where maintenance of the same scale is desirable, firms can often borrow to finance any increased cost. Still, it would be frivolous to belittle the importance of the replacement need. The question is whether it is a function of income.

If we agree with Dr. *Gynther* that the test of accounts is their ability to give information that helps us with decision, then we must ask what information is provided more clearly by the special

[5] The quotations are all from Ernest Barker, *Church, State, and Study*, London 1930, pages 160–3.

[6] L. Robbins, *The Nature and Significance of Economic Science*, London 1949, pp. 46–7.

index than by the general index method. On costs and assets, the latter (modified as in Table II) gives the same information as the former. On money, it seems better. On income, it seems much better; by switching the limelight onto holding gains, it gives information that must surely be useful to managers as well as shareholders.

One wonders whether the special index man would still abide by his rules in extreme situations. Suppose the product of a machine becomes unsalable. We should learn more from accounts if the machine is written off than if it is not — even though its physical shape is as good as ever.

Because Dr. *Gynther's* contribution to the special index argument is so interesting, I have concentrated on it, and failed to mention the many other useful and important things that his book includes. And perhaps I have, despite the many quotations from him, failed to state his case properly. If so, I apologise. I hope that he will now put us further in his debt by strengthening his argument; this he could best do by comparing the performance of the two methods as aids in solving detailed management problems[7].

[7] I am greatly indebted to Mr. M. *Bromwich* for help with this article.

Indexation Générale ou Particulière? - Le Maintien du Capital en cas de Variation de Prix

Traduction de l'article rédigé en anglais par le professeur W. T. Baxter de l'Université de Londres

Le livre du Dr. Ray S. *Gynther** (Chef de la Section Comptabilité de l'Université de Queensland) donne une bonne vue d'ensemble sur les incidences de la variation des prix. Mais il pousse plus loin encore son développement en exposant les divergences existant entre les deux principales théories d'indexation. Celles-ci s'accordent pour affirmer que la comptabilité classique, dans sa recherche du maintien du capital nominal, n'est pas adaptée à nos besoins. Mais elles s'opposent lorsqu'il s'agit de trouver ce qui peut remplacer le capital nominal. L'une souhaite le maintien du capital dans le cadre d'un pouvoir d'achat général, l'autre préconise le maintien de la composition physique de l'actif.

Définition du profit

Ces deux théories définissent le profit comme l'excédent du capital qui a été revalorisé pour tenir compte de la variation des prix. Mais la première nous suggère de revaloriser le capital (c'est-à-dire le total de l'actif net, y compris les réserves etc.) à l'aide d'un indice général. La seconde propose que le réajustement soit effectué par l'établissement d'une réserve de réévaluation égale au total des changements de valeurs de chacun des actifs, après que ces valeurs aient été revues de manière spécifique, ou par l'utilisation d'un indice applicable à chaque nature de biens. Le Docteur *Gynther* baptise donc la première catégorie de théoriciens «Théoriciens de l'indice général» et la seconde «Théoriciens de l'indice spécifique». Il ne cache pas qu'il se considère lui-même comme un représentant enthousiaste de l'indice spécifique.

Les deux systèmes

Dans sa préface, il précise que notre expérience peut, effectivement, influencer nos idées sur ce sujet. «Il semble que le point de vue que l'on adopte varie selon que l'on étudie une société de l'intérieur ou de l'extérieur, et ceci dépend de sa propre situation.» L'auteur ayant été pendant douze années cadre-comptable, secrétaire général et «controller» d'une société, c'est un «théoricien de l'intérieur». Il est persuadé que le but de la comptabilité est de tenir des comptes principalement pour chaque groupe ou entreprise, puisque, dans notre monde, les activités sont exercées par des groupes (entreprises, associations, organismes gouvernementaux, etc.). Notre point de vue est modifié par notre milieu et «par les idées sous-jacentes que l'on a sur la destination de la comptabilité» (page 44) c'est-à-dire selon que l'on considère la santé d'une société avec les

* (v. note page 173).

yeux d'un observateur extérieur ou avec ceux d'un de ses membres. Dans le sens commun, la comptabilité tend à la fois à protéger les intérêts des actionnaires et à veiller à maintenir l'indexation générale. La comptabilité, dans les affaires, raisonne en fonction d'indices spécifiques.

Le Dr. *Gynther* souhaite que chaque actionnaire puisse calculer son revenu en tenant compte de l'indice général. Mais, affirme-t-il, le comptable d'une société n'est pas le comptable de ses propriétaires. Pour la compagnie, il est, avant tout, important de maintenir la consistance des actifs; les adeptes de l'indice particulier «comprenant les observateurs qui étudient la société de l'intérieur, ne pensent pas aux actionnaires en premier lieu. Ils veulent voir *l'entité* (total des actifs de la compagnie et des capacités de production) maintenue avant d'accéder aux bénéfices, — conduisant ainsi à l'utilisation d'indices particuliers. Ils désirent voir le capital «s'accroître» régulièrement de façon à rester en rapport constant avec la hausse des prix des biens formant l'actif de la compagnie. Leur intérêt principal est l'intérêt même de la société» (p. 46).

La position du Dr. *Gynther* est en partie due à la nécessité, pour une entreprise, de disposer de chiffres permettant de prendre des décisions jour après jour — c'est-à-dire pour une comptabilité de gestion par opposition au calcul du bénéfice annuel. C'est là que réside la force de sa position; le critère principal de la valeur d'un système comptable (conventionnel ou rectifié), est sa capacité de réponse à des questions posées aussi bien par des directeurs devant chaque jour prendre des décisions que par l'investisseur ou le contrôleur fiscal.

Exemple chiffré — Bilans

La meilleure façon d'illustrer les arguments de ces deux écoles est de montrer un exemple (adaption de l'un de ceux utilisés par le Dr. *Gynther* p. 47).

Supposons qu'une société débute avec un capital de $ 1000 en caisse et l'utilise pour acheter des marchandises destinées à la revente. La marchandise est, par la suite, vendue au détail $ 2000 alors que son coût de remplacement au prix de gros est de $ 1550 (c'est-à-dire que l'indice particulier est passé de 100 à 155). Au cours de cette même période, l'indice général des prix n'est passé que de 100 à 120.

Ces chiffres doivent être tout d'abord étudiés à l'aide de bilans successifs. On prendra ces bilans aux dates suivantes:

1. au début de l'opération.
2. au cours de cette opération, juste après l'accroissement du coût de remplacement du bien et de l'indice général.
3. fin de l'opération, après réalisation de la vente.

Les bilans établis à ces trois dates sont repris au tableau I. Pour permettre toutes les comparaisons, on a repris, au début, son déroulement en comptabilité classique.

Tableau I

Actif et Passif selon les diverses méthodes

	(1) Début	(2) En cours d'opération (après augmentation)	(3) Fin
I Comptabilité classique			
Actif	$	$	$
Espèces	1,000		2,000
Actif au prix d'achat		1,000	
Passif			
Capital	1,000	1,000	1,000
Bénéfice			1,000
			2,000
II Comptes réévalués			
Actif			
Espèces	1,000		2,000
Actif à la valeur de remplacement		1,550	
Passif			
(a) *Indice Général*			
Capital initial	1,000	1,000	1,000
Capital — ajustement pour inflation		200	200
Gain dû à la rétention de l'actif		350	
Bénéfice dégagé			800
	1,000	1,550	2,000
(b) *Indice Particulier*			
Capital initial	1,000	1,000	1,000
Capitalisation due à la réévaluation		550	550
Bénéfice			450
	1,000	1,550	2,000

VALUATION OF A PRACTISING ACCOUNTANT'S WORK-IN-PROGRESS

Valuation of a Practising Accountant's Work-in-progress—I

W. T. Baxter

Income Tax Position

A case recently before the Special Commissioners dealt with the value of the work-in-progress of a firm of practising accountants. Such cases are of course private, and the decision does not form a binding precedent for other taxpayers. But the issues canvassed during the hearing are important both for tax and theory, and the decision—presumably circulated to Inspectors—is likely to influence the official attitude to future assessments of the same kind. So an informal account of these informal proceedings may be useful. It fills Part I of my article (published with the kind consent of the firm concerned). Part II goes on to discuss relevant theory.[1]

Facts

The facts of the case are as follows. The firm of professional accountants had for decades allowed for work-in-progress in its annual accounts. The work-in-progress is valued by multiplying the actual hours spent on work by a cost rate. A deduction is made for doubtful debts.

The case hinged on whether the cost rate—call it x shillings per hour—gave a proper value, and hence a proper profit figure.

When the point was raised by an Inspector in 1959 (for the first time, or the first time in many years), x had been used, without revision, for perhaps ten years. When originally adopted (still earlier), x may well have reflected average hourly salaries—indeed, dim memories suggested that once at least there had been an increase in the rate to mirror salary increases. But admittedly x was by 1959 a notional cost, no longer in line with current rates. Nevertheless the Inspector then wrote that he was 'prepared to settle'; and the rate of x was used for several more years.

In 1962, the firm decided, on its own initiative, to change from the notional to an actual cost rate. The new rate is found by dividing total direct salaries, and other variable expenses, for the given year by the number of hours worked; the rate turned out to be about $2x$ in 1962 (and thereafter would automatically rise or fall with actual salaries).

In its profit and loss account for the year to 31 March 1962, the firm applied the new method both to opening and closing work-in-progress. The 'uplift' in the former was at first credited to partners' current accounts; then, to stress that this sum was not available in cash for drawings, it was transferred to capital accounts.

The firm told the Inspector of the change, before the 1961/62 assessment was made, suggesting that the new basis should be adopted by him for the year to 31 March 1962, i.e. for the 1962/63 assessment—with the proviso that both opening and closing work-in-progress for the accounting year should be adjusted to the new rate. The change would of course tend to raise tax in both 1962/63 and later years, since the increased rate would be applied to a (normally) increasing number of hours, and also end rates are slightly higher (because of salary rises) than opening rates.

[1] I have to thank Mr J. F. Flower for his generous help with this article.

The Inspector rejected the proviso. At the hearing of the case, he claimed that the assessments should instead be as follows:

1963/64 onwards. New basis.

1962/63. New basis for closing work-in-progress, old basis for opening—i.e. the whole appreciation for many years should be taxed in this year.

Alternatively, if the 1962/63 opening work-in-progress was valued at new rates, then (he argued) the process of rate revision should be extended backwards, i.e.:

1961/62. The first assessment should be on the new basis.

1957/58–1960/61. Additional assessments should now be made (following 'discovery'), using the new rates. And

1956/57. To round off the six-year revision, an additional assessment should be made. Closing work-in-progress should be valued at the new rate, opening at the old (i.e. x). The latter rate was correct at that date—the Inspector maintained—because there were then changes in the partners and 'discontinuance and new business' treatment was applied, so that there was a 'purchase' of the work-in-progress by the new firm from the old.

Relevant Law

There are no clear legal rules on the points at issue. The relevant (or least irrelevant) are:[1]

Statute law

Section 122, ITA 1952 states that tax is to be charged in respect of annual profits or gains arising or accruing.

Section 127, ITA 1952 states that the profit assessable for a particular year of assessment is the full amount of the profits or gains of the year preceding the year of assessment.

Section 5 (3), ITMA 1964 deals with 'discovery'. If an Inspector discovers that any income which ought to have been assessed has not been assessed, he may make an assessment on the further amount.

Case law

Appendix I (page 19) gives the cases cited during the hearing.

Counsel for the firm stressed the *Duple* and the *Ahmedabad* cases. In the former (it will be remembered) the House of Lords held that a manufacturer may use either the direct cost method or the overhead method of valuing stock; in the latter, the Privy Council held that, at a change of valuation basis, the opening and closing figures should both be put on the new basis. The Inspector stressed the *Broadstone* case (rejecting the base stock method), and the *Anaconda* case (rejecting Lifo).

[1] See also John E. Talbot, 'Tax Aspects of Stock Valuation' and 'Stock in Trade and the Auditor', *British Tax Review*, respectively September 1957 and March 1962.

Practice

During the hearing, it was stated that recognised accounting methods used by professional firms include:

Cash basis

This ignores both debtors and work-in-progress.

The result of their omission is, of course, to postpone the recognition of profit to a later year. The point is illustrated in an imaginary arithmetical example in Appendix II. This shows incidentally that the methods are listed here in order of diminishing conservatism, i.e. the cash basis is the tardiest in profit recognition.

Bills delivered

Work-in-progress is ignored.

Work-in-progress, valued at cost

Here there are various possibilities:

Direct cost.

This may be notional, as in the case here discussed; it may be a fraction (as little as one-eighth was mentioned in relation to one case) of total annual salaries plus lunch vouchers, etc. It may be found from actual hours and actual rates of salary of professional staff; in some accounting firms, it is expanded to include typists' work. Sometimes the valuation may consist of a round sum, left unaltered for many years; presumably this sum becomes very conservative in the end.

Cost plus.

Valuation may be at direct cost plus a percentage for overheads.

Fees minus gross profit.

Here the firm works backwards, i.e. discounts the full fee by a profit percentage.

Work-in-progress, including some profit

The profit may take the form of a charge, based on time records, for partners' salaries. There is an obvious convenience in building up job costs in this way; otherwise there would be an awkward break in continuity when say work is switched from a partner to a senior member of the staff. But the Inspector stated that the Revenue would never insist on the inclusion of partners' salaries.

Or the value may be found by multiplying hours by the full rate to be charged as fees (instead of a cost rate), or by a fraction (say two-thirds) of the fee rate.

It was pointed out that not all professional fees are charged on a time basis. There may be an official scale. The charge may be *ad valorem*; thus architects commonly charge a percentage of the cost of the building, etc., and even accountants have been known in the past to charge a percentage of cash transactions (e.g. for some types of insolvency work).

It was also stated that the *lower of cost or market* rule is used widely, to provide a ceiling for work-in-progress and debtors. A common procedure is to make specific provision for debts that are likely to prove bad, or for work that for other reasons may never be rewarded (e.g. after an interim audit, a firm may be asked to resign, in which circumstances probably little or no fee could be recovered). For some kinds of work (e.g. charities) the fee may be nominal or nothing.

Incidentally, recommendation N.22 of the Institute of Chartered Accountants of England and Wales, on the valuation of stock and work-in-progress, states that its scope includes manufacturers and merchants, but not professional firms. Thus, although it was quoted at some length during the case, it could not be regarded as directly applicable. (One may, however, reasonably suppose that economic principles applicable to firms handling goods must normally hold for firms supplying services.)

Firm's Arguments

Counsel for the firm submitted that, as a wide range of interpretations of 'cost' is found in practice and is quite proper, a wide range of corresponding 'profit' measurements must also be proper. The firm's 'old method' of valuation fell within the permitted range. Equally, the firm was entitled to change to its 'new method'; indeed, cases show that the Revenue can on occasion demand a change of method.

Profit is found in somewhat artificial ways—by a host of technical rules that may give answers remote from everyday views. And absolute truth is unobtainable. As Lord Simonds said in the *Duple* case, different amounts of profit may be reached by different methods. (But Lord Reid was puzzled by the view that 'either method will produce a true figure'. He thought that, taking a particular business for a single year, very different figures cannot both be true. The view may mean that both methods will for a whole period—several years—produce the same aggregate profit; or it may mean that one or other method will produce a true figure depending on the nature of the business.)

It followed in the present case that neither the old nor the new basis produces absolute truth. The old was applied consistently, and (for all that anyone knows) may have produced better profit figures than the new. In particular, an auditor's costs are subject to 'jointness', so that the direct cost of a given bit of work (defined in terms of addition to total cost due to doing that work) may be small, as well as hard to find; despite the name 'direct cost', it thus seems to fit in with paragraph 7 (*b*) of the Institute's recommendation N.22, approving the use in suitable circumstances of a limited 'marginal' cost[1] basis for stock valuation.

The notional cost of the old basis was admittedly not an 'actual' figure, but neither, for example, is standard cost. And, in the *Broadstone Mills* case, even the approved new basis allowed the application of an arbitrary 40 per cent factor to actual cost.

[1] 'That is to say that part of the cost of production of the period which has been incurred only because the stock remaining on hand was acquired or produced; all other expenses . . . arise irrespective of the quantity of stock which remains on hand at the end of the period and therefore are not an element in its cost.'

In the *Duple* case, Lord Simonds said that a first principle of tax law is that the taxpayer is entitled to debit his expenditure in the year of assessment even if it may be recoverable in another; the Crown is not entitled to anticipate profit, as it might do if too high a value were put on stocks. But this principle must be harmonised with another, viz. that at any rate *some* value must be placed on stock. Lord Reid said that all expenses (not excluded by the Act) may be included in the expenditure of the year, and therefore the problem is what expenditure it is proper to exclude from the account by setting against it a figure representing stock or work-in-progress.

The change of basis, counsel maintained, should apply to both opening and closing stock. Even in the well-known cases where a taxpayer had been made to change his stock basis (e.g. *Broadstone Mills* and *Anaconda*), he was permitted to do so both at the beginning and end of the transition year; nor had anyone there suggested that earlier years should be revised too. The *Ahmedabad* rule should be applied generally, as otherwise 'profit' will include more than the profit of the given year.[1]

On the subject of discovery, counsel argued that, if an Inspector decides a first assessment is too low, he must justify his change of view before he can make an additional assessment. The onus lies with him. He must point to something that demonstrates positively that undercharge took place.

Witnesses on both sides mentioned—with varying degrees of enthusiasm—evidence given by Sir Henry Hancock (then Chairman, Board of Inland Revenue) to the Committee of Public Accounts.[2] He there said that the cash basis has judicial recognition, and that an Inspector can refuse to allow it only in the first three years at the commencement of a profession. Between

[1] Inland Revenue practice with regard to change in the basis of stock valuation is set out in a note published in *The Accountant*, 17 November 1962, page 648. The note may be summarised thus:

Change in basis

The Revenue accepts any 'valid basis' recognised by the accountancy profession, so long as it does not violate the taxing statutes. The phrase 'non-valid basis' denotes a basis that fails to accord with this standard, and includes a valuation which, although in form made on a recognised basis, pays insufficient regard to the facts. Because of the consistency principle, there would need to be good reason for changing a valid basis (e.g. alteration in the nature of the trade, absorption by a group).

Change from one valid basis to another valid basis

Here opening stock of the year of change is valued on the same basis as closing stock. Valuations of earlier years are seldom revised.

It is convenient not to regard every change in method as a change of basis. Changes which involve no more than refinement are not a change of basis, and do not call for amendment of opening value.

Change from a non-valid basis to a valid basis

The new basis is applied to both opening and closing values of the year of change. Also a review is made of past liabilities, but (in the absence of fraud, etc.) the Revenue would not seek tax on an amount greater than the uplift in the opening stock of the year of change.

[2] *Reports from Committees*, 1957, IV, Minutes of Evidence, 18 December 1956, p. 7.

the cash basis and the earnings basis there is a complete spectrum of practices, all in accordance with recognised accountancy principles; here convention is so strong that it virtually has the force of law.

Revenue's Arguments

For the Inland Revenue, the Inspector argued that Section 127 applies to both Cases I and II, so that the rules for commerce apply also to the professions. The Revenue has the right to insist on use of an earnings basis, in order that the Act's 'full amount of the profits' can be found. Thus, in the present case, even if the use of a rigid cost rate was wholly satisfactory by ordinary accounting tests, the Revenue could reject it. For convenience, rough-and-ready methods (such as the cash basis) are indeed often accepted; but they can in law be put aside by the Inspector if he cares to attack them.

The Revenue (he maintained) may be willing to accept a change of basis—but not where this leads to chaos. 'Cost', if chosen as the basis, must mean actual (i.e. historical) cost. When two or more ways of measuring profit are available, the right way is the one that most nearly fits the facts (*Anaconda* case). Two tests must be applied: the chosen method must satisfy ordinary commercial principles, and it must not violate the law.

The *Broadstone Mills* decision stated that stock must not be brought in at an arbitrary figure. Yet there (in contrast to the present case) some at least of the stock was valued for tax purposes at current prices. In the *Duple* case, both the rates in question were at least varied from year to year, i.e. were at an 'actual', so that dispute centred on the choice between 'actuals'.

Further, once a firm chooses its factors for valuation, it must be ready to re-apply them to all years. In this case, the firm had not for many years explained or been asked to explain its valuation procedure, so that the Revenue did not know what was happening prior to 1959; therefore the Revenue had now the right to make additional assessments.

The Inspector interpreted the decisions on 'discovery' as stretching the word to cover a change of view. Thus discovery occurs if an Inspector (perhaps on taking over another district) finds out that an error in law has been made. The word may at times mean no more than that the Inspector 'has reason to believe'; the only limitation on his change of mind is that he must not act blindly or officiously. He can discover without proving, i.e. once discovery has been made, the onus of proof is on the taxpayer.

A witness for the Revenue said that in his view a wide spectrum of methods—ranging from the cash basis to full earnings—exists. The extremes are legitimate, but the 'in-betweens', though often accepted, are mainly concessions; and, if they are used, they must be 'worked properly'. Whether or not work-in-progress should be included, and the method of valuing it, depends on the Inspector's view on whether such work is relevant to profit. It is likely to be relevant where the firm is growing. The witness knew of many cases of stock-at-end being raised without a corresponding rise in opening stock, i.e. the *Ahmedabad* decision, if applicable, dealt with a complete change of method and not with an adjustment of existing basis.

The Decision

The Special Commissioners decided in favour of the Inland Revenue.

Their opinion may be summarised as follows:

Discovery

Fresh facts came to the Inspector's knowledge in 1959 after the making of the original assessments for 1956/57, 1957/58 and 1958/59, and thus there was clearly a discovery although the Inspector did not then act on it. As regards 1959/60 and 1960/61, there was a genuine change of view, and this amounted to discovery; and there was no binding agreement between the appellants and the Inspector on the 1956/60 assessments.

Basis of valuing work-in-progress

There is no dispute between the parties that 'the revised basis' of valuation, adopted for both opening and closing work-in-progress for the year to 31 March 1962, is preferable for the years of assessment 1962/63 *et seq.* There is a wide choice of method in valuing work-in-progress; but the continued use of the old basis in the earlier years led to an increasing inaccuracy in computing profits for income tax purposes. The revised basis produces a more accurate estimate of profits, and ought to be applied in principle throughout the period.

Moreover, the revised basis is not fundamentally different from the old basis; in both, a specific hourly cost rate is applied to recorded hours of work. Therefore the value of work-in-progress at 31 March 1961 should be computed on the revised basis, but the evidence did not enable the Commissioners to say what would be the effect of substituting the revised basis in the earlier years, and the parties should agree the amounts on the basis of the decision in principle.

[Note: The *Ahmedebad* principle was in fact applied in settling the final adjustments with the Inland Revenue. Thus both opening and closing revised valuations were incorporated in the assessments based on profits for the year to 31 March 1962 and each earlier year until the earliest date was reached, i.e. the date of purchase by the 'new firm' from the 'old firm' following the 'discontinuance and new business adjustments'—see page 4 above.]

Appendix I

Case law

The cases cited by counsel for the firm were *Whimster & Co.* v. *I.R. Comrs.*, (1925) 12 TC 813, and *Regent Oil Co., Ltd.* v. *Strick*, [1965] 3 WLR 636 (ordinary principles of commercial accounting should normally govern profit measurement); *Duple Motor Bodies Ltd.* v. *Ostime*, (1959) 39 TC 537 (a manufacturer may at his discretion use either the direct cost or overhead method for valuing stock); *I.R. Comrs.* v. *Morrison*, (1932) 17 TC 325 (a professional firm may switch from an earnings to a cash basis, but may not switch back in a later year when large debts are collected); *D. and G. R. Rankine* v. *I.R. Comrs.*, (1952) 32 TC 520 (fees received after the dissolution of a professional firm, working on a cash basis, may not be charged retrospectively on earlier years for which the assessments had become final and conclusive, but the first assessment on the broken final year may be made on the earnings basis); and *Bombay Commissioner of Income Tax* v. *Ahmedabad New Cotton Mills Co., Ltd.*, (1929) 46 TLR 68 PC (at a change of stock valuation basis, both opening and closing figures should be raised to the new basis. As this is an Indian case, it may not apply in Britain; but a witness for the Inland Revenue said that body is becoming more favourable to the decision.)

The chief additional cases cited by the Inspector were *Minister of National Revenue (Canada)* v. *Anaconda American Brass Ltd.*, [1956] 1 All ER 20, and *Patrick* v. *Broadstone Mills Ltd.*, (1953) 35 TC 44 (respectively rejecting the LIFO and base stock methods, i.e. rejecting the rules of commercial accounting in certain circumstances), and *Wetton, Page & Co.* v. *Attwooll*, [1963] 1 All ER 166 (a change to an earnings basis—for a firm of accountants—was correctly made).

On the onus of proof, the Inspector cited *I. Haythornthwaite & Sons, Ltd.* v. *Kelly*, (1927) 11 TC 657, and *Commercial Structures, Ltd.* v. *Briggs*, (1948) 30 TC 477 ('the word "discover" . . . may be taken simply to mean "find out" ').

Appendix II

Numerical illustration to valuation methods of professional firms

Data

A firm is created specially to carry out two consultancy jobs, A and B. Both are done during Year 1. The firm then stops working, and is later wound up.

The following are the relevant figures (£000 omitted):

		£
Year 0	Initial capital paid in	150
Year 1	Costs incurred. Direct—Job A ..	40
	B ..	60
		100
	Indirect	50
		150
	Bill delivered, and cash received, for A	60
Year 2	Bill delivered for B	140
Year 3	Cash received for B	140

The fee for B is (proportionately to direct costs) higher than that for A because the firm's responsibilities, etc., are higher.

Problem

What is the firm's income, for years 1, 2 and 3, on the following alternative bases:

(*a*) Cash received.
(*b*) Bills delivered.
(*c*) Work-in-progress, valued at direct cost.
(*d*) Work-in-progress, valued at full cost, taken as direct cost plus 50 per cent.
(*e*) Work-in-progress, valued at selling price less the average net margin (25 per cent of selling price).
(*f*) Work-in-progress, valued at selling price?

Solution

The following table shows the assets at each stage (so far as this firm recognises them) by each method in turn. The growth in the total gives the profit for the year.

Date	*0*	*1*	*2*	*3*
a Cash basis				
Cash	150	60	60	200
Profit ..		−90	—	140
b Bills delivered				
Cash	150	60	60	200
Debtor.. ..			140	
	150	60	200	200
Profit ..		−90	140	—
c W.I.P. (direct cost)				
Cash	150	60	60	200
Debtor.. ..			140	
W.I.P.		60		
	150	120	200	200
Profit ..		−30	80	—
d W.I.P. (full cost)				
Cash	150	60	60	200
Debtor.. ..			140	
W.I.P.		90		
	150	150	200	200
Profit ..		—	50	—
e W.I.P. (net selling price)				
Cash	150	60	60	200
Debtor.. ..			140	
W.I.P.		105		
	150	165	200	200
Profit ..		15	35	—

f W.I.P. (selling price)							
Cash	150	60		60		200	
Debtor.. ..				140			
W.I.P.		140					
	150	200		200		200	
Profit ..			50		—		—

The table shows the forward shift in the timing of profit recognition as we move from the more to the less conservative values. At the top, under the conservative rules of bases (*a*) and (*b*), year 1 shows a loss of £90, and profit is postponed till later years; at the foot of the table (base *f*), year 1 claims the whole profit of £50.

It is an accident that (*d*) gives Year 1 a profit of *nil*; for instance, if A's fee were £65 instead of £60, profit would be £5. But the accident is useful, since it makes us remember that valuation at full cost is an attempt to postpone all profit (positive or negative) on the work-in-progress; it also underlines the point that, where there are joint costs, A's profit depends on B's valuation.

Valuation of a Practising Accountant's Work-in-progress—II

W. T. Baxter

Discussion on Theory

The case described in Part I is disturbing, in that it shows up the vagueness of accounting theory, and our sorry lack of any logical apparatus with which to sweep away uncertainty and to reach one convincing and inescapable 'profit'. So perhaps we should now turn from the particular case, and remind ourselves of the relevant principles.

Income Theory

Testing income measures

What do we mean when we say that one income figure is better than another?

When we find fault with a method of measuring income—say, a firm's profit—we are usually prompted by a feeling that the resulting figure is at odds with what we already know about the firm's progress, or fails to tell us something that we should like to know about it. Thus we rate the various methods by their ability to give us sound information—to answer our questions about how wealth is growing.

If this view is right, then 'trueness' is here a function of information; the ideal with which we (perhaps unwittingly) compare any given profit figure is one that gives us a sounder picture of the firm's progress.

However, just as a child's mark in a single examination may 'fail to do him justice', so too any one basis of profit measurement may give a blinkered view of the firm's progress. It will highlight some aspects and shut out others. Probably we are asking for too much if we suppose that any single figure can reflect all aspects of a firm's performance. We struggle in vain for the ideal measure.

To give another analogy, a motorist would doubtless be most happy if a single dial told him all that he wants to know about his car's running—speed, miles, oil pressure, petrol, etc; but in fact no composite index can sum up such diverse matters, and he must look at several dials. Similarly we expect profit figures to summarise too much—to answer such diverse questions as (by the owner):

(*a*) 'how much cash can I safely withdraw?' (i.e. liquidity problems)

(*b*) 'how well are my new manager's methods doing?' (efficiency problems)

(*c*) 'should I plough back money in this firm rather than invest it in another?' (alternative investments)

and

(*d*) (probably most important) 'how much can I afford to consume?' (extent and time-pattern of consumption)

No figure can answer such diverse questions, and so there is no perfect profit.

Further, we must confine our search for the ideal to what is practicable. The chosen measure must be fairly free from uncertainty, and not demand too much work. A judge could hardly say 'Profit figure *A* is truer than *B* because it takes fewer man-hours to find,' but this consideration must in fact weigh at the back of our minds.

Income tax has introduced an extra factor in our quest for the ideal. A firm's income is no longer merely a statistical abstraction; it is also what determines the tax payment. This is bound to colour our views of the ideal. At the least, we now must give more weight to the type of measure that reduces argument with the Inspector of Taxes; in addition, there is a strong temptation to prefer the type that lessens or postpones tax payments. Thus the tail threatens to grow more powerful than the dog; a fragile statistical concept is being made to carry a weight than it can hardly bear.

Possible measures

In my view, the simplest and best approach to income theory is to define income (including profit) in terms of increase in wealth. If total wealth, measured in some acceptable way and adjusted for drawings, is £10 on 1 January and £18 on 31 December, then the year's profit is £8. The trouble starts when we try to define the acceptable way of measurement.

The only bases that are tolerably sound in logic are the forward-looking ones: income is here the increase in the firm's value as a whole, found by a capital budgeting exercise on discounted cash flow. But such an approach (though probably used by most of us, often in an almost unrecognisably rough-and-ready form, in our private decisions on comsumption and investment) is wholly alien to formal practice. It involves guesswork on such a magnificent scale as to rule it out whenever more than one person shares the profit.

If we may not look forward, we must look at the present and past. What we see are the separate assets. So we adopt some form of balance sheet approach, i.e. we draw up an inventory of the net assets. (Normally we in fact start with a profit and loss account. But this interlocks exactly with the balance sheet, e.g. asset depreciation must be written off. So one can properly tackle income measurement *via* the balance sheet; and this is helpful because assets tend to be more concrete and familiar than costs and revenue.)

When we try to list assets, we still face problems on what to include, and how to value. I propose to side-step the first problem (inclusion) as being of less importance for our present ends than the second (valuation).

Current values of assets

If we try to value assets in current terms, two bases suggest themselves: replacement cost and sale price. Both get their authority from the market. They are sometimes debatable or hard to find; and in certain contexts (e.g. where an asset would no longer be replaced by an identical physical substitute) the definitions need a lot of refining. But at least the concepts seem firmly rooted in current economic reality, and capable of logical discussion and development.

Current market values are used in accounting to a small—perhaps growing—extent. But no-one can pretend that their use is typical. Normally we reject current values and turn to the past.

The realisation basis and historical cost

The differences between various profit concepts hinge largely on the *time*—i.e. the stage in the cycle of production and sale—at which they concede that wealth has increased. (The point was illustrated in Appendix II, to the first part of this article; page 156, March). Accountants usually prefer not to recognise a gain until it meets the test of realisation. This, we maintain, is of over-riding importance, because it tends both to give objective proof of growth and to result in cash now or in the near future; so it removes the risks of guesswork and of paying out dividends and tax before enough cash is to hand.

Our balance sheets accordingly reject current market values (since these fail to meet the realisation test) and ignore appreciation until it is realised. In consequence, most of the assets in a balance sheet are left at their historical costs. Our caution is admirable; yet alas it starts us sliding down a slippery slope that ends in a logical Wonderland.

There seem (for our present purpose) to be three reasons for dissatisfaction with the realisation basis:

(1) This basis compares badly with the ideal, in that it often gives a less complete and convincing view of economic growth than do other bases—e.g. its timing of gains may seem haphazard and misleading in comparison with the time-patterns of the market bases.

(2) Its caution is a personal matter, adopted by different accountants with differing degrees of thoroughness.

(3) It forces us to split the firm's wealth into artificial sections (the various costs to be matched against the sales of the given or later years); and this division is often an absurdity.

Let us look at each reason a little more closely.

Drawbacks of Realisation Basis

(1) *Incomplete view of income*

Realised income is apt to give poor answers to most of the questions listed on page 239. It may indeed often give the safest answer to question (*a*) (though a budget of the firm's cash needs might sometimes be still safer). It gives less good answers to the other questions; and its failure may be plain to anyone in close touch with the firm.

For example, in the early years of a new factory, while stocks are being built up, etc., the realisation basis will tend to give a depressing picture. Yet other signs may assure the proprietor that he is coming along well. Accounts drafted on a less cautious basis would catch the cheerful overtones, and serve him as more useful guides for some kinds of decision—e.g. suggesting that he can now afford to increase his home consumption, or that he can advantageously borrow to expand the firm.

Again, the profits of the realisation basis are apt to strike us as being too jerky and chancy. Suppose a dealer has two pictures, *X* and *Y*. *X* (a lucky buy) cost £10; *Y* cost £80; each can be sold for £100. A customer comes in on 31 December, and dithers between them. If he chooses *X*, the year's profit includes £90; if he chooses *Y*, £20. These contrasting profit figures are useful as post mortem comment on the dealer's buying skill, but poor guides to his comsumption decisions. For the latter, it would be far more helpful to value the remaining picture on a market basis.

(2) *Arbitrariness of realisation test*

The second drawback of the realisation basis is that we are

not agreed on the point in time when realisation takes place.

In general, accounting text-books suggest that the contract of sale marks the time of realisation. At the moment of sale, they argue, the firm is justified in boosting asset values; now the bird has left the bush and is in the hand (or very nearly), and its change of position is verified objectively by the agreement with an outsider.

But the sale test does not in fact yield hard-and-fast values, since there is still latitude about provisions for discount, bad debts, etc. Given enough caution and respect for compound interest, the firm can legitimately expand these provisions till it is working on a cash basis (as is implied for instance by the retail method of valuing hire-purchase sales).

For each degree of caution, there is yet another profit figure. The realisation basis, despite its objectivity, offers many alternatives (and its own logic can scarcely help us to choose between them). The example in Appendix II to Part I shows how varying shades of caution can alter the time-pattern of profit recognition by a professional firm.

Rather oddly, the 'bills delivered' approach seems at variance with the contract test, and to be less objective. A professional firm can choose its own time for sending out bills. And the contract is made, not when the bill is sent, but when the firm first agrees to work for its client; the client in return agrees to pay a 'reasonable' but perhaps undetermined fee. When the client gets the bill, he may still object to it, and—if it is not based on an official scale—perhaps prove that it is unreasonable.

This second drawback is capable of cure, in the sense that tax law or general agreement could force us all to use much the same test of realisation. But probably cash receipt is the sole test that would be generally applicable. The price of this reform would for most firms be a most uninformative 'profit'.

(3) *Aberrations of historical charges against revenue*
If book figures for asset values can be increased at realisation only, then unrealised assets must either be left at their original size or reduced. We rarely reduce them; and so they normally stand at their historical cost of first acquisition until they become charges in the income statement. And then the 'expensing' of historical cost involves us in fresh uncertainties.

Historical cost may stand up well in the ultra-simple circumstance envisaged when we first start to spell out our theory. For instance, a merchant puts his £10 opening capital into a single unit of stock (i.e. he has only one cost and one asset). It is not sold till Year 2. He can till then suspend judgement on the venture—by valuing stock at its historical cost of £10 in the intervening accounts at the close of Year 1. By freezing book-values in this way, he seems to fulfil the conventional accounting aim of matching cost with revenue in Year 2.

But things go haywire as soon as assumptions become in the least realistic. The £ may change in value during the stock-turn period. This could have at least a mild effect on professional firms. For instance, the firm described in Part I of this article expects each year to put up its revised rate for valuing work-in-progress; to the extent that the increase is due to inflation, the resulting profit increase is illusory. (This is as much as I shall say about price-level change. It is a major cause of dissatisfaction with historical cost; but an adequate treatment would expand the article to unendurable length.)

Another trouble arises when there is a common pool of costs or assets. Then we meet the snag that is sometimes called 'jointness'. It thwarts us in two ways:

(*a*) Sequence troubles.
Under this head come the familiar questions posed by fifo, lifo, hifo, nifo, average cost, etc. The short answer to the questions must surely be that prior physical sequence—real or conceptual—cannot in its own right give economic significance to assets.

Sequence is unlikely to worry a professional firm, because each item of such a firm's stock has identity.

(*b*) Ingredient troubles.
What is to be included in 'cost', and what left out? Our usual example is a manufacturer's stock; should he charge the direct ingredients only, or should some or all of the works and general oncost be put in too? Where jointness obtrudes, we can hardly give a sensible answer. Cost is then incurred for a group of varied products or of units of the same product, and there may be no defensible way of splitting it. The extreme example is that in which the products emerge in fixed proportions; something approaching this obtains in oil refining, where attempts to split the cost of crude among the resulting products (by weight, etc.) have attracted so much ridicule that they have now been largely abandoned.

With some kinds of problem, we can reasonably expect that time will bring a solution. But not here. Greater understanding will (I suspect) merely make us appreciate more clearly that a slice of joint cost is meaningless.

Only the variable part of a firm's costs can, with some show of reason, be linked to specific products. But how are we to find that part? The refinements of management accounting perhaps point the way—by defining 'variable' in terms of cause-and-effect: if doing a given job makes expense rise, this increase is the job's cost; if expense stays the same, the job is costless. This is quite different from telling a cost clerk to use some routine mode of classification—say, treat direct wages (itself an arbitrary figure) as a product cost, and indirect wages as a period cost. A firm of accountants, hard-pressed for staff, would be unlikely to dismiss clerks if it lost one small audit; it would prefer (if no other job were to hand) to send them home to work for their exams at full pay. By the canons of management accounting, their wages are not part of the audit's cost. So 'cost' in this sense would often lead to low stock values. Moreover it is very subjective, in that it can be found only from estimates (by a knowledgeable person, not a subordinate) about each job's impact. Therefore management accounting's cost cannot serve as income accounting's cost without some re-definition. Income accounting is in need of a convincing test—beyond that of routine classification, often misleading—for determining the right historical cost ingredients in stock.

We tend in this dilemma to pick ingredients by reference to our imaginary ideal, or to some other basis. In the accounts of the new factory on page 240 for instance, we may include full oncost in stock values because this raises profit—and thus gets nearer to the more informative profit that would result from use of a market or a forward-looking basis; so here we justify one interpretation of the realisation basis by appeal to something that is remote from the logic of realisation.

Information instead of intrinsic logic as criterion

Similarly, in the tax case described in Part I, it was noteworthy that the change in method of valuing work-in-progress, from notional cost to full direct cost, was generally regarded as an improvement; the new form was described for instance as more sensitive. As the figures in Appendix II show, such a change tends to bring smoother and earlier profits (particularly in a growing firm). Yet this change within the realisation basis cannot be justified by any realisation test; on the contrary, the new figures were a shade less objective and sure. Nor does it seem justifiable on any intrinsic logic of historical cost. Approval was again due to promptings from something external—the ability of the changed figures to give better answers to key questions.

Anyone who criticises a realised profit figure is in a sense comparing it with quantities found by other bases. Thus we test, often without appreciating what we are doing, the working of one basis by using the results of others. It would be reasonable for us to compare the results of bases *X* and *Y*, and then to abandon *X* for *Y* if *Y* is better; but we accountants stick to *X* (realisation), and merely change its sub-procedures in whatever way will push its results nearer to those of *Y*. Given the constraints of practice, this rather timid mode of progress is perhaps sensible enough, and may indeed be the only route to improvement. But it results in mental muddle, and helps to explain why our descriptions and defence of the realisation basis, and of any of its sub-procedures, can sound remarkably lame.

If we do in fact habitually select the sub-procedures that lead to the most helpful profit figures, then we should recognise this step, and include it in our reasoning. Our discussions of principle should centre round information, and neglect the sterile problems of historical cost.

True, this change of approach would bring a risk—that unscrupulous people would be able to substitute propaganda for information. However, the present rules of valuation afford considerable latitude to such people, so perhaps the dangers would be not much greater than they are already.

Conclusions on realisation test

Earlier paragraphs suggest that many assets cannot be given uncontentious values if we insist on using the realisation basis plus historical cost. Moreover, the profit figures produced by this basis are apt to be uninformative.

Because this basis involves so many conceptual and practical troubles, it is hardly surprising that we run into great difficulties when we try to argue logically about the relevant procedures.

The Replacement Cost Basis

It is instructive to ask why replacement cost might do a better job than historical cost.

The 'new firm' approach to replacement

Like historical cost, replacement cost is by no means free from conceptual and practical troubles. But we can perhaps be more hopeful about reducing its troubles to manageable size.

A useful approach is to interpret 'replacement' by asking how much finance would be needed by a new firm, resembling the given firm in function and size, to acquire and hold a similar asset. This approach lets us work with current buying prices, and so gets rid of out-of-date values and sequence troubles. It puts the hypothetical costs onto a leisurely and long-term basis. It does not surmount the troubles of jointness in stock manufacture, but probably lessens them.

The compensation analogy

Except where jointness is an awkward factor, the analogy of compensation may also give clarity to this approach. To use the analogy, one must imagine that the firm is deprived of the asset, and then ask how much money would be needed to 'make the firm whole' again, i.e. how much is needed to replace the firm in its old position (or one equally acceptable).

But the compensation analogy must not be pushed too far. If a professional firm was deprived of work-in-progress by some freakish catastrophe, i.e. if staff had to repeat the whole of its work to date on a big unfinished job, then the extra cost and disruption might be enormous. Such dramatic possibilities hardly point to values that would be informative in normal circumstances.

Conclusions

Inevitable vagueness of profit

This survey (by no means exhaustive) has no doubt made disheartening reading. Accounting profit is not a thing of intellectual beauty; on the contrary, it depends in good part on whim, convention, and clerical accident. Other bases might give better figures, but even these would have their faults. In any case, the ideal may be something that fluctuates with the informational needs of the given firm.

When we try to learn about profit from our text-books and *Recommendations*, we may be struck by their lack of forthright rules. However, if this article is sound, we should not be surprised at such hesitancy: it is entirely proper when our choice lies between such misty concepts, and the tests by which we assess their rival claims are so vague. The authorities seem at fault here only in failing to stress that their rules must of necessity be nebulous, and that the problem is perhaps insoluble.

On this view, profit (at least when cut into yearly sums) just is not a suitable subject for tax. If we insist on taxing on an annual basis, then we must accept that the results will at times be muddled and unfair. I can see no easy alternative to letting each taxpayer choose his own conventions, and making tax law accept these, for better or worse, so long as they do not violate elementary rules of honesty and consistency.

On this view, too, we cannot expect help from judicial rules, and should not be surprised if these become an ossifying influence. Where measurement is concerned, precedent may soon be at odds with good current practice. One is tempted to use the analogy of physical science: last year's most accurate method of measuring may be bettered this year. But the analogy is not very apt. With physical measurement, there may presumably be some ideal method to which each year's refinements bring us nearer. Wealth and income are however a matter of mental attitudes, which are likely to vary with time; so the thing being measured is not fixed. Perhaps the law on obscenity provides a better analogy, for here too mental attitudes are important and changeable; a society's views on what is obscene vary with its *mores*, education, etc., and the law should follow suit. Juries may be better than judges for deciding what is nowadays obscene. Perhaps the same holds for what is nowadays income.

Practical steps

This *non possumus* attitude may be the height of wisdom in an academic setting. But the accountant has to get on with his job; he must decide that one of the measures is best, apply it, and be ready to defend it.

The Inland Revenue (we may suppose) reluctantly accepts the view that it must put up with the crude cash basis, but prefers a much more refined basis (e.g. one that brings in work-in-progress at a high cost). It is prepared on occasion to attack a compromise between these extremes—and (odd though this seems to the non-lawyer) may succeed in having the semi-crude rejected though the crude is accepted.

To many professional firms, the most important reason for measuring profit is to fix the tax liability; what started as a by-product has become the main product. This being the case, a cynical but sensible view is that the firm should choose the basis which minimises the tax burden. The cash basis tends at least to postpone tax payments; accordingly, firms that already use this basis should cling to it, and new firms should try to adopt it as early as possible.

Where the cash basis is not in use, there are strong grounds for selecting whichever other basis will best serve the firm's internal ends. The figures can then be judged by their success in giving helpful information.

One test fastens on the certainty of the eventual receipt of cash. If debts and stocks are often not realised in full, the firm has good grounds for valuing such assets at low rates. But fortunately this line of thought is unlikely to be important for most professional firms.

A very important test is that the figures should show trends clearly—for instance in a way that seems fair to both the old and new partners at a change in the partnership. They may well fail to do so (i.e. profit fluctuates unduly) if they depend on such accidents as whether bills have been delivered or large jobs finished. By this smoothness test, the accounts should indeed allow for both debtors and work-in-progress.

DEBTORS

The valuation of debtors at face value cannot be justified on grounds of complete realisation. The justification presumably lies in the smoothness test, and in the commonsensical view—among laymen as well as accountants—that a description of a firm's wealth would be uninformative if it did not include debts at a high value. General experience is that debtors pay in full, and fairly soon. Even where the firm renders professional services, and so cannot base its expectations on contracts, face value (less any bad debt provision that the circumstances warrant) seems solid enough to be put into the balance sheet.

WORK-IN-PROGRESS

The smoothness test suggests also that accounts should allow for work-in-progress where this varies from year to year, and that the work should be valued at a rate adequate to iron out the bulk of accidental fluctuation in profit.

The precise valuation rate cannot be settled by realisation logic. But perhaps we are entitled to argue from the analogy of the replacement cost basis. If we ask how much extra finance would be required by a 'new firm' because it needs to carry work-in-progress at a given level, the answer may often be something remarkably like conventional full cost. The direct costs of such work in the long-term budget of a new firm must usually be close to the direct costs of historical job records. And the long-term budget could make at least a rough guess at the extra sum needed to finance overhead during the turnover period of the work-in-progress, thus giving a defensible overhead rate.

General

In some firms, other informational needs may outweigh the smoothness criterion, etc., and demand different sub-procedures. If the preceding pages are right, a suitable change in the sub-procedures should then be made: we should openly recognise that information is a better guide than cost logic.

Should opening stock be revalued at a change of basis?

How far does this discussion help with the subsidiary question raised by the tax case—of whether, given that one is right to switch methods of valuing closing stock, one is entitled to revalue opening stock too?

If it is reasonable to judge a profit figure by its usefulness for decision-making, then revaluation of opening stock is surely justifiable and indeed necessary (whether the change is one of basis or mere detail). Without such revaluation, the given year's profits will tend to make a violent jump. This will blur trends, and impair decisions.

However, at a firm's discontinuance the stock is (for tax purposes) revalued at market value. A firm that had already raised both opening and closing stock to high figures (in the closing or any other year) could escape tax on this appreciation. Perhaps an upward adjustment of taxable profit here is equitable.

DEPRECIATING ASSETS

1938 in the 94th H.A.A. Regiment, and his professional career was interrupted by the war, when in December 1939 he was commissioned into the 32nd L.A.A. Regiment. During the remainder of the war he served with that Regiment in Malta and from Normandy into Germany. By the end of the war he was second-in-command of his Regiment and had been "mentioned in dispatches". He carried his interest in the welfare of his men back into civilian life and for many years he has been Honorary Treasurer of the British Legion, Scotland and Secretary and Treasurer of the Scottish National War Memorial. His firm is also Secretary and Treasurer of the Society for Employment of Ex-Regular Soldiers, Sailors and Airmen. The long list of other charitable and voluntary work with which he and his firm are associated shows his deep interest in helping his neighbour. As his father had done before him he has always taken a deep interest in the affairs of the Institute. He was a member of the Edinburgh Local Committee from 1958 to 1961 and from 1962 to 1967, serving as Convener in 1962-63. He served on the Council of the Institute from 1962 to 1967, during which period he also had the responsible task of Convener of the Finance and General Purposes Committee.

While the office of President is one of great honour, it also carries heavy responsibilities demanding much hard work and leadership. Owing to circumstances quite beyond the control of the Institute, Geoffrey has become President without the normal "running in" period as Vice-President. He is, however, a man of charming personality and sound common sense and he has the ability to get on well with everyone he meets. He also has a great sense of responsibility and service to others, and there is no doubt that he will carry out his duties as President with dignity and distinction.

His chief recreation is golf and he is well known at Muirfield, where he has served on the Committee, and when the Open Championship was held there in 1966 he was in charge of the difficult and very responsible task of organising "crowd control" and the stewarding of the course. He has regularly attended the Moore Cup gatherings at Gleneagles and has been responsible for the very pleasant social golf meetings which have been held there in the autumn in recent years.

The European Congress of Accountants held in Edinburgh in 1963 again saw Geoffrey very much involved—as a member of the Organisation Committee and as Convener of both the Exhibition and Finance Sub-Committees.

He is married and has two sons. His wife Fay has already had a foretaste of the social duties which befall the President's wife as she was on the Committee which so successfully made the arrangements for the ladies who were in Edinburgh for the European Congress of Accountants.

Geoffrey is never a man to blow his own trumpet, but if he can be caught in the right mood he can still play a very good saxophone, although the dance band which he ran in his youth is now a distant memory!

Depreciating Assets: the Forward-looking Approach to Value

Professor W. T. BAXTER, B.COM., C.A., J.DIP.M.A.

London School of Economics

This paper was originally presented at a conference held at Fontainebleau by the European Institute of Business Administration (INSEAD) in 1970. It has already been published in ABACUS *(December 1970), to whose Editor we are grateful for permission to print it here.*

Diagram 1 shows the life story of a depreciating asset. We can all recognise MC, the asset's purchase price. We can all recognise too its scrap proceeds, KK′. But mostly we are remarkably vague about the rest of the diagram. What sort of path does the value curve CK′ follow between dates M and K? For that matter, how do we know what is the length of the best life-span MK?

Diagram 1 in fact shows three of the possible value curves between C and K′. They are found by three of the accounting methods for measuring depreciation:—

Diagram 1

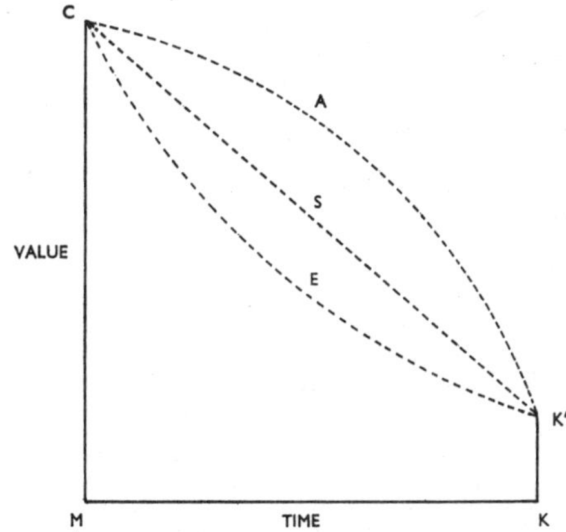

Some possible value curves of a depreciating asset

(1) the straight-line method—giving CSK′;

(2) the " fixed percentage of the diminishing balance ", or exponential, method—giving CEK′; and

(3) the annuity method—giving CAK′.

The choice of method here results in very different annual values and costs.[1] And there are other methods (*e.g.*, those based on units of physical service, and on a fixed charge to cover both repair outlays and depreciation) that could lead to more variation. Can we find principles with which to test the merits of these rival figures, and perhaps to suggest better ones?

Value Concepts

Depreciation is merely a part of the larger subject of asset valuation, and one's treatment of depreciation thus depends on one's general attitude to that subject. A writer on depreciation should start off with a statement of his preferred concept—*e.g.*, historical cost or current value, such as sale or replacement price.

One can classify the various concepts into two main groups: backward-looking and forward-looking. The historical costs of the ledger clearly belong to the former. Buyers and sellers are more concerned with expectations, and so market prices belong to the latter.

The historical cost approach does not seem to give any logical basis for finding the value curve of a depreciating asset. Its apologists usually claim that it " matches costs and revenues " in a " systematic and equitable " manner. I have yet to see a convincing explanation of what these fine words mean. Perhaps the trouble lies partly in the bastard mixture of past cost with estimates of future life and scrap proceeds. A clean divorce from the past may be better. So this article asks how forward-looking accounts would meet the problem. From the various forward-looking bases, it selects one which (for reasons that will appear later) I call *deprival value*. Usually this is much the same thing as replacement cost; so for simplicity the article deems the value of depreciating assets to be a function of the current replacement cost of a similar but new asset. However, the main part of the article assumes that prices are stable; so the figures will be much the same as those used by the historical cost approach, and the argument may by analogy help the latter over its stiles.

If value is forward-looking, serious discussion of our subject is impossible unless we concede that some estimate, however rough, must be made of the cash flows of the asset's whole life. (And the usual rule-of-thumb methods in fact rely on sweeping assumptions about the future—all the more dangerous because they are hidden.)

[1] The exact shapes of CEK′ and CAK′ are affected by the length of life; that of CAK′ depends too on the rate of cost-of-capital. The diagram takes a perhaps not unrealistic life of about 20 years, and a cost-of-capital rate of 14%.

Preliminaries

Before one can get to grips with the main problem, various preliminary points must be cleared up.

Time-assets and use-assets

The lives of some assets end when the asset is worn out by use; but more often, perhaps, lives end for reasons that have little to do with use, *e.g.* obsolescence. So it is often helpful to distinguish two kinds of cost—use-depreciation and time-depreciation. But this article will for the most part assume that assets are time-assets.

Relevant cash flow

Depreciation bookkeeping is a matter of ironing out the lumps—of converting the asset's erratic cash flows into smooth annual costs. The well-known methods put most of their stress on only two kinds of flow—initial price and final scrap proceeds. But any other erratic flows must in logic call for the same smoothing; depreciation theory should concern itself with the whole set of outlays (and sometimes revenues) that vary with, and because of, the asset's age. Repairs are the example that comes most readily to mind, and so this article will treat variation in repair outlays as the typical flows.

Primary and secondary assets

The argument will run most easily if it concentrates on the history of a single depreciating asset—the " primary asset ". But capital maintenance demands that, as fast as the depreciating asset loses value, the owner should build up a stock of other assets—the " secondary assets ", sometimes called the " depreciation fund investments ". Normally these will be liquid at first, but they will in time spread throughout the asset structure; occasionally they are kept separate in the form of financial securities and are labelled " sinking fund investments ".

Cost-of-capital rates

To find the whole yearly cost of a proposed investment in an asset, one must allow for interest on the capital to be sunk in it. One must therefore ask how its purchase is to be financed. A special loan may be raised for this purpose only; then the loan interest is one of the asset's costs. More likely perhaps, the firm may dip into some of its general funds; where these might instead be put to other good uses, their investment in the given asset squeezes out those other uses; what is squeezed out or foregone (*i.e.* potential net gains) is the opportunity cost of the capital. In one or other of these ways, the purchase gives rise to an annual sacrifice that is very real if not always very obvious.

But, as the secondary assets accumulate, they tend to lighten the sacrifice, for they will not be left idle. They may for instance be used to repay the loan, or to add to plant, stores, etc. Their earnings (or cost savings) should grow at a compound rate and increasingly offset the annual sacrifice of interest or opportunity cost. If all goes well, by the end of the primary asset's life the sacrifice is quite neutralised, and costs are back in the same net position as at the start. The growth of the secondary assets is thus part-and-parcel of the depreciating asset's story. Somewhat surprisingly, their earnings rate affects the depreciation calculation. The " interest " of the annuity method should presumably be interpreted as reflecting these sacrifices and secondary earnings. Here the phrase " cost-of-capital " (normally employed in a rather different sense) will be used for the net sacrifice.

Present Values and Annual Equivalents

When one comes to tackle the arithmetic of depreciation, often one can (with the help of the cost-of-capital rate, or a discount rate derived from it) re-state the relevant cash flows of an asset in equivalent forms that are more convenient. Some of these are:—

(1) Present value of the complete sets of flows for the asset's whole life.[2]

(2) Annual equivalent of (1) above, *i.e.* a figure that one might call rental cost.[3] If the firm hired the asset from an outside owner, the " rent " would cover interest as well as depreciation (and such repair costs as fell on the owner). Typically the cost-of-capital must be a big part of " rent "; with rates of not less than 8%, and lives of 20 years or more, one can say not too inaccurately that cost-of-capital for most of the life exceeds depreciation.[4] Under the annuity method, the firm's operating department in effect hires the asset from the firm itself; the " rent " charge, if it allows for cost-of-capital at a realistic rate, is a shadow-price that measures the full yearly sacrifice of ownership, and its inclusion in the department's income statement helps management to see whether the decision to buy was wise.

(3) Present value of the annual equivalent ((2) above) in perpetuity. Just as the firm might arrange to provide itself always with a hired asset by paying an annual rent, so too it might do so (conceptually at least) by paying a very large initial lump sum in lieu of all the annual rents ((2) above) or periodic replacement prices, etc. ((1) above). In other words, it could pay £x now to secure the services of one asset after another for a very long time—as far forward as the mind can reach. £x would then measure the burden that an owner shoulders when he decides to obtain the services of the given kind of asset from now onwards. He can equally well be regarded as assuming a burden of £x when he decides to obtain those services by the usual route of buying an asset and replacing it as often as is necessary thereafter. He can find the value of x, the size of his notional burden, by discounting a perpetual series of the actual flows, or of the notional yearly rents ((2) above) at his cost-of-capital rate.[5] With long lives and stiff discount rates, x is apt to prove not much more than the price of the first asset.

The notion that the costs of ownership constitute a perpetual burden is foreign to everyday thought. But it is handy for depreciation arithmetic and gives a helpful framework for exposition, so that this article will make much use of it.

Diagram of Burden

The idea of the perpetual burden can perhaps be best developed in diagrams. In Diagram 2 (on page 162), OX shows time. OY shows the burden's size; as a burden is a negative form of benefit, it is measured below OX.

Where the asset in question does not depreciate (*e.g.* land), a single payment suffices to get the flow of services for good. For instance, if such a payment is made at date C′, it can be shown as M′C′; and if it is made instead at F′, it can be shown as G′F′. Then the " burden line ", *i.e.* the cost of buying this asset at any given date, is P′N′.

If, on the other hand, that payment must be made again and again for each of a perpetual series of depreciating assets (*e.g.* a machine and its replacements), the burden will be graver, and the burden line will lie farther from OX. For instance, if the firm decides at date C′ henceforth to own a certain type of machine, it is assuming a perpetual burden whose present value is, say, MC′; if it makes the decision at F′, the burden's value is GF′; the line has fallen to PN.

Deprival Value

One way of looking at the benefit of owning an asset is to say that ownership postpones (for the rest of the

[2] Let V_0 = initial price,
i = relevant cost-of-capital rate,
v = present value factor—that is $\frac{1}{1+i}$
k = number of years in the whole life,
$O(k)$ = sum of the present values of the various repair outlays, etc., during the life,
Sv^k = present value of the scrap proceeds.
Then A, the present value of all these flows, is found from:—

$$A = V_0 + O(k) - Sv^k \quad \text{.......(1)}$$

For fuller treatment see A. J. MERRETT and ALLEN SYKES: The Finance and Analysis of Capital Projects; *Longmans Green*, London, 1963; Chapters 1, 18 and 19.

[3] This rent, U, is found from: $U = A \times \frac{i}{1 - v^k}$ ....(2)

[4] A good rule-of-thumb for finding the approximate rent is to add together:—

(*a*) the straight-line depreciation charge; and
(*b*) interest for a year on two-thirds of the asset's price.

[5] P, the burden, is found from: $P = \frac{U}{i}$ ....(3)

or from: $P = \frac{A}{1 - v^k}$ ....(4)

asset's life) the need to shoulder the full burden. This breathing-space creates the asset's value.

We can measure the benefit by comparing the owner's actual position with what his position would be if he were deprived of the asset. Deprival value is thus the difference between the present values of cash flows in two alternative budgets:—

(1) *The " Have Not " budget*

This shows the full burden, *i.e.* the cash flow facing a deprived owner.

(2) *The " Have " budget*

This shows the lighter burden that actually faces the owner; it discounts and sums any flows for the rest of the asset's life, and the full burden at the next replacement date. Possession of the present asset makes the total less than that of (1).

Diagram 2 can be used to illustrate this comparison. Suppose an asset is bought at date C′, and its optimum life is C′K′. To value it at, say, date A′, one must compare the " Have Not " line, BN (which shows the full burden BA′ that at once faces a deprived owner), with the " Have " line, AK (which is found by discounting the full burden of the next replacement date, K′K).

At date A′ the difference between the two lines is BA. Accordingly this measures the deprival value then. In the same way, GF is the deprival value at F′, and MC (= price) is the deprival value at C′. We have found what seems a logical way of measuring the value of the depreciating asset; the complete value curve for the whole life is MCFAK.

Diagram 2

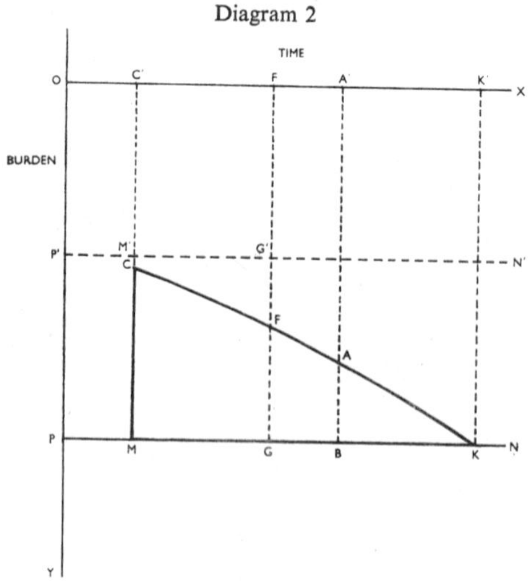

Perpetuity approach to asset value

Value Pattern—No Varying Repairs, etc.

Examining this curve, one sees that it is concave to M. It is in fact the same kind of curve as that produced by the annuity method; this suggests that the latter method is the correct one to use under the conditions assumed in Diagram 2. These are that the relevant outlay series will contain no varying items (such as rising repairs) during the asset's life, and that the cost-of-capital is not negligible.

With the lowering of cost-of-capital rates, the curve would flatten out and look more and more like a straight line. This suggests that the straight-line method is the correct one if repairs do not vary and the cost-of-capital rate is negligible.

The area MCK can be lifted out of the perpetuity framework and shown alone, in the style of Diagram 1. This has the advantage of simplicity, but fails to provide any rationale for the values, *e.g.* Diagram 1 fails to show that CAK′, the humped curve of the annuity method, is the best of the three curves, on the given assumptions about the cash flow pattern.

Value Curve—with Repairs, etc.

The perpetuity approach will readily produce fresh value curves under more complex assumptions. Consider an instance where the cash flow of each successive asset ends with scrap receipts, and contains a varying item (such as the outlay for a major overhaul) some two-thirds through the life. Then the curves must be re-drawn as in Diagram 3. Here the axes are the same as in 2. MC is again the price, and MK the optimum life. Just as payment of the price improves the vista and so creates value, any other useful outlay—such as AD for the overhaul at date B—must push up the value curve. Conversely the scrap receipts KE signal a fall in value. The value curve is now MCADEK—falling faster till date B, then restored somewhat by the overhaul, then falling fast to scrap level.

Diagram 3

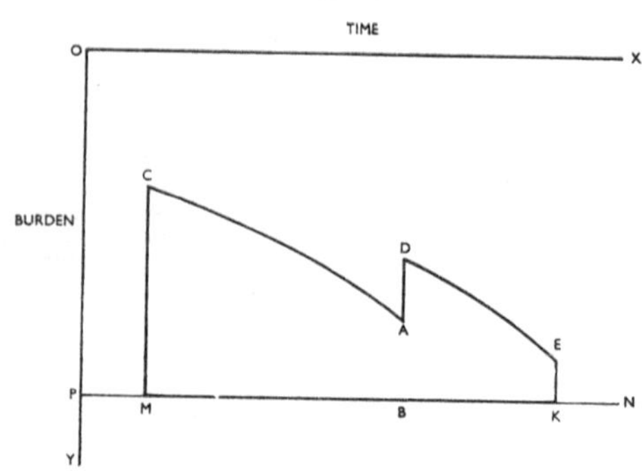

Perpetuity approach—asset with varying outlays

Exponential Method

With imagination, one can perhaps see what would happen to CADE if a series of rising repair outlays, stretching over the whole life, is substituted for the one big overhaul. Such a pattern of mounting outlays tends to result in a shape like CEK' in Diagram 1.

In other words, accountants are right in saying that the exponential method caters for rising repairs. But of course a curve begotten by a general mathematical formula need not be a close fit for a given repair pattern. A curve specially tailored to each asset would be safer.

Methods Tailored to the Given Asset's Needs

There seems no good reason, where a firm knows from experience what the outlay pattern of a given asset is likely to be, why it should not devise a depreciation formula specially for that asset.

Something approaching this is already done if the firm uses the method that charges a fixed annual provision to cover both depreciation and repairs. But this method should be extended to allow for other varying outlays (*e.g.* revenue that falls with age), for cost-of-capital, and (with use-assets) for physical usage during each year.[6]

Cost-of-capital and Depreciation Methods

The effect of recognising cost-of-capital is not so much to produce additional depreciation methods as to add an extra dimension to the familiar methods. Thus the normal illustrations to the annuity method (and its variants such as the sinking fund method) show that it is in fact the straight-line method with cost-of-capital superimposed; in Diagram 1, as I have already pointed out, the straight-line curve CSK' becomes the annuity curve CAK' if cost-of-capital is recognised. And there is no reason why the exponential or any other value curve should not be given the extra dimension. The arithmetic is not too forbidding. The only question is whether this refinement yields enough information to justify the additional work.

It gives information on two matters—asset values and annual cost.

Results of Recognising Cost-of-capital

(1) *Higher asset values*

Let us assume the firm's revenues and costs to be such that, if it paid a fixed rent for the depreciating asset, profit would be constant: and that all profit is at once paid out as dividend. If it in fact buys the asset in the ordinary way, it will, as a consequence of providing for depreciation, accumulate secondary assets. Their earnings and cost savings improve the net cash receipts of each year, at a compound rate, throughout the depreciating asset's life; at replacement date, however, secondary assets and their earnings vanish; and the cycle is repeated in each successive life. A thoughtful owner, anxious to find income figures that will serve as a guide to questions of consumption, etc., must look askance at such undulations. A constant figure will here give him the most helpful information (and what better grounds than this have we for deciding what income is?).

Let us then envisage a set of balance sheets covering this asset's life. Each must show the same yearly growth in wealth; and this growth is earmarked to be paid out at once as dividends, leaving a constant total. Despite this fixed ceiling, the secondary assets rise each year at a compound pace. Therefore the primary asset must fall in a complementary way; its value sinks slowly at first, fast later, so that its value curve is humpy, as in Diagram 2.

This pattern is not just a quirk of bookkeeping, but matches the facts. A man with a high cost-of-capital rate recoils from imminent outlays. He is relatively indifferent to remote ones: a small provision now will take care of them, thanks to the high growth rate. He thus deems replacement a matter of small concern in the asset's early years, and of great concern in the final years. In other words, depreciation is small at first, and big later.

It is often said that fixed asset values are not of major importance to business. But the figures are sometimes helpful, notably in studies of the efficiency with which assets are being used. Tests such as the ratio of earnings to assets will then be applied; and undervaluation will warp the tests' results. If, say, the directors of a holding company want to watch the efficiency of each subsidiary, they should insist on the assets being valued realistically.

(2) *Better cost information*

Some firms that own premises, wagons, etc., charge each department with a suitable rent for the use of these assets. In consequence, each department's section of the income statement is made more searching, and its manager's demands for extra resources are checked. As the charges are also credited to some non-departmental section of the income statement (*e.g.* interest), their net effect on the profit of the whole firm is *nil*.

In the same way, the annuity system charges each department with an annual rent that covers the full sacrifice of owning a depreciating asset (see page 161)—cost-of-capital as well as the asset's decline in value over the year. Such a charge makes the departmental section of the income statement a far more rigorous test of performance, and helps to show whether the decision to acquire an asset has proved sound. As the cost-of-capital part of the rent is credited to another section of the income statement, the profit of the whole firm is reduced only by a net depreciation cost (the decline in value). The rising pattern of this cost confers yet another benefit: it offsets the rising secondary earnings, and so makes for

[6] The accountant would have to take the following steps:—

(1) At the start of life, find the notional rent, U, per unit of time (or of use, if the asset is a use-asset).

(2) Each year, increase the asset's value by debiting it with:

(*a*) The varying outlays (*e.g.*, overhaul costs).

(*b*) "Appreciation"—at the cost-of-capital rate on the opening balance;

and reduce by crediting:

(*c*) The notional rent found from U—with time-assets, a constant each year.

(*d*) Any revenues varying because of the asset's age.

smoother profits (in the way just explained under (1) above).

The nature of the charges, and the contrast between them and those of the straight-line method, are best shown by a diagram. Number 4 illustrates the story of a not untypical asset: life is 20 years, and the cost-of-capital rate is 14%. Time is again measured on the OX axis, and annual cost on the OY axis. SL is the annual charge by the straight-line method; AA′ is the whole rent or gross depreciation by the annuity method; and DD′ is the net depreciation (*i.e.* the fall in value between the start and end of each successive year, found from a value curve such as CAK′ in Diagram 1). The vertical distance between AA′ and DD′ thus shows the cost-of-capital in any year. DF shows the charges under the sinking fund method—which seems to me to give an indefensibly low figure.

Some of the things revealed by Diagram 4 seem rather startling. The full cost that should be charged to the department (AA′) is more than three times the orthodox straight-line cost (SL). DD′ grows greatly over the life, from a negligible amount to a substantial one, and could thus be a useful corrective to the profit pattern of a new or newly-expanded firm.

Optimum Life Span

The preceding pages assume that the owner has found the optimum life span, *i.e.* that PN lies as close as possible to OX in Diagram 2. How does he find this life?

If price were the main outlay to be considered, then his burden could be lightened (*i.e.* PN could be raised) by keeping each asset longer. But a longer life must at some point entail disadvantages such as higher repairs and lower scrap values. These will make for a heavier burden (*i.e.* push PN down).

Thus the owner must weigh two conflicting forces and try to find the compromise that minimises his burden. By drafting alternative budgets for a series of different life-spans (*i.e.* using a marginal approach), he can discover which life gives the lowest perpetual burden (and annual equivalent); or he may find it simpler in some types of calculation to remember that the increasing rate of yearly outlays (repairs plus fall in scrap value) must in the last year of the optimum life rise to the level of the replacement's annual equivalent ((2) on page 161).

Diagram 4

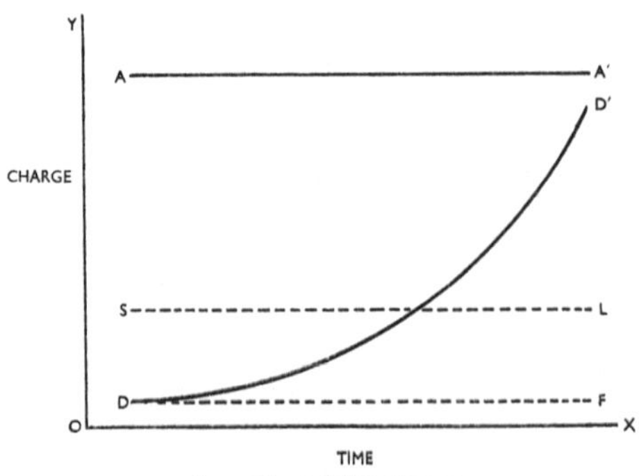

Annual depreciation charges

Price Changes

So far, the argument has assumed that the asset will be replaced by another with the same cash flows. But in fact these are likely to alter, because of price-change. This can be analysed in two steps:—

(1) *General change in the value of money*

One should start by assuming that the asset's flows move exactly in step with the general change. Thus, in inflation, the asset's value and annual depreciation costs should be raised with a general index factor. The raising of the asset's value does not betoken any real rise in the owner's wealth, and the corresponding credit is not income but a nominal adjustment to capital. But the raising of annual depreciation costs in income statements leads to a better measure of income, if this is defined as the growth of the owner's real wealth.

(2) *Real change*

The future flows are in fact not likely to move in ways that exactly match the general index. Thus, when the general level of prices is rising, perhaps maintenance costs may rise faster still, while the price of new assets may rise more slowly because of technological improvement. The gaps between such " special " change and the general change are important for the owner's wealth. So the second step is to revalue the asset further, to reflect the special change; the corresponding extra credit represents a genuine (if at this stage an unrealised) profit. In decision budgets, etc., depreciation costs too should be adjusted for special change. But whether the extra cost should be used to reduce the balance on the income statement is highly debatable: if special depreciation is debited in the income statement, then surely a credit must also be introduced for the corresponding real appreciation (which has now been realised), thus keeping income at the general index level of (1) above.

Curves such as those in Diagram 1 can be readily adapted for price-changes. Diagram 5 shows what may happen when there is a single and unexpected real change —caused, say, by the appearance of a cheaper model (" cheaper " covering both price and repairs, etc.). Let us call the two models Old and New. Old's value curve was expected to be CFK′K (whose path reflects rising repairs). New appears at date E. At once the burden of perpetual ownership is eased—and the advantage of possessing Old is thereby lessened. Old's value curve falls vertically from F. If the comparison of Old with New gives New a moderate advantage only, the drop may be to some such point as G, and the revised curve may be

CFGL′L, *i.e.* the optimum life is shortened to L. But there is a range of other possibilities: Old's value and life now depend on the gap between Old's future annual outlays and New's annual equivalent; if at E the former already exceed the latter, Old will be scrapped at once (*i.e.* L coincides with E) as its value is less than its scrap price; if they remain lower till K, Old's earlier life estimate still holds (*i.e.* L coincides with K) though its value curve is beneath FK′.

If New's price, etc., are above Old's, the book-value should be raised, and Old's life will tend to be extended. Its revised value pattern may for instance be like CFHM′M. Any real appreciation is in my view a part of the year's income (though it may reasonably be labelled " unrealised ").[7]

Conclusion

The forward-looking approach thus suggests that no rigid method is likely to suit the outlay patterns of all assets, and that even a specially-tailored formula must allow for market movements. The ideal method would be fluid enough to match all kinds of ups and downs. It would for instance show the value pattern of a cow—rapid up-surge in youth, a summit at maturity, and gentle fall thereafter. Canning [8] reasoned in this way long ago, and no one has yet proved him wrong.

[7] Its treatment when it first occurs, and when the asset depreciates later, is described in E. O. EDWARDS and P. W. BELL: The Theory and Measurement of Business Income; *University of California Press*, Berkeley, 1961.

[8] JOHN B. CANNING: Economics of Accountancy; *Ronald Press*, New York, 1929.

Diagram 5

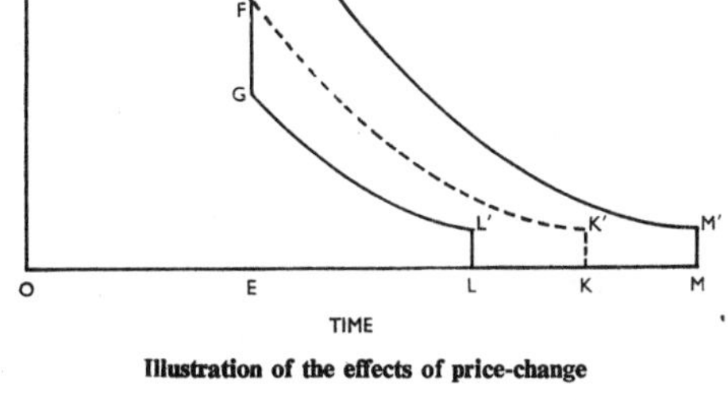

Illustration of the effects of price-change

The Harmonisation of European Practices in the Presentation of External Financial Accounts

Drs W. SCHATTINGA

This article, by a member of the Nederlands Instituut van Registeraccountants deals, without going into too much detail, with the main points in the proposals for harmonising the presentation of annual accounts in the E.E.C.

We are indebted to the author, and to the Editor of DE ACCOUNTANT, *the journal of the Dutch Institute, for permission to reproduce this article, which originally appeared, in English, in the issue 3/70 (November) of that journal.*

(1) Introduction

The European Commission, the main executive body of the European Economic Community, ensures among other things that the provisions of the Treaty of Rome are carried out. One of these provisions is the harmonisation of legislation as far as this is considered to be essential for the proper functioning of the Common Market. One of the elements of legislation considered to be of importance in this respect is the proper presentation of the financial position and results of companies established in the Common Market.

The Commission asked its department " Direction générale du Marché Intérieur " to take measures for this purpose. Consequently this " Direction " asked representatives of our profession five years ago to draw up proposals for harmonising the legal requirements for annual accounts. This was done by representatives from Belgium, France, Germany, Italy and The Netherlands in a committee under the able chairmanship of Dr W. Elmendorff, of Dusseldorf. The committee submitted its proposals to the " Direction générale " which, after consulting mainly legal advisers, sent a draft to the member states for consideration. I am commenting on this draft, which is not identical to the proposals of the Elmendorff committee of which I was a member. In view of the changes that have been made, our committee cannot be considered responsible for the present draft proposals.

Upon starting its work our committee had to consider the legal requirements then in force in the member states, the Bills pending in several countries to improve these requirements, the generally accepted accounting principles and good business practice in the member states and also in other countries of the Western world.

These related to the presentation and layout of the balance sheet and the profit and loss account, to the valuation of assets and liabilities and the principles of profit determination. With regard to the last there was little scope for the " economic concept of profit " put forward in an important paper [1] presented by Professor Palle Hansen of Denmark, at the Seventh International Congress of Accountants in Amsterdam in 1957. It is necessary to try to value a company in cases of acquisitions and mergers, but to ascertain annual profits as the difference between the valuations of the company at the beginning and the end of a year (plus withdrawals) would inevitably involve too many subjective expectations about the future. We believe that we had to adhere to the accounting *ex post* concept of profit (even though elements of subjective judgment remain).

I mention this point because it brings me to the limitations governing annual accounts. We should not expect from them more than they can provide. For *internal* management purposes they have less value than the annual operating plans (the estimates for one or more years of turnover, costs, results, yield on capital employed and prospective source and use of funds statements). These are more in line with Professor Hansen's *ex ante* thinking. The annual accounts cannot disclose much to the management that they did not already know from periodical statements of results and turnover, cash flow statements, etc.

Nevertheless annual accounts continue to be of major importance, especially for *external* reporting. The management has to give an account of its stewardship to shareholders and information to other interested parties such as potential new shareholders, bondholders, creditors in general, employees, the government and the public at large. In the annual report the management can give some forecast about the future, but in the annual accounts it shows what has happened in the past, albeit that this is more than merely the recording of past events.

Valuation and profit determination include elements of judgment and the application of thinking in the field of business economics. Basically, the annual accounts are interim reports during the overall life of the company, in which revenues and costs are matched as well as possible for the particular year. Our committee was aware that the annual accounts cannot provide answers to all questions such as the value of the company, yield positions in detail or development of future liquidity, but they can give material with which the interested parties are able, with the support of investment analysts and the financial press, to form a reasonably reliable opinion of the state of the company's affairs.

(2) Basic Concepts

Article 2 of the draft proposals reads, freely translated into English: The annual accounts consist of the balance sheet, the profit and loss account and explanatory notes which form an indivisible entity. They must comply with normal accounting procedures.

The annual accounts shall be drawn up clearly to give, in accordance with the rules of valuation and presentation, as true and fair a view as is possible of the shareholders' funds (capital and reserves), and the company's financial position and results.

These main rules are of overriding importance; the rest can be regarded as implementing these targets.

(3) Layout of Balance Sheet and Profit and Loss Account

To comply with these targets, minimum requirements were drawn up for the presentation of the accounts. Reproduced at pages 167 and 169 are Schedules 1 and 2, the layout of the balance sheet and one of the four possible specimens for the profit and loss account. I shall not go into detail but will confine myself to a few remarks.

(*a*) The presentation of the accounts relates to industrial and trading companies and not, for instance, to banks and insurance companies.

Departure from the standard forms is permitted if this leads to greater information value (*e.g.* for mining companies and shipping).

(*b*) It may be said that the layout of the balance sheet and profit and loss account is too rigid and does not leave enough latitude. A more flexible system would allow more possibility of adapting the layout to a company's particular needs. The viewpoints of the members of our committee differed considerably in this respect, and the outcome was a compromise between even more rigid rules and greater flexibility as proposed especially by the Dutch delegation.

The " Direction générale " increased the number of headings. It should, however, be observed that not all headings will occur in practice, and there are safety valves to enable more concise and readable presentation, that is to say:—

> The information required for the accounts can be shown in the balance sheet and profit and loss account *or* in the notes; to show it in the notes improves the presentation of the former.
>
> Member states are free to stipulate that items in the balance sheet and profit and loss account preceded by arabic numerals can be grouped together when their amounts are immaterial in relation to the size of the company.
>
> Companies with a balance sheet total of less than U.S.A.$ 1 million can start the profit and loss account with the gross trading profit.
>
> Publication of condensed statements is allowed when this is explicitly stated and reference is made to where the complete accounts can be consulted.

[1] " Ascertainment of Profit in Business ".

DEPRECIATION, REPLACEMENT PRICE, AND COST OF CAPITAL

W. T. Baxter and N. H. Carrier

Depreciation, Replacement Price, and Cost of Capital

W. T. BAXTER AND N. H. CARRIER*

The Problem

It is generally accepted that, when prices change, the costs charged in ordinary accounts (being historical) tend to lag behind current costs and revenue, with various ill results. The operating costs most subject to the time lag are those for materials and depreciation.

Reformers say this error can be corrected by adjusting historical charges to current levels, either by direct revaluation or by use of a suitable price index. The aim of our paper is not to challenge the logic and desirability of reform—far from it—but to examine the values at stake and to ask how far its arithmetic is right.

In a sense, the answer to our question is plain enough. If, when assets subject to the time lag are consumed, their replacements are in fact bought at current price, the proposed correction achieves its aim. If however the replacement is not bought at the current level but later, as is usual with depreciating assets, the correction is not obviously adequate. We shall try to analyze this possible shortfall. To do so, we must distinguish between various types of account, of asset, and of price change.

COST IN BUDGETS AND IN INCOME STATEMENTS

Cost measurement is likely to be important in two contexts. First, the cost of inputs may be wanted for budgets to aid management decision—for instance, to find whether the cost of a job is likely to be less than its revenue. It may be wanted too for post mortem accounts to test whether the decision to do the job was justified.

* Professor and Reader, London School of Economics and Political Science. The authors wish to thank Mrs. S. Dev and Professor J. Flower for their helpful criticisms.

Second, the firm's costs for the year are needed for the income statement. But these costs need not agree with those of the decision budget (e.g., such a budget should confine itself to the marginal cost of the given job, whereas the income statement must include also costs that are fixed so far as each job goes).

"USE DEPRECIATION" AND "TIME DEPRECIATION"

When the asset in question consists of direct materials, its conversion into input causes a physical shrinkage. So there is here a cause-and-effect link between using up and the need for the replacement outlay, and the latter is clearly an avoidable sacrifice of the job.

With some depreciating assets, an analogous process seems to exist: the asset's life will end only when a certain amount of physical use has taken place. So its use on a job normally entails an avoidable replacement cost; and such use depreciation is a cost for purposes alike of decision and income measurement.

With other depreciating assets, however, use has no effect on the date of the replacement outlay, as this is governed by factors such as obsolescence, a contract, etc. Therefore the use of such assets on a job causes no sacrifice, and depreciation should be left out of the job's budget. But the passage of time does bring the outlays nearer, and so time-depreciation is a proper charge in income statements.

No doubt many depreciating assets have both a use and a time component in their yearly cost.

GENERAL VERSUS SPECIAL PRICE-INDEX ADJUSTMENT

Price change may be either general (affecting a wide range of commodities and services, as during inflation), special (peculiar to the given asset) or, more usually, a mixture of both. Advocates of reform in accounts differ in their stress on the two forms of change, and thus divide into two camps. Though both reject the conventional view that income is the excess after money capital has been maintained, they dispute over the alternative definitions of capital. One group argues for the maintenance of real capital (usually defined in terms of the owner's standard of living), the other for the maintenance of physical capital. Their tools for correcting cost and income are therefore respectively the general index and the special index.

General index. The "general index man" holds that where inputs are kept long enough for their price to change, their historical costs in the income statement should be updated with a suitable index of general purchasing power, so that they will be expressed in \$s of the same value as the revenue \$s.

Special index. The "special index man" aims to adjust the inputs' historical cost to their current market value (on the grounds that the latter is also replacement cost, and income is the surplus after providing for this cost).[1] He finds current value by adjusting historical cost with a special index for the particular type of asset, or by direct revaluation.

NATURE OF COST

When anything more than a record of stewardship is wanted, cost measurement should be forward-looking. Just as value is a matter of expected future benefits, so too cost is a matter of future sacrifices. The cost to a firm of a given job is the job's effect in worsening the future cash flow. Thus, when the firm turns an existing asset into input for the job, typically the adverse consequence is that the firm will pay cash to replace the asset; so the cost of using up this asset is its replacement price. (There are some exceptions to this rule, but they need not concern us here.)

Moreover, the obvious costs of acquiring inputs (purchase price, freight, etc.) may need to be augmented. When the asset is bought ahead of needs, ownership involves also less obvious (but no less real) sacrifices such as storage of the assets and cost of capital on the sum invested. With cheap assets and a quick turnover, these unobtrusive costs may well be trivial, and they are seldom added to the asset's book value. But cost of capital must play an essential part in discussions of principle since one cannot compare outlays of different dates without discounting. In what follows, we have no option but to accord more weight to depreciation methods that allow for "interest" (e.g. the annuity method) than their use in practice warrants. It is a pity that practice neglects them so; particularly when rates are high, cost of capital must have a marked effect on depreciation cost and the values of depreciating assets.

Stable Prices

CURRENT AND REMOTE REPLACEMENT COST

Replacement cost is easy to measure if inputs are replaced promptly and in lots whose physical size can vary with needs. These conditions are often met when the input consists of materials. Thus the decision to use up x lbs. of stores may well lead to the outlay of the current replacement cost of x lbs.

Measurement becomes less easy, even with stable prices, where inputs are not replaced within the accounting period, e.g., where they are bought in lots whose size exceeds the needs of a given job, etc. This situation is not unusual; for instance, there may be a saving in buying materials in large lots. Depreciating assets would seem, from the standpoint of the economic realities, to be merely large lots of input bought ahead of needs.

[1] The issues are described, and case for the special index approach put, by R. S. Gynther, *Accounting for Price-Level Changes* (Oxford: Pergamon Press, 1966).

DEPRECIATION AS THE WORSENING OF CASH PROSPECTS

Where input is bought in large lots, the use of part of the lot will affect the date of a future replacement; indeed, if the using-up of one lot is always the signal for buying another, it will affect the whole chain of future replacements. So today's cost, and the value of the remaining asset, depend on a change in budget prospects. Suppose, for instance, that the firm buys stores in 100 ton lots, ahead of needs, and normally uses 25 tons a year. It buys a lot at the close of 1970. If it happens to use no stores in 1971, the replacement dates will be 1975, 1979, and so on; if it duly uses 25 tons, the dates will be 1974, 1978, etc. The cost of using the 25 tons in 1971 is this shift in the chain—the worsening of the cash prospect. It can be found by comparing the present values of the two chains of future payments; presumably, in the absence of special circumstances, these stretch to a far-off time horizon and so are best treated as perpetuities.

It may be objected that this view must be nonsense because the inherent uncertainties of remote prediction make accurate measurement impossible. The answer surely is that the cost is real enough even though its dimensions are not precisely known. One must accept the use of estimates or else abandon reason. And here, as in many other situations, a careful analysis of uncertain forces may often help sound judgment even though the sensible man will sometimes decide in the end to cut the corners by working on very simple assumptions.

VALUE AS THE POTENTIAL WORSENING OF CASH PROSPECT BY DEPRIVAL

For most accounting purposes, value too can perhaps be defined most serviceably as the gap between two prospects—those facing an owner and a deprived owner. In other words, it is the compensation that should in normal circumstances be paid to a deprived owner to make good his loss. It can be found by comparing the future outlays in what may be called the "Have" and "Have-not" budgets. A deprived owner would have to pay for a new asset forthwith, for a replacement at the end of that asset's life, and so on, i.e., he would be faced with the immediate burden of a perpetuity-due of replacement payments. An undeprived owner need not make a replacement payment till his asset reaches the end of its life; then he too will face the burden of a perpetuity-due. The difference between these two budget prospects is the benefit of ownership, i.e., "deprival value," or "opportunity value."

Prices in the second-hand market will not affect deprival value except when the asset is on the point of being scrapped; if the firm always buys an input in large lots, the price of small lots is irrelevant. Thus the firm may prefer new to second-hand trucks, i.e., may think that ton-miles come cheaper in large lots (in some broad sense that covers not only price but factors such as availability and reliability). Then depreciation has nothing to do with the buying prices of second-hand trucks; it has everything to do with unit costs derived from the outlays on a new truck. Replacement cost here has a specialized meaning that does not match everyday speech.

DIAGRAMMATIC TREATMENT OF LONG-RUN REPLACEMENT COST

In Figure 1, OX shows time, and $Y'OY$ value. As the main cash flows in question constitute a burden rather than a benefit, values are shown below OX. OP is the present value of the perpetuity-due of replacement payments at date O; and, with stable prices, a horizontal line PQ traces the burden that faces a would-be owner at any later date, e.g., KK' at time K.

Suppose the owner buys the asset at time M' and it lasts till K'. Ownership at once makes his long-term burden less onerous, reducing it to CM', the present value of KK'. But the relief evaporates as the years pass and replacement looms nearer; by time D', for instance, the present vƒlue of

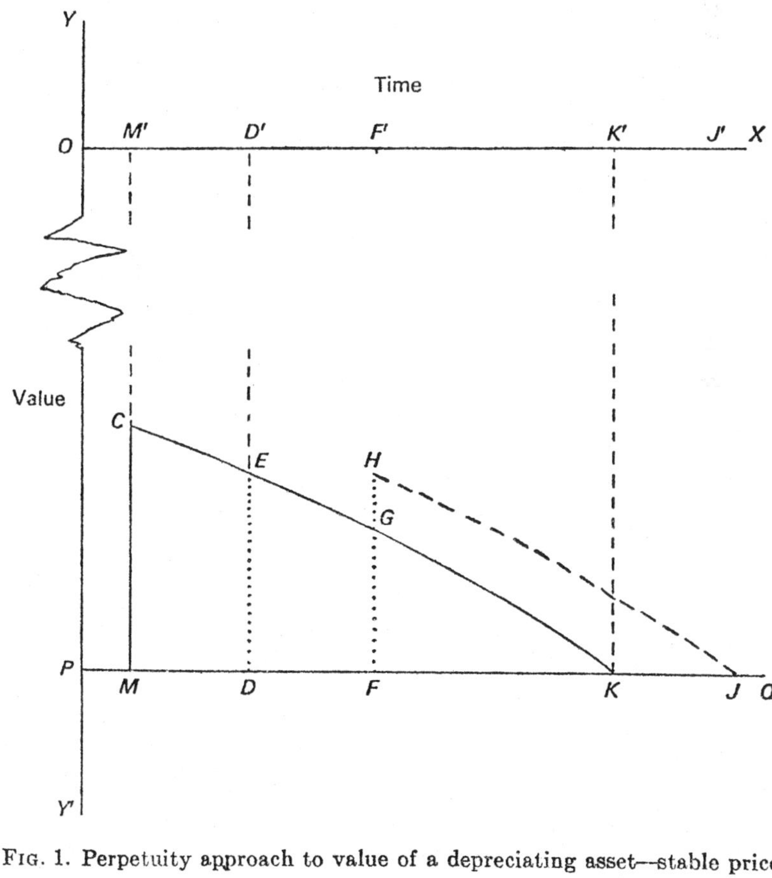

FIG. 1. Perpetuity approach to value of a depreciating asset—stable prices.

KK' has grown to ED'. The pattern of burden over the asset's life is the falling line CK.

CK thus traces the values found in Have budgets and MK those in Have-not budgets. The vertical distances between them give the deprival values at different dates; MC, for instance, is the value at acquisition (equal to initial price), and DE at D'. Thus MCK is the asset's value curve. It here assumes that the cash flow does not include uneven outlays for repairs, etc., or a final receipt for scrap. For instance, between the two dates D' and F' the asset's value sinks from DE to FG; depreciation is GH. A backward-looking approach tries to describe GH in terms of fall in the original cost MC and is hard put to justify its size. Our forward-looking approach regards DE and FG as contrasts between budgets, and depreciation as the worsening of these contrasts. With stable conditions, one can say that the value of the asset's future services would, but for the lapse of the period or use during it, still be the same at F as at D; replacement would thus be postponed from K to J, and at date F the Have curve would be HJ instead of GK: so use etc., causes a fall in value of FH-FG, i.e., GH. Here the forward-looking and the historical approaches both lead to the same answer, but they might not do so if prices changed.

The area MCK can be lifted from the perpetuity framework and shown as OCK in the simpler and more familiar style of Figure 2. Again OY shows value and OX time; CK is the value curve, and GH is the fall in value between D and F. But, whether they are made explicit, the perpetuities give the logical basis for the simpler figure.

COMPARISON WITH THE ANNUITY METHOD

With stable prices, the asset values of the figures agree with those found by the annuity method of depreciation. But though this method yields the

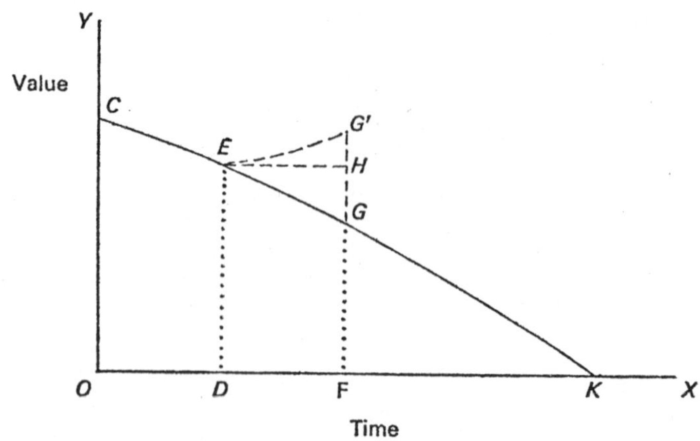

FIG. 2. Value curve of a depreciating asset—stable prices.

same net annual charge as the figures, it throws in extra information by:

(a) charging operations with the whole cost of ownership for the year—what we call the "full servicing charge" for the investment in the asset. This has two components:
   (1) the forward-looking cost already considered (e.g., *GH* in the figure) which might be labelled the "replacement charge" or "net depreciation"; and
   (2) imputed interest (which we prefer to call "cost of capital") for the year on the opening value.

(b) crediting (2) to another section of the income statement (say, that for interest charges).

Profit is the same whether the gross or the net cost is charged in the income statement (since, if the gross sum (a) is debited, the imputed interest (b) must be credited, as in the example below). But the gross figure shows the full annual sacrifice caused by the decision to own and employ the asset. It may be likened to a notional rent charged by the firm, as a test of efficiency, to the department using the asset.

CONFLICTING PULLS: DEPRECIATION VERSUS APPRECIATION DUE TO COST OF CAPITAL

The two steps of the annuity method serve to show that there are two conflicting pulls on a depreciating asset's value. On the one hand, cost of capital tends to raise the value; if discounting makes a remote benefit less valuable, then the obverse is that the benefit must appreciate as time brings it closer. On the other hand, the asset's conversion into input must more than offset this appreciation. The rival pulls can be illustrated diagrammatically if the input is assumed to be left undisturbed till near the end of each year. Thus Figure 2 shows them for the year between *D* and *F*. Value first appreciates at the cost-of-capital rate (the addition of "interest" by the annuity method) from *E* to *G'*. At year-end, when the input is taken, value falls abruptly. With a time-asset, this fall is from *G'* to *G*. With a use-asset, the fall is also from *G'* to *G* if the planned amount of input is duly consumed, but is only to *H* if some hitch postpones using up the input till next year. The full servicing charge of the annuity method is *GG'*, while the replacement charge is *GH*.

Even with use-assets, the cost-of-capital part of the full service charge (*HG'*) would seem to be an unavoidable cost of jobs. If the job is not done, the value curve of Figure 1 becomes *HJ*, and nothing higher; value must in Figure 2 drop from *G'* to *H*. Undesired delay can hardly raise value. So the cost-of-capital ingredient is a fixed cost of the period; as long as one is measuring cost for job budgets, not income statements, this appreciation within each year should be omitted. To make the point, the income statement might be drafted along these lines.

Section for operating department		
Depreciation:		
Avoidable cost:		
Replacement charge for use-assets		$50
Fixed cost:		
Replacement charge for time-assets	$50	
Cost of capital on both types of asset	20	70
Full servicing charge		$120
Section for interest charges		
Deduct:		
Cost of capital charged to operations		$20
Net writedown in value		$100

SECONDARY ASSETS, COST OF CAPITAL, AND EVENTUAL REPLACEMENT COST

The long-run cost of capital has important effects on the value pattern, producing the curvature of *CK* in the diagrams. Thus it also affects the replacement charge pattern.

Suppose a man at the end of year 1 holds stores whose price is $100, and that if he used them on a job now, he would have to buy another batch for $100 at the end of year 2. The sacrifice caused by the job in year 1 would not be $100 but only the present value of the future payment of $100; use-cost is here replacement price reduced by cost of capital. The same answer can be reached by saying that the man will maintain his capital if, on doing the job in year 1, he sets aside enough "secondary assets" to make good the "primary asset" in 12 months' time; as these secondary assets will themselves add to earnings, they can start at below $100.

The primary asset is the depreciating asset that is being measured. The secondary assets are the additional assets that the firm acquires as a result of providing for the depreciation of the primary asset. These additions may at first take the form of cash. But later the cash will probably be put to some fruitful use. Thus it may be used to repay loan and so reduce cost of capital, or to buy all manner of other assets, perhaps including other depreciating assets. In one shape or another, these additions will in time cut costs or swell revenues or appreciate. Thus the depreciation provisions engender a stream of extra benefits. These change the replacement charges in the way described in the preceding paragraph, i.e., they are just as relevant to the value of the primary asset as, say, its repairs.

The further away the replacement date and the higher the secondary earnings, the less the depreciation cost during the early years of life. High secondary earnings make for late depreciation cost; it is these earnings that impart the curvature to a depreciating asset's value pattern and which justify the annuity method's addition of imputed interest. To be pedantically precise, one should talk about the rate of secondary earnings rather than of interest or cost of capital.

ARITHMETIC OF DEPRECIATING ASSETS

Despite our liking for the annuity method, we propose not to use its formulas; their algebra may deal well enough with the stable prices but does not generalize readily for other situations. We shall use instead formulas that link with the burden of perpetual ownership. This approach generalizes well, as it covers the otherwise troublesome problems of dealing with a decision's future repercussions (possibly after prices have changed). Admittedly the notion of perpetual ownership is unfamiliar; but, just as the common way of getting an asset's services (purchase of one asset for an initial price) is sometimes replaced by hire at an annual rent, so too it might—in theory at least—be replaced by purchase now of the whole succession of assets for a bigger initial sum. This sum would be the present value of a perpetuity of yearly rents and also of a perpetuity-due of prices for successive assets.

Operations are deemed to start with the buying of an asset, or the perpetual use of an asset, at time $t = 0$.

A' = outlay on the asset. With materials, A' is the asset's price. With depreciating assets, there may be many relevant outlays (e.g., price and varying annual repairs), while final scrap proceeds constitute a negative outlay; then A' must be interpreted as the present value, at the start of life, of a complete set of the relevant outlays over a life. In the following formulas, A' for simplicity assumes initial price to be the only outlay.

P = present value of A' in perpetuity, just before the first payment (in advance).

k = the asset's life span, from purchase to scrapping. The possibility of k being changed by technology, etc., is excluded.

i = the earnings rate on the secondary assets.

v = $1/(1 + i)$, the discounting factor.

Transactions take place at time t (when the asset has a remaining life of m), and accounts are then drawn up for the preceding 12 months, i.e., for the period since $t - 1$, when the asset had a life of $m + 1$.

The perpetuity. Let P = the present-value of the burden of perpetual ownership. Using the above terms, one can by definition obtain it as:

$$\begin{aligned} P &= A' + A'v^k + A'v^{2k} + \cdots \\ &= A'/(1 - v^k). \end{aligned} \tag{1}$$

Asset value. $V(m, t)$ is the deprival value of an asset at time t, when the remaining life is expected to be m years. Without the asset, a firm wanting perpetual use of an asset must immediately incur a burden of P (traced over time by PQ in Figure 1). But if at time t it already owns an asset with m more years of life, the burden is deferred for m years and has a present value of $v^m P$ (in the figure, ED' at D'). The balance, namely $P - v^m P$, is the value of the partially worn asset (DE in the figure).[2]

Thus

$$V(m, t) = P(1 - v^m). \tag{2}$$

Replacement charge. If at date t the owner works a use-asset to the planned extent, he is left with a burden whose present value is Pv^m. Without use, the burden would be only Pv^{m+1}. The cost of use (or, with time-assets, of the passage of the year) is the difference. Thus:

$$\text{Replacement charge} = P(1 - v)v^m \tag{3}$$

or this may be expressed as $V(m + 1, t) - V(m, t)$, or as $A'(1 - v)v^m/(1 - v^k)$.

(3) contains only one term that depends on m, namely v^m. At the end of the first year, remaining life will be 1 less than a complete life, i.e., $m = k - 1$. A year later, remaining life will have fallen to $k - 2$. Thus the expressions for the replacement charges for successive years will contain factors $v^{k-1}, v^{k-2}, \cdots, v^2, v$ and 1. Since v is less than unity, these form an increasing series, i.e., the charge (in the absence of disturbing forces such as rising repairs) grows as the asset ages. In the figure, this is reflected by CK's increasing rate of fall.

Full servicing charge. This is the yearly cost of the decision to acquire the asset. Suppose the firm has a capital P which it will use to buy the perpetual use of an asset at either time $t - 1$ or t. If it opts for t, the capital can continue to earn in some secondary use and so grows to $(1 + i)P$; if it opts for $t - 1$, it loses these earnings. Thus the cost of ownership for the year is $(1 + i)P - P$, i.e.,

$$\text{Full servicing charge} = iP. \tag{4}$$

The argument remains valid for all the years of life. If ownership is deferred from time 0 to any time $t - 1$, the saving at $t - 1$ is $P[(1 + i)^{t-1} - 1]$; if it is deferred from 0 to t, the saving at time t rises to $P[(1 + i)^t - 1]$. The difference is the cost of the tth year of ownership; valued at time t, it is:

$$P[(1 + i)^t - 1] - (1 + i)P[(1 + i)^{t-1} - 1] = iP,$$

as before. This fits in with everyday experience of a rent being constant.

[2] Where the asset's varying annual outlays and scrap value are big enough to merit consideration, they will change P and formula (2). At t, let the present values of the remaining outlays and scrap value be $O(m)$ and Sv^m respectively. Formula (2) then becomes:

$$V(m, t) = P(1 - v^m) - O(m) + Sv^m.$$

An analogous formula is developed in A. J. Merrett and Allen Sykes, *The Finance and Analysis of Capital Projects* (London: Longmans, 1962), p. 470.

Components of full servicing charge. Figure 1 shows how the burden of ownership can be treated as a whole or as two parts: thus, at date D' the whole burden is DD', which is made up of ED' and DE—respectively the amount needed to earn future replacements and the asset's value.

The yearly equivalent of the burden can likewise be treated as a whole (the full servicing charge, the constant iP), or as two parts:

Replacement charge (with stable real prices, the same thing as *net write-down in the asset's value*). Formula (3) in effect expresses this in terms of i and the part of P needed to provide replacements.

Cost-of-capital charge. This can be expressed[3] as $iP(1 - v^{m+1})$, i.e., as cost of capital on the asset's opening value for the year.

Thus all three quantities can be expressed in terms of i and P or its components.

Since the full charge is constant and net cost of use rises over the years, cost of capital must be a falling charge.

An arithmetical example that illustrates the use of the formulas is given in Appendix 2.

General Price Change

We must now consider what happens when prices change before replacement. Let us first suppose that the change is general and affects the money values of all the firm's assets at the same rate which implies that the yearly depreciation provisions of our model are never left as money assets, but are promptly invested in secondary assets whose money values can go up and down. In these convenient circumstances (it is reasonable to suspect), change in money values cannot by itself change real values one whit: the owner is no better or worse off than if prices had stayed stable.

It is necessary to choose an income concept on which to base the new formulas. We assume that income statements are drafted largely with the aim of helping the collective owners with their consumption decisions. If the income figure is to have meaning, the charges for wealth lost as input should be measured in the same $s as wealth gained as revenue, and (in view of the statement's aim) this equivalence is probably best defined in

[3] From formulas (3) and (2), the replacement charge plus cost of capital on opening value can be written:

$$
\begin{aligned}
& P(1 - v)v^m + iP(1 - v^{m+1}) \\
&= P[v^m - v^{m+1} + i - iv^{m+1}] \\
&= P[i + v^m - v^{m+1}(1 + i)] \\
&= P[i + v^m - v^m] \\
&= iP \\
&= \text{full servicing charge by formula (4).}
\end{aligned}
$$

terms of the owners' purchasing power. So cost subject to a time-lag should be updated with the general index.

ASSUMPTION OF CONSTANT RATE OF PRICE-CHANGE

One can simplify a first approach to the problem in a way that perhaps is in the long run not too unrealistic by assuming that the price change occurs at a steady rate, g. As A' is the price of an asset at the time 0, $A'(1 + g)$ will be the price at 1, $A'(1 + g)^2$ at 2, and so on g may be positive (where prices rise) or negative (where they fall).

REVISED FIGURE FOR PERPETUITY APPROACH

Figure 1 changes under the influence of g, and Figure 3 shows the revised curves. PQ, the burden of deciding to own an asset in perpetuity, is no longer a horizontal straight line but becomes concave to Y'; here it has been given a downward slope, implying that prices are assumed to be rising, i.e., that g is positive. If g were negative, PQ would slope upward but would still be concave.

MC is again the initial price. CK again assumes the particular asset to have no varying cash flow (on repairs etc.) during its life; any point on CK can be found by discounting the full burden at K back to the given date. Vertical distances between MK and CK measure the benefit of ownership and hence value, e.g., DE and FG are values at dates D and F.

MODIFICATION OF ALGEBRA FOR CHANGING PRICES

To deal with changing prices, the algebra must be modified.

$A'(t)$ = the price of the asset at time t. For brevity, the price of the first asset $[A'(0)]$ will be written simply A'.

$P(t)$ = the cost of the perpetual use of the asset at time t. The cost at 0 will be written P.

Real and illusory cost of-capital rates. With general price change, the secondary earnings rate, i, will probably seem to change. During inflation, for instance, these secondary assets will appreciate; if i was .1 p.a. in a stable preliminary period, and then prices rise at the rate of .06 p.a., an equity investment of \$1 will in one year grow to \$1.166, so that the growth rate may loosely be described as .166, whereas (as the capital of 1 opening \$ is equivalent to 1.06 of the depreciated closing \$s) the real rate is still $[(1.166/1.06) - 1] = .1$.

One must thus distinguish two versions of the rate. We shall use i for the illusory rate (.166 in the example) found from \$s of different values. Where the real rate is relevant, we shall use i^* instead; $i^* = (1 + i)/(1 + g) - 1 = (i - g)/(1 + g)$. This rate is not altered by general price change and so in the example stays at .1.

The formulas of earlier pages use i, and so their v is here based on the illusory rate. Where a real discount rate is more convenient, we shall now use q instead of v; that is:

$$q = v(1 + g).$$

The formulas can be adapted to general price change as follows. The perpetuity [see formula (1)]

$$P = A' + A'(1+g)^k v^k + A'(1+g)^{2k} v^{2k} \cdots$$
$$= A'/1 - q^k. \quad (5)$$

As q is the unchanging real discount rate, based on i^*, the burden is the same whether or not general prices will change; the owner of nonmoney assets is indifferent to such change. In Figure 3, OP is the same whether PQ is horizontal or curves.

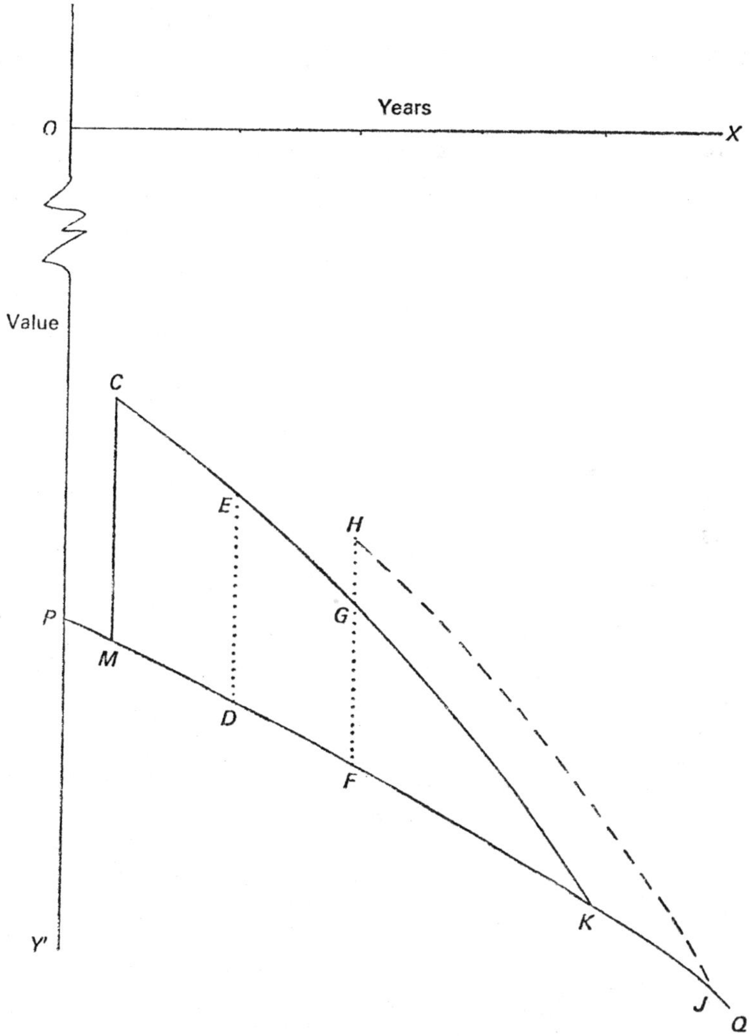

FIG. 3. Perpetuity approach to value of a depreciating asset—rising prices.

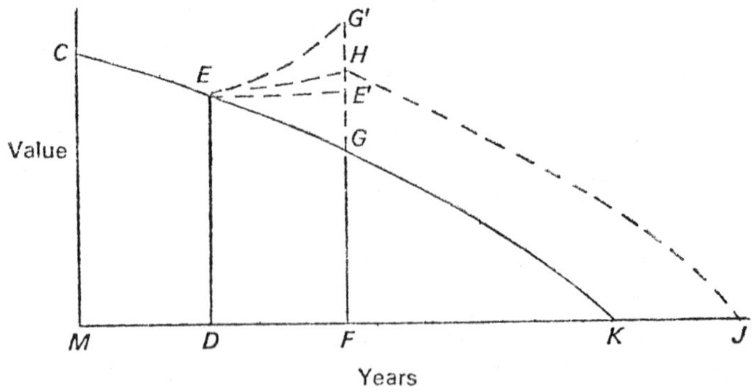

FIG. 4. Annual movements in the value of a depreciating asset—rising prices.

Asset value. The argument of formula (2) can be adapted to show that

$$\begin{aligned} V(m, t) &= P(t) - P(t + m)v^m \\ &= P(1 + g)^t(1 - q^m). \end{aligned} \tag{6}$$

Formula (6) enables one to measure how far the current value has departed from historical book value.

The whole value pattern can be derived from Figure 3 by measuring vertical distances between MK and CK. Figure 4 shows this pattern as MCK. A comparison of such patterns with those for like assets under stable prices (e.g., OCK in Figure 2) would reveal that a positive rate of g leads to a higher hump in the curve[4] (just as if, with stable prices, the rate i increased). The rising cost of future replacements causes growth in the deprival value of a partly worn asset.

Replacement charge. Adapting formula (3), one finds the charge for the year to (and in the money of) t becomes

$$P(1 + g)^t(1 - q)v^m \tag{7}$$

or

$$A'(1 + g)^t(1 - q)q^m/(1 - q^k).$$

Thus in current money terms the charge grows proportionately to the price change.

The same thing can be explained from the figures. In Figures 1 and 2, the omission to employ a use-asset at time F shifted the Have curve CK to the right; value, instead of falling from DE to FG, stayed at FH; thus, use

[4] To establish this, it has to be shown that $(1 + g)^{k-m}(1 - q^m)/(1 - q^k)$ is an increasing function in g, with $m < k$ and $q < 1$. Taking logarithms and differentiating, after some algebraic manipulation it is found necessary to show that $k/(1 - q^k) - m/(1 - q^m)$ is positive, i.e., that $x/(1 - q^x)$ is an increasing function in x for positive x. This can be shown by differentiating, putting $1 - y$ for q^x and expanding the logarithm of $(1 - y)$, for $0 < y < 1$.

causes a replacement charge of GH for the period. In Figures 3 and 4, similarly, the charge is GH. In Figure 3, however, the vertical distances between HJ and FJ are greater[5] than in 1. Thus GH is greater than when prices are constant; the replacement charge goes up because of the remote future rise in prices.

This is perhaps merely saying that when he perceived that prices are likely to rise, the man who has already bought a stock of scarce[6] inputs will congratulate himself on the acquisition. They appreciate at his moment of perception. But if he now decides to use some of them, the sacrifice is correspondingly greater.

Full servicing charge (*GG' in Figure 4*). This can still be simply expressed as $i^*P(t)$. Or one can substitute

$$P(1+g)^t(1-q)/q. \tag{8}$$

THE ADEQUACY OF GENERAL INDEX REFORM

The replacement charge in stable times [formula (3)] is $A'(1-v)v^m/(1-v^k)$. If, when prices begin to change, the accountant still uses historical costs, he is in effect rewriting the formula as $A'(1-q)q^m/(1-q^k)$, i.e., he retains the real[7] cost-of-capital rate i^*. The general index man corrects this in year t to $A'(1+g)^t(1-q)q^m/(1-q^k)$. But the latter is precisely the desired charge of formula (7); his reform is vindicated triumphantly.

Moreover, the correction satisfies a further test. Thanks to the appreciation of the secondary assets each year at the rate g, the cumulative provisions will mount up over the life to exactly the replacement cost; there is no need to burden the later years with supplements to the charges of earlier years.

All of this strengthens the view that general price change is a mere effervescence that will (other things being equal) leave real wealth untouched. Accounts ought to show this underlying reality, and simple adjustment enables them to do so.

ARTIFICIALITY OF GENERAL PRICE-CHANGE ASSUMPTIONS

But the notion of a completely general price change plainly is artificial in the extreme. In real life, the prices of all the assets in a business are unlikely to move precisely in step with a general index; the cost-of-capital rate is also unlikely, for reasons both internal and external to the firm, to change precisely as a textbook demands. So the question is whether general

[5] This follows from the argument developed in the preceding footnote.

[6] Figure 3 assumes scarcity in the sense that loss of input at date D cannot be made good till K at earliest. This is realistic enough of many depreciating assets whose owners will not stock up with replacements ahead of needs because of storage difficulties and the risk of deterioration and obsolescence.

[7] If he instead uses the changing illusory rate, correction tends to overcompensate for the price change.

index reform still works well when the change in the future replacement price of the primary asset will diverge from the change in general prices.

Special Price Change

The simplest plan is to concentrate on the divergence, i.e., on the real change. This can best be done by assuming in the first instance that general prices remain constant. Therefore, in this section a firm is envisaged whose assets, except for the depreciating asset, have stable values throughout.

Reform can be concerned with several things—asset values, costs for decision budgets, and income measurement. We are at one with the special index man in holding that special prices govern asset values and decision costs; our arithmetic may improve his measurement of these where replacement is remote. But we are skeptical of his approach to income, sometimes shown by endorsement of LIFO as well as special index depreciation. We venture to suggest that when the general index is stable, historical cost depreciation is better; and our formulas are based on this view.

A cost budget is concerned with two alternative courses that face the planner at a given date; the cost of using an asset is the difference between two prospects at that moment, i.e., is swayed by the special replacement price of the asset. The income statement tries to measure change in the net assets between two different dates. We think it helpful to the owners to treat real holding gain on the inputs as part of this change. But the special index man, because of concern to protect the firm's level of physical activity, does not treat holding gains on input as revenue, though he includes them in the charges.

THE SPECIAL INDEX VIEW OF INCOME

In essence, the problem here is whether a $100 appreciation in asset *A* should, when *A* becomes input and needs to be replaced, seem a lesser sacrifice to the owner than a $100 gain in the shape of a physically separate asset *B*. We can discern little difference. And if the owner decides to maintain the business thereafter at its new level, we think that he is in both cases financing expansion (in the economic sense) by voluntarily ploughing back $100 of earnings; whereas the special index man (judging by his physical yardstick) thinks in the case of *A* that there is no expansion and that the owner is merely maintaining his original capital. We agree that replacement will demand extra resources but hold that the treasurer's problem here is the one that arises when any form of economic expansion is to be paid for, i.e., it is one of future finance but not of current income measurement.

COMBINING SPECIAL INDEX COST WITH HISTORICAL INCOME

It may be objected that if special index correction gives the best asset values and decision costs, there are grounds of convenience for showing special costs in the income statement: they would tie in better than historical costs with a revalued balance sheet and would be better guides to the costs of rival firms with new assets, etc.

Though this argument is entirely sound, it is not conclusive for income measurement. One can indeed charge special index cost in the income statement and yet, by also crediting the holding gain (i.e., the appreciation on assets while waiting to become input) end up with an unchanged profit.[8] This procedure has the further advantage of analyzing the components of income.

As an example, suppose a use-asset to be bought for $100 and to have a 2-year life, and that i is .1. With stable prices, for year 1 the replacement charge is about $47.6 and the full servicing charge $57.6. With price rising at a rate of .03, the year 1 net charge (based on future replacement prices) rises to about $49.81; and so jobs should not be accepted unless their margin exceeds this. The operating department is presumably responsible too for the fixed cost of "interest," still $10. On the other hand, its investment has earned a holding gain of $3. So the statement might run:

Section for operating department	
Depreciation:	
Avoidable cost of use (replacement charge)	$49.81
Fixed cost of capital	10.00
Total	59.81
Less: Holding gain	3.00
Full servicing charge	$56.81
Section for finance	
Interest charges:	
Deduction for charge to operations	$10.00
Net write-off from asset's value	$46.81

Note that the replacement charge and the net write-off in the asset's value are no longer the same thing. Therefore it is necessary to distinguish between a full charge that includes holding gain ($59.81 here) and one that excludes such gain ($56.81 here).

Holding gain may of course be negative (and where assets are subject to technological improvement, loss may well be more usual than gain). The above form of statement implies that loss such as obsolescence is charged against the department that invested in the asset.

MEASUREMENT

We shall use s for the rate of special price change and again assume change to be constant. Where A' covers not merely price but also present values of

[8] Our argument clearly owes much to E. Edwards and P. Bell, *The Theory and Measurement of Business Income* (Berkeley: University of California Press, 1961).

varying repairs, etc., s must be a composite for the cash flows of the whole life of each successive vintage of assets. s must in our calculations be less than i; if it exceeds i, the perpetuity arithmetic gives infinite or negative present values and so becomes futile.

Discounting. When present values are calculated, the growth due to s must partly offset the discounting due to i. The net discount factor is called p $(= v(1 + s))$.

The perpetuity. Figure 3 still gives a picture of the perpetuity curve. And, using the earlier reasoning, one finds

$$P = A'/(1 - p^k). \tag{9}$$

Value. This can again be described as in Figure 3. The formula becomes

$$V(m, t) = P(1 + s)^t(1 - p^m). \tag{10}$$

Holding gain. Figure 4 shows a year's gain as $E'H$, which is $sV(m + 1, t - 1)$.

Cost of capital. Figure 4 shows a year's cost as HG', which is $iV(m + 1, t - 1)$.

Replacement charge. This is GH in Figure 4. It can be calculated as:

$$P(1 + s)^t(1 - p)p^m \tag{11}$$

or as

$$A'(1 + s)^t(1 - p)p^m/(1 - p^k).$$

Full servicing charge. This is shown as GG' in Figure 4, i.e.:

$$(1 + i)V(m + 1, t - 1) - V(m, t) \tag{12}$$

and reduces to $(i - s)P(t - 1)$.

RESULTS OF ADAPTING TO SPECIAL CHANGE

Examples may help to show the effects of these formulas. One should compare the Appendix 2 figures for stable prices with those for special change (with falling prices), or the curves in Figure 5 (rising prices).

The values, etc., found by the forward-looking formulas (9)–(11) vary in all years from those of stable prices, i.e., the annuity figures. Thus the formulas yield suitable replacement charges for decisions. But as their income concept aims only to maintain the initial investment, over the whole life the sum of their value write-offs is still A'. In other words, if the income statement uses forward-looking replacement cost but credits holding gain, the net effect over the whole life is *nil*, and the extra cost of replacement is *not* set aside. Even if the holding gains are voluntarily accumulated as a replacement allowance, they will not match the extra cost. (To reach this figure, the accumulations would have to be topped up with sums found by calculating how much the secondary assets would appreciate if the special index applied to them.)

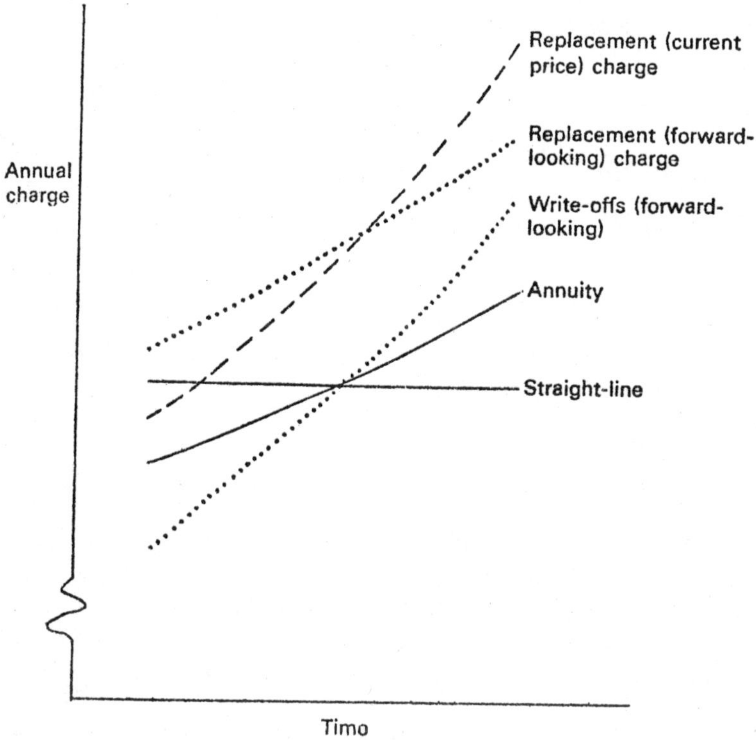

FIG. 5. Depreciation charges by various methods (with special change).

THE INADEQUACY OF SPECIAL INDEX REFORM

Formula (11), second version, puts the forward-looking replacement charge at $A'(1 + s)^t(1 - p)p^m/(1 - p^k)$. The special index man would instead adjust the annuity charge (3) with the current special index to $A'(1 + s)^t(1 - v)v^m/(1 - v^k)$.

The two patterns are by no means the same. They start and end very differently: the current charges understate the effects of change in the early years, and overstate them towards the end. The two curves intersect near mid-life, and so (given normal rates of s and i) their life totals may come quite close.

The cumulative provision of the special index man fails in the end to equal replacement price;[9] it will be less when prices rise and more when they fall. To achieve equality, he must each year adjust the charges of earlier years. With rising prices, this task may prove beyond the firm's means.

[9] If the firm has a stable group of like assets and replaces the same number of assets each year, the yearly replacement outlay equals the year's total of the special index man's charges for the individual assets. Some large and stable firms may come near to this theoretical model: their group of assets resembles the promptly replaced materials (page 191) rather than a single asset with a remote replacement date.

POLICY IMPLICATIONS

Where depreciation is a big part of a firm's costs, special price change can affect total cost and profit in ways that may seem rather odd. Thus a negative s (as with creeping obsolescence) means that firms which buy the expensive assets of an early date may face price cutting when other firms buy cheap assets later. Our formulas deal with this situation: their treatment of holding loss somewhat shifts the weight of the full servicing charge and net writedown to the start of life. Presumably a public utility could justly tilt its pattern of charges to consumers in the same way, though its spokesman might have some little trouble in explaining why the hope of cheaper assets in the future results in higher prices now.[10] Conversely, the prospect of rising replacement prices should tilt a public utility's charges in favor of today's consumers.

Mixture of General and Special Change

Lastly comes the realistic situation that combines both general and special change. Here again it is necessary to choose an income concept on which to base new formulas. The reasoning of the previous two sections suggests that asset values and decision costs should be updated with the special index, but that income should be measured by the general index approach. In other words, the way to unravel the new figures is to adjust the assets with the special index, and the owner's capital, etc., with the general index. The difference (real holding gain) is in our view a form of profit.

MEASUREMENT

Let the separate general and real (special) forces produce, when both are active, a total price change at the steady rate of c per annum; thus $(1 + c) = (1 + s)(1 + g)$. For discounting, let $(1 + c)/(1 + i) = r$, where i is the illusory rate produced by general appreciation.[11]

The perpetuity:

$$P = A'/(1 - r^k). \tag{13}$$

Value:

$$V(m, t) = P(t)(1 - r^m). \tag{14}$$

Replacement charge:

$$V(m + 1, t) - V(m, t). \tag{15}$$

[10] See Ralph Turvey, *Optimal Pricing and Investment in Electricity Supply* (London: Allen & Unwin, 1968), p. 56, and James C. Bonbright, *Principles of Public Utility Rates* (New York: Columbia University Press, 1961), p. 213.

[11] See M. Bromwich, "Inflation and the Capital Budgeting Process," *Journal of Business Finance*, Autumn, 1969, p. 39.

Full servicing charge:

$$(1 + i)V(m + 1, t - 1) - V(m, t). \tag{16}$$

RESULTS

These formulas, like (9)–(12), yield informative values and decision costs. But their net charges in the income statement are content to service the initial real capital: the cumulative write-offs mount up to the initial capital adjusted with the general index (and not to the special replacement price). Specimen figures, for rising general prices but falling real prices, are given at the end of Appendix 2. The relationship between our replacement charges and those of the special index man stays much as in the previous section. The special charges are inadequate for their task and do not in the end match replacement price.

If the income statement charges special cost, real holding gain should be credited, as in the example on page 205. Then the balance is still that of the general index concept.

In practice, there may well be real holding gains on *secondary* assets too. But such gains are analogous to the general index gains (see p. 203), in that they change the cost-of-capital rate and so do not upset the formulas. The firm may of course set the gains aside to help with final replacement; on our assumptions, they then constitute retained earnings and do not change income.

Conclusions

Our analysis suggests that reform will not be as facile as one could wish. Where the asset is not replaced till after the accounting date, charges should depend on prices that will be paid at a long series of future dates. Guesswork about the future is needed for finding values and use-costs; if rule-of-thumb procedures seem to avoid such guesswork, they must in fact rely on implicit assumptions that may be doubly dangerous because they are not recognized. One can derive workable expressions by assuming constant rates of price change where the rates are not expected to be constant, or results may still suggest the wisest strategy.

Our results confirm that inflation does nothing fundamental to non-money wealth. The obvious solution is here the right one: errors can be corrected by working in real terms. This vindicates the general index reformer who is in effect doing just that.

When there is change in the asset's real cost, reform is not obvious. The special index man's faith in current cost has not led him wildly astray in the measurement of avoidable cost, but has done so elsewhere. For income statements, if maintenance of the owner's purchasing power is the proper criterion, general index correction of historical cost will serve much better. With a little ingenuity, the accountant can draft an income statement that will both adjust cost with special indexes and end with the income figure of the general index.

APPENDIX 1

Derivation of Algebraic Expressions

Introduction

It is necessary to establish solutions only for the general case combining general and special price change. The particular cases of stable prices, or of general or special change alone, may then be derived by setting the rates of change of irrelevant prices at zero. However, the algebra of the particular cases can usually be simplified by working from first principles.

Notation

The notation of the text is used. If $g = 0$, i becomes a real rate, as does c.

Assumptions

The vital assumptions are the constancy of the rates of interest and price change.

Preliminary Equations

From fundamental principles

$$(1 + i^*)(1 + g) = (1 + i) \tag{A1}$$

$$(1 + s)(1 + g) = (1 + c) \tag{A2}$$

from which expressions for i^* in terms of i, and s in terms of c, or vice versa, may readily be derived.

Basic Equations

$$A'(t) = A'(1 + c)^t \tag{A3}$$

$$\begin{aligned} P(t) &= A'(t) + v^k A'(t + k) + v^{2k} A'(t + 2k) + \cdots \\ &= A'(t)/(1 - r^k). \end{aligned}$$

Hence

$$P = A'/(1 - r^k) \tag{A4}$$

and

$$P(t) = P(1 + c)^t \tag{A5}$$

$$\begin{aligned} V(m, t) &= P(t) - v^m P(t + m) \\ &= P(t)(1 - r^m). \end{aligned} \tag{A6}$$

Charges for the period $t - 1$ to t (evaluated at time t)

The full service charge is $(1 + i)P(t - 1) - P(t)$, which is easily reduced to $(i - c)P(t - 1)$. (A7)

It is sometimes convenient to use the form

$$(1 + i)V(m + 1, t - 1) - V(m, t). \quad \text{(A8)}$$

This is easily shown to be the same as (A7) by replacing the V-values, using (6).

Real cost-of-capital charge is $i^*V(m + 1, t - 1)$, measured in the currency of time $t - 1$, and thus

$$i^*(1 + g)V(m + 1, t - 1) \quad \text{in the currency of time } t. \quad \text{(A9)}$$

Value at the beginning of the year at time $t - 1$ is $(1 + g)V(m + 1, t - 1)$ measured in the currency of time t; and hence the value to be written off, in the currency of time, t, is

$$(1 + g)V(m + 1, t - 1) - V(m, t). \quad \text{(A10)}$$

If the cost of capital and writedown in value are added together, and $(1 + i^*)(1 + g)$ is replaced by $(1 + i)$, the expression is seen to be the same as the full service charge in form (A9). Holding gain, like cost of capital, is first expressed in terms of $t - 1$ currency and, after conversion to t currency, is

$$s(1 + g)V(m + 1, t - 1). \quad \text{(A11)}$$

Replacement charge is

$$V(m + 1, t) - V(m, t). \quad \text{(A12)}$$

This readily reduces to

$$P(t)(1 - r)r^m. \quad \text{(A13)}$$

A convenient way of evaluating the replacement charge may sometimes be to add the holding gain to the amount available to write value down. Adding them together [from (A10) and (A11)] gives

$$s(1 + g)V(m + 1, t - 1) + (1 + g)V(m + 1, t - 1) - V(m, t)$$

and, replacing $(1 + s)(1 + g)$ by $(1 + c)$, gives

$$(1 + c)V(m + 1, t - 1) - V(m, t).$$

Using (A6), one sees this to be the same as (A12).

The arithmetic can be made simple, as in Appendix 2. But the algebraic derivation of the expressions is necessary to justify the arithmetic.

APPENDIX 2

Arithmetical Example

Stable Prices

$A' = 100; k = 6; i = 0.1; v = 1/(1 + i) = 0.909{,}091; v^6 = 0.564{,}473;$ $1 - v^6 = 0.435{,}527; P = A'/(1 - v^6) = 229.607; iP = 22.961.$

Year	Value of asset at beginning of year (1)	Full service charge (2)	Cost of capital (3)	Replacement charge (= value write-off) (4)	Value of asset at end of year (5)
1	100.000	22.961	10.000	12.961	87.039
2	87.039	22.961	8.704	14.257	72.782
3	72.782	22.961	7.278	15.683	57.099
4	57.099	22.961	5.710	17.251	39.848
5	39.848	22.961	3.985	18.976	20.872
6	20.872	22.961	2.087	20.874	−0.002

Derivation

Column (1) first row: given
remaining rows: column (5) of row before
(2) initial calculation (values here all the same, but not in other cases)
(3) column (1) × i
(4) column (2) − column (3)
(5) column (1) − column (4).

General Price Change Only

$A' = 100; k = 6; i = 0.155; g = 0.05; i^* = (i - g)/(1 + g) = 0.1;$ $q = (1 + g)/(1 + i) = 0.909{,}091; q^6 = 0.564{,}473; 1 - q^6 = 0.435{,}527;$ $P = A'/(1 - q^6) = 229.607.$

Full service charge for first year $= (i - g)P = 24.109.$

Year	Value of asset at beginning of year in currency of		Full service charge (3)	Cost of capital (4)	Replacement charge (= value write-off) (5)	Value of asset at end of year, in end of year currency (6)
	beg. year (1)	end year (2)				
1	100.000	105.000	24.109	10.500	13.609	91.391
2	91.391	95.961	25.314	9.596	15.718	80.243
3	80.243	84.255	26.580	8.425	18.155	66.100
4	66.100	69.405	27.909	6.940	20.969	48.436
5	48.436	50.858	29.304	5.086	24.218	26.640
6	26.640	27.972	30.769	2.797	27.972	0

Derivation

Column (1) first row: given
remaining rows: column (6) of row before
(2) column (1) × (1 + g)
(3) first row: initial calculation
remaining rows: row before × (1 + g)

(4) column (2) × i^*
(5) column (3) − column (4)
(6) column (2) − column (5).

Special Price Change Only

$A' = 100$; $k = 6$; $i = 0.1$; $s = -0.04$; $p = (1 + s)/(1 + i) = 0.872,727$; $p^6 = 0.441,845$; $1 - p^6 = 0.558,155$; $P = A'/(1 - p^6) = 179.162$.

Full service charge for first year $= (i - s)P = 25.083$.

Year	Value of asset at beginning of year (1)	Full service charge (2)	Cost of capital (3)	Value write-off (4)	Holding loss (5)	Replacement charge (6)	Value of asset at end of year (7)
1	100.000	25.083	10.000	15.083	4.000	11.083	84.917
2	84.917	24.080	8.492	15.588	3.397	12.191	69.329
3	69.329	23.117	6.933	16.184	2.773	13.411	53.145
4	53.145	22.192	5.314	16.878	2.126	14.752	36.267
5	36.267	21.304	3.627	17.677	1.451	16.226	18.590
6	18.590	20.452	1.859	18.593	0.744	17.849	−0.003

Derivation

Column (1) first row: given
remaining rows: column (7) of row before
(2) first row: initial calculation
remaining rows: row before × (1 + s)
(3) column (1) × i
(4) column (2) − column (3)
(5) column (1) × s (gain if s positive, loss if negative)
(6) column (4) + column (5) if gain, − column (5) if loss
(7) column (1) − column (4).

General and Special Price Changes

$A' = 100$; $k = 6$; $i = 0.155$; $g = 0.05$; $c = 0.008$; $i^* = (i - g)/(1 + g) = 0.1$; $s = (c - g)/(1 + g) = -0.04$; $r = (1 + c)/(1 + i) = 0.872,727$; $r^6 = 0.441,845$; $1 - r^6 = 0.558,155$; $P = A'/(1 - r^6) = 179.162$.

Full service charge for first year $= (i - c)P = 26.337$.

Year	Value of asset at beginning of year in currency of: beg. year (1)	end year (2)	Full service charge (3)	Cost of capital (4)	Value write-off (5)	Holding loss (6)	Replacement charge (7)	Value of asset at end of year, in end of year currency (8)
1	100.000	105.000	26.337	10.500	15.837	4.200	11.637	89.163
2	89.163	93.621	26.548	9.362	17.186	3.745	13.441	76.435
3	76.435	80.257	26.760	8.026	18.734	3.210	15.524	61.523
4	61.523	64.599	26.974	6.460	20.514	2.584	17.930	44.085
5	44.085	46.289	27.190	4.629	22.561	1.852	20.709	23.728
6	23.728	24.914	27.408	2.491	24.917	0.997	23.920	−0.003

Derivation

Column (1) first row: given
remaining rows: column (8) of row before
(2) column (1) $\times$ $(1 + g)$
(3) First row: initial calculation
remaining rows: row before $\times$ $(1 + c)$
(4) column (2) $\times$ i^*
(5) column (3) − column (4)
(6) column (2) $\times$ s (gain if s positive, loss if negative)
(7) column (5) + column (6) if gain, − column (6) if loss
(8) column (2) − column (5).

MONETARY CORRECTION

Article

Monetary Correction

ADJUSTMENTS TO INFLATION IN THREE SOUTH AMERICAN COUNTRIES

by

W T BAXTER

The author was Professor of Accounting in the London School of Economics, 1947–73, and is now Emeritus Professor. This article follows a four-month study tour in South America last year.

THIS ARTICLE tries to describe how inflation affects firms and households in three South American countries — Argentina, Brazil and Chile. All three have known inflation for many years, often at high rates. Last year, Brazil's rate was about 29%, but it has been through much worse spells. Argentina's was almost 335%, and Chile's, which in 1973 reached over 500%, sank to about 340%.

With rates like these, one would expect to find general distrust of money, and attempts to substitute more reliable units. But money serves several functions, and in fact the extent of substitution has varied from one function to another. As the medium of exchange, money persists in use; to abandon it would be difficult, since foreign currency is not easy to come by, and barter is awkward. It persists likewise as the medium of value, *eg* for expressing today's prices. But it tends to drop out of use whenever a time-lag is involved: it fails as a serviceable unit of account, even more as a standard for deferred payments and a store of value. These functions are increasingly being served by new units, linked with money by an ever-shifting exchange rate.

Monetary correction, or indexation, is sometimes interpreted as a product of ineptitude: a country admits its inability to halt inflation, and turns instead to devices for living comfortably with it. However, the country must have vigour to make the system work: the effectiveness and timing of monetary correction mirror the political scene. In Brazil, correction started soon after the revolution of 1964; the measures are comprehensive, closely enforced, and subject to fréquent amendment. Chile developed some of the corrective devices nearly twenty years ago, but full-blooded versions had to wait for the *coup d'état* of September 1973, and so have come into effect only recently. In Argentina, correction is fragmentary and not fully implemented, and is less the child of government than of private initiative.

The Brazilian measures have been much publicized. Chile's new measures imitate those of Brazil, but try to go one better; they deserve publicity too.

Monetary correction covers a range of measures stretching from indexation of investments to the 'crawling-peg' exchange-rate system. All the measures accept that the money unit becomes treacherous when used over any length of time, and they in effect replace it with a constant basket of things-in-general; they do so by raising the last period's money figure (in a contract, account, etc) to this period's equivalent, with the aid of a general price index. Some of the measures achieve full correction, and others stop somewhat short.

FULL CORRECTION

Indexed bonds and other credits

The Brazilian government began to issue readjustable treasury bonds (ORTN) in 1964. The annual interest rate on a five-year bond is 6%. This is a real rate: the interest payments rise quarterly in step with a general index (of wholesale prices), and the sum repaid at redemption rises likewise, by an amount that is tax-free. In time, the government extended indexation to other obligations. An much-cited example is the severance indemnity fund:* employers pay 8% of wages into a individual bank account for each employee, to be used for retirement and unemployment benefits; these forced savings and their accumulated interest are indexed. Another example is the account with savings banks: the balance in a savings book (*caderneta de poupança*) is indexed, and has the further attraction, especially for the wealthy, that depositors may deduct 6% of their average balance from their income-tax liability. All these adjustables have become popular, and attract a great volume of saving.† Loans to companies and institutions are for the most part also indexed; a state bank may lend to a Brazilian (as distinct from a foreign-owned) company at a real annual rate of 3%, but the normal private loan, probably raised through an investment bank, costs up to 12% (real).

* Fundo de Garantia do Tempo de Serviço (FGTS).

† See, for instance, 'Inflation Control and Economic Growth', Paper 4 issued by the Brazilian Embassy in London, 1974.

Where the loan is for only six months or less, full monetary correction is not used: instead, a high predetermined rate of interest is charged — say nearly 30% a year by an investment bank; commercial banks charge less, but tie costly strings to the transaction.*

Argentina too has issued state adjustable bonds. There are three types; all have shortish lives (five to seven years), during which each bond is redeemed in yearly or half-yearly slices. *Valores nacionales ajustables* are expressed in pesos, with annual interest at 7%; the nominal figures are adjusted according to the wholesale-price index (agricultural products excluded). *Bonos nacionales para inversión y desarrollo* are expressed in pesos, with interest at 8%; the nominal figures are adjusted to the US dollar exchange rate — but at the unrealistic official rate. *Bonos externos* are expressed in US dollars, and so need no adjustment; the interest rate is set slightly above the London interbank eurodollar rate. All three are quoted on the Buenos Aires stock exchange, at prices that stick fairly closely to their theoretically correct values. Non-government adjustables are still rare; and (probably as a result) long-term loans have almost vanished from company balance sheets. Instead, thanks to easy-going monetary policy, banks give loans readily (at only some 30% annually) for 180 days, and these loans are normally renewed. Private lenders charge higher rates — sometimes over 100%; the legal maximum is 36%, so the difference must be paid 'under the counter' or in disguised forms.

Indexed bonds have been known in Chile for some twenty years; the Government's issues yield about 7% real annual interest. Indexation has been further popularized by the vigorous savings and loans associations (*cf* Britain's building societies). Their savings and deposit accounts are used alike by business and the small saver, and are indexed and tax-free. During the worst period of inflation their interest payments were pushed up by the index to 20% or more *per month*, and the consequent rush to invest accounted for about half of total savings by the end of 1974; then the Government, embarrassed by the size of the interest payments, placed a ceiling on withdrawals, and the associations lost ground. The state savings banks also index their accounts, and companies, etc, issue indexed bonds. The interest rate (unindexed) on short-term loans has been volatile — for instance 16% a month in mid-1975 and only 10–11% when the inflation rate declined three months later — so lenders are gambling on whether or not they receive a positive real rate.

Rents

Rents have been indexed in Brazil for many years. Until recently, they were linked to the minimum wage, but a more broadly-based index has been substituted. The increases are accepted by tenants as tolerable while the inflation rate is

* Control on bank interest rates has recently been lifted; see this issue, page 202.

declining, but become burdensome when it is rising. Argentina's system allows increases in small jumps, geared to the minimum wage. Chile has decontrolled office rents, but house rents are still controlled, at 11% of the value of the property; this is reappraised each year by officials, and then rents suddenly jump to perhaps three times their former size — an increase that distresses tenants but may fail to match inflation.

Miscellaneous contracts

Once the idea of indexation became familiar, it was adapted to many contracts that involved future payments. Thus, if a farm is to be sold at a price paid in monthly instalments, these will be indexed. Sometimes contracts are priced instead in foreign currency, though this is illegal in some countries; for instance, rents and hotel bills may be geared to the US dollar, and a lawyer may quote his fees in dollars.

Brazilian contracts may use the ORTN instead of the cruzeiro. There is also a standard unit for building and personal loans, the *unidade de poder constante* (UPC). One borrows so many units, and their cruzeiro value changes quarterly in line with the index for the previous quarter. These units make for easier calculation (*eg* of schedules of interest and capital redemption), especially where a computer is used.

Chilean law and indexation

Law has everywhere tended to lag behind practice. In Chile, for example, the legal code (which dates from last century) still does not deal with indexation. Until some three years ago, the courts did not recognize it; the most they would do to compensate for delayed payment was to allow a trivial rate of interest. Contracts could indeed be couched in terms of foreign currency, but the actual payment had to be in a local-currency equivalent based on the official exchange rate (at one point, only a fifteenth of the black-market rate); in consequence many contracts were made surreptitiously, with payment by transfer abroad.

The courts were in time forced to soften their attitude. Somewhat unexpectedly, the thin end of the wedge was a concession in the tax rules. When the price of property was paid by indexed instalments, the rules originally treated the increases as taxable interest. This was so harsh that it caused widespread evasion: a contract would ostensibly require immediate payment, but in fact the parties would agree to instalment payments 'under the desk'. In the end, in hope of collecting tax on at least the true interest, the authorities exempted the indexed capital. The law was further modified by the indexation rules for savings and loan associations and adjustable bonds. The main relaxation took place some three years ago, however, following the price explosion. The courts would probably now recognize indexation where contracts clearly agree to it, and would include it in their awards for damages (such as for motor accidents, from the date of the accident to that of payment).

In all countries with indexed bonds, the problem of estimating just compensation, to cover future living costs of an injured person, is of course much simplified; the victim is in a far happier position than his counterpart elsewhere.

Wills

With stiff inflation, the man who is drawing up his will tends to make bequests in the form of non-money assets such as houses. If he bequeaths fixed sums of money instead, he puts himself under pressure to revise his will often; a better plan is to quantify the money with some unit other than that of his own currency. The US dollar is an obvious choice. In Brazil, his will may allot a sum in 'cruzeiros equivalent to *x* ORTN'. The bequest of an annuity can be defined in terms of interest on indexed bonds, or so many times the minimum wage.*

Insurance

Life insurance is an early victim of inflation. During the 1940s, many Argentine life offices cancelled their policies and paid out the surrender values. Where this has not been done, the policies are now almost worthless.

When indexed bonds and real estate are available to life offices as investments, one might suppose that a new breed of life policies would emerge, geared to some non-money base (*cf* the unit-linked policy in Britain). And in fact such policies are at least permissible in Brazil and Argentina, and the Chilean government insists that all new life policies should take this form. Yet the new policies have not caught on: the once-bitten-twice-shy reaction is no doubt to blame, and the growth of social insurance may have made private policies look superfluous.

In Brazil, group insurance to some extent fills the place of traditional life insurance; it accounts for at least 90% of all life business. Company employees pay a premium that is geared to their salaries. The cover is very short-term (almost monthly), has no endowment element, and ceases when the employee moves to another job; the unit is the minimum wage.

* Brazil now forbids the latter formula.

Accident insurers try to keep up with inflation by raising premiums often. Where the inflation rate is low, yearly rises are adequate; where it is high, the rises must come quarterly or even more frequently. Thus Chilean policies may contain a clause that stipulates for quarterly adjustment based on indices of general prices or building costs; the office sends an extra premium demand to its large clients each quarter. In Argentina, an alert client may raise his cover with each 10% jump in prices, paying an extra charge perhaps each month. The small insurer tends to have too little cover, and suffers from the 'average clause'.

Taxation

Where there is steep inflation, normally the taxpayer has the strongest inducement to postpone payment — and thereby increases the government's deficit, and probably stokes up the inflation. Before the 1964 reforms, the Brazilian taxpayer could reckon that any conceivable penalties for delay were outweighed by the whittling down of his real tax burden. The Argentine taxpayer still can do so. Moreover, inflation gives the taxpayer two extra grounds for holding that non-payment is justified — fiscal drag (the government's failure to raise personal allowances in step with earnings) and the artificial profits of historical accounts. Thus in Argentina, which has yet to overhaul its tax system, workers can with some truth protest that tax allowances are cruelly low, while businessmen maintain that firms may be paying some 200% tax on real profit.

Indexation makes tax-gathering faster and fairer. In Brazil and Chile, the tax due at a given date is subject to monetary correction thereafter, plus interest and fines. More remarkable, amounts overpaid to the tax-collector are refunded with correction; perhaps more than anything else, this opened people's eyes to the fact that the government was in earnest. In Chile, a firm now pays tax each month, on its provisional estimates of the current month's profit; this has led to a marked speed-up in accounting procedures (hitherto often in arrear). Brazil has added an ingenious touch to its controls: each taxpayer has been given a tax number, which he must quote when entering on any big transaction such as buying a car or a ticket for foreign travel; this has caught many persons in the tax net for the first time.

However, the new rules also make tax more equitable. In Chile, the personal allowances are defined in tax units, whose size in pesos rises each month, so that fiscal lag is still-born. Both Brazil and Chile require firms to reform their accounts (see below). They give tax concessions for saving: thus Brazil's fiscal incentives consist of tax deductions for firms that invest in the north-east and Amazon regions, and to individuals who pay into savings accounts and blocked accounts with mutual funds.

PARTIAL CORRECTION

In some of its forms, correction is (or is popularly believed to be) less than complete. Examples of what might be called partial correction follow.

The 'crawling peg'

In 1964, the Chilean authorities had to decide whether to let the exchange rate float down. They decided this would cause too many shocks and (in the absence of a developed forward market) fluctuations. So they decided instead on frequent minor changes, and claim to be the inventors of the 'crawling peg'. This system was discontinued under the Allende administration but reintroduced by the present military government; its operations have been successful, in that the black market in foreign exchange seems now to have shrunk to negligible size. The peg's crawlings do not exactly match general index movements; this is to allow for fluctuations in the balance-of-payments position.

Brazil copied Chile in 1968. At present, its peg crawls every two or three weeks without prior notice, to baffle speculators. The rate is supposed to reflect the difference between Brazil's price index and the corresponding indices of its chief trading partners. But many other variables affect the rate, such as the rising export subsidies and import restrictions; and even the casual tourist may be able to buy cruzeiros below the official rate.

Wages

In Brazil, there is a minimum wage, now fixed by an elaborate legal formula that embraces last year's real wage and half the rates of expected productivity and inflation.* The wage rises once a year. It varies in different regions, tending to increase as one travels down the road from the North-East to the big cities of the South, where costs are higher. Since April 1975 the minimum wage has not been used as a direct factor for calculating monetary correction in other fields.

* Details in Albert Fishlow, 'Indexing Brazilian Style: Inflation without Tears?', Brooklyn Papers on Economic Activity 1: 1974.

There is a widespread belief that wages have lagged behind inflation; it has been estimated that between 1964 and 1968, before the introduction of the present system, there was a 30% drop in real wages. However, if the family, and not the individual, is taken as the earning unit, the average standard of living has probably not fallen, since there are now more people at work, especially women.

Many wages, especially in the more prosperous South, are above the minimum level, and so not subject to direct indexation. In part, the increases are due to awards by labour courts (often the same percentage rise as that of the minimum wage), but they must spring in part from a demand effect, in the absence of militant union activity.

Though Brazilian wages seem low by some foreign standards, their nominal size is eked out by a substantial fringe. A thirteenth month's wage, at the December level, is paid as supplement for holidays and Christmas. Then there are the 8% contribution for retirement, and any other sums for company insurance against accidents and other mishaps. Further, workers participate in profits, in the sense of receiving credits in government funds* to which employers pay a percentage of sales; this device gives workers some share in the general prosperity, yet neatly avoids quarrels over the true size of their own company's profits — quarrels that have soured Peru's experiments with worker cooperatives. A liberal employer may find that the extras add nearly 50% to his wages bill.

In Chile, too, there is a minimum wage. It rises at least quarterly, catching up briefly with the general index; but many employers feel impelled to give rises even more often.

The Argentine government has awarded sporadic general increases. The most publicized was that of June 1975, when wages were pushed up by at least 100%; there have been many since. Sailors, backed by one of the powerful unions, have received a 400% rise. But, to quote from the graffiti, 'prices go up by the lift, wages by the stairs'.

ACCOUNTING PROCEDURES

Accounting reform

Traditional accounting uses historical costs of assets to measure wealth and its increase. So, when inflation occurs, the accounting figures drift apart from today's realities. The two main statements — the balance sheet and the profit-and-loss account — are both damaged. The former values non-money assets, especially fixed assets, at antiquated figures that are far below current market prices. The latter commits sins of both omission and commission: it neglects to show the *appreciation on non-money assets* (in either money terms or real terms),

* The Programa de Integração Social (PIS) and the Programa de Formação do Patrimônio do Servidor Público (Pasep).

as well as the inflation *loss from holding money assets* or the corresponding gain from being in debt; and it shows a layer of unreal profit because of its *time-lag error*, *ie* the subtraction of former costs of input (goods and depreciation) from current sales.

South American countries have been pioneers in substituting inflation accounting for traditional methods. Normally they have not done this by frontal assaults, such as changes in the company law on accounts; instead they have amended their tax rules (for instance, to allow depreciation on modernized values for fixed assets), and then insisted that firms must in return use the corrected figures in their own books.

Reform has been achieved in two stages. The first step was to make firms revalue their fixed assets, with a general price index. This in turn led to correspondingly larger depreciation charges, and lower profits.

Argentina has not yet got beyond this first step. Its institute of public accountants has worked manfully for further advances, and to this end has issued a far-reaching 'standard' of good practice; but the government has failed to give it support, and the standard is largely unhonoured.

The next step was to tackle the time-lag error on stocks ('inventory profit') and the loss on holding money. Brazil combines the two things by making firms provide for the 'maintenance of working capital'. This is done with a single adjustment in the profit-and-loss account. The adjustment is calculated on the opening balances of stock and net money assets, in accordance with the wholesale-price index. Thus it fails to allow for these assets' variations during the year, or to give information on these two very different ingredients.

Comments on reforms

This system must strike the onlooker as something of a patchwork. It does not produce a comprehensive set of updated figures; the owners' capital, retained earnings, etc, stay at historical levels. And, by ignoring the current prices of the various assets, it does not allow for their different cash demands at replacement. Brazilian accountants say that the rules have been promulgated in the past without adequate consultation with practical men, and that the incessant flow of amendments demands much hard study. Remarkably few people understand the government's worksheets on which firms must calculate depreciation. The sheets are adorned with such terms as 'revaluation of cost', 'depreciation of revaluation', and 'revaluation of depreciation'; not surprisingly, the total of these tinkerings does not accord with the answer to a straightforward sum.

Chile's system, which came into force last year, is more elegant, being largely the brain-child of academic accountants who built on Brazilian experience. It is very thorough-going, in the sense of updating all historical figures — even the owners' capital. Though it relies mainly on the general index, it uses specific values for a few assets, *eg* old stock must be revalued at replacement cost, and shares at their quoted price. Many debts due to or by the firm are of course subject to automatic revaluation, thanks to indexation. Unfortunately, the net total of all the value changes (not only loss of working capital but appreciation on fixed assets) is carried as a cost or gain to the profit-and-loss account. Inflation accounting is normally expected to lessen taxable profits (by raising costs, to cut out the time-lag error); but this Chilean device seems apt to increase them, especially where money liabilities exceed money assets.

It is usually bad accounting to lump diverse items together. The fusion of such contrasting items as loss on money and the time-lag error, in both Brazil and Chile, conceals useful information; managers and shareholders should see the separate figures. And it is by no means clear that the different items merit the same tax treatment. Brazil and Chile give semi-hidden relief to firms that suffer loss on money. Private taxpayers, denied such relief on the cash in their pockets, may well feel that the government is over-indulgent to firms. Businessmen in northern countries have not yet even dared to ask for such privileged treatment.

One can thus criticize the failure in Brazil and Chile to unravel useful information, and — in Brazil's case — to update all the figures. Nevertheless, future historians of accounting will surely accord these countries a glowing chapter for pioneering in inflation adjustment, and for showing that the new methods can, with government pressure, be put into general use. Their model is built on an intellectually respectable concept — real-capital maintenance — and allows for inflation's erosion of money assets (two areas where Britain's own Sandilands report is weak).

Management accounts

Companies deal with inflation in very different ways when they draft forecasts. Some use today's figures in their budgeted income statements, arguing that price changes will affect both costs and revenues to much the same degree; others bring in estimates of inflation, for at least the next month or two; yet others use foreign-currency units. Firms that are sophisticated enough to test investment projects (with discounted cash-flow budgets) are normally also sophisticated enough to use monetary correction or foreign currency.

Costing systems tend to break down under serious inflation. Some firms cling to them, but look on the figures mainly as guides to physical efficiency. With 'standard costs', the figures for material must be revised continually, to replacement level. One benefit from such current figures is that they help with the uphill task of educating sales staff to keep changing their prices.

Conclusion

Critics of monetary correction argue that it may itself feed inflation, and also — by making the latter more tolerable — may weaken the will to regain stability. The contrary argument is that a counter-inflation policy brings unfortunate side-effects, such as unemployment, and monetary correction can soften these and thereby help the policy.* South American experience hardly yields firm evidence on the curing of inflation; rather it suggests that monetary correction is useful because it lessens the worst effects of continuing inflation, namely personal suffering and the misallocation of resources.

* Milton Friedman, *Monetary Correction*, Occasional Paper 41, Institute of Economic Affairs, London 1974.

THE DEVELOPMENT OF CONTEMPORARY ACCOUNTING THOUGHT

An Arno Press Collection

Baldwin, H[arry] G[len]. **Accounting for Value As Well as Original Cost** *and* Castenholz, William B. **A Solution to the Appreciation Problem.** 2 Vols. in 1. 1927/1931

Baxter, William. **Collected Papers on Accounting.** 1978

Brief, Richard P., Ed. **Selections from Encyclopaedia of Accounting, 1903.** 1978

Broaker, Frank and Richard M. Chapman. **The American Accountants' Manual.** 1897

Canning, John B. **The Economics of Accountancy.** 1929

Chatfield, Michael, Ed. **The English View of Accountant's Duties and Responsibilities.** 1978

Cole, William Morse. **The Fundamentals of Accounting.** 1921

Congress of Accountants. **Official Record of the Proceedings of the Congress of Accountants.** 1904

Cronhelm, F[rederick] W[illiam]. **Double Entry by Single.** 1818

Davidson, Sidney. **The Plant Accounting Regulations of the Federal Power Commission.** 1952

De Paula, F[rederic] R[udolf] M[ackley]. **Developments in Accounting.** 1948

Epstein, Marc Jay. **The Effect of Scientific Management on the Development of the Standard Cost System** (Doctoral Dissertation, University of Oregon, 1973). 1978

Esquerré, Paul-Joseph. **The Applied Theory of Accounts.** 1914

Fitzgerald, A[dolf] A[lexander]. **Current Accounting Trends.** 1952

Garner, S. Paul and Marilynn Hughes, Eds. **Readings on Accounting Development.** 1978

Haskins, Charles Waldo. **Business Education and Accountancy.** 1904

Hein, Leonard William. **The British Companies Acts and the Practice of Accountancy 1844-1962** (Doctoral Dissertation, University of California, Los Angeles, 1962). 1978

Hendriksen, Eldon S. **Capital Expenditures in the Steel Industry, 1900 to 1953** (Doctoral Dissertation, University of California, Berkeley, 1956). 1978

Holmes, William, Linda H. Kistler and Louis S. Corsini. **Three Centuries of Accounting in Massachusetts.** 1978

Horngren, Charles T. **Implications for Accountants of the Uses of Financial Statements by Security Analysts** (Doctoral Dissertation, University of Chicago, 1955). 1978

Horrigan, James O., Ed. **Financial Ratio Analysis—An Historical Perspective.** 1978

Jones, [Edward Thomas]. **Jones's English System of Book-keeping.** 1796

Lamden, Charles William. **The Securities and Exchange Commission** (Doctoral Dissertation, University of California, Berkeley, 1949). 1978

Langer, Russell Davis. **Accounting As A Variable in Mergers** (Doctoral Dissertation, University of California, Berkeley, 1976). 1978

Lewis, J. Slater. **The Commercial Organisation of Factories.** 1896

Littleton, A[nanias] C[harles] and B[asil] S. Yamey, Eds. **Studies in the Historv of Accounting.** 1956

Mair, John. **Book-keeping Moderniz'd.** 1793

Mann, Helen Scott. **Charles Ezra Sprague.** 1931

Marsh, C[hristopher] C[olumbus]. **The Theory and Practice of Bank Book-keeping.** 1856

Mitchell, William. **A New and Complete System of Book-keeping by an Improved Method of Double Entry.** 1796

Montgomery, Robert H. **Fifty Years of Accountancy.** 1939

Moonitz, Maurice. **The Entity Theory of Consolidated Statements.** 1951

Moonitz, Maurice, Ed. **Three Contributions to the Development of Accounting Thought.** 1978

Murray, David. **Chapters in the History of Bookkeeping, Accountancy & Commercial Arithmetic.** 1930

Nicholson, J[erome] Lee. **Cost Accounting.** 1913

Paton, William Andrew and Russell Alger Stevenson. **Principles of Accounting.** 1918

Pixley, Francis W[illiam]. **The Profession of a Chartered Accountant and Other Lectures.** 1897

Preinreich, Gabriel A. D. **The Nature of Dividends.** 1935

Previts, Gary John, Ed. **Early 20th Century Developments in American Accounting Thought.** 1978

Ronen, Joshua and George H. Sorter. **Relevant Financial Statements.** 1978

Shenkir, William G., Ed. **Carman G. Blough: His Professional Career and Accounting Thought.** 1978

Simpson, Kemper. **Economics for the Accountant.** 1921

Sneed, Florence R. **Parallelism in Two Disciplines.** (M.A. Thesis, University of Texas, Arlington, 1974). 1978

Sorter, George H. **The Boundaries of the Accounting Universe** (Doctoral Dissertation, University of Chicago, 1963). 1978

Storey, Reed K[arl]. **Matching Revenues with Costs** (Doctoral Dissertation, University of California, Berkeley, 1958). 1978

Sweeney, Henry W[hitcomb]. **Stabilized Accounting.** 1936

Van de Linde, Gérard. **Reminiscences.** 1917

Vatter, William J[oseph]. **The Fund Theory of Accounting and Its Implications for Financial Reports.** 1947

Walker, R. G. **Consolidated Statements.** 1978

Webster, Norman E., Comp. **The American Association of Public Accountants.** 1954

Wells, M. C., Ed. **American Engineers' Contributions to Cost Accounting.** 1978

Worthington, Beresford. **Professional Accountants.** 1895

Yamey, Basil S. **Essays on the History of Accounting.** 1978

Yamey, Basil S., Ed. **The Historical Development of Accounting.** 1978

Yang, J[u] M[ei]. **Goodwill and Other Intangibles.** 1927

Zeff, Stephen Addam. **A Critical Examination of the Orientation Postulate in Accounting, with Particular Attention to its Historical Development** (Doctoral Dissertation, University of Michigan, 1961). 1978

Zeff, Stephen A., Ed. **Selected Dickinson Lectures in Accounting.** 1978